# Django Unleashed

# Django Unleashed

Andrew Pinkham

**SAMS** | 800 East 96th Street, Indianapolis, Indiana 46240 USA

**Django Unleashed**

Copyright © 2016 by Pearson Education, Inc.

All rights reserved. No part of this book shall be reproduced, stored in a retrieval system, or transmitted by any means, electronic, mechanical, photocopying, recording, or otherwise, without written permission from the publisher. No patent liability is assumed with respect to the use of the information contained herein. Although every precaution has been taken in the preparation of this book, the publisher and author assume no responsibility for errors or omissions. Nor is any liability assumed for damages resulting from the use of the information contained herein.

ISBN-13: 978-0-321-98507-1
ISBN-10: 0-321-98507-9

The Library of Congress cataloging-in-publication data is available at http://lccn.loc.gov/2015033839.
Printed in the United States of America
First printing, October 2015

**Trademarks**

All terms mentioned in this book that are known to be trademarks or service marks have been appropriately capitalized. Sams Publishing cannot attest to the accuracy of this information. Use of a term in this book should not be regarded as affecting the validity of any trademark or service mark.

**Warning and Disclaimer**

Every effort has been made to make this book as complete and as accurate as possible, but no warranty or fitness is implied. The information provided is on an "as is" basis. The author and the publisher shall have neither liability nor responsibility to any person or entity with respect to any loss or damages arising from the information contained in this book or programs accompanying it.

**Special Sales**

For information about buying this title in bulk quantities, or for special sales opportunities (which may include electronic versions; custom cover designs; and content particular to your business, training goals, marketing focus, or branding interests), please contact our corporate sales department at corpsales@pearsoned.com or (800) 382-3419.

For government sales inquiries, please contact governmentsales@pearsoned.com.
For questions about sales outside the U.S., please contact international@pearsoned.com.

**Editor-in-Chief**
Mark L. Taub

**Acquisitions Editor**
Debra Williams Cauley

**Development Editor**
Chris Zahn

**Managing Editor**
John Fuller

**Project Editor**
Elizabeth Ryan

**Copy Editor**
Carol Lallier

**Indexer**
John S. Lewis

**Proofreader**
Linda Begley

**Editorial Assistant**
Kim Boedigheimer

**Cover Designer**
Mark Shirar

**Compositor**
DiacriTech

# Contents

# Preface

In early 2013, a startup in Austin, Texas, approached me to work on a banking application using Django. My experience with Django was limited: I had tried to use the tool in 2009 but felt that the learning curve was steep. I wanted to give Django a try but did not have enough time to learn how to use it given the project's time constraints (which was fine: we were forced to use PHP anyway). When I looked at Django again in 2013, I discovered that it had become far more accessible. For certain, those four years had seen Django improve by leaps and bounds. However, I had also gained key knowledge working with web frameworks.

At the end of the project in 2013, I was asked by a different group to take what I had learned and teach its engineers how to program Django. I liked the work enough that I started creating a series of videos based on the material. During a test showing of the videos, one of my reviewers casually commented that the material would be more suitable and more approachable as a book. I still have a hard time believing that such an innocent comment resulted in a year and a half of such intense work, but that is the origin of this book: an off-hand comment.

This book is the book I wish I'd had in 2009 and in 2013. It is a how-to book that teaches you how to build a webpage from scratch using Django. The first part of the book (the first 12 chapters) are for my 2009 self. It answers the basic questions that I had when I started learning Django, and it explains the basics of web frameworks and websites. I think of the remaining chapters as a response to my 2013 self. They address the needs of more experienced users. Related materials are available at `https://django-unleashed.com`. I hope you find this book useful.

## Is This Book for Me?

This book is meant for two types of people:

1. Programmers who have never built a website before and do not know how web frameworks operate
2. Programmers who have dabbled or used the basics of Django, and who would like to hone their skills and take advantage of Django's intermediate features

The book thus caters to both beginners and intermediate users. The only knowledge assumed is basic programming knowledge and Python.

## What This Book Contains

This book is a hands-on, single example: we build and deploy a fully functional website over the course of the 30 chapters. Each chapter covers a single part of Django and is the logical next step to building our website while learning how to use Django.

**Part I, Django's Core Features,** is an introduction to websites, web frameworks, and Django. We assume knowledge of programming and Python, but absolutely no knowledge of the internals of back-end web programming. In these first 12 chapters, we use the core parts of Django—the parts used in (almost) every website—to create the basics of our website. This includes interacting with a database, sending HTML to visitors, and accepting user input in a safe manner.

**Part II, Django's Contributed Library,** examines the tools provided by Django that are helpful when building a website but that are not necessary to every site. Effectively, we will be adding features to our website to modernize the site and make it full-featured. From Chapter 13 through Chapter 23, we will see how to integrate CSS into our website, shorten our code through generic behavior, and add user authentication to our website.

**Part III, Advanced Core Features,** expands on Django's basics, detailing how to improve their use. We see how to take full control of our site, shortening code, optimizing our site for speed, and expanding behavior. We then deploy our website to the Internet, hosting the website on Heroku's managed cloud. Finally, in Chapter 30, we consider what we would have done differently in our project had we known at the beginning what we now know at the end of the book.

## Conventions Used in This Book

This book is written with a bottom-to-top approach, meaning we start with a lower level of abstraction (more details) and gradually move up the abstraction ladder (shorter but more opaque code). If you would prefer to learn with a top-to-bottom approach, I recommend reading Chapter 12 after Chapter 1, and starting each chapter with the last section of the chapter, titled "Putting It All Together" throughout the book.

This book features quite a few asides (sometimes called admonitions) meant to help you understand Django or else to add tidbits of information to your programming toolkit.

**Info**    An aside with basic information that extends or adds to the current content.

**Warning!**    Gotchas, errors, and things to watch out for: these warnings are here to make your life easier by helping you avoid common mistakes.

**Documentation**    Links to documentation from Django, Python, and other resources, which enable you to continue to learn material on the subject at hand.

**Code Repository**    This book is heavily tied to the website found at `https://django-unleashed.com`, as is the project code found throughout the book and provided in full on github. Each example from the project has the git commit hash printed with it (and is a link to the digital version), allowing you to access each commit by adding `https://dju.link/` before the commit hash (this may in turn be followed by a file path). Even so, every so often a particular commit is worth noting, and these asides will point you toward the code in the repository.

**Ghosts of Django Past and Future**   The project in this book uses Django 1.8, the latest version, to create a website. However, it is not uncommon to find earlier versions of Django in the wild or at your new workplace. These asides aim to give you knowledge of changes between Django 1.4 and Django 1.8 so you can more easily navigate the various versions of Django if need be (that said, any new project should strive to use the latest version of Python and Django).

# Acknowledgments

I have been blessed with an incredible family. I could not have done this without them.

A huge thank you to Amber Gode and Anna Ossowski, both of whom read and reviewed large portions of this book and without whom this would be a very different product. Thanks to Wendell Smith, James Oakley, Dave Liechty, Jacinda Shelly, and Andrew Farrell for all of their hard work and feedback on both the code and the writing. Special thanks to Amy Bekkerman for always knowing the right question to ask. Thanks to Harry Percival for catching problems with the code. Thanks to Sasha Méndez for her feedback and particularly to Debra Williams Cauley of Pearson. She shared my enthusiasm for this project and enabled me to get this book going. Thank you to Sarah Abraham, Matt Kaemmerer, and Blake West, who were my very first guinea pigs (in the class that eventually gave rise to this book). Thanks to Paul Phillips for always grabbing a beer and listening to me complain about the sometimes frustrating, blinding work of coding and writing.

Finally, I want to acknowledge the Django and Python Communities. They are an amazing group of individuals, and I would not have written such an extensive book without their openness and support.

# About the Author

**Andrew Pinkham** is a software engineer who grew up in Paris and currently resides in Austin, Texas. Andrew runs a consulting business called JamBon Software, which specializes in web and mobile products and also offers Python and Django training. He prides himself on being an engineer who can communicate complex ideas in simple ways and is passionate about security and distributed systems. In his free time, Andrew writes fiction and swims. He is a 2009 graduate of Dartmouth College and can be found online at andrewsforge.com, or afrg.co for short.

## We Want to Hear from You!

As the reader of this book, *you* are our most important critic and commentator. We value your opinion and want to know what we're doing right, what we could do better, what areas you'd like to see us publish in, and any other words of wisdom you're willing to pass our way.

We welcome your comments. You can email or write to let us know what you did or didn't like about this book—as well as what we can do to make our books better.

*Please note that we cannot help you with technical problems related to the topic of this book.*

When you write, please be sure to include this book's title and author as well as your name and email address. We will carefully review your comments and share them with the author and editors who worked on the book.

Email: errata@informit.com

Mail:

Sams Publishing
ATTN: Reader Feedback
330 Hudson Street
7th Floor
New York, New York 10013

## Reader Services

Visit our website and register this book at informit.com/register for convenient access to any updates, downloads, or errata that might be available for this book.

# Django's Core Features

"Begin at the beginning," the King said, very gravely, "and go on till you come to the end: then stop."

*Alice in Wonderland*
by Lewis Carroll

# Starting a New Django Project: Building a Startup Categorizer with Blog

## In This Chapter

- The difference between static and dynamic websites
- The difference between the front end and back end of websites
- The HTTP request/response cycle
- The nature of a framework and how it differs from a library
- What it means to be a Python web framework (e.g., Django)
- The outline of the project we will build in Parts I, II, and III

## 1.1 Introduction

We have a lot to do and a lot to learn, but instead of jumping right in, let's take a moment to understand what we're doing.

Part I is an example meant to demonstrate the core features of Django. Part I is intended to be read linearly. Jump between chapters at your own peril!

This first chapter is a general introduction to the modern world of building dynamic websites. We start by introducing web technologies and jargon before taking a look at Django. Our introduction to Django focuses on what Django is and appropriate ways to use it. We then outline the project we'll build, scoping out the content for not only Part I but also Parts II and III. This overview gives us the opportunity to use Django to generate a basic project that we'll use throughout the book.

### Warning!

This book assumes knowledge of Python (but not web technologies)! While the appendix supplies a very short review of Python, this book will not teach you to code in Python.

> **Info**
>
> This book is heavily tied to a git repository, which contains all of the project code and much of the example code found in this book:
>
> https://github.com/jambonrose/DjangoUnleashed-1.8/
>
> If you are reading the digital version of this book, the file paths and commit hashes in the project examples of this book are actually links that will take you directly to relevant commit on Github.
>
> If you are reading a physical copy of this book, I have provided the `dju.link` shortlink domain. The link http://dju.link/9937ef66c0 will redirect you to the Github commit diff for the project, just as http://dju.link/9937ef66c0/helloworld/views.py will redirect you to the `views.py` file as it exists in the `9937ef66c0` hash.
>
> Additional content may be found on the book's website:
>
> http://django-unleashed.com/

> **Info**
>
> To get started with this book, you only really need to have Python and Django installed. However, having tools like git, virtualenvwrapper, and pip will make your life significantly easier. For install instructions and the full list of tools helpful for building Django projects, please see Appendix G.

## 1.2  Website Basics

Before talking about how we build websites, it's important to understand what a website is and how it operates.

When we open our browser and enter a URL such as `http://google.com`, our computer uses HTTP (the scheme in the URL) to talk to the computer (or set of computers) found at the `google.com` domain. The goal of this computer is to give us information that we are asking for.

A **website** is a resource stored on a server. A **server** is simply a computer whose job is to provide a resource (a website in this case) or service and *serve* it to you. A website comprises one or more webpages. A **webpage** is a discrete entity that contains data. The core functionality of a website is to send these webpages to people who ask for them. To do this, we use a protocol (a means of communication) called Hyper Text Transfer Protocol (HTTP). Formally, a user's browser sends an **HTTP request** to a website. The website then sends an **HTTP response** containing a webpage. The process is illustrated in Figure 1.1.

Each webpage is uniquely identifiable, usually by using a Uniform Resource Locator (URL). A URL is a string with specific information, split according to the following (specified in RFC 3986):[1] `scheme://network_location/path?query#fragments`. For example, Figure 1.2 shows the breakdown for a real URL.

The network location, or authority, is typically either an IP address (such as `127.0.0.1`) or a domain name, as shown in Figure 1.2. The scheme tells the browser not only what to

---

1. https://dju.link/rfc3986

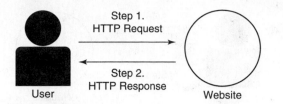

**Figure 1.1:** HTTP Request/Response Cycle Diagram

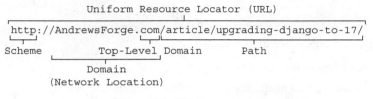

**Figure 1.2:** URL Components

get but how to get it. The URL `https://google.com/` tells the browser to use the HTTPS protocol (Secure HTTP) to go to the Google website and ask for the webpage found at / (the last slash on the URL is the path; if omitted, the slash is added implicitly).

In Part I, we only need to use scheme, network location, and path portions of our URLs. In Chapter 14: Pagination: A Tool for Navigation, we'll see how to make use of the query with Django. We won't make use of fragments, as they're typically used directly in HTML as anchors (links) internal to a single webpage.

The request/response loop of the HTTP protocol and the URL are the basis of *every* website. Originally, it was the only part of the website. Today, websites are more full-featured and more complex.

## 1.3   Understanding Modern Websites

HTTP is a stateless protocol: it doesn't know who you are or where you've been. It knows only what you've just asked it for. In the early days of the Internet, each webpage on a site was a file, such as a text file or a PDF. Websites were **static**.

Today, many websites are **dynamic**. We now interact with websites: instead of just asking the server to send us a file, we write comments on videos, blog about the best web framework ever, and tweet cat pictures to our friends. To enable these activities, webpages must be generated (computed) for each user based on new and changing data. We've had to add a number of technologies on top of HTTP to determine state (such as sessions, which we'll see in Chapter 19: Basic Authentication), and we now have entire languages and systems (like Django!) to make the dynamic generation of webpages as easy as possible. Our original HTTP loop now has an extra step between the request and response, as shown in Figure 1.3.

This dynamic generation of webpages is referred to as **back-end** programming, as opposed to **front-end** programming. Front-end programming involves creating the

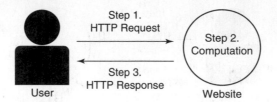

**Figure 1.3:** HTTP Request/Response Cycle Diagram

behavior of the webpage once it has already been generated by the back end. We can think of the combined experience in four steps:

1. A user's browser issues a request for a page.

2. The server (or back end) generates a markup file (typically HTML) based on recorded information and information provided by the user; this file in turn points the user to download associated content such as JavaScript, which defines behavior, and Cascading Style Sheets (CSS), which define style such as color and fonts. The entire set of items defines the webpage.

3. The server responds to the user's browser with this markup file (typically causing the browser to then ask for the other content such as CSS and JavaScript).

4. The user's browser uses the information to display the webpage. The combination of HTML (content and structure), CSS (style), and JavaScript (behavior) provides the front-end part of the website.

While front-end programming certainly provides for a dynamic experience, the words *dynamic webpage* typically refer to a webpage that is computed on the back end. It can be difficult to distinguish the difference between front-end and back-end programming because modern websites strive to blur the difference to create a more seamless user experience. In particular, websites known as **single-page applications** blur this line to the point that step 2 is seriously mangled. However, the distinction is still important, as the HTTP protocol remains between the user and the server and the tools for front-end and back-end programming are typically quite different.

Furthermore, this book does not cover front-end programming. We will see how to serve static content such as CSS and JavaScript in Chapter 16: Serving Static Content with Django, but we will not write a single line of either. This book is dedicated entirely to back-end programming and generating dynamic webpages with Django.

## 1.4   Building Modern Websites: The Problems That Frameworks Solve and Their Caveats

Very few people program dynamic websites from scratch anymore (i.e., without relying on other people's code). It is a difficult, tedious process, and it is typically not a good use of time. Instead, most developers rely on frameworks.

A framework is a large codebase, or collection of code, meant to provide universal, reusable behavior for a targeted project. For example, a mobile framework, such as those provided by Apple and Google for their mobile phones or smartphones, provides key functionality for building mobile apps. Consider the many touch actions on the iPhone: a user can tap his or her screen or hold, slide, turn with two fingers, and more. Developers do not need to worry about figuring out what touch action the user has performed: Apple's framework handles that task for developers.

Using frameworks offers enormous advantages. The most obvious is the removal of tedious and repetitive tasks: if iPhone apps require specific behavior, then the framework will provide it. This saves time for developers not only because of the provided functionality, which allows developers to avoid coding entirely, but also because the code provided is tested by many other developers on a wide variety of projects. This widespread testing is particularly important when it comes to security—a group of developers working on a framework are more likely to get sensitive components right than is any single developer.

Frameworks are different from other external codebases, such as libraries, because they feature **inversion of control**. Understanding inversion of control is key to properly using frameworks. Without a framework, the developer controls the flow of a program: he or she creates behavior or pulls behavior into the code project by calling functions from a library or toolkit. By contrast, when using a framework, the developer adds or extends code in specific locations to customize the framework to the program's requirements. The framework, which is essentially the base of the program, then calls those functions implemented by the developer. In this way, the framework, not the developer, dictates control flow. This is sometimes referred to as the Hollywood principle: "Don't call us, we'll call you." We can easily demonstrate the difference in pseudocode (Example 1.1).

**Example 1.1: Python Code**

```
# Using a Library
def my_function(*args):
    ...
    library.library_function(*args)
    ...


# Using a framework
def my_function(*args):
    ...


framework.run(my_function)
```

Inversion of control may seem counterintuitive or even impossible. How may the robot choose its behavior? Remember: the framework is built by other developers, and they are the ones who specify the behavior followed by the framework. As a developer using a framework, you are simply adding to or directing the behavior provided by other developers.

Using a framework has a few caveats. A framework may offer significant time savings, reusability, and security and may encourage a more maintainable and accessible codebase, but only if the developer is knowledgeable about the framework. A developer cannot fill in all the gaps (by adding or extending code) expected by the framework until he or she understands where all the gaps are. Learning a framework can be tricky: because a framework is an interdependent system, using a part of the framework may require understanding another part of the system (we'll see this in Chapter 6: Integrating Models, Templates, Views and URL Configurations to Create Links between Webpages), which requires knowledge and tools from the three chapters preceding it. For this reason, using a framework requires investing significant overhead in learning the framework. In fact, it will take all of Part I of this book to explain the core inner workings of Django and to gain a holistic understanding of the framework. But once there, we'll be off to the races.

Despite this overhead, it is in your interest to use a framework and to spend the time to learn how to use it properly. Colloquially, developers are told, "Don't fight the framework."

## 1.5   Django: Python Web Framework

As outlined in Section 1.3, a website must always

1. Receive an HTTP request (the user asks for a webpage)
2. Process the request
3. Return the requested information as an HTTP response (the user sees the webpage)

Django is a free and open-source Python back-end web framework that removes the tedium of building websites by providing most of the required behavior. Django handles the majority of the HTTP request and response cycle (the rest is handled by the server Django runs on top of). Developers need only focus on processing the HTTP request, and Django provides tools to make even that easy.

All Django projects are organized in the same way, largely because of the framework's inversion of control but also because it makes navigating existing Django projects much easier for developers who, for instance, maintain the code or step into a job mid-project.

Django's project structure is most often described according to the Model-View-Controller (MVC) architecture because it makes the framework easier to learn. Originally, MVC was a very specific architecture, but it has become an umbrella term for libraries that are patterned after the following idea (illustrated in Figure 1.4):

- The Model controls the organization and storage of data and may also define data-specific behavior.
- The View controls how data is displayed and generates the output to be presented to the user.
- The Controller is the glue (or middleman) between the Model and View (and the User); the Controller will always determine what the user wants and return data to the user, but it may also optionally select the data to display from the Model or use the View to format the data.

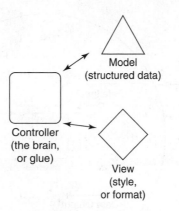

**Figure 1.4:** MVC Architecture Diagram

Most often, literature will state that different pieces of Django map to different pieces of MVC. Specifically,

- Django models are an implementation of MVC Models (Chapter 3: Programming Django Models and Creating a SQLite Database).
- Django templates map to MVC Views (Chapter 4: Rapidly Producing Flexible HTML with Django Templates).
- Django views and URL configuration are the two pieces that act as the MVC Controller (Chapter 5: Creating Webpages with Controllers in Django).

## Warning!

Django and MVC use the word *view* to mean different things.

- The View portion of MVC determines how data is displayed.
- In Django, a view refers to something that builds a webpage and is part of the implementation of MVC Controllers.

Django views and MVC Views are unrelated. Do not confuse them.

The truth is a little bit more complicated. Django projects aren't truly MVC, especially if we abide by the original definition. We will discuss this topic in much more depth in Chapter 12: The Big Picture, once we have a better grasp of all of the moving pieces. For the moment, because it can help beginners organize the framework, we continue to use the (more modern and vague version of) MVC architecture to make sense of the framework.

If we combine our diagrams of the HTTP request/response loop and MVC architecture as in Figure 1.5, we get a much better picture of how Django works.

The Controller, the subject of Chapter 5, represents the heart of Django and is the only part of the MVC architecture that is necessary to generate a webpage. However, most

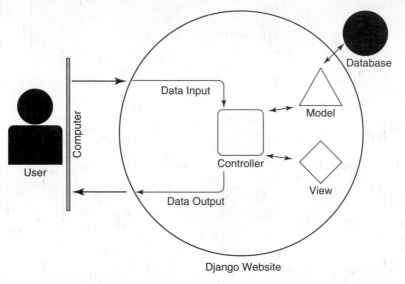

**Figure 1.5:** Application of MVC Architecture Diagram

browsers expect data to be returned by the server in specific formats, such as XML, HTML, or HTML5. The View encapsulates the tools Django supplies for easily outputting such data and is the subject of Chapter 4. Finally, we typically need to use persistent data when generating content in the Controller. The Model section represents the tools for structuring and storing data and is the subject of Chapter 3.

> **Info**
>
> You may have noticed that the popular format JSON is missing from the list of formats that the View section of Django outputs (XML, HTML, HTML5). Django doesn't need to supply a tool for outputting JSON because Python, which Django is built in, provides a JSON serializer.

You'll note that the Model section is connected to a database. The Model itself does not store data but instead provides tools for communicating with databases. We discuss the merits of databases in more depth in Chapter 3. For the moment, just note that Django provides the tools to communicate with several different databases, including SQLite, MySQL, PostgreSQL, and Oracle, which is yet another huge time-saver for us.

Django provides many more tools to make building websites easy. For instance, database schema migrations (Chapter 3 and Chapter 10: Revisiting Migrations), which help with managing models, and an authentication system (Chapter 19 and Chapter 22: Overriding Django's Authentication with a Custom User) are built in. What's more, Django is Python code, allowing developers to use any standard or third-party Python library. Python libraries afford developers an enormous amount of power and flexibility.

Django prides itself on being the "web framework for perfectionists with deadlines." Django provides the functionality needed for every website. The framework also comes with tools to make common website features easy to implement. This "batteries included" approach is why tens of thousands of developers use Django. Released into the wild in 2005, Django powers many websites, including Instagram, Pinterest, Disqus, and even *The Onion*. The core team of Django developers rigorously and regularly test Django, making it both fast and safe.

Django follows the Don't Repeat Yourself (DRY) principle. You will never need to repeat your code if you don't want to (of course, Django won't stop you if you do). Additionally, Django adheres to the Python philosophy that explicit is better than implicit. Django will never assume what you want and will never hide anything from you. If there is a problem, Django will tell you.

As mentioned in Section 1.3, despite all of the things Django will do for you, it will not build or help build front-end behavior for you (this is the purview of JavaScript apps and the browser). Django is a back-end framework, only one half of the equation for building a modern website. It allows you to dynamically create HTML for the front end (Chapter 4) and to intelligently provide the content necessary for a modern front end (Chapter 16), but it does not provide the tools to build dynamic browser behavior for the user. However, before you toss this book in a corner and walk away from Django forever, note that *a back end is necessary before a front end can exist*. A back end may be only half of the equation, but it is the first half: without the request/response loop, there is no website.

## 1.6  Defining the Project in Part I

The purpose of *Django Unleashed* is to teach Django by example. The goal of Part I of this book is to teach you the core fundamentals of Django, the parts of the system required by every website, and how MVC (mostly) applies to that system. To accomplish these tasks, we begin building a website that is self-contained to Django: we purposefully avoid any external libraries built for Django in order to better focus on the framework itself. At each step of the building process, you are introduced to a new Django feature, providing insight into the framework. By the end of Part I, these insights will allow you to see exactly how Django operates and adheres to MVC. Note that the book builds on this project all the way through Part III. Even then, the goal is not to build a production-quality website but rather to teach you via example. We nonetheless discuss how to begin and build a production website in Chapter 30.

### 1.6.1  Selecting Django and Python Versions

Django 1.8 is the latest and greatest Django version and is what every new project should use. Although this book includes informative notes about older versions, please do not use deprecated versions for new projects because these versions do not receive security updates.

Django 1.8 supports Python 2.7 and Python 3.2+ (Python 3.2, Python 3.3, and Python 3.4). When starting a new project, developers are left with the choice of which Python version to use for their project. The choice, unfortunately, is not as simple as picking the latest version.

Python 3 is the future, as Python 2.7 is officially the last Python 2 version. For a website to work for as long as possible, it becomes desirable to create Django websites in Python 3. However, Python 2 is still commonly used, as Django has only officially supported Python 3 since version 1.6, released in November 2013. What's more, enterprise Linux systems still ship with Python 2 as the default, and tools and libraries built for Django may still require Python 2 (as our site in Parts I, II, III is self-contained to Django, we do not need to worry about this decision yet, but we return to the issue in Chapter 30).

When creating reusable tools for a Django project, the gold standard is thus to write code that works in both Python 3 and Python 2. The easiest way to do this is to write code intended for Python 3 and then make it backward compatible with Python 2.7.

Our project is a simple website not aimed at being reused. In light of this and the many guides written about writing Python code that runs in both 2 and 3, our project will be built to run only in Python 3. Specifically, we use Python 3.4 (there is no technological reason to choose 3.2 or 3.3 over 3.4). This will further allow us to focus on Django itself and not get distracted by compatibility issues.

## 1.6.2   Project Specifications

Website tutorials have gone through phases. Tutorials started by teaching developers how to build blogs. Some disparaged these yet-another-blog tutorials as being passé. Writers switched first to building forums, then polls, and finally to-do lists.

In the real world, if you needed any of these applications, you would download an existing project such as WordPress or sign up for a service such as Medium. Rather than weeks of development, you would have a website by the end of an afternoon. It might not be as you envisioned your perfect site, but it would be good enough.

One of Django's major strengths is its precision. Django allows for the rapid creation of unusual websites that work exactly as the developer desires. It is in your interest for this book to build a website that is not available on the Internet already. The difficulty with building an unusual website is that the material tends to be less accessible.

Given the approachable nature of a blog, we will build a blog with special features. A blog is a list of articles, or **blog posts**, published on a single site and organized by date. Blog authors may choose to write about anything in each post, but they usually stick to a general theme throughout the entire blog. Our blog focuses on news relating to technology startup businesses. The goal is to help publicize startups to blog readers.

The problem with most blogs is that their topics are not well organized. Blogging platforms typically label blog posts with tags, leading writers to create tags for each item they blog about. A blog about startups would likely have a tag for each startup written about. We use Django to improve our blog's topic organization.

In our website, we expand blog functionality by codifying the creation of startups. Each startup will be its own object, not a tag. The advantage of making startups their own objects is that it allows us to add special information about them. We can now display information related to the business. We can list a description and a date, and we can even link to external articles written about the startup. These capabilities would not be possible if the startup were simply a tag.

Furthermore, we may organize startups with the same tags we use to label the blog posts. For example, we may label Startup A with the Mobile and Video Games tags. We could then tag Startup B with Mobile and Enterprise. These categories make organizing data simple but flexible. If we browse to the Mobile tag, the website uses that tag to list both Startup A and Startup B as well as any blog posts with the tag. For our website, we also enable blog posts to be directly connected to startup objects. Blog posts will thus exist for news about the site itself or to announce news about startups in our system. Our website makes startups far more discoverable than a regular blog website would.

In Part I, we focus on the most basic features. We create the blog, startup, and tagging system in Django. The goal is to make Django's core, features necessary to every website, as evident as possible.

In Part II, we allow authenticated users to log in. The public will be able to read any of the content of the website. Authenticated users will be able to submit articles, startups, and tags. These content suggestions will be reviewable by you, the site administrator.

In Part III, we allow for tag inheritance. If we write a blog post about Startup A, the tags labeling the startup will now also label the blog post.

It benefits us to list the webpages we will build in Part I:

1.  A page to list tags
2.  A page to list startups
3.  A page to list blog posts
4.  A page for each tag
5.  A page for each startup
6.  A page for each blog post (which also lists news articles)
7.  A page to add a new tag
8.  A page to add a new startup
9.  A page to add a new blog post
10. A page to add and connect news articles to blog posts

# 1.7  Creating a New Django Project and Django Apps

In the following section, we create a new Django project in preparation for the website laid out in the last section. We then create Django apps, which are like small libraries within our project (we go over them in detail when we create them). By the end, we will be ready to start coding our website.

We do not cover how to install Django here. The official website has an excellent and updated guide[2] to do this. Just in case, however, I have supplied my own writing on the subject in Appendix G.

---

2. https://dju.link/18/install

## 1.7.1   Generating the Project Structure

Inversion of control means that Django already provides most of the code required to run a website. Developers are expected to supplement or extend the existing code so that the framework may then call this code; by placing code in key places, developers instruct the framework how to behave according to the developers' desires. Think of it as creating a building: even though many of the tools and contractors are supplied, the developer must still give these contractors orders, and the process requires a very specific scaffolding. Originally, building the scaffolding was a real pain, as developers had to manually account for framework conventions. Luckily, modern frameworks supply tools that generate the correct scaffolding for us. Once this scaffolding is in place, we can instruct the various contractors to behave in specific ways.

With Django correctly installed (please see Appendix G), developers have access to the `django-admin` command-line tool. This command, an alias to the `django-admin.py` script, provides subcommands to automate Django behavior.

### Ghosts of Django Past

If you are using a version of Django prior to 1.7, then the alias `django-admin` will be unavailable. You will instead have to invoke the actual script, `django-admin.py`.

Our immediate interest with `django-admin` is the `startproject` subcommand, which automatically generates correct project scaffolding with many, but not all, of the expected Django conventions. To create a project named **suorganizer** (start **up organizer**), you can invoke the command shown in Example 1.2.

**Example 1.2: Shell Code**

```
$ django-admin startproject suorganizer
```

Inside the new folder by the name of our new project, you will find the folder structure shown in Example 1.3.

**Example 1.3: Shell Code**

```
$ tree .            # in .../suorganizer
.
├── manage.py
└── suorganizer
    ├── __init__.pyr
    ├── settings.py
    ├── urls.py
    └── wsgi.py

1 directory, 5 files
```

Please note the existence of two directories titled suorganizer. To avoid confusion between the two directories, I distinguish the top one as root, or /, throughout the rest of the book. As such, instead of writing suorganizer/manage.py, I will refer to that file by writing /manage.py. Importantly, this means /suorganizer/settings.py refers to suorganizer/suorganizer/settings.py. What's more, all commands executed from the command line will henceforth be run from the root project directory, shown in Example 1.4.

**Example 1.4: Shell Code**

```
$ ls
manage.py     suorganizer
```

Let's take a look at what each file or directory does.

- / houses the entire Django project.
- /manage.py is a script much like django-admin.py: it provides utility functions. We will use it in a moment. Note that it is possible to extend manage.py to perform customized tasks, as we will see in Part II.
- /suorganizer/ contains project-wide settings and configuration files.
- /suorganizer/__init__.py is a Python convention: it tells Python to treat the contents of this directory (/suorganizer/) as a package.
- /suorganizer/settings.py contains all of your site settings, including but not limited to
  - timezone
  - database configuration
  - key for cryptographic hashing
  - locations of various files (templates, media, static files, etc)
- /suorganizer/urls.py contains a list of valid URLs for the site, which tells your site how to handle each one. We will see these in detail in Chapter 5.
- /suorganizer/wsgi.py stands for Web Server Gateway Interface and contains Django's development server, which we see next.

## 1.7.2 Checking Our Installation by Invoking Django's runserver via manage.py

While Django has only created a skeleton project, it has created a *working* skeleton project, which we can view using Django's testing server (the one referenced in /suorganizer/wsgi.py). Django's /manage.py script, provided to every project, allows us to quickly get up to speed.

Django requires a database before it can run. We can create a database with the (somewhat cryptic) command `migrate` (Example 1.5).

**Example 1.5: Shell Code**

```
$ ./manage.py migrate
```

You should be greeted with the output (or similar output) shown in Example 1.6.

**Example 1.6: Shell Code**

```
Operations to perform:
  Synchronize unmigrated apps: staticfiles, messages
  Apply all migrations: contenttypes, auth, admin, sessions
Synchronizing apps without migrations:
  Creating tables...
    Running deferred SQL...
  Installing custom SQL...
Running migrations:
  Rendering model states... DONE
  Applying contenttypes.0001_initial... OK
  Applying auth.0001_initial... OK
  Applying admin.0001_initial... OK
  Applying contenttypes.0002_remove_content_type_name... OK
  Applying auth.0002_alter_permission_name_max_length... OK
  Applying auth.0003_alter_user_email_max_length... OK
  Applying auth.0004_alter_user_username_opts... OK
  Applying auth.0005_alter_user_last_login_null... OK
  Applying auth.0006_require_contenttypes_0002... OK
  Applying sessions.0001_initial... OK
```

We'll see exactly what's going on here starting in Chapter 3 and in detail in Chapter 10. For the moment, let's just get the server running by invoking the `runserver` command shown in Example 1.7.

**Example 1.7: Shell Code**

```
$ ./manage.py runserver
Performing system checks...

System check identified no issues (0 silenced).
May 2, 2015 - 16:15:59
Django version 1.8.1, using settings 'suorganizer.settings'
Starting development server at http://127.0.0.1:8000/
Quit the server with CONTROL-C.
```

## Ghosts of Django Past

In versions prior to Django 1.7, the command above will not work, as `manage.py` does not have execute permissions. Run `chmod +x manage.py` to give `manage.py` the needed permission, or else execute it by invoking it through Python. For example: `python manage.py runserver`

If you navigate your browser to `http://127.0.0.1:8000/`, you should be greeted with the screen printed in Figure 1.6.

Django is running a test server on our new project. As the project has nothing in it, Django informs us we need to create an app using `/manage.py`.

To quit the server, type `Control-C` in the terminal.

### 1.7.3 Creating New Django Apps with `manage.py`

In Django nomenclature, a project is made of any number of apps. More expressly, a project is a website, while an app is a feature, a piece of website functionality. An app may be a blog, comments, or even just a contact form. All of these are encapsulated by a project, however, which is the site in its totality. An app may also be thought of as a library within the project. From Python's perspective, an app is simply a package (Python files can be modules, and a directory of modules is a package).

We have two features in our site: (1) a structured organization of startups according to tags and (2) a blog. We will create an app for each feature.

As with a project, Django supplies a way to easily create the scaffolding necessary to build an app. This time, we invoke `/manage.py` to do the work for us, although we could just as easily have used `django-admin`. Let's start with the central focus of our site, our startup organizer, and create an app called **organizer**, as shown in Example 1.8.

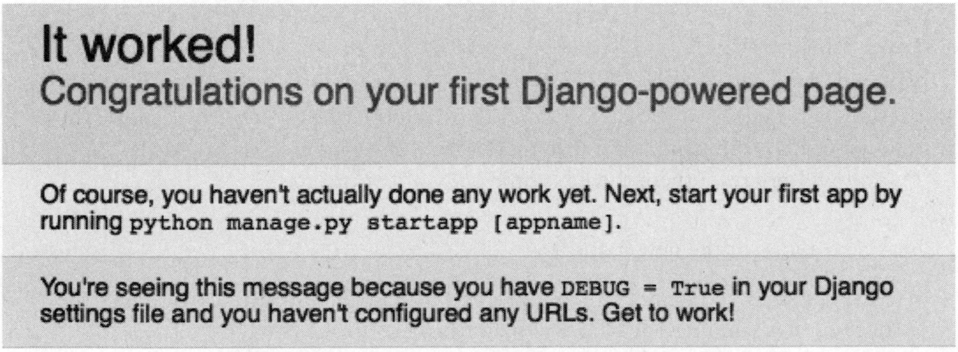

## It worked!
## Congratulations on your first Django-powered page.

Of course, you haven't actually done any work yet. Next, start your first app by running `python manage.py startapp [appname]`.

You're seeing this message because you have `DEBUG = True` in your Django settings file and you haven't configured any URLs. Get to work!

**Figure 1.6:** Runserver Congratulations Screenshot

**Example 1.8: Shell Code**

```
$ ./manage.py startapp organizer
```

The directory structure of the project should now be as shown in Example 1.9.

**Example 1.9: Shell Code**

```
$ tree .
.
├── manage.py
├── organizer
│   ├── __init__.py
│   ├── admin.py
│   ├── migrations
│   │   └── __init__.py
│   ├── models.py
│   ├── tests.py
│   └── views.py
└── suorganizer
    ├── __init__.py
    ├── settings.py
    ├── urls.py
    └── wsgi.py

3 directories, 11 files
```

## Ghosts of Django Past

Prior to version 1.7, Django did not supply a migration system, and thus the `migrations` directory in projects older than that version will not appear, or will actually belong to a tool called South. Be careful about this when using projects built in early Django versions!

## Info

You will likely also find files ending in `.pyc`. These are compiled Python files and can be safely ignored. However, if you find them as distracting as I do, you can use the following shell command to remove them: `find . -name '*.pyc'-delete`. Python will re-create them the next time your run your site.

Let's take a look at the new items.

- `/organizer/` contains all the files related to our new **organizer** app. Any file necessary to running our blog will be in this directory.

- `/organizer/__init__.py` is a Python convention: just as for `/suorganizer/__init__.py`, this file tells Python to treat the contents of this directory (`/organizer/`) as a package.

- `/organizer/admin.py` contains the configuration necessary to connect our app to the Admin library supplied by Django. While Admin is a major Django feature, it is not part of Django's core functionality, and we will wait until Part II to examine it, along with the rest of the Django Contributed Library (apps included with Django's default install). If you are very impatient, you should be able to jump to Chapter 23: The Admin Library as soon as you've finished reading Chapter 5.

- `/organizer/migrations/` is a directory that contains data pertaining to the database tables for our app. It enables Django to keep track of any structural changes the developer makes to the database as the project changes, allowing for multiple developers to easily change the database in unison. We will see basic use of this database table in Chapter 3 and revisit the topic in Chapter 10.
- `/organizer/migrations/__init__.py` marks the `migration` directory as a Python package.
- `/organizer/models.py` tells Django how to organize data for this app. We do see how this is done in the next chapter.
- `/organizer/tests.py` contains functions to unit test our app. Testing is a book unto itself (written by Harry Percival), and we do not cover that material.
- `/organizer/views.py` contains all of the functions that Django will use to process data and to select data for display. We make use of views starting in Chapter 2 but won't fully understand them until Chapter 5.

Django encapsulates data and behavior by app. The files above are where Django will look for data structure, website behavior, and even testing. This may not make sense yet, but it means that when building a site with Django, it is important to consider how behavior is organized across apps. Planning how your apps interact and which apps you need, as we did earlier in this chapter, is a crucial step to building a Django site.

We can create our **blog** app in exactly the same way as the **organizer** app, as shown in Example 1.10.

**Example 1.10: Shell Code**

```
$ ./manage.py startapp blog
```

Note that the directory structure and all the files generated are exactly the same as for our **organizer** app.

## 1.7.4 Connecting Our New Django Apps to Our Django Project in `settings.py`

Consider for a moment the difference between `/organizer/` (or `/blog/`) and `/suorganizer/`. Both encapsulate data, the former for our **organizer** (or **blog**) app and the second for our project-wide settings, a phrase that should mean more now that we know the difference between an app and a project (reminder: a project is made up of one or more apps).

We must now connect our new apps to our project; we must inform our project of the existence of **organizer** and **blog**. On line 33 of `/suorganizer/settings.py`, you will find a list of items titled `INSTALLED_APPS`. Currently enabled in our project are a list of

Django contributed apps (you can tell because these items all start with `django.contrib`), some of which we examine in Part II. We append the list with our new apps, as shown in Example 1.11.

**Example 1.11:** Project Code
`suorganizer/settings.py` in `ba014edf45`

```
33    INSTALLED_APPS = (
34        'django.contrib.admin',
35        'django.contrib.auth',
36        'django.contrib.contenttypes',
37        'django.contrib.sessions',
38        'django.contrib.messages',
39        'django.contrib.staticfiles',
40        'organizer',
41        'blog',
42    )
```

**Info**

While the order of `INSTALLED_APPS` typically does not matter, there are instances in which apps listed prior to others will be given precedence. We see an instance of this in Chapter 24.

Let's run our test server again (Example 1.12).

**Example 1.12:** Shell Code

```
$ ./manage.py runserver 7777
Performing system checks...

System check identified no issues (0 silenced).
February 10, 2015 - 19:09:25
Django version 1.8.3, using settings 'suorganizer.settings'
Starting development server at http://127.0.0.1:7777/
Quit the server with CONTROL-C.
```

**Info**

Note that this time, I've run the server with an extra parameter that specifies which port I want to run on. Instead of the default port `8000`, the server may now be accessed on port `7777` via URL `http://127.0.0.1:7777/`. By convention, `http://127.0.0.1` will always point to your own computer. Any port may be specified, but a port number below `1024` may require superuser privileges (which are typically attained via `sudo`). The ability to specify a port is useful when the `8000` port is already taken. For instance, you may be testing another Django website at the same time or have another program that defaults to `8000`. To make the server publicly available on port 80 (the standard port for HTTP; a very dangerous thing to do), you could use the command `sudo ./manage.py runserver 0.0.0.0:80`.

Navigating to the page in your browser, you should be greeted by exactly the same page in your browser, telling you once again to

1. Create a new App
2. Configure our site URLs

We have successfully done item 1 and will demonstrate item 2 in our Hello World example in the next chapter.

We will return to our main project in Chapter 3, where we organize our data and create a database. In Chapter 4, we create templates to display data. In Chapter 5, we build our URL configuration (expanding on item 2 above) and the rest of the MVC Controller. These activities will effectively reveal how Model-View-Controller theory maps to Django.

# 1.8   Putting It All Together

The chapter outlined the project to be built in Parts I, II, and III of the book and introduced Django.

Django is a Python web framework based on MVC architecture, which signifies that Django removes the tedium of building websites by supplying a universal, reusable codebase. This approach saves developers time in the long run but creates an overhead cost of having to learn the interdependent system. Like any framework, Django works on the principle of inversion of control, sometimes called the Hollywood principle ("Don't call us, we'll call you"), which explains why we write code in locations dictated by Django convention. Specifically, in keeping with MVC architecture, we know that we need only worry about the Models, Views, and Controllers and that Django will glue them together and handle everything else.

In this chapter, we used `django-admin` to generate the project scaffolding necessary for Django. This scaffolding allows us to add code in specific locations, according to inversion of control.

We not only generated a Django project but also created the apps necessary for any project: a project is a website, whereas an app is a feature, a piece of website functionality. The site we've set out to build is a startup categorization system paired with a blog. Given the two features, we created two apps using Django's `manage.py` tool. We then used this tool to run a test server, checking our work. The test server informed us that, now that we have our apps created and connected to our project via `settings.py`, we should configure our site URLs. We take a quick look at this in the next chapter, but we wait until Chapter 5 before we really get there.

This book seeks to teach Django by example. Part I teaches Django's core, or the pieces of the framework that are typically required for every project. Django organizes project data according to MVC theory. Chapters 3, 4, and 5 each demonstrate a core Django feature, each an aspect of MVC. In Chapter 3, we organize our data and create a database.

In Chapter 4, we create the display output for our data. In Chapter 5, we connect our data to our display, creating webpages by programming Django views, pointed to by URL configurations.

Before we jump into MVC, however, Chapter 2: Hello World: Building a Basic Webpage in Django illustrates a basic Django site, which sheds light on the power of MVC.

# 2

# Hello World: Building a Basic Webpage in Django

## In This Chapter

- Create an app (again)
- Build a webpage that displays "Hello World"
- Take a peek at Django views and URL configurations, which make up the Controller
- Remove an app

## 2.1 Introduction

The goal, when using the web framework, is to add code to the Model, View, and Controller sections to give life to the website you wish to build. I stated in Chapter 1 that every developer would need all three of these tools to build a functional website. However, a close look at Figure 2.1 shows that it is possible to build a website using only the Controller portion of Django.

In this chapter, we build a single webpage in Django using only the Controller (Chapter 5: Creating Webpages with Controllers in Django) to demonstrate that the diagram is technically correct. However, in doing so, we will see that the Model (Chapter 3: Programming Django Models and Creating a SQLite Database) and View (Chapter 4: Rapidly Producing Flexible HTML with Django Templates) portions of Django are crucial when building a full-features website, but we do not use them here.

Hello World, the traditional programming example, is typically quite short and simple in a programming language. Django is a framework, and building a webpage to display "Hello World" is a little more involved than it would be with a programming language. The goal is not to understand every detail but to get a first global view of the framework. It should seem a little magic.

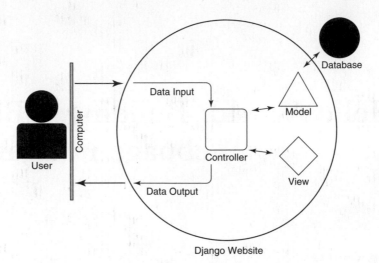

**Figure 2.1:** Application of MVC Architecture Diagram

## 2.2    Creating and Integrating a New App

For the sake of time, we reuse our **suorganizer** project. For the sake of repetition, we create (and then destroy) a new app.

As seen in Chapter 1, interacting with Django via the shell always starts with an invocation to `manage.py`. We start by creating a new app, **helloworld**, using the `startapp` command shown in Example 2.1.

**Example 2.1: Shell Code**

```
$ ./manage.py startapp helloworld
```

The file directory is exactly the same as for **organizer** and **blog**, as discussed in Chapter 1, Section 1.7.3. Just as before, we must now connect or integrate our app to our project. We append the name of our app to a list of installed apps in the project settings file. Open `/suorganizer/settings.py`, find the tuple of installed apps at line 33, and append the name of our **helloworld** app. The resulting code is shown in Example 2.2.

**Example 2.2: Project Code**
`suorganizer/settings.py` in 84b2c91a94

```
33    INSTALLED_APPS = (
34        'django.contrib.admin',
35        'django.contrib.auth',
36        'django.contrib.contenttypes',
37        'django.contrib.sessions',
38        'django.contrib.messages',
```

```
39          'django.contrib.staticfiles',
40          'organizer',
41          'blog',
42          'helloworld',
43      )
```

With our app created and integrated, we can now turn our attention to the Controller.

# 2.3 Building Hello World

In Chapter 1, Section 1.2, we discussed how every website was originally a collection of webpages, each identified by a URL. Each webpage is thus two things: the data that the webpage contains and gives back to the user and the URL that identifies the webpage.

Django uses this construction to its advantage and splits the theoretical Controller into two parts. To build a webpage, we first need to define what data the webpage returns and then define the URL for the webpage.

## 2.3.1 Webpage Data

Webpage data are typically stored in the views.py file of any app. This may seem confusing, given the Model-**View**-Controller architecture. For the moment, remember that Django views and MVC Views are unrelated concepts!

Open the file found at /helloworld/views.py. Erase the contents of the file and replace them with the code shown in Example 2.3.

**Example 2.3: Project Code**
helloworld/views.py **in** 9937ef66c0

```
1   from django.http import HttpResponse
2
3
4   def greeting(request):
5       return HttpResponse('Hello World!')
```

Our webpage is simply a Python function called greeting(). Given our understanding of HTTP request/response, we can already see how Django handles this for us. Django gives our function a request, which we ignore above, and we simply return a response, which Django then sends back to the user. Django terms greeting() a **function view** (a Python function that fulfills the role of a Django view). In Example 2.3, our response is simply Hello World, as you should expect of this chapter.

## 2.3.2 Webpage URL

Now that our webpage has data, we must create a URL for it. In Chapter 5, we see how to create URLs for each app separately. For the moment, however, we simply use the project-wide URL configuration.

To tell Django of the existence of the webpage created by `greeting()`, we must make changes to `/suorganizer/urls.py`. Open the file and import our new function by adding `from helloworld.views import greeting` to the end of the import list, just as you would import any Python function. We then direct Django to our webpage by adding an item to the `urlpatterns` list. The argument we add is `url(r'^$', greeting)`. The contents of the file should now be as shown in Example 2.4.

**Example 2.4: Project Code**
`suorganizer/urls.py` **in** 98a8ef0d11

```
16    from django.conf.urls import include, url
17    from django.contrib import admin
18
19    from helloworld.views import greeting
20
21    urlpatterns = [
22        url(r'^admin/', include(admin.site.urls)),
23        url(r'^$', greeting),
24    ]
```

## Info

If you open `/suorganizer/urls.py` yourself, you will discover that the first 15 lines of the document provide instructions on how to build URLs. We've just used the first of these methods. We'll see the rest in Chapter 5.

Given the two–part nature of a webpage, it should seem natural that the call to `url()` has two arguments. The first is our URL, as a regular expression string, and the second is the webpage itself. For the moment, understand that we are using the regular expression to match nothing, the root of the website. If our website domain is `django-unleashed.com`, then the URL `http://django-unleashed.com/` will display our `greeting()` webpage. Stated differently, if a user requests `http://django-unleashed.com/`, Django will use `urlpatterns`, the URL configuration above, to first find and then run the `greeting()` function, returning its contents to the user as an HTTP response.

## 2.4   Displaying Hello World

With webpage data and URL defined, we can now see the fruits of our labor. In Example 2.5, we again turn to `manage.py` to make our life easy.

**Example 2.5: Shell Code**

```
$ ./manage.py runserver
```

**Warning!**

If you did not run the `migrate` command in Chapter 1, Section 1.7.2, you must do so before you can invoke `runserver`, as shown in Example 2.6.

**Example 2.6: Shell Code**

```
$ ./manage migrate
```

Open your browser and navigate to `http://127.0.0.1:8000/`. Django will greet you with "Hello World." We have successfully created a single webpage using only MVC's Controller.

## 2.5 Controller Limitations: The Advantages of Models and Views

The Controller is very powerful: with only three lines, Django has allowed us to create a basic webpage.

The Controller is, however, also very limited. Consider that our webpage is currently plain text. We are not building an HTML page, as all browsers expect us to. We could manually build out an HTML page, but doing so becomes cumbersome, as we shall discover in the beginning of Chapter 4.

Even more problematic is that we are only building static content right now. If we want to change the content, we have to add or change it manually. Instead, we want the ability to dynamically generate pages. Imagine being able to tell Django to print `"Hello {object}".format(object=a_python_variable)` and to feed it data from the database. Suddenly, if we have five data items in the database, we have five webpages!

Being able to build and communicate with a database thus becomes crucial and will be the focus of Chapter 3. The combination of content in Chapter 3 (Models) and Chapter 4 (Views) will allow us to reexamine and use the Controller to build dynamic webpages in Chapter 5.

## 2.6 Removing Our Helloworld App from Our Project

Before we move on, we should remove our **helloworld** app, as we no longer need it.

Due to Django's clean encapsulation of apps, the removal of an app is very straightforward. We must first delete the URL pattern, remove the app from `settings.py`, and then simply delete the app's directory.

It is important to stress the utility of app encapsulation. Due to an app's nature as a Python package, the organization offered by Django apps is potentially one of Django's more salient features, especially when building a large, complex website. It allows for the rapid and clean addition or removal of apps or features. However, clean app encapsulation is not enforced by Django (it would be impossible to do so) and can be quite difficult to create and maintain. While it is important to strive to create self-contained apps, perfect app encapsulation is not always possible: consider our own site, where the **blog** relies on tag data stored in the **organizer**. This book encapsulates as best as possible but does not focus on the issue or explore how to make an app independent (typically necessary when releasing an app to the world).

In the `/suorganizer/urls.py` file, delete the lines we added. The entire file is printed in Example 2.7 for convenience (we had added an import after line 18 and a line of code after line 20).

**Example 2.7: Project Code**
`suorganizer/urls.py` **in** 7321276c34

```
16   from django.conf.urls import include, url
17   from django.contrib import admin
18
19   urlpatterns = [
20       url(r'^admin/', include(admin.site.urls)),
21   ]
```

Find the `INSTALLED_APPS` tuple on line 33 of `/suorganizer/settings.py` and remove the string referencing our app. The tuple should now read as shown in Example 2.8.

**Example 2.8: Project Code**
`suorganizer/settings.py` **in** a2ec249174

```
33   INSTALLED_APPS = (
34       'django.contrib.admin',
35       'django.contrib.auth',
36       'django.contrib.contenttypes',
37       'django.contrib.sessions',
38       'django.contrib.messages',
39       'django.contrib.staticfiles',
40       'organizer',
41       'blog',
42   )
```

I choose to remove the app files via the command line, as in Example 2.9, but you could easily do it via your operating system's file browser.

**Example 2.9: Shell Code**

```
$ rm -r helloworld/
```

With that done, there are no traces of our **helloworld** app. Again, please take a moment to note that this process was simple only because all of our app files were stored in a single directory, according to clean app encapsulation.

# 2.7 Putting It All Together

It is normal to be a little overwhelmed at this point. The key takeaways here are as follows:

- Everything in this chapter is Python. Django is Python (the exception being Django templates, which are the View portion of MVC and the topic of Chapter 4).

- A webpage is a Python callable called a **view** (of no relation to MVC View). We named our function view `greeting()`.

- The developer directs Django to views via a list of URLs called the **URL configuration**. When a user requests the URL, Django calls the view (which may be a function or any other Python callable) that the URL configuration points to.

- The views and URL configuration comprise the Controller from MVC theory. Chapter 5 is dedicated to this material.

- Inversion of control, inherent to a framework, is evident. We did not code any main loop or program to handle webpages. We only directed Django to our code and let it handle everything for us.

- Django encapsulates and abstracts code and data according to app structure. It is therefore important to consider what an app will be used for.

Chapter 2 is meant as a sneak preview into the heart of Django. It will take us all of Part I to holistically understand Django as a framework. By then you'll be able to return to Chapter 2, and waltz through the content. But until then—hold on tight! The next few chapters are the hard ones, the crucial ones, the content you will use on *every* website you build with Django.

# 3

# Programming Django Models and Creating a SQLite Database

## In This Chapter

- Learn about basic database principles
- Structure the data on our website using Django models and model fields
- Write model methods to create behavior for our data
- Generate a SQLite3 database
- Discover migrations, the better way to keep track of changes to your database structure
- Learn about and use the ORM to interact with the database

## 3.1  Introduction

In Chapter 1: Starting a New Django Project, we specified the design of our Startup Organizer project based on behavior. To be able to implement this behavior, however, we must know what data we need. Typically, the first step to building a website in Django is to define how the data are organized and then to use this work to build the database. Django models are a direct application of Models from MVC (Model-View-Controller) theory: they encapsulate the organization of data and the communication with the database. Django models are the topic of Chapter 3.

> **Info**
> *Model* from Model-View–Controller is capitalized, while *model* in Django's code is not capitalized. The same rule applies to *View* and *view*.

We start by establishing what data we expect to be in the database and then use Django models to specify and organize the data. This allows us to automatically generate a SQLite database. We use Django to communicate with the database, demonstrating how to add, query, and delete content from the database. This last section is instrumental in demonstrating the results of the code we write throughout the chapter.

This chapter assumes basic knowledge of databases and relations. If you feel hazy about primary keys, foreign keys, or many-to-many relationships, please refer to Appendix C: Relational Database Basics. Understanding these concepts is crucial to understanding why Django generates the database the way it does.

## 3.2   Why Use a Database?

Many beginning web developers are unclear as to why websites use a database. More experienced web developers often forget to explain the reason because databases are such a staple of building modern web applications.

A short answer to why we need a database is that the combination of Django's core functionality and a database allows us to avoid hardcoding content because a database provides rapid access to persistent, normalized data.

Like any other computer application, a website is simply a system process. A process is typically quite volatile: should the process or computer terminate unexpectedly, all of the data in memory is lost. In the case of a process like a website, we want the ability to start the process after a crash and still have access to all of the data published by the site (e.g., startups and blog posts) and all of the data provided by users (e.g., usernames and passwords). Being able to store data **persistently**, maintaining state beyond the start and stop of the process, is thus crucial in a website. Stated differently, we split our website into discrete stateful (the data) and stateless (the process) parts.

If our only goals were persistent data and dynamic content, we could simply store all of our data in files on disk. However, this solution would be slow, would make searching difficult, and would become completely unwieldy as the data grow. We could begin to structure the data (**normalize** them), load them into memory at runtime (for rapid access), index them (even more rapid access), and perform writes from memory to the file to maintain state, but at that point we would have effectively reprogrammed a database.

Consequently, to ensure rapid access to consistent, persistent, normalized data, databases have become a staple of modern dynamic websites. What's more, the separation of data from behavior allows for multiple computers to act as a single website, separating state (data and database) from stateless aspects (the code) of the project. This becomes crucial when deploying and scaling a website, as we discuss in Chapter 26: Optimizing Our Site for Speed and Chapter 29: Deploy!.

In Part I, we build our website using SQLite, the simplest of databases available to Django. However, in Chapter 30: Starting a New Project Correctly, we discuss how to start a project while using PostgreSQL, a far more powerful database better suited to websites.

For more on databases and key relations, please read Appendix C: Relational Database Basics.

## 3.3   Organizing Our Data

Before coding the actual models, let's establish what data we need. As outlined in Chapter 1, we want the following behaviors:

- List startup organizations
- Organize startups (by tags or labels)

- Link to external news sources about startups
- Write blog posts about startups

To achieve these behaviors, we need to store information about four entities: startups, tags, news links, and blog posts.

Each of these entities will contain information about itself. For example, a blog post is made up of a title, a date, and text. We can make a list of these attributes in our database:

- Tag
  - tag name
- Startup
  - name of company
  - description or purpose
  - date founded
  - contact email
  - website
- News Link
  - title or headline
  - link to article
  - publication date
- Blog Post
  - post title
  - post text or description
  - publication date

In the context of a database, each entity above is a table and each attribute is a column. The table for Startup might look like Table 3.1.

In the context of a web framework, each entity in the list above is a model, and each attribute belonging to a model is a field. Therefore, the Blog Post model has three fields—title, description, and date—with the implication that models map to database tables and model fields map to database columns. The Startup model stores data in the startup table, and the Startup model description field is the description column in the startup table. When we create or add actual data, we will be creating model instances, which will create rows in the database. In Table 3.1, Jambon Software is a row in the database but a model instance to Django.

**Table 3.1:** Database Table for Startup Data

| PK | Name | Description | Founded | EMail | Website |
|----|------|-------------|---------|-------|---------|
| 1 | Boundless Soft | No task is too perilous... | 2013-01-01 | sl@bou... | boundlesssoft... |
| 2 | Jambon Software | Web and Mobile Consulting | 2013-01-18 | django@... | jambonsw.com |

If we were outlining these data with the intent of manually building a database, we would need to supply more information before the database would work properly. We would first need to add a primary key to each table (shown as leftmost column in Table 3.1), then add relations between the tables, and finally create indexes to ensure speed.

Relations in databases are based on primary keys and foreign keys. A primary key is an identifier for a row in the database table. A foreign key is the primary key of another row in the database. One-to-many relationships are expressed by the creation of foreign keys in a column of a table. Many-to-many relationships are expressed with a separate two-column table, where each column contains foreign keys. Primary keys are thus a necessity in any relational database.

Luckily, Django abstracts and removes a lot of the work for us by automatically adding an indexed primary key to each model, which we can access as the pk field. A new developer might expect to use the pk field to build relationships, as he or she would use it to manually build a database. But again, Django abstracts and eases the process by providing fields for each relation, all while automatically indexing columns containing keys. Therefore, *we need only concern ourselves with the abstract relations between our models rather than adding entire tables to our list*, again simplifying our work.

The easiest relationship is that of news links and startups. A news link may belong to only one startup, but a startup may have multiple news links, meaning we seek to create a one-to-many relationship. A news link points at a startup: a news link has a foreign key to a startup.

Each startup will have multiple tags, and each tag may belong to multiple startups. This is a many-to-many relationship. Similarly, each blog post will be associated with tags via a many-to-many relationship.

Finally, we want to be able to write blog posts about startups. Each blog post may be about multiple startups, and each startup may be written about multiple times, another many-to-many relationship.

In conclusion, we must add the following relationships to our models:

- A one-to-many relationship pointing news links to startups
- A many-to-many relationship between startups and tags
- A many-to-many relationship between blog posts and tags
- A many-to-many relationship between blog posts and startups

## 3.3.1  Accessing Data: Understanding Django's Slug

When organizing data for a website, a developer should always ask how the data will be accessed and, more specifically, how the user will request these data.

A website is accessed with a URL, or Uniform Resource Locator, which identifies data held by the website. For URLs to work correctly, the resources that they identify must be **uniquely identifiable**. To find a resource, we must have an unambiguous method by which to refer to it. If we do not, then it becomes possible to request a URL and to end up with two or more potential resources. Can you imagine asking Amazon for a page about a movie and half of the time receiving a page about a different movie of the same name?

Websites would become unusable. Unique identification of that data is necessary for clear access to website data via a URL.

Suppose we have a startup with the name "Boundless Software LLC" and the primary key of 1. Given our outline in Section 3.3, this startup will be a model instance in Django and a row in our startup database table. We need to provide a unique URL for users to access the webpage with information about this startup. We could build a URL using the primary key, as it is by definition a unique identifier. Sir Tim Berners-Lee—inventor of the World Wide Web and current director of the World Wide Web Consortium (W3C)—recommends the creation of human-readable and memorable URLs. If we use the primary key, our URL will look like `http://site.django-unleashed.com/startup/1/`, a URL that is not easy to remember and tells us very little about the resource we are requesting. Using the title is a step in the right direction, but because of the way URLs are encoded, our startup would now be accessed via `http://site.django-unleashed.com/startup/Boundless%20Software%20LLC`, which is unhelpful and potentially tricky (consider what happens if the name is capitalized differently). Instead, a URL such as `http://site.django-unleashed.com/startup/boundless-software/` would be more desirable.

In Django, the string `boundless-software` in the URL above is called a **slug**. A slug is a unique string that identifies data. Using a slug allows for the customizable creation of clean and human-friendly URLs. While developers can define a slug however they wish, Django supplies tools to make the process simple, both limiting and enforcing the behavior of a slug. To make the slug string safe to use in URLs, Django makes sure that slug strings contain only alphanumeric characters, dashes, and underscores; a slug may not contain spaces or any other special characters that result in encoding. While not directly enforced by Django, it is considered good practice to make slugs case insensitive to avoid user confusion: asking for `Boundless-Software` and `boundless-software` should result in the same webpage. As such, we store slugs in the database as lowercase strings.

Slugs are typically only part of a URL; they are generally a part of a unique identifier rather than the entire unique identifier. Blog posts, which are effectively news articles, are typically associated with a date. Most blog software uses both the date and the slug as the unique identifier for a post. Using the URL `http://site.django-unleashed.com/blog/2015/4/more-django-info/` as an example, the unique identifier for this blog post is the year (2015), month (April, or 4), and slug (`more-django-info`) of the post. Uniqueness of a slug can be dependent on other pieces of data. For this reason, Django allows developers to explicitly set how the slug interacts with other data and defaults to not making the slug unique at all.

The only cost of using a slug is the addition of a new field in the data model, and the benefit is clarity and ease of use. In anticipation of the creation of clean URLs, we should consider which of our models need to have slug fields. In Chapter 1, we designed the site so that each blog post, startup, and tag has its own webpage, leaving news links to be listed on the startup page with which they are associated. We must now add a slug field to our models for blog posts, startups, and tags. In the case of startups and tags, the slug will act as the unique identifier, while blog posts will use the year and month in addition to the slug.

# 3.4  Specifying and Organizing Data in Django Using Models

We have now completely listed the data we require to build our website. The updated list is as follows:

- Tag
  - tag name
  - slug
- Startup
  - name of company
  - slug
  - description or purpose
  - date founded
  - contact email
  - website
- News Link
  - title or headline
  - link to article
  - publication date
  - foreign key to Startup
- Blog Post
  - post title
  - slug
  - post text or description
  - publication date
- Many-to-Many Relationships
  - startup and tag
  - blog post and tag
  - blog posts and startup

## 3.4.1  A First Look at Django Models and Fields

The goal of this section is to transform the preceding list into code that Django understands. Django will handle communication with the database for us, going so far as to generate a database. It will allow us to abstract database queries and data validation for input. Overall, we will save an enormous amount of time by avoiding writing all of the code necessary for these tasks and simplifying code throughout the project. The trick is to maintain app encapsulation and to put the code in the right place.

Specifying how data is organized in Django is simple and one of Django's most exciting features. Django provides declarative syntax for the purpose of understanding models, based on Python classes. We begin by turning our basic blog post data into a model.

Because we are coding this for the blog, we write the code into the `models.py` file of our **blog** app. We start by creating a `Post` model for our blog post data. To create a model, we can simply create a Python class that inherits from `models.Model`, as shown in Example 3.1. That's it!

**Example 3.1: Project Code**

`blog/models.py` in dfb719fa8c

```
1    from django.db import models
.        . . .
8    class Post(models.Model):
9        pass
```

While this code is quite powerful, we cannot demonstrate any of this power without model fields. Fields are (instances of) the Python classes that validate and contain actual data. The model is just a means for organizing fields together. For our blog post, we want the following fields:

- Post title
- Slug field (for clean, unique URL)
- Post text or description
- Publication date

The code to add fields to our model is quite simple, as you can see in Example 3.2.

**Example 3.2: Project Code**

`blog/models.py` in c21873ba69

```
8    class Post(models.Model):
9        title = models.CharField(max_length=63)
10       slug = models.SlugField()
11       text = models.TextField()
12       pub_date = models.DateField()
```

The power provided by `models.Model` is now much easier to describe. The model and fields behave just like any other Python code: given a `Post` instance p, we can manipulate the title of our blog post via `p.title`. However, unlike vanilla Python code, the superclass affords us a huge amount of functionality, such as communication with the database via an object-relational mapper (ORM), as we shall see shortly. The inheritance also allows us to define our class attributes according to specific field classes. Each field provides behavior: it specifies (1) how the data is stored in the database, (2) which Python type the data will be manipulated in, (3) how to validate the data when submitting it to the website, and (4) how to display the data in certain contexts such as forms, which we will see starting in Chapter 7: Allowing User Input with Forms.

The first data attribute we define is the `title` field. We set it as an instance of a `CharField`. Take note! Both models and model fields are Python classes. These classes allow for both the models and fields to exist in Python and the database. When passing its value to Python, a `Charfield` becomes a string (type `str` in Python 3, type `unicode` in Python 2). When in SQLite, a `CharField` becomes a `varchar`, which is why we must always supply a `max_length` parameter to the class. `CharFields` are not validated: Django does not check or validate what values are given to a `CharField`. Incidentally, a `CharField` is the basis for all other string-based fields.

The second data attribute of the `Post` model class is `slug`, set to an instance of Django's `SlugField`. A `SlugField` is just a `CharField` with validation: Django does check the value passed to the `SlugField`, ensuring that it contains only valid characters. As discussed in the previous section, a slug must include only lowercase alphanumeric characters and dashes, and Django's validator returns an error in the event that the string passed to this field does not meet that requirement.

The third class attribute is a `TextField`. In Python, this field is simply another string, but in the database it is a `text` field, which is more flexible and allows for more text than a `varchar`. Like the `CharField`, it does not have any validation. If you can use a `CharField` instead of a `TextField`, then you should, as it is economical for the database in both speed and space. However, as we do not know how long each blog post text will be, we opt for `TextField` in this case.

The final attribute is the `pub_date` field, which is a `DateField`. Python uses the `datetime.date` class to represent data from this field, and SQLite stores the data as a `date` type. Django validates data passed to `pub_date`, ensuring that only valid dates are stored and avoiding silly mistakes such as February 31.

With no more effort than simply declaring what we want, we can make Django understand exactly what kind of data we intend to use. Again, the trick is not only to use the supplied `Model` superclass but also to put the code in the right place.

## 3.4.2   Completing Our Django Models

With our `Post` model firmly defined in our **blog** app, we can now write the models necessary to run the startup organizer section. Consider again that the basic (no relations) data we intend to use are the following:

- Tag
  - tag name
  - slug field (for clean URL)
- Startup
  - name of company
  - slug field (for clean URL)
  - description or purpose

- date founded
- contact email
- website
- News Link
  - title or headline
  - link to article
  - publication date

To start, we need to create the model classes for each of the data structures. We do so in the `/organizer/models.py` file, shown in Example 3.3.

**Example 3.3: Project Code**
`organizer/models.py` in `342fdb6a6b`

```
1    from django.db import models
2
3
4    # Model Field Reference
5    # https://docs.djangoproject.com/en/1.8/ref/models/fields/
6
7
8    class Tag(models.Model):
9        pass
10
11
12   class Startup(models.Model):
13       pass
14
15
16   class NewsLink(models.Model):
17       pass
```

We can then add fields to each and every model. Each field is simply an instance of a class defined as an attribute of our model, which in turn is just a class. We start with our Tag model, shown in Example 3.4.

**Example 3.4: Project Code**
`organizer/models.py` in `893db45794`

```
8    class Tag(models.Model):
9        name = models.CharField(max_length=31)
10       slug = models.SlugField()
```

We can then define the fields for our Startup model, as in Example 3.5.

**Example 3.5: Project Code**
organizer/models.py **in** 4fa5544dd5

```
13    class Startup(models.Model):
14        name = models.CharField(max_length=31)
15        slug = models.SlugField()
16        description = models.TextField()
17        founded_date = models.DateField()
18        contact = models.EmailField()
19        website = models.URLField()
```

The code in Example 3.5 contains only two new fields instances: `EmailField` and `URLField`. Each one is actually a `CharField` with specific validation by regular expression. The `EmailField` ensures that data submitted to it look like a valid email address, while the `URLField` ensures that data submitted to it look like a valid URL. While instances of `CharField` require a `max_length`, `EmailField` and `URLField` do not. However, as we'll discover in a moment, it's sometimes better to define the option anyway.

We can finish by declaring the fields on our `NewsLink` model, as in Example 3.6.

**Example 3.6: Project Code**
organizer/models.py **in** 83e7cade96

```
22    class NewsLink(models.Model):
23        title = models.CharField(max_length=63)
24        pub_date = models.DateField()
25        link = models.URLField()
```

### 3.4.3  Adding Relational Fields to Our Models

When we wrote our models in the two previous sections, we did not include the relationships between models that we had so carefully defined. In this section, we connect our models.

We had outlined the following:

- A one-to-many relationship pointing news links to startups
- A many-to-many relationship between startups and tags
- A many-to-many relationship between blog posts and tags
- A many-to-many relationship between blog posts and startups

This is a first look at relationships, and it can be a little confusing if you've never seen them before. We take a closer look at them in Section 3.6.2.2 later in this chapter, which should help crystalize some of that knowledge in case this section doesn't quite get you there.

Creating a one-to-many relationship is straightforward. We simply add a `ForeignKey` field to our `NewsLink` model in `/organizer/models.py`, linking it—or pointing it—to the `Startup` model, as in Example 3.7.

**Example 3.7: Project Code**

`organizer/models.py` **in** `a0bb9cbcb2`

```
22   class NewsLink(models.Model):
.        ...
26       startup = models.ForeignKey(Startup)
```

Creating a many-to-many relationship is just as simple but perhaps a little less intuitive. In Example 3.8, we create a relationship between startups and tags with the addition of a single field.

**Example 3.8: Project Code**

`organizer/models.py` **in** `304a7da030`

```
13   class Startup(models.Model):
.        ...
20       tags = models.ManyToManyField(Tag)
```

This code is not intuitive, because the way it is written implies a direction between `Startup` and `Tag` objects, just as there is with one-to-many relationships. However, there is no direction with many-to-many relationships. We could have just as easily created this relationship in the `Tag` model by adding an attribute `startups` that was a `ManyToManyField(Startup)`. You'll note that we have not done this: we need add only a single field to a single model to create a full relationship. The model you pick to add this field is entirely up to you and will not affect the relationship.

This leads us to a fairly intriguing question: if a developer may code a `ManyToManyField` in either of the models that are being related, how does he or she pick the model in which to place the code (we can add the field in *one* of the models, not both)? When choosing the model to add a `ManyToManyField`, I try to think of the objects in terms of attributes and ownership. Tags are attributes, or metadata, and I therefore place the field defining the relationship in the models that own those data. In the case of the many-to-many relationship between blog posts and startups, I think that the blog post is about the startup, which makes the startup an attribute of the blog post. As such, I create that relationship as a field in the `Post` model, found in `/blog/models.py`, shown in Example 3.9. Remember to import `Tag` and `Startup`.

**Example 3.9: Project Code**

`blog/models.py` **in** `737fa51dc3`

```
3    from organizer.models import Startup, Tag
.        ...
10   class Post(models.Model):
.        ...
15       tags = models.ManyToManyField(Tag)
16       startups = models.ManyToManyField(Startup)
```

You may disagree with my decision and choose to do it the other way. And that's just fine.

### 3.4.4   Controlling Model Field Behavior with Field Options

It is possible to pass options to model fields. These field options can constrain behavior or provide defaults to our data, allowing us to write less code later. As model fields are (instances of) Python classes, we are simply passing parameters to the instantiation of field classes.

One of the most powerful options available is the ability to tell Django and the database that certain values are unique. This is particularly useful for slugs, which we know must be unique (`SlugField` instances do not default to being unique because of the many options available, as we shall see in Chapter 10: Revisiting Migrations). In the case of our `Tag` model, in `/organizer/models.py`, we set both the name and slug fields to be unique, as shown in Example 3.10.

**Example 3.10:** **Project Code**
`organizer/models.py` **in** `4c76a99e1d`

```
 8   class Tag(models.Model):
 9       name = models.CharField(
10           max_length=31, unique=True)
11       slug = models.SlugField(
12           max_length=31,
13           unique=True,
14           help_text='A label for URL config.')
```

By simply passing `unique=True`, both Django and the database will know that our slug field is unique (as we shall see shortly).

We've also set another parameter, `help_text`, providing some quick information about what a slug is. This field option will come into play when we automatically generate forms in Chapter 7.

On top of help text, we can also provide full names to our fields, as we've done below with the `NewsLink` model by passing a `verbose_name` argument. The `verbose_name` parameter may be set explicitly or may be passed as the first unnamed argument, as demonstrated in Example 3.11 (`'date published'`). Once again, we see this in action in Chapter 7.

**Example 3.11:** **Project Code**
`organizer/models.py` **in** `159d09e18d`

```
27   class NewsLink(models.Model):
 .       ...
29       pub_date = models.DateField('date published')
```

We should also take the opportunity to set the `max_length` of the `URLField`. By default, Django sets the `max_length` of any `URLField` to 200, despite that the host portion of the URL alone may be up 255 characters. The Uniform Resource Identifier

RFC[1] encourages URI producers to conform to domain name system (DNS) syntax, which is where the number comes from, but this is only a recommendation, and URLs may be up to 2,000 characters long. Despite the fact that we may not be able to store longer URLs (we will see what happens if we try to exceed `max_length` in Chapter 7), I will nevertheless set the length of the field to 255 characters, as shown in Example 3.12.

**Example 3.12: Project Code**
`organizer/models.py` in 159d09e18d

```
27    class NewsLink(models.Model):
 .        ...
30        link = models.URLField(max_length=255)
```

## Ghosts of Django Past

If you are working in a version prior to Django 1.8, you will also want to override the `max_length` option on any `EmailField`. As noted by Dominic Sayers in the errata of RFC 3696[2], an email may be 254 characters long because of limitations in Simple Mail Transfer (RFC 2821)[3]. Django's default prior to version 1.8 is set to 75, which is substantially smaller.

Our `Startup` model, shown in Example 3.13, uses all of the parameter options described previously as well as the `db_index` option. Fields with this option set to `True` will be indexed in the database (fields with the `unique` option are automatically indexed, so we don't use `db_index` on any `SlugField`). In our case, setting this now is actually a needless pre-optimization and is meant purely for demonstration purposes. We talk more about optimizations in Chapter 26.

**Example 3.13: Project Code**
`organizer/models.py` in 6d816ac65c

```
17    class Startup(models.Model):
18        name = models.CharField(
19            max_length=31, db_index=True)
20        slug = models.SlugField(
21            max_length=31,
22            unique=True,
23            help_text='A label for URL config.')
24        description = models.TextField()
25        founded_date = models.DateField(
26            'date founded')
27        contact = models.EmailField()
28        website = models.URLField(max_length=255)
29        tags = models.ManyToManyField(Tag)
```

---

1. https://dju.link/rfc3986
2. https://dju.link/rfc3696
3. https://dju.link/rfc2821

Our `Post` model, in `/blog/models.py`, features some of the options found above but is a little more complicated (Example 3.14). Our slug is unique only according to the month, and our publication date is automatically added. Most notably, however, is the related name option we've passed to our relationship fields.

**Example 3.14: Project Code**
`blog/models.py` **in** e9df485863

```
10    class Post(models.Model):
11        title = models.CharField(max_length=63)
12        slug = models.SlugField(                    # Unique only when month is included
13            max_length=63,
14            help_text='A label for URL config',
15            unique_for_month='pub_date')            @
16        text = models.TextField()
17        pub_date = models.DateField(
18            'date published',
19            auto_now_add=True)                      ⓑ
20        tags = models.ManyToManyField(
21            Tag, related_name='blog_posts')         ⓒ
22        startups = models.ManyToManyField(
23            Startup, related_name='blog_posts')
```

ⓐ  Let's start with the unique option. Recall that we want the URLs associated with blog posts to involve a date so that they resemble `http://site.django-unleashed.com/blog/2015/4/more-django-info/`. It no longer matters if slugs are completely unique, because the year and month are part of the URL. We do not care if blog posts with the same slug but written during different months of different years are in conflict, because we would still have unique URLs, such as `http://site.django-unleashed.com/blog/2015/4/more-django-info/` and `http://site.django-unleashed.com/blog/2013/07/more-django-info/`. We only care if there is a conflict with slugs for blog posts published in the same month. As such, instead of assigning uniqueness across the table in the database using `unique=True`, we tell Django to check for uniqueness only with slugs also published that same month. We do so using `unique_for_month`, making sure to pass it a valid `DateField` or `DateTimeField` attribute variable belonging to our model, resulting in `unique_for_month='pub_date'`.

ⓑ  In `pub_date` we've enabled the `auto_now_add` parameter, which means that the field will be automatically set to the current date the first time it is submitted to the database. If we had instead used the `auto_now` parameter, our field would be updated each and every time the model is modified (as opposed to just the first time).

ⓒ  Finally, in both of our many-to-many relationships, we have passed the `related_name` parameter. In theory, there are two equal sides to every relation: a post has tags associated with it just as a tag has posts associated with it. However, in Django we only ever specify symmetric relations in a single place. The `related_name` parameter is what defines the other side of a relation. Concretely, given a `Post` instance p, the tags associated with this post are accessible via `p.tags`, as defined by the preceding model. However, given a `Tag` instance `t`, we had not explicitly defined a variable to access `Post` objects. Thanks to the `related_name` option, we may now access the list of blog posts related to the tag `t` via the `blog_posts` attribute, as in `t.blog_posts`. Similarly, given a `Startup` instance `s`, we can now access related `Post` objects via `s.blog_posts`.

The `related_name` parameter is actually an option. If we do not set it, Django automatically creates the other side of the relation for us. In the case of the `Tag` model, Django would have created a `post_set` attribute, allowing access via `t.post_set` in our example. Similarly, a `Startup` named `s` would have accessed related blog posts via `s.post_set`. The formula Django uses is the name of the model followed by the string `_set`. The `related_name` parameter thus simply overrides Django's default rather than providing new behavior.

Understanding the use and interaction of related fields can be difficult without seeing them in action. We will see this more concretely several times before the end of the chapter and again throughout the rest of Part I.

### 3.4.5 Adding Methods to Django Models

Because Django models are Python classes, developers can add behavior to the model by writing class methods. Doing so is as straightforward as writing any Python method because fields act like class attributes within Python.

For the moment, we will not expand on the behavior of any of our models. The entire purpose of Part I is to learn how Django works at its core, and expanding Django functionality this early in the game would detract from this goal.

However, it is possible to write methods that supplement model behavior. Django actually expects and encourages developers to write two such methods for each model. We wait until Chapter 6 to see the second method but we write the first, the string method, right now.                                           181  get_absolute_url()

The string method is actually a Python method, meant to give an instance a string representation. Without it, Python typically represents an object by simply referring to it by its class, like so: `<Startup: Startup object>`. When dealing with several objects, however, this becomes confusing (a list of `Startup` objects will look like `[<Startup: Startup object>,<Startup: Startup object>]`), and so Python offers the convention of writing `__str__` so that the object will instead be represented like so: `<Startup: Boundless Software LLC>`. Django makes use of this convention and encourages developers to supply the method to all models.

#### Ghosts of Python Past

We are currently writing code in Python 3.4 for Django 1.8. If we were writing code in Python 2.7, the `__str__` method would be named `__unicode__`. In Python 3, all strings are 32-bit Unicode by default, and so the `__unicode__` method was removed in favor of `__str__`.

In /organizer/models.py, we add the code in Examples 3.15 and 3.16 to our tag and startup models:

**Example 3.15: Project Code**
organizer/models.py in 0e04297d98

```
 8    class Tag(models.Model):
 .        ...
16        def __str__(self):
17            return self.name
```

**Example 3.16: Project Code**
organizer/models.py in 9e3bbdfc0f

```
20    class Startup(models.Model):
 .        ...
34        def __str__(self):
35            return self.name
```

When referring to a Tag or Startup instance, the name of the object will be listed. This is possible because even though the class attribute name is an instance of a CharField, we can treat it just as we would any Unicode string in Python.

When listing NewsLink instances, however, we want to show not only the headline of the link but also which Startup object the link is related to. We therefore return a string that is formatted to display both pieces of information, as in Example 3.17.

**Example 3.17: Project Code**
organizer/models.py in 43dd0d1a35

```
38    class NewsLink(models.Model):
 .        ...
44        def __str__(self):
45            return "{}:{}".format(
46                self.startup, self.title)
```

When self.startup is accessed, Python actually calls the string representation method for the object, which we just coded. We could also have written self.startup.name, which would have been equivalent in this case (as that is what Startup.__str__() returns).

In /blog/models.py, we add a string representation method to our Post model, as in Example 3.18. In this case, we format the string returned to display the title of the Post instance as well as the time the blog post was published.

**Example 3.18: Project Code**
blog/models.py **in** d3baa05f7d

```
10   class Post(models.Model):
 .       ...
25       def __str__(self):
26           return "{} on {}".format(
27               self.title,
28               self.pub_date.strftime('%Y-%m-%d'))
```

As with CharField and strings, instances of DateField act like datetime.date objects in Python. This allows us to call strftime on our pub_date class attribute, formatting our date into a desired string, and then using this string to format the output of the method.

While the string representation method is quite helpful, as we shall rapidly discover, the true takeaway here is that all fields are easily manipulated because Django is Python.

### 3.4.6  Controlling Model Behavior with Nested Meta Classes

While the ability to write methods to add behavior to a model is quite useful, the ability to affect existing behavior is perhaps even more important. Django allows developers control of how the system interacts with models by providing configurable options, customizable in a nested class titled Meta.

For example, we can tell Django that we want to order our Tag model alphabetically by the model's name field by adding the code in Example 3.19 to /organizer/models.py.

**Example 3.19: Project Code**
organizer/models.py **in** 3c8067a1b8

```
 8   class Tag(models.Model):
 .       ...
16       class Meta:
17           ordering = ['name']
```

Django will look for the Meta class in the Tag class and then search for known options, affecting the behavior of Tag instances or groups of Tag instances.

In our Startup model, we tell Django to order lists of Startup objects by name but specify that the latest Startup should be the object with the most recent founded_date field (Example 3.20).

**Example 3.20: Project Code**
organizer/models.py **in** 7fc4e73826

```
23   class Startup(models.Model):
 .       ...
37       class Meta:
38           ordering = ['name']
39           get_latest_by = 'founded_date'
```

This allows two different types of behavior. Should we choose to list `Startups`, Django will automatically order them alphabetically. However, should we want to show the most recent `Startup`, we also have that option.

In many cases, developers will want to use the date for two purposes: for ordering lists and for getting the latest objects. The `ordering` attribute only enables the first, while the `get_latest_by` attribute only enables the latter. In Example 3.21, in the `NewsLink` model, we use `pub_date` to both order `NewsLink` lists and to provide the latest `NewsLink` instance. The `verbose_name` attribute defines the way Django displays instances of our models.

**Example 3.21: Project Code**
`organizer/models.py` in `1ac385de63`

```
45    class NewsLink(models.Model):
.         ...
51        class Meta:
52            verbose_name = 'news article'          @
53            ordering = ['-pub_date']
54            get_latest_by = 'pub_date'
```

The dash in front of the string in our ordering defines the direction of ordering. Instead of `ordering = ['pub_date']`, we have written `ordering = ['-pub_date']`. The dash switches the ordering from ascending to descending. Instead of listing dates from oldest to newest, Django will order items from newest to oldest if the dash is provided.

When Django displays the name of a class (such as with the Admin app, seen in Chapter 23: The Admin Library), it will change a camel case name and add spaces. Effectively, `NewsLink` will become *news link* when displayed. In turn, Django uses context to capitalize this information when desired.

Much like the `verbose_name` option in Django fields, the option above allows us to change the display string of a class. In Example 3.21, *news link* is overridden by *news article* in our `Meta` class.

Django also uses this information when displaying lists or sets of model instances. It does so by simply appending an *s* to the `verbose_name`, whether generated or provided. The `verbose_name_plural` is thus very useful, as it allows developers to override the plural name of the class. We don't need this for any of our classes, but with a model named `Pony`, we would need to use `verbose_name_plural` to tell Django to use the string *Ponies* when displaying lists of the model.

In Example 3.22, in `/blog/models.py`, we give `Post` behavior similar to that of `NewsLink`.

**Example 3.22: Project Code**
`blog/models.py` in `e2e1ea416d`

```
10    class Post(models.Model):
.         ...
25        class Meta:
26            verbose_name = 'blog post'
27            ordering = ['-pub_date', 'title']
28            get_latest_by = 'pub_date'
```

As with `NewsLink`, lists of `Post` instances will be ordered from newest to oldest using the publication date of the object. However, with `Post` objects, we further order objects according to the title of the blog post.

# 3.5 Using Django to Automatically Create a SQLite Database with `manage.py`

Now that we've structured our data in Django, we can ask Django to build a database for us. Creating or modifying a database is a two-step process. We must first create a migration file and then the actual database. We start by examining why migrations are crucial to any project. We then generate a migration file and examine what it does. Finally, we use the migration file to build a database.

You should always use Django to build your database. One of the biggest mistakes beginners make is to try to create the database separately from Django, either before or after creating their Django models. This is a very clear instance of developers "fighting the framework." Not only is it an unproductive use of time, it is actually counter-productive. You will always want to define models in Django and then make Django generate the database for you.

## 3.5.1 Understanding Migrations

Models allow us to define the structure, relations, and behavior of the data we use on our website. The behavior we've defined will have a direct effect on our use of the data in Python (as we shall see in the next section), but the structure we've created is just an abstraction for how the data will be stored in the database. In Django, models and the database schema are reflections of one other. Any modification of one must result in the modification of the other. In a fully deployed team project, this can be quite tricky. If one developer makes a change to his or her local test database, he or she needs a way to share these changes with other developers and the various servers running the website(s) in a repeatable and version-controlled manner. If the change turns out to be in error, the developer should also have an easy way to undo his or her changes. Finally, if two developers are working on the same area of the code and make conflicting changes, it should be easy to recognize the issue and resolve the problem.

Migrations solve these problems by providing a controlled, predictable system for altering a database. The typical workflow with Django is to

1. Create or change a model in Django,
2. Generate a migration file,      *djadm make migrations <app>*     50
3. Use the migration file to create/alter the database.    *djadm migrate*     53

The migration file contains the instructions to alter the database and to roll back (or revert) those alterations. The advantage of keeping these instructions in a file is that this file may be easily run (applied) and shared among developers. Migration files may be considered version control for the database, although the analogy is imperfect. The advantage of having these changes as files (and where the analogy breaks down) is the ability to store and share these files using a standard version-control system.

Migrations are a key part of every Django project, as they help avert major headaches and save time.

## 3.5.2   Creating Migrations

Migration generation, like most other interactions with Django, occurs thanks to the `manage.py` script.

Before actually generating a migration, run the check command, shown in Example 3.23. Django will warn you if there are any typos or problems with your models.

**Example 3.23: Shell Code**

```
$ ./manage.py check
System check identified no issues (0 silenced).
```

Satisfied with the output of check, we can then run the `makemigrations` command. In Example 3.24, I run the command twice, specifying each app.

**Example 3.24: Shell Code**

```
$ ./manage.py makemigrations organizer
Migrations for 'organizer':
  0001_initial.py:
    - Create model NewsLink
    - Create model Startup
    - Create model Tag
    - Add field tags to startup
    - Add field startup to newslink
$ ./manage.py makemigrations blog
Migrations for 'blog':
  0001_initial.py:
    - Create model Post
```

We do not need to specify the name of each app (I did so purely for demonstration). We can invoke `makemigrations` with no arguments, as in Example 3.25. If we did this right now (after having already generated migration files), Django would tell us that we've not made any changes to the models: the migration files reflect the state of our models and, therefore, so would the database we create.

**Example 3.25: Shell Code**

```
$ ./manage.py makemigrations
No changes detected
```

Django has created instructions for the migration tool in each app, under the `migrations` folder. If you open `/blog/migrations/0001_initial.py`, you will be treated to a declarative, human-readable set of instructions to create a database table. Despite its readability, it is also quite dense. Let's break it down.

The overall structure of the file is the `Migration` class, which is imported from `django.db`, as shown in Example 3.26.

**Example 3.26: Project Code**
`blog/migrations/0001_initial.py` **in** ed26b9aae0

```
4    from django.db import migrations, models
5
6
7    class Migration(migrations.Migration):
```

The class defines the `dependencies` attribute, shown in Example 3.27. In this instance, our migration depends on the migration in **organizer**. This makes sense: our `Post` model has many-to-many fields to both `Tag` and `Startup` and requires Tag and Startup to exist before this migration file can be applied.

**Example 3.27: Project Code**
`blog/migrations/0001_initial.py` **in** ed26b9aae0

```
 9       dependencies = [
10           ('organizer', '0001_initial'),
11       ]
```

The core of the `Migration` class is the `operations` attribute, shown in Example 3.28. Migration operations are the actions Django takes to make the database reflect the content of our model classes. Django uses instances to build the information it needs before using it, and the order in which these objects are instantiated in the `operations` list matters. In this case, Django is only instantiating `CreateModel` and using the information passed to it to prepare for the migration.

**Example 3.28: Project Code**
`blog/migrations/0001_initial.py` **in** ed26b9aae0

```
13       operations = [
14           migrations.CreateModel(
15               name='Post',
16               fields=[
 .               ...
40               ],
41               options={
 .                   ...
46               },
47           ),
48       ]
```

In this example, the migration operation `CreateModel` creates a new model called `Post`, adds the fields in the `fields` list (not printed—more information later), sets model options based on our `Meta` class in `options` (not printed—more information later), and inherits `models.Model` in the `bases` tuple.

The `fields` list is not printed because it is quite long and contains exactly what you would expect: the field classes we instantiated in `/blog/models.py`. Example 3.29, for instance, is the slug field, appearing with exactly the attributes we gave it.

**Example 3.29:** **Project Code**
`blog/migrations/0001_initial.py` in ed26b9aae0

```
25                      ('slug',
26                       models.SlugField(
27                           max_length=63,
28                           unique_for_month='pub_date',
29                           help_text='A label for URL config')),
```

Many-to-many fields appear in a similar format, as demonstrated in Example 3.30.

**Example 3.30:** **Project Code**
`blog/migrations/0001_initial.py` in ed26b9aae0

```
37                      ('tags', models.ManyToManyField(
38                           to='organizer.Tag',
39                           related_name='blog_posts')),
```

As mentioned earlier, Django automatically creates primary keys for all of our models, allowing us to forgo their definition while still taking advantage of their use via relations. Our migration file, as shown in Example 3.31, allows us to see what type of fields Django will create for our primary key.

**Example 3.31:** **Project Code**
`blog/migrations/0001_initial.py` in ed26b9aae0

```
17                      ('id',
18                       models.AutoField(
19                           serialize=False,
20                           verbose_name='ID',
21                           auto_created=True,
22                           primary_key=True)),
```

Finally, the migration defines the options for the model (Example 3.32). These are the attributes we defined in the nested `Meta` class.

**Example 3.32:** **Project Code**
`blog/migrations/0001_initial.py` in ed26b9aae0

```
41                  options={
42                      'ordering': [
43                          '-pub_date', 'title'],
```

```
44                         'verbose_name': 'blog post',
45                         'get_latest_by': 'pub_date',
46                     },
```

Migration files are instrumental to building a website, particularly when working with a team. We return to their use in later parts of the book.

### 3.5.3  Applying Migrations to Create or Modify a Database

The command to run the code in the migrations files, colloquially called applying a migration, is `migrate`. If you've been following closely, you already used the command in Chapter 1, before we used the `runserver` command. Calling the command created a default SQLite database, which Django requires to run on a server.

Regardless of whether you already have a database, you will now call `migrate` again, as in Example 3.33.

**Example 3.33: Shell Code**

```
$ ./manage.py migrate
```

If you don't already have a database, Django will create one named `db.sqlite3`, as specified on line 64 of `/suorganizer/settings.py`. Django will also produce the output shown in Example 3.34.

**Example 3.34: Shell Code**

```
Operations to perform:
  Synchronize unmigrated apps: messages, staticfiles
  Apply all migrations: blog, auth, admin, organizer, sessions,
                        contenttypes
Synchronizing apps without migrations:
  Creating tables...
    Running deferred SQL...
  Installing custom SQL...
Running migrations:
  Rendering model states... DONE
  Applying contenttypes.0001_initial... OK
  Applying auth.0001_initial... OK
  Applying admin.0001_initial... OK
  Applying contenttypes.0002_remove_content_type_name... OK
  Applying auth.0002_alter_permission_name_max_length... OK
  Applying auth.0003_alter_user_email_max_length... OK
  Applying auth.0004_alter_user_username_opts... OK
  Applying auth.0005_alter_user_last_login_null... OK
  Applying auth.0006_require_contenttypes_0002... OK
  Applying organizer.0001_initial... OK
  Applying blog.0001_initial... OK
  Applying sessions.0001_initial... OK
```

If you already have a database, Django will modify your database to account for the changes outlined in the migration files we just generated. Instead of the text in Example 3.34, Django will output a subset, as it is doing a subset of the work (Example 3.35).

**Example 3.35: Shell Code**

```
Operations to perform:
  Synchronize unmigrated apps: staticfiles, messages
  Apply all migrations: organizer, sessions, blog, auth, admin,
                    contenttypes
Synchronizing apps without migrations:
  Creating tables...
    Running deferred SQL...
  Installing custom SQL...
Running migrations:
  Rendering model states... DONE
  Applying organizer.0001_initial... OK
  Applying blog.0001_initial... OK
```

In either case, your database is identical in structure, which is the purpose of migrations.

If you're curious about what, exactly, Django is telling the database to do, you can use the sqlmigrate command to ask Django. For instance, the command ./manage.py sqlmigrate blog 0001 asks Django for the SQL code it uses when applying the first migration of the **blog** app. The result is printed in Example 3.36.

**Example 3.36: SQL Code**

```
BEGIN;
CREATE TABLE "blog_post" (
    "id" integer NOT NULL PRIMARY KEY AUTOINCREMENT,
    "title" varchar(63) NOT NULL,
    "slug" varchar(63) NOT NULL,
    "text" text NOT NULL,
    "pub_date" date NOT NULL);
CREATE TABLE "blog_post_startups" (
    "id" integer NOT NULL PRIMARY KEY AUTOINCREMENT,
    "post_id" integer NOT NULL
        REFERENCES "blog_post" ("id"),
    "startup_id" integer NOT NULL
        REFERENCES "organizer_startup" ("id"),
    UNIQUE ("post_id", "startup_id"));
CREATE TABLE "blog_post_tags" (
    "id" integer NOT NULL PRIMARY KEY AUTOINCREMENT,
    "post_id" integer NOT NULL
        REFERENCES "blog_post" ("id"),
    "tag_id" integer NOT NULL
        REFERENCES "organizer_tag" ("id"),
    UNIQUE ("post_id", "tag_id"));
CREATE INDEX "blog_post_2dbcba41" ON "blog_post" ("slug");
CREATE INDEX "blog_post_startups_f3aa1999"
    ON "blog_post_startups" ("post_id");
```

```
CREATE INDEX "blog_post_startups_99f77c8c"
    ON "blog_post_startups" ("startup_id");
CREATE INDEX "blog_post_tags_f3aa1999"
    ON "blog_post_tags" ("post_id");
CREATE INDEX "blog_post_tags_76f094bc"
    ON "blog_post_tags" ("tag_id");
COMMIT;
```

The `CreateModel` operation in the **blog** migration file we generated results in all of the SQL code listed in Example 3.36. When we invoke `migrate`, Django uses the data in the instance of `CreateModel` to generate this SQL, which it then applies to the database. The creation of the `blog_post` table is thus expected. Take note again of the `id` primary key, automatically created for us but not specified in our models. A little more tricky is the creation of the `blog_post_startups` and `blog_post_tags` tables, which are the result of the many-to-many field seen in both our models and the migration file. Finally, Django creates indexes to allow rapid access to all of the keys, both primary and related.

The key takeaway from all of this is that models allow Django to automatically create and modify databases thanks to migrations. Django is quite intelligent about this process and focuses on shortening code. Django automatically supplies a primary key to models and sets up indexes for these keys. Furthermore, Django allows us to avoid the tedious and repetitive process of defining many-to-many relations as full tables and instead provides a field to shorten our code and the process.

## Info

One of the most common questions on the Internet with relation to Django's many-to-many relations is, *How do I customize or add information to the relation?* For instance, given a many-to-many relation between hotel rooms and guest, how would one store the reservation number for each relation? The answer is that Django allows developers to create their own models for relations. To use the model (replacing Django's generated table), use the `through` parameter when instantiating a `ManyToManyField`. This is Django's recommended method and results in the same SQL as if you had manually built a many-to-many relationship using nothing but foreign keys (don't do this—it's a lot of extra work for nothing).

We are now in a position to start adding data to the website.

## Ghosts of Django Past

Prior to Django 1.7, Django did not provide migrations natively. If you're working with migrations in Django 1.6 or earlier, you are likely using an app called South. South does not work with Django 1.7 or later, and so we do not cover its use in this book. However, the principle is exactly the same.

If you're working in Django 1.6 or earlier and you don't have migrations, then you will be interested in the `syncdb` and `sqlall` commands. That said, I urge you to add South to your project. If you change your models without a migration system, you will be forced to edit your database manually or else to throw it out and regenerate it.

# 3.6   Manipulating Data in the Database: Managers and QuerySets

With our data organized and a place to put it, we can now begin manipulating data.

## Code Repository

As of commit a06fc61b0e[4], the code repository contains an IPython notebook that allows you to run all of the code in the following section (without having to copy and paste any of it!). For IPython notebooks to work, you need IPython and the django-extensions package installed and in the INSTALLED_APPS list. As Example 3.37 shows, you may use the requirements.txt file in the repository for the purpose of installing, thanks to the pip tool:

**Example 3.37: Shell Code**

```
$ pip install -r requirements.txt
```

You will have to add the django-extensions package to INSTALLED_APPS yourself. To get the code running, simply run the command shown in Example 3.38.

**Example 3.38: Shell Code**

```
$ ./manager.py shell_plus --notebook
```

This command will open your browser. Click on the file titled Chapter_3_Model_Managers_and_QuerySets.ipynb, and all of the code here will be at your disposal.

At this stage, many tutorials will turn to Django's Admin library to add data to the database. This is certainly the easiest way to add data to the database and exciting for beginners. However, it doesn't help beginners learn how to interact with the database in Python, which becomes crucial in Chapter 5. The goal of this section is thus not to add data but to familiarize you with Django's ORM. If we were simply adding data with the ORM, this section would be much shorter.

## 3.6.1   Basic Database Interaction via Models

We can interact quite powerfully with Django's ORM in the Python interpreter. This is useful not only because it will help us learn Django on the fly but also because it is a tool we will continue to use throughout our careers in Django. Using the interpreter to test queries as you write them can help speed the development process.

---

4. https://dju.link/a06fc61b0e

Rather than invoke Python and then import the necessary Django tools, Django provides a shortcut. We can invoke `./manage.py shell`, which runs the Python interpreter (or IPython, if you have it installed) and fetches the bare minimum for Django to work. From there we can begin loading in our own project code, as shown in Example 3.39.

**Example 3.39: Python Interpreter Code**

```
Python 3.4.3 (default, Mar 10 2015, 14:53:35)
[GCC 4.2.1 Compatible Apple LLVM 6.0 (clang-600.0.56)] on darwin
Type "help", "copyright", "credits" or "license" for more information.
>>> from datetime import date
>>> from organizer.models import Tag, Startup, NewsLink
>>> from blog.models import Post
```

Django is Python. Consequently, we can instantiate our models just as we would any Python classes, as shown in Example 3.40.

**Example 3.40: Python Interpreter Code**

*note: lower case*

```
>>> edut = Tag(name='Education', slug='education')
```

Note that we treat model fields just as we would any other Python class attribute.

As Example 3.41 shows, we can also see the output of `__str__()`, as it will be printed as the representation of an object in the interpreter.

**Example 3.41: Python Interpreter Code**

```
>>> edut
<Tag: Education>
```

**Info**

Note that the second line in the shell only works because we implemented `__str__`. Were this not the case, calling `edut` would simply print the object as `<Tag: Tag object>`.

At this point, the object exists only in the computer's memory. To save it to the database, we can use the `save()` method, shown in Example 3.42, which the object inherits from Django's `models.Model`.

**Example 3.42: Python Interpreter Code**

```
>>> edut.save()
```

The `Model` superclass also allows us to call `delete()` to remove the `Tag` from the database, as shown in Example 3.43.

**Example 3.43: Python Interpreter Code**

```
>>> edut.delete()
```

Note, however, that while the object no longer exists in the database, the object still exists in the interpreter's memory, as shown in Example 3.44.

**Example 3.44: Python Interpreter Code**

```
>>> edut
<Tag: Education>
```

While this capability is incredibly practical and powerful, it is only the tip of the iceberg. As it turns out, Django supplies entire classes for interacting with the database, most notably managers and querysets.

## 3.6.2   Database Interaction via Managers

Django attaches an object called a **manager** to every model class. The manager helps interaction with the database in complicated ways: it is a key part of Django's ORM (which is hinted at by the db in the path below) and is the most common way Django developers will interact with data in the database. Effectively, it is one of the most powerful tools inherited through `models.Model` and one with which we will be very familiar by the end of the book.

By default, Django automatically generates a manager for each model and assigns it to the `objects` attribute. As shown in Example 3.45, we can use the Python `type()` built-in to see what the object is.

**Example 3.45: Python Interpreter Code**

```
>>> type(Tag.objects)
django.db.models.manager.Manager
```

Much like models, managers can create and delete objects, but rather than taking two steps (instantiation and then `save()`), the manager uses a single command, as shown in Example 3.46.

**Example 3.46: Python Interpreter Code**

```
>>> Tag.objects.create(name='Video Games', slug='video-games')
<Tag: Video Games>
```

But why stop there? As you can see in Example 3.47, the manager can create multiple objects in a single command!

**Example 3.47: Python Interpreter Code**

```
>>> Tag.objects.bulk_create([
...     Tag(name='Django', slug='django'),
...     Tag(name='Mobile', slug='mobile'),
...     Tag(name='Web', slug='web'),
... ])
[<Tag: Django>, <Tag: Mobile>, <Tag: Web>]
```

*.bulk_create()*

Unlike a model, however, a manager can get data from the database, as shown in Example 3.48. Any call to `objects` will provide the most updated version of the data.

**Example 3.48: Python Interpreter Code**

```
>>> Tag.objects.all()
[<Tag: Django>,
 <Tag: Mobile>,
 <Tag: Video Games>,
 <Tag: Web>]
```

*.all()*

The return value from a manager looks like a list, acts like a list, but is not a list. It is a queryset object, as shown in Example 3.49.

**Example 3.49: Python Interpreter Code**

```
>>> Tag.objects.all()[0]
<Tag: Django>
>>> type(Tag.objects.all())
django.db.models.query.QuerySet
```

Managers are attached to the model **class** but not to model instances. If you try to access `objects` on an object, Django will error, as shown in Example 3.50.

**Example 3.50: Python Interpreter Code**

```
>>> try:
...     edut.objects
... except AttributeError as e:
...     print(e)
Manager isn't accessible via Tag instances
```

There are many methods available on managers and querysets, and we simply don't have the time to see them all. The Django documentation[5] supplies all the information you'll need. Instead, we focus on the tools we will use most often: the tools to get items from the database.

We've already seen one: the `all()` manager method displays all of the objects of that model. I also use the `count()` method in Example 3.51 as a quick demonstration.

**Example 3.51: Python Interpreter Code**

```
>>> Tag.objects.all()
[<Tag: Django>,
 <Tag: Mobile>,
 <Tag: Video Games>,
 <Tag: Web>]
>>> Tag.objects.count()
4
```

To be more selective about which object we want, we can use the `get()` method, shown in Example 3.52, which expects keyword arguments in which each key is a field in the model.

**Example 3.52: Python Interpreter Code**

```
>>> Tag.objects.get(slug='django')
<Tag: Django>
```

The `get()` method, shown in Example 3.53, is one of the few manager methods that does not return a queryset. Instead, it just returns the model object.

**Example 3.53: Python Interpreter Code**

```
>>> type(Tag.objects.all())
django.db.models.query.QuerySet
>>> type(Tag.objects.get(slug='django'))
organizer.models.Tag
```

The values passed to `get()` are case sensitive by default, as shown in Example 3.54.

**Example 3.54: Python Interpreter Code**

```
>>> try:
...     Tag.objects.get(slug='Django')
... except Tag.DoesNotExist as e:
...     print(e)
Tag matching query does not exist.
```

---

5. https://dju.link/18/querysets

However, managers and querysets come with a feature called **lookups**. A field name followed by two underscores and then a lookup will allow modification of the behavior of the method. For instance, to make the `get()` method case insensitive, we can use the `iexact` lookup, shown in Example 3.55.

**Example 3.55: Python Interpreter Code**

```
>>> Tag.objects.get(slug__iexact='DJANGO')
<Tag: Django>
```

*·get(<field name>__ <lookup> = <val> ) = <vals>*

The behavior in Example 3.55 is exactly how we want to handle `slug` fields. Slugs are unique case-insensitive identifiers. The ability to browse for "django" and "Django" and get the same data is crucial when handling URLs, and Django supplies the ability to act appropriately out of the box.

Django comes with a large number of lookups and even allows you to create your own (starting in Django 1.7). Once again, we won't be able to see each and every one, as that is the reference documentation's job. However, Example 3.56 shows two more just to whet your appetite.

**Example 3.56: Python Interpreter Code**

```
>>> Tag.objects.get(slug__istartswith='DJ')
<Tag: Django>
>>> Tag.objects.get(slug__contains='an')
<Tag: Django>
```

You'll note that all of the examples with `get()` are crafted to return only a single object. This is by design because the `get()` method will only ever return a single object. If you query it with information that matches more than one object, as shown in Example 3.57, Django will throw an exception.

**Example 3.57: Python Interpreter Code**

```
>>> try:
        # djangO, mObile, videO-games
...     Tag.objects.get(slug__contains='o')
... except Tag.MultipleObjectsReturned as e:
...     print(e)
get() returned more than one Tag -- it returned 3!
```

*· filter( )*

Due to the `get()` method's behavior, the other commonly used method is the `filter()` method (Example 3.58), which does exactly what it sounds like. Like the `all()` method, it returns a queryset.

**Example 3.58: Python Interpreter Code**

```
>>> Tag.objects.filter(slug__contains='o')
[<Tag: Django>, <Tag: Mobile>]
>>> type(Tag.objects.filter(slug__contains='o'))
django.db.models.query.QuerySet
```

Most manager methods return a queryset object, just as most queryset methods return queryset objects. We can chain calls to querysets, allowing us to filter and control the results to get exactly what we're looking for. In Example 3.59, we first filter the results and then order them.

.order_by()

**Example 3.59: Python Interpreter Code**

```
>>> Tag.objects.filter(slug__contains='o').order_by('-name')
[<Tag: Mobile>, <Tag: Django>]
```

The advantage to chaining these calls is that the database will be called only once. The topic of reducing the number of database calls really belongs in Chapter 26, but it is worth noting here that managers and querysets are both lazy: they try to wait until they must display or return data before they actually ask the database for that data. This delay can be quite powerful but also confusing if you don't expect that behavior.

The methods found on querysets are overloaded on the manager, meaning that if we can call it on the queryset we can call it on the manager. (The opposite is usually also true, but not always). For instance, we can call order_by on the Tag manager, as in Example 3.60.

**Example 3.60: Python Interpreter Code**

```
>>> # on a manager
>>> Tag.objects.order_by('-name')
[<Tag: Web>,
 <Tag: Video Games>,
 <Tag: Mobile>,
 <Tag: Django>]
>>> # on a queryset
>>> Tag.objects.filter(slug__contains='e').order_by('-name')
[<Tag: Web>, <Tag: Video Games>, <Tag: Mobile>]
```

By default, Django orders objects in querysets according to their primary key. However, as we defined an ordering in the Meta subclass of Tag, our Tag objects have been listed alphabetically. The query in Example 3.60—reverse alphabetical order—is thus the opposite of the default we set earlier in this chapter.

Finally, on top of get() and filter(), there are the values() and values_list() methods. The two are fairly similar, so I only demonstrate the second one. In Example 3.61, rather than returning a queryset with model objects, Django returns a queryset with tuples!

**Example 3.61: Python Interpreter Code**

```
>>> Tag.objects.values_list()
[(3, 'Django', 'django'),
 (4, 'Mobile', 'mobile'),
 (2, 'Video Games', 'video-games'),
 (5, 'Web', 'web')]
>>> type(Tag.objects.values_list())
django.db.models.query.ValuesListQuerySet
```

*values_list()*

The neat thing about values() and values_list() is the ability to quickly select which model fields we want to get, as shown in Example 3.62.

**Example 3.62: Python Interpreter Code**

```
>>> Tag.objects.values_list('name', 'slug')
[('Django', 'django'),
 ('Mobile', 'mobile'),
 ('Video Games', 'video-games'),
 ('Web', 'web')]
```

More often than not, however, we'll be using the methods to get a single value for a list. As Example 3.63 shows, this leads to a queryset of singletons (single-item tuples), which is far from great for unpacking.

**Example 3.63: Python Interpreter Code**

```
>>> Tag.objects.values_list('name')
[('Django',),
 ('Mobile',),
 ('Video Games',),
 ('Web',)]
```

Luckily, as Example 3.64 shows, the method accepts the flat keyword, which when set to True (with a single field passed) will return a queryset of strings.

**Example 3.64: Python Interpreter Code**

```
>>> Tag.objects.values_list('name', flat=True)
['Django', 'Mobile', 'Video Games', 'Web']
```

Just to be clear: this is still a queryset, not a list (Example 3.65)!

**Example 3.65: Python Interpreter Code**

```
>>> type(Tag.objects.values_list('name', flat=True))
django.db.models.query.ValuesListQuerySet
```

### 3.6.2.1   Data in Memory vs Data in the Database

As discussed in Section 3.3, a key concept when building models is that the Python class will map directly to a database table. Each field attribute in the class becomes a database column, and every object instantiated and saved becomes a row. For instance, the call to the `Startup` manager, in Example 3.66, creates a database row for Startup data (Table 3.2).

**Example 3.66: Python Interpreter Code**

```
>>> jb = Startup.objects.create(          # Create row in db table
...     name='JamBon Software',                organizer_startup
...     slug='jambon-software',
...     contact='django@jambonsw.com',
...     description='Web and Mobile Consulting.\n\n'
...                 'Django Tutoring.\n',
...     founded_date=date(2013, 1, 18),
...     website='https://jambonsw.com/',
... )
>>> jb
<Startup: JamBon Software>
```

Please note that the primary key (PK) I have selected in Table 3.2 is arbitrary and will be automatically assigned by your database. Also, the `founded_date` field expects an instance of `date` and will error if given anything else.

The nuance here is that the database will save data only when it is told to. We saw this with the educational tag earlier, but it bears repeating because it is a common beginner mistake. For instance, let's take the `date` field on our Startup (Example 3.67).

**Example 3.67: Python Interpreter Code**

```
>>> jb.founded_date
datetime.date(2013, 1, 18)
```

If we reassign it to a different date, as in Example 3.68, it will register correctly in Python, as expected.

**Example 3.68: Python Interpreter Code**

```
>>> jb.founded_date = date(2014,1,1)
>>> jb.founded_date
datetime.date(2014, 1, 1)
```

**Table 3.2: Database Table for Startup Data**

| PK | Name | Description | Founded | EMail | Website |
|---|---|---|---|---|---|
| 3 | Jambon Software | Web and Mobile Consulting | 2013-01-18 | django@... | jambonsw.com |

However, if we do not run `save()` on the `jb` object, then the database will never know of this change. We can see this in Example 3.69 when we retrieve the data from the database.

**Example 3.69: Python Interpreter Code**

```
>>> jb = Startup.objects.get(slug='jambon-software')
>>> jb.founded_date
datetime.date(2013, 1, 18)
```

Always remember to save your data!

### 3.6.2.2  Connecting Data through Relations

When talking about the ORM, we've focused entirely on simple fields. But many of our models have relation fields with many-to-one and many-to-many relationships.

Our `Post` object is connected to both tags and startups. We can easily create a `Post` (as in Example 3.70), but we cannot assign relations using `create()` on the model manager.

**Example 3.70: Python Interpreter Code**

```
>>> djt = Post.objects.create(
...     title='Django Training',
...     slug='django-training',
...     text=(
...         "Learn Django in a classroom setting "
...         "with JamBon Software."),
)
>>> djt
<Post: Django Training on 2015-06-09>
```

*djt: Post instance*

The date is automatically assigned at creation because of `auto_now_add`. We can override it as in Example 3.71.

**Example 3.71: Python Interpreter Code**

```
>>> djt.pub_date = date(2013, 1, 18)
>>> djt.save()
>>> djt
<Post: Django Training on 2013-01-18>
```

*relation managers*

Model managers are not the only managers available in Django. When dealing with relations, Django uses a manager to connect data. For example, the tags field in our `Post` model is actually a manager for many-to-many relationships and comes with many of the same functions as a model manager. We can verify this by first creating a `Post` and then using the Python `type()` built-in, as shown in Example 3.72.

*p 44*

**Example 3.72: Python Interpreter Code**

*Post 44*

```
>>> type(djt.tags)
django.db.models.fields.related.create_many_related_manager.<locals>
    .ManyRelatedManager
>>> type(djt.startups)
django.db.models.fields.related.create_many_related_manager.<locals>
    .ManyRelatedManager
```

Just as we can model managers, we can call the `all()` method to see all of the objects the manager can access. The calls in Example 3.73 show all of the tags associated with the post, followed by all of the startups associated with the post (none in both cases).

**Example 3.73: Python Interpreter Code**

```
>>> djt.tags.all()
[]
>>> djt.startups.all()
[]
```

Relation managers come with an `add()` method, which allows for objects to be connected. In Example 3.74, we connect the Django tag to our new blog post.

**Example 3.74: Python Interpreter Code**

```
>>> django = Tag.objects.get(slug__contains='django')
>>> djt.tags.add(django)
>>> djt.tags.all()
[<Tag: Django>]
```

We started to learn about how many-to-many relationships are structured in Django in Section 3.4.3 but only skimmed the surface. Let's take a moment to review that material and add to it our newfound knowledge of managers.

Consider the code in Example 3.75.

**Example 3.75: Python Code**

```
Student(models.Model):
    classes = models.ManyToManyField(          " forward relation " @67
        SchoolClass)
```

Given objects `timmy` and `physics`, for example, instances of `Student` and `SchoolClass` respectively, the classes being taken by `timmy` are `timmy.classes.all()`, and the students taking `physics` are `physics.student_set.all()`. The attributes `timmy.classes` and `physics.student_set` are relational managers, and both return `QuerySet` objects. Even though a many-to-many relationship is symmetric (if someone is your friend, you are his or her friend, too), many talk about the forward and backward relation of the relationship because the relationship is defined in only one place. In this example, `timmy.classes` is the forward relation (because the field is defined on *@ 66* Student), whereas `physics.student_set` is the reverse relation because Django automatically sets it for us.

When we set the `related_name` attribute of a relationship field, as in Example 3.76, we are changing the name of the variable Django creates for the relation on the other model (the reverse relation).

**Example 3.76: Python Code**

```
Student(models.Model):
    classes = models.ManyToManyField(
        SchoolClass,
        related_name='students')
```

With the code in Example 3.76, instead of `physics.student_set.all()`, we access the related manager of students with `physics.students.all()`. The call to *✗* `timmy.classes.all()` remains unchanged.

I must stress: despite some of the vocabulary around many-to-many relations, there is no real "forward" or "reverse" relation. The relationship is symmetric, and the vocabulary exists only as a means of talking about where the field is defined in Django.

Let's return to our site code. In Example 3.77, we can use that to call the reverse relation between the Django tag and the blog post we just connected.

**Example 3.77: Python Interpreter Code**

```
>>> django.blog_posts.all()        django is a Tag instance
[<Post: Django Training on 2013-01-18>]
```

Had we not overridden the name of the manager to `blog_posts` in our `Post` model, the call in Example 3.77 would instead have been to `post_set`. We can see this with the `Startup<->Tag` many-to-many relationship. With a `Startup` object, we can use the variable `tags` to get the related manager. With a `Tag` object, as in Example 3.78, we instead use `startup_set` for the same relation.

*Startup  43*

**Example 3.78: Python Interpreter Code**

```
>>> django.startup_set.add(jb)   # a "reverse" relation     jb is a Startup instance
>>> django.startup_set.all()
[<Startup: JamBon Software>]
>>> jb.tags.all()   # the "forward" relation
[<Tag: Django>]
```

Let's see it one more time, just to be clear. In Example 3.79, we take our new blog post and use the `ManyToManyField` defined in the `Post` model to access the related manager and add the JamBon Software startup.

**Example 3.79:** Python Interpreter Code

```
>>> djt
<Post: Django Training on 2013-01-18>
>>> djt.startups.add(jb)
>>> djt.startups.all()
[<Startup: JamBon Software>]
```

We can then use the reverse related manager on the `Startup` object to see that the JamBon Software startup and blog post are now connected. Because we defined the `related_name` option on the startups `ManyToManyField` defined in the `Post` model, we access the related manager through `blog_posts` instead of through `post_set` in Example 3.80.

**Example 3.80:** Python Interpreter Code

```
>>> jb.blog_posts.all()
[<Post: Django Training on 2013-01-18>]
```

Take a step back for a second. We've covered a lot of ground, and not all of this is going to sink in right away. The good news is that it doesn't have to: this is material that will keep coming back throughout the book because it is crucial to using Django.

## 3.7  String Case Ordering

Note that when we created our data in Section 3.8, all of the strings for each field met the same capitalization criteria. As Example 3.81 shows, when we created `Tag` data, the first letter of the name field of the tag was always capitalized, while the `slug` field was always all lowercase, as discussed in the beginning of the chapter.

**Example 3.81:** Python Interpreter Code

```
>>> Tag.objects.values_list('name','slug').order_by('name')
[('Django', 'django'),
 ('Education', 'education'),
 ('Mobile', 'mobile'),
 ('Video Games', 'video-games'),
 ('Web', 'web')]
```

It is important to pick a case and stick to it for all values because the case of a string may affect the order of the values. For instance, if we create a new Tag object with the name andrew in all lowercase, most developers would assume that it would appear as the first object in the queryset when ordering by the name field. However, as you can see in Example 3.82, you would be wrong: it is possible, depending on your environment, for the new Tag to appear last.

**Example 3.82: Python Interpreter Code**

```
>>> Tag.objects.create(name='andrew', slug='ZEBRA')
<Tag: andrew>
>>> Tag.objects.values_list('name','slug').order_by('name')
[('Django', 'django'), ('Education', 'education'),
('Mobile', 'mobile'), ('Video Games', 'video-games'),
('Web', 'web'), ('andrew', 'ZEBRA')]
```

Similarly, an uppercase slug will change the ordering, as you can see in Example 3.83. Given the slug field ZEBRA, developers might expect the object to be last in the list and be surprised to discover otherwise.

**Example 3.83: Python Interpreter Code**

```
>>> Tag.objects.values_list('name','slug').order_by('slug')
[('andrew', 'ZEBRA'), ('Django', 'django'),
('Education', 'education'), ('Mobile', 'mobile'),
('Video Games', 'video-games'), ('Web', 'web')]
```

As you may have gathered, uppercase letters appear before lowercase letters in the environment used above. This is part of the reason that slug values are typically all lowercase, which ensures correct ordering.

Therefore, a project developer must make a conscious decision about the case of strings in the project database. In light of this information, we may choose to make the names of all tags lowercase. We can make this change very easily because of Django's ORM, as demonstrated in Example 3.84.

**Example 3.84: Python Interpreter Code**

```
>>> for tag in Tag.objects.all():
...     tag.name = tag.name.lower()
...     tag.save()
>>> Tag.objects.values_list('name')
[('andrew',), ('django',), ('education',),
 ('mobile',), ('video games',), ('web',)]
```

However, all `Tag` objects are now listed in lowercase, as shown in Example 3.85.

**Example 3.85: Python Interpreter Code**

```
>>> Tag.objects.all()
[<Tag: andrew>, <Tag: django>, <Tag: education>,
 <Tag: mobile>, <Tag: video games>, <Tag: web>]
```

Example 3.86 shows that we can change the default string representation of our object by changing the `__str__` method to capitalize the name field by default.

**Example 3.86: Project Code**
`organizer/models.py` in `b2f9fea554`

```
 8    class Tag(models.Model):
 .       ...
19        def __str__(self):
20            return self.name.title()
```

Consider that we will have to remember to capitalize our `Tag` objects when displaying them publicly in Chapter 4 as well. We can see the change in our `__str__` method if we reload the Django shell (to quit the shell, hit Control-C; to reload it, invoke it again via `\.manage.py` shell) and then run the code in Example 3.87.

**Example 3.87: Python Interpreter Code**

```
>>> Tag.objects.all()
[<Tag: Andrew>, <Tag: Django>, <Tag: Education>,
 <Tag: Mobile>, <Tag: Video Games>, <Tag: Web>]
>>> Tag.objects.values_list('name')
[('andrew',), ('django',), ('education',),
 ('mobile',), ('video games',), ('web',)]
```

We could make a similar change to our `Startup` objects, ensuring that any list of `Startup` objects is ordered correctly. However, the case of a string is not only about organization but may also affect the display of a string. Should we take the same steps as above, the startup named JamBon Software would be stored as jambon software and displayed as Jambon Software in the shell. This is an error: the *B* in *JamBon* should be capitalized (a shortcoming in our website that we will discuss, but never actually have the opportunity to fix). If we affect the case of the string, we have no way of knowing that the *b* in the name should be capitalized, as the business desires. Changing the case for our startups is thus undesirable, as it will irreparably change how the information is displayed. We return to this issue in Part II and ensure that startups are ordered correctly, with the understanding that lists of `Startup` objects in Part I may not be ordered as we want.

Before moving on, you should delete the `Tag` object we created in this section, as shown in Example 3.88.

**Example 3.88: Python Interpreter Code**

```
>>> Tag.objects.get(name__iexact='Andrew').delete()
```

Consider that, at the moment, there is nothing stopping another developer from adding a `Tag` object in the database in all caps. Preventing such an action involves data validation, which we touch on in Chapter 7.

# 3.8 Putting It All Together

In Chapter 3, we saw how Django handles data. Django maps the Models of MVC (Model-View-Controller) directly on models, providing a way to organize and manipulate data.

Django models and model fields are simply Python classes. Django sets up very precise conventions, expecting class attributes of models to be instances of Django fields. Because Django is simply Python, however, developers can interact with models and fields just as they would with classes and attributes. Developers may in turn add methods to these models. What's more, Django provides simple declarative syntax via field options and nested `Meta` classes to customize field and model behavior without needing to write complicated code.

By convention, Django models that are to be identified by URLs are expected to have a `slug` field or attribute. A `slug` is a unique lowercase human-readable identifier that developers and the site may use to find a model, allowing for the creation of clean and simple URLs.

Developer-written models also inherit an ORM from `models.Model`, called a **manager**, which allows for direct manipulation of data in the database and is a part of Django we will keep coming back to because of its utility. In turn, managers produce querysets, which provide flexibility when handling groups of data.

As such, Django models allow for the automatic creation and alteration of databases. A key factor here is that Django expects to generate and alter a database (using migration files, seen here rapidly and in more depth in Chapter 10). Developers should not start a project by defining a database schema and then trying to mirror their schema in Django. This goes against the Django philosophy: don't fight the framework! Start with an outline of your desired data, create it declaratively in Django, and then let Django do the work of creating a database.

All in all, there is a lot of content in Chapter 3, and there is no way to remember it all on the first go, especially given the number of manager and queryset methods and the number of fields. Following are the key parts to understand:

- Models are simply Python classes with inherited behavior.
- Models are made up of fields.

- Fields are Python objects and behave like types.
- Models each have a model manager, which enables communication with the database.
- Each database relation creates two related managers, one for each model of the relation.
- Managers produce querysets, which feature many of the same methods of managers.

We will continue to come back to this information to help familiarize you with it as we use managers and querysets to build our site throughout Part I.

4

# Rapidly Producing Flexible HTML with Django Templates

## In This Chapter

- Learn the utility of templates
- Create templates in the Django Template Language (DTL) to display the data in our models
- Use template filters and tags to output exactly what you want
- Inherit template functionality to adhere to the DRY principle
- Integrate Django's external templates in our Python code

## 4.1 Introduction

Now that we have structured and created data, we must determine how the user will see these data. In this chapter, we create Django templates, which Django uses to display data and which act as the View in MVC architecture.

We begin the chapter by revisiting the Hello World example originally seen in Chapter 2: Hello World: Building a Basic Webpage in Django. By doing so, we gain perspective on what Django templates must achieve to easily and quickly display data. Once the goals are established, we build our templates. Finally, we see how Django allows us to interact with templates.

This chapter assumes basic understanding of HTML. The book does not provide a primer on the subject, as entire books have been written on the topic and free resources are available online. That said, if you understand the idea behind HTML tags and know that the <a> (anchor) tag creates hyperlinks, you are probably all set.

# 4.2   Revisiting Hello World: The Advantages of Templates

In Chapter 2, we built a single webpage that displayed the text `Hello World!` to the user. Building a webpage was a two-step process: we first defined what the webpage would display, and then we defined the URL that identified that webpage. Both of these steps are part of MVC architecture's Controller, which we examine in Chapter 5: Creating Webpages with Controllers in Django.

In Chapter 2, Section 2.5, we discussed the fact that a dynamic website needs to use all three MVC components. In particular, we discussed the ability to generate webpages automatically based on data in a database. We can now communicate with a database, and to best illustrate the utility of the MVC View component, we will try again to build a dynamic webpage.

Because we destroyed our **helloworld** app at the end of Chapter 2, we cannot simply return to our code. Rather than create a new Django app, we will use our **organizer** app to create a webpage.

As before, creating a webpage is a two-step process. We first define the data that the webpage will display. This is simply a Python function in this case, called a **function view** in Django, which returns a certain kind of data. Open `/organizer/views.py` and replace the contents with the code in Example 4.1.

**Example 4.1: Project Code**

`organizer/views.py` in ef2c075c3f

```
1   from django.http.response import HttpResponse
2
3
4   def homepage(request):
5       return HttpResponse('Hello (again) World!')
```

While the exact significance of the `request` parameter or the `HttpResponse` call should still seem a bit mysterious, you should be aware that this is Django's representation of the HTTP request/response loop, as discussed in Chapter 1: Starting a New Django Project. What's more, we know from experience that any text passed to and returned by `HttpResponse` will be printed on the webpage.

The second step is to create a URL that identifies the webpage. As in Chapter 2, we use the project-wide URL configuration in `/suorganizer/urls.py` to inform Django of the existence of our function view, called `homepage()` this time. The pair of values passed to `url()` denote the URL and the Python function that builds the website. In this case, the call `url(r'^$', homepage)` informs Django that the root webpage will call the `homepage()` view. Remember to first import the function into the file. The contents of `/suorganizer/urls.py` should now read as in Example 4.2.

**Example 4.2: Project Code**

`suorganizer/urls.py` **in** 95b20c151b

```
16    from django.conf.urls import include, url
17    from django.contrib import admin
18
19    from organizer.views import homepage
20
21    urlpatterns = [
22        url(r'^admin/', include(admin.site.urls)),
23        url(r'^$', homepage),
24    ]
```

We can immediately see the fruit of our labors. In the terminal, use `manage.py` to run Django's test server, as in Example 4.3.

**Example 4.3: Shell Code**

```
$ ./manage.py runserver
```

Open a browser and navigate to `http://127.0.0.1:8000/` to see the page. You will be greeted by the text `Hello (again) World!` in your browser.

Now that we have models, we can do better than a simple hardcoded Hello World. We can make our page dynamic! Let's return to `/organizer/views.py` and display actual data on our page (Example 4.4). Specifically, let us list all of the `Tag` objects that exist in the database.

**Example 4.4: Project Code**

`organizer/views.py` **in** c4a0b6a5b4

```
1    from django.http.response import HttpResponse
2
3    from .models import Tag
4
5
6    def homepage(request):
7        tag_list = Tag.objects.all()
8        output = ", ".join([tag.name for tag in tag_list])
9        return HttpResponse(output)
```

## Info

The code `from .models import Tag` is called an **explicit relative import**. It's equivalent to `from organizer.models import Tag`. However, as we are already in the `organizer` package, we do not need to specify it. If we ever choose to change the name of the package by renaming the `organizer/` directory, we won't need to change a relative import, whereas we would with an absolute import.

We first add a relative import to our `Tag` model. In our `homepage()` function, we use the model manager to request all `Tag` objects. On line 6, we use a list comprehension to create a list of all of the tag names and `join` this list into a string, delineating each item with a comma and a space, which we assign to the `output` variable. On line 7, we pass our `output` variable, containing our string of `Tag` names, to the `HttpResponse` object, and return it, effectively passing the `Tag` data to Django to become a webpage.

Reload the page in your browser (or browse back to `http://127.0.0.1:8000/`) to see the change take place. You will see the list of the names of the `Tag` objects we inputted in the database Chapter 3, which (depending on how closely you're following along) will output the code in Example 4.5.

**Example 4.5: HTML Code**

```
django, education, mobile, video games, web
```

This is a great start! If we add an item to the database, our `homepage()` view will automatically show it for us. It's like Django is automatically updating the content for us. As powerful as this is, it is too simple. Browsers expect our website to return a markup language such as HTML or JSON. At the moment, we would have to format this markup directly in our view. For example, a simple page listing the names of our tags might look something like Example 4.6.

**Example 4.6: Project Code**
`organizer/views.py` in dd5e4e1a71

```
 6   def homepage(request):
 7       tag_list = Tag.objects.all()
 8       html_output = "<html>\n"
 9       html_output += "<head>\n"
10       html_output += "  <title>"
11       html_output += "Don't Do This!</title>\n"
12       html_output += "</head>\n"
13       html_output += "<body>\n"
14       html_output += "  <ul>\n"
15       for tag in tag_list:
16           html_output += "    <li>"
17           html_output += tag.name.title()
18           html_output += "</li>\n"
19       html_output += "  </ul>\n"
20       html_output += "</body>\n"
21       html_output += "</html>\n"
22       return HttpResponse(html_output)
```

The code in Example 4.6 is cluttered and terrible, and it would be even worse for longer, more complicated HTML. Imagine being able to simply pass data to a pre-prepared document, which would format and present the data as desired. Imagine no more: this decoupling of presentation and logic is the reason that MVC splits View and Controller and why Django implements MVC Views as Django templates.

## 4.3 Understanding Django Templates and Their Goals

In the real world, such as in metalworking, a template is a mold used to shape or pattern a material. In computing, typically in the context of a word processor, a template is a file that comes with a preset format and preset content, which the user then fills in with more content.

Django templates take elements from both real-world templates and word-processing templates. A Django template is an external file or document that acts as a guide or blueprint for data, while also providing preset content. These blueprints, written by the developer, allow Django to quickly generate markup content to be returned to the user.

An easy way to think about templates is to liken them to fill-in-the-blank exercises. Each template provides content and structure with intentional blanks. We carefully identify each blank, giving it a purpose or some meaning. We then tell Django to assemble webpages using data and a template, making use of the purpose or meaning assigned to each blank in the template to properly fill it in with data.

If we return to our metallurgy analogy for (a very loose) comparison, the template is the mold and the data are the metal we are pouring. However, the mold here provides not just structure but also elements of the final item we are creating, and the metal we are pouring can be selectively poured or ignored.

Templates are thus external to Django: they are a document Django fills in. In fact, they are the only part of the framework that is not in Python. Templates are markup-language agnostic: a developer may output HTML, JSON, YAML, or any other imaginable text format. This is because the developer may write the template in any format and simply have Django fill in the blanks the developer leaves and indicates.

An important implication of templates' external nature is that Django has a method for importing the data from the document into Django, allowing Django to then identify the gaps the developer has left and fill them in. The Django template loader is an important piece of the puzzle, as we shall see by the end of the chapter.

## 4.4 Choosing a Format, an Engine, and a Location for Templates

The templates we are going to build for our website will be written in HTML 5, which has become the standard markup language for webpages.

> **Info**
>
> Other choices of markup language are HTML 4 and JSON. HTML 4 is still used on older sites, but HTML 5 is now widely adopted and is safe to use. JSON is used in the context of sites with powerful JavaScript front ends. Rather than retransmit the format of the page each time, some websites (like Twitter) opt to provide a single HTML page coupled with a JavaScript front end, allowing the website to transmit more compact data in the form of JSON. This means less bandwidth usage but increased processing for the user. This method is considered advanced and should only be used on sites that need to (quite drastically) optimize their bandwidth.

A template engine is a system that loads and renders a template into markup and therefore defines the language used to write the template. Starting in Django 1.8, Django enables the use of external template engines. Django's own template engine, called the Django Template Language (DTL), was the only option in Django 1.7 and earlier. As of Django 1.8, you are no longer tied to the DTL and can pick another template engine such as Jinja2. For simplicity's sake, this book uses the DTL exclusively and does not consider other options.

Given that templates are external to Django, we need a specific location to store them. In both our **organizer** and **blog** app directories, create a new directory named `templates`. Django automatically checks this directory for templates.

You could store all of your app templates in these two directories, but doing so leads to a potential problem. When loading a template, Django treats all of the `template` directories as a single directory. Consequently, file name conflicts may result, as `/organizer/templates/template.html` and `/blog/templates/template.html` look like the same file to Django. Given this behavior, Django recommends the convention of adding a subdirectory to `template/` by the name of the app, effectively creating a namespace for the app. You should thus create `organizer/` and `blog/` directories, resulting in paths `/organizer/templates/organizer/` and `/blog/templates/blog/`.

> **Info**
>
> You could, in theory, store **organizer** templates in the **blog** app under the directory `/blog/templates/organizer/`, but it would break clean app encapsulation.

## 4.5    Building a First Template: A Single `Tag` Object

In the following section, we create our first template, which will display information related to a single `Tag` object stored in the database. We build the template step by step, identifying and learning different parts of the DTL.

### 4.5.1    Coding the Foundation of the Template in HTML

Let's write the HTML for the body of the webpage that will display a tag. Create a new file `/organizer/templates/organizer/tag_detail.html`, and write the code shown in Example 4.7.

**Example 4.7: Project Code**
`organizer/templates/organizer/tag_detail.html` in db859e6f4b

```
1    <h2>  </h2>
2      <section>
3        <h3>Startups</h3>
```

```
 4            <ul>
 5
 6            </ul>
 7        </section>
 8            <section>
 9                <h3>Blog Posts</h3>
10                <ul>
11
12                </ul>
13            </section>
```

## Info

The indentation in my project templates are a little strange, because they reflect the indentation levels of the HTML elements as they appear at the end of the project. This makes performing diffs on templates—or seeing changes between commits in the repository on Github—much easier, at the cost of some odd indentation.

The code from the previous example is HTML and should make sense to you. This book does not provide a primer or an appendix on the topic, as it is outside the scope of a back-end framework. If you do not know HTML, reading the guide[1] provided by W3Schools is a good start.

The goal of the page is to show a single Tag object and to list all of the startups and blog posts associated with it. If we were having a human fill in this information, we could add the HTML comments shown in Example 4.8 to try and direct them.

**Example 4.8: Project Code**
`organizer/templates/organizer/tag_detail.html` in dd856e76ce

```
 1      <h2> <!-- name of tag --> </h2>
 2        <section>
 3          <h3>Startups</h3>
 4          <ul>
 5            <!-- list of startups related to tag -->
 6          </ul>
 7        </section>
 8          <section>
 9              <h3>Blog Posts</h3>
10              <ul>
11                <!-- list of posts related to tag -->
12              </ul>
13          </section>
```

The omission of the <html> and <body> tags is intentional. We will add them later.

---

1. https://dju.link/html

## 4.5.2  Filling in Content with Template Variables

The HTML comments in our template would be very helpful to a human, but Django needs a little bit more help figuring out what to fill in. With (most) templates, we must assume we will give Django at least one object with a name of our choosing (we do so in Chapter 5). Django uses such objects to fill in the blanks left in the template. In this instance, we want to supply Django with tag information. We therefore plan to give the template we are currently building a `Tag` model object, creatively named `tag`. In Django nomenclature, we pass a `Tag` instance to the `tag` template variable.

Django templates allow us to handle Python objects just as we would in Python via a domain-specific language. Practically speaking, given a `Tag` instance named `tag`, we can access object data and object methods as we would in Python, by calling attributes such as `tag.name` and `tag.slug` (fields we specified in Chapter 3: Programming Django Models and Creating a SQLite Database).

We must also help Django figure out where the blanks are. To do so, we surround our blanks with double brackets. Instead of simply calling `tag.name`, we must call `{{ tag.name }}`. The double-brackets are called **delimiters**: they help Django know whether it should process the text or leave it alone. In our template, we can thus replace the first comment with `{{ tag.name }}`, as in Example 4.9. When a view passes a tag to this template (next chapter), Django knows to fill in the blank with the name attribute of the Tag.

**Example 4.9: Project Code**
`organizer/templates/organizer/tag_detail.html` in a5247adb70

```
1    <h2>{{ tag.name }}</h2>
```

If a developer provides an attribute that doesn't exist, such as `tag.imaginary_variable`, Django does not error: Django simply doesn't print anything. If you are missing a value in your template, it is either because the value is empty or because you've coded the wrong variable name. This may sound frustrating, but it can also be useful, as seen in Chapter 8: Displaying Forms in Templates).

One of the key features of printing variables in Django templates is that text is escaped according to HTML rules (which may be frustrating if you are attempting to output a different markup). For instance, imagine we wish to print the value `I <3 Django` in a variable. This might be problematic, as `<` is symbol with meaning in HTML (used for opening tags such as `<strong>`). The Django template system will automatically escape this value for us, replacing it with `&lt;`. As such, should our variable contain the value `I <3 Django`, Django will actually output `I &lt;3 Django`, which in turn will be properly rendered by the browser back into `I <3 Django`, which is what site users will see. Escaping is thus typically useful and desirable but can cause unexpected problems in certain cases. Moreover, while I've presented this as a convenience feature, it is actually a security feature and something you want.

> **Info**
>
> Starting in Django 1.8, Django supplies the ability to use other templating systems. These templating systems may or may not behave as described above. For instance, the popular Jinja2 templating system does not escape values by default! Always be sure to read the documentation.

### 4.5.3 Adding Logic with Template Tags

To iterate and print the lists of startups and blog posts associated with a `Tag` object, we need something a little more powerful than simple variables. We need a loop.

Just as Django allows for variables through the {{ }} delimiters, Django provides template tags, which are delimited by {% %}. Template tags allow for conditional logic, loops, and evaluation of functions and methods, meaning that we can run and evaluate Python in our template.

> **Info**
>
> On top of the {{ variable }} and {% expression %} delimiters, Django supplies {# #}, which is used to write comments in templates. The utility of using template comments over markup-specific comments is that they will not appear in the output of the rendered templates. This further allows for a separation of comments specific to the template code from comments specific to markup code.

We first consider how to get a list of startups, how to iterate through them, and then how to display this information in the template. We then repeat the process for the list of blog posts.

#### 4.5.3.1 Iterating through a QuerySet in a Template to Print a List of Startup Objects

Recall from Chapter 3 that our many-to-many relationship can be directly accessed as a manager object via the related name variable: the manager that provides the set of `Startup` objects associated with our `Tag` object can be accessed via `tag.startup_set`. The manager method we use here is `all()`, meaning we are calling `tag.startup_set.all()`.

The `all()` manager method returns a `QuerySet` object, which can act like a Python list and allows us to iterate through it using a Python `for` loop. Valid Python code would be `for startup in tag.startup_set.all()`. In Django templates, we remove the parentheses from the method, meaning that a valid template tag of the loop above is `{% for startup in tag.startup_set.all %}`. Unlike variables, template tags provide scope, and therefore we must limit the scope by closing template tags. In this case, we do so with `{% endfor %}`. Anything in scope, including markup and other logic, will be repeated because of our loop. As in Python, our loop gives us access to the `startup` object referenced to in the `for` loop, allowing us to print the name of the startup object with `{{ startup.name }}`.

We can thus use the unordered list HTML tag <ul> with list item <li> to print a list of Startup objects, as in Example 4.10.

**Example 4.10: Project Code**

`organizer/templates/organizer/tag_detail.html` in b9feddf8e3

```
 1    <h2>{{ tag.name }}</h2>
 2      <section>
 3        <h3>Startups</h3>
 4        <ul>
 5          {% for startup in tag.startup_set.all %}
 6            <li><a href="">
 7              {{ startup.name }}
 8            </a></li>
 9          {% endfor %}
10        </ul>
11      </section>
```

Take a moment to consider that our call to tag.startup_set.all() results in a database query.

In Chapter 5, we write the view (as seen in our Hello World example) that will pair Tag object data to this view. When we ask for the *django* Tag, it will result in the code (omitting the blog post list) shown in Example 4.11.

**Example 4.11: HTML Code**

```
<h2>django</h2>
<section>
  <h3>Startups</h3>
  <ul>
    <li><a href="">JamBon Software</a></li>
  </ul>
</section>
<!-- blog post section omitted -->
```

This is exactly what we want, unless the Tag object is not associated with any startups. For instance, our *web* Tag is unassociated with any content. This leads to the code in Example 4.12 being output.

**Example 4.12: HTML Code**

```
<h2>web</h2>
<section>
  <h3>Startups</h3>
  <ul>
  </ul>
</section>
<!-- blog post section omitted -->
```

This is obviously undesirable. Thankfully, we can control this behavior with conditional logic. Like the `for` tag, Django provides an `if` tag in addition to basic Boolean logic operators (and, or, ==, !=, >, etc.). We don't need any operators in our case, however: we just need to know whether there is any content in the queryset returned by `tag.startup_set.all()`. Luckily, because querysets behave like Python lists, we can simply ask if the list exists, remembering to provide expression delimiters with our conditional logic: `{% if tag.startup_set.all %}`. This is equivalent to `{% if tag.startup_set.all > 0 %}`. We close the tag with `{% endif %}`. Anything in the scope of the tag is processed only if the condition is met. Our code now reads as in Example 4.13.

**Example 4.13: Project Code**

`organizer/templates/organizer/tag_detail.html` **in** ed4f0664d9

```
 1     <h2>{{ tag.name }}</h2>
 2     {% if tag.startup_set.all %}
 3       <section>
 4         <h3>Startups</h3>
 5         <ul>
 6         {% for startup in tag.startup_set.all %}
 7           <li><a href="">
 8             {{ startup.name }}
 9           </a></li>
10         {% endfor %}
11         </ul>
12       </section>
13     {% endif %}
```

If we print our page for the *web* `Tag`, we'll output the code in Example 4.14.

**Example 4.14: HTML Code**

```
<h2>web</h2>
<section>
  <h3>Blog Posts</h3>          # No startups section
  <ul>
    <!-- list of posts related to tag -->
  </ul>
</section>
```

That's a very lonely piece of HTML. Let's inform the user that the tag isn't currently associated with any `Startup` objects. We can do this by providing an `else` condition to our `if` condition above, as in Example 4.15.

**Example 4.15: Project Code**

`organizer/templates/organizer/tag_detail.html` **in** 1038c236e3

```
 1     <h2>{{ tag.name }}</h2>
 2     {% if tag.startup_set.all %}
```

```
 3        <section>
 4          <h3>Startups</h3>
 5          <ul>
 6            {% for startup in tag.startup_set.all %}
 7              <li><a href="">
 8                {{ startup.name }}
 9              </a></li>
10            {% endfor %}
11          </ul>
12        </section>
13      {% else %}
14        <p>This tag is not related to any startups.</p>
15      {% endif %}
```

### 4.5.3.2   Iterating through a `QuerySet` in a Template to Print a List of `Post` Objects

We can now follow the same steps we saw with `Startup` to print the blog posts list. Recall that in our `Post` model we specified a `related_name` option to our many-to-many field, as shown in Example 4.16.

**Example 4.16:** Project Code
blog/models.py **in** 67f70808d7

```
10    class Post(models.Model):
 .        ...
20        tags = models.ManyToManyField(
21            Tag, related_name='blog_posts')
```

Instead of `tag.post_set.all`, our related name attribute gives us access to the `Tag` objects associated with `Post` objects via `tag.blog_posts.all`.

Just as before, we can loop throughout the `QuerySet` returned by this call, encompassing the entire process in an `if` block. The code we create in the first step is shown in Example 4.17.

**Example 4.17:** Project Code
organizer/templates/organizer/tag_detail.html **in** 67f70808d7

```
16            <section>
17              <h3>Blog Posts</h3>
18              <ul>
19                {% for post in tag.blog_posts.all %}
20                  <li><a href="">
21                    {{ post.title }}
22                  </a></li>
23                {% endfor %}
24              </ul>
25            </section>
```

In the second step, we surround the code with that shown in Example 4.18.

**Example 4.18: Project Code**

`organizer/templates/organizer/tag_detail.html` in ea6fec30c2

```
16          {% if tag.blog_posts.all %}
  .           ...
27          {% else %}
28            <p>This tag is not related to any blog posts.</p>
29          {% endif %}
```

Consider that our code may print a rather unappealing page. For example, the *web* `Tag` currently in our database results in the output shown in Example 4.19.

**Example 4.19: HTML Code**

```
<h2>web</h2>
<p>This tag is not related to any startups.</p>
<p>This tag is not related to any blog posts.</p>
```

It would be prettier if the template only printed a message about missing content if neither list prints any content. As such, we can remove both of the `else` blocks and add a third `if` statement at the end of the template. The full code thus reads as in Example 4.20.

**Example 4.20: Project Code**

`organizer/templates/organizer/tag_detail.html` in 963f1a5ce9

```
 1      <h2>{{ tag.name }}</h2>
 2      {% if tag.startup_set.all %}
 3        <section>
 4          <h3>Startups</h3>
 5          <ul>
 6            {% for startup in tag.startup_set.all %}
 7              <li><a href="">
 8                {{ startup.name }}
 9              </a></li>
10            {% endfor %}
11          </ul>
12        </section>
13      {% endif %}
14          {% if tag.blog_posts.all %}
15          <section>
16            <h3>Blog Posts</h3>
17            <ul>
```

```
18                  {% for post in tag.blog_posts.all %}
19                    <li><a href="">
20                        {{ post.title }}
21                    </a></li>
22                  {% endfor %}
23                </ul>
24              </section>
25          {% endif %}
26          {% if not tag.startup_set.all and not tag.blog_posts.all %}
27            <p>This tag is not related to any content.</p>
28          {% endif %}
```

Just as in Python, we negate the Boolean value of a variable using the not keyword in the if condition in the template.

## 4.5.4   Controlling the Output of Variables with Template Filters `title`, `length`, and `pluralize`

We are now outputting the correct data, but it's not very pretty: consider how neither *django* nor *web* is capitalized. Remember from Chapter 3 that, for alphabetization reasons, all of our tags are stored in the database in lowercase. When we display them to the user, we clearly don't want to display them this way. We need to capitalize our content.

In addition to printing variables and providing template tags for logic, templates provide the ability to interact with variables via template filters. Template filters allow developers to sort, modify, and count lists; to format a Python date object into a pretty string; and to modify strings, such as to change their case.

Django template filters may be applied to a variable by appending a vertical bar character, or *pipe*, to the variable followed by the name of the filter (and any arguments the filter might take): {{ variable|filter }}. Spaces between the variable, vertical bar, and filter name are not welcome. In our case, we are most interested in the title filter, which capitalizes the first letter of each word in a string and lowercases every other character. In Example 4.21, in our Tag detail template, we change {{ tag.name }} to {{ tag.name|title }} and {{ post.title }} to {{ post.title|title }}. We do not add the filter to {{ startup.name }}, as we allow those to be capitalized at will, allowing for names such as *JamBon Software* (with the title filter, this would become *Jambon Software*, which is an error because the *B* is intentionally capitalized; we discuss this topic again in Chapter 27: Building Custom Template Tags and Chapter 30: Starting a New Project Correctly).

**Example 4.21: Project Code**
organizer/templates/organizer/tag_detail.html **in** 937466728c

```
1    <h2>{{ tag.name|title }}</h2>
     ...
20                {{ post.title|title }}
```

When displaying information for our *django* `Tag` object, Django now outputs the code shown in Example 4.22.

**Example 4.22: HTML Code**

```
<h2>Django</h2>
<section>
  <h3>Startups</h3>
  <ul>
    <li><a href="">JamBon Software</a></li>
  </ul>
</section>
<section>
  <h3>Blog Posts</h3>
  <ul>
    <li><a href="">Django Training</a></li>
  </ul>
</section>
```

> **Info**
>
> The `capfirst` is typically the first filter new developers turn to when seeking to capitalize a string. The problem with this filter is that it only capitalizes the first letter in a string rather than the first letter of every word in the string. If we apply the `capfirst` filter on the string video games, then the filter will return "Video games," which is less nice than the "Video Games" string returned by the `title` filter (note the first *g* in *Games* in both outputs).

*| capfirst*

Template filters not only can modify strings for display but also can help make text more readable. Let's start in Example 4.23 by using the `length` filter, which counts the number of items in a list.

**Example 4.23: Project Code**

`organizer/templates/organizer/tag_detail.html` in `201dffbdd3`

```
5        <p>
6            Tag is associated with
7            {{ tag.startup_set.all|length }}
8            startups.
9        </p>
```

*| length*

Once we have tags associated with multiple startups, this will look great. However, our *django* tag is currently associated with only a single startup, which means we will be printing the text "Tag is associated with 1 startups." The *s* that pluralizes *startups* is awkward in English when used for a single item. Luckily, there is a template filter, `pluralize`, that will print an *s* if the number passed to the filter is greater than one. We can chain filters, which

*| pluralize*
*(expects a number)*

means we can get the number of items from our `length` filter as before and pass the result to `pluralize`, like so: `{{ tag.startup_set.all|length|pluralize }}`. This technique is demonstrated in Example 4.24.

**Example 4.24: Project Code**
`organizer/templates/organizer/tag_detail.html` in `69fb156e6d`

```
6            Tag is associated with
7            {{ tag.startup_set.all|length }}
8            startup{{ tag.startup_set.all|length|pluralize }}.
```

> **Info**
>
> Should you need to pluralize a word that doesn't end with an *s* character, you can still pass the desired output to `pluralize`. For example, `witch{{ witch_num |pluralize:"es" }}`. It is also possible to provide both the singular and plural endings of a word, such as `pon{{ pony_num|pluralize:"y,ies" }}`.

With our new filters applied, the code above prints "Tag is associated with 1 startup" as well as "Tag is associated with 2 startups," making the site more readable and polished.

The code in Example 4.24 demonstrates the use of the `length` filter as well as the ability to chain template filters. However, it is not the best code we could write at this point in time. The first improvement we can make is to remove the `length` filter. The `pluralize` filter is very intelligent and may be applied to numbers, lists, and `QuerySet` objects. The call `{{ tag.startup_set.all|pluralize }}` will output the same results as our original call.

Our call is still very inefficient. When we invoke a manager in a template, we are also making a call to the database. This is expensive—interaction with the database is typically the first thing to optimize to make a website run more quickly. The fewer database queries, the better. The next optimization is to fetch only the data necessary. Consider that our call to `tag.startup_set.all` fetches all of the `Tag` objects in our database even though we are only interested in the number of tags in the database. Recall from Chapter 3 that model manager objects and queryset objects provide a `count()` method, which returns the number of objects in a database query. Every instance of `{{ tag.startup_set .all|length }}` can thus be replaced with `{{ tag.startup_set.count }}`, as in Example 4.25.

**Example 4.25: Project Code**
`organizer/templates/organizer/tag_detail.html` in `8a160f295b`

```
6            Tag is associated with
7            {{ tag.startup_set.count }}
8            startup{{ tag.startup_set.count|pluralize }}.
```

Any database query for count() is faster than a database query for all(), particularly for large datasets. Our code is thus faster, but not the fastest it could be. In Chapter 26, we optimize the preceding code (and code introduced in Chapter 5) to further improve the speed of our website.

To finish up, we can also apply our pluralize filter to the <h2>Startups</h2> and <h2>Blog Posts</h2> subheadings, resulting in <h2>Startup{{ tag .startup_set.count|pluralize }}</h2> and <h2>Blog Post{{ tag .blog_posts.count|pluralize }}</h2>. Our final code for the template (in this chapter) is shown in Example 4.26.

**Example 4.26: Project Code**
`organizer/templates/organizer/tag_detail.html` in 37255170a3

```
1    <h2>{{ tag.name|title }}</h2>
2    {% if tag.startup_set.all %}
3      <section>
4        <h3>Startup{{ tag.startup_set.count|pluralize }}</h3>
5        <p>
6          Tag is associated with
7          {{ tag.startup_set.count }}
8          startup{{ tag.startup_set.count|pluralize }}.
9        </p>
10       <ul>
11         {% for startup in tag.startup_set.all %}
12           <li><a href="">
13             {{ startup.name }}
14           </a></li>
15         {% endfor %}
16       </ul>
17     </section>
18   {% endif %}
19     {% if tag.blog_posts.all %}
20       <section>
21         <h3>Blog Post{{ tag.blog_posts.count|pluralize }}</h3>
22         <ul>
23           {% for post in tag.blog_posts.all %}
24             <li><a href="">
25               {{ post.title|title }}
26             </a></li>
27           {% endfor %}
28         </ul>
29       </section>
30     {% endif %}
31     {% if not tag.startup_set.all and not tag.blog_posts.all %}
32       <p>This tag is not related to any content.</p>
33     {% endif %}
```

Observe again that we have not coded the <html>, <head>, or <body> HTML tags and that Django does not provide them. We will include these for all templates before the end of the chapter. For the moment, let's build the rest of the body of our templates.

## 4.6    Building the Rest of Our App Templates

With a fundamental understanding of template variables, filters, and tags, we are now in a position to build the templates for all of the webpages we anticipated building in Chapter 1. We start with the templates in our **organizer** app and finish with our **blog** app before we move on to template inheritance and loading and rendering templates in the next sections.

### 4.6.1    Template for a List of `Tag` objects

Create a new template at /organizer/templates/organizer/tag_list.html. In Example 4.27, as you may have guessed from the file name, we will list all of our Tag objects. In Chapter 5, we will put a list of tags to the tag_list variable.

**Example 4.27: Project Code**
organizer/templates/organizer/tag_list.html in b4fb40ec0c

```
1    <h2>Tag List</h2>
2    <ul>
3      {% for tag in tag_list %}
4        <li>
5          <a href="">
6            {{ tag.name|title }}</a>
7        </li>
8      {% endfor %}
9    </ul>
```

As before, we use a for loop to iterate through the tag_list that we assume the template is provided with. This loop gives us access to a tag object, which we print the name of using {{ tag.name|title }}. Take note of the title template filter that we use to correctly capitalize the text. We surround this in HTML markup to ensure correct viewing and indicate the end of the for loop using {% endfor %}.

Given our template and the Tag models entered in Chapter 3, the page created from our template will generate the code in Example 4.28.

**Example 4.28: HTML Code**

```
<h2>Tag List</h2>
<ul>
  <li><a href="">Django</a></li>
  <li><a href="">Mobile</a></li>
  <li><a href="">Video Games</a></li>
  <li><a href="">Web</a></li>
</ul>
```

In our last template, we accounted for the possibility that a Tag object might not have any Startup objects associated with it, creating an if tag to check whether any existed.

To make this template robust, we should also account for the possibility that there are no Tag objects in the database, meaning that tag_list is empty. We could write the code shown in Example 4.29.

**Example 4.29: Project Code**
organizer/templates/organizer/tag_list.html **in** 47d7f1f91b

```
 1    <h2>Tag List</h2>
 2    {% if tag_list %}
 3    <ul>
 4      {% for tag in tag_list %}
 5        <li>
 6          <a href="">
 7            {{ tag.name|title }}</a>
 8        </li>
 9      {% endfor %}
10    </ul>
11    {% else %}
12      <p><em>There are currently no Tags available.</em></p>
13    {% endif %}
```

However, more often than not, tag_list will contain items, meaning that the preceding code will incur the cost of an if statement for nothing.

Instead of using an if statement, we can use the {% empty %} tag in our template, as shown in Example 4.30. This tag allows for the check to be done by the for loop, resulting in shorter code and potentially less processing.

**Example 4.30: Project Code**
organizer/templates/organizer/tag_list.html **in** 29b62a27cc

```
 1    <h2>Tag List</h2>
 2    <ul>
 3      {% for tag in tag_list %}
 4        <li>
 5          <a href="">
 6            {{ tag.name|title }}</a>
 7        </li>
 8      {% empty %}
 9        <li><em>There are currently no Tags available.</em></li>
10      {% endfor %}
11    </ul>
```

{% empty %}

Note that the {% empty %} tag infers scope from the {% endfor %} and does not require its own close tag.

The code with the if statement and the code with the empty tag are not actually equivalent. In the first case, the template will output the code in Example 4.31.

**Example 4.31: HTML Code**

```
<h1>Tag List</h1>
<p><em>There are currently no Tags available.</em></p>
```

The second case ({% empty %} variant) will output the code in Example 4.32.

**Example 4.32: HTML Code**

```
<h1>Tag List</h1>
<ul>
  <li><em>There are currently no Tags available.</em></li>
</ul>
```

Our new code (using {% empty %}) is thus actually equivalent to the code in Example 4.33.

**Example 4.33: Project Code**
organizer/templates/organizer/tag_list.html in 8c701bd0ed

```
1    <h2>Tag List</h2>
2    <ul>
3    {% if tag_list %}
4      {% for tag in tag_list %}
5        <li>
6          <a href="">
7              {{ tag.name|title }}</a>
8        </li>
9      {% endfor %}
10   {% else %}
11     <li><em>There are currently no Tags available.</em></li>
12   {% endif %}
13   </ul>
```

We are simply shortening it to the code in Example 4.34.

**Example 4.34: Project Code**
organizer/templates/organizer/tag_list.html in e9bd61448b

```
1    <h2>Tag List</h2>
2    <ul>
3      {% for tag in tag_list %}
4        <li>
5          <a href="">
6              {{ tag.name|title }}</a>
```

```
 7        </li>
 8        {% empty %}
 9        <li><em>There are currently no Tags available.</em></li>
10        {% endfor %}
11     </ul>
```

The code in Example 4.34 is more elegant and potentially faster, but we are making a tradeoff. Printing a single-item list in the event of an empty list is typically frowned upon, and some perfectionists will squirm at our markup in the latter case. However, our reasoning for choosing the code with the `empty` tag over the code with the `if` tag is still sound: we have opted to prioritize speed and elegance in anticipated cases by forgoing the `if` statement at the cost of printing unclean markup in the case of unanticipated output. Stated differently, our choice only makes sense under the assumption that the unclean markup is printed in the event of an error. Consider that the reason we are making any change to this code is to increase the robustness and usability of the application.

You may have noticed that we built our template with anchor tags (`<a>`) where the text value is defined but the `href` attribute is not, and we will continue to do so throughout this chapter. We will provide the `href` attribute values in Chapter 6 because correctly creating a URL link requires a holistic understanding of MVC architecture as implemented in Django.

## 4.6.2  Template for a Single `Startup` Object

Create a new file at `/organizer/templates/organizer/startup_detail.html`. In the template, we list information associated with a single `Startup` object using an HTML definition list, as shown in Example 4.35. We assume that our template is given a `startup` object, from which we will derive all data: we will list all of the fields, or data attributes, of our `Startup` model class passed to the `startup` variable (which we shall code in Chapter 5).

**Example 4.35: Project Code**
`organizer/templates/organizer/startup_detail.html` **in** 5cc3cf5880

```
 1    <article>
 2
 3      <h2>{{ startup.name }}</h2>
 4      <dl>
 5        <dt>Date Founded</dt>
 6          <dd>{{ startup.founded_date }}</dd>
 7        <dt>Website</dt>
 8          <dd>{{ startup.website }}</dd>
 9        <dt>Contact</dt>
10          <dd>{{ startup.contact }}</dd>
11
12        <dt>Tag{{ startup.tags.count|pluralize }}</dt>
13          {% for tag in startup.tags.all %}
```

```
14              <dd><a href="">
15                  {{ tag.name|title }}
16              </a></dd>
17          {% endfor %}
18
19      </dl>
20
21      <p>{{ startup.description }}</p>
22
23          {% if startup.newslink_set.all %}
24              <section>
25                  <h3>Recent News</h3>
26                  <ul>
27                  {% for newslink in startup.newslink_set.all %}
28                      <li>
29 (external link)       <a href="{{ newslink.link }}">
30                          {{ newslink.title|title }}</a>
31                      </li>
32                  {% endfor %}
33                  </ul>
34              </section>
35          {% endif %}
36
37          {% if startup.blog_posts.all %}
38              <section>
39                  <h3>Blog Post{{ startup.blog_posts.all|pluralize }}</h3>
40                  <ul>
41                  {% for post in startup.blog_posts.all %}
42                      <li>
43                          <a href="">
44                              {{ post.title|title }}</a>
45                      </li>
46                  {% endfor %}
47                  </ul>
48              </section>
49          {% endif %}
50
51      </article>
```

The code in Example 4.35 does not introduce anything new, and you should be comfortable reading it. For the sake of clarity, however, we will now quickly walk through it.

Lines 3, 6, 8, and 10 print (respectively) the name, foundation date, website, and contact email of the startup, using (respectively) `startup.name`, `startup.founded_date`, `startup.website`, and `startup.contact`. We also print the full text description of the `startup` object on line 21. We print all of these values using the template variable delimiters: {{ variable }}.

We have three loops using a `Startup`-related manager and the `for` template tag delimited by {% expression %}. The first loop, starting at line 13 and ending at line 17, iterates through all of the `Tag` objects related to the `Startup` object passed to our template. We print the name of each `Tag` object, capitalizing the first letter of every word in the string with the `title` template filter. The second loop iterates through `NewsLink` objects associated with the `startup` variable on lines 27 through 32, printing the URL and headline of the news piece in a simple HTML link (using the anchor tag `<a>`). We apply the `title` filter to the `Newslink` headline. The third loop, from lines 41 to 46, displays related blog posts.

Observe that we close scope using `{% endfor %}` for all of our loops. Anything in scope, or between the start and end tag, will be repeated for each iteration of the loop, including printing of markup.

Unlike with our `Tag` templates, we use neither an `if` template tag nor the `{% else %}` tag to verify the existence of `Tag` objects. We are thus assuming that a `Startup` will always be associated with one `Tag` object.

We can improve the display above in three ways. We can

1. Customize the display of the foundation date of the startup.
2. Provide a link directly to the `Startup` website.
3. Properly format the description of the startup.

### 4.6.2.1  Using the `date` Template Filter to Customize Output

While we treat the `startup.founded_date` value on line 4 as a string, it is in fact a Python `datetime.date` object. Given the code above, should you render the page for our 'JamBon Software' startup, the page will print "Jan. 18, 2013" for the date value.

Django automatically applies the `date` filter. `{{ startup.founded_date }}` is equivalent to `{{ startup.founded_date|date }}`. The `date` filter allows us to customize the way in which the date is printed. By default, it applies the `"DATE_FORMAT"` argument, meaning that `{{ startup.founded_date }}` is equivalent to `{{ startup.founded_date|date }}`, which in turn is equivalent to `{{ startup.founded_date|date:"DATE_FORMAT" }}`. The `date` filter also accepts three other pre-prepared date formats: `"SHORT_DATE_FORMAT"`, `"DATETIME_FORMAT"`, and `"SHORT_DATETIME_FORMAT"`. Our variable is a `DateField`, not a `DateTimeField`, which means we cannot use the `"DATETIME_FORMAT"` or `"SHORT_DATETIME_FORMAT"` arguments. However, `{{ startup.founded_date|date:"SHORT_DATE_FORMAT" }}` will output "01/18/2013" instead of the default "Jan. 18, 2013" provided by the `"DATE_FORMAT"` argument.

In turn, it is possible to customize the date output by specifying a format string in which each character in the string has a special meaning in relation to the date. For example, `{{ startup.founded_date|date:"SHORT_DATE_FORMAT" }}`, which will output "01/18/2013," could also be written `{{ startup.founded_date|date:"d/m/Y" }}`. Alternatively, `{{ startup.founded_date|date:"DATE_FORMAT" }}` can be written `{{ startup.founded_date|date:"N j, Y" }}`, outputting "Jan. 18, 2013." Django provides 40 case-sensitive characters to allow for date customization. It would not benefit us to look at each one, so instead we examine the ones we intend to use for our own `datetime` object.

Our call to `date` will use the F, j, S, and Y format characters. F will print the full month, j will print the day of the month as an integer, S will add a suffix to the number (such as *st*), and Y will print the year as a four-digit number. As such, our call to `{{ startup.founded_date|date:"F jS, Y" }}` will output "January 18th, 2013" for the JamBon Startup.

For the full list of template `date` format characters, please see the official reference guide, found on the official Django documentation page.[2]

### 4.6.2.2  Automatic Linking with the `urlize` Template Filter

Currently, we are printing the URL of the startup's website as a string. It would be easier for the user if we provided this as a link, allowing them to simply click the link rather than having to copy and paste it.

There are two ways to do this. The first is to code the necessary HTML, as in Example 4.36.

**Example 4.36:** Django Template Language Code

```
<a href="{{ startup.website }}">{{ startup.website }}</a>
```

Observe that we have done something very similar for our `NewsLink` object in Example 4.37.

**Example 4.37:** Django Template Language Code

```
<a href="{{ newslink.link }}">{{ newslink.title|title }}</a>
```

Our second option is to use the `urlize` template filter on the current variable: `{{ startup.website|urlize }}`. In the case our website, if `http://jambonsw.com`, then the `urlize` filter will print `<a href="http://jambonsw.com" rel="nofollow">http://jambonsw.com</a>`.

We should always consider the two options because `urlize` adds the `rel="nofollow"` attribute to our anchor tag. Search engines use the number of links to a website as a way of determining a site's importance, but links with the `rel="nofollow"` attribute do not contribute to the ranking algorithms. The attribute was introduced as a way for blog writers to limit the effect of spam links posted in comments, effectively telling search engines that those links were not official. As such, the attribute, and therefore `urlize`, is very useful in some but not all contexts.

In this context we must ask ourselves who is providing the information about each startup. As the final goal is to have it be community driven, and therefore out of our direct control, I will choose to use the `urlize` filter, as I think the `rel="nofollow"` attribute is potentially warranted. However, this is a subjective choice, and you may disagree with it.

---

2. https://dju.link/18/date-tag

> **Info**
>
> It is helpful to remember that a URL has the following components:
>
> `scheme://network_location/path?query#fragments`
>
> A network location may be a domain name with top-level domain (TLD) or else an IP address. In `google.com`, `google` is the domain name and `com` is the TLD.

The `urlize` filter is a finicky filter. The scheme of the URL is optional, but in the event that it is not specified, the domain of the URL must have one of the following TLDs: `.com`, `.edu`, `.gov`, `.int`, `.mil`, `.net`, and `.org`.

> **Ghosts of Django Past**
>
> In versions prior to Django 1.8, the `urlize` filter would not recognize URLs that had a path but not a scheme. You could not specify `docs.djangoproject` `.com/en/1.8/` and instead had to ensure the value of the field in the model was `https://docs.djangoproject.com/en/1.8/`

If we pass the string `lemonde.fr` to the `urlize` filter, it will not print an HTML anchor tag. Instead, we must provide `http://lemonde.fr` to `urlize`.

While knowing about the potential pitfalls of various template filters is useful, this section is also a prelude to Chapter 7: Allowing User Input with Forms. We return to this filter then to consider the issue in full.

### 4.6.2.3  Using the `linebreaks` Filter to Correctly Format a Paragraph

One of the features of HTML is that it ignores whitespace. Formatting such as paragraph breaks and multiple spaces are simply ignored. Instead, HTML is supposed to be formatted using the paragraph tag `<p>` and the line break tag `<br />`.

The description we have for our `Startup` objects is not currently formatted in HTML, nor would we want it to be. Providing a markup-agnostic format allows us to output to whatever we want. However, it also means that printing it the way we are now will result in multiple paragraphs being squashed together.

For example, take the following paragraph:

```
This is the first paragraph.

This is the second.
This is not quite its own.
```

While the spacing will be correctly printed in the HTML page, the browser will render it as:

```
This is the first paragraph. This is the second. This is not quite its own.
```

Luckily, Django provides the `linebreaks` filter, which converts a newline (a single carriage return) to a `<br />`, and two to a `<p>`. This capability allows regular formatting to be preserved in our HTML output. To apply it, we simply change line 21, shown in Example 4.38, to read as shown in Example 4.39.

**Example 4.38: Django Template Language Code**

```
<p>{{ startup.description }}</p>
```

**Example 4.39: Django Template Language Code**

```
{{ startup.description|linebreaks }}
```

Note that the surrounding paragraph tags have been removed. The filter will provide them for us. Given our example, the output will now be as shown in Example 4.40.

**Example 4.40: HTML Code**

```
<p>This is the first paragraph.</p>
<p>This is the second.<br />This is not quite its own.</p>
```

This approach effectively retains any formatting we may provide in our `Startup` description field.

Incorporating all of our changes from the last three subsections, our final template code is shown in Example 4.41.

**Example 4.41: Project Code**

`organizer/templates/organizer/startup_detail.html` in edf261b0c7

```
 1   <article>
 2
 3     <h2>{{ startup.name }}</h2>
 4     <dl>
 5       <dt>Date Founded</dt>
 6         <dd>{{ startup.founded_date|date:"F jS, Y" }}</dd>
 7       <dt>Website</dt>
 8         <dd>{{ startup.website|urlize }}</dd>
 9       <dt>Contact</dt>
10         <dd>{{ startup.contact }}</dd>
11
12       <dt>Tag{{ startup.tags.count|pluralize }}</dt>
13         {% for tag in startup.tags.all %}
14           <dd><a href="">
15             {{ tag.name|title }}
16           </a></dd>
17         {% endfor %}
18
19     </dl>
20
21     {{ startup.description|linebreaks }}
22
23       {% if startup.newslink_set.all %}
24         <section>
25           <h3>Recent News</h3>
```

```
26              <ul>
27                 {% for newslink in startup.newslink_set.all %}
28                   <li>
29                     <a href="{{ newslink.link }}">
30                       {{ newslink.title|title }}</a>
31                   </li>
32                 {% endfor %}
33               </ul>
34             </section>
35           {% endif %}
36
37           {% if startup.blog_posts.all %}
38             <section>
39               <h3>Blog Post{{ startup.blog_posts.all|pluralize }}</h3>
40               <ul>
41                 {% for post in startup.blog_posts.all %}
42                   <li>
43                     <a href="">
44                       {{ post.title|title }}</a>
45                   </li>
46                 {% endfor %}
47               </ul>
48             </section>
49           {% endif %}
50
51  </article>
```

### 4.6.3  Template for a List of Startup Objects

We can now create a template to list our startups. As shown in Example 4.42, create a new file /organizer/templates/organizer/startup_list.html.

**Example 4.42: Project Code**

organizer/templates/organizer/startup_list.html **in** 13ce1870d0

```
1    <h2>Startup List</h2>
2    <ul>
3      {% for startup in startup_list %}
4        <li>
5          <a href="">
6            {{ startup.name }}</a>
7        </li>
8      {% empty %}
9        <li><em>No Startups Available</em></li>
10     {% endfor %}
11   </ul>
```

In Chapter 5, we pass a list of startups to the startup_list template variable. The template iterates through the list using the for template tag loop, making sure to provide an {% empty %} condition. We simply print the name of the startup with {{ startup.name }}.

### 4.6.4  Template for a Single Blog Post

Create a new file /blog/templates/blog/post_detail.html, as shown in Example 4.43. We plan to pass data to a post variable.

**Example 4.43:** Project Code

blog/templates/blog/post_detail.html **in** b04022d368

```
 1  <article>
 2
 3    <header>
 4      <h2>{{ post.title|title }}</h2>
 5      <p>
 6        Written on
 7        <time datetime="{{ post.pub_date|date:"Y-m-d" }}">
 8          {{ post.pub_date|date:"l, F j, Y" }}
 9        </time>
10      </p>
11    </header>
12
13    {{ post.text|linebreaks }}
14
15    {% if post.startups.all or post.tags.all %}
16      <footer>
17
18        {% if post.startups.all %}
19          <section>
20            <h3>Startup{{ post.startups.count|pluralize }}</h3>
21            <ul>
22              {% for startup in post.startups.all %}
23                <li><a href="">
24                  {{ startup.name }}
25                </a></li>
26              {% endfor %}
27            </ul>
28          </section>
29        {% endif %}
30
31        {% if post.tags.all %}
32          <section>
33            <h3>Tag{{ post.tags.count|pluralize }}</h3>
34            <ul>
35              {% for tag in post.tags.all %}
36                <li><a href="">
37                  {{ tag.name|title }}
38                </a></li>
39              {% endfor %}
40            </ul>
41          </section>
42        {% endif %}
43
44      </footer>
```

```
45    {% endif %}
46
47  </article>
```

There are a couple of things here you may not recognize.

First, we are using HTML5 semantic tags, such as the `article` tags encapsulating the entire content, the `header` tags encapsulating metadata about the blog post (title and time), and the `time` HTML tag on line 7.

The `time` HTML tag is a way to make sure dates are understood not only by humans but also by robots. The attribute is for robots, while the value between the opening and closing tags is for humans. We can use the `time` HTML tag in tandem with the `date` template filter to display `post.pub_date` and inform both users and robots of when the blog post was written. For the robots, we must keep to a strict format, so we output a four-digit year, a two-digit month, and a two-digit day, with two dashes between the values but passing the format string `"Y-m-d"`. For humans, we can print something more friendly: `"l, F jS, Y"`. The format character `l` will print the full name of the day, such as *Monday*, `F` will print the full name of the month, `j` will print a one- or two-digit day, `S` will print a suffix for the number, such as *st*, and `Y` will print a four-digit year. Effectively, this might print "Thursday, January 2nd, 2014" on the page, which robots will see as "2014-01-02."

The rest of the code should be familiar. We provide a list of `Tag` and `Startup` objects by iterating through a related manager using the `for` template tag between lines 22 and 26 as well as 35 and 39. On lines 20 and 33 we use the `pluralize` filter, ensuring proper grammar for our text, and `linebreaks` on line 13 to ensure proper formatting for the text of our blog post.

## 4.6.5  Template for a List of Blog Posts

Create a new file `/blog/templates/blog/post_list.html`, as shown in Example 4.44. The variable we pass data to is named `post_list`.

**Example 4.44: Project Code**
`blog/templates/blog/post_list.html` in 597bfb94f4

```
1     {% for post in post_list %}
2       <article>
3         <header>
4           <h2>
5             <a href="">
6               {{ post.title|title }}</a>
7           </h2>
8           <p>
9             Written on:
10            <time datetime="{{ post.pub_date|date:"Y-m-d" }}">
11              {{ post.pub_date|date:"l, F j, Y" }}
12            </time>
13          </p>
```

```
14              </header>
15              <p>{{ post.text|truncatewords:20 }}</p>
16              <p>
17                <a href="">
18                  Read more&hellip;</a>
19              </p>
20            </article>
21          {% empty %}
22            <p><em>No Blog Posts Available</em></p>
23          {% endfor %}
```

| **Info**

The &hellip; HTML code stands for **HTML ellip**sis, and will print . . . in the browser.

As with our other list templates, we loop over the provided variable using the `for` template tag, closing the scope at the end and providing content in case the variable is empty via `{% empty %}`. Our semantic HTML5 `header` tag provides the title of the blog post as well as the date the blog post was published, which we make available to humans and robots using the `time` HTML tag, which we build with the help of the `date` template filter, as discussed in the previous section.

The only new filter is the `truncatewords` filter on line 15, which must be passed an integer (we pass the integer 20). As you may have guessed, the filter will take a string and truncate it to the number of words passed in as an argument. As such, in our case, any blog post will be truncated to 20 words. Observe that we have not used this new filter in conjuction with `linebreaks`. One of the features of `truncatewords` is that it removes any newlines from the string, resulting in a single paragraph, which is perfect when presenting a list of items but makes `linebreaks` unnecessary.

# 4.7 Using Template Inheritance for Design Consistency

Currently, should we use our templates, we would only be providing partial HTML. We do not provide open or close `<html>` tags, nor a `<head>`, or even a `<body>`. We have programmed only the content, and we have done so in anticipation of this section.

Typically, a website provides webpages with repeated code. To preserve the look and feel of the site, each webpage is similarly structured and styled. If we had programmed this in each template, it would mean that—should we desire a structure change—we would have to change code in each and every template. Instead, we can use a single structure and connect it to the templates we have already programmed, creating a single place to change site-wide HTML structure.

### 4.7.1 Informing Django of the Existence of Site-wide Templates

While Django knows to look in each app folder for the `template/` directory, Django does not have a default folder to check for templates that are not built for a specific app. We can therefore place these templates anywhere.

To keep things simple, I recommend creating a `templates/` directory in the root project directory.

*[handwritten: dir for site-wide templates (a)]*

We now need to inform Django of the existence of our new directory. In `/suorganizer/settings.py`, we can find the `TEMPLATES` setting, which contains all of the settings for templates. We're going to override the `DIRS` key, which is currently an empty list. We need to give `DIRS` an absolute path to our `template` directory. We can create this absolute path by using the `os.path.join()` method with the `BASE_DIR` variable provided by `settings.py` on line 16 in Example 4.45.

**Example 4.45: Project Code**

`suorganizer/settings.py` **in** `8ffd4f666e`

```
16   BASE_DIR = os.path.dirname(os.path.dirname(os.path.abspath(__file__)))
```

The override to `TEMPLATES` is shown in Example 4.46.

**Example 4.46: Project Code**

`suorganizer/settings.py` **in** `8ffd4f666e`

```
58   TEMPLATES = [{
59       'BACKEND': 'django.template.backends.django.DjangoTemplates',
60       'DIRS': [
61           os.path.join(BASE_DIR, 'templates'),
62       ],
63       'APP_DIRS': True,
64       'OPTIONS': {
65           'context_processors': [
66               'django.template.context_processors.debug',
67               'django.template.context_processors.request',
68               'django.contrib.auth.context_processors.auth',
69               'django.contrib.messages.context_processors.messages',
70           ],
71       },
72   }]
```

*[handwritten: (a)]*

### Ghosts of Django Past

The `TEMPLATES` setting is new in Django 1.8. Prior to this version, Django had the various settings related to templates in separate variables. If you are in Django 1.7 or earlier, you will be interested in overriding `TEMPLATE_DIRS`. It accepts the same input as `DIRS`.

## Warning!

In some cases, you will see people pass DIRS or TEMPLATE_DIRS a tuple instead of a list. Take heed when passing either of them a tuple with a single item! Single-item tuples must be defined with a comma: (item,) is a tuple, whereas (item) is simply encapsulated by parentheses.

## Ghosts of Django Past

In versions prior to Django 1.7, settings.py does not provide a BASE_DIR variable, and TEMPLATE_DIRS is already defined as an empty tuple in the file. If you are using a previous version, make sure that you are not defining the setting twice and that you are providing an absolute path. You may provide an absolute path either by writing it out from the system root (not the project root!) or by copying the definition of BASE_URL in newer versions of Django and then using the code in Example 4.46. This last choice was the official recommendation, even if not the provided default.

## 4.7.2  Building the Site-wide Generic Template

Now that Django knows where to find the template, we can finally create it. Create a new file /templates/base.html and start by coding a basic HTML page, as shown in Example 4.47.

**Example 4.47: Project Code**

templates/base.html **in** 507d342e9c

```
 1   <!DOCTYPE html>
 2   <html lang="en">
 3
 4     <head>
 5       <meta charset="utf-8">
 6       <title>
 7           Startup Organizer
 8       </title>
 9       <meta http-equiv="X-UA-Compatible" content="IE=edge,chrome=1">
10       <meta name="viewport" content="width=device-width, initial-scale=1">
11       <!--[if IE]><script
12         src="http://html5shiv.googlecode.com/svn/trunk/html5.js">
13       </script><![endif]-->
14     </head>
15
16     <body>
17
18       <div><!-- container -->
19         <header>
20             <h1>Startup Organizer</h1>
21         </header>
22         <main>
23             This is default content!
24         </main>
```

```
25        </div><!-- container -->
26
27        <footer>
28          <p>
29            &copy; 2015
30            <a href="https://AndrewsForge.com/">
31              Andrew Pinkham</a>
32          </p>
33          <p>
34            Created for
35            <a href="https://Django-Unleashed.com/">
36              Django Unleashed</a>
37          </p>
38        </footer>
39
40      </body>
41
42    </html>
```

### Info

The &copy; HTML entity produces a copyright symbol, ©, when rendered in the browser.

Unlike our other templates, base.html is not namespaced within the template virtual directory. We will always refer to it simply as base.html as opposed to something like site/base.html.

Before connecting the template with our existing templates, we need to tell Django which parts of the template we will be replacing. We can do so using the block template tag. As expected, the tag is delineated by {% %} delimiters. The tag expects a single parameter, separated by a space: the name of the block. Closing the scope of the block is done with {% endblock %}.

We create two blocks in Example 4.48: one for the title of the page and one for the content of the page.

*{% extends <name.html> %}*

*{% block <name> %}*

**Example 4.48: Project Code**
templates/base.html **in** 4913d63374

```
 6        <title>
 7          {% block title %}
 8            Startup Organizer
 9          {% endblock %}
10        </title>
 .          ...
24        <main>
25          {% block content %}
26            This is default content!
27          {% endblock %}
28        </main>
```

In the event we choose not to override a block, Django will use the content provided in Example 4.48. This is fine for the title block, but we should make sure to always override the content block.

### 4.7.3   Using the Generic Template in Our `Tag` List Template

We now have a site-wide template that provides the HTML structure we want and defines blocks for us to override. We now need to edit our site templates to inherit this generic template and override the blocks we've defined.

Let's start with our `Tag` list template, found in `/organizer/templates/organizer/tag_list.html`. We first tell the template to inherit the generic template by using the `extends` template tag followed by the location of the file: `{% extends "base.html" %}`.

With the generic template inherited, we simply wrap the content we wrote previously with the `block` template tags. We should also take care to override the title block by coding `{% block title %}{{ block.super }} - Tag List{% endblock %}`. The `{{ block.super }}` allows us to refer to what exists in the parent block. As the generic template defined `{% block title %}Startup Organizer{% endblock %}`, the preceding code effectively prints *Startup Organizer - Tag List*.

What previously read as shown in Example 4.49.

**Example 4.49:** Project Code

`organizer/templates/organizer/tag_list.html` **in** e9bd61448b

```
 1    <h2>Tag List</h2>
 2    <ul>
 3      {% for tag in tag_list %}
 4        <li>
 5          <a href="">
 6            {{ tag.name|title }}</a>
 7        </li>
 8      {% empty %}
 9        <li><em>There are currently no Tags available.</em></li>
10      {% endfor %}
11    </ul>
```

now reads as shown in Example 4.50.

**Example 4.50:** Project Code

`organizer/templates/organizer/tag_list.html` **in** 60f1b7ff0f

```
 1    {% extends "base.html" %}
 2
 3    {% block title %}
 4    {{ block.super }} - Tag List
 5    {% endblock %}
 6
 7    {% block content %}
```

```
 8      <h2>Tag List</h2>
 9      <ul>
10        {% for tag in tag_list %}
11          <li>
12            <a href="">
13               {{ tag.name|title }}</a>
14          </li>
15        {% empty %}
16          <li><em>There are currently no Tags available.</em></li>
17        {% endfor %}
18      </ul>
19    {% endblock %}
```

We have in no way changed the content, simply wrapped it after adding the extends tag. The extends tag must appear as the first tag in the file or else template inheritance will not occur.

When we listed the Tag objects before, we created the code shown in Example 4.51 (the HTML has had newlines removed to shorten the output).

**Example 4.51: HTML Code**

```
<h2>Tag List</h2>
<ul>
  <li><a href="">Django</a></li>
  <li><a href="">Mobile</a></li>
  <li><a href="">Video Games</a></li>
  <li><a href="">Web</a></li>
</ul>
```

With our inheritance and override of both content and title blocks, our page now outputs the code shown in Example 4.52 (again, the HTML below has had newlines removed).

**Example 4.52: HTML Code**

```
<!DOCTYPE html>
<html lang="en">
  <head>
    <meta charset="utf-8">
    <title>Startup Organizer - Tag List</title>
    <meta http-equiv="X-UA-Compatible" content="IE=edge,chrome=1">
    <meta name="viewport" content="width=device-width, initial-scale=1">
    <!--[if IE]><script
      src="http://html5shiv.googlecode.com/svn/trunk/html5.js">
    </script><![endif]-->
  </head>
```

```
<body>
  <div><!-- container -->
    <header>
        <h1>Startup Organizer</h1>
    </header>
    <main>
      <h2>Tag List</h2>
      <ul>
        <li><a href="">Django</a></li>
        <li><a href="">Mobile</a></li>
        <li><a href="">Video Games</a></li>
        <li><a href="">Web</a></li>
      </ul>
    </main>
  </div><!-- container -->
  <footer>
    <p>&copy; 2015
      <a href="https://AndrewsForge.com/">
      Andrew Pinkham</a></p>
    <p>Created for
      <a href="https://Django-Unleashed.com/">
      Django Unleashed</a></p>
  </footer>
</body>
</html>
```

This is exactly what we want, but we can make a small tweak to our code to clean it up. At the moment, we are passing `extends` a constant: `"base.html"`. While this is what a lot of examples use, consider that this magic string cannot be overridden. Instead, it would be preferable to use a variable and then provide a default to the variable. This technique allows the Django Controller the possibility of overriding the template's inheritance scheme without requiring the developer to specify a base template every time this template is used. We can do so using the `default` filter. Our code now reads as in Example 4.53.

**Example 4.53: Project Code**
`organizer/templates/organizer/tag_list.html` in 95a55c55e3

```
1   {% extends parent_template|default:"base.html" %}
```

## 4.7.4    Building the App-Generic Templates

Typically, developers do not inherit app templates directly from the base template. Instead, each app defines an intermediary template, which inherits from the base. This allows apps to define their own behavior. A template thus first inherits from the app base template, which in turn inherits from the project base template.

At the moment, we don't actually have anything to place in the app base template, so this may seem silly. However, following this convention can save you time in the long run, as we shall see in Chapter 16: Serving Static Content with Django.

To start, we can create a base template for our **organizer** app: `organizer/templates/organizer/base_organizer.html`. The contents at this point are very simple, as shown in Example 4.54.

**Example 4.54: Project Code**
`organizer/templates/organizer/base_organizer.html` in `4791ef1567`

```
1  {% extends parent_template|default:"base.html" %}
```

The blog base template `blog/templates/blog/base_blog.html` is identical, as shown in Example 4.55.

**Example 4.55: Project Code**
`blog/templates/blog/base_blog.html` in `27aebdc2e2`

```
1  {% extends parent_template|default:"base.html" %}
```

This allows us to go back to `organizer/templates/organizer/tag_list.html` and change the inheritance, as shown in Example 4.56.

**Example 4.56: Project Code**
`organizer/templates/organizer/tag_list.html` in `b0c05bc701`

```
1  {% extends parent_template|default:"organizer/base_organizer.html" %}
```

Note that our `Tag` list webpage has not changed. We've simply changed the inheritance structure to make our lives easier in the long run.

## 4.7.5  Using the Generic Templates in the Rest of the App Templates

For the sake of brevity, we look at only one more example of how to integrate the generic template with our app template, in this case the list of `Startup` objects.

There are three steps to properly configuring each app template:

1. Surround the content in the file with `{% block content %}` and `{% endblock %}`.

2. Extend the app base template.

3. Override the title by using the `block` template tag.

The truth is that doing so for each and every app template is tedious and straightforward. In a normal project, we would typically start with the site-wide generic template before programming the app templates (where, in turn, we'd start with the app base templates). We did so in reverse to make the topic more approachable: it is easier to print a single variable than it is to inherit pre-existing templates.

Open /organizer/templates/organizer/startup_list.html. Example 4.57 shows the current file.

**Example 4.57: Project Code**

organizer/templates/organizer/startup_list.html **in** 13ce1870d0

```
1    <h2>Startup List</h2>
2    <ul>
3      {% for startup in startup_list %}
4        <li>
5          <a href="">
6            {{ startup.name }}</a>
7        </li>
8      {% empty %}
9        <li><em>No Startups Available</em></li>
10     {% endfor %}
11   </ul>
```

We start by surrounding the content with `block` template tags. To properly invoke the override, the name of the block in our startup list template must be the same as the name of the block in the site-wide generic template, so we name the block in Example 4.58 `content`.

**Example 4.58: Project Code**

organizer/templates/organizer/startup_list.html **in** 9d05732bbc

```
7    {% block content %}
8      <h2>Startup List</h2>
9      <ul>
10       {% for startup in startup_list %}
11         <li>
12           <a href="">
13             {{ startup.name }}</a>
14         </li>
15       {% empty %}
16         <li><em>No Startups Available</em></li>
17       {% endfor %}
18     </ul>
19   {% endblock %}
```

This approach works only if we inherit the app base template (which inherits the project base template), so in Example 4.59, we use the `extends` template tag to do so.

**Example 4.59: Project Code**

organizer/templates/organizer/startup_list.html **in** 9d05732bbc

```
1   {% extends parent_template|default:"organizer/base_organizer.html" %}
```

We may then override the title of our HTML page by again using the `block` template tag, this time referencing the title block, as shown in Example 4.60. You may optionally use the {{ `block.super` }} variable to refer to the value of the parents block.

**Example 4.60: Project Code**

organizer/templates/organizer/startup_list.html **in** 9d05732bbc

```
3   {% block title %}
4   {{ block.super }} - Startups
5   {% endblock %}
```

The final result is shown in Example 4.61.

**Example 4.61: Project Code**

organizer/templates/organizer/startup_list.html **in** 9d05732bbc

```
1    {% extends parent_template|default:"organizer/base_organizer.html" %}
2
3    {% block title %}
4    {{ block.super }} - Startups
5    {% endblock %}
6
7    {% block content %}
8      <h2>Startup List</h2>
9      <ul>
10       {% for startup in startup_list %}
11         <li>
12           <a href="">
13              {{ startup.name }}</a>
14         </li>
15       {% empty %}
16         <li><em>No Startups Available</em></li>
17       {% endfor %}
18     </ul>
19   {% endblock %}
```

Consider that the content within the title block can be variable. For instance, in the single `Tag` object template, /organizer/templates/organizer/tag_detail.html, our title could be set as in Example 4.62.

**Example 4.62: Project Code**

`organizer/templates/organizer/tag_detail.html` in 0c87eb4aed

```
3   {% block title %}
4   {{ block.super }} - {{ tag.name|title }}
5   {% endblock %}
```

Remember that all of the code used in the book is available on GitHub, so you can see exactly what changes I've made for each file, should you wish to. However, following the three steps just outlined allows you to code correctly, even if we make different choices with regard to the title of the page.

# 4.8  Using Templates in Python with the `Template`, `Context`, and `loader` Classes

MVC's View, Django's template system, is the only part of Django to feature code that is not Python. It's a safe bet that Django provides a way to import these template files into Python and to interact them with the other parts of Django. We now explore how to first **load** the template files we have written and then to output or **render** content.

## 4.8.1  Using Templates in the Shell

To interact with the system, we return to the Django shell. The shell or terminal can be a little uncomfortable to beginners, but using the shell shortens the code creation feedback loop and is a great tool to learn and use regularly. The alternative would be to create a Python file, add or edit code, run the code, and view the output. By going directly to the shell, we are provided with output far more quickly, allowing us to dabble with code. Furthermore, if we wanted to use the template system in the context of Django, we would be writing views, and that content is reserved for Chapter 5.

As seen in Chapter 3, we can invoke the shell thanks to /manage.py (Example 4.63).

**Example 4.63: Shell Code**

```
$ ./manage.py shell
```

Let's start in Example 4.64 by importing the `Template` and `Context` classes from the `template` package in Django.

**Example 4.64: Python Interpreter Code**

```
>>> from django.template import Template, Context
```

A `Template` object is just what you'd expect: it contains markup with the the template variables, tags, and filters we've been using throughout this chapter. We can create the markup by instantiating a new object, as shown in Example 4.65.

**Example 4.65: Python Interpreter Code**

```
>>> template = Template('Hi, my name is {{ name }}.')
```

Throughout the chapter, we've been assuming that we will pass in a value to each template to fill in the gaps we've left. This is the function of the Context class: it defines a dictionary of values to fill in a `Template`. Given our single {{ name }} variable in Example 4.65, we can instantiate a `Context` object to fill in the value by passing in a dictionary where the key is the name of the template variable, and the value of the key is the string we want to display. We can then render the template using the aptly named `render()` method, as in Example 4.66.

**Example 4.66: Python Interpreter Code**

```
>>> template = Template('Hi, my name is {{ name }}.')
>>> context = Context({'name': 'Andrew'})
>>> template.render(context)
'Hi, my name is Andrew.'
```

*— Create Template instance*
*— Create Context instance*
*— invoke render() on the template instance, passing the context instance*

Once a `Template` is loaded, it can be rendered as many times as desired (without needing to be reloaded), as shown in Example 4.67.

**Example 4.67: Python Interpreter Code**

```
>>> context = Context({'name': 'Ada'})
>>> template.render(context)
'Hi, my name is Ada.'
```

Note that if the `Context` does not provide a value, the renderer will not error (Example 4.68).

**Example 4.68: Python Interpreter Code**

```
>>> template.render(Context())
'Hi, my name is .'
```

Similarly, if the names of the keys passed to `Context` are in any way different from those the `Template` expects, then the `Template` will not render as you expect. To demonstrate this, in Example 4.69, I first render the `Template` with the correct `Context` key but then change the key to have an uppercase letter, resulting in nothing being printed.

**Example 4.69:** Python Interpreter Code

```
>>> template.render(Context({'name': 'Andrew'}))
'Hi, my name is Andrew.'
>>> template.render(Context({'Name': 'Andrew'}))
'Hi, my name is .'
```

It is thus important to make sure the `Context` we create for each `Template` matches the expected variable names of the `Template`.

Given a variable with attributes, the template language allows access to those attributes, as shown in Example 4.70.

**Example 4.70:** Python Interpreter Code

```
>>> template = Template(
...     '{{ ml.exclaim }}!\n'
...     'she said {{ ml.adverb }}\n'
...     'as she jumped into her convertible {{ ml.noun1 }}\n'
...     'and drove off with her {{ ml.noun2 }}.\n'
... )
>>> mad_lib = {
...     'exclaim':'Ouch',
...     'adverb':'dutifully',
...     'noun1':'boat',
...     'noun2':'pineapple',
... }
>>> context = Context({'ml': mad_lib})
>>> template.render(context)
'Ouch!
she said dutifully
as she jumped into her convertible boat
and drove off with her pineapple.'
```

Naturally, creating the `Template` as in the preceding examples is not what we wish to do. We would prefer to load the files we have created as `Template` objects. To ease the process of doing so, as shown in Example 4.71, Django provides another class in the `template` package named `loader`, which in turn provides the `get_template()` method, which is exactly what we want.

**Example 4.71:** Python Interpreter Code

```
>>> from django.template import loader
>>> template = loader.get_template('organizer/tag_list.html')
>>> best_list = [
```

1 Overall: from django.template import Template, Context, loader

2 Instead of creating a Context instance, call loader.get-template() to fetch on

```
...      {'name': 'Pirates'},
...      {'name': 'Ninjas'},
...      {'name': 'Cowboys'},
... ]
>>> context = Context({'tag_list': best_list})
>>> template.render(context)
```

The call results in a Unicode string, formatted for readability in Example 4.72.

**Example 4.72: HTML Code**

```html
<!DOCTYPE html>
<html lang="en">
  <head>
    <meta charset="utf-8">
    <title>Startup Organizer - Tag List</title>
    <meta http-equiv="X-UA-Compatible" content="IE=edge,chrome=1">
    <meta name="viewport" content="width=device-width, initial-scale=1">
    <!--[if IE]><script
      src="http://html5shiv.googlecode.com/svn/trunk/html5.js">
    </script><![endif]-->
  </head>
  <body>
    <div><!-- container -->
      <header>
          <h1>Startup Organizer</h1>
      </header>
      <main>
        <h2>Tag List</h2>
        <ul>
          <li><a href="">Pirates</a></li>
          <li><a href="">Ninjas</a></li>
          <li><a href="">Cowboys</a></li>
        </ul>
      </main>
    </div><!-- container -->
    <footer>
      <p>&copy; 2015
        <a href="https://AndrewsForge.com/">
        Andrew Pinkham</a></p>
      <p>Created for
        <a href="https://Django-Unleashed.com/">
        Django Unleashed</a></p>
    </footer>
  </body>
</html>
```

We're not actually interested in providing a list of our own creation, especially not to our tag list template. We really want to use the data in our database. In Example 4.73, we first import our Tag model and then ask for all of the data in the database using the model manager.

**Example 4.73: Python Interpreter Code**

```
>>> from organizer.models import Tag
>>> Tag.objects.all()
[<Tag: Django>, <Tag: Education>, <Tag: Mobile>,
 <Tag: Video Games>, <Tag: Web>]
```

The model manager returns a QuerySet object of all the tags. Remember that a QuerySet is not the same as a list object, but it knows how to behave like one. The shell allows us to test this immediately, as in Example 4.74.

**Example 4.74: Python Interpreter Code**

```
>>> template = loader.get_template('organizer/tag_list.html')
>>> context = Context({'tag_list': Tag.objects.all()})
>>> template.render(context)
```

The resultant output by the shell is not particularly readable. For better results, we can use the print() functions, as shown in Example 4.75.

**Example 4.75: Python Interpreter Code**

```
>>> print(template.render(context))
```

## 4.8.2  Using Templates in Views

Using the shell is a fantastic way to prototype code. If you made any typos in the last section, you were immediately alerted to them, and any problematic code got sorted out on the fly. However, the shell alone doesn't build you a website.

Let's return to our view example from the beginning of the chapter. As a refresher, your /organizer/views.py should currently read as shown in Example 4.76.

**Example 4.76: Project Code**
organizer/views.py **in** dd5e4e1a71

```
1    from django.http.response import HttpResponse
2
3    from .models import Tag
4
5
6    def homepage(request):
7        tag_list = Tag.objects.all()
```

```
 8        html_output = "<html>\n"
 9        html_output += "<head>\n"
10        html_output += "  <title>"
11        html_output += "Don't Do This!</title>\n"
12        html_output += "</head>\n"
13        html_output += "<body>\n"
14        html_output += "  <ul>\n"
15        for tag in tag_list:
16            html_output += "    <li>"
17            html_output += tag.name.title()
18            html_output += "</li>\n"
19        html_output += "  </ul>\n"
20        html_output += "</body>\n"
21        html_output += "</html>\n"
22        return HttpResponse(html_output)
```

We begin by importing the necessary tools, notably `Context` and `loader`, as in Example 4.77. We do not need to call `Template` directly because of `get_template()`.

**Example 4.77: Project Code**
`organizer/views.py` in 614a996dd8

```
2    from django.template import Context, loader
```

The goal is to render our tag list template with the actual `Tag` object data in the database. We can take all of the code we just saw in the Python interpreter and add it directly to our function view, as in Example 4.78.

**Example 4.78: Project Code**
`organizer/views.py` in 614a996dd8

```
 7    def homepage(request):
 8        tag_list = Tag.objects.all()
 9        template = loader.get_template(
10            'organizer/tag_list.html')
11        context = Context({'tag_list': tag_list})
12        output = template.render(context)
13        return HttpResponse(output)
```

It's all right if some of this code is still a little magic—we'll sort that out before the end of Chapter 5. For the moment, our focus is not on the view but on running the template code listed in section 4.8.1. Let's review.

Starting on line 9, we load our template, passing in a path relative to the `templates/` directory. The path is namespaced to the app only because we created the `/organizer/templates/organizer/` directory.

We wrote the template so that it expects a `Context` with the key `tag_list`. Similarly, we have a variable with the list of `Tag` objects named `tag_list`. We thus create a `Context` object by invoking: `context = Context({'tag_list': tag_list})` on line 11. For clarity, this is: `context = Context({'template_variable': python_variable})`.

Finally, we render the `Template` with the `Context` by calling `render()` and pass the text output of the function to `HttpResponse`, which we return.

You can see the results of this code by running the development server. In the terminal, run the server by invoking the code in Example 4.79.

**Example 4.79: Shell Code**

```
$ ./manage.py runserver
```

Direct your browser to `http://127.0.0.1:8000/` to be greeted by the HTML page we predicted in the previous section. We have successfully used a Django template in a view: we used an MVC View in an MVC Controller.

## 4.9   Putting It All Together

In this chapter, we discovered how Django implements the View portion of the Model-View-Controller architecture. Django allows the developer to easily create data to be displayed via the template system. The system comprises two parts: the actual template files and the template loader and renderer.

Template files are documents external to Django that act as a blueprint or mold for data. Templates allow the developer to write documents in a markup language, such as HTML, with gaps in them, which Django fills in. The developer instructs Django on how to fill these gaps via a domain-specific template language. The Django template language includes variables, template filters to modify the variables, and template tags to perform conditional and loop logic. Template documents are the only part of Django not in Python.

The Django template language is delineated from the markup of the developer's choice via `{{ variable }}`, `{% expression %}`, and `{# comments #}` (which we only saw in an aside).

A variable may have data attributes accessed just as in Python via a period: `{{ variable.attribute }}`. Additionally, filters, which are functions dedicated to formatting or modifying variables, may be applied with a vertical bar (with no spaces in between): `{{ variable|filter }}`. Some filters allow or expect a single argument, which may be passed in with a colon and enclosed in quotations if the argument is not an integer: `{{ variable|filter:"arg" }}`. Filters may also be chained: `{{ variable|filter1|filter2 }}`.

The `{% expression %}` code is referred to as a **template tag**. A template tag may be a command, a condition, or a loop. Template tag commands, unlike filters, may take any number of arguments, separated by spaces. Like filters, template tag arguments must be enclosed in quotation marks if they are not integers. We saw an example of this with the `extends` tag, which allows templates to inherit markup from another template.

Template tag conditions and loops typically create scope, meaning they must be closed. In this chapter, we used the `for` template tag extensively and saw the `if` template tag on

occasion. Both work the same way they do in Python, but they must be closed with
{% endfor %} and {% endif %}, respectively. We discussed the use of {% empty %}, a
tag that imitates the else condition of a for loop in Python, in that it allows for the
condition of an empty list passed to for.

We shall discover the url tag in Chapter 6. Django supplies many more template filters
and tags for the developer to use. For reference material on the subject, please visit the
official Django documentation.[3]

The template documents may be loaded and rendered in Django through the use of the
template package. With the package, Django may call get_template(), creating a
Template object, which the developer can then render() into a string by passing in a
Context object, built from a dictionary of values. This rendered string may then be passed
to HttpResponse and returned to the user in a view, as we discuss in depth in the
Chapter 5.

---

# Creating Webpages with Controllers in Django: Views and URL Configurations

**In This Chapter**

- Build webpages with views and URL patterns
- Learn the purpose behind views and URL configurations
- Build views using both Python functions and objects
- Learn the differences between function and class-based views
- Make programming quicker with Django shortcuts
- Connect URL configurations to encapsulate behavior by app
- Preview webpage redirection

## 5.1   Introduction

In Chapter 2: Hello World: Building a Basic Webpage in Django, we saw that the Controller is the only part of Django actually required to make a webpage (the relevant diagram is reprinted in Figure 5.1). However, we immediately ran into problems: we had no way to easily fetch and format data. Because the main function of websites revolves around data, the Controller is often described as the glue between Model and View despite the Controller's independence.

In this chapter, we return to the Controller, seen earlier in Chapter 2 and Chapter 4: Rapidly Producing Flexible HTML with Django Templates. We first re-examine how the two parts of the Controller, URL configurations and views, interact. We then use the cumulative knowledge we have gained to build dynamic webpages.

The Controller is central to Django and comes with a number of options. Once we have the basics, we look at how to handle problems that occur in views. We then look at ways to more rapidly code views (at the cost of developer control). Coding views enable us to very quickly build all the webpages for our site.

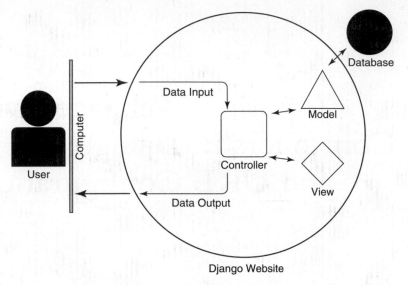

**Figure 5.1:** Application of MVC Architecture Diagram

Before we finish the chapter, we also examine two special methods for creating Controllers, which become important later in the book.

This chapter assumes knowledge of HTTP and regular expressions. Primers on both are provided in Appendix A and Appendix E, respectively.

## 5.2    The Purpose of Views and URL Configurations

A webpage consists of (1) the data contained in the webpage and (2) the URL (location) of the webpage. Django follows this abstraction by splitting the Controller into two parts. Django views give Django the data of the webpage. The URL associated with each view is listed in the URL configuration.

> **Warning!**
>
> For many beginners, the name of the Controller causes confusion: Django views are **unrelated** to MVC architecture's View. Django views are one half of the Controller. Django templates map to MVC's Views. To differentiate between the two, I capitalize *View* when referring to MVC and use lowercase *view* when referring to Django.

In the rest of this section, we expand on the nature and purpose of the URL configuration and views. To make the material more tangible, we then step through what happens when Django receives a request, detailing the actions the Controller takes.

## 5.2.1 Django URL Configurations

As discussed in Chapter 1, Section 1.2, webpages were originally quite basic. The webpage's data were contained in a flat file (a text file, an HTML file, or a PDF file, for instance). The URL was literally the location of the file on the server. If a user directed his or her browser to `http://awebsite.com/project1/important.pdf`, the `awebsite.com` server would go to the `project1` directory and fetch the `important.pdf` file to give to the user's browser.

Because modern web frameworks generate webpages dynamically, URLs have ceased to be the actual path to the data. A URL is now an abstraction, and it represents the logical path to data. For instance, the path `/startup/jambon-software` obviously requests information about the JamBon Software startup, whereas the path `/blog/2013/1/django-training/` is clearly a request for a blog post about Django classes published in January 2013.

The name *Uniform Resource Locator* is thus not quite right anymore, as we are not actually requesting the location of the data. Instead, we are simply identifying it. Appropriately, URLs are a direct subset of Uniform Resource Identifiers (URIs), as illustrated in Figure 5.2.

While there is some confusion surrounding the difference between URLs and URIs, RFC 3986[1] is quite clear on the topic (effectively superseding RFC 3305)[2]:

> A URI can be further classified as a locator, a name, or both. The term "Uniform Resource Locator" (URL) refers to the subset of URIs that, in addition to identifying a resource, provides a means of locating the resource by describing its primary access mechanism (e.g., its network "location").

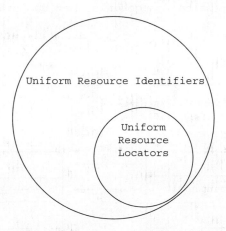

**Figure 5.2:** URLs are a subset of URIs

1. https://dju.link/rfc3986
2. https://dju.link/rfc3305

Every URL is thus a URI. However, a URL must specify a scheme to access the data, such as `http` or `https`, while a URI does not have to. According to this definition, the string `/blog/2013/1/django-training/` is a URI, but the string `http://site.django-unleashed.com/blog/2013/1/django-training/` is a URL despite the fact that the URL path is not an actual location. For this reason, Django continues to refer to URLs instead of URIs.

Because of the Hollywood principle (inversion of control), the URL configuration acts as a way to direct both users *and* Django to data. The URL configuration connects URLs to views: Django uses the URL configuration to find views. Django does not know the existence of any view without the URL configuration.

The URL configuration is a list of URL pattens. The URL pattern represents the two parts of a webpage: it maps a URI (the route/location/identifier) to a view (the data). Formally, the URI is a regular expression pattern, whereas the view is a Python callable. A URL configuration can also point to another URL configuration instead of a view, as we discuss in more depth in Section 5.7.1.

In Figure 5.3, each arrow is a URL pattern. Multiple URIs may point to a single view, but a single URI may not be defined more than once. The regular expression pattern in each URL pattern is how Django performs its matching. When Django receives an HTTP request, it tries to match the URL of the request to each and every regular expression pattern in each and every URL pattern. Upon finding a match, Django calls the view that the regular expression pattern maps to. Django uses the first match, meaning that the order of the list of URL patterns matters if there are several potential matches. If Django does not find a match, it returns an HTTP 404 error.

In the example provided by Figure 5.3, if a user requested the URI `/startup/`, perhaps in a URL such as `http://site.django-unleashed.com/startup/`, then Django

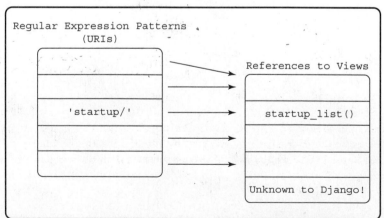

**Figure 5.3:** URL Configuration

would call the startup_list() function view. Django automatically strips the root slash of the URL path (to Django, /startup/ becomes startup/).

We first coded a URL pattern in Chapter 2 and then again in Chapter 4. This last one, shown in Example 5.1, should still exist in suorganizer/urls.py.

**Example 5.1: Project Code**
suorganizer/urls.py **in** 95b20c151b

```
23        url(r'^$', homepage),
```

Requesting the root path of our website causes Django to call homepage(), coded in organizer/views.py. We walk through exactly how Django does this shortly.

> **Info**
>
> A word of caution: there are *URL patterns*, and there are *regular expression patterns*. Simply referring to a pattern is ambiguous and should be avoided.

## 5.2.2 Django Views

The view is where webpage data is generated. The developer uses the view to interact with the database, load and render the template, and perform any other logic necessary to displaying a webpage.

A Django view is any Python callable (function, class, or object) that meets the following two requirements:

- Accepts an HttpRequest object as argument
- Returns an HttpResponse object

An HttpRequest object contains all of the information about the page requested, any data the user is passing to the website, and any data the browser is sending about the user. The HttpResponse returns an HTTP code (please see Appendix A for information about HTTP codes) as well as any data the developer chooses to return to the user.

Because the nature of a view depends solely on its input and output, any Python callable can be a view. Typically, however, you will be using either functions or Django's supplied classes to create views. For the moment, we build views using functions and wait until the end of the chapter to look at Django's class-based views.

Developers often refer to Django views as **view functions**. This is rather confusing, as views are not limited to being functions (this was not the case historically, which is where the vocabulary originates). In this book, I refer to any callable that builds a webpage as a **view**. Any view that is built using a function is called a **function view**, and any view that is an object is called a **class-based view** (following the documentation's nomenclature).

We currently have a function view coded in organizer/views.py, shown in Example 5.2.

**Example 5.2: Project Code**
`organizer/views.py` in `f0d1985791`

```
 7   def homepage(request):
 8       tag_list = Tag.objects.all()
 9       template = loader.get_template(
10           'organizer/tag_list.html')
11       context = Context({'tag_list': tag_list})
12       output = template.render(context)
13       return HttpResponse(output)
```

We can see how the function in Example 5.2 adheres to view requirements: it accepts an `HttpRequest` object as the `request` argument and returns an `HttpResponse` object with the output of a rendered template. It is also clearly dynamic, generating content based on data in the database.

In this chapter, we focus on using the database to generate dynamic pages. In Chapter 9: Controlling Forms in Views, we generate dynamic pages based on not only the database but also the contents of the `HttpRequest` object. In Chapter 15: Creating Webpages with Django Flatpages, we also discuss the ability to make static/flat pages with views.

## 5.3  Step-by-Step Examination of Django's Use of Views and URL Configurations

Nothing clarifies programming quite like walking through each step the code takes. Let's find out what happens when we run our web server and navigate to `http://127.0.0.1:8000/`.

Before we can go to the webpage, we have to start Django. We do so with Example 5.3.

**Example 5.3: Shell Code**

```
$ ./manage.py runserver
```

Django loads the settings in `suorganizer/settings.py`, configuring itself. It then loads all of the URL patterns in the URL configuration into memory, which allows Django to match URLs quickly. Once set up, we can type `http://127.0.0.1:8000/` into our browser.

Our browser begins by finding the server with the network location `127.0.0.1`. That's easy: that IP address always refers to the machine you're using. Once it knows that, it looks at the scheme and path of the URL and sends an HTTP request for the path `/` to itself on port 8000. Django receives this request.

> **Info**
> If we had requested just `http://127.0.0.1:8000` (without the last slash), the browser would still request the path `/`. It is implicit in this case.

Django first translates the actual HTTP request (raw data) into an `HttpRequest` object (Python). Having this object in Python makes it easy for us and the framework to manipulate any information the browser is passing our site, as we shall discover in Chapter 9. Django takes the path in the `HttpRequest` object—currently /—and strips it of the first /. In this case, we are left with the empty string. *Our new path is the empty string* ".

Django's next goal is to select a URL pattern. Django has the list of URL patterns in the URL configuration it loaded into memory when it first started up. Each URL pattern consists of at least two things: a regular expression pattern and a view. To select a URL pattern, Django tries to match the requested path—the empty string in this case—to each regular expression pattern of each URL pattern. Given our URL configuration, Django currently has only two options, shown in Example 5.4.

**Example 5.4: Project Code**
`suorganizer/urls.py` in 95b20c151b

```
16    from django.conf.urls import include, url
17    from django.contrib import admin
18
19    from organizer.views import homepage
20
21    urlpatterns = [
22        url(r'^admin/', include(admin.site.urls)),
23        url(r'^$', homepage),
24    ]
```

Each call to `url()` in Example 5.4 is a URL pattern. Django tries to match the empty string, derived from the URL path, to each of the regular expression patterns in the URL patterns above. The empty string very clearly does not match the text `admin/`. However, Django will select the second URL pattern because the regular expression `r'^$'` matches the empty string:

- The `r` informs Python the string is raw, meaning it does not escape any of the characters in the string.
- The `^` matches the beginning of a string.
- The `$` matches the end of a string.

With the URL pattern `url(r'^$', homepage)` selected, Django calls the Python function the URL pattern points to. In this case, the URL pattern points to the `homepage()` Python function, imported via the call `from organizer.views import homepage` on line 19. When Django calls the view, it passes the `HttpRequest` object to the view.

We coded the view such that it loads tag data from the database, loads the tag list template, and renders the template with the `Tag` object data. We then pass this output to an `HttpResponse` object and return it to Django. Django translates this object into a real HTTP response and sends it back to our browser. Our browser then displays the webpage to us.

To clarify, the regular expression `r'^a$'` would match a request to
`http://127.0.0.1:8000/a`. If we were to change the URL pattern from `url(r'^$',`
`homepage)` to `url(r'^home/$', homepage)`, we would now need to navigate to
`http://127.0.0.1:8000/home/` to run the `homepage()` function and display a
list of tags.

Inversion of control should be apparent. We are not controlling Django. It translates
HTTP requests and responses for us and handles the entire URL matching process. We are
simply providing it with the data to use in these matches and telling it what to use to build
the webpage (the view). And even then, we are relying heavily on the tools Django provides.

If we were to ask Django for a webpage that did not exist, such as
`http://127.0.0.1:8000/nonexistent/`, Django would try to match
`nonexistent/` to the regular expression patterns in our URL configuration. When it did
not find one, it would error. In production, Django would send back an HTTP 404
response. However, because we have `DEBUG=TRUE` in our `suorganizer/settings.py`
file, Django instead tries to warn us of the problem and shows us a list of valid URL paths.

## 5.4    Building Tag Detail Webpage

To reinforce what we already know and expand our knowledge of URL patterns, we now
create a second webpage. Our webpage will display the information for a single `Tag` object.
We call our function view `tag_detail()`. Let's begin by adding a URL pattern.

In Chapter 3, we specifically added `SlugField` to our `Tag` model to allow for the
simple creation of unique URLs. We intend to use it now for our URL pattern. We want
the request for `/tag/django/` to show the webpage for the *django* Tag and the request for
`/tag/web/` to show the webpage for the *web* Tag.

This is the first gap in our knowledge. How can we get a single URL pattern to
recognize both `/tag/django/` and `/tag/web/`? The second gap in our knowledge is that
we have no easy way to use the information in the URL pattern. Once we've isolated *django*
and *web*, how can we pass this information to the view so that it may request the data from
the database?

To make the problem more concrete, let's start with the `tag_detail()` view.

### 5.4.1   Coding the `tag_detail()` Function View

Open `/organizer/views.py` and program the bare minimum functionality of a view
(accept an `HttpRequest` object, return an `HttpResponse` object), as shown in
Example 5.5.

**Example 5.5: Project Code**
`organizer/views.py` **in** `f0d1985791`

```
16   def tag_detail(request):
17       return HttpResponse()
```

Our first task is to select the data for the `Tag` object that the user has selected. For the moment, we will assume that we have somehow been passed the unique slug value of the `Tag` as the variable `slug`, and we use it in our code (but Python will yell at you if you try to run this). We use the `get()` method of our `Tag` model manager, which returns a single object. We want our search for the `slug` field to be case insensitive, so we use the `iexact` field lookup scheme. Our lookup is thus `Tag.objects.get(slug__iexact=slug)`, as shown in Example 5.6.

**Example 5.6: Project Code**
`organizer/views.py` in ba4f692e00

```
16    def tag_detail(request):
17        # slug = ?
18        tag = Tag.objects.get(slug__iexact=slug)
19        return HttpResponse()
```

We may now load the template we wish to render, `organizer/tag_detail.html`. When we wrote the template, we wrote it to use a variable named `tag`. We thus create a `Context` object to pass the value of our Python variable named `tag` to our template variable `tag`. Recall that the syntax is `Context({'template_variable_name': Python_variable_name})`. We thus extend our view code as shown in Example 5.7.

**Example 5.7: Project Code**
`organizer/views.py` in 2fdb78366f

```
16    def tag_detail(request):
17        # slug = ?
18        tag = Tag.objects.get(slug__iexact=slug)
19        template = loader.get_template(
20            'organizer/tag_detail.html')
21        context = Context({'tag': tag})
22        return HttpResponse(template.render(context))
```

We have what would be a fully working function view if not for the problem we are now forced to confront: the `slug` variable is never set. The value of the slug will be in the URL path. If Django receives the request for /tag/django/, we want the value of our `slug` variable to be set to `'django'`. Django provides two ways to get it.

The first way is terrible and inadvisable: we can parse the URL path ourselves. The `request` variable, an `HttpRequest` object, contains all the information provided by the user and Django, and we could access `request.path_info` to get the full path. In our example above, `request.path_info` would return `'tag/django/'`. However, to get the slug from our URL path, we would need to parse the value of `request.path_info`, and doing so in each and every view would be tedious and repetitive, in direct violation of the Don't Repeat Yourself (DRY) principle.

The second method, the recommended and easy solution, is to get Django to send it to us via the URL configuration, as we shall discover in the next section. To accommodate this solution, we simply add `slug` as a parameter to the function view.

Our final view is shown in Example 5.8.

**Example 5.8: Project Code**
`organizer/views.py` in 84eb438c96

```
16   def tag_detail(request, slug):
17       tag = Tag.objects.get(slug__iexact=slug)
18       template = loader.get_template(
19           'organizer/tag_detail.html')
20       context = Context({'tag': tag})
21       return HttpResponse(template.render(context))
```

## 5.4.2   Adding a URL Pattern for `tag_detail`

With our `tag_detail()` function view fully programmed, we now need to point Django to it by adding a URL pattern to the URL configuration. The pattern will be in the form of `url(<regular_expression>, tag_detail)`, where the value of `<regular_expression>` is currently unknown. In this section, we need to solve two problems:

1. We need to build a regular expression that allows for multiple inputs. For example, `/tag/django/` and `/tag/web/` must both be valid URL paths.

2. We must pass the value of the slug in the URL path to the detail view.

The answer to both of these problems is to use regular expressions groups.

To solve the first case, we first begin by building a static regular expression. Remember that our regular expressions patterns should not start with a `/`. To match `/tag/django/` we can use the regular expression `r'^tag/django/$'`. Similarly, `r'^tag/web/$'` will match `/tag/web/`. The goal is to build a regular expression that will match all slugs. As mentioned in Chapter 3, a `SlugField` accepts a string with a limited character set: alphanumeric characters, the underscore, and the dash. We first define a regular expression character set by replacing `django` and `web` with two brackets: `r'^tag/[]/$'`. Any character or character set inside the brackets is a valid character for the string. We want multiple characters, so we add the `+` character to match at least one character: `r'^tag/[]+/$'`. In Python, \w will match alphanumeric characters and the underscore. We can thus add \w and - (the dash character) to the character set to match a valid slug: `r'^tag/[\w\-]+/$'`. This regular expression will successfully match `/tag/django/`, `/tag/web/`, and even `/tag/video-games/` and `/tag/video_games/`.

> **Info**
>
> In the code above we opted to specify `[\w\-]+` for the slug match, instead of `[\w-]+` or `[-\w]+`. Python will accept and work correctly with `[\w-]+` or `[-\w]+`, but the

character set is imprecise. The - character is reserved for specifying ranges, such as [A-Z]+, which will match any capital alphabet character. To specify the - character, we have to escape it with a slash: the [A\-Z]+ pattern will match a string of any length than contains only the letters A, Z, or -. However, as you may have guessed, if the dash is specified at the the beginning or end of a character set, Python is smart enough to realize that you mean the character rather than a range. Even so, this can be ambiguous to other programmers, and it's best to always escape the dash when you want to match the - character.

This regular expression matches all of the URLs we actually want, but it will not pass the value of the slug to the tag_detail() function view. To do so, we can use a named group. Python regular expressions identify named groups with the text (?P<name>pattern), where name is the name of the group and pattern is the actual regular expression pattern. In a URL pattern, Django takes any named group and passes its value to the view the URL pattern points to. In our case, we want our named group to use the pattern we just built— [\w\-]+—and to be called slug. We thus have (?P<slug>[\w\-]+).

Our full regular expression has become r'^tag/(?P<slug>[\w\-]+)/$'. This regular expression will match a slug and pass its value to the view the URL pattern points to. We can now build our URL pattern.

We are building a URL pattern for our tag_detail() view, which exists in the views.py file in our **organizer** app. We first import the view via a Python import and then create a URL pattern by calling url() and passing the regular expression and the view. Example 5.9 shows the resulting URL configuration in suorganizer/urls.py.

**Example 5.9:** Project Code
suorganizer/urls.py **in** 5b18131069

```
16    from django.conf.urls import include, url
      ...
19    from organizer.views import homepage, tag_detail
      ...
24        url(r'^tag/(?P<slug>[\w\-]+)/$',        # RE like (?P<name> pattern )
25            tag_detail,
26            ),
```

If we request http://127.0.0.1:8000/tag/django or the Django runserver, Django will select our new URL pattern and call tag_detail(request, slug='django').

The regular expression pattern and view pointer are not the only parameters we can pass to url(). It is possible, and highly recommended, to specify the keyword argument name for URL patterns. The utility of specifying name is the ability to refer to a URL pattern in Django, a practice we discuss in Chapter 6: Integrating Models, Templates, Views, and URL Configurations to Create Links between webpages. This practice not only is useful in Django but also allows me to refer to URL patterns in the book without ambiguity.

It is possible to name a URL pattern whatever you wish. However, I strongly recommend you namespace your names, allowing for easy reference without conflict across your site. In this book, I use the name of the app, the name of the model being used, and the display type for the object type. We thus name the URL pattern `organizer_tag_detail`. Our final URL pattern is shown in Example 5.10.

**Example 5.10: Project Code**
`suorganizer/urls.py` in `79c8d40d8a`

```
24        url(r'^tag/(?P<slug>[\w\-]+)/$',
25            tag_detail,
26            name='organizer_tag_detail'),
```

> ### Info
> When I refer to namespaces, I mean it in an informal sense: it's simply a string that we structure in a particular way. I am not referring to the actual URL namespace tool Django provides that we will use in Chapter 19: Basic Authentication.

Consider all the code we have avoided writing by writing our URL pattern intelligently. At the end of Section 5.4.1, we were considering parsing the raw URL path string (passed to the view via `request.path_info`) to find the slug value of our tag. Thanks to Django's smart URL configuration, simply by providing a named group to our regular expression pattern, we can pass values in the URL directly to the view.

## 5.5   Generating 404 Errors for Invalid Queries

As things stand, we can use the command line to start our development server (Example 5.11) and see the fruits of our labor.

**Example 5.11: Shell Code**

```
$ ./manage.py runserver
```

If you navigate to the address of a valid `Tag`, you will be greeted by a simple HTML page built from our template. For example, `http://127.0.0.1:8000/tag/django/` will display a simple page about our Django tag. However, what happens if you browse to a URL built with an invalid tag slug, such as `http://127.0.0.1:8000/tag/nonexistent/?`

You'll be greeted by a page of Django debug information, as shown in Figure 5.4.

Django is displaying a page informing you that Python has thrown an exception. The title of the page, "DoesNotExist at /tag/nonexistent/," tells us that the URL we asked for does not exist. The subtitle, "Tag matching query does not exist" tells us that the database query for our `Tag` could not find a row in the database that matched what we desired (in this case, we queried `Tag.objects.get(slug__iexact='nonexistent')`). What's more, below the initial readout presented in Figure 5.4, you'll find a Python traceback, shown in Figure 5.5, where Django informs us that the Python exception type being raised is DoesNotExist.

Of the four functions in the traceback, three are in Django's source code and therefore (most likely) are not the problem. The second item in the traceback, however, is in /organizer/views.py and reveals that the code throwing the exception is tag = Tag.objects.get(slug__iexact=slug), on line 17. This does not mean the code is wrong (it isn't!), simply that the problem originates there. The problem, as stated in the top half of the page, is that there is no Tag object with slug "nonexistent" in the database.

This message is obviously not what we want users to be greeted with in the event of a malformed URL. The standard return for such in websites is an HTTP 404 error. Let us

## DoesNotExist at /tag/nonexistent/

Tag matching query does not exist.

| | |
|---|---|
| Request Method: | GET |
| Request URL: | http://127.0.0.1:8000/tag/nonexistent/ |
| Django Version: | 1.8.3 |
| Exception Type: | DoesNotExist |
| Exception Value: | Tag matching query does not exist. |
| Exception Location: | /Users/magus/.virtualenvs/book_code/lib/python3.4/site-packages/django/db/models/query.py in get, line 334 |
| Python Executable: | /Users/magus/.virtualenvs/book_code/bin/python |
| Python Version: | 3.4.3 |
| Python Path: | ['/Users/magus/Development/book_code', |
| | '/Users/magus/.virtualenvs/book_code/lib/python34.zip', |
| | '/Users/magus/.virtualenvs/book_code/lib/python3.4', |
| | '/Users/magus/.virtualenvs/book_code/lib/python3.4/plat-darwin', |
| | '/Users/magus/.virtualenvs/book_code/lib/python3.4/lib-dynload', |
| | '/opt/local/Library/Frameworks/Python.framework/Versions/3.4/lib/python3.4', |
| | '/opt/local/Library/Frameworks/Python.framework/Versions/3.4/lib/python3.4/plat-darwin', |
| | '/Users/magus/.virtualenvs/book_code/lib/python3.4/site-packages'] |
| Server time: | Thu, 30 Jul 2015 00:00:05 +0000 |

**Figure 5.4:** Django Error Message

**Traceback** Switch to copy-and-paste view

/Users/magus/.virtualenvs/book_code/lib/python3.4/site-packages/django/core/handlers/base.py in get_response

    132.                        response = wrapped_callback(request, *callback_args,
    **callback_kwargs)
    ▶ Local vars

/Users/magus/Development/book_code/organizer/views.py in tag_detail

    17.                tag = Tag.objects.get(slug__iexact=slug)
    ▶ Local vars

/Users/magus/.virtualenvs/book_code/lib/python3.4/site-packages/django/db/models/manager.py in manager_method

    127.                return getattr(self.get_queryset(), name)(*args, **kwargs)
    ▶ Local vars

/Users/magus/.virtualenvs/book_code/lib/python3.4/site-packages/django/db/models/query.py in get

    334.                self.model._meta.object_name
    ▶ Local vars

**Figure 5.5:** Django Error Traceback

return to our function view in /organizer/views.py and augment it so that it returns a proper HTTP error rather than throwing a Python exception.

Django supplies two ways to create an HTTP 404 error. The first is with the HttpReponseNotFound class, and the second is with the Http404 exception.

The HttpReponseNotFound class is a subclass of the HttpResponse class. Like its superclass, HttpReponseNotFound expects to be passed the HTML content it is asked to display. The key difference is that returning an HttpResponse object results in Django returning an HTTP 200 code (Resource Found), whereas returning a HttpReponseNotFound object results in an HTTP 404 code (Resource Not Found).

The Http404 is an exception and as such is meant to be raised rather then returned. In contrast to the HttpReponseNotFound class, it does not expect any data to be passed, relying instead on the default 404 HTML page, which we build in Chapter 29: Deploy! when we deploy our site.

Consider that our code is currently raising a DoesNotExist. We therefore have to catch this exception and then proceed with an HTTP 404 error. It is thus more appropriate and more Pythonic to use an exception, meaning our code in Example 5.12 will use the Http404 exception. Start by importing this in the file, by adding Http404 to the second import line (the one for HttpResponse). The import code should now read as shown in Example 5.12.

**Example 5.12: Project Code**
organizer/views.py **in** 294dabd8cc

```
1    from django.http.response import (
2        Http404, HttpResponse)
```

To catch the DoesNotExist exception, we surround our model manager query with a Python try...except block. Should the query raise a DoesNotExist exception for a Tag object, we then raise the newly imported Http404. This leaves us with the code shown in Example 5.13.

**Example 5.13: Project Code**
organizer/views.py **in** 294dabd8cc

```
17    def tag_detail(request, slug):
18        try:
19            tag = Tag.objects.get(slug__iexact=slug)
20        except Tag.DoesNotExist:
21            raise Http404
22        template = loader.get_template(
23            'organizer/tag_detail.html')
24        context = Context({'tag': tag})
25        return HttpResponse(template.render(context))
```

Had we opted to use HttpReponseNotFound, we might have coded as in Example 5.14.

**Example 5.14: Python Code**

```python
# this code not optimal!
try:
    tag = Tag.objects.get(slug__iexact=slug)
except Tag.DoesNotExist:
    return HttpReponseNotFound('<h1>Tag not found!</h1>')
```

Raising an exception rather than returning a value is considered better Python practice because `raise()` was built explicitly for this purpose. What's more, it allows us to create a single 404.html page in Chapter 29, further maintaining the DRY principle.

Note that some developers might try to use the code shown in Example 5.15.

**Example 5.15: Python Code**

```python
# this code is incorrect!
tag = Tag.objects.get(slug__iexact=slug)
if not tag:
    return HttpReponseNotFound('<h1>Tag not found!</h1>')
```

The code is incorrect: it will not catch the `DoesNotExist` exception raised by the model manager query. A `try...except` block is required.

If you browse to `http://127.0.0.1:8000/tag/nonexistent` on the development server now, you will be treated to an HTTP 404 page, which is our desired behavior.

The error in this section is different from a nonmatching URL. If you browse to `http://127.0.0.1:8000/nopath/`, Django will tell you it couldn't match the URL to a URL pattern and, in production, will return a 404 error automatically. The issue we solved here was when the URL did match but the view did not behave as expected.

## 5.6   Shortening the Development Process with Django View Shortcuts

We now have a two-function view in `/organizer/views.py`, which currently reads as shown in Example 5.16.

**Example 5.16: Project Code**

`organizer/views.py` in 294dabd8cc

```python
1  from django.http.response import (
2      Http404, HttpResponse)
3  from django.template import Context, loader
```

```
4
5    from .models import Tag
6
7
8    def homepage(request):
9        tag_list = Tag.objects.all()
10       template = loader.get_template(
11           'organizer/tag_list.html')
12       context = Context({'tag_list': tag_list})
13       output = template.render(context)
14       return HttpResponse(output)
15
16
17   def tag_detail(request, slug):
18       try:
19           tag = Tag.objects.get(slug__iexact=slug)
20       except Tag.DoesNotExist:
21           raise Http404
22       template = loader.get_template(
23           'organizer/tag_detail.html')
24       context = Context({'tag': tag})
25       return HttpResponse(template.render(context))
```

That is a lot of code for two simple webpages. We also have a lot of duplicate code in each function, which is not in keeping with the DRY philosophy. Luckily for developers, Django provides shortcut functions to ease the development process and to significantly shorten code such as the preceding.

## 5.6.1   Shortening Code with `get_object_or_404()`

Our first shortcut, `get_object_or_404()`, is a complete replacement for the `try...except` block that currently exists in our `tag_detail()` function.

Let's start by importing it into our `/organizer/views.py` file, as in Example 5.17.

**Example 5.17: Project Code**
`organizer/views.py` in 5705e49877

```
2    from django.shortcuts import get_object_or_404
```

We can then delete the following lines, as in Example 5.18.

**Example 5.18: Project Code**
`organizer/views.py` in 294dabd8cc

```
18       try:
19           tag = Tag.objects.get(slug__iexact=slug)
20       except Tag.DoesNotExist:
21           raise Http404
```

We replace the content in Example 5.18 with the code in Example 5.19.

**Example 5.19: Project Code**

`organizer/views.py` **in** 5705e49877

```
18        tag = get_object_or_404(
19            Tag, slug__iexact=slug)
```

The `get_object_or_404()` shortcut expects to have the model class and the desired query passed as arguments and will return the object if it finds one. If not, it raises `Http404`, just as we had programmed before. Because we are passing in the `Tag` object and using exactly the same query, the behavior of our shortened code is exactly the same as that of our original code.

Our `tag_detail()` thus reads as in Example 5.20.

**Example 5.20: Project Code**

`organizer/views.py` **in** 5705e49877

```
17    def tag_detail(request, slug):
18        tag = get_object_or_404(
19            Tag, slug__iexact=slug)
20        template = loader.get_template(
21            'organizer/tag_detail.html')
22        context = Context({'tag': tag})
23        return HttpResponse(template.render(context))
```

## 5.6.2 Shortening Code with `render_to_response()`

Most views must do the following:

1. Load a template file as a `Template` object.
2. Create a `Context` from a dictionary.
3. Render the `Template` with the `Context`.
4. Instantiate an `HttpResponse` object with the rendered result.

Django supplies not one but two shortcuts to perform this process for us. The first is the `render_to_response()` shortcut. The shortcut replaces the behavior that we currently have in our views, performing all four tasks listed above. Let's start by importing it, adding it to the end of our pre-existing shortcut import, as shown in Example 5.21.

**Example 5.21: Project Code**

`organizer/views.py` **in** 5ff3dee4fa

```
1    from django.shortcuts import (
2        get_object_or_404, render_to_response)
```

We can now use render_to_response() to shorten our code. In our homepage() view, for instance, we can remove the code shown in Example 5.22.

**Example 5.22: Project Code**
organizer/views.py **in** 5705e49877

```
 7    def homepage(request):
 8        tag_list = Tag.objects.all()
 9        template = loader.get_template(
10            'organizer/tag_list.html')
11        context = Context({'tag_list': tag_list})
12        output = template.render(context)
```

The code in Example 5.22 is easily replaced with the code in Example 5.23.

**Example 5.23: Project Code**
organizer/views.py **in** 5ff3dee4fa

```
 7    def homepage(request):
 8        return render_to_response(
 9            'organizer/tag_list.html',
10            {'tag_list': Tag.objects.all()})
```

Observe how we pass in the same path to the template and a simple dictionary with the (identical) values to populate the template. The shortcut does the rest for us: the behaviors in the preceding two code examples are exactly the same.

The process to shorten tag_detail() is exactly the same. We start by removing the code in Example 5.24.

**Example 5.24: Project Code**
organizer/views.py **in** 5705e49877

```
20        template = loader.get_template(
21            'organizer/tag_detail.html')
22        context = Context({'tag': tag})
23        return HttpResponse(template.render(context))
```

Then, in Example 5.25, we write a call to render_to_response(), passing in the same values seen in the previous code: the same template path and the same dictionary passed to our Context instantiation.

**Example 5.25: Project Code**

`organizer/views.py` in `5ff3dee4fa`

```
16          return render_to_response(
17              'organizer/tag_detail.html',
18              {'tag': tag})
```

Our entire file has been reduced to the code shown in Example 5.26.

**Example 5.26: Project Code**

`organizer/views.py` in `5ff3dee4fa`

```
1   from django.shortcuts import (
2       get_object_or_404, render_to_response)
3
4   from .models import Tag
5
6
7   def homepage(request):
8       return render_to_response(
9           'organizer/tag_list.html',
10          {'tag_list': Tag.objects.all()})
11
12
13  def tag_detail(request, slug):
14      tag = get_object_or_404(
15          Tag, slug__iexact=slug)
16      return render_to_response(
17          'organizer/tag_detail.html',
18          {'tag': tag})
```

The code in Example 5.26 was the original way to shorten code and, while still frequently seen on the Internet and in older projects, is no longer the best way to shorten a simple view. Instead, you'll want to use `render()`.

### 5.6.3  Shortening Code with `render()`

Before introducing the `render_to_response()` shortcut, our `/organizer/views.py` read as shown in Example 5.27.

**Example 5.27: Project Code**

`organizer/views.py` in `4d36d603db`

```
1   from django.http.response import HttpResponse
2   from django.shortcuts import get_object_or_404
3   from django.template import Context, loader
```

```
4
5    from .models import Tag
6
7
8    def homepage(request):
9        tag_list = Tag.objects.all()
10       template = loader.get_template(
11           'organizer/tag_list.html')
12       context = Context({'tag_list': tag_list})
13       output = template.render(context)
14       return HttpResponse(output)
15
16
17   def tag_detail(request, slug):
18       tag = get_object_or_404(
19           Tag, slug__iexact=slug)
20       template = loader.get_template(
21           'organizer/tag_detail.html')
22       context = Context({'tag': tag})
23       return HttpResponse(template.render(context))
```

Example 5.27 is sufficient for the simple views we are currently building but will prove to be inadequate in the long run. Specifically, we are not using Django context processors.

At the moment, our views are rendering `Template` instances with `Context` instances and passing the result to an `HttpResponse` object. The problem with this approach is that sometimes Django needs to make changes to the values within the `Context` objects. To enable Django to make changes to data that render a `Template`, we must use a `RequestContext` instead of a `Context` object. When a `Template` renders with a `RequestContext`, Django uses the `HttpRequest` object to add data to the `RequestContext`, providing information not available to `Context`. To do so, Django calls the context processors, which are simply functions that are listed in the `TEMPLATES` options of `/suorganizer/settings.py` (Example 5.28).

**Example 5.28: Project Code**
`suorganizer/settings.py` **in** 4d36d603db

```
58   TEMPLATES = [{
.        ...
64       'OPTIONS': {
65           'context_processors': [
66               'django.template.context_processors.debug',
67               'django.template.context_processors.request',
68               'django.contrib.auth.context_processors.auth',
69               'django.contrib.messages.context_processors.messages',
70           ],
71       },
72   }]
```

At the moment, enabling context processors is of no use to us, but in Chapter 9, we build views and templates that rely on Django context processors. However, it behooves us to examine them now, as they provide insight into our new shortcut.

To make the change to using context processors, we need only change each use of `Context` to `RequestContext`. The only difference is that `RequestContext` needs the `HttpRequest` object, as it intends to pass it to all the context processors. We therefore pass `request` to `RequestContext` before the dictionary of values. Our code now reads as shown in Example 5.29.

**Example 5.29: Project Code**

`organizer/views.py` in c392ab707a

```
1   from django.http.response import HttpResponse
2   from django.shortcuts import get_object_or_404
3   from django.template import RequestContext, loader
4
5   from .models import Tag
6
7
8   def homepage(request):
9       tag_list = Tag.objects.all()
10      template = loader.get_template(
11          'organizer/tag_list.html')
12      context = RequestContext(
13          request,
14          {'tag_list': tag_list})
15      output = template.render(context)
16      return HttpResponse(output)
17
18
19  def tag_detail(request, slug):
20      tag = get_object_or_404(
21          Tag, slug__iexact=slug)
22      template = loader.get_template(
23          'organizer/tag_detail.html')
24      context = RequestContext(
25          request,
26          {'tag': tag})
27      return HttpResponse(template.render(context))
```

Understanding and using `RequestContext` or `Context` has a direct effect on our choice of shortcuts. Prior to Django 1.3, developers would force the `render_to_response()` shortcut to use the `RequestContext` object by coding as shown in Example 5.30.

**Example 5.30: Python Code**

```
return render_to_response(
    'path/to/template.html',
    data_dictionary,
    context_instance=RequestContext(request))
```

Many examples online and older projects continue to use this method. However, starting in Django 1.3 (released March 2011), developers should instead use the render() shortcut, which is identical to render_to_response() except that it uses a RequestContext object instead of a Context object and therefore takes the HttpRequest object as a third argument. Specifically, render() does the following:

1. Loads a template file as a Template object
2. Creates a RequestContext from a dictionary (with HttpRequest)
3. Calls all the context processors in the project, adding or modifying data to the RequestContext
4. Renders the Template with the RequestContext
5. Instantiates an HttpResponse object with the rendered result

The render() shortcut thus replaces the project code from Example 5.30, taking three arguments: request, the path to the template file, and the dictionary used to build the RequestContext object. We can follow the same replacement steps used for render_to_response() in the case of render(). Example 5.31 shows the resulting /organizer/views.py.

**Example 5.31: Project Code**
organizer/views.py **in** d2ecb7f70d

```
1   from django.shortcuts import (
2       get_object_or_404, render)
3
4   from .models import Tag
5
6
7   def homepage(request):
8       return render(
9           request,
10          'organizer/tag_list.html',
11          {'tag_list': Tag.objects.all()})
12
13
14  def tag_detail(request, slug):
15      tag = get_object_or_404(
16          Tag, slug__iexact=slug)
17      return render(
18          request,
19          'organizer/tag_detail.html',
20          {'tag': tag})
```

Using RequestContext is slower than using Context, and therefore render() is slower than render_to_response() (when without the context argument). Nonetheless, most developers now use render() out of the box, choosing to prioritize ease of programming over performance. Using Context or render_to_response(), particularly in young projects with few users, could be considered a pre-optimization, limiting functionality in favor of performance. In addition, context processors are not typically the bottleneck on a website. By the same token, if a context processor is ever needed on a view using `Context` or `render_to_response()`, more work will be required to get the context processor working, particularly if the developer is unclear as to where the problem lies. It is therefore not a bad idea to start with `RequestContext` and `render()` and replace them if necessary (and if possible!). We reinforce this notion in Chapter 19 when we opt to use variables created by context processors on every webpage.

In keeping with this logic and with current trends, the rest of the book relies on `render()` as the de facto view shortcut.

As we move forward, please keep in mind that while similar, `render_to_response()` and `render()` have very different uses, and many of the examples online should be using `render()` instead of `render_to_response()`, making this latter shortcut a common pitfall for beginners when building forms (Chapter 9) or when using the contributed library.

# 5.7 URL Configuration Internals: Adhering to App Encapsulation

We currently have two function views, now masterfully shortened, and two URL patterns, creating two webpages. However, our URL configuration is in direct violation of app encapsulation in Django. The URL patterns that direct users to the two webpages generated by the **organizer** app exist in a file that is for the project: the URLs are in a file under `suorganizer/`, as opposed to a file within the `organizer/` directory.

The practical goal of this section is to refactor our URL configuration so that our Django website adheres to the app encapsulation standard. However, to do so, we must learn much more about the URL configuration. The instructional goal of this section is to teach you exactly how URL patterns are used and built in Django.

## 5.7.1 Introspecting URL Patterns

We've discovered that a URL configuration is a list of URL patterns, stored by convention in a variable named `urlpatterns`. What I (and others) casually refer to as a *URL pattern* is actually a `RegexURLPattern` object. Each call to `url()` instantiates a `RegexURLPattern`; a URL configuration is thus a list of `RegexURLPattern` objects stored in a variable named `urlpatterns`.

Each `RegexURLPattern` is instantiated by a call to `url()` (see Example 5.32), which takes as mandatory arguments (1) a regular expression pattern and (2) a reference to a view. As an optional argument, it's possible to pass (3) a Python dictionary, where each key value is passed to the view as keyword arguments. We will see this in action before the end of the chapter and then again in Chapter 19. Finally, `url()` will accept (4) a named argument `name`, where we can specify the name of the `RegexURLPattern`. We've named our second URL pattern `organizer_tag_detail`, but the utility of names won't be clear until Chapter 6.

**Example 5.32: Python Code**

```
url(regular_expression,
    view,
    optional_dictionary_of_extra_values,
    name=a_name)
```

## Ghosts of Django Past

Prior to Django 1.8, it was possible to point to a view using a string that acted as a Python namespace (similar to imports). For example, we could have used the line in Example 5.33.

**Example 5.33: Python Code**

```
url(r'^$', 'organizer.views.homepage')
```

What's more, while the `urlpatterns` variable was still a simple list, it was convention (but not necessary) to create and process the list using a call to the `patterns()` function, as in Example 5.34.

**Example 5.34: Python Code**

```
urlpatterns = patterns('',
    url(regular_expression, view),
')
```

The first argument to `patterns` was the string prefix, which worked in tandem with namespace strings. For instance, the URL configurations in Example 5.35 and Example 5.36 are equivalent.

**Example 5.35: Python Code**

```
urlpatterns = patterns('',
    url(regular_expression,
        'organizer.views.homepage'),
)
```

**Example 5.36: Python Code**

```
urlpatterns = patterns('organizer.views',
    url(regular_expression,
        'homepage'),
)
```

The use of `patterns` and namespace strings in URL patterns are deprecated and should not be used. Use direct Python imports (what we are currently using) instead.

Django uses the ROOT_URLCONF setting in settings.py to find the URL configuration for the project. It does so as soon as the server starts (along with settings). This makes Django fast, as the entire regular expression pattern-matching scheme is stored in memory once, but it also means that if you change the URL configuration or any settings, you must restart the Django server (unless you're running the development server, which anticipates changes).

Because a URL configuration is a list, the order of URL patterns matters, particularly when the URLs matched by regular expression patterns overlap. In Chapter 6, we will see an example of overlapping URLs and how order comes into play.

While we now understand the basics of URL patterns and configurations, we're still missing a key concept: how to connect different URL configurations.

## 5.7.2 Using include to Create a Hierarchy of URL Configurations

The second argument passed to url() need not point at a view: it can point at another URL configuration, thanks to the include() function. This capability allows us to create a separate URL configuration in each Django app and have a URL pattern in the site-wide URL configuration point to each one. In effect, the full URL configuration is not a simple list but is actually a tree, where the leaves of the tree are webpages (see Figure 5.6).

When a URL pattern points to a URL configuration, the regular expression pattern acts as a URI prefix. For instance, if the path r'^blog/' points to a URL configuration, then all of the URL patterns in that URL configuration will effectively have that URI prefixed to their own regular expression.

This functionality comes with an important pitfall: regular expression patterns in URL patterns that point to URL configurations must be treated as partial regular expression patterns: we cannot use the $ character to close the pattern, or it will prevent the use of the ensuing patterns. If a URL pattern with the regular expression pattern r'^first/$' points

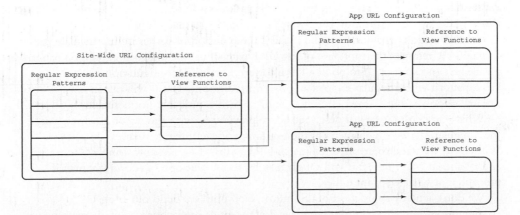

**Figure 5.6:** URL Configuration Tree

to a URL configuration with the regular expression pattern `r'^second/$'`, Django will *effectively* (but not actually, as we'll discuss shortly) combine them for the result of `r'^first/$second/$'`. Instead of matching `/first/second/` as desired, Django will only match `/first/`. To properly build this URL pattern, the first regular expression must remove the $, reading `r'^first/'`, so that the combination results in `r'^first/second/$'`, as in Example 5.37.

**Example 5.37: Python Code**

```python
# app/urls.py
urlpatterns = patterns(
    url(r'^second/$',
        a_view),
)

# project/urls.py
import app.urls as app_url_config

urlpatterns = patterns(
    url(r'^first/',  # there is no '$' here!
        include(app_url_config)),
)
```

Django is not actually combining regular expressions but rather truncating the URL path it receives. For this reason, the ^ can still be used in `r'^second/$'`. When a user requests `/first/second/`, Django removes the first `/`, resulting in a request for `first/second/`. Django then uses regular expression pattern `r'^first/'` to match `first/second/`. This explains why we cannot use the $: `r'^first/'` will match `first/second/`, but `r'^first/$'` will not. Once Django has selected this URL pattern, it uses the regular expression pattern `r'^first/'` to truncate the path from `first/second/` to `second/`, allowing the regular expression pattern `r'^second/$'` to match this new path.

Given Django's behavior, a second pitfall is the omission of slashes in intermediate paths. Django only removes the root slash of any URL path. If we use a regular expression pattern `r'^first'` (no slash or $) to point a URL pattern to a URL configuration containing a URL pattern with a regular expression pattern `r'^second/$'`, it will match not `/first/second/` but instead `/firstsecond/`, which is probably not desirable.

What's more, the behavior described above provides us with the reason to always use the ^ regular expression character at the beginning of every regular expression pattern. Without it, we stand to erroneously match URL paths. If we are now using `r'^first/'` and `r'second/$'` (no ^), it will validly match `/first/whoops/second/`, which is probably not what we want either.

We don't actually apply most of this information until we build our **blog** URL configuration. For our **organizer** app, we don't want to prefix our path with anything yet. (We will in Chapter 11: Bending the Rules: The Contact Us Webpage when we want the path /tag/ and /startup/, not /organizer/tag/ or /organizer/startup/.) The prefix we use now is therefore empty.

Start by creating a new file, /organizer/urls.py. In it, we create a new URL configuration. We import the url() function to create RegexURLPattern objects. We then create a urlpatterns list to allow Django to find our URL configuration. We can then call url() with the same parameters as the ones currently in /suorganizer/ urls.py. We end up with a /organizer/urls.py file which reads as in Example 5.38.

**Example 5.38: Project Code**

organizer/urls.py in 18f1a2d3bc

```
1    from django.conf.urls import url
2
3    from .views import homepage, tag_detail
4
5    urlpatterns = [
6        url(r'^$', homepage),
7        url(r'^tag/(?P<slug>[\w\-]+)/$',
8            tag_detail,
9            name='organizer_tag_detail'),
10   ]
```

*url config for organizer app*

To direct Django to this new URL configuration, we need to point our root URL configuration file to this new file using the include() function, already included in the Python imports. To start, we need to import the URLs from our **organizer** app. To avoid name-space clashes, we use the as keyword to rename the urls module organizer_ urls. We can then simply point include() to this Python reference. We do this by using the ^ regular expression pattern character, shown in Example 5.39.

**Example 5.39: Project Code**

suorganizer/urls.py in 18f1a2d3bc

```
16   from django.conf.urls import include, url
17   from django.contrib import admin
18
19   from organizer import urls as organizer_urls
20
21   urlpatterns = [
22       url(r'^admin/', include(admin.site.urls)),
23       url(r'^', include(organizer_urls)),
24   ]
```

*url config for root*

If you are still running the development server, it will automatically detect the changes made and reload your URL configuration. If not, restart it by invoking runserver on the command line, as shown in Example 5.40.

**Example 5.40: Shell Code**

```
$ ./manage.py runserver
```

With the development server running, you can now browse to `127.0.0.1:8000` to see our `homepage()` view and `127.0.0.1:8000/tag/mobile/` to demonstrate our `tag_detail()` view. Consider that while our URL configuration has changed, the URLs we are able to use have not. We have refactored code, not added new behavior.

# 5.8  Implementing the Views and URL Configurations to the Rest of the Site

We now have a fundamental understanding of URL configurations and views and have two fully functional webpages using the best tools at our disposal. With these tools, we will now build the rest of the webpages in our site.

## 5.8.1  Restructuring Our `homepage()` View

Before we build out new views, it is in our best interest to change our `homepage()` view to give it a more sensible name and URL path.

Given that it is a list of `Tag` objects, we should replace the URL pattern so that it matches `tag/` as the URL path and provide it with a name, `organizer_tag_list`, as demonstrated in Example 5.41 in `/organizer/urls.py`.

**Example 5.41: Project Code**
`organizer/urls.py` **in** `1f86398a5e`

```
1   from django.conf.urls import url
2
3   from .views import tag_detail, tag_list
4
5   urlpatterns = [
6       url(r'^tag/$',
7           tag_list,
8           name='organizer_tag_list'),
9       url(r'^tag/(?P<slug>[\w\-]+)/$',
10          tag_detail,
11          name='organizer_tag_detail'),
12   ]
```

Note that we use `^` and `$` in the URL pattern starting on line 6 to carefully define the start and end of the URL path.

In our `/organizer/views.py` file, we thus need to rename our `homepage()` view to `tag_list()`, as in Example 5.42. We make no other changes.

**Example 5.42: Project Code**
`organizer/views.py` **in** `1f86398a5e`

```
16   def tag_list(request):
17       return render(
18           request,
19           'organizer/tag_list.html',
20           {'tag_list': Tag.objects.all()})
```

Given our changes, `http://127.0.0.1:8000/` is no longer a valid URL. Django notes the result of our changes by displaying the list of valid URL patterns, indicating that we may browse to `http://127.0.0.1:8000/tag/` or `http://127.0.0.1:8000/tag/<slug>/`, such as `http://127.0.0.1:8000/tag/mobile/`, to display valid pages.

## 5.8.2  Building a `Startup` List Page

In `/organizer/urls.py`, we begin by creating a URL pattern for a startup list page, as shown in Example 5.43. Our new URL pattern will direct requests for URL path `startup/` to the function view `startup_list()`.

**Example 5.43: Project Code**
`organizer/urls.py` **in** `69767312bf`

```
3    from .views import (
4        startup_list, tag_detail, tag_list)
.        ...
6    urlpatterns = [
7        url(r'^startup/$',
8            startup_list,
9            name='organizer_startup_list'),
.        ...
16   ]
```

In `/organizer/views.py`, we may follow the example of our `Tag` object list view when building one for `Startup` objects. In Example 5.44, we load and render the template we built for this purpose and pass in all of the `Startup` objects in the database to the name of the template variable, which we earlier named `startup_list`.

**Example 5.44: Project Code**
`organizer/views.py` **in** `69767312bf`

```
4    from .models import Startup, Tag
.        ...
7    def startup_list(request):
8        return render(
9            request,
10           'organizer/startup_list.html',
11           {'startup_list': Startup.objects.all()})
```

Remember to add the imports, as shown in Examples 5.43 and 5.44!

### 5.8.3  Building a `Startup` Detail Page

As we did for our `tag_detail()` view, we will now build a `startup_detail()` view. The function will show a single `Startup` object, directed to in the URL by the `slug` field of the model. Our function view thus must take not only a `request` argument but also a `slug` argument. In `/organizer/views.py`, enter the code shown in Example 5.45.

**Example 5.45: Project Code**
`organizer/views.py` **in** bb3aa7eb88

```
 7   def startup_detail(request, slug):
 8       startup = get_object_or_404(
 9           Startup, slug__iexact=slug)
10       return render(
11           request,
12           'organizer/startup_detail.html',
13           {'startup': startup})
```

As before, we use the `slug` value passed by the URL configuration to query the database via the Django-provided `get_object_or_404`, which will display an HTTP 404 page in the event the `slug` value passed does not match one in the database. We then use `render()` to load a template and pass the `startup` object yielded by our query to the template, to be rendered via the template variable of the same name.

In `/organizer/urls.py`, we direct Django to our new view by adding the URL pattern shown in Example 5.46.

**Example 5.46: Project Code**
`organizer/urls.py` **in** bb3aa7eb88

```
 3   from .views import (
 4       startup_detail, startup_list, tag_detail,
 5       tag_list)
 .       ...
 7   urlpatterns = [
 .       ...
11       url(r'^startup/(?P<slug>[\w\-]+)/$',
12           startup_detail,
13           name='organizer_startup_detail'),
 .       ...
20   ]
```

Note again the `^` and `$` characters that define the beginning and end of our URL path and how our use of regular expression named groups allows us to pass the slug portion of the URL directly to our view as a keyword argument. We make sure, as always, to name the URL pattern.

### 5.8.4  Connecting the URL Configuration to Our Blog App

We've created the four display webpages in our **organizer** app. We will now build two pages in our **blog** app. To maintain app encapsulation, we must first create an app-specific URL configuration file and then point a URL pattern in the site-wide URL configuration to it.

Start by creating /blog/urls.py and coding the very basic requirements for a URL configuration. This will yield the code shown in Example 5.47.

**Example 5.47: Project Code**
blog/urls.py in 02dabec093

```
1   urlpatterns = [
2   ]
```

In /suorganizer/urls.py we can direct Django to our **blog** app URL configuration thanks to include(), as shown in Example 5.48.

**Example 5.48: Project Code**
suorganizer/urls.py in 02dabec093

```
19    from blog import urls as blog_urls
 .        ...
22    urlpatterns = [
 .        ...
24        url(r'^blog/', include(blog_urls)),
 .        ...
26    ]
```

Remember that the full URL configuration is actually a tree. If a URL pattern points to another URL configuration, Django will pass the next URL configuration a truncated version of the URL path. We can thus continue to use the ^ regular expression character to match the beginning of strings, but we cannot use the $ to match the end of a string. When the user requests the blog post webpage, he or she will request /blog/2013/1/django-training/. Django will remove the root slash and match the URL path in the request to the URL pattern above, as the regular expression r'^blog/' matches the path. Django will use the regular expression pattern r'^blog/' to truncate the path to 2013/1/django-training/. This is the path it will forward to the **blog** URL configuration and is what we want our post detail view to match.

Before we create a blog post detail view, let us first program a list view for posts.

### 5.8.5  Building a Post List Page

With our **blog** app connected via URL configuration, we can now add URL patterns. Let's start with a list of blog posts.

In /blog/views.py, our function view is straightforward, as you can see in Example 5.49.

**Example 5.49: Project Code**
blog/views.py **in** 928c982c03

```
1    from django.shortcuts import render
2
3    from .models import Post
4
5
6    def post_list(request):
7        return render(
8            request,
9            'blog/post_list.html',
10           {'post_list': Post.objects.all()})
```

We wish to list our blog posts at /blog/. However, this is already the URL path matched by our call to include in suorganizer/urls.py. When a user requests /blog/, Django will remove the root /, and match the URL pattern we just built. Django will then use r'^blog/' to truncate the path from blog/ to the empty string (i.e., nothing). We are thus seeking to display a list of blog posts when Django forwards our **blog** app the empty string. In Example 5.50, we match the empty string with the regular expression pattern r'^$'.

**Example 5.50: Project Code**
blog/urls.py **in** 928c982c03

```
1    from django.conf.urls import url
2
3    from .views import post_list
4
5    urlpatterns = [
6        url(r'^$',
7            post_list,
8            name='blog_post_list'),
9    ]
```

## 5.8.6   Building a Post Detail Page

The final view left to program is our detail view of a single Post object. Programming the view and URL pattern for this view is a little bit trickier than our other views: the URL for each Post object is based not only on the slug but also on the date of the object, making the regular expression pattern and query to the database a little more complicated. Recall that we are enforcing this behavior in our Post model via the unique_for_month attribute on the slug.

Take http://site.django-unleashed.com/blog/2013/1/django-training/ as an example. After include() in our root URL configuration truncates `blog/` from the URL path, our **blog** app URL configuration will receive `2013/1/ django-training/`. Our regular expression pattern must match a year, month, and slug and pass each one as a value to our view.

The year is four digits, and our named group is thus `(?P<year>\d{4})`. A month may have one or two digits, so our named group is `(?P<month>\d{1,2})`. Finally, and as before, our slug is any set of alphanumeric, underscore, or dash characters with length greater than one, so we write our named group as `(?P<slug> [\w-] +)`. We separate each part of the URL path with a `/` and wrap the string with `^` and `$` to signify the beginning and end of the URL path to match. The string containing our regular expression is thus `r'^(?P<year>\d{4})/(?P<month>\d{1,2})/(?P<slug> [\w-] +)/$'`.

To direct Django to a view in `/blog/views.py`, we may write the call in Example 5.51 to `url()`.

**Example 5.51: Project Code**
`blog/urls.py` in cb5dd59383

```
3    from .views import post_detail, post_list
.       ...
5    urlpatterns = [
.       ...
9        url(r'^(?P<year>\d{4})/'
10           r'(?P<month>\d{1,2})/'
11           r'(?P<slug>[\w\-]+)/$',
12           post_detail,
13           name='blog_post_detail'),
14   ]
```

## Warning!

In Example 5.51, we are passing **one regular expression pattern**, despite that there appears to be three. Python allows strings to be split into string fragments as long as there is only whitespace between the string fragments. Note how lines 9 and 10 do not end with a comma, while line 11 does. This is because the strings on lines 9, 10, and 11 are all a single string to Python, split this way to fit on the pages of this book. The r preceding the string fragments makes each fragment a raw string.

Our function view will thus accept four parameters: `request`, `year`, `month`, and `slug`.

In Example 5.52, in `/blog/views.py`, start by changing the import to include `get_object_or_404`, which we will need for our detail page.

**Example 5.52: Project Code**
`blog/views.py` in cb5dd59383

```
1    from django.shortcuts import (
2        get_object_or_404, render)
```

We must now build a query for the database. Our `Post` model contains a `pub_date` field, which we could compare to a `datetime.date`, but we don't have the necessary information to build one (we lack the day). For the occasion, Django provides `DateField` and `DateTimeField` objects with special field lookups that break each field down by its constituents, allowing us to query `pub_date__year` and `pub_date__month` to filter results. In the case of our example URL, `http://site.django-unleashed.com/blog/2013/1/django-training/`, this functionality allows us to write the query shown in Example 5.53.

**Example 5.53: Python Code**

```
Post.objects
    .filter(pub__date__year=2014)
    .filter(pub__date__month=11)
    .get(slug__iexact='django-training')
```

While the query to our `Post` model manager will work, it is more desirable to use the `get_object_or_404` to minimize developer-written code. Recall that `get_object_or_404` wants a model class and a query string as parameters. Django does not limit the number of query strings passed to `get_object_or_404`, allowing developers to pass as many as necessary. Given *n* arguments, the first *n*-1 will call `filter()`, while the *n*th will result in a call to `get()`. Practically, this means Django will re-create the query in Example 5.53 for us exactly, with the call shown in Example 5.54.

**Example 5.54: Project Code**
`blog/views.py` in cb5dd59383

```
 8        post = get_object_or_404(
 9            Post,
10            pub_date__year=year,
11            pub_date__month=month,
12            slug=slug)
```

The rest of our view is exactly like any other. The view passes the `HttpRequest` object, a dictionary, and a string to `render()`. The `render()` shortcut uses the `HttpRequest` object and the dictionary to build a `RequestContext` object. The string passes a path to the template file, allowing `render()` to load the template and render the template with the `RequestContext` object. The shortcut then returns an `HttpResponse` object to the view, which the view passes on to Django. Our final view is thus shown in Example 5.55.

**Example 5.55: Project Code**
`blog/views.py` in cb5dd59383

```
 7    def post_detail(request, year, month, slug):
 8        post = get_object_or_404(
```

```
 9           Post,
10           pub_date__year=year,
11           pub_date__month=month,
12           slug=slug)
13     return render(
14           request,
15           'blog/post_detail.html',
16           {'post': post})
```

# 5.9 Class-Based Views

## Warning!

This section deals with Python *methods* and *HTTP methods*. I will refer to Python methods simply as *methods* and to HTTP methods as *HTTP methods*, typically referring to the actual HTTP method in capitals (such as the HTTP GET method or the HTTP OPTIONS method).

Any Python callable that accepts an `HttpRequest` object as argument and returns an `HttpResponse` object is deemed a view in Django. So far, we've stuck exclusively to using Python functions to create views. Prior to Django 1.3, this was the only recommended way to create views. However, starting in version 1.3, Django introduced a class to allow developers to create view objects.

Django introduced a class to create view objects because coding the class for the view is actually rather tricky and prone to security issues. For this reason, despite the ability to use any Python callable as a view, developers stick to using the Django recommended class or else simply use functions.

The class itself is simply called `View`, and developers refer to classes that inherit `View` as class-based views (CBVs). These classes behave exactly like function views but come with several unexpected benefits.

To begin, let's replace our `Post` list function view with a class-based view. Example 5.56 shows our current view.

### Example 5.56: Project Code
`blog/views.py` in cb5dd59383

```
19   def post_list(request):
20       return render(
21           request,
22           'blog/post_list.html',
23           {'post_list': Post.objects.all()})
```

We are not going to change the logic of the function. However, the function must become a method belonging to a class (which implies the addition of the `self` parameter, required for Python methods). We may name the class whatever we wish, so we shall call it

`PostList`, but for reasons discussed shortly, the name of the method must be `get()`, as shown in Example 5.57.

**Example 5.57: Project Code**
`blog/views.py` **in** d9b8e788d5

```
3   from django.views.generic import View
    . . .
20  class PostList(View):
21
22      def get(self, request):
23          return render(
24              request,
25              'blog/post_list.html',
26              {'post_list': Post.objects.all()})
```

The import of `View` typically causes beginners confusion because it implies that `View` is generic, leading people to confuse `View` and class-based views with *generic* class-based views (GCBVs). *GCBVs are not the same as CBVs, and making a distinction between the two is crucial.* We wait until Chapter 17 and Chapter 18 to deal with GCBVs. For the moment, know that we are building CBVs and that they are different from GCBVs.

Our `PostList` class inherits from the `View` class we imported, imbuing it with (currently unseen) behavior.

The significance of the name of the method `get()` is that it refers to the HTTP method used to access it (a primer on HTTP methods is provided in Appendix A). Therefore, our method will be called only if the user's browser issues an HTTP GET request to a URL that is matched by our URL pattern. To contrast, if an HTTP POST request is made, Django will attempt to call the `post()` method, which will result in an error because we have not programmed such a method. We'll come back to this shortly.

In `/blog/urls.py`, import the `PostList` class and then change the URL pattern pointer to the pattern shown in Example 5.58.

**Example 5.58: Project Code**
`blog/urls.py` **in** d9b8e788d5

```
3   from .views import PostList, post_detail
    . . .
.   urlpatterns = [
        . . .
.       url(r'^$',
.           PostList.as_view(),
.           name='blog_post_list'),
        . . .
.   ]
```

The `as_view()` method is provided by the inheritance of the `View` superclass and ensures that the proper method in our CBV is called. When Django receives an HTTP

GET request to a URL that matches the regular expression in our URL pattern, as_view() will direct Django to the get() method we programmed. We'll take a much closer look at exactly how shortly.

## 5.9.1 Comparing Class-Based Views to Functions Views

A CBV can do everything a function view can do. We've not seen the use of the URL pattern dictionary previously, and so we'll now take the opportunity to use a dictionary in both a function view and a CBV to demonstrate similarities. The practical purpose of our dictionary is to override the base template of our view (which we defined in Chapter 4 in the template as parent_template), and the learning purpose is to familiarize you with the URL pattern dictionary and CBVs.

To start, we add the dictionary to both **blog** URL patterns, as shown in Example 5.59.

**Example 5.59: Project Code**
blog/urls.py in d3030ee8d3

```
 5    urlpatterns = [
 6        url(r'^$',
 7            PostList.as_view(),
 8            {'parent_template': 'base.html'},
 9            name='blog_post_list'),
10        url(r'^(?P<year>\d{4})/'
11            r'(?P<month>\d{1,2})/'
12            r'(?P<slug>[\w\-]+)/$',
13            post_detail,
14            {'parent_template': 'base.html'},
15            name='blog_post_detail'),
16    ]
```

*(handwritten annotations: (1) re, (2) view, (3) dict, (4) name, Optional dict in url ( ))*

In our post_detail function view, shown in Example 5.60, we must add a named parameter that's the same as the key in the dictionary (if we had several keys, we'd add several parameters).

**Example 5.60: Project Code**
blog/views.py in d3030ee8d3

```
 8    def post_detail(request, year, month,
 9                    slug, parent_template=None):
```

*(handwritten annotation: change to view def)*

To follow through with our example, we need to pass the argument to our template. In Example 5.61, we add parent_template to the context dictionary defined in the render() shortcut.

**Example 5.61: Project Code**
`blog/views.py` in d3030ee8d3

```
15          return render(
16              request,
17              'blog/post_detail.html',
18              {'post': post,
19               'parent_template': parent_template})
```

The process for using the dictionary is almost identical to a CBV. We first add a new parameter to the `get()` method and then pass the new argument to `render()`, as shown in Example 5.62.

**Example 5.62: Project Code**
`blog/views.py` in d3030ee8d3

```
22      class PostList(View):
23
24          def get(self, request, parent_template=None):
25              return render(
26                  request,
27                  'blog/post_list.html',
28                  {'post_list': Post.objects.all(),
29                   'parent_template': parent_template})
```

The modification illustrates a key point with CBVs: the view is entirely encapsulated by the class methods. The CBV is a container for multiple views, organized according to HTTP methods. At the moment, illustrating this more directly is impossible, but we revisit the concept in depth in Chapter 9. The bottom line at the moment is that any modification you might make to a function view occurs at the method level of a CBV.

We're not actually interested in overriding the base templates of our views and so should revert the few changes we've made in this section.

### 5.9.2   Advantages of Class-Based Views

The key advantages and disadvantages of CBVs over function views are exactly the same advantages and disadvantages that classes and objects have over functions: encapsulating data and behavior is typically more intuitive but can easily grow in complexity, which comes at the cost of functional purity.

A staple of object-oriented programming (OOP) is the use of instance variables, typically referred to as **attributes** in Python. For instance, we can usually better adhere to DRY in classes by defining important values as attributes. In `PostList`, we replace the string in `render()` with an attribute (which contains the same value), as shown in Example 5.63.

**Example 5.63: Project Code**
`blog/views.py` in ac3db8b26b

```
20    class PostList(View):
21        template_name = 'blog/post_list.html'    # a class attribute
22
23        def get(self, request):
24            return render(
25                request,
26                self.template_name,
27                {'post_list': Post.objects.all()})
```

At the moment, this does us little good on the DRY side of things, but it does offer us a level of control that function views do not offer. Quite powerfully, CBVs allow for existing class attributes to be overridden by values passed to as_view(). Should we wish to change the value of the `template_name` class attribute, for example, we need only pass it as a named argument to as_view() in the `blog_post_list` URL pattern, as shown in Example 5.64.

**Example 5.64: Project Code**
`blog/urls.py` in 78947978fd

```
6        url(r'^$',
7            PostList.as_view(
8                template_name='blog/post_list.html'),
9            name='blog_post_list'),
```

Even if the `template_name` attribute is unset, the view will still work as expected because of the value passed to as_view(), as shown in Example 5.65.

**Example 5.65: Project Code**
`blog/views.py` in 78947978fd

```
20    class PostList(View):
21        template_name = ''
```

However, if the `template_name` attribute is undefined (we never set it in the class definition), then as_view will ignore it.

In the event that `template_name` is unset and the developer forgets to pass it, we should be raising an `ImproperlyConfigured` exception. We will see its use in Chapter 17.

Once again, we're not actually interested in the advantages presented by the changes made in this section, and so I will revert all of the changes made here in the project code.

### 5.9.3  `View` Internals

CBVs also come with several much subtler advantages. To best understand these advantages, it's worth diving into the internals of `View` and seeing exactly what we're inheriting when we create a CBV.

The easiest place to start is with `as_view()`. In a URL pattern, we use `as_view()` to reference the CBV. Example 5.66 shows an example generic URL pattern.

**Example 5.66: Python Code**

```
url(r'^(?P<slug>[\w\-]+)/$',
    CBV.as_view(class_attribute=some_value),
    {'dict_key': 'dict_value'},
    name='app_model_action')
```

The `as_view()` method is a static class method (note that we call `PostList.as_view()` and not `PostList().as_view()`) and acts as a factory; `as_view()` returns a view (a method on the instance of `PostList`). Its main purpose is to define a (nested) function that acts as an intermediary view: it receives all the data, figures out which CBV method to call (using the HTTP method), and then passes all the data to that method, as shown in Example 5.67.

**Example 5.67: Python Code**

```
# grossly simplified for your benefit
@classonlymethod
def as_view(cls, **initkwargs)
    def view(request, *args, **kwargs)
        # magic!
    return view
```

In Example 5.67, the `cls` parameter will be the CBV. In our `blog_post_list` URL pattern, `as_view()` will be called with `cls` set to `PostList`. When we passed `template_name` to `as_view()` in `blog_post_list`, `initkwargs` received a dictionary in which `template_name` was a key. Example 5.68 shows the result.

**Example 5.68: Python Code**

```
as_view(
    cls=PostList,
    initkwargs={
        'template_name': 'blog/post_list.html',
    })
```

To best behave like a view, the nested `view()` method first instantiates the CBV as the `self` variable (demonstrating exactly how flexible Python is as a language). The `view()` method then sets a few attributes (removed from the example code) and calls the `dispatch()` method on the newly instantiated object, as shown in Example 5.69.

**Example 5.69: Python Code**

```
# still quite simplified
@classonlymethod
def as_view(cls, **initkwargs)
    def view(request, *args, **kwargs)
        self = cls(**initkwargs)
        ...
        return self.dispatch(request, *args, **kwargs)
    return view
```

For clarity's sake, I want to reiterate that passing undefined attributes to `as_view()` will result in problems because `as_view()` specifically checks for the existence of these attributes and raises an `TypeError` if it cannot find the attribute, as shown in Example 5.70.

**Example 5.70: Python Code**

```
# still quite simplified
@classonlymethod
def as_view(cls, **initkwargs)
    for key in initkwargs:
        ...
        if not hasattr(cls, key):
            raise TypeError(...)
    def view(request, *args, **kwargs)
        self = cls(**initkwargs)
        ...
        return self.dispatch(request, *args, **kwargs)
    return view
```

If `as_view()` is the heart of `View`, then `dispatch()` is the brain. The `dispatch()` method, returned by `view()`, is actually where the class figures out which method to use. `dispatch()` anticipates the following developer-defined methods: `get()`, `post()`, `put()`, `patch()`, `delete()`, `head()`, `options()`, `trace()`. In our `PostList` example, we defined a `get()` method. If a `get()` method is defined, `View` will automatically provide a `head()` method based on the `get()` method. In all cases, `View` implements an `options()` method for us (the HTTP OPTIONS method is used to see which methods are valid at that path).

In the event the CBV receives a request for a method that is not implemented, then `dispatch()` will call the `http_method_not_allowed()` method, which simply returns an `HttpResponseNotAllowed` object. The `HttpResponseNotAllowed` class is a subclass of `HttpResponse` and raises an HTTP 405 "Method Not Allowed" code, informing the user that that HTTP method is not handled by this path.

This behavior is subtle but very important: by default, function views are not technically compliant with HTTP methods. At the moment, all of our views are programmed to handle GET requests, the most basic of requests. However, if someone were to issue a PUT or TRACE request to our pages, *only the `PostList` CBV will behave correctly* by raising a 405 error. All of the other views (function views) will behave as if a GET request had been issued.

*(on function views)*

If we wanted, we could use the `require_http_methods` function decorator to set which HTTP methods are allowed on each of our function views. The decorator works as you might expect: you tell it which HTTP methods are valid, and any request with other methods will return an HTTP 405 error. For example, to limit the use of GET and HEAD methods on our `Post` detail view, we can add the decorator, as demonstrated in Example 5.71.

**Example 5.71: Project Code**
`blog/views.py` in `34baa4dfc3`

```
 3   from django.views.decorators.http import \
 4       require_http_methods
 .       ...
10   @require_http_methods(['HEAD', 'GET'])
11   def post_detail(request, year, month, slug):
```

> ### Info
> The use of `@require_http_methods(['GET', 'HEAD'])` is common enough that Django provides a shortcut decorator called `require_safe` to help shorten your code by just a bit.

Even so, the decorator doesn't provide automatic handling of OPTIONS, and organizing multiple views according to HTTP method results in simpler code, as we shall see in Chapter 9.

### 5.9.4   Class-Based Views Review

A CBV is simply a class that inherits `View` and meets the basic requirements of being a Django view: a view is a Python callable that always accepts an `HttpRequest` object and always returns an `HttpResponse` object.

The CBV organizes view behavior for a URI or set of URIs (when using named groups in a regular expression pattern) according to HTTP methods. Specifically, `View` is built such that it expects us to define any of the following: `get()`, `post()`, `put()`, `patch()`, `delete()`, `trace()`. We could additionally define `head()`, `options()`, but `View` will automatically generate these for us (for `head()` to be automatically generated, we must define `get()`).

Internally, the CBV actually steps through multiple view methods for each view. The as_view() method used in URL patterns accepts initkwargs and acts as a factory by returning an actual view called view(), which uses the initkwargs to instantiate our CBV and then calls dispatch() on the new CBV object. dispatch() selects one of the methods defined by the developer, based on the HTTP method used to request the URI. In the event that the method is undefined, the CBV raises an HTTP 405 error.

In a nutshell, as_view() is a view factory, while the combination of view(), dispatch(), and any of the developer-defined methods (get(), post(), etc.) are the actual view. Much like a function view, any of these view methods must accept an HttpRequest object, a URL dictionary, and any regular expression group data (such as slug). In turn, the full combined chain (view(), dispatch(), etc.) must return an HttpResponse object.

At first glance, CBVs are far more complex than function views. However, CBVs are more clearly organized, allow for shared behavior according to OOP, and better adhere to the rules of HTTP out of the box. We will further expand on these advantages, returning to the topic first in Chapter 9.

Our understanding of views will change in Chapter 9 and Chapter 17, but at the moment, the rule of thumb is as follows: if the view shares behavior with another view, use a CBV. If not, you have the choice between a CBV and a function view with a require_http_methods decorator, and the choice is pure preference. I personally stick with CBVs because I find the automatic addition of the HTTP OPTIONS method appealing, but many opt instead to use function views.

# 5.10    Redirecting the Homepage

If you run Django's development server and navigate to the root of the website, you'll discover that we've missed a spot, as shown in Example 5.72.

**Example 5.72: Shell Code**

```
$ ./manage.py runserver
```

Browsing to http://127.0.0.1:8000/ will display an error page telling us the URL configuration doesn't have a route for this page. While we've created a very detailed and clean URL configuration for all of our URLs, we've omitted the homepage, the root of our website.

We want to show the list of blog posts on the homepage. There are several ways we can go about doing so.

## 5.10.1    Directing the Homepage with URL Configurations

The first and perhaps most obvious way would be to create a new URL pattern to send the route to the view we have already built. In /suorganizer/urls.py, we could add the URL pattern shown in Example 5.73 to the URL configuration.

**Example 5.73: Project Code**

`suorganizer/urls.py` in `3ddb5f3810`

```
20    from blog.views import PostList
  .       ...
23    urlpatterns = [
24        url(r'^$',
25            PostList.as_view()),
  .       ...
29    ]
```

The regular expression pattern: `^` starts the pattern, while `$` ends the pattern. This matches `''`, which is what the root of the URL is to Django, given that it always strips the first `/`.

Similarly, given that the `PostList` view is the root of the **blog** URL configuration, the URL pattern could also be as shown in Example 5.74.

**Example 5.74: Project Code**

`suorganizer/urls.py` in `4dc1d03a79`

```
23        url(r'^$', include(blog_urls)),
```

Neither of the solutions presented above is desirable, as they both corrupt the cleanliness and simplicity of our site URLs. In the first instance, `http://site.django-unleashed.com/blog/` and `http://site.django-unleashed.com/` are now exactly the same. In the second case, we have created an entire branch of URLs, which is far worse. Not only are `http://site.django-unleashed.com/blog/` and `http://site.django-unleashed.com/` the same page, but so is `http://site.django-unleashed.com/blog/2013/1/django-training/` and `http://site.django-unleashed.com/2013/1/django-training/` (note the missing `blog/` in the second URL path). This will effectively create a duplicate of every URL the **blog** already matched.

Our website should maintain a clean URL scheme. Short of creating a separate homepage view, directing our homepage to an existing view as above is undesirable.

## 5.10.2   Redirecting the Homepage with Views

Rather than simply displaying a webpage on our homepage, we will instead redirect the user to the desired URL. In this instance, `http://site.django-unleashed.com/` will redirect to `http://site.django-unleashed.com/blog/`, which is the `post_list()` view.

To redirect a URL, we need a view. This creates a minor problem: we are redirecting our site-wide homepage with a view, which at this point exists only in app directories. However, this code does not belong in either our **organizer** or **blog** apps. Although Django does not anticipate the need for site-wide `views.py`, nothing is stopping us from creating `/suorganizer/views.py`. Inside, we write the code shown in Example 5.75.

*site-wide views*

**Example 5.75: Project Code**
suorganizer/views.py **in** 2e8036623d

*NB This way of redirecting will be replaced by a better way in chapt 17*

```
1  from django.http import HttpResponseRedirect
2
3
4  def redirect_root(request):
5      return HttpResponseRedirect('/blog/')
```
@

The `HttpResponseRedirect` class is a subclass of `HttpResponse` with special properties, just like `HttpResponseNotFound`. Given a URL path, it will redirect the page using an HTTP 302 code (temporary redirect). Should you wish for an HTTP 301 code (permanent redirect), you could instead use `HttpResponsePermanentRedirect`. Note that doing so in development can result in unexpected behavior because the browser will typically cache this response, resulting in difficulties should you change the behavior.

*@ 241*

In `/suorganizer/urls.py`, we can import the new view and replace our previous URL pattern with the one in Example 5.76.

**Example 5.76: Project Code**
suorganizer/urls.py **in** 2e8036623d

*site-wide urls*

```
22  from .views import redirect_root
23
24  urlpatterns = [
25      url(r'^$', redirect_root),
.       ...
29  ]
```

Running the deployment server with `$ ./manage.py runserver` and navigating a browser to `http://127.0.0.1:8000/` will result in a redirect to `http://127.0.0.1:8000/blog/`.

The behavior is what we desire, but our implementation could be improved. Instead of using `HttpResponseRedirect`, we can use a Django shortcut, `redirect()`. Our `/suorganizer/views.py` will now look like Example 5.77.

**Example 5.77: Project Code**
suorganizer/views.py **in** 5fb0dff63a

```
1  from django.shortcuts import redirect
2
3
4  def redirect_root(request):
5      return redirect('/blog/')
```

The code in Example 5.77 will work exactly as if we were still using `HttpResponseRedirect`, with an HTTP 302 code. Should we wish to switch to an HTTP 301 code, we could pass `permanent=True` to the shortcut, as in: `redirect('/blog/', permanent=True)`.

The advantage to `redirect()` is that, unlike HttpResponseRedirect, it does not need a URL path (currently used in Example 5.77). To better adhere to the DRY principle, we can instead use the name of the URL pattern we wish to redirect to, as shown in Example 5.78.

**Example 5.78: Project Code**
`suorganizer/views.py` **in** ba8c7c5e89

```
4   def redirect_root(request):
5       return redirect('blog_post_list')
```

The shortcut in Example 5.78 is exactly what we want, but it may be a little opaque. Unlike the shortcuts we've seen before, we don't currently understand everything going on under the hood. Specifically, we don't know how the shortcut builds a proper URL path from the URL pattern. We will see exactly how to do this in the next chapter and revisit this shortcut then.

Note that our way of redirecting, with a site-wide function view, is not the way you would redirect in an actual project. Our method is in direct violation of DRY, but we won't be able to fix that until Chapter 17.    GCBV  383 ff

In short, the behavior above is exactly what we want, and the code is the best we can write given our current knowledge. Please keep this function and behavior in mind going forward, as we will revisit it in Chapter 6 and replace it in Chapter 17.

# 5.11   Putting It All Together

In Chapter 5, we examined Django views and URL configurations, which make up the Controller of Django's Model-View-Controller architecture. The Controller acts as the glue between the Model and View. In Django, the Controller receives, selects, processes, and then returns data.

A Django view is any callable that receives an `HttpRequest` object (with any other additional arguments) and returns an `HttpResponse` object. Originally, Django recommended using functions as views, but modern Django also provides a canonical way of creating classes to create object views.

To make writing views easier, Django supplies shortcut functions. We saw three shortcuts, starting with `get_object_or_404()`, which gets an object according to a model class and query while accounting for the possibility that the query will not match a row in the database, in which case it raises a `Http404` exception. We then saw the `render_to_response()` and `render()`. Both load a template, render the template with a context, and instantiate an `HttpReponse` object with the result. However, the `render()` shortcut uses a `RequestContext` instead of a `Context` object, allowing Django to run context processors on the `RequestContext`, effectively adding values for the template to use during the rendering phase. This added functionality is key to certain views and functionality, and thus `render()` has become the favored shortcut, even if it is marginally slower than `render_to_response()`.

To direct Django to the views the developer writes, Django provides the URL configuration mechanism. The URL configuration is contained in a file pointed to by the project settings. Inside the file, Django expects (by convention) to find the `urlpatterns` variable, which is a list of `RegexURLPattern` objects. Each `RegexURLPattern` object is created by a call to `url()`, which expects at the very least (1) a regular expression pattern and (2) a reference to a Python callable. A call to `url()` may also optionally be called with (3) a dictionary of values that are passed as keywords to the view that the resulting `RegexURLPattern` points to. Finally, `url()` can receive (4) the keyword argument `name`, which sets the name of the `RegexURLPattern`, a feature that will become crucial in the next chapter.

URL configurations may be connected using `include()`. A URL pattern may include another URL configuration, allowing for the creation of a URL scheme that is a tree, where the root URL configuration specified in the Django project settings is the root of the tree. This feature furthermore allows for app encapsulation, allowing each app to define its own URL patterns, extending those of the project, which `include()` achieves by truncating the regular expression match from the URL path requested of Django.

In short, the URL configuration directs Django to the view thanks to URL pattens, which contains the logic required to make a webpage.

# Integrating Models, Templates, Views, and URL Configurations to Create Links between Webpages

**In This Chapter**

- Link webpages
- Generate HTML hyperlinks by *reversing* URL patterns
- Adhere to DRY in views and templates while linking
- Revisit webpage redirection

## 6.1   Introduction

Hyperlinks, casually called **links**, are *the* key feature of the web. The ability to click on text or an image to navigate to a new webpage is a basic necessity for any website. Without this functionality, you would have to enter a URL for each and every webpage you wished to view.

For the most part, our website does not make use of links. We have skeleton links: HTML anchor `<a>` tags without the `href` attribute defined (the exception being the links in the `Newslink` model, but these links point to external sources, not our own webpages).

Building a link in HTML is trivial. To create a link to our tag list webpage, we could simply code `<a href="/tag/">`. However, maintaining the Don't Repeat Yourself (DRY) principle in Django while generating hyperlinks is a little trickier. This is the first time we will see various parts of Django work interdependently, which is why the content of this chapter was unavailable to us until now and why a full chapter is dedicated to something as simple as links.

After we examine the principle of link creation and the methods at our disposal, we will enable site navigation and connect all our pages with links.

# 6.2    Generating URLs in Python and Django Templates

While the practical goal of this chapter is to generate links, the actual goal is to focus on using multiple parts of Django and enforcing DRY.

The goal of DRY is to only ever define any piece of information once. We already have all of our links defined in the URL configuration, which means that we do not want to code links in raw HTML. If we change the regular expression pattern of a URL pattern, we should not have to make any other changes: we do not want to have to change links in each and every template.

The issue, of course, is that we are trying to accomplish the very opposite of what a regular expression pattern typically does: we are not interested in matching a string, we are interested in generating a string that matches a specific regular expression pattern. In Django, we refer to this generation as "reversing a URL." We are reversing the regular expression pattern in a URL pattern because we are generating a string instead of matching.

## 6.2.1    Reversing URL Patterns

If we take a regular expression pattern without character sets or groups (named or otherwise), then reversal is simple. Our `organizer_tag_list` URL pattern has `r'^tag/$'` for its regular expression pattern. The URL path `/tag/` is the only string that matches this regular expression pattern and therefore the string we want to generate.

As with everything else, Django makes our lives easy by supplying a tool to do exactly what we want, helpfully called `reverse()`. We can simply import the `reverse()` function from `django.core.urlresolvers`. We then pass `reverse()` the name attribute of a URL pattern. To test this functionality, we step into the Python interpreter (or IPython) with `./manager.py shell`, as shown in Example 6.1.

**Example 6.1: Python Interpreter Code**

```
>>> from django.core.urlresolvers import reverse
>>> reverse('organizer_tag_list')
'/tag/'
```

Our Python code is not the only place where URL reversal will prove useful. The Django Template Language supplies the `url` template tag, which works exactly like `reverse()` (because it uses `reverse()` internally). Once again, as shown in Example 6.2, we only need to pass the name of a URL pattern to reverse its regular expression pattern.

**Example 6.2: Django Template Language Code**

```
{% url 'organizer_tag_list' %}
```

Like any other template tag, the `url` tag is expressed via `{% expression %}` and expects any string arguments to be encompassed by single or double quotes and separated by spaces. In Example 6.3, we can see it in action in the shell.

**Example 6.3: Python Interpreter Code**

*test url tag in the shell.*

```
>>> from django.template import Template, Context
>>> code = "{% url 'organizer_tag_list' %}"
>>> template = Template(code)
>>> template.render(Context())
'/tag/'
```

## 6.2.2 Reversing Regular Expression Patterns with Character Sets

Things get trickier with regular expression patterns that contain character sets, such as the `organizer_tag_detail` URL pattern, which has the regular expression pattern `r'^tag/(?P<slug>[\w\-]+)/$'`. When matching URL paths, the character set is useful because it allows both `/tag/django/` and `/tag/web/` to be matched. However, when reversing a URL, the character set becomes an unknown.

In this instance, URL reversal works like a template (or like a Mad Lib). Django expects us to provide the name of the URL pattern as well as any of the values that it needs to fill in the unknowns. To generate `/tag/django/` from `r'^tag/(?P<slug>[\w\-]+)/$'`, we must pass `organizer_tag_detail` and `'django'` to `reverse()` or the `url` template tag. We have the choice to pass in `'django'` as part of a set of arguments or as a set of keyword arguments. In Example 6.4, I demonstrate URL reversal in the Django shell (invoked by `$ ./manage.py shell`).

*full url pattern: @178*

**Example 6.4: Python Interpreter Code**

```
>>> from django.core.urlresolvers import reverse
>>> reverse('organizer_tag_detail', args=['django'])
'/tag/django/'
>>> reverse('organizer_tag_detail', kwargs={'slug': 'django'})
'/tag/django/'
```

*URL name*

*reverse*

A key aspect of URL reversal is that it works on the basis of regular expression groups and not on character sets. At the moment, this doesn't matter to us, as each of our (named) groups features only a single character set. However, this won't always be the case (starting in Chapter 19: Basic Authentication).

More concretely, if we had the regular expression pattern shown in Example 6.5, we would pass only a single variable to `reverse()` and `url`, as there is only a single group despite there being two character sets.

**Example 6.5: Python Code**

```
# matches dragon-slayer
url(r'(?P<hyphenated_word>[\w]+-[\w]+)', view)
```

The syntax is slightly different in templates, but the principle remains the same, as shown in Example 6.6.

**Example 6.6: Python Interpreter Code**

```
>>> from django.template import Template, Context
>>> code = "{% url 'organizer_tag_detail' 'web' %}"
>>> template = Template(code)
>>> template.render(Context())
'/tag/web/'
>>> code = "{% url 'organizer_tag_detail' slug='web' %}"
>>> template = Template(code)
>>> template.render(Context())
u'/tag/web/'
```

For both reverse() and the url template tag, the keyword arguments only work because the [\w\-]+ character set is in a named group called slug: (?P<slug>    ). If the regular expression of organizer_tag_detail did not use a named group, we would be unable to use keyword arguments.

Of course, while passing strings such as web and django is nice, we want to be sure to use data that actually exists in the database (to avoid generating a URL for a page that doesn't exist). With Django, ensuring the data exist is simple because data are represented in Python as objects and can be used directly in a similar fashion in templates. In Example 6.7, we load a Tag and use its slug value to generate the output.

**Example 6.7: Python Interpreter Code**

```
>>> from django.core.urlresolvers import reverse
>>> from organizer.models import Tag
>>> django_tag = Tag.objects.get(slug__iexact='django')
>>> reverse(
...     'organizer_tag_detail',
...     kwargs={'slug': django_tag.slug})
'/tag/django/'
```

We do the same thing with the url template tag in Example 6.8.

**Example 6.8: Python Interpreter Code**

```
>>> from django.template import Template, Context
>>> from organizer.models import Tag
>>> django_tag = Tag.objects.get(slug__iexact='django')
>>> context = Context({'tag': django_tag})
>>> code = "{% url 'organizer_tag_detail' tag.slug %}"
>>> template = Template(code)
>>> template.render(context)
'/tag/django/'
```

This is a great start to adhering to DRY, but we can take it one step further.

### 6.2.3   Canonical Model URLs

Each of our model objects is displayed only on a single webpage, which means that each model object effectively has a single, canonical URL to access its full information. Our website will display the `Tag` titled `Django` if and only if a user requests the URL path `/tag/django/`.

Instead of calling `reverse()` with `tag.slug`, it is easier to ask the model for its URL directly. It results in shorter code, better adheres to DRY, and is what Django recommends.    ✗

In fact, Django not only recommends having a method on each model to create a canonical URL but expects us to name this method `get_absolute_url()`. Once we have it programmed, it allows us to code as shown in Example 6.9.    ✗

**Example 6.9:** Python Interpreter Code

*in the shell*

*get-absolute-url()*
*in code*

```
>>> from organizer.models import Tag
>>> django_tag = Tag.objects.get(slug__iexact='django')
>>> django_tag.get_absolute_url()
'/tag/django/'
```

We also can use this method in templates, as shown in Example 6.10.

**Example 6.10:** Python Interpreter Code

*get-absolute-url*
*in template*

```
>>> from django.template import Template, Context
>>> from organizer.models import Tag
>>> django_tag = Tag.objects.get(slug__iexact='django')
>>> context = Context({'tag': django_tag})
>>> code = "{{ tag.get_absolute_url }}"
>>> template = Template(code)
>>> template.render(context)
'/tag/django/'
```

With `get_absolute_url()`, we don't need to remember that a `Tag` object takes a `slug` or any other arguments. If we change the regular expression pattern to `organizer_tag_detail`, we need only change the code in the `Tag` model method `get_absolute_url()`. In the long run, implementing `get_absolute_url()` saves us time, and naming it so becomes useful in Chapter 9: Controlling Forms in Views and Chapter 17: Understanding Generic Class-Based Views, where we'll see that inversion of control yet again saves us time.    ✗

Note that `get_absolute_url()` is helpful only for detail pages. For list pages, we'll continue to use `reverse()` and the `url` template tag.    ∫

Before we use this knowledge, let's take a quick peek at what happens if we make a mistake while reversing a URL pattern.

## 6.2.4  The `NoReverseMatch` Exception

When URL reversal doesn't work, Django raises a `NoReverseMatch` exception. In Example 6.11, we ask for a URL pattern name that doesn't exist.

**Example 6.11: Python Interpreter Code**

```
>>> from django.core.urlresolvers import reverse
>>> reverse('no_such_url_pattern')
```

Django outputs the stack trace for the error, as shown in Example 6.12. The important bit is at the very end of the output (formatted in the example for convenience).

**Example 6.12: Python Code**

```
django.core.urlresolvers.NoReverseMatch:
    Reverse for 'no_such_url_pattern'
    with arguments '()'
    and keyword arguments '{}'
    not found.
    0 pattern(s) tried: []
```

Django could not find a URL pattern by that name, and so it tried to generate our request using zero patterns!

Django uses the same exception if the URL pattern being reversed necessitates arguments, but the error string is slightly different, as you can see in Example 6.13.

**Example 6.13: Python Interpreter Code**

```
>>> # this needs a tag.slug values passed to args or kwargs!
>>> reverse('organizer_tag_detail')
```

The command in the previous example will lead to the error displayed in Example 6.14.

**Example 6.14: Python Code**

```
django.core.urlresolvers.NoReverseMatch:
    Reverse for 'organizer_tag_detail'
    with arguments '()'
    and keyword arguments '{}'
    not found.
    1 pattern(s) tried: ['tag/(?P<slug>[\\w\\-]+)/$']
```

Here, we can see that it found the `organizer_tag_detail` URL pattern, but it was unable to reverse the pattern because it received no arguments and no keywords.

Debugging URL reversal can be a little tricky. If and when you receive output because of a `NoReverseMatch`, it is important to read the full error message, as the same exception is raised for a number of issues. Take time to consider the pattern Django is using, make sure it is the right pattern, and then consider whether you are passing in the right number of arguments and whether your keyword arguments and named groups are spelled correctly.

# 6.3   Using the `url` Template Tag to Build a Navigation Menu

Before we generate the URLs for the links we have already left blank, we're going to add to the work we must do.

A standard design feature of modern websites is a navigation menu. Navigation menus allow for easier site navigation and are typically necessary to provide a good user experience. In this section, we create a navigation menu and then use the `url` template tag to generate the links in the menu.

Had we programmed every template independently, we would now be faced with the task of changing every template. However, because we built our templates with inheritance via the `extends` template tag, we can make a single change to our site-wide template, found in `/templates/base.html`.

Let's start with the basic HTML for the menu. We then hardcode the links in the menu as a means of showing how easy that could be. We then use the `url` template tag to generate the links so that our site correctly adheres to DRY.

## 6.3.1   Building the `<nav>` Menu in HTML and Hardcoding Our Links

The HTML we start with to create our navigation is shown in Example 6.15.

**Example 6.15: Project Code**
`templates/base.html` in ddc1da1f62

```
24        <nav>
25         <ul>
26          <li>
27           <a href="">
28             Blog</a></li>
29          <li>
30           <a href="">
31             Startups</a></li>
32          <li>
33           <a href="">
34             Tags</a></li>
35         </ul>
36        </nav>
```

We have a three-item list, each of which is a link to one of our list pages. As with our HTML anchor tags before, we have left the `href` attributes unspecified. Our URL configuration for the list of startup objects is shown in Example 6.16.

**Example 6.16: Project Code**

organizer/urls.py in ddc1da1f62

```
 8        url(r'^startup/$',
 9            startup_list,
10            name='organizer_startup_list'),
```

Should we wish to hardcode the navigation link to our startup list, we could write the code `<a href="/startup/">Startups List</a>`. By looking at the other URL patterns for our list webpages, we could hardcode all of our links to be as shown in Example 6.17.

**Example 6.17: Project Code**

templates/base.html in 7ccb77ef9e

```
24        <nav>
25          <ul>
26            <li>
27              <a href="/blog/">
28                Blog</a></li>
29            <li>
30              <a href="/startup/">
31                Startups</a></li>
32            <li>
33              <a href="/tag/">
34                Tags</a></li>
35          </ul>
36        </nav>
```

This example, of course, is not how you should do this task. Let's improve our code.

## 6.3.2   Using the `url` Template Tag to Create URL Paths for the Navigation Menu

I'm not going to harp about DRY much longer: hopefully you know the drill. Using the `url` template tag is the name of the game here.

With regular expressions that lack character sets, we can use `url` with only the name of a URL pattern. To generate the links in our navigation, our code (replacing the hard links) is pretty straightforward, as shown in Example 6.18.

**Example 6.18: Project Code**

templates/base.html in afd3be6931

*equiv*
*@ 177*

```
27              <a href="{% url 'blog post list' %}"> Blogs </a>
  .
  ...
30              <a href="{% url 'organizer_startup_list' %}"> Startups </a>
  .
  ...
33              <a href="{% url 'organizer_tag_list' %}"> Tags </a>
```

This code outputs exactly what we previously hardcoded (printed in Example 6.19 for convenience and accessible directly via the development server).

**Example 6.19: Project Code**

`templates/base.html` in `7ccb77ef9e`

```
24          <nav>
25           <ul>
26            <li>
27             <a href="/blog/">
28              Blog</a></li>
29            <li>
30             <a href="/startup/">
31              Startups</a></li>
32            <li>
33             <a href="/tag/">
34              Tags</a></li>
35           </ul>
36          </nav>
```

If we were to change the regular expression pattern of `organizer_startup_list` from `r'^startup/$'` to `r'^startup_list/$'`, we would have no more work to do! It's more work for Django but less work for us.

# 6.4   Linking List Pages to Detail Pages

Now that we can navigate to the list pages for all of our objects, we should generate the links on these list pages.

We have three list pages, in each of which we must link at least one detail page.

In `/organizer/templates/organizer/tag_list.html` we must fill in the code shown in Example 6.20.

**Example 6.20: Project Code**

`organizer/templates/organizer/tag_list.html` in `afd3be6931`

```
12          <a href="">
13            {{ tag.name|title }}</a>
```

In `/organizer/templates/organizer/startup_list.html` we must fill in the code shown in Example 6.21.

**Example 6.21: Project Code**

`organizer/templates/organizer/startup_list.html` in `afd3be6931`

```
12          <a href="">
13            {{ startup.name }}</a>
```

In /blog/templates/blog/post_list.html, we created two links: the title link and a read more link, as shown in Example 6.22.

**Example 6.22: Project Code**
blog/templates/blog/post_list.html **in** afd3be6931

```
12                    <a href="">
13                      {{ post.title|title }}</a>
 .                      ...
24                <a href="">
25                  Read more&hellip;</a>
```

In the following section, we correctly link all of the preceding anchor tags.

## 6.4.1   Using `url` to Create Detail Page Links

Let's pretend for a moment that we don't know about `get_absolute_url()` and that we're going to stick to using the `url` template tag directly.

All of our detail pages are dynamic pages with at least one regular expression named group. To reverse a URL pattern with such regular expressions, we saw earlier that we could treat the regular expression pattern like a template and pass the value we want to fill in the character set directly to either `reverse()` or the `url` template tag.

### 6.4.1.1   Using `url` with `Tag` Detail

The URL pattern `organizer_tag_detail` currently reads as shown in Example 6.23.

**Example 6.23: Project Code**
organizer/urls.py **in** 0a66a80be9

```
17        url(r'^tag/(?P<slug>[\w\-]+)/$',
18            tag_detail,
19            name='organizer_tag_detail'),
```

In our `Tag` list template, Django currently outputs the HTML code shown in Example 6.24.

**Example 6.24: HTML Code**

```
<ul>
  <li><a href="">Django</a></li>
  <li><a href="">Mobile</a></li>
  <li><a href="">Video Games</a></li>
  <li><a href="">Web</a></li>
</ul>
```

We want it to output HTML anchor tags with `href` attributes that point to the detail pages of each `Tag` object, and we do so in Example 6.25.

**Example 6.25: HTML Code**

```html
<ul>
  <li><a href="/tag/django/">Django</a></li>
  <li><a href="/tag/mobile/">Mobile</a></li>
  <li><a href="/tag/video-games/">Video Games</a></li>
  <li><a href="/tag/web/">Web</a></li>
</ul>
```

Given the `organizer_tag_detail` URL pattern, we therefore need to tell Django the value of the `slug` named group when reversing this URL pattern.

To link to the `Tag` detail page from the `Tag` list page, we can open the list template and use the `url` tag. On line 12 of Example 6.26, we give the `url` tag the name of the URL pattern as well as the value of the tag's `SlugField`, made accessible to us by the `for` loop on line 10.

**Example 6.26: Project Code**

`organizer/templates/organizer/tag_list.html` **in** `0a66a80be9`

```
10        {% for tag in tag_list %}
11          <li>
12            <a href="{% url 'organizer_tag_detail' tag.slug %}">
13              {{ tag.name|title }}</a>
14          </li>
15        {% empty %}
16          <li><em>There are currently no Tags available.</em></li>
17        {% endfor %}
```

I want to reiterate that the use of `reverse()` and the `url` template tag is highly desirable as a means of maintaining the DRY principle. If we wanted to switch the regular expression pattern of `organizer_tag_detail` to `r'^label/(?P<slug>[\w\-]+)/$'`, we would currently be able to do so with a single change to the regular expression pattern! No other work would be required. Imagine if we had instead used the code shown in Example 6.27 (code I have seen in the wild).

**Example 6.27: Django Template Language Code**

```html
<!-- this is not wrong, but it is very bad -->
<a href="/tag/{{ tag.slug }}/">{{ tag.name|title }}</a>
```

*Bad, bad! Yowza*

If we changed the regular expression pattern to `r'^label/(?P<slug>[\w\-]+)/$'`, we would still have to make changes in all of our templates if we were using the code in

Example 6.27. Not only is full reversal of URLs (along with `get_absolute_url`) recommended, it should be the only way you link pages internally.

### 6.4.1.2  Using `url` with `Startup` Detail

The process is exactly the same with the `organizer_startup_detail` URL pattern. We start by examining the actual pattern, shown in Example 6.28.

**Example 6.28:** Project Code

`organizer/urls.py` in 2e4bf4eec8

```
11        url(r'^startup/(?P<slug>[\w\-]+)/$',
12            startup_detail,
13            name='organizer_startup_detail'),
```

To reverse the URL pattern, we need to fill in the `slug` named group of the regular expression pattern, as shown in Example 6.29. We thus pass the slug value of the `Startup` to the `url` template tag on line 12 within the main loop of the `Startup` list page to link to `Startup` detail pages. In this instance, we can also take the opportunity to use keyword arguments with `url`, specifying the name of the group by adding `slug=` before the value we want filled in.

**Example 6.29:** Project Code

`organizer/templates/organizer/startup_list.html` in 2e4bf4eec8

```
10        {% for startup in startup_list %}
11          <li>
12            <a href="{% url 'organizer_startup_detail'
   .                     slug=startup.slug %}">
13              {{ startup.name }}</a>
14          </li>
15        {% empty %}
16          <li><em>No Startups Available</em></li>
17        {% endfor %}
```

### 6.4.1.3  Using `url` with `Post` Detail

Linking to `Post` detail pages from `Post` list pages is slightly trickier; instead of a single group, the `blog_post_detail` URL pattern has three, as you can see in Example 6.30.

**Example 6.30:** Project Code                *(P?< re > patt )*

`blog/urls.py` in 16f672d967

```
 9        url(r'^(?P<year>\d{4})/'
10            r'(?P<month>\d{1,2})/'
11            r'(?P<slug>[\w\-]+)/$',
12            post_detail,
13            name='blog_post_detail'),
```

In this case, the `url` template tag will need the year, month, and slug values of a `Post`, making our calls to `url` rather long. Once again, access to `post` and relevant values is made available by the `for` loop on line 8 in Example 6.31 (but not printed here).

**Example 6.31: Project Code**
`blog/templates/blog/post_list.html` in 16f672d967

```
12              <a href="{% url 'blog_post_detail'
 .                        post.pub_date.year post.pub_date.month
 .                        post.slug %}">
13              {{ post.title|title }}</a>
```

> **Warning!**
>
> Django template tags must appear on a single line: they may not be split across multiple lines in your code. The calls to template tags in this book are formatted to fit on the page, which sometimes requires adding newlines to the code. The actual code in the git repository does not feature these newlines, as Django will not parse template tags split across multiple lines.

The preceding example is hideous, but as Example 6.32 shows, it's even worse if we use keyword arguments.

**Example 6.32: Project Code**
`blog/templates/blog/post_list.html` in 16f672d967

```
24              <a href="{% url 'blog_post_detail' year=post.pub_date.year
 .                        month=post.pub_date.month slug=post.slug %}">
25              Read more&hellip;</a>
```

Replacing the code in Example 6.32 with calls to `get_absolute_url()` is going to feel great.

## 6.4.2 Replacing Detail Page Links with `get_absolute_url()`

The ultimate way to adhere to DRY while generating links is to provide a `get_absolute_url()` method to each model class, allowing for the quick retrieval of each model object's canonical URL path.

### 6.4.2.1 `get_absolute_url` in `Tag`

Let's focus on our `Tag` model class first. To reverse a URL in Python, we need the `reverse()` method, and so we start by importing it in Example 6.33.

**Example 6.33: Project Code**
`organizer/models.py` in dbcee003de

```
1   from django.core.urlresolvers import reverse
```

We can then focus on creating the method. The `organizer_tag_detail` URL pattern reads as in Example 6.34.

**Example 6.34: Project Code**
`organizer/urls.py` in dbcee003de

```
17        url(r'^tag/(?P<slug>[\w\-]+)/$',
18            tag_detail,
19            name='organizer_tag_detail'),
```

We need to fill in the slug name group of the regular expression, and so when we call `reverse()` for `organizer_tag_detail`, we also pass in the value of the slug for that model object. In Example 6.35, I opt to do so using keyword arguments.

**Example 6.35: Project Code**
`organizer/models.py` in dbcee003de

```
 9    class Tag(models.Model):
 .        ...
23        def get_absolute_url(self):
24            return reverse('organizer_tag_detail',
25                            kwargs={'slug': self.slug})
```

This code allows us to return to our `Tag` list template and replace our links to `Tag` detail templates with the code in Example 6.36.

**Example 6.36: Project Code**
`organizer/templates/organizer/tag_list.html` in b47ee007a0

```
12        <a href="{{ tag.get_absolute_url }}">
13            {{ tag.name|title }}</a>
```

Make sure you change the template delimiters from {% %} to {{ }}. The first are used only for template tags, while the second are used for any attribute access, even if that attribute is actually a Python callable.

A key advantage once we have `get_absolute_url()` programmed is that we no longer need to keep considering the URL pattern for our model object's detail webpage. We can simply call the method and be assured that it will generate the proper URL.

As a quick aside, while I will always opt to use keyword arguments in `get_absolute_url`, we saw earlier that this was not our only option. Example 6.37 is an example of reversing the `organizer_tag_detail` with arguments instead of keyword arguments.

**Example 6.37: Project Code**

`organizer/models.py` in `a50f4126c7`

```
23        def get_absolute_url(self):
24            return reverse('organizer_tag_detail',
25                           args=(self.slug,))
```

### 6.4.2.2 `get_absolute_url` in `Startup`

The process for replacing the links in our `Startup` list page with `get_absolute_url` is practically identical. We need to pass the value of the `Startup` slug to `reverse()`, and again, in Example 6.38, I opt to use keyword arguments.

**Example 6.38: Project Code**

`organizer/models.py` in `91c56cdbfc`

```
28    class Startup(models.Model):
      ...
49        def get_absolute_url(self):
50            return reverse('organizer_startup_detail',
51                           kwargs={'slug': self.slug})
```

If we return to the `Startup` list template, we can replace our call to the `url` template tag with our newly implemented `get_absolute_url()`, as in Example 6.39.

**Example 6.39: Project Code**

`organizer/templates/organizer/startup_list.html` in `255669e31e`

```
12        <a href="{{ startup.get_absolute_url }}">
13            {{ startup.name }}</a>
```

### 6.4.2.3 `get_absolute_url` in `Post`

The code that will be most simplified in our template is that of the `Post` detail links. For convenience (and because of its complexity), the `blog_post_detail` is reproduced in Example 6.40.

**Example 6.40: Project Code**

`blog/urls.py` in `275c8f41c6`

```
9         url(r'^(?P<year>\d{4})/'
10            r'(?P<month>\d{1,2})/'
11            r'(?P<slug>[\w\-]+)/$',
12            post_detail,
13            name='blog_post_detail'),
```

The URL pattern has three named groups that we need to specify with reverse() to properly generate a valid URL path, as shown in Example 6.41.

**Example 6.41:** Project Code

blog/models.py in 275c8f41c6

```
 1    from django.core.urlresolvers import reverse
 .        ...
11    class Post(models.Model):
 .        ...
36        def get_absolute_url(self):
37            return reverse(
38                'blog_post_detail',
39                kwargs={'year': self.pub_date.year,
40                        'month': self.pub_date.month,
41                        'slug': self.slug})
```

The calls to get_absolute_url in the Post list template are far simpler than the call to url, as you can see in Example 6.42.

**Example 6.42:** Project Code

blog/templates/blog/post_list.html in cecd1fa0c8

```
12                <a href="{{ post.get_absolute_url }}">
13                    {{ post.title|title }}</a>
 .        ...
24                <a href="{{ post.get_absolute_url }}">
25                    Read more&hellip;</a>
```

In the case of both url and get_absolute_url(), Django is quite smart about URL reversal. Remember that the blog/ URL path is a prefix in the root URL configuration. Nevertheless, Django will properly output /blog/2013/1/django-training/ as opposed to /2013/1/django-training/ (where the blog/ prefix is missing, an error I have seen humans make). The use of reverse(), url, and get_absolute_url() should be the *only* way you generate internal links on your webpages.

# 6.5   Creating Links on the Object Detail Pages

Our navigation menu links to list pages on every page, and our list pages link to detail pages, but we still have links on detail pages that need work:

- /organizer/templates/organizer/tag_detail.html;
- /organizer/templates/organizer/startup_detail.html;
- /blog/templates/blog/post_detail.html.

Following are the links for which we need to provide an `href` attribute value:

- The `Tag` detail template lists `Startup` objects associated with each `Tag`.
- The `Startup` detail template lists all of the `Tag` objects associated with each `Startup`.
- The `Post` detail template lists all of the `Tag` and `Startup` objects associated with the `Post`.

If we were still using the `url` template tag to create links, this would be a tedious and potentially tricky process. We would have to look at each URL pattern, determine which named groups exist in the regular expression pattern, and then pass the appropriate class attributes to the `url` tag. Or we could copy and paste our previous calls, a direct example of how we are breaking the DRY principle.

However, because we have programmed `get_absolute_url()` for each of these objects, the task of creating all of these links becomes quick and painless.

In `/organizer/templates/organizer/tag_detail.html`, we use `{{ startup.get_absolute_url }}` and `{{ post.get_absolute_url }}`, resulting in the code shown in Example 6.43.

**Example 6.43: Project Code**
`organizer/templates/organizer/tag_detail.html` **in** `88d19beed0`

```
19              <li><a href="{{ startup.get_absolute_url }}">
20                  {{ startup.name }}
 .                      ...
31                  <li><a href="{{ post.get_absolute_url }}">
32                      {{ post.title|title }}
```

In `/organizer/templates/organizer/startup_detail.html`, we use `{{ tag.get_absolute_url }}` and `{{ post.get_absolute_url }}`, resulting in the code shown in Example 6.44.

**Example 6.44: Project Code**
`organizer/templates/organizer/startup_detail.html` **in** `7a32b2af63`

```
21              <dd><a href="{{ tag.get_absolute_url }}">
22                  {{ tag.name|title }}
 .                      ...
50                      <a href="{{ post.get_absolute_url }}">
51                          {{ post.title|title }}</a>
```

In `/blog/templates/blog/post_detail.html`, we can use both `{{ tag.get_absolute_url }}` and `{{ startup.get_absolute_url }}`, resulting in the code shown in Example 6.45.

**Example 6.45: Project Code**

blog/templates/blog/post_detail.html **in** 55f5e3c8be

```
30              <li><a href="{{ startup.get_absolute_url }}">
31                  {{ startup.name }}
  .                 ...
43              <li><a href="{{ tag.get_absolute_url }}">
44                  {{ tag.name|title }}
```

With this very simple and straightforward method of linking pages, we have almost effortlessly changed our templates to correctly link all our pages together.

# 6.6   Revisiting Homepage Redirection

In Chapter 5: Creating Webpages with Controllers in Django, we saw how to use the HttpResponseRedirect class and redirect shortcut to redirect a URL pattern to another URL path and pattern (respectively) via a function view. At the time, we did not understand how Django was reversing the URL pattern into a URL. The redirect shortcut should now be much clearer. For the sake of clarity, let's walk through the process again.

We started with the code shown in Example 6.46 in /suorganizer/views.py.

**Example 6.46: Project Code**

suorganizer/views.py **in** 2e8036623d

```
1    from django.http import HttpResponseRedirect
2
3
4    def redirect_root(request):
5        return HttpResponseRedirect('/blog/')
```

This approach is undesirable because we are violating DRY. We should instead redirect to a known and valid URL pattern. In this instance, we want to redirect to the list of blog posts, which is the post_list() function view via the blog_post_list URL pattern. With our newfound knowledge, we can use reverse() to build the URL path to this view, as shown in Example 6.47.

**Example 6.47: Project Code**

suorganizer/views.py **in** 720db559ab

```
1    from django.core.urlresolvers import reverse
2    from django.http import HttpResponseRedirect
3
4
5    def redirect_root(request):
6        url_path = reverse('blog_post_list')
7        return HttpResponseRedirect(url_path)
```

*equiv to @187*

The call to the redirect() shortcut in Example 6.48 is equivalent to the code in Example 6.47.

**Example 6.48: Project Code**

`suorganizer/views.py` in `fcf043125e`                    *equiv to.*
                                                          *@ 1.86*

```
1  from django.shortcuts import redirect
2
3
4  def redirect_root(request):
5      return redirect('blog_post_list')
```

The `redirect()` shortcut uses the `reverse()` method on the name of the URL pattern and then uses this value to redirect the page via a `HttpResponseRedirect`.

The `permanent=True` keyword argument may be passed to `redirect()` to use a `HttpResponsePermanentRedirect` instead, resulting in an HTTP 301 (Moved Permanently) code instead of HTTP 302 (Found – Temporary Redirect). What's more, the `redirect()` shortcut also allows the developer to pass in an absolute URL path, which must start with a /, as in `return redirect('/blog/')`.

While the use of `redirect()` in a view is perfectly acceptable, we're currently doing more work than we ought to. We'll return to redirecting in Chapter 17 and replace this content, deleting `suorganizer/views.py` entirely.

# 6.7 Putting It All Together

When organizing code in Django, many beginners ask, *Where do I put this*? Experienced developers answer cryptically: use fat models, thin views, and thinner templates. We followed this advice in this chapter. We could have coded URL reversal functionality in the template, but it might cost us extra work down the line. It is far better for us to remove that code and keep it in our models. We are in effect fattening our model in favor of slimming our templates.

The central goal, of course, was not to fatten our models or slim our templates, but to add hyperlink functionality in such a way as to make our life easy in the long run by adhering to DRY. We could only do this because we had a mostly implemented Model-View-Controller architecture in place.

Django generates URL paths by using the information already stored in the URL configuration. The process of building these URLs is called *reversing URL patterns*, or simply *reversing URLs*.

In Python, Django supplies the `reverse()` function to reverse URLs. In templates,    ✗
Django supplies the `url` template tag, which just calls `reverse()`.

At its most basic, the reversal functions require the name of a URL pattern. If the regular expression pattern of the URL pattern contains only a string literal, then Django can perform the reversal with no extra information. Reversing `organizer_startup_list`, which has the regular expression pattern `r'^startup/$'`, will always generate the string `/startup/`.

If the regular expression pattern contains grouped characters sets, then Django needs to be told what values to replace the groups with. The regular expression pattern acts like a template in this instance, where groups such as `([\w\-]+)` are variables to be replaced. The use of regular expression named groups allows us to refer to these as variables: we can talk about the `slug` value in the regular expression pattern `r'^startup/(?P<slug>[\w\-]+)/$'`.

Similarly, `reverse()` and the `url` template tag allow us to provide the values of both unnamed and named groups.

In the event of both named and unnamed groups, `reverse()` accepts a list passed to the `args` parameter, filling in the character sets in the order the `args` are passed. Similarly, `url` takes all of the unnamed arguments after the name attribute of the URL pattern and passes them to `reverse()` as the `args` parameter. We saw this in action when implementing `get_absolute_url()` for our `Tag` model (shown here in Example 6.49).

**Example 6.49: Project Code**
`organizer/models.py` **in** a50f4126c7

```
 9    class Tag(models.Model):
 .        ...
23        def get_absolute_url(self):
24            return reverse('organizer_tag_detail',
25                            args=(self.slug,))
```

However, as Example 6.50 shows, for extra precision, we can pass a dictionary to the `kwargs` parameter or `reverse()`, where the keys of the dictionary are the names of the regular expression named groups (this will not work with unnamed groups, as the keys of the dictionary won't refer to anything!). The `url` template takes any keyword parameters after the name attribute of the URL pattern and passes them to `reverse()` as the `kwargs` parameter.

**Example 6.50: Project Code**
`organizer/models.py` **in** dbcee003de

```
 9    class Tag(models.Model):
 .        ...
23        def get_absolute_url(self):
24            return reverse('organizer_tag_detail',
25                            kwargs={'slug': self.slug})
```

When invoking `reverse()` or the `url` template tag with arguments, you should always ask yourself: *Can I put this code in a model class?* If the answer is yes, you should implement the `get_absolute_url()` method (or similar, as we shall see in Chapter 9). In this chapter, using the method allowed us to shorten our code and replace multiple instances of `url`. Using the model method is also the best way of adhering to DRY.

We did not code `get_absolute_url()` for `NewsLink`, as the model is displayed with `Startup` objects and does not have its own webpage. This seems reasonable at the moment, but in Chapter 9 we discover this is actually a mistake. While not the official recommendation, I am of the opinion that `get_absolute_url()` should be defined for most if not all models.

# Allowing User Input with Forms

## In This Chapter

- Build Django forms
- Divide and conquer forms as finite-state machines
- Temporarily store user data for validation
- Safely add user data to the database

## 7.1  Introduction

First coined by Darcy DiNucci in 1999 and popularized in the mid–2000s by others, the (marketing) term *Web 2.0* has largely referred to websites that allow for user input and interaction. At the moment, our website only displays data and is therefore distinctly Web 1.0. For the next three chapters, we focus on fixing this shortcoming.

Much in the same way that Chapter 3: Programming Django Models and Creating a SQLite Database, Chapter 4: Rapidly Producing Flexible HTML with Django Templates, and Chapter 5: Creating Webpages with Controllers in Django are linked, the next three chapters are heavily interconnected.

When dealing with data, developers usually consider how data is created, read, updated, and deleted, or CRUD. At the moment, our website handles displaying or reading data just fine. We need to take care of the rest, because the Django shell (demonstrated in Chapter 3) is currently the only way to add, update, or delete data, and our users will not have access to it.

The ultimate goal is thus to create webpages that allow users to create, update, and delete data from our website. More precisely, we will allow users full interaction with `Tag`, `Startup`, `NewsLink`, and `Post` objects.

We are thus talking about adding three (CUD) webpages for each object, which will result in twelve new views, twelve new URL patterns, and twelve new templates. Before building templates or pages, we will use this chapter to create Django forms. Django forms are tools to handle creating and updating data, and we will therefore only need a single form for each of our objects. In a nutshell, Django forms (as opposed to HTML forms) allow for temporary storage and validation of data input by the user.

In Chapter 8: Displaying Forms in Templates, we build templates to display forms, and in Chapter 9: Controlling Forms in Views, we build views to interact with forms (mirroring Chapter 4 and Chapter 5). In this chapter (which mirrors Chapter 3), we start with the fundamentals of form, and then see how to reduce our code to maintain the Don't Repeat Yourself (DRY) principle (making for a bottom-up approach).

While the Model-View-Controller (MVC) architecture has largely helped us understand the moving parts of Django so far, this is the first chapter where we will see that Django does not truly follow the guidelines set forth by MVC.

## 7.2   Django Forms as State Machines

Django forms and models are often confused by beginners. Whereas a model is a representation of data in the database and is used to communicate with the database with the object-relational mapper (ORM), a form is a temporary container for data, meant to process the data it is given before passing it along to another part of Django. Django refers to the act of giving data to the form as the act of *binding data to the form*. Typically the form passes the data along to the model, but the data could be returned to the user or sent in an email. Practically speaking, the developer could do whatever he or she wishes with the data provided to the form by the user.

This flexibility can make forms a little bit difficult to understand. The classical computer science approach to make large systems easy to understand is to divide and conquer the system. Specifically, we deal with forms as **automatons**, or **finite-state machines**. If you've not heard of these terms, they sound a little daunting. They're actually quite straightforward. For instance, flipping a coin is a two-state finite automata: you get heads (1) or tails (2). The process of rolling a six-sided die is a six-state finite automata: there is one state for every number on the die.

In this chapter, we will build all of the forms for our site. We start by manually building a basic form for our Tag class—TagForm—and then demonstrate how to interact with the form in the shell. We establish form behavior as a finite-state machine and dive into data validation. We then see how to connect TagForm to Tag directly, not only shortening our code but also helping secure it. We finish the chapter by using the culmination of our knowledge to build the rest of our site forms.

## 7.3   Creating `TagForm`, a Form for `Tag` Objects

Django forms mirror the declarative syntax seen in Django models. Consider the Tag model class in `/organizer/models.py`, shown in Example 7.1.

**Example 7.1: Project Code**
`organizer/models.py` in 4484e55751

```
 9    class Tag(models.Model):
10        name = models.CharField(
11            max_length=31, unique=True)
```

```
12        slug = models.SlugField(
13            max_length=31,
14            unique=True,
15            help_text='A label for URL config.')
16
17      class Meta:
18          ordering = ['name']
19
20      def __str__(self):
21          return self.name.title()
22
23      def get_absolute_url(self):
24          return reverse('organizer_tag_detail',
25                          kwargs={'slug': self.slug})
```

The form we create, `TagForm`, with the intent of creating a new `Tag` model, must mirror the model fields in our class. We thus create a new class that acts as a Django form and create the same name and `slug` fields as found in `Tag`. In a new file `/organizer/forms.py`, we code as shown in Example 7.2.

**Example 7.2: Project Code**
`organizer/forms.py` **in** 4484e55751

```
1   from django import forms
2
3
4   class TagForm(forms.Form):
5       name = forms.CharField(max_length=31)
6       slug = forms.SlugField(
7           max_length=31,
8           help_text='A label for URL config')
```

*Tag Form*

*Tag Form*

*@ 39*

In Example 7.2, we create a class `TagForm`, inherit the `forms.Form` class supplied by Django, which gives our `TagForm` class much of the behavior needed to act like a form. As we do in our models, we then create fields with field options by instantiating Python classes. Observe that instead of `models.FieldName`, we are instantiating classes from `forms` via `forms.FieldName` as fields. This is crucial: fields for models and fields for forms are quite different.

Both model and form fields

- Map to a Python type
- Validate their data

However, a model field knows how to represent data in a database, whereas a form field does not. A form field is associated with a Django widget, which is nothing more than an HTML field element, such as `<input>` and `<textarea>` and radio lists. This association allows Django forms to be represented as an HTML form in a template.

Both model and form fields may represent their data in HTML output. Both model and form fields are associated with a Python type, allowing both to be printed in templates, as we saw in Chapter 4. Therefore, Django forms have the ability to be represented in two ways in templates: as the data passed to them (like models in Chapter 4), or as the HTML forms expecting data (as we shall see when we create form templates in Chapter 8).

### 7.3.1   Implementing the `save()` Method for `TagForm`

To best take advantage of inversion of control, Django recommends that developers implement the `__str__()` and `get_absolute_url()` model methods. This convention is not mandatory but makes models easier to work with both for developers and other key parts of the framework (we saw how `__str__()` clarified our interactions in the shell in Chapter 3, and we will see that `get_absolute_url()` makes our life easier in both Chapter 9 and Chapter 17: Understanding Generic Class-Based Views).

Django forms follow a similar convention with the `save()` method. The convention of implementing this method is by no means mandatory, but becomes highly useful. It also reveals that forms are typically considered a gateway to the database via models and model managers: forms will *save* data to the database. The name of the method is pure convention, and the method can be named anything else. If instead of saving data to the database the form sends data in an email, we could just as easily call the method `send()` or `process()`. However, even in these cases, it is not uncommon for developers to alias these methods to the attribute `save()` by coding `save = self.process` within the form class.

Implementing the `save()` method (or any method with similar purposes) comes with an important caveat. *The* key tenet of security on the Internet is: **don't trust your users**. While most of our users are perfectly trustworthy, it takes only a single malicious user to steal or destroy our database or to hack other users and websites via our own. When we bind a form (give the form data), we do not know whether that data is valid. There are two possibilities. Perhaps the user has made a mistake, for instance by submitting a string when we want a number. Or, the user could be trying to find a security hole in our website. In either case, we want to ensure the data is correct and safe. In Django, this safe data is referred to as **cleaned data**, because the data is **validated** and then sanitized, or cleaned.

In the next section, we see how to bind data and then how to clean this data. Once we have done so, we call our `save()` method. We will want to access this cleaned data via the `self.cleaned_data['attribute_name']` dictionary, created automatically by Django during the cleaning process. When writing `save()`, we should never directly access an attribute, such as `self.name`, as this data, termed **raw data**, may not be safe. We should always instead access `self.cleaned_data['name']`. Note that if validation on any form attribute fails, this data will not be added to this dictionary. We will explore the validation and cleaning process shortly, and see how to extend and modify it to our purposes.

In our case, the `save()` method for our `TagForm` class is simply going to create a new `Tag` object. To do this, we need access to the `Tag` model manager, and we first import it from our local `models.py` module. When we create the new object, we use cleaned data, not raw data: we pass `self.cleaned_data['name']` and `self.cleaned_data['slug']` to the `create()` model manager method, as shown in Example 7.3.

**Example 7.3: Project Code**

`organizer/forms.py` in 5014777e7e

```
3    from .models import Tag
     ...
6    class TagForm(forms.Form):
     ...
12       def save(self):                    @ 192            ⓑ 202
13           new_tag = Tag.objects.create(           # results in db insertion
14               name=self.cleaned_data['name'],
15               slug=self.cleaned_data['slug'])
16           return new_tag
```

One last part of the `save()` convention is the act of returning the new object. This step ✗
allows developers to use and manipulate the new data in other locations, as we shall in our
new views.

An implication of the way we write `save()` methods is that a form takes by default the ← 1
input of a single object. Django provides a tool called formsets[1] for when you might want to
take data for multiple objects, but we will unfortunately not have time to explore them in
this book.

## 7.3.2  Using `TagForm` in the Django Shell

To demonstrate the use of `TagForm`, including the validation and binding data to the form,
we can turn to the Django shell (available from your terminal with `./manage shell`). In
Example 7.4, we invoke the shell, import `TagForm`, and instantiate the class.

**Example 7.4: Python Interpreter Code**

```
>>> from organizer.forms import TagForm
>>> tform = TagForm()                    # create TagForm instance : no data
```

As with models, the inheritance of `forms.Form` affords us all of the behavior Django
expects forms to have. Notably, we can see if the form has been given data thanks to the
`is_bound` data attribute, and we can check whether this data has been correctly validated
and cleaned thanks to the `is_valid()` method, shown in Example 7.5.

**Example 7.5: Python Interpreter Code**

```
>>> tform.is_bound
False
>>> tform.is_valid()
False
```

formsets

---

1. https://dju.link/18/formsets

1   Create an HTML Form containing several Django forms?

The is_bound Boolean attribute is very straightforward: the form either does or does not have data. The is_valid() method is a little more subtle, as calling the method actually causes Django to validate and clean the data. If all of the data validates correctly, Django returns True. If not, it returns False.

The two attributes are conceptually related. Data can only ever validate correctly if that data exists. If is_bound is false, if there is no data, then is_valid() will always return False. It is impossible for is_valid to return True if is_bound returns False. If is_valid returns True, then is_bound is also True: there must be data bound to the form for the data to validate. However, not all data will be valid. We can represent the two states as a three-state finite machine, as shown in Table 7.1.

When is_valid() validates and cleans data, it creates the cleaned_data dictionary (and explains why is_valid() is a method rather than an attribute). However, should we attempt to access tform.cleaned_data before invoking 'is_valid()', we will be greeted with AttributeError: 'TagForm' object has no attribute 'cleaned_data'.

We can bind data to a form by passing a dictionary as argument when instantiating a form class. In Example 7.6, we pass an empty dictionary to TagForm. This is technically the act of binding data to the form, even if the data is an empty dictionary. We can then validate this data.

We see that while our dictionary contains no data, the form acknowledges that it is nonetheless bound with data: tform is a bound form. We also see that cleaned_data is available after we call is_valid(). The cleaned_data dictionary thus only exists when a form is bound and after is_valid() has been called.

Let's bind the form with correct data, as shown in Example 7.7.

**Table 7.1: Potential Function Outputs**

| is_bound() | is_valid() |
|------------|------------|
| False | False |
| True | False |
| True | True |

**Example 7.6: Python Interpreter Code**

```
>>> tform = TagForm({})
>>> tform.is_bound
True
>>> tform.cleaned_data
Traceback (most recent call last):
  File "<console>", line 1, in <module>
AttributeError: 'TagForm' object has no attribute 'cleaned_data'
>>> tform.is_valid()
False
>>> tform.cleaned_data
{}
```

**Example 7.7: Python Interpreter Code**

```
>>> tagdata = {
...    'name':'new tag',
...    'slug':'new_tag',
... }
>>> tform = TagForm(tagdata)          # Create TagForm Instance w/ OK data
>>> tform.is_bound
True
>>> tform.is_valid()
True
>>> tform.cleaned_data                # cleaned_data is a dict
{'name':'new tag', 'slug':'new_tag'}
```

We can see that both `is_bound` and `is_valid()` return `True` and that `cleaned_data` contains all of the values we passed in.

In addition to `cleaned_data`, forms supply the `errors` dictionary, which is a dictionary in which the key is the field that has not validated correctly, and the value is the nature of the error. In this case, because our form is valid, we have no errors, as you can see in Example 7.8.

**Example 7.8: Python Interpreter Code**

```
>>> tform.errors
{}
```

Unlike `cleaned_data`, `errors` does not need to have `is_valid()` called before it is accessed. If the validation process has not already occurred when `errors` is referenced, it will cause the form data to be cleaned, building `cleaned_data` in the process. Django allows for this behavior because of the difference in how views and templates handle these variables. You should not write Python code that avoids calling `is_valid()` entirely (explicit is better than implicit!), despite having the ability to do so, as demonstrated in Example 7.9.

**Example 7.9: Python Interpreter Code**

```
>>> tform = TagForm(tagdata)
>>> tform.errors
{}
>>> tform.cleaned_data
{'name':'new tag', 'slug':'new_tag'}
```

In views (Python), we always call `is_valid()` before accessing `cleaned_data` or `errors`.

Let's bind the form with data that we know will not validate, shown in Example 7.10. For instance, our name field must be a string. Instead, we pass in None, which will result in an error.

**Example 7.10:** Python Interpreter Code

```
>>> errordata = {
...     'name':None,
...     'slug':'new_tag',
... }
>>> tform = TagForm(errordata)
>>> tform.is_bound
True
>>> tform.is_valid()
False
>>> tform.cleaned_data
{'slug':'newtag'}
>>> tform.errors
{'name': ['This field is required.']}
```

Quite notably, the tform.cleaned_data contains only correct data. The errors dictionary correctly informs us that we must provide a value to the name field.

Powerfully, starting in Django 1.7, the forms supply multiple ways of outputting the errors in different formats. It is possible to call form.errors.as_data(), demonstrated in Example 7.11, which returns a dictionary with ValidationError objects instead of text. This may be useful for gaining more precise information about the errors causing the form to fail validation.

**Example 7.11:** Python Interpreter Code

```
>>> tform.errors.as_data()
{'name': [ValidationError(['This field is required.'])]}
```

That said, Django is quite smart about these errors. For instance, our name field has a maximum length of 31 characters. Should we pass in a string that is too long, Django correctly warns us of the error, as shown in Example 7.12.

**Example 7.12:** Python Interpreter Code

```
>>> errordata2 = {
...     'name':'abcdefghijklmnopqrstuvwxyzabcdef',
...     'slug':'new_tag',
... }
```

```
>>> len(errordata2['name'])
32
>>> tform = TagForm(errordata2)
>>> tform.is_valid()
False
>>> tform.cleaned_data
{'slug':'new_tag'}
>>> tform.errors
{'name':
    ['Ensure this value has at most 31 characters (it has 32).']}
```

In conclusion, if we treat a form as a finite-state machine where is_bound and is_valid() dictate the states of the machine, then a form has three states, as shown in Table 7.2.

It is impossible for data to be valid if the form is unbound, which is why forms do not have four states.

Understanding the states in which the form may exist will help when using them in a view, as it will become easier to establish behavior surrounding their use.

### 7.3.3  Form Validation Techniques in Django

Ensuring correct user input is referred to as **input validation**. One of the major features of Django forms is the ability to customize validation, making is_valid() do exactly as the developer desires. Django provides two validation methods: validator and clean methods.

1. A validator is a simple regular expression to which Django matches a value. A validator is therefore a Boolean check: Does the value passed to the field match the regular expression?

2. A clean method is a function that takes as input some value, processes it, and is expected to return a new, *cleaned* value or else to raise a `ValidationError` exception if the value could not be cleaned.

Validators are associated with both model fields and form fields and are typically only programmed when creating custom fields (a topic far outside the scope of this book). Clean methods, by contrast, are part of model fields, form fields, models, and forms. In models and forms, clean methods typically come in two flavors: field specific, and form/model specific. The purpose of the latter is to handle any validation that requires access to multiple fields.

**Table 7.2: Form States**

| Data | Validity |
| --- | --- |
| Unsubmitted | Invalid |
| Submitted | Invalid |
| Submitted | Valid |

**Table 7.3: Validation Methods**

| Type | Owner | Acts On | Typically Overridden? |
|---|---|---|---|
| Validator | Field | Field (itself) | No |
| Clean method | Field | Field (itself) | No |
| Clean method | Form/model | Single field | Yes |
| Clean method | Form/model | Form/model (multiple fields) | Yes |

A form field (or model field) therefore has a validator, its own clean method, and the clean method a form (or model) will run on it (shown in Table 7.3). Typically, developers will not override validators or clean methods owned by fields and will instead override the form clean methods (both the field specific and form specific methods). Occasionally, developers will also override the model clean methods (which may also be field or model specific).

The form `is_valid()` method causes data validation, leading to the creation of the `cleaned_data` dictionary. When `is_valid()` is called, it runs the validation methods in the order in Table 7.3 (conceptually—the truth is more complicated). Each field has its own validator and clean method called. The form then runs its own field-specific clean methods, and finishes the process by running the form clean method. As such, when building forms, developers are typically only interested in the third and fourth items in Table 7.3.

In the event a field validator or clean method raises an exception, the validation process stops and returns the `errors` and `cleaned_data` dictionaries. The form clean methods are thus run only if the fields validate correctly and pass the form clean methods cleaned values. This is important, and we revisit it in a moment.

Our `Tag` model has only two fields for us to consider, but as luck would have it, both of these fields require custom validation, which we build in the next subsections.

### 7.3.4   Creating a Clean Method for the `Tag` Model `name` Field

Recall that in Chapter 3, we decided that our tag name field should all be lowercase because of database alphabetization. There is, at this point, nothing stopping a user from submitting a tag name in all caps. In the following subsection, we ensure that any string value submitted to our form will be submitted to the database in all lowercase.

In forms and models, field-specific clean methods come in the form of `clean_<fieldname>()`. We can create a custom clean method in our `TagForm` for the name field by implementing the `clean_name()` method. The goal of the clean method is to ensure that the value being passed is lowercase. In `/organizer/forms.py`, we code as shown in Example 7.13.

**Example 7.13: Project Code**
`organizer/forms.py` **in** d4999958a4

```
 6    class TagForm(forms.Form):
 .        ...
12        def clean_name(self):
13            return self.cleaned_data['name'].lower()
```

Observe that `clean_name()` is not passed a value but that the new clean value is returned. The developer is expected to get the value of the field directly from the `cleaned_data` dictionary and to return the new value (but not insert it in the dictionary!). Further note that we access the dictionary without verifying the existence of the key (such as with `self.cleaned_data.get('name')`. Remember that form clean methods are run only if the field clean methods have not raised an exception for that field. Said differently, a field-specific clean method of a form is run only if the field value exists in the `cleaned_data` dictionary. The code in Example 7.13 is therefore safe.

When using a `clean_<fieldname>()` method, you should only ever access the `cleaned_data` key for that field. In `clean_name()`, you should only access `self.cleaned_data['name']`, which is guaranteed to exist. Should you attempt to access `self.cleaned_data['slug']` from within `clean_name()`, you might cause an error, as there is no guarantee that `self.cleaned_data['slug']` exists. The purpose of field-specific field-cleaning methods in forms is to handle a single field (hence the term field-specific). In the event use of multiple fields is necessary, developers should use the form-specific clean method `clean()`. Note that in `clean()`, none of the fields are guaranteed to exist, and therefore, using safe dictionary access methods such as `get()` become necessary (i.e., `self.cleaned_data.get('slug', None)`).

## 7.3.5  Preparing to Build a Clean Method for the Tag Model `slug` Field

Before diving into the code of `clean_slug()`, it is worth considering what action we must take. For clarity's sake, we decided that our URLs should be case insensitive, meaning by proxy that `slug` fields should be case insensitive, and that as such, we would store all slugs as lowercase strings in the database. We should then write a `clean_slug()` method similar to `clean_name()`.

However, the `slug` field of our `Tag` model comes with another constraint. Much like when building our models, looking ahead to our URL configuration can save us programming time in the long run. At the moment, our `organizer_tag_detail` URL pattern reads as shown in Example 7.14.

**Example 7.14: Project Code**
`organizer/urls.py` in 30726ed0ed

```
17      url(r'^tag/(?P<slug>[\w\-]+)/$',
18          tag_detail,
19          name='organizer_tag_detail'),
```

It should be obvious now that requesting the `/tag/django/` URL will attempt to find the `Tag` object with the slug `django`.

We would like to display `TagForm` when the URL `/tag/create/` is requested. This creates a URL conflict: `/tag/create/` will either (1) display the form or (2) attempt to find a `Tag` with the `slug` value `create`. Of course, it cannot do both, and so we must pick which action this request will take. We pick the first of the two possibilities listed. When we build the view and `organizer_tag_create` URL pattern to display TagForm, we will be very careful and make sure that the `organizer_tag_create` URL pattern takes precedence over `organizer_tag_detail`.

Consider that, given our decision to make a request to `/tag/create/` to display a `TagForm`, any `Tag` with the `slug` value `create` will *never* be displayed: the URL to access such a `Tag` would be `/tag/create/`, which is already our URL for our `TagForm`. As such, we must ensure than no `Tag` object with the `slug` value `create` is ever allowed to be created. In our form, we must ensure correct user input; we must ensure the user of the form never submits `create` to the `slug` field.

### 7.3.6   Creating a Clean Method for the `Tag` Model `slug` Field

Our `slug` field clean method, `clean_slug()`, must do two things:

1. Ensure that `slug` is lowercase (to prevent alphabetization and conflicts).

2. Ensure `slug` is not `create` (to prevent URL path collision).

Item 1 is straightforward, as we saw in the `clean_name()` method. However, in the event that item 2 fails, there is no clear and simple course of action to rectify the problem. Following Python's explicit nature, we should therefore raise an error. As such, we must first import the `ValidationError` exception, which Django expects developers to raise in the event a value cannot be validated. In `/organizer/forms.py`, we add the import `from django.core.exceptions import ValidationError`. We can then code as shown in Example 7.15.

**Example 7.15: Project Code**
`organizer/forms.py` in 30726ed0ed

```
 2    from django.core.exceptions import ValidationError
  .       . . .
 7    class TagForm(forms.Form):          cf Tag model, 190
  .       . . .
16        def clean_slug(self):
17            new_slug = (
18                self.cleaned_data['slug'].lower())      # work w cleaned_data only
19            if new_slug == 'create':
20                raise ValidationError(     # causes is_valid() to return False
21                    'Slug may not be "create".')
22            return new_slug
```

As before, we access the `cleaned_data` dictionary directly for the field value, assured that the key exists if the method is being called. If our lowercase value is `create`, we then raise an exception. Effectively, this exception causes `is_valid()` to return `False`, leading our view to redisplay the form, this time bound with data. Powerfully, raising the exception as we do causes the `slug` key to be removed from `cleaned_data` and instead to be added to the `errors` dictionary, with the text we pass to `ValidationError` as the error text value. This allows the bound form in the template to display the error text we pass to `ValidationError`. We shall see this in action shortly. In the event our new lowercase slug value is not `create`, we return it, ensuring that the new value is then properly inserted into `cleaned_data`.

Our `clean_slug()` function is this simple only because of all the other work being done by Django. Our form uses a `SlugField` field class and sets `max_length=31`. When Django validates the value passed to the field, it first checks that a value actually has been passed and that it has not received an empty string. It then passes the value to field validators, which ensure that the value matches the regular expression `r'^[-a-zA-Z0-9_]+$'` and that the length of the string does not exceed 31 characters. Django is doing a lot of heavy lifting for us, enabling us to write very targeted code for our specific needs.

[`SlugField def`]
191

### 7.3.7 Using `ModelForm` Inheritance to Connect `TagForm` to `Tag`

We could now move on to our other forms, as our `TagForm` is fully functional. However, consider that to create our `TagForm` class, we reproduced the structure of our `Tag` model with form fields. Should we add or modify a field in `Tag`, we would need to mirror our actions in `TagForm`. We can avoid this scenario and maintain DRY if we connect `TagForm` to `Tag`. By changing the inheritance of `TagForm` from `forms.Form` to `forms.ModelForm` and connecting `TagForm` to `Tag` via a `Meta` nested class attribute, not only can we remove the list of declared form fields, but we can also remove the `save()` method, as it is now automatically provided to us. In `/organizer/forms.py`, we would thus have the code shown in Example 7.16.

@

**Example 7.16: Project Code**
organizer/forms.py **in** d61714022e

```
1    from django import forms
2    from django.core.exceptions import ValidationError
3
4    from .models import Tag
5
6
7    class TagForm(forms.ModelForm):          @
8        class Meta:
9            model = Tag
10           fields = '__all__'
11
12       def clean_name(self):
13           return self.cleaned_data['name'].lower()
14
15       def clean_slug(self):
16           new_slug = (
17               self.cleaned_data['slug'].lower())
18           if new_slug == 'create':
19               raise ValidationError(
20                   'Slug may not be "create".')
21           return new_slug
```

} new_name = self.cleaned-data['name'].lower()
} return new_name

*(b) 193 →*

There is a key difference between our implementation of save() and the implementation provided by the ModelForm superclass. Our implementation always assumed we were creating an object. With ModelForm, we gain the ability to both create and update an object. We'll come back to this shortly.

Inheriting ModelForm allows for Tag model fields to be mapped to form fields. Recall that form fields do not have representations in the database and that model fields are not connected to form widgets. The fields option in the Meta nested class tells ModelForm which model fields to use in the form. This mapping is quite powerful, as it will include many of the attributes we programmed, such as verbose_name and help_text, which will prove useful when creating our form templates next chapter.

To use all of the fields in Tag, we passed the string __all__ to the fields attribute of Meta. However, we could just as easily have specified the code in Example 7.17.

**Example 7.17: Project Code**
organizer/forms.py **in** 0155c27199

```
 7   class TagForm(forms.ModelForm):
 8       class Meta:
 9           model = Tag
10           fields = ['name', 'slug']
```

If we wanted our TagForm to accept new values for only the name of a Tag, we would specify only the name field, leaving out the slug field. The fields attribute is thus a white-list system. If you would prefer a black-list system, then the exclude attribute is for you, allowing you to specify exclude = ['slug'] to make TagForm work with only the name field. The exclude equivalent of fields = '__all__' is thus an empty list or tuple, is shown in Example 7.18.

**Example 7.18: Project Code**
organizer/forms.py **in** 53469d97da

```
 7   class TagForm(forms.ModelForm):
 8       class Meta:
 9           model = Tag
10           exclude = tuple()        # empty tuple ⇒ exclude nothing
```

You should favor fields = '__all__' over the code in Example 7.18, as it is considered cleaner, and it is what we use in the project code.

We've kept both clean methods to clean our name and slug fields, just as before. With a ModelForm, form validation works exactly as previously described: the form fields are validated and cleaned using their own clean methods, and then the form has any field-specific clean methods run and finishes with a form-specific clean method named clean().

**Info**

We do not need to rename the clean method names, because the names of our fields in the form and the model are the same. Had we previously used form fields with different names, we would need to modify the names of the clean methods to reflect the names of the model fields in `Tag`.

### 7.3.8   Understanding `ModelForm` Validation

One of Django's central gotchas revolves around misunderstanding validation in forms inheriting `ModelForm`.

Much like a regular Django form, a `ModelForm` runs all of the clean and validator methods associated with the form (which is why we keep `clean_name()` and `clean_slug()`). However, a `ModelForm` also uses model validation.

That's right: models also provide validation! Models supply a `full_clean()` method, which is similar to the form's `is_valid()` method. Model validation is very similar to form validation. The model starts by validating individual fields with validators and clean methods. The model itself may supply field-specific clean methods, just as the form does, and the model may also similarly supply a model-specific method to clean multiple fields, similarly called `clean()`. Finally (but unlike the form), the model checks the database for uniqueness constraints, ensuring that data marked as unique (by field or date) truly is.

It is important to know: *model validation is not used by default*. The model method `full_clean()` is not called when saving a model directly via `save()` or even when using a model manager, such as with `Model.objects.create()`. However, with a `ModelForm`, we get the added benefit of model validation. In a `ModelForm`, the `full_clean()` method is never actually explicitly called, but all of the behaviors of `full_clean()` are replicated by the `ModelForm` methods. Using a `ModelForm` is therefore not only shorter and cleaner (in terms of DRY) but also safer.

Many developers are surprised by the lack of default model validation, and some do not believe the claim. For your benefit, I will demonstrate how models do not validate data properly without an explicit call to `full_clean()`. Consider our `Post` model. The `slug` field is unique according to the month of the `pub_date` field, thanks to the attribute `unique_for_month='pub_date'`. This cannot be enforced by the database: running `$ ./manage.py sqlall blog` in the shell reveals that our SQLite database stores the slug as `"slug" varchar(63) NOT NULL`. Contrast this with the `slug` for `Tag` and `Startup` models, which is stored as `"slug" varchar(31) NOT NULL UNIQUE` thanks to the `unique=True` attribute. As such, whereas the database will (additionally) check for slug uniqueness for `Tag` and `Startup` objects, it is up to Django to check for `Post` model `slug` uniqueness conflicts according to date. In my version of the database, the Django Training blog post has `pub_date=datetime.date(2013, 1, 18)` and `slug='django-training'`. We can create a conflict by invoking the shell with `$ ./manage.py shell` and creating a new item with the same `slug` and `pub_date` values, as shown in Example 7.19.

**Example 7.19: Python Interpreter Code**

```
>>> from datetime import date
>>> from blog.models import Post
>>> conflict = Post.objects.create(
... title='Conflict',
... slug='django-training',
... pub_date=date(2013,1,18),
... text='This object will cause problems.',
... )
>>> conflict
<Post: Conflict on 2015-03-27>
>>> # auto_now_add=True has overriden our pub_date
>>> # we therefore reset the date again
>>> conflict.pub_date = date(2013,1,18)
>>> conflict.save()
>>> conflict
<Post: Conflict on 2013-1-18>
```

Running the development server with ./manage.py runserver and navigating to http://127.0.0.1:8000/blog/2013/1/django-training/ will result in Django printing an error page, where the MultipleObjectsReturned exception prints that get() returned more than one Post -- it returned 2!

In Example 7.19, I used the model manager create() method, but using the code in Example 7.20 results in exactly the same problem.

**Example 7.20: Python Interpreter Code**

```
>>> conflict = Post(
... title='Conflict 2: The Return',
... slug='django-training',
... pub_date=date(2013,1,18),
... text='More Problem Behavior in Theaters Soon!',
... )
>>> conflict
<Post: Conflict 2: The Return on 2013-1-18>
>>> conflict.save()
>>> conflict
<Post: Conflict 2: The Return on 2015-03-27>
>>> # auto_now_add=True has overriden our pub_date
>>> conflict.pub_date = date(2013,1,18)
>>> conflict.save()
>>> conflict
<Post: Conflict 2: The Return on 2013-1-18>
```

In fact, browsing to the conflict page on the development server will now print get() returned more than one Post -- it returned 3! All of this can be avoided, as shown in Example 7.21, either by using a `ModelForm` for user input or by explicitly calling `full_clean()`.

**Example 7.21: Python Interpreter Code**

```
>>> conflict.full_clean()
Traceback (most recent call last):
  File "<console>", line 1, in <module>
  File "django/db/models/base.py", line 950, in full_clean
    raise ValidationError(errors)
ValidationError:
    {'slug': ['Slug must be unique for Date Published month.']}
```

To clean up the database, the code in Example 7.22 may be used.

**Example 7.22: Python Interpreter Code**

```
>>> Post.objects.all()
[<Post: Conflict on 2013-1-18>,
 <Post: JamBon Software: Games and Utilities on 2013-1-18>,
 <Post: Conflict 2: The Return on 2013-1-18>]
>>> Post.objects.filter(title__icontains='conflict').delete()
>>> Post.objects.all()
[<Post: JamBon Software: Games and Utilities on 2013-1-18>]
```

Model validation is thus not the norm and can lead to problems if you are anticipating the automatic use of these features. However, *using `ModelForm` class inheritance enforces model validation*, ensuring that both the form and the model constraints are respected when the user inputs data in the site. We will verify this as soon as we have a form webpage for our `Post` model.

### 7.3.9  Updating Objects with `ModelForm`

When we inherited `ModelForm`, we were able to remove our implementation of `save()`, because `ModelForm` provides its own. However, unlike our simple implementation, the `ModelForm` version of `save()` allows for objects to be created and updated.

The inheritance of `ModelForm` allows us to pass objects to the subclassed form via the `instance` attribute, as shown in Example 7.23.

**Example 7.23: Python Interpreter Code**

```
>>> django_tag = Tag.objects.get(slug='django')
>>> form = TagForm(instance=django_tag)
```

At the moment, if we run `save()`, nothing will happen because the data has not changed, and neither has the state of the form, as shown in Example 7.24.

**Example 7.24: Python Interpreter Code**

```
>>> form.is_bound
False
>>> form.is_valid()
False
```

The result of `is_valid()` (Example 7.25) might seem confusing at first: after all, the data in our `django_tag` instance is perfectly valid. However, remember that for `is_valid()` to be `True`, `is_bound` also must be true.

**Example 7.25: Python Interpreter Code**

```
>>> error_tag = Tag(name='will_error', slug='%%%')
>>> form = TagForm(
...     {'name': 'will_throw_exception'},
...     instance=error_tag,
... )
>>> form.is_valid()
False
>>> form.errors
{'slug': ['This field is required.']}
```

Not what you were expecting? The `instance` attribute *does not directly contribute to the data being saved*. Its utility is entirely in redisplaying data to the user. When updating an object, the form expects the entirety of the data to be resubmitted. It will not use the `instance` data during a call to `save()`, as shown in Example 7.25.

Without knowledge of how our template or views work, this section might seem a little opaque. We won't be able to fully expand on the utility of these tools until Chapter 9.

# 7.4   Building the Forms for `Startup`, `Newslink`, and `Post` Models

We now have a fundamental understanding of forms, form fields, form validation, and `ModelForm` inheritance. We can now create the forms for `Startup`, `Newslink`, and `Post` models.

## 7.4.1   Creating `PostForm`

We use a `ModelForm` to connect to our `Post` tag in Example 7.26. We also make sure to lower the case on the `slug` field value via the field-specific clean method, remembering to return the value for proper processing.

**Example 7.26: Project Code**
`blog/forms.py` in `afcd636772`

```
 1   from django import forms
 2
 3   from .models import Post
 4
 5
 6   class PostForm(forms.ModelForm):
 7       class Meta:
 8           model = Post
 9           fields = '__all__'
10
11       def clean_slug(self):
12           return self.cleaned_data['slug'].lower()
```

Unlike what we do for our other forms, we don't need to write the `clean_slug()` method to ensure that `create` is never submitted as the `slug` field value. Uniqueness for the `slug` field in `Post` does not work like the rest of our model classes. Let's review.

In our `Post` model class, we create the `slug` field such that it enforced uniqueness according to the month and year of the `pub_date` field, as shown in Example 7.27.

**Example 7.27: Project Code**
`blog/models.py` in `afcd636772`

```
11   class Post(models.Model):
 .       ...
13       slug = models.SlugField(
14           max_length=63,
15           help_text='A label for URL config',
16           unique_for_month='pub_date')
 .       ...
18       pub_date = models.DateField(
19           'date published',
20           auto_now_add=True)
```

Imagine we published a blog post in April 2015 with the string `pycon` as the slug. If we try to publish another post with the same slug in April, then Django will refuse to submit the data to the database. However, if we publish another post in June 2015 with the same slug, Django will accept the new `Post` object in the database. Uniqueness is dependent upon two fields. However, this means that `Post` objects may have identical `slug` field values. For instance, in the example above, we have two `Post` objects with `pycon` as the `slug` (one for April 2015 and one for June 2015). This is in contrast to `Tag` and `Startup` objects, where their tags are (respectively) unique: a `Tag` with the string `django` as slug will always be the only `Tag` to have `django` as slug.

Because URLs are unique identifiers, the behavior described above forced us to use the year, month, and slug when creating a URL pattern for blog posts, as shown in Example 7.28.

**Example 7.28: Project Code**
`blog/urls.py` in `afcd636772`

```
 9        url(r'^(?P<year>\d{4})/'
10            r'(?P<month>\d{1,2})/'
11            r'(?P<slug>[\w\-]+)/$',
12            post_detail,
13            name='blog_post_detail'),
```

Our `PostForm` will be displayed on the webpage generated when users visit `/blog/create/`, which does not in any way conflict with any potential blog detail URL, such as `/blog/2015/5/create/`. We need only lower the case of the `slug` field value. A quick check of our URL configuration has once again saved us from doing extra work!

## 7.4.2   Creating `StartupForm` and `NewsLinkForm`

As with `PostForm`, we can use `ModelForm` inheritance to quickly create the forms for `Startup` and `Newslink` model classes in `/organizer/forms.py`, shown in Example 7.29.

**Example 7.29: Project Code**
`organizer/forms.py` in `e90ec17deb`

```
 4    from .models import NewsLink, Startup, Tag
 5
 6
 7    class NewsLinkForm(forms.ModelForm):
 8        class Meta:
 9            model = NewsLink
10            fields = '__all__'
11
12
13    class StartupForm(forms.ModelForm):
14        class Meta:
15            model = Startup
16            fields = '__all__'
```

Note that we are going to need to clean the `slug` field in our `StartupForm` just as we did for `TagForm`. In Example 7.30, we copy and paste the function from `TagForm` into `StartupForm`.

**Example 7.30: Project Code**
`organizer/forms.py` in `c97fc1c40e`

```
13    class StartupForm(forms.ModelForm):
 .        ...
18        def clean_slug(self):
19            new_slug = (
```

```
20                  self.cleaned_data['slug'].lower())
21          if new_slug == 'create':
22              raise ValidationError(
23                  'Slug may not be "create".')
24          return new_slug
```

This code should ring all sorts of alarms. We have just copied a function from one method to another. Worse: *we did so in the same file.* This is a blatant violation of DRY. Both `TagForm` and `StartupForm` implement `clean_slug()` in exactly the same way. Django does not supply a way to adhere to DRY, because Python does—class inheritance!

To enable both the `TagForm` and `StartupForm` classes to have the same `clean_slug()` method, we can create a third class from which both `TagForm` and `StartupForm` can inherit. Python developers typically refer to these classes as *mixins* because they mix a method or piece of functionality into other classes. It's typically considered good practice to have the word Mixin at the end of such classes.

As shown in Example 7.31, we thus create a new class called `SlugCleanMixin` and copy the `clean_slug()` method from either `TagForm` or `StartupForm` into `SlugCleanMixin`.

### Example 7.31: Project Code
`organizer/forms.py` **in** 1153f3e8b7

```
13      class SlugCleanMixin:
14          """Mixin class for slug cleaning method."""
15
16          def clean_slug(self):
17              new_slug = (
18                  self.cleaned_data['slug'].lower())
19              if new_slug == 'create':
20                  raise ValidationError(
21                      'Slug may not be "create".')
22              return new_slug
```

In Example 7.32, we add the new class to the inheritance list of `TagForm`, and `StartupForm` (`StartupForm(forms.ModelForm)` becomes `StartupForm (SlugCleanMixin, forms.ModelForm)`. This allows us to remove the `clean_slug()` method from both `TagForm` and `StartupForm`.

### Example 7.32: Project Code
`organizer/forms.py` **in** 4a33718213

```
25      class StartupForm(
26              SlugCleanMixin, forms.ModelForm):
  .         ...
32      class TagForm(
33              SlugCleanMixin, forms.ModelForm):
```

Because `TagForm` and `StartupForm` inherit from `SlugCleanMixin`, they still have the method defined and will still call `clean_slug()` during the data-cleaning process. However, the method is now defined in only a single place in our code, meaning any changes we make occur in only one place.

## 7.5   Putting It All Together

When first confronted by forms, many beginners try to fit the new tool under the umbrella of the Model-View-Controller (MVC) architecture. Because forms handle data, it's common for beginners to associate forms with the Model portion of MVC. With a loose definition of MVC, where Models are simply any part of the framework that store and structure data, this is not wrong: the purpose of a form is to temporarily store data. However, the form is also meant to clean the data to ensure validity and secure the website and then to process it in some way (typically by adding it to the database), both of which are actions outside of Models purview. With the original, rather strict definition of MVC, forms don't belong anywhere.

Forms are complex beasts and are best dealt with as finite-state machines. When dealing with forms, we ask about whether the form is *bound* (whether it has data) and whether it is *valid* (whether the data is correct and safe). Once data is bound, we can use the `is_valid()` method to check whether the data is valid. In all cases, the validity check will result in the creation of a `cleaned_data` dictionary. In the event a form is bound but invalid, the form will create an `errors` dictionary, informing us (and the user) what is wrong with the data.

Forms are classes with attributes to other objects, called *form fields*. Form fields are similar to but different from model fields, notably because they cannot be represented in the database but are associated with a widget, which is simply Django's term for HTML form fields. Very often, forms will be declared as `ModelForm` objects and directly associated with Django models, allowing for simple adherence to the DRY principle.

When implementing forms that interact with models, developers should opt to inherit from `ModelForm` instead of `Form`. This switch provides many form utilities that automatically interact with the model that the form is associated with. In particular, `ModelForm` subclasses inherit a `save()` method, which will create or update an object in the database. `ModelForm` subclasses can also be instantiated with the `instance` attribute, which allows developers to pass an existing object in the database to the subclass.

Django's forms are incredibly powerful and one of the framework's more salient features, but they can take some getting used to. What's more, their importance only becomes truly apparent when combined with templates and views. It will take the next two chapters to fully appreciate their utility and to get our site into a state where users can finally interact with it.

8

# Displaying Forms in Templates

## In This Chapter

- Build templates to display Django forms
- Learn to control form output in a myriad of ways
- Follow best practice and adhere to DRY in templates
- Reconsider template inheritance, and avoid common pitfalls

## 8.1 Introduction

In this chapter, we build templates to display the Django forms we built in Chapter 7: Allowing User Input with Forms. We start by programming our `TagForm` template manually in HTML, without any use of the context variables passed to the template. We introduce `RequestContext` variables and slowly replace pieces of our HTML with these variables (the variables will output exactly what we coded). The first solution we examine requires the most work but affords us the most control. Our final solution requires the least amount of work, but also affords us less control. In between the first and final solutions, we will iterate through a number of options, gradually relinquishing control in favor of less code.

The templates we build will allow us to prompt the user to create, update (modify), and delete objects. All in all, we will create 12 templates: three for each kind of object (`Tag`, `Startup`, `NewsLink`, and `Post`).

While dealt with separately, template and views rely heavily on each other, and in an actual development setting, you would probably develop the template, view, and URL pattern to a single webpage all at once rather than program all of the templates first. This approach, however, is not conducive to learning new material, which is why we focus solely on templates in this chapter.

This chapter assumes knowledge of HTML and HTML forms.

## 8.2 Creating a New Template to Create Tag Objects

To accept data into a view to be processed by a Django view, we need to prompt the user to give us this data. We use an HTML form to do this (if you don't know what this is, please refer to an HTML textbook).

Create the file /organizer/templates/organizer/tag_form.html, and code as shown in Example 8.1.

**Example 8.1: Project Code**

organizer/templates/organizer/tag_form.html **in** d3f0583ad0

```
1   {% extends parent_template|default:"organizer/base_organizer.html" %}
2
3   {% block title %}
4   {{ block.super }} - Create Tag
5   {% endblock %}
6
7   {% block content %}
8     <form
9         action="{% url 'organizer_tag_create' %}"
10        method="post">
11      {% csrf_token %}
12      <p>
13        <label for="id_name">Name:</label>
14          <input id="id_name" maxlength="31"
15              name="name" type="text" />
16      </p>
17      <p>
18        <label for="id_slug">Slug:</label>
19          <input id="id_slug" maxlength="31"
20              name="slug" type="text" />
21        <span class="helptext">
22          A label for URL config
23        </span>
24      </p>
25      <button type="submit">
26        Create Tag</button>
27    </form>
28  {% endblock %}
```

Most of the code in Example 8.1 should be straightforward. We extend the base app template on the first line, making sure to override both the title and content blocks.

In the content block, we create an HTML form, pointing it to submit data to a URL pattern via the url template tag. We create this URL pattern and the associated view in the next chapter. We also notably specify that the method the form will use is "post", signifying that the form will request the page and submit data via the HTTP POST verb.

The call to {% csrf_token %} on line 11 is the only new code. CSRF refers to cross-site request forgery, which is a malicious attack to inject data into a site via an authenticated user. To mitigate the possibility of data injection, Django expects any request that submits data, such as those issued with the HTTP POST or HTTP PUT methods, to provide a unique identifier, called a **token**, to verify that the submission is coming from a user visiting our actual site. Django thus needs us to present this token to the user before the user can submit data and therefore expects every form submitted to have the CSRF

token. Django uses *context processors* to build the CSRF token (in tandem with
middleware), which means that Django necessitates the use of `RequestContext` objects
(and therefore the `HttpRequest` object) when rendering templates for forms. The
`render()` shortcut is thus far more desirable than the `render_to_response()` shortcut,
as per our discussion of the topic in Chapter 5: Creating Webpages with Controllers in
Django.                                                                    @ 142

In short,          *action is Post, put*

- A template with a form must have a CSRF token, generated by a context processor.                ✗

- To enable use of context processors, a view must use a `RequestContext` object
  instead of a `Context` object.

For more on the subject of CSRF, please see Appendix D.

### 8.2.1   Using Template Variables to Make the `TagForm` Template Dynamic

The HTML form we manually coded in our template is exactly what we want users to see
when we present an unbound `TagForm`. However, our code makes us unable to present a
bound form with errors or any kind of dynamic content. What's more, our code is in direct
violation of DRY, as any change to `TagForm` will result in a change to our template.

In the following sections, we will see how to use template variables to replace the current
HTML version. This change is mandatory, not only because of our desired adherence to
DRY but also because our current form is terrible in terms of usability. Consider that our
inability to output form errors, meant to prompt the user into action, is a serious usability
problem.

To better understand the issue, we need to enter invalid information in the form. This is
sometimes easier said that done. For instance, creating an error for the `name` field is not
straightforward: the field accepts any Unicode character, and we cannot trigger an error in
relation to the `max_length=31` field validator because we carefully coded our HTML
`input` field with the attribute `maxlength="31"`. The easiest way to create an error with
the `name` field is therefore to simply leave it empty. Triggering a validation error with our
`slug` field is simpler: we have the option to pass the value `create`, or any character that is
not alphanumeric, such as a dash or an underscore.

Run the development server with `./manage.py runserver`, and browse to
`http://127.0.0.1:8000/tag/create/`. Leave the name field empty, and enter either
`'create'` or `'%%%'` in the `slug` field, and press submit. You will be greeted by an empty
form with no errors: it is identical to our first load. In terms of usability, this is terrible.

In the next subsections, we use template variables to display errors and then to
automatically fill bound form fields with submitted data. These two steps will solve our
usability problem. We will then ensure that our form adheres to the DRY principle.

### 8.2.2   Displaying Form Errors in `tag_form.html`

Recall that our template `RequestContext` is passed the unbound or bound `form` variable.
In the case of a bound `form`, we have access to a dictionary named `errors`, which allows
us to print an error by using the name of the field as attribute. For example, should our

name field have an error, we can print the error text with {{ form.errors.name }}. Further recall that a template will not error in the event we call a template variable that does not exist. Consequently, we can call or reference values of form without checking for their existence.

Consider that we can check all of these values in the interpreter, accessed in the command line by ./manage.py shell, as shown in Example 8.2.

**Example 8.2: Python Interpreter Code**

```
>>> from organizer.forms import TagForm
>>> tf = TagForm({'slug':'create'})    # omits a value for name
>>> tf.errors
{'name': ['This field is required.'],
 'slug': ['Slug may not be "create".']}
```

It is also possible, as shown in Example 8.3, to output JSON thanks to form.errors.as_json, where the value of every key in the dictionary returned will be JSON.

**Example 8.3: Python Interpreter Code**

```
>>> tf.errors.as_json()
{'name': [{'code': 'invalid',
           'message': 'This field is required.'}],
 'slug': [{'code': 'invalid',
           'message': 'Slug may not be "create".'}]}
```

Typically, however, developers use none of the options presented above. The form variable makes form field errors available not only as an independent dictionary but also in relation to the form fields. Rather than form.errors.slug, developers generally use form.slug.errors.

We can thus create a loop to print the errors for the slug field, as shown in Example 8.4.

**Example 8.4: Project Code**

organizer/templates/organizer/tag_form.html in 0e36ff2586

```
31        {% if form.slug.errors %}
32          <ul class="custom_error_list">
33            {% for error in form.slug.errors %}
34              <li><em>{{ error }}</em></li>
35            {% endfor %}
36          </ul>
37        {% endif %}
```

We can print errors for the name field in exactly the same way, as shown in Example 8.5.

**Example 8.5: Project Code**
`organizer/templates/organizer/tag_form.html` **in** 0e36ff2586

```
19        {% if form.name.errors %}
20          <ul class="custom_error_list">
21            {% for error in form.name.errors %}
22              <li><em>{{ error }}</em></li>
23            {% endfor %}
24          </ul>
25        {% endif %}
```

In the event a field is left empty, one of the form field errors will print a field-required message, as shown in Example 8.6.

**Example 8.6: HTML Code**

```
<ul class="errorlist">
  <li>
    This field is required.
  </li>
</ul>
```

Passing `'%%%'` to the slug input field yields the message shown in Example 8.7.

**Example 8.7: HTML Code**

```
<ul class="errorlist">
  <li>
    Enter a valid 'slug' consisting of letters, numbers,
        underscores or hyphens.
  </li>
</ul>
```

Finally, if we pass `'create'` to the slug input field, we are greeted by the text we passed to the ValidationError exception we raised in `clean_slug()`, as shown in     @ 215
Example 8.8.

**Example 8.8: HTML Code**

```
<ul class="errorlist">
    <li>
        Slug may not be "create".
    </li>
</ul>
```

Consider that because `clean_slug()` starts with the process to lower the case of `slug`, passing in `'create'`, `'CREATE'`, and `'cReAtE'` all cause the error behavior above, which is as desired because our URL paths are case insensitive.

While not implemented, recall that forms are also capable of a form-specific clean method called `clean()`. We can print any exceptions raised in `clean()` by looping over `form.non_field_errors`, as shown in Example 8.9. A `non_field_error` is any error not associated with a field: it is an error that arises from a combination of fields or from the form itself.

**Example 8.9: Project Code**
`organizer/templates/organizer/tag_form.html` in `0e36ff2586`

```
12        {% if form.non_field_errors %}
13          <ul class="custom_error_list">
14            {% for error in form.non_field_errors %}
15              <li><em>{{ error }}</em></li>
16            {% endfor %}
17          </ul>
18        {% endif %}
```

## 8.2.3    Redisplaying Bound Form Values in `tag_form.html`

We currently display errors in our `TagForm`, which is a strong first step for usability, but we are not currently providing field values. If a user fills in our form with invalid data and submits it, the bound form the site displays does not provide the values the user submitted. Concretely, if the user provides the `name` and `slug` fields with *Creation* and *create*, the form will return, informing the user that the `slug` field may not be "create," but both the `name` and `slug` fields will be empty, requiring the user to retype the entire form. Screenshots of this behavior are provided in Figure 8.1.

Bound form values are available in the template `Context` as `{{ form.field.value }}`. With our `slug` field, we could check the existence of the value and print it with `{{ form.slug.value }}` as demonstrated in Example 8.10.

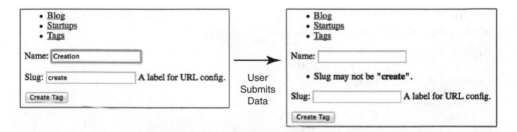

**Figure 8.1:** Behavior without Redisplay

**Example 8.10: Project Code**

`organizer/templates/organizer/tag_form.html` **in** 9375258880

```
46        {% if form.slug.value %}
47          <input id="id_slug" maxlength="31"
48              name="slug" type="text"
49              value="{{ form.slug.value }}" />
50        {% else %}
51          <input id="id_slug" maxlength="31"
52              name="slug" type="text" />
53        {% endif %}
```

*[handwritten note: display bound form field value if it exists]*

If the user submits invalid data, the form will now provide the `slug` value the user submitted, as shown in Figure 8.2.

To solve the same problem with our name field, we can add the condition shown in Example 8.11 to our template.

**Example 8.11: Project Code**

`organizer/templates/organizer/tag_form.html` **in** 9375258880

```
28        {% if form.name.value %}
29          <input id="id_name" maxlength="31"
30              name="name" type="text"
31              value="{{ form.name.value }}" />
32        {% else %}
33          <input id="id_name" maxlength="31"
34              name="name" type="text" />
35        {% endif %}
```

While this condition solves our usability problem, it adds a lot of repetitive code to our template. In the next section, we shorten all our code and maintain the DRY principle.

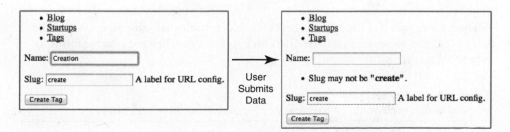

**Figure 8.2:** Behavior with Redisplay

## 8.2.4   Maintaining the DRY Principle in `tag_form.html`

Our understanding of displaying forms in templates has focused entirely on minute control of the form. However, we have done so at the cost of the DRY principle. In the following subsection, we significantly shorten the code used to display forms—at the cost of control of our HTML.

### 8.2.4.1   Replacing Loops and Conditions with Variables

One of the key shortcuts Django provides is the ability to call variables directly to provide looping behavior. For example, we are currently looping over `form.non_field_errors` (form errors not specific to any field), `form.name.errors`, and `form.slug.errors`. The latter is displayed in Example 8.12.

**Example 8.12:** Project Code

`organizer/templates/organizer/tag_form.html` in 0e36ff2586

```
31        {% if form.slug.errors %}
32          <ul class="custom_error_list">
33            {% for error in form.slug.errors %}
34              <li><em>{{ error }}</em></li>
35            {% endfor %}
36          </ul>
37        {% endif %}
```

Rather than loop over the variable, we can simply call the variable, and Django will loop over it for us. We can therefore remove all of our error loops and simply call the variables shown in Example 8.13 instead (the code replaces three loops).

**Example 8.13:** Project Code

`organizer/templates/organizer/tag_form.html` in c2f0ea0c4d

```
12        {{ form.non_field_errors }}
13        {{ form.name.errors }}
  .       ...
25        {{ form.slug.errors }}
```

Django also provides conditional checks for values. In the last subsection, we introduced an `if` condition to provide submitted data back to the user when redisplaying forms, as shown in Example 8.14.

**Example 8.14:** Project Code

`organizer/templates/organizer/tag_form.html` in 9375258880

```
28        {% if form.name.value %}
29          <input id="id_name" maxlength="31"
30              name="name" type="text"
```

```
31              value="{{ form.name.value }}" />
32          {% else %}
33            <input id="id_name" maxlength="31"
34                name="name" type="text" />
35          {% endif %}
     .      ...
46          {% if form.slug.value %}
47            <input id="id_slug" maxlength="31"
48                name="slug" type="text"
49                value="{{ form.slug.value }}" />
50          {% else %}
51            <input id="id_slug" maxlength="31"
52                name="slug" type="text" />
53          {% endif %}
```

We can replace the entire if block with a single variable {{ form.slug }}, as shown in Example 8.15. Recall from Chapter 7 that a form field is associated with a Django widget, which is nothing more than an HTML input type. By calling {{ form.slug }}, Django will print the form field widget, with or without a bound value, exactly as we had done manually. The code in Examples 8.14 and 8.15 are thus equivalent.

**Example 8.15: Project Code**
organizer/templates/organizer/tag_form.html in c1709af9e0

```
16          {{ form.name }}
     .      ...
21          {{ form.slug }}
```

On top of the actual HTML input fields, we can also replace the help text with a variable, as shown in Example 8.16.

**Example 8.16: Project Code**
organizer/templates/organizer/tag_form.html in c1709af9e0

```
22          <span class="helptext">
23            {{ form.slug.help_text }}
24          </span>
```

The help text may be defined in a form, but because we are using a ModelForm, Django will print the help_text attribute we defined in our Tag model back in Chapter 3. The implication, of course, is that the text descriptions provided to the model are available via the form in a template, demonstrating a great example of the DRY principle.

All in all, our form now reads as shown in Example 8.17.

**Example 8.17: Project Code**
`organizer/templates/organizer/tag_form.html` **in** c1709af9e0

*compare 212*
*221*

```
 8   <form
 9       action="{% url 'organizer_tag_create' %}"
10       method="post">
11   {% csrf_token %}
12   {{ form.non_field_errors }}
13   {{ form.name.errors }}
14   <p>
15       <label for="id_name">Name:</label>
16       {{ form.name }}
17   </p>
18   {{ form.slug.errors }}
19   <p>
20       <label for="id_slug">Slug:</label>
21       {{ form.slug }}
22       <span class="helptext">
23           {{ form.slug.help_text }}
24       </span>
25   </p>
26   <button type="submit">
27       Create Tag</button>
28   </form>
```

### 8.2.4.2   Generating Field IDs and Labels

We are manually outputting both the `id` attribute and the value of the HTML `label` tag. This is unnecessary, as Django can actually generate the IDs and labels for fields, replacing each ID with {{ form.field_name.id_for_label }} and each label with {{ form.field_name.label }}, as shown in Example 8.18.

**Example 8.18: Project Code**
`organizer/templates/organizer/tag_form.html` **in** b17d0c1860

```
13       {{ form.name.errors }}
14       <p>
15         <label for="{{ form.name.id_for_label }}">
16             {{ form.name.label }}:
17         </label>
18         {{ form.name }}
19       </p>
20       {{ form.slug.errors }}
21       <p>
22         <label for="{{ form.slug.id_for_label }}">
23             {{ form.slug.label }}:
24         </label>
```

```
25        {{ form.slug }}
26        <span class="helptext">
27           {{ form.slug.help_text }}
28        </span>
29     </p>
```

Thanks to our use of `ModelForm` inheritance, any model fields that had the verbose_name attribute provided will use that value when printing the label in the form above. As a refresher, Example 8.19 is code from our `Startup` model.

**Example 8.19: Project Code**
`organizer/models.py` in b17d0c1860

```
28    class Startup(models.Model):
 .        ...
36        founded_date = models.DateField(
37            'date founded')
```

Without the verbose_name option (implicitly declared if it's the first argument to a field), Django would generate a label for the field that read `Founded Date`. However, because of our option, Django will instead capitalize the first letter of each word in our string and output `Date Founded` as a label. In the case of our `Tag` model, we did not specify any verbose_name options, and so the name and slug fields will automatically generate labels that read `Name` and `Slug`.

This is a great first step, but even this can be improved. To output both the `id_for_label` and the `label`, Django provides each field with `label_tag`, allowing us to further shorten our code with the same output, as shown in Example 8.20.

**Example 8.20: Project Code**
`organizer/templates/organizer/tag_form.html` in de023ca38f

```
12        {{ form.non_field_errors }}
13        {{ form.name.errors }}
14     <p>
15        {{ form.name.label_tag }}
16        {{ form.name }}
17     </p>
18        {{ form.slug.errors }}
19     <p>
20        {{ form.slug.label_tag }}
21        {{ form.slug }}
22        <span class="helptext">
23           {{ form.slug.help_text }}
24        </span>
25     </p>
```

Compare 220
222

## 8.2.5    Looping over Form Fields

The worst error we are making here is probably the most subtle to beginners. We are manually declaring each and every field in our form: we reference name and slug fields directly. This is fine on a small form like TagForm, but on a larger form, it becomes unwieldy. What's more, any changes to TagForm's fields will result in changes in our template, which we never, ever want. We can entirely avoid this unwieldy result by creating a form loop to iterate through all of the fields in our form, entirely replacing our code with that shown in Example 8.21.

**Example 8.21: Project Code**

organizer/templates/organizer/tag_form.html **in** f48adbb1a2

compare 221

```
13        {% for field in form %}
14            {{ field.errors}}
15        <p>
16            {{ field.label_tag }}
17            {{ field }}
18            {% if field.help_text %}
19              <span class="helptext">
20                  {{ field.help_text }}</span>
21            {% endif %}
22        </p>
23        {% endfor %}
```

Example 8.21 is the first template example in this chapter that you might actually use in a production environment. All of the previous examples were meant to demonstrate variable use and shortening, to help lead us to this template—but it is not actually what you want in a template. The key difference is the loop. All of the variables seen previously are valid: using {{ form.field.label_tag }} or customizing HTML via <label for= "{{ form.field.id_for_label }}">{{ form.field.label }}:</label> are both valid options. However, these variables should always be used in tandem with a loop iterating over the form fields, as opposed to referencing each form field by name.

To that effect, the form offers variables such as {{ form.hidden_fields }} and {{ form.visible_fields }} for the developer to loop over. The impetus to loop over fields is also why errors are made available not only as part of the errors dictionary, but also as an attribute of each field, as seen on line 14 in Example 8.21.

## 8.2.6    Printing Forms Directly

Using a loop to iterate over form fields is not actually the shortest way to print a form. Django provides the loop {{ form.as_p }} as a single command, reducing our entire template to that shown in Example 8.22.

**Example 8.22: Project Code**

organizer/templates/organizer/tag_form.html **in** 1a77ff0b15

```
1    {% extends parent_template|default:"organizer/base_organizer.html" %}
2
3    {% block title %}
```

```
4   {{ block.super }} - Create Tag
5   {% endblock %}
6
7   {% block content %}
8     <form
9         action="{% url 'organizer_tag_create' %}"
10        method="post">
11      {% csrf_token %}
12      {{ form.as_p }}
13      <button type="submit">
14        Create Tag</button>
15    </form>
16  {% endblock %}
```

Note that it is always necessary to provide the HTML `<form>` tags, the `{% csrf_token %}` tag, and the submit button.

Django also provides the `{{ form.as_ul }}` and `{{ form.as_table }}`, should developers wish to automatically print forms as lists and tables. In each case, Django expects the developer to provide their own `<ul>` or `<table>` tags (respectively), and to then call the template attributes above. For example, `{{ form.as_ul }}` is shown in Example 8.23.

**Example 8.23: Django Template Language Code**

```
<ul>
{{ form.as_ul }}
</ul>
```

In conclusion, Django allows for a myriad of ways to print a form in a template, and it should now be clear why Django advertises itself as "the perfectionist's web framework." All the methods available present a spectrum from most control to most simple. Typically, developers start with a template that simply prints the form with `{{ form.as_p }}`. As Cascading Style Sheet (CSS) designers need more control or specific changes, the template developer then customizes the form output as needed. To maintain the DRY principle and usability, always (1) program the form as a loop iterating over fields and errors, and (2) ensure that any value afforded by the `form` is used as a variable: this includes not only errors but also the value of a bound field and even the widget of a field. Abiding by these two rules will save you time down the road.

Before we go in Example 8.24, let's add some HTML around the form, in anticipation of the CSS we'll create in Chapter 16: Serving Static Content with Django.

**Example 8.24: Project Code**
`organizer/templates/organizer/tag_form.html` in `ec18b33c7e`

```
7   {% block content %}
8     <div>
9       <div>
10        <form
11            action="{% url 'organizer_tag_create' %}"
12            method="post">
```

```
13              {% csrf_token %}
14              {{ form.as_p }}
15              <button type="submit">
16                Create Tag</button>
17          </form>
18        </div>
19      </div>
20    {% endblock %}
```

## 8.3   Creating a New Template to Update Tag Objects

The form template to update Tag objects is nearly identical to the form template to create Tag objects. The key differences are (1) the HTML form action attribute, where we call a get_update_url() method on the Tag object, and (2) the value of the submit button on the HTML form.

We thus start like any other template, by first extending the base app template, and overriding the title and content blocks, as in Example 8.25.

**Example 8.25: Project Code**

organizer/templates/organizer/tag_form_update.html **in** 0874cb22bf

```
1    {% extends parent_template|default:"organizer/base_organizer.html" %}
2
3    {% block title %}
4    {{ block.super }} - Update Tag
5    {% endblock %}
6
7    {% block content %}
.      ...
20   {% endblock %}
```

In the content block in Example 8.26, we start by anticipating our CSS from Chapter 16.

**Example 8.26: Project Code**

organizer/templates/organizer/tag_form_update.html **in** 0874cb22bf

```
7    {% block content %}
8      <div>
9        <div>
.        ...
18       </div>
19     </div>
20   {% endblock %}
```

The form itself needs the HTML form tag with the action and method attributes specified. We then make sure we include the csrf_token, generated by the context processors in our `RequestContext` object, and print the actual Django form by simply calling {{ `form.as_p` }}. Finally, we add a submission button and close the HTML `form` tag, as in Example 8.27.

**Example 8.27: Project Code**
`organizer/templates/organizer/tag_form_update.html` **in** `0874cb22bf`

```
10          <form
11              action="{{ tag.get_update_url }}"
12              method="post">
13          {% csrf_token %}
14          {{ form.as_p }}
15          <button type="submit">
16              Update Tag</button>
17          </form>
```

The key difference between the `tag_form_update.html` and `tag_form.html` template is not the action of the form or even the value of the button (although those are useful), but how we will use the Django form in the template.

In Chapter 7, we saw that we could pass model instances to `ModelForm` subclasses via the `instance` attribute. This does not affect the bound state of the form or the validation process of the form. What it does do, however, is change the output of `as_p()` (and other display methods). The `ModelForm` subclass takes the values of the model instance and prefills the HTML form with existing data, thanks to the `value` attribute of HTML `input` fields. The output of `TagForm` with the `django` tag as an instance is displayed in Example 8.28.

158 ...
↳ 205-6

**Example 8.28: HTML Code**

```
<p>
  <label for="id_name">Name:</label>
  <input
      id="id_name"
      maxlength="31"
      name="name"
      type="text"
      value="django" />
</p>
<p>
  <label for="id_slug">Slug:</label>
  <input
      id="id_slug"
      maxlength="31"
      name="slug"
      type="text"
      value="django" />
  <span class="helptext">A label for URL config.</span>
</p>'
```

We will, of course, return to this topic in Chapter 9.

## 8.4    Creating a New Template to Delete `Tag` Objects

Unlike the template for creating or deleting Tag objects, the form for deleting `Tag` objects doesn't need to take any information and therefore doesn't need to display `TagForm`. Instead, we're creating a template that asks the user for confirmation of the removal of data.

We start by extending the base app template, and overriding the `title` and `content` blocks, as shown in Example 8.29.

**Example 8.29: Project Code**

`organizer/templates/organizer/tag_confirm_delete.html` **in** 7a857b7c54

```
 1    {% extends parent_template|default:"organizer/base_organizer.html" %}
 2
 3    {% block title %}
 4    {{ block.super }} - Delete Tag
 5    {% endblock %}
 6
 7    {% block content %}
 .        ...
24    {% endblock %}
```

We then wrap the actual HTML form in two `div` tags, as shown in Example 8.30.

**Example 8.30: Project Code**

`organizer/templates/organizer/tag_confirm_delete.html` **in** 7a857b7c54

```
 7    {% block content %}
 8      <div>
 9        <div>
 .          ...
22        </div>
23      </div>
24    {% endblock %}
```

Finally, in Example 8.31, we create an HTML form that asks confirmation from the user. The `action` attribute—like the `tag_form_update.html`—is a new method on the `Tag` class, which we will program in Chapter 9. Unlike for our other forms, we actually supply two options: a button to submit the form (and delete the tag) or a cancel link to go back to the Tag Detail page.

**Example 8.31: Project Code**

`organizer/templates/organizer/tag_confirm_delete.html` **in** 7a857b7c54

```
10        <form
11            action="{{ tag.get_delete_url }}"
12            method="post">
13          {% csrf_token %}
```

```
14        <p>
15          Are you sure you want to delete
16          tag {{ tag.name }}?
17        </p>
18        <a href="{{ tag.get_absolute_url }}">
19          Cancel</a>
20        <button type="submit">Delete Tag</button>
21      </form>
```

## 8.5 Creating Templates for `StartupForm`, `NewsLinkForm`, and `PostForm`

The process for building our templates is very straightforward. We begin by inheriting our app base template, and then override the title and content blocks. In our content block, we must:

1. create an HTML form tag

2. invoke the creation of the CSRF tag via {% csrf_token %}

3. display the form variable passed to the template RequestContext

4. display a submit button.

If we follow the steps above, our template for StartupForm, coded in /organizer/templates/organizer/startup_form.html, will look like the code in Example 8.32.

**Example 8.32: Project Code**
organizer/templates/organizer/startup_form.html **in** 42175702d5

```
1   {% extends parent_template|default:"organizer/base_organizer.html" %}
2
3   {% block title %}
4   {{ block.super }} - Create Startup
5   {% endblock %}
6
7   {% block content %}
8     <div>
9       <div>
10        <form          ①
11          action="{% url 'organizer_startup_create' %}"
12          method="post">
13          {% csrf_token %}      ②
14          {{ form.as_p }}       ③
15          <button type="submit">      ④
16            Create Startup</button>
17        </form>
18      </div>
19    </div>
20  {% endblock %}
```

The templates for creating `Startup`, `Post`, and `NewsLink` objects are all virtually identical, as you can see in Example 8.33. Even the templates for updating objects are near identical.

**Example 8.33: Project Code**
`organizer/templates/organizer/tag_form_update.html` in `0874cb22bf`

```
1   {% extends parent_template|default:"organizer/base_organizer.html" %}
2
3   {% block title %}
4   {{ block.super }} - Update Tag
5   {% endblock %}
6
7   {% block content %}
8     <div>
9       <div>
10        <form
11           action="{{ tag.get_update_url }}"
12           method="post">
13          {% csrf_token %}
14          {{ form.as_p }}
15          <button type="submit">
16            Update Tag</button>
17        </form>
18      </div>
19    </div>
20  {% endblock %}
```

If you compare this example with our `TagForm` template, you'll note that it's very similar. What's more, so is our `PostForm` template, coded in `/blog/templates/blog/post_form.html` in Example 8.34.

**Example 8.34: Project Code**
`blog/templates/blog/post_form.html` in `f6b11ed351`

```
1   {% extends parent_template|default:"blog/base_blog.html" %}
2
3   {% block title %}
4   {{ block.super }} - Create Blog Post
5   {% endblock %}
6
7   {% block content %}
8     <div>
9       <div>
10        <form
11           action="{% url 'blog_post_create' %}"
12           method="post">
13          {% csrf_token %}
14          {{ form.as_p }}
```

```
15            <button type="submit">
16                Create Blog Post</button>
17            </form>
18        </div>
19    </div>
20  {% endblock %}
```

Our NewsLinkForm template, /organizer/templates/organizer/
newslink_form.html, might as well be identical, as shown in Example 8.35.

**Example 8.35: Project Code**
organizer/templates/organizer/newslink_form.html **in** cb19646720

```
 1  {% extends parent_template|default:"organizer/base_organizer.html" %}
 2
 3  {% block title %}
 4  {{ block.super }} - Link News Article to Startup
 5  {% endblock %}
 6
 7  {% block content %}
 8    <div>
 9      <div>
10        <form
11            action="{% url 'organizer_newslink_create' %}"
12            method="post">
13          {% csrf_token %}
14          {{ form.as_p }}
15          <button type="submit">
16              Link Article</button>
17        </form>
18      </div>
19    </div>
20  {% endblock %}
```

# 8.6   Reconsidering Template Inheritance

Our templates for displaying forms are nearly identical. We have oodles of duplicate code, in violation of DRY and common sense, and it may seem like a very good idea to create a template at the site-level to inherit from in all of these templates. **Do not do it—it's a trap.**

The recommended structure for templates is what we have at the moment, and is most easily visualized as in Figure 8.3.

If we were to add a base_form.html template, we would be duplicating the structure above, but only for templates, as shown in Figure 8.4.

This, in and of itself, doesn't seem so bad. However, if you combine it with the first inheritance structure and organize it according to Django apps (which is how it will be organized on disk), as in Figure 8.5, you can see that this actually complicates things quite a bit, even in a project as simple as ours.

As any project scales, this solution will grow out of hand very quickly.

Implementing a full set of templates to reduce the amount of code we have is a mistake. The solution to our problem is to create our own template tags (like `url` or `block`) to add the HTML form code into each of these templates. This is very much an advanced feature, however, which we explore in Chapter 27. Until then, we have to forego DRY in our HTML form templates.

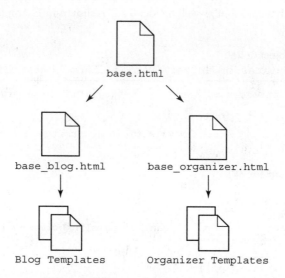

**Figure 8.3:** Current Template Inheritance

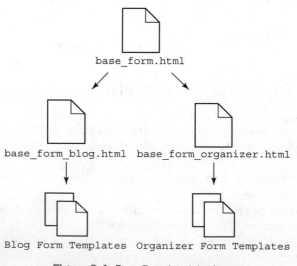

**Figure 8.4:** Form Template Inheritance

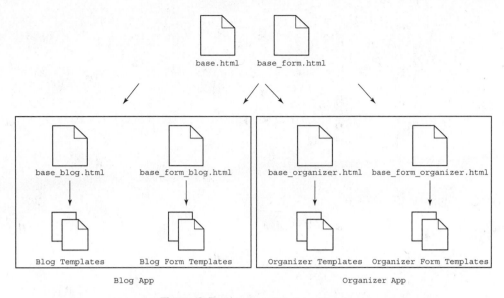

**Figure 8.5:** Form Template Inheritance

## 8.7   Putting It All Together

Django supplies a huge amount of flexibility when outputting a form in a template. It is possible to customize the output of bound form data, the form widgets, errors in the form, and any associated data (such as help_text in the model if the form is a ModelForm). This can be quite overwhelming, however. The simplest way to start is to use form.as_p, making sure to write the HTML form tag, submit button, and CSRF token out manually, and then customize as needed.

When building an HTML form in a template, developers must declare the actual HTML form tag, which details the webpage the data will be sent to (action) and how that information is being sent (method). We further need to supply a csrf_token template tag, so that the user will submit data (via HTTP POST, PUT, or other method) with the token, allowing Django to mitigate CSRFs. To submit the data, we declare an HTML submission button as well. Finally, we need to remember to output the actual Django form, using any of the methods available.

If you're feeling underwhelmed or overwhelmed by our templates, I recommend coming back to this chapter after going through Chapter 9. Because all of this content is so heavily interconnected, having a holistic understanding of the system can help clarify the display choices we made in this chapter.

# Controlling Forms in Views

## In This Chapter

- Implement views to create, update, and delete objects
- Use class inheritance to shorten our view code
- Build URL patterns for all of our views
- Provide model methods to reverse (most) of our new URL patterns
- Modify templates from last chapter to link to our new webpages

## 9.1 Introduction

We have our Django forms, and the templates to display the forms—it is time to build our views and URL patterns to put it all together.

Previously programmed views had a single goal: display information to the user. Views built with forms are more complicated, as the user must interact with the form and therefore with the view. The view must now display a form, accept data, and potentially display a form with errors.

We start by implementing views for the webpages meant to create objects. We then move on to webpages to update objects and finish with the pages meant to delete objects. By the end of Chapter 9, we will have fully implemented CRUD (create, read, update, delete) on our website.

## 9.2 Webpages for Creating Objects

We start by using the forms we programmed in Chapter 7: Allowing User Input with Forms to create objects in webpages. We first implement a function view, `tag_create()`, and we do so slowly, because programming a view with a form can be tricky, and getting it wrong can result in a lot of debugging. While not my favored method for implementing form-handling views, the code in the `tag_create()` view is commonly seen in material related to Django, because it is the code that Django's documentation uses to introduce form handling in views. Fully understanding this code is thus very useful and serves as a stepping-stone to implementing `TagCreate`, which uses more explicit code to handle forms and user data.

With a fundamental understanding of what we are building, we move directly into creating `PostCreate`, `StartupCreate`, and `NewsLinkCreate`.

Before we dive into the code, however, we must establish expected user behavior. We treat the form as a finite-state machine, matching it to user behavior, to ensure we account for all cases when building our view.

## 9.2.1   Understanding Expected Form Behavior

Manipulating forms in views is based primarily on expected user behavior. Typically, with an HTML form to create new objects, web developers and designers expect very strict behavior on the part of the web form, visualized in Figure 9.1. *The states in Figure 9.1 detail form states for creating objects.* We deal with updating and deleting objects later in this chapter.

We need to use our forms and views in tandem to allow for the user behavior described in Figure 9.1. Without proper preparation and planning, this is a process that many beginners find nightmarish. However, if we treat the system as a finite-state machine, we can greatly simplify our task. Remember that we already know from Chapter 7 that a form may exist in three states. For convenience, the form state table is reprinted in Table 9.1.

When we code our views, we thus know that we have to handle forms in three different ways. Combining Table 9.1 with Figure 9.1 allows us to determine what action we should take in each case, creating Table 9.2.

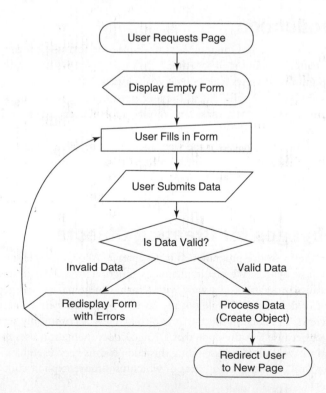

**Figure 9.1:** Diagram for Expected User Interaction

In Chapter 7, section 7.2, we discussed how binding data to a form in Python means giving data to the form. This makes two states obvious: a form with data and without data. In Figure 9.1, we display the form without data, or when the data submitted is invalid. This accounts for states 1 and 2 in Table 9.2. We can improve Table 9.2 by specifying the state of the form, yielding Table 9.3.

There is an added complication to the state table: the HTTP method. There are multiple ways to submit data to a website, but the two big ones are via the GET and POST HTTP methods. Naively, our states could multiply to the 6 possibilities shown in Table 9.4, where GET and POST may each deal with the three states in Table 9.3.

**Table 9.1: Form States**

| Data | Validity |
|------|----------|
| Unsubmitted | Invalid |
| Submitted | Invalid |
| Submitted | Valid |

**Table 9.2: Form States with Typical Action**

| # | Data | Validity | Typical Action |
|---|------|----------|----------------|
| 1 | Unsubmitted | Invalid | Display form in template |
| 2 | Submitted | Invalid | Display form in template |
| 3 | Submitted | Valid | Process and redirect |

**Table 9.3: Form States with (Precise) Typical Action**

| # | Data | Validity | Typical Action |
|---|------|----------|----------------|
| 1 | Unsubmitted | Invalid | Display unbound form in template |
| 2 | Submitted | Invalid | Display bound form in template |
| 3 | Submitted | Valid | Process and redirect |

**Table 9.4: Form States with Typical Action and HTTP methods**

| # | Method | Data | Validity | Typical Action |
|---|--------|------|----------|----------------|
| 1 | GET | Unsubmitted | Invalid | Display unbound form in template |
| 2 | GET | Submitted | Invalid | Display bound form in template |
| 3 | GET | Submitted | Valid | Process and redirect |
| 4 | POST | Unsubmitted | Invalid | Display unbound form in template |
| 5 | POST | Submitted | Invalid | Display bound form in template |
| 6 | POST | Submitted | Valid | Process and redirect |

We can vastly simplify Table 9.4, as (1) state 4 is impossible, while (2) states 2 and 3 are undesirable. Let's examine the reasons for each simplification.

Remember when operating on forms in the shell, we discovered that initializing the form with any data, even empty data, resulted in a bound form, as shown in Example 9.1.

**Example 9.1: Python Interpreter Code**

```
>>> f = TagForm({})
>>> f.is_bound
True
```

The situation provided by the shell code in Example 9.1 applies directly to our use of the POST method. When submitting a request via the POST method, there is always data submitted, even if it is empty. Therefore, every POST request results in a bound form. State 4 in Table 9.4 is thus impossible.

States 2 and 3 are valid but undesirable. Consider that passing data via GET, as we do in states 2 and 3, puts all of the information in the URL. This practice is not safe, as it means another user on the same computer will have access to any information sent by the first user. For that reason, passing data via GET is typically frowned upon. We will make sure that data is passed only via POST. When we built our templates, we actually ensured this by specifying `method="post"` in the HTML form tag. We therefore remove states 2 and 3 from consideration.

As such, only states 1, 5, and 6 are possible. We know we cannot simplify our state machine any further, as our original form state table (Table 9.3) had three states. The final states and behaviors our views must account for are listed in Table 9.5.

By treating the form as a finite-state machine, we have just saved ourselves a lot of work. But we're not done!

Given that a Django form has three states, we know that the minimum number of states we must deal with is three. What's more, from our preceding word, we also know that we don't need any more states than the ones we have defined.

However, our state table currently has three attributes for each action: method, data, and validity. Each attribute has two choices. This means we could define a maximum of $2^3$ actions: eight actions. If we had only two attributes, we would be able to define four states ($2^2 = 4$), which is more than what we need. However, if we reduce to one attribute, we are left with two states. As such, we should see if we can reduce the number of attributes to two.

Sure enough, if you examine Table 9.5, you'll notice that the states between the method and data attributes line up. We can't forgo the use of the HTTP methods: they are central to

**Table 9.5: Shortened Form States**

| # | Method | Data | Validity | Typical Action |
|---|--------|------|----------|----------------|
| 1 | GET | Unsubmitted | Invalid | Display unbound form in template |
| 2 (orig. 5) | POST | Submitted | Invalid | Display bound form in template |
| 3 (orig. 6) | POST | Submitted | Valid | Process and redirect |

**Table 9.6: Final Form States**

| # | Method | Validity | Typical Action |
|---|--------|----------|----------------|
| 1 | GET | Invalid | Display unbound form in template |
| 2 | POST | Invalid | Display bound form in template |
| 3 | POST | Valid | Process and redirect |

building websites. Views depend on the knowledge, and our desire to ensure the user doesn't submit data via GET means we are also using HTTP methods for security purposes. We can, however, remove the data attribute. Our new (and final!) form state table is printed in Table 9.6.

The effect of this simplification is that when programming our views, we will never need to check is_bound. For security purposes, if we receive a GET request, we always return an unbound form (and we ensure our site never uses GET requests with data in templates). In the case of POST requests, because POST always technically provides data (even if it's empty!), it's safe to assume that all POST request result in forms where is_bound will be true. Our assumption is also quite safe: as seen in Chapter 7, Section 7.3.2, for is_valid() to return True, is_bound must be true. It is therefore safe to only check is_valid() in our view and to forgo is_bound entirely if we rely on HTTP methods instead.

Given all of the information above, our first attempt to write the pseudocode for our view could be as shown in Example 9.2.

**Example 9.2: Pseudocode**

```
if HTTP method is GET:
    show unbound HTML form
else if HTTP method is POST:
    bind data to form
    if the data is valid:
        create new object from data
        show webpage for new object
    else: # empty data or invalid data
        show bound HTML form with data and errors
```

The pseudocode is not incorrect, but it has a pitfall: we have accounted for HTTP GET and POST, which are the two most used methods. However, what happens if we use another method? Our view will not return any data. We could raise an HTTP 405 error in these cases, as shown in Example 9.3.

**Example 9.3: HTML Code**

```
if HTTP method is GET:
    show unbound HTML form
else if HTTP method is POST:
    bind data to form
```

```
    if the data is valid:
        create new object from data
        show webpage for new object
    else: # empty data or invalid data
        show bound HTML form with data and errors
else
    raise HTTP 405 (method not allowed)
```

While this would be my preferred method, it is not how the official Django documentation introduces forms. Instead, the documentation introduces a form that only checks for the POST method, and then behaves in all other instances as if a GET request had been received (Example 9.4).

**Example 9.4: HTML Code**

```
if HTTP method is POST:
    bind data to form
    if the data is valid:
        create new object from data
        show webpage for new object
    else: # empty data or invalid data
        show bound HTML form
else: # HTTP method is GET or other, but not POST
    show unbound HTML form
```

The pseudocode is subject to several implicit behaviors that should now be very clear. We are assuming knowledge about the is_bound variable, and we are accounting (somewhat erroneously) for more HTTP methods than is initially obvious. The actual code for the function view will prove to be (unfortunately) even more implicit, as we will discover shortly.

We start by programming a view to follow the official pseudocode recommendation. However, because of better compliance with HTTP (specifically, raising an HTTP 405 error when appropriate) and the innate organization it enables, we will quickly opt to use class-based views for our form views.

## 9.2.2   Implementing a Webpage to Create Tags

We now understand the behavior necessary for creating webpages that interact with Django forms. In the next two subsections, we create a view based on the pseudocode we just built, followed by the creation of a URL pattern for our view.

### 9.2.2.1   Implementing `TagCreate`

We can now program a function view for creating a Tag object by translating the pseudocode from the end of last section into Python. Open /organizer/views.py and create a basic function view called tag_create(), as shown in Example 9.5.

**Example 9.5: Project Code**

`organizer/views.py` **in** `25b7d634af`

```
23  def tag_create(request):
24      pass
```

We can take the pseudocode from the last section and fill in the view with comments. Our first goal is to figure out which HTTP method was used. Unsurprisingly, Django stores this information in the `HttpRequest` object passed to every view, under the `method` attribute. We can thus immediately replace the HTTP method check with an actual Python condition, as shown in Example 9.6.

**Example 9.6: Project Code**

`organizer/views.py` **in** `224478e0d6`

```
23  def tag_create(request):
24      if request.method == 'POST':
25          # bind data to form
26          # if the data is valid:
27              # create new object from data
28              # show webpage for new object
29          # else: (empty data or invalid data)
30              # show bound HTML form (with errors)
31          pass
32      else:  # request.method != 'POST'
33          # show unbound HTML form
34          pass
```

Django also stores any POST data sent to the server as the `POST` attribute of the `HttpRequest` object. The `POST` attribute is a dictionary, which means we can directly use the value to instantiate and bind our form (line 26 in Example 9.7).

To validate the form, we can call `form.is_valid()`, creating `errors` and `cleaned_data` in the process. As discussed in the previous section, we don't need to use `form.is_bound`, as our use of HTTP methods covers the same cases.

**Example 9.7: Project Code**

`organizer/views.py` **in** `34de57fa2a`

```
4   from .forms import TagForm
    ...
24  def tag_create(request):
25      if request.method == 'POST':
26          form = TagForm(request.POST)      # instantiate y bind form from POST dict
27          if form.is_valid():
28              # create new object from data
29              # show webpage for new object
30              pass
```

```
31              else:  # empty data or invalid data
32                    # show bound HTML form (with errors)
33                    pass
34          else:  # request.method != 'POST'
35                # show unbound HTML form
36                pass
```

Our first task is to create a new `Tag` object. We want to use `TagForm` for this task.
Currently, `TagForm` reads as shown in Example 9.8.

**Example 9.8: Project Code**
`organizer/forms.py` **in** `34de57fa2a`

```
32  class TagForm(
33          SlugCleanMixin, forms.ModelForm):
34      class Meta:
35          model = Tag
36          fields = '__all__'
37
38      def clean_name(self):
39          return self.cleaned_data['name'].lower()
```

Because `TagForm` inherits from `forms.ModelForm`, we know that `TagForm` instances
provide a `save()` method. This method works very similarly to the one we programmed
before inheriting from `form.ModelForm`. As a reminder, the `save()` method we
programmed, which is a simplified version of the one provided by `form.ModelForm`, is
printed in Example 9.9.

**Example 9.9: Project Code**
`organizer/forms.py` **in** `5014777e7e`

```
6   class TagForm(forms.Form):
    .       ...
12      def save(self):
13          new_tag = Tag.objects.create(
14              name=self.cleaned_data['name'],
15              slug=self.cleaned_data['slug'])
16          return new_tag
```

We can thus simply call `new_tag = form.save()`.

We now want to redirect to the webpage of this new `Tag` object. We have seen
redirection multiple times, either through the instantiation of `HttpResponseRedirect` or
through calls to `redirect()`. We also know that we can use the `get_absolute_url()`
method we implemented for the `Tag` model class to return the URL path of this new
object. You might imagine using the code in Example 9.10.

**Example 9.10: Python Code**

```
tag_url = new_tag.get_absolute_url()
return redirect(tag_url)
# or alternatively:
# return HttpResponseRedirect(tag_url)
```

Thanks to inversion of control, we can avoid the preceding code and simplify our redirection to the line of code in Example 9.11

**Example 9.11: Python Code**

```
return redirect(new_tag)
```

Recall that Django expects model classes that have webpages to provide the get_absolute_url(). Thanks to our use of this convention and inversion of control, Django knows to call get_absolute_url() if we pass the redirect() shortcut a model instance.

## Info

Our knowledge of the shortcut is increasing. We now know that redirect() will accept the following as arguments:

1. A URL path

2. The name of a URL pattern

3. A model object (as long as the get_absolute_url() method is implemented)

Our code now reads as in Example 9.12.

**Example 9.12: Project Code**
organizer/views.py **in** b06f0e1754

```
 1   from django.shortcuts import (
 2       get_object_or_404, redirect, render)
 .       ...
24   def tag_create(request):
25       if request.method == 'POST':
26           form = TagForm(request.POST)
27           if form.is_valid():
28               new_tag = form.save()
29               return redirect(new_tag)
30           else:  # empty data or invalid data
31               # show bound HTML form (with errors)
32               pass
33       else:  # request.method != 'POST'
34           # show unbound HTML form
35           pass
```

We have two things left to do: display a bound form with errors and display an unbound form if an HTTP request method other than POST was used. In both cases, we want to show a webpage with an HTML representation of TagForm. In both cases, we can thus use render() to load and render a template.

In the case of our form views, we do not have a choice of shortcut: we must use render() over render_to_response. As discussed in Chapter 5, Section 5.6.3, render() uses a RequestContext to render templates, allowing Django to inject data into our template context. In the case of the templates we built in Chapter 8: Displaying Forms in Templates, the use of RequestContext is mandatory because of our use of the csrf_token.

To display our unbound and invalid forms, we load the tag_form.html template in the organizer app namespace, created in Chapter 8.

We've already created a bound form with users' input on line 26, so we can simply pass this to render starting on line 31, as shown in Example 9.13.

**Example 9.13: Project Code**
organizer/views.py **in** 9291344de2

```
24   def tag_create(request):
25       if request.method == 'POST':
26           form = TagForm(request.POST)
27           if form.is_valid():
28               new_tag = form.save()
29               return redirect(new_tag)
30           else:  # empty data or invalid data
31               return render(
32                   request,
33                   'organizer/tag_form.html',
34                   {'form': form})
35       else:  # request.method != 'POST'
36           # show unbound HTML form
37           pass
```

Finally, we need to show an empty, unbound form in the event the webpage has not been requested via the POST method. We thus need to create an unbound form and pass it to render() in a dictionary, as in Example 9.14.

**Example 9.14: Project Code**
organizer/views.py **in** 61c87b6542

```
24   def tag_create(request):
25       if request.method == 'POST':
26           form = TagForm(request.POST)
27           if form.is_valid():
28               new_tag = form.save()
29               return redirect(new_tag)
```

```
30                else:  # empty data or invalid data
31                    return render(
32                        request,
33                        'organizer/tag_form.html',
34                        {'form': form})               # form is bound
35            else:  # request.method != 'POST'
36                form = TagForm()
37                return render(
38                    request,
39                    'organizer/tag_form.html',
40                    {'form': form})                    # form is unbound
```

We can verify our code to be a correct translation of our pseudocode by comparing it to our state machine, shown in Table 9.7.

We have three states and three behaviors:

1. `redirect()` on line 29 for valid data (POST)

2. `return render()` on lines 31 through 34 for invalid data (POST)

3. `return render()` on lines 37 through 40 for no data (GET or other)

The code in Example 9.14 is not actually what the Django documentation recommends, as it is possible to combine the calls to `render()`, making the difference implicit.

While the calls to `render()` on lines 31 through 34 and lines 37 through 40 look identical, they are different because the `form` variable passed to each `RequestContext` is different. In the first call to `render()`, the form passed is instantiated on line 26 and has `is_valid()` called on line 27, meaning the `errors` and `cleaned_data` dictionaries will be available to the template. By contrast, the form passed via dictionary to the second call to `render()` is instantiated on line 36 and is unbound, providing neither the `errors` nor `cleaned_data`.

Although the two calls to `render()` fulfill different behaviors, the code is identical, and therefore it is possible to move and merge the two into a single call outside of the `if` condition. This leads us to the final version of our code, and what Django's documentation gives as the example for using forms in function views (but not CBVs!). The code in Example 9.15 is equivalent to the code in Example 9.14.

**Table 9.7: Form States with Typical Action**

| # | Method | Validity | Typical Action |
|---|--------|----------|----------------|
| 1 | GET | Invalid | Display unbound form in template |
| 2 | POST | Invalid | Display bound form in template |
| 3 | POST | Valid | Process and redirect |

**Example 9.15: Project Code**

`organizer/views.py` **in** 9723360390

```
24    def tag_create(request):
25        if request.method == 'POST':
26            form = TagForm(request.POST)
27            if form.is_valid():
28                new_tag = form.save()
29                return redirect(new_tag)
30        else:  # request.method != 'POST'
31            form = TagForm()
32        return render(
33            request,
34            'organizer/tag_form.html',
35            {'form': form})
```

*equiv to
@ 242*

The call to `render()` on lines 32 through 35 thus fulfills the behavior for two of the three expected states for our form. The form passed in may either be the unbound form now instantiated on line 31 or the bound form instantiated on line 26. In this last case, the bound form will always have errors.

The function view we have built is the way Django introduces form handling in views. It is common to see this code in other material and is well worth understanding. However, it is not my favored way of handling forms in views because of the multiple cases of implicit behavior and the way it handles HTTP methods. Before we can sort this all out, however, we should build a URL pattern for the view and make sure our code actually works.

### 9.2.2.2    Adding a URL Pattern and Hyperlink

Creating a URL pattern for our view is deceptively simple. In `/organizer/urls.py`, code the URL pattern shown in Example 9.16.

**Example 9.16: Project Code**

`organizer/urls.py` **in** cc75d1162f

```
 3    from .views import (
 4        startup_detail, startup_list, tag_create,
 5        tag_detail, tag_list)
 .        ...
 7    urlpatterns = [
 .        ...
17        url(r'^tag/create/$',
18            tag_create,
19            name='organizer_tag_create'),
 .        ...
23    ]
```

Consider, however, the URL pattern for the `organizer_tag_detail` URL pattern shown in Example 9.17.

**Example 9.17: Project Code**

`organizer/urls.py` in cc75d1162f

```
20      url(r'^tag/(?P<slug>[\w\-]+)/$',
21          tag_detail,
22          name='organizer_tag_detail'),
```

As discussed when building the form class in Chapter 8, the URL path `/tag/create/` will validly match the regular expression `r'^tag/(?P<slug>[\w\-]+)/$'` in the `organizer_tag_detail` URL pattern. Requesting `/tag/create/` causes a match conflict, and as such, we must give precedence to the `organizer_tag_create` URL pattern. The order of a URL configuration confers precedence over patterns, and as such, the order of the `organizer_tag_create` and `organizer_tag_detail` is important.

If the `organizer_tag_create` URL appears **after** `organizer_tag_detail`, then running the server and requesting `/tag/create/` will call the `tag_detail()` view instead of the `tag_create()` view. It will result in an HTTP 404 page informing us the "create" tag does not exist (switch the code to see for yourself!). The `organizer_tag_create` URL pattern thus becomes inaccessible.

The `organizer_tag_create` URL patterns must appear **before** the `organizer_tag_detail` URL pattern to work. The URL configuration is partially printed in Example 9.18.

**Example 9.18: Project Code**

`organizer/urls.py` in cc75d1162f

```
 3   from .views import (
 4       startup_detail, startup_list, tag_create,
 5       tag_detail, tag_list)
 .       ...
 7   urlpatterns = [                        reg'd order
 .       ...
17       url(r'^tag/create/$',                   1
18           tag_create,
19           name='organizer_tag_create'),
20       url(r'^tag/(?P<slug>[\w\-]+)/$',        2
21           tag_detail,
22           name='organizer_tag_detail'),
23   ]
```

Finally, we need to provide a link to our new webpage. In our `tag_list.html` template, we can use the `url` template tag to link to our form view, as shown in Example 9.19.

**Example 9.19: Project Code**

`organizer/templates/organizer/tag_list.html` **in** fa52634a9e

```
8     <h2>Tag List</h2>
9     <div>
10      <a href="{% url 'organizer_tag_create' %}">
11        Create New Tag</a>
12    </div>
```

### 9.2.2.3   Replacing `tag_create()` with `TagCreate`

Our `tag_create()` function view has become the quintessential beginner's view for
handling forms that create views, and it is code you will become familiar with as you spend
more time with Django.

In Chapter 5: Creating Webpages with Controllers in Django, Section 5.9, we switched
our view for listing `Post` objects from a function view to a CBV. We saw that a CBV is a
class that instantiates an object that acts as a view. The class has multiple methods that act as
views, each of which is intended to handle a different HTTP method.

By using a CBV to replace `tag_create()`, we gain all of the advantages we spoke of in
Chapter 5 (adherence to HTTP and the use of object-oriented programming), while also
making our code less implicit (my biggest gripe with our view at the moment).

Our object creation form views have three behaviors to account for, as relisted in
Table 9.8.

For convenience, the function view `tag_create()` we created based on Table 9.8 and
on Django's official documentation as shown in Example 9.20.

**Table 9.8: Form States**

| # | Method | Validity | Typical Action |
|---|--------|----------|----------------|
| 1 | GET    | Invalid  | Display unbound form in template |
| 2 | POST   | Invalid  | Display bound form in template |
| 3 | POST   | Valid    | Process and redirect |

**Example 9.20: Project Code**

`organizer/views.py` **in** cc75d1162f

```
24    def tag_create(request):
25        if request.method == 'POST':
26            form = TagForm(request.POST)
27            if form.is_valid():
28                new_tag = form.save()
29                return redirect(new_tag)
30        else:  # request.method != 'POST'
31            form = TagForm()
32        return render(
33            request,
34            'organizer/tag_form.html',
35            {'form': form})
```

The implicit behavior in Example 9.20 is as follows:

- The return of `render()` fulfills two behaviors (item 1 and 2 in Table 9.8).
- The HTTP POST method is handled separately, while all other methods are handled as if a GET method had been issued.

We could easily build a function view that does not have these issues, but I find that the organization structure of a CBV helps developers write explicit code, and is more helpful to beginners.

In Example 9.21, open `/organizer/views.py` and add a new class, `TagCreate`, with two attributes, and that inherits from `View`.

**Example 9.21: Project Code**

`organizer/views.py` **in** a30e354253

```
 3    from django.views.generic import View
 .        . . .
25    class TagCreate(View):
26        form_class = TagForm
27        template_name = 'organizer/tag_form.html'
```

The `form_class` is the form we will use to create and update this data. The `template_name` is the string pointing to the template we will load and render with our `form_class`.

Remember that, despite the import path, a CBV is *not* a generic class-based view. We will wait until Chapter 17: Understanding Generic Class-Based Views to discuss the difference in full.

In Table 9.8, our state machine dictates that we handle the GET and POST HTTP methods. We thus need to program the `get()` and `post()` methods of our class.

Our `get()` method is incredibly straightforward, as we only need to output an unbound form. We can use our `form_class` class attribute to instantiate an unbound form and then render it in our template (with a `RequestContext` for the `csrf_token`), as shown in Example 9.22.

**Example 9.22: Project Code**

`organizer/views.py` **in** a30e354253

```
25    class TagCreate(View):
26        form_class = TagForm
27        template_name = 'organizer/tag_form.html'
28
29        def get(self, request):
30            return render(
31                request,
32                self.template_name,
33                {'form': self.form_class()})
```

Our post() method needs to cover two behaviors:

1. If data is invalid, then we display a bound form with errors.

2. If data is valid, we create a new Tag and then redirect to its detail page.

Example 9.23 handles our POST request according to our state machine diagram.

**Example 9.23: Project Code**

organizer/views.py **in** a30e354253

```
25   class TagCreate(View):
26       form_class = TagForm
27       template_name = 'organizer/tag_form.html'
 .       ...
35       def post(self, request):
36           bound_form = self.form_class(request.POST)
37           if bound_form.is_valid():
38               new_tag = bound_form.save()
39               return redirect(new_tag)
40           else:
41               return render(
42                   request,
43                   self.template_name,
44                   {'form': bound_form})
```

In /organizer/urls.py, we can import our new view by adding it to our existing imports. We can then modify the organizer_tag_create URL pattern to read as shown in Example 9.24.

**Example 9.24: Project Code**

organizer/urls.py **in** a30e354253

```
3    from .views import (
4        TagCreate, startup_detail, startup_list,
5        tag_detail, tag_list)
6
7    urlpatterns = [
 .       ...
17       url(r'^tag/create/$',
18           TagCreate.as_view(),
19           name='organizer_tag_create'),
 .       ...
23   ]
```

Personally, this new code makes me quite happy: as there are three return statements, our adherence to the finite-state machine table is quite clear, making it easier for others to read and understand our code.

**Table 9.9:** View States

| # | Method | Validity | Typical Action |
|---|--------|----------|----------------|
| 1 | GET | Invalid | Display unbound form in template |
| 2 | POST | Invalid | Display bound form in template |
| 3 | POST | Valid | Process and redirect |

For the most part, our `TagCreate` CBV is a complete refactor of the `tag_create` function view. In theory, we have not added or changed behavior. Given our discussion of CBVs in Chapter 5, Section 5.9, you know that's not *quite* right.

CBVs are host to some implicit behavior. By design, a CBV handles *only* the HTTP verbs that are defined, providing an implementation of `options()` by default, as well as `head()` if `get()` is defined. In all other cases, the CBV issues an HTTP 405 error, informing the issuer of the request that the HTTP method is not allowed (i.e., it's not implemented or supported).

If a browser requests `/tag/create/` using GET or POST, `TagCreate` and `tag_create()` behave identically. However, if a browser requests the webpage using PUT or OPTIONS, then the two views behave differently. The function view behaves as if a GET method had been used, while `TagCreate` returns an HTTP 405 error.

To be crystal clear: `TagCreate` has behavior defined for HTTP requests using the HEAD, GET, POST, and OPTIONS methods. Every other method will raise an HTTP 405 error.

There is no question that we could build a function view to behave exactly as `TagCreate` does, but I find that it takes more effort in the long run. What's more, because CBVs organize HTTP methods according to class method, I find the use of CBVs for interacting with Django forms to be ideal. In the rest of the chapter, we default to using CBVs for our form handling.

### 9.2.3 Creating `Post` Objects in a View with `PostForm`

Let's use our view for creating `Post` objects to review what we learned in the last section.

Our `PostCreate` will implement `get()` to handle state one of Table 9.9, a reprint of our finite-state machine for views that create objects using Django forms. States 2 and 3 will be handled by the `post()` method.

As in `TagCreate`, we use class attributes to keep elements used in both views easily accessible in a single place, as shown in Example 9.25.

**Example 9.25: Project Code**
`blog/views.py` in `639cc39b30`

```
1   from django.shortcuts import (
2       get_object_or_404, redirect, render)
.       ...
7   from .forms import PostForm
.       ...
```

```
11   class PostCreate(View):
12       form_class = PostForm
13       template_name = 'blog/post_form.html'
14
15       def get(self, request):
16           return render(
17               request,
18               self.template_name,
19               {'form': self.form_class()})
20
21       def post(self, request):
22           bound_form = self.form_class(request.POST)
23           if bound_form.is_valid():
24               new_post = bound_form.save()
25               return redirect(new_post)
26           else:
27               return render(
28                   request,
29                   self.template_name,
30                   {'form': bound_form})
```

The URL pattern to point Django to our view, as with any CBV, makes use of the as_view() class method, shown in Example 9.26.

**Example 9.26: Project Code**
blog/urls.py **in** 639cc39b30

```
 3   from .views import (
 4       PostCreate, PostList, post_detail)
 .       ...
10   url(r'^create/$',
11       PostCreate.as_view(),
12       name='blog_post_create'),
```

Finally, in Example 9.27, we can link to our new webpage form the list of Post objects webpage.

**Example 9.27: Project Code**
blog/templates/blog/post_list.html **in** 2bbba65237

```
 8           <div>
 9               <a href="{% url 'blog_post_create' %}">
10                   Write New Blog Post</a>
11           </div>
```

### 9.2.4  Creating `Startup` Objects in a View with `StartupForm`

It should come as no surprise that the views to interact with `StartupForm` and
`NewsLinkForm` to create new objects will be almost identical to `TagCreate` or
`PostCreate`.

For `StartupCreate`, as you can see in Example 9.28, the only differences are these:

1. The value of the class attribute `template_name`

2. The value of the class attribute `form_class`

**Example 9.28: Project Code**

`organizer/views.py` in 59bb59cf69

```
 5    from .forms import StartupForm, TagForm
 .        ...
 9    class StartupCreate(View):
10        form_class = StartupForm
11        template_name = 'organizer/startup_form.html'
12
13        def get(self, request):
14            return render(
15                request,
16                self.template_name,
17                {'form': self.form_class()})
18
19        def post(self, request):
20            bound_form = self.form_class(request.POST)
21            if bound_form.is_valid():
22                new_startup = bound_form.save()
23                return redirect(new_startup)
24            else:
25                return render(
26                    request,
27                    self.template_name,
28                    {'form': bound_form})
```

The URL for our view should look and feel really boring at this point, as shown in
Example 9.29.

**Example 9.29: Project Code**

`organizer/urls.py` in 59bb59cf69

```
 3    from .views import (
 4        StartupCreate, TagCreate, startup_detail,
 5        startup_list, tag_detail, tag_list)
 .        ...
```

```
 7   urlpatterns = [
 .      ...
11       url(r'^startup/create/$',
12           StartupCreate.as_view(),
13           name='organizer_startup_create'),
 .      ...
26   ]
```

Even the link is run of the mill, as you can see in Example 9.30.

**Example 9.30: Project Code**

`organizer/templates/organizer/startup_list.html` **in** 19b4cdad76

```
 9       <div>
10         <a href="{% url 'organizer_startup_create' %}">
11           Create New Startup</a>
12       </div>
```

Let's get our `NewsLinkCreate` view programmed and then take another look at this.

## 9.2.5  Creating `NewsLink` Objects in a View with `NewsLinkForm`

In most respects, `NewsLinkCreate` is identical to our other object creation views. However, the `post()` method in `NewsLinkCreate` comes with an interesting quirk. Ignoring the difference in variable names (`new_newslink` instead of `new_startup`), we find ourselves unable to use `redirect()` in the same way as we previously did. That makes sense: Django convention only allows for this behavior because a model has a `get_absolute_url()` method. The problem is that our `NewsLink` class doesn't! We could circumvent by redirecting to the page the `NewsLink` is displayed at: the `Startup` page, causing Django to call the `get_absolute_url()` method of the `Startup` object pointed to by our new `NewsLink` object. We do so in Example 9.31.

**Example 9.31: Project Code**

`organizer/views.py` **in** 3e4f9be0f5

```
 5   from .forms import (
 6       NewsLinkForm, StartupForm, TagForm)
 .      ...
10   class NewsLinkCreate(View):
11       form_class = NewsLinkForm
12       template_name = 'organizer/newslink_form.html'
```

```
13
14      def get(self, request):
15          return render(
16              request,
17              self.template_name,
18              {'form': self.form_class()})
19
20      def post(self, request):
21          bound_form = self.form_class(request.POST)
22          if bound_form.is_valid():
23              new_newslink = bound_form.save()
24              return redirect(new_newslink.startup)
25          else:
26              return render(
27                  request,
28                  self.template_name,
29                  {'form': bound_form})
```

That's functional but not great. It's far easier, as shown in Example 9.32, to simply define get_absolute_url() on NewsLink (and, in fact, all our models) and not have to worry about details like this.

**Example 9.32: Project Code**
organizer/models.py **in** a32e2298de

```
54    class NewsLink(models.Model):
  .       ...
69        def get_absolute_url(self):
70            return self.startup.get_absolute_url()
```

As Example 9.33 shows, this allows us to change our redirect to the simplest option available, and to maintain the idea of fat models.

**Example 9.33: Project Code**
organizer/views.py **in** a32e2298de

```
10    class NewsLinkCreate(View):
  .       ...
20        def post(self, request):
  .           ...
22            if bound_form.is_valid():
  .               ...
24                return redirect(new_newslink)
```

As before, we then create a URL pattern for our new view using as_view(), as shown in Example 9.34.

**Example 9.34: Project Code**

`organizer/urls.py` **in** `3e4f9be0f5`

```
 3   from .views import (
 4       NewsLinkCreate, StartupCreate, TagCreate,
 5       startup_detail, startup_list, tag_detail,
 6       tag_list)
 .       ...
 8   urlpatterns = [
 9       url(r'^newslink/create/$',
10           NewsLinkCreate.as_view(),
11           name='organizer_newslink_create'),
```

We then link to the new page, this time from our startup detail page, as shown in Example 9.35.

**Example 9.35: Project Code**

`organizer/templates/organizer/startup_detail.html` **in** `c2d119723b`

```
33                      <p>
34                          <a href="{% url 'organizer_newslink_create' %}">
35                          Add Article</a></p>
```

## 9.2.6   Shortening Organizer Views

At this point, the last four views we have programmed are virtually identical. Your DRY Pavlov response should be through the roof. It's time to refactor!

In this section, we create a class mixin for `TagCreate`, `StartupCreate`, and `NewsLinkCreate`. We won't integrate this mixin with `PostCreate` because we want to maintain app encapsulation. If this bothers you, I'll let you in on a secret: the content of Chapter 17 will allow us to remove *all* of this code.

Recall from Chapter 7 that a **class mixin** is an abstract class that is intended to simply provide behavior to other classes and is never meant to be instantiated itself. The use of this mixin class comes with an important, desirable caveat. The class we are about to create is a simple Python class that *does not inherit from View*. We cannot use the mixin as a CBV and therefore cannot use it in a URL pattern. This caveat is desirable: it means that other developers cannot accidentally use it in a webpage (what's more, having the word `Mixin` at the end of the class helps clarify this). We therefore create a new file, `organizer/utils.py`, to store the mixin class, as it's not a view and does not belong in `organizer/views.py`.

Our `ObjectCreateMixin` will thus provide the core behavior of each of our views. It's really easy: we just need to copy and paste the `get()` and `post()` methods from any class, and then rename the variable in `post()` to `new_object` (instead of `new_tag` or `new_startup`), as in Example 9.36.

**Example 9.36: Project Code**

organizer/utils.py **in** 453d154264

```
1   from django.shortcuts import redirect, render
2
3
4   class ObjectCreateMixin:
5       form_class = None
6       template_name = ''
7
8       def get(self, request):
9           return render(
10              request,
11              self.template_name,
12              {'form': self.form_class()})
13
14      def post(self, request):
15          bound_form = self.form_class(request.POST)
16          if bound_form.is_valid():
17              new_object = bound_form.save()
18              return redirect(new_object)
19          else:
20              return render(
21                  request,
22                  self.template_name,
23                  {'form': bound_form})
```

With our get() and post() methods removed from all our CBVs, we need to inherit the ObjectCreateMixin class. We keep the template_name and form_class attribute to override the empty values in ObjectCreate, as in Example 9.37. If the advantage to these attributes was not clear originally, hopefully it is now.

**Example 9.37: Project Code**

organizer/views.py **in** 4048860156

```
8   from .utils import ObjectCreateMixin
    . . .
11  class NewsLinkCreate(ObjectCreateMixin, View):      # Mixin must be first
12      form_class = NewsLinkForm                        # so this code applies
13      template_name = 'organizer/newslink_form.html'   #
    . . .
16  class StartupCreate(ObjectCreateMixin, View):
17      form_class = StartupForm
18      template_name = 'organizer/startup_form.html'
    . . .
37  class TagCreate(ObjectCreateMixin, View):
38      form_class = TagForm
39      template_name = 'organizer/tag_form.html'
```

Our organizer app now has three CBVs for creating objects and a mixin class. We have drastically shortened our code with little effort, making effective use of the fact that our views are class-based rather than functions. Note that our URL patterns, and in turn our links, do not need to change at all.

Some very astute readers may point out that we could keep going. Instead of using a mixin, we could use a single CBV and pass the class attributes as key-word arguments to `as_view()`, a feature we saw in Chapter 5, Section 5.9.2. These readers are right, but doing so here is a rabbit hole that we will wait until Chapter 17 to jump down.

For the moment, we turn our attention to views that modify objects and views that delete objects.

## 9.3   Webpages for Updating Objects

The behavior in a view that updates an object is very similar to that of a view that creates an object. In fact, the only difference is that the instance of the model class must already exist and be saved in the database.

The implication is that we will need to identify this object. While the URL patterns for views that created objects were not important, we now have to focus on the URL patterns, as this is how the user will identify the data. In many ways, views for updating objects are a combination of detail views and object creation views.

The state machine for view is only subtly modified, as listed in Table 9.10.

In Chapter 7, Section 7.3.9, we saw that we could pass an instance to a form, giving it knowledge of that object, as shown in Example 9.38.

In Chapter 8: Displaying Forms in Templates, Section 8.3, we saw that the effect of passing an instance to a form was principally on the HTML code that the form would output, as shown in Example 9.39.

**Table 9.10: View States for Updating Objects**

| # | Method | Validity | Typical Action |
|---|--------|----------|----------------|
| 1 | GET | Invalid | Display form in template with instance data |
| 2 | POST | Invalid | Display form in template with instance and errors |
| 3 | POST | Valid | Process and redirect |

**Example 9.38: Python Interpreter Code**

```
>>> django_tag = Tag.objects.get(slug='django')
>>> form = TagForm(instance=django_tag)
>>> form.is_bound
False
```

**Example 9.39: HTML Code**

```html
<p>
  <label for="id_name">Name:</label>
  <input
      id="id_name"
      maxlength="31"
      name="name"
      type="text"
      value="django" />
</p>
<p>
  <label for="id_slug">Slug:</label>
  <input
      id="id_slug"
      maxlength="31"
      name="slug"
      type="text"
      value="django" />
  <span class="helptext">A label for URL config.</span>
</p>
```

The use of the `instance` attribute is crucial to allowing our view to update an object. The key differences between a view that updates and a view that creates are as follows:

- The URL pattern for an object update view must identify an object (via `slug` or other).
- The view must fetch that object from the database, and pass the object as the `instance` attribute to the form, regardless of whether the form is unbound or bound (thus affecting both `get()` and `post()`).

## 9.3.1 Creating a View to Modify `Post` Objects

To uniquely identify a `Post`, we need a year, a month, and a slug. However, if we simply identify the object, we will be in conflict with our `blog_post_detail` URL pattern. We need to differentiate our new `blog_post_update` URL from `blog_post_detail`, so we append the `/update/` path segment to the regular expression pattern, anticipating the creation of `PostUpdate`, as shown in Example 9.40.

**Example 9.40: Project Code**
`blog/urls.py` **in** `3fc0ec56de`

```
3    from .views import (
4        PostCreate, PostList, PostUpdate, post_detail)
.        ...
6    urlpatterns = [
.        ...
18       url(r'^(?P<year>\d{4})/'
19           r'(?P<month>\d{1,2})/'
20           r'(?P<slug>[\w\-]+)/'
```

```
21            r'update/$',
22            PostUpdate.as_view(),
23            name='blog_post_update'),
24    ]
```

If we look ahead for a moment, we can see that we won't ever want to use the url template tag with blog_post_update, for exactly the same reasons we don't want to use url with the blog_post_detail URL pattern: it's long and prone to typos. Instead, we can define a new method on our model class to provide the URL reversal for us on each object, as shown in Example 9.41.

**Example 9.41: Project Code**
blog/models.py **in** 3fc0ec56de

```
11   class Post(models.Model):
.        ...
43       def get_update_url(self):
44           return reverse(
45               'blog_post_update',
46               kwargs={'year': self.pub_date.year,
47                       'month': self.pub_date.month,
48                       'slug': self.slug})
```

Note that while get_absolute_url() is a method that Django looks for by convention, get_update_url() is not. It is our invention, but helpful nonetheless.

In blog/views.py, we can start by creating a new CBV called PostUpdate, as shown in Example 9.42.

**Example 9.42: Project Code**
blog/views.py **in** 3fc0ec56de

```
55   class PostUpdate(View):
56       form_class = PostForm
57       model = Post
58       template_name = 'blog/post_form_update.html'
```

The form_class and template_name attributes serve the same purpose as the views earlier in this chapter. The new model attribute tells us which model class to use to find the instance data we are updating.

We have a three-state machine that we implement in get() and post() methods of our CBV. In both cases, we need to fetch the Post object that we are updating. In get(), we will display PostForm with the Post instance. In post(), we will validate the data submitted by the user thanks to PostForm. In the event the data is invalid, we will redisplay the form, combining the data the user submitted with the instance data from the database. In the event the data is valid, we update the Post object by calling save() on the form.

Our get() method is thus incredibly similar to the get() methods for our object creation views. The sole difference is the code at the very beginning, which finds the instance we are updating and then passes that instance to our form, as shown in Example 9.43.

**Example 9.43: Project Code**
blog/views.py in 3fc0ec56de

```
55    class PostUpdate(View):
56        form_class = PostForm
57        model = Post
58        template_name = 'blog/post_form_update.html'
59
60        def get(self, request, year, month, slug):
61            post = get_object_or_404(
62                self.model,
63                pub_date__year=year,
64                pub_date__month=month,
65                slug=slug)
66            context = {
67                'form': self.form_class(
68                    instance=post),
69                'post': post,
70            }
71            return render(
72                request, self.template_name, context)
```

Our post() method sees a very similar modification. We must first find the object we are updating and then pass it as the instance attribute to the form, this time along with any data the user has submitted, as shown in Example 9.44. The rest of it is exactly like the object creation views.

**Example 9.44: Project Code**
blog/views.py in 3fc0ec56de

```
55    class PostUpdate(View):
56        form_class = PostForm
57        model = Post
58        template_name = 'blog/post_form_update.html'
.         ...
74        def post(self, request, year, month, slug):
75            post = get_object_or_404(
76                self.model,
77                pub_date__year=year,
78                pub_date__month=month,
79                slug=slug)
80            bound_form = self.form_class(
81                request.POST, instance=post)
82            if bound_form.is_valid():
83                new_post = bound_form.save()
84                return redirect(new_post)
```

```
85              else:
86                  context = {
87                      'form': bound_form,
88                      'post': post,
89                  }
90                  return render(
91                      request,
92                      self.template_name,
93                      context)
```

By design, the beginning of the get() and post() methods are identical. I originally programmed it this way to make the previous two examples as clear as possible. However, we don't want to keep duplicate code like that around. While CBVs anticipate the implementation of methods according to the names of HTTP methods, there is nothing stopping us from defining our own methods. As such, we split the object-fetching code into it's own method, called get_object(), as shown in Example 9.45.

**Example 9.45: Project Code**

`blog/views.py` **in** 59bf691794

```
55  class PostUpdate(View):
56      form_class = PostForm
57      model = Post
58      template_name = 'blog/post_form_update.html'
59
60      def get_object(self, year, month, slug):
61          return get_object_or_404(
62              self.model,
63              pub_date__year=year,
64              pub_date__month=month,
65              slug=slug)
```

This technique allows both get() and post() to call much simpler code, as shown in Example 9.46.

**Example 9.46: Project Code**

`blog/views.py` **in** 59bf691794

```
55  class PostUpdate(View):
56      form_class = PostForm
57      model = Post
58      template_name = 'blog/post_form_update.html'
    .   ...
67      def get(self, request, year, month, slug):
68          post = self.get_object(year, month, slug)
    .   ...
77      def post(self, request, year, month, slug):
78          post = self.get_object(year, month, slug)
```

Finally, we can turn to our templates and link to our new webpage using our new model method. We do this first in our `post_detail.html` template, as shown in Example 9.47.

**Example 9.47: Project Code**

`blog/templates/blog/post_detail.html` in d810a0cf51

```
12      <ul>
13       <li>
14        <a href="{{ post.get_update_url }}">
15          Edit Post</a></li>
16       </ul>
```

For usability purposes, we also add a link from the `post_list.html` template, as shown in Example 9.48.

**Example 9.48: Project Code**

`blog/templates/blog/post_list.html` in 60fe18085c

```
19          <ul>
20           <li>
21            <a href="{{ post.get_update_url }}">
22              Edit Post</a></li>
23           </ul>
```

## 9.3.2 Creating a View to Modify `NewsLink` Objects

In Chapter 3: Programming Django Models and Creating a SQLite Database, I mentioned that we would regret not adding a `slug` to our `NewsLink` model class. That time is now.

When we built the model, we (pretended that we) had only considered the fact that we were displaying news on the startup's page, meaning we didn't need a slug for the URL. The problem we are faced with now is that we need to identify `NewsLink` objects in the URL, and we don't have a good way to do it.

The purpose of this exercise is to provide an example of using the primary key of an object to identify it. The URL pattern and view we use makes use of the `id` column in the database, aliased as `pk` in Django's object-relational mapping (ORM), to identify each `NewsLink` object. This will also allow for us to dive into the topic of migrations in Chapter 10: Revisiting Migrations.

In our new `organizer_newslink_update` URL pattern, we mirror the regular expression pattern for `organizer_newslink_create`, changing the `create` to `update` and adding a character set after that to match the primary key digits, as shown in Example 9.49.

**Example 9.49: Project Code**

`organizer/urls.py` **in** `17264da6ff`

```
 8   urlpatterns = [
 9       url(r'^newslink/create/$',
10           NewsLinkCreate.as_view(),
11           name='organizer_newslink_create'),
12       url(r'^newslink/update/(?P<pk>\d+)/$',
13           NewsLinkUpdate.as_view(),
14           name='organizer_newslink_update'),
 .       ...
33   ]
```

Following DRY, we opt to create a `get_update_url()` method on the `Post` model to make reversing object URLs as painless as possible, as shown in Example 9.50.

**Example 9.50: Project Code**

`organizer/models.py` **in** `17264da6ff`

```
54   class NewsLink(models.Model):
 .       ...
72       def get_update_url(self):
73           return reverse(
74               'organizer_newslink_update',
75               kwargs={'pk': self.pk})
```

The process for building `NewsLinkUpdate` is the same as for `PostUpdate`. We implement `get()` and `post()` similarly to an object create view, adding code at the beginning to fetch the `NewsLink` we are changing and making sure to pass it to our `NewsLinkForm` as the `instance` attribute.

For `PostUpdate`, we opted to define three attributes. Given that these choices are entirely at our discretion, to mix things up a bit I use only the `form_class` and `template_name` attributes in `NewsLinkUpdate`, as shown in Example 9.51.

**Example 9.51: Project Code**

`organizer/views.py` **in** `17264da6ff`

```
16   class NewsLinkUpdate(View):
17       form_class = NewsLinkForm
18       template_name = (
19           'organizer/newslink_form_update.html')
```

There's also no real need for `get_object()` method, as the call to `get_object_or_404()` is quite short, as shown in Example 9.52.

**Example 9.52: Project Code**

`organizer/views.py` in `17264da6ff`

```
16    class NewsLinkUpdate(View):
17        form_class = NewsLinkForm
18        template_name = (
19            'organizer/newslink_form_update.html')
20
21        def get(self, request, pk):
22            newslink = get_object_or_404(
23                NewsLink, pk=pk)
24            context = {
25                'form': self.form_class(
26                    instance=newslink),
27                'newslink': newslink,
28            }
29            return render(
30                request, self.template_name, context)
```

The implementation of `post()`, with understanding of the new requirements for update behavior, is similarly straightforward, as shown in Example 9.53.

**Example 9.53: Project Code**

`organizer/views.py` in `17264da6ff`

```
16    class NewsLinkUpdate(View):
17        form_class = NewsLinkForm
18        template_name = (
19            'organizer/newslink_form_update.html')
  .       ...
32        def post(self, request, pk):
33            newslink = get_object_or_404(
34                NewsLink, pk=pk)
35            bound_form = self.form_class(
36                request.POST, instance=newslink)
37            if bound_form.is_valid():
38                new_newslink = bound_form.save()
39                return redirect(new_newslink)
40            else:
41                context = {
42                    'form': bound_form,
43                    'newslink': newslink,
44                }
45                return render(
46                    request,
47                    self.template_name,
48                    context)
```

In the case of `NewsLink` objects, we have only a single place to add a link to our new form update webpage: the startup detail webpage, where associated news is displayed, as shown in Example 9.54.

**Example 9.54: Project Code**

`organizer/templates/organizer/startup_detail.html` **in** abe3ab5a91

```
41                       <ul>
42                           <li>
43                               <a href="{{ newslink.get_update_url }}">
44                                   Edit Link</a></li>
45                       </ul>
```

### 9.3.3   Webpages to Update `Startup` and `Tag` Objects

We could build `StartupUpdate` and `TagUpdate` independently of each other, but if we did, we'd find that they are nearly identical. Objects of both classes are identified in views by `SlugField` values, meaning that the arguments passed and the functions called internally will be identical. Similar to our `ObjectCreateMixin` seen earlier in this chapter, we now build a class called `ObjectUpdateMixin` to provide both `StartupUpdate` and `TagUpdate` with their behavior.

As we did for `ObjectCreateMixin`, we define the new mixin class in the `organizer/utils.py` file.

We can anticipate the needs of our class, creating the `form_class`, `model`, and `template_name` attributes we've previously used, as shown in Example 9.55.

**Example 9.55: Project Code**

`organizer/utils.py` **in** d87fc101f2

```
 1   from django.shortcuts import (
 2       get_object_or_404, redirect, render)
 .       ...
27   class ObjectUpdateMixin:
28       form_class = None
29       model = None
30       template_name = ''
```

Our `get()` method uses the `slug` value passed to it from the URL pattern to fetch the object we're updating, passing that object as the `instance` attribute, and then displaying the unbound form with the instance data in our template, as shown in Example 9.56.

**Example 9.56: Project Code**

`organizer/utils.py` **in** d87fc101f2

```
27   class ObjectUpdateMixin:
28       form_class = None
29       model = None
30       template_name = ''
31
32       def get(self, request, slug):
33           obj = get_object_or_404(
34               self.model, slug__iexact=slug)
```

```
35          context = {
36              'form': self.form_class(instance=obj),
37              self.model.__name__.lower(): obj,
38          }
39          return render(
40              request, self.template_name, context)
```

The post() method also uses the slug value to fetch the object and configure the form defined in the form_class attribute. As do all of our form views so far, it then checks to see if the data submitted by the user is valid and acts accordingly, as shown in Example 9.57.

**Example 9.57: Project Code**
organizer/utils.py in d87fc101f2

```
27  class ObjectUpdateMixin:
28      form_class = None
29      model = None
30      template_name = ''
    ...
42      def post(self, request, slug):
43          obj = get_object_or_404(
44              self.model, slug__iexact=slug)
45          bound_form = self.form_class(
46              request.POST, instance=obj)
47          if bound_form.is_valid():
48              new_object = bound_form.save()
49              return redirect(new_object)
50          else:
51              context = {
52                  'form': bound_form,
53                  self.model.__name__.lower(): obj,
54              }
55              return render(
56                  request,
57                  self.template_name,
58                  context)
```

### 9.3.3.1 Updating Tag Objects in a View with TagForm

To use the mixin to create a webpage for updating Tag objects, we start with the URL pattern: identical to organizer_tag_detail with the /update/ path segment appended, as shown in Example 9.58.

**Example 9.58: Project Code**
organizer/urls.py in 980c97c8e6

```
33      url(r'^tag/(?P<slug>[\w\-]+)/update/$',
34          TagUpdate.as_view(),
35          name='organizer_tag_update'),
```

We immediately take the opportunity to implement get_update_url(), as shown in Example 9.59.

**Example 9.59: Project Code**
organizer/models.py **in** 980c97c8e6

```
 9   class Tag(models.Model):
 .       ...
27       def get_update_url(self):
28           return reverse('organizer_tag_update',
29                           kwargs={'slug': self.slug})
```

The actual implementation of TagUpdate, thanks to ObjectUpdateMixin, is simply a question of overriding the right class attributes, as shown in Example 9.60.

**Example 9.60: Project Code**
organizer/views.py **in** 980c97c8e6

```
 8   from .utils import (
 9       ObjectCreateMixin, ObjectUpdateMixin)
 .       ...
94   class TagUpdate(ObjectUpdateMixin, View):
95       form_class = TagForm
96       model = Tag
97       template_name = (
98           'organizer/tag_form_update.html')
```

### 9.3.3.2   Updating Startup Objects in a View with StartupForm

The process for using ObjectUpdateMixin to help implement StartupUpdate is identical to TagUpdate's process. Before following along with the book, see if you can mimic the process yourself!

Start with the URL pattern, mimicking organizer_startup_detail but differentiating between the two by appending /update/, as shown in Example 9.61.

**Example 9.61: Project Code**
organizer/urls.py **in** 5b9d4bfeb4

```
25       url(r'^startup/(?P<slug>[\w\-]+)/update/$',
26           StartupUpdate.as_view(),
27           name='organizer_startup_update'),
```

Don't forget to implement get_update_url(), as shown in Example 9.62, to make all future linking easier.

**Example 9.62: Project Code**

`organizer/models.py` **in** 5b9d4bfeb4

```
32   class Startup(models.Model):
 .      ...
57       def get_update_url(self):
58           return reverse('organizer_startup_update',
59                         kwargs={'slug': self.slug})
```

As you can see in Example 9.63, the view code is the easiest part, thanks to our mixin.

**Example 9.63: Project Code**

`organizer/views.py` **in** 5b9d4bfeb4

```
73   class StartupUpdate(ObjectUpdateMixin, View):
74       form_class = StartupForm
75       model = Startup
76       template_name = (
77           'organizer/startup_form_update.html')
```

### 9.3.3.3 Adding Links for `TagUpdate` and `StartupUpdate`

Our new webpages won't be accessible if we don't link to them. Thanks to `get_update_url()` on both models, creating links is trivial.

In both cases, we want to be able to update an object directly from the detail page of that object. Example 9.64 shows the code to link to `organizer_tag_update` from `tag_detail.html`.

**Example 9.64: Project Code**

`organizer/templates/organizer/tag_detail.html` **in** 43ae84a609

```
 9       <ul>
10         <li>
11           <a href="{{ tag.get_update_url }}">
12             Edit Tag</a></li>
13       </ul>
```

The code in Example 9.65 links `organizer_startup_update` from `startup_detail.html`.

**Example 9.65: Project Code**

`organizer/templates/organizer/startup_detail.html` **in** 58b5ee384e

```
11       <ul>
12         <li>
13           <a href="{{ startup.get_update_url }}">
14             Edit Startup</a></li>
15       </ul>
```

This is a great start, but it's also nice to be able to jump directly to editing an object from a list view. In Example 9.66, therefore, we add a link to `organizer_tag_update` in `tag_list.html`.

**Example 9.66: Project Code**
`organizer/templates/organizer/tag_list.html` **in** 9ebe8ae7e1

```
18            <ul>
19              <li>
20                <a href="{{ tag.get_update_url }}">
21                  Edit Tag</a></li>
22            </ul>
```

We mimic this in `startup_list.html`, using the startup's `get_update_url()` method to point to `organizer_startup_update`, as shown in Example 9.67.

**Example 9.67: Project Code**
`organizer/templates/organizer/startup_list.html` **in** 2023a756d9

```
18            <ul>
19                <li>
20                  <a href="{{ startup.get_update_url }}">
21                    Edit Startup</a></li>
22            </ul>
```

# 9.4    Webpages for Deleting Objects

To delete an object, we need to identify it. That's it. There's no data validation, and no need for a form. Our webpages are thus much simpler and won't use any of the forms we programmed in Chapter 7.

Our webpages to delete objects implement a two-step process. When the user requests the webpage (via the HTTP GET method), identifying the object via the URL, we first prompt the user to confirm his or her desire to delete the object. This HTML form then requests the page again, this time using the HTTP POST method, causing our view to delete the object. Our state machine for our view is printed in Table. 9.11.

It's worth being security minded here. Have we just opened up our website to attack? (The answer is yes, as we won't implement authentication until Chapter 19: Basic Authentication, but barring that. . . ) What happens if a user or a robot begins issuing POST requests to all of our webpages? Can the user or robot delete all of the data on the website?

It will be impossible for users to avoid the first step—the GET request—because the cross-site request forgery (CSRF) token is required by Django for any POST request. If a user were to issue a POST request to the webpage without a CSRF request, Django would simply refuse to comply. This ensures that the user is submitting the POST request after having already visited the page Django displays after the GET request. Without authentication, we're still vulnerable, even with this step in place, but it's a start.

**Table 9.11:** View States for Deleting Objects

| # | Method | Action |
|---|--------|--------|
| 1 | GET | Confirm deletion ("Are you sure?") |
| 2 | POST | Delete object |

Much like the process for our update views, the process for building these webpages involves focus on the URL pattern for each view, as we must identify each object to be able to delete.

## 9.4.1 Creating a Webpage to Delete `Post` Objects

Much like `blog_post_update`, our `blog_post_delete` will replicate the path segment used to identify `Post` objects found in `blog_post_detail`. However, to differentiate `blog_post_delete` from either `blog_post_detail` or `blog_post_detail`, our new URL pattern will append the `/delete/` path segment to our regular expression pattern, as shown in Example 9.68.

**Example 9.68: Project Code**
`blog/urls.py` in 459a101fa0

```
19        url(r'^(?P<year>\d{4})/'
20            r'(?P<month>\d{1,2})/'
21            r'(?P<slug>[\w\-]+)/'
22            r'delete/$',
23            PostDelete.as_view(),
24            name='blog_post_delete'),
```

Much like with the update URLs, it is in our interest to build a method on our models to reverse the URL pattern in a single place, shortening any future work we might need to do, as shown in Example 9.69.

**Example 9.69: Project Code**
`blog/models.py` in 459a101fa0

```
11    class Post(models.Model):
 .        ...
43        def get_delete_url(self):
44            return reverse(
45                'blog_post_delete',
46                kwargs={'year': self.pub_date.year,
47                        'month': self.pub_date.month,
48                        'slug': self.slug})
```

As you can see in Example 9.70, the definition of our `PostDelete` class is simple: we declare a class that inherits `View`. No attributes required.

**Example 9.70: Project Code**
blog/views.py **in** 459a101fa0

```
33   class PostDelete(View):
```

The implementation of get() is simply the implementation of get() on PostDetail, but with a different template, as shown in Example 9.71.

**Example 9.71: Project Code**
blog/views.py **in** 459a101fa0

```
33   class PostDelete(View):
34
35       def get(self, request, year, month, slug):
36           post = get_object_or_404(
37               Post,
38               pub_date__year=year,
39               pub_date__month=month,
40               slug__iexact=slug)
41           return render(
42               request,
43               'blog/post_confirm_delete.html',
44               {'post': post})
```

We could shorten this code or use inheritance to combine behavior from PostDetail and PostDelete (and even PostUpdate), but this won't be worth it in the long run (foreshadowing for Chapter 17).

The implementation of post() is also terribly simple, as you can see in Example 9.72. We identify and fetch the Post in question, and if we find it, we delete it. We then redirect to the list of blog posts.

**Example 9.72: Project Code**
blog/views.py **in** 459a101fa0

```
33   class PostDelete(View):
     ...
46       def post(self, request, year, month, slug):
47           post = get_object_or_404(
48               Post,
49               pub_date__year=year,
50               pub_date__month=month,
51               slug__iexact=slug)
52           post.delete()
53           return redirect('blog_post_list')
```

You'll note that we haven't touched the CSRF token. Django handles this for us: if the POST request is issued without a proper token (i.e., one generated by Django and presented to the user in the form in our tag_delete.html template), then Django automatically errors, returning a 403 error code response to the user.

Certain that our code is safe, we can add links to our new webpage. We can first call get_delete_url() on our Post object in the post_detail.html, as shown in Example 9.73.

**Example 9.73: Project Code**

blog/templates/blog/post_detail.html in 23397f50d5

```
16          <li>
17            <a href="{{ post.get_delete_url }}">
18              Delete Post</a></li>
```

We also add a link in post_list.html so that users looking at the list can take immediate action rather than clicking through to the detail page first, as shown in Example 9.74.

**Example 9.74: Project Code**

blog/templates/blog/post_list.html in 5e8f967d97

```
23                  <li>
24                    <a href="{{ post.get_delete_url }}">
25                      Delete Post</a></li>
```

### 9.4.2  Creating a Webpage to Delete `NewsLink` Objects

Our NewsLinkDelete view suffers from the same quirk that our NewsLinkUpdate view does. Because we don't have a URL-safe string unique identifier for NewsLink objects, we are forced to use the primary key of the row in the database, contrary to the principle of readable URLs. We sort this all out in Chapter 10, but for the moment, we build a rather unfriendly URL pattern, as shown in Example 9.75.

**Example 9.75: Project Code**

organizer/urls.py in cd1e78c2bd

```
13      url(r'^newslink/delete/(?P<pk>\d+)/$',
14          NewsLinkDelete.as_view(),
15          name='organizer_newslink_delete'),
```

Even without a unique identifier, we still take the opportunity to define a get_delete_url() method, allowing for reversal of the new URL pattern, as shown in Example 9.76.

**Example 9.76: Project Code**

organizer/models.py in cd1e78c2bd

```
62    class NewsLink(models.Model):
  .         ...
80        def get_delete_url(self):
81            return reverse(
82                'organizer_newslink_delete',
83                kwargs={'pk': self.pk})
```

We can then turn our attention to the view itself.

If it weren't for the actual signature of the methods, we would largely be able to reuse the code from `PostDelete`. As shown in Example 9.77, the `get()` method finds the object and then displays a template with an HTML form to prompt the user (we built this template in Chapter 8).

**Example 9.77: Project Code**
`organizer/views.py` in cd1e78c2bd

```
17    class NewsLinkDelete(View):
18
19        def get(self, request, pk):
20            newslink = get_object_or_404(
21                NewsLink, pk=pk)
22            return render(
23                request,
24                'organizer/'
25                'newslink_confirm_delete.html',
26                {'newslink': newslink})
```

The `post()` method finds the object and then remembers which startup the news link is associated with, as shown in Example 9.78. This allows us to first delete the object and then redirect to the page that had been displaying the news link.

**Example 9.78: Project Code**
`organizer/views.py` in cd1e78c2bd

```
17    class NewsLinkDelete(View):
 .        ...
28        def post(self, request, pk):
29            newslink = get_object_or_404(
30                NewsLink, pk=pk)
31            startup = newslink.startup
32            newslink.delete()
33            return redirect(startup)
```

We can finish by linking to our new webpage from the `startup_detail.html` template, as shown in Example 9.79.

**Example 9.79: Project Code**
`organizer/templates/organizer/startup_detail.html` in 118db89c56

```
50                    <li>
51                        <a href="{{ newslink.get_delete_url }}">
52                        Delete Link</a></li>
```

### 9.4.3  Webpages to Delete `Startup` and `Tag` Objects

We implemented `ObjectCreateMixin` and `ObjectUpdatedMixin`. It should come as no surprise that we're about to implement `ObjectDeleteMixin` (also in `organizer/utils.py`).

Whereas implementing `ObjectCreateMixin` and `ObjectUpdatedMixin` was straightforward, `ObjectDeleteMixin` requires a little bit more thought.

As shown in Example 9.80, we first need to be able to identify what kind of object we are deleting, so we start by defining a `model` attribute on the class. In the case of `get()`, we need to render a template, so we add the `template_name` attribute to our class too. For the `post()` method, we won't be using the template, because our object has been deleted. We instead need a page to redirect to, so we can create the `success_url` attribute.

**Example 9.80: Project Code**
`organizer/utils.py` in 8191bf6813

```
28    class ObjectDeleteMixin:
29        model = None
30        success_url = ''
31        template_name = ''
```

Both `Startup` and `Tag` objects are uniquely identified by `slug`, so we can use this to our advantage (and the `model` attribute) to find whichever model object we need. We then provide this object to `RequestContext` used by `render()`, as shown in Example 9.81.

**Example 9.81: Project Code**
`organizer/utils.py` in 8191bf6813

```
28    class ObjectDeleteMixin:
29        model = None
30        success_url = ''
31        template_name = ''
32
33        def get(self, request, slug):
34            obj = get_object_or_404(
35                self.model, slug__iexact=slug)
36            context = {
37                self.model.__name__.lower(): obj,
38            }
39            return render(
40                request, self.template_name, context)
```

The `post()` method will similarly use the `slug` to identify the object and then promptly delete it. Instead of using `redirect()` to direct the user to a new page, we'll opt to return an `HttpResponseRedirect` object. This is a basic optimization: the `redirect()` function always first needs to figure out what it has been given: a URL pattern name, a URL path, or a model instance. In our case, we know that `success_url` is a URL, so we can circumvent all of the work `redirect()` would be doing and simply give the URL path to a `HttpResponseRedirect` object, as shown in Example 9.82.

**Example 9.82: Project Code**
`organizer/utils.py` **in** 8191bf6813

```
 1   from django.http import HttpResponseRedirect
 .      ...
28   class ObjectDeleteMixin:
29       model = None
30       success_url = ''
31       template_name = ''
 .      ...
42       def post(self, request, slug):
43           obj = get_object_or_404(
44               self.model, slug__iexact=slug)
45           obj.delete()
46           return HttpResponseRedirect(
47               self.success_url)
```

### 9.4.3.1  Deleting `Tag` Objects in a View

With a mixin for our behavior, we can dive right into creating the webpage to delete tags.

For the URL pattern, we copy the regular expression pattern from `organizer_tag_detail` and append the `/delete/` path segment, as shown in Example 9.83.

**Example 9.83: Project Code**
`organizer/urls.py` **in** dc53479077

```
41       url(r'^tag/(?P<slug>[\w-]+)/delete/$',
42           TagDelete.as_view(),
43           name='organizer_tag_delete'),
```

With the creation of a URL pattern that requires arguments at reversal, we immediately add a method to the appropriate model. In Example 9.84, we create the `get_delete_url()` method on our `Tag` model class.

**Example 9.84: Project Code**
`organizer/models.py` **in** dc53479077

```
 9   class Tag(models.Model):
 .      ...
27       def get_delete_url(self):
28           return reverse('organizer_tag_delete',
29                       kwargs={'slug': self.slug})
```

Much like `TagCreate` and `TagUpdate`, the actual implementation of `TagDelete` is based entirely on simply overriding class attributes, thanks in this case to inheritance from `ObjectDeleteMixin`, as shown in Example 9.85.

**Example 9.85: Project Code**
`organizer/views.py` **in** dc53479077

```
 9   from .utils import (
10       ObjectCreateMixin, ObjectDeleteMixin,
11       ObjectUpdateMixin)
 .       ...
106  class TagDelete(ObjectDeleteMixin, View):
107      model = Tag
108      success_url = reverse_lazy(
109          'organizer_tag_list')
110      template_name = (
111          'organizer/tag_confirm_delete.html')
```

### 9.4.3.2  Adding Links for `TagDelete` and `StartupDelete`

We can link to `organizer_tag_delete` thanks to the `get_delete_url()` method in both `tag_detail.html` and `tag_list.html`. The code is identical; the additions to the first file are listed in Example 9.86.

**Example 9.86: Project Code**
`organizer/templates/organizer/tag_detail.html` **in** 2b28c9c737

```
13           <li>
14             <a href="{{ tag.get_delete_url }}">
15               Delete Tag</a></li>
```

We can link the `Startup` delete page from the detail and list pages in the same manner in both `startup_detail.html` and `startup_list.html`. The code to the latter is shown in Example 9.87.

**Example 9.87: Project Code**
`organizer/templates/organizer/startup_list.html` **in** 39fb99eb9a

```
22             <li>
23               <a href="{{ startup.get_delete_url }}">
24                 Delete Startup</a></li>
```

### 9.4.3.3  Deleting `Startup` Objects in a View

You know the drill: to create a webpage, we create a URL pattern and a view. We start in this case with the URL pattern, as shown in Example 9.88.

**Example 9.88: Project Code**

`organizer/urls.py` **in** 6a7f71b15c

```
29       url(r'^startup/(?P<slug>[\w\-]+)/delete/$',
30           StartupDelete.as_view(),
31           name='organizer_startup_delete'),
```

As the reversal of our URL pattern will require arguments, we create a model method to put all of that logic in a single place, as shown in Example 9.89.

**Example 9.89: Project Code**

`organizer/models.py` **in** 6a7f71b15c

```
36    class Startup(models.Model):
  .       ...
61        def get_delete_url(self):
62            return reverse('organizer_startup_delete',
63                           kwargs={'slug': self.slug})
```

We then declare our view class, inheriting both `ObjectDeleteMixin` and `View` and overriding the attributes defined in `ObjectDeleteMixin`, as shown in Example 9.90.

**Example 9.90: Project Code**

`organizer/views.py` **in** 6a7f71b15c

```
78    class StartupDelete(ObjectDeleteMixin, View):
79        model = Startup
80        success_url = reverse_lazy(
81            'organizer_startup_list')
82        template_name = (
83            'organizer/startup_confirm_delete.html')
```

# 9.5   Putting It All Together

The end of Chapter 9 is the culmination of the last three chapters. In this chapter, we used the forms from Chapter 7 and the templates from Chapter 8 to create webpages that users can interact with, creating, modifying, and deleting content from the site.

We built webpages to create, update, and delete objects. We saw that when creating a view to use a form to create or update an object, the view must account for the three states a form may exist in. As such, views handling forms are typically also finite-state machines with three states. CBVs become very useful in this case because they make all three states of both the view and the form very simple to understand. Similarly, to properly handle CSRF (by enabling the CSRF context processor), a view must render templates with a `RequestContext` object rather than a `Context` object. This favors the use of `render()`

over `render_to_response()` and is a large reason many developers simply ignore the latter shortcut when building a website in modern Django versions.

The last three chapters have been difficult and detail-oriented chapters. Our webpages only make sense when seen in the context of interaction between forms, views, and templates, and this can make them daunting when seen at first. Remember that forms are far simpler when dealt with as simple finite-state machines, and that building a form with all the shortcuts we saw can actually be very little work:

1. Create a form class that inherits `ModelForm`.

2. Implement any necessary clean functions for the fields of the form.

3. Create a CBV with `get()` and `post()` methods exactly as detailed in the chapter, making sure to specify any desirable attributes (`form_class`, `model` and `template_name`, being the most common).

4. Create a template that

   a. Defines an HTML form tag, `<form method="post" action=".">`, replacing the `action` attribute value with a value computed by the `url` template tag or that calls a model method to reverse a URL pattern

   b. Defines the `submit` button: `<button type="submit">Submit Button!</button>`

   c. Creates a CSRF token: `{% csrf_token %}`

   d. Generates the form: `{{ form.as_p }}`

# 10

# Revisiting Migrations

## In This Chapter
- Learn about data and schema migrations
- Use data migrations to add content to the website
- Use schema migrations to enhance and fix existing behavior

## 10.1  Introduction

In Chapter 3: Programming Django Models and Creating a SQLite Database, Section 3.5 we saw that Django provides a mechanism, called *migrations*, to automate interactions with the database.

In this chapter, we revisit the concept of migrations and use Django's system to fix several problems with our website. Most notably, we do the following:

- Create data in the database.
- Add a `SlugField` to `NewsLink`.
- Create a unique identifier for `NewsLink`.
- Allow `Post` objects to be created without being associated with a `Tag` or `Startup` object.

## 10.2  Last Week's Episode (Reviewing Chapter 3)

*A migration is simply a script that changes our database.* It acts as version control for our database.

Migrations can change anything about the database. Given that a database is structured data, developers typically talk about modifying the structure, or **schema**, of the database, or else about changing the data in the database. Of course, it is also possible to do both at the same time.

Migration use is closely tied to the Don't Repeat Yourself (DRY) principle. Generally, we make a change in our model and then want to reflect the change in the structure of our database (because a model is an abstract representation of data, whereas the database is the actual storage of this data). Migrations are often generated directly by Django and always stored as part of the project.

The utility of a migration should not be underestimated. Imagine you are working with your teammate Laura. You've split the work, and while Laura fixes a bug in one of your project's views, it's your job to change one of the models and then the database. By creating a migration, you are allowing any changes you make to the database to be easily replicated. When you share your changes with Laura, she will be able to use the migration file to replicate your changes exactly. Contrast this with a system without migrations: Laura would be forced to try and mirror your changes by hand, which is time-consuming and prone to error.

We've already seen migrations in action. Both the **organizer** and **blog** apps have a single migration, each of which creates the database structure defined by our models. If you open these migrations, it's very easy to become overwhelmed, as there is a lot of unfamiliar code. Instead of trying to make it through these Django-generated scripts, we will instead write our own migrations.

## Warning!

This book doesn't deal with testing in Django, as an entire book could be written on the topic (in fact, it has been written: it's called *Test-Driven Development with Python* and is written by Harry Percival).

It is nonetheless worth noting that this chapter has a major effect on testing. When running tests, Django by default uses migrations to build a temporary test database, which includes all data migrations. This means that the test database will have whatever data we add in these sections, which could potentially cause problems if you are unaware of this behavior.

# 10.3    Data Migrations

The concept of a data migration is simple: it's a migration that changes the data within the database and makes no changes to the schema.

Data migrations are strange beasts. For many websites, they're not particularly useful, or else are applied very minimally. For instance, it may be useful to add the list of countries to your database. They certainly don't fit the narrative of this book. However, for a project meant to teach Django, they are wonderful. From here on out, any time you use the project code available on Github, you won't need to add data—it will already exist in the database—allowing you to focus on using/changing the code in the website to better learn Django.

## 10.3.1    Tag Data

In this section, we add data in our database for our `Tag` objects.

To begin, we need to create a new migration file. If you try to use the command we saw in Chapter 3, Section 3.5, Django will inform you there's no migration needed, as shown in Example 10.1.

**Example 10.1: Shell Code**

```
$ ./manage.py makemigrations
No changes detected
```

You can force it to create a new migration for a particular app by passing the `--empty` flag, as shown in Example 10.2.

**Example 10.2: Shell Code**

```
$ ./manage.py makemigrations --empty organizer
Migrations for 'organizer':
  0002_auto_20150515_2300.py
```

By default, Django will name the migration file according to the date and time in Coordinated Universal Time (UTC), which is not particularly helpful for us or other developers. It's in your interest to rename it, so that you know what the purpose of the migration is. In Example 10.3, I opt to rename the file `0002_tag_data.py`.

**Example 10.3: Shell Code**

```
$ cd organizer/migrations/
$ mv 0002_auto_20150515_2300.py 0002_tag_data.py
```

We can now dive into the migration itself. The file is fairly short, as shown in Example 10.4.

**Example 10.4: Project Code**

`organizer/migrations/0002_tag_data.py` in fed5331c72

```
 1   # -*- coding: utf-8 -*-
 2   from __future__ import unicode_literals
 3
 4   from django.db import migrations, models
 5
 6
 7   class Migration(migrations.Migration):
 8
 9       dependencies = [
10           ('organizer', '0001_initial'),
11       ]
12
13       operations = [
14       ]
```

The migration script is embodied entirely by the `Migration` class. The `dependency` attribute on line 9 tells Django what other migrations need to be run before this one can be used, while the `operations` attribute on line 13 is where the actual work is done.

We are simply adding data to our `Tag` object, and so we don't need to change or add any dependencies—the `0001_initial` migration in the `organizer` app is the migration that creates the `organizer_tag` table in our database, effectively mirroring the `Tag` class in our `organizer/models.py` file.

All of the migration work we need to do happens in the `operations` list. As of version 1.8, Django offers 16 built-in migration operations and allows developers to create new ones if these don't suit their purposes. We are most interested in the `RunPython` operation, which allows us to use Python callables to change the database. In our case, we use functions.

`RunPython` expects us to define two functions: a forwards function and a backwards function. The idea is that for any change we make to the database, we need to be able to undo it. The backwards function is thus the opposite of the forwards function.

Like the rest of Django, the functions we build are subject to the Hollywood principle: Don't call us, we'll call you. When Django's migration system uses `RunPython` to call our functions, it passes in two instances, one instance of `Apps` and one instance of `SchemaEditor`, as shown in Example 10.5.

**Example 10.5: Project Code**
`organizer/migrations/0002_tag_data.py` **in** d8725d0bf2

```
 7    def add_tag_data(apps, schema_editor):
 8        pass
 .        ...
11    def remove_tag_data(apps, schema_editor):
12        pass
```

The `SchemaEditor` is the part of the migration system that actually communicates with databases. It knows how to take the migration operations and turn them into SQL for whichever database Django is currently communicating with.

The instance of `Apps` is exactly what it sounds like: it's a list of all the apps (**organizer** and **blog** in our case) available to the project and is called an **app registry**. An app registry is a list of `AppConfig` instances, which are automatically created for each app (we'll program our own in `AppConfig` classes in Chapter 25: Handling Behavior with Signals after seeing them again in Chapter 19: Basic Authentication and Chapter 23: The Admin Library).

In the case of migrations, the instance of `Apps` is not what currently exists in the project but what existed when the migration was created. This is because we are interested in the **historical model**, sometimes called the **frozen model**, when using the migration system. Developers routinely ask the migration system whether there are any changes that need to be made to the database based on changes in their models (the `makemigrations` command). The problem is that Django cannot reliably use the database to figure out what has changed. There's no guarantee that the database exists or even what state the database is in (it might be several migrations behind the model!). To figure out what has changed, Django uses previous migrations to determine what state the database should be in (the historical models) and then compares that state to the current models.

The utility of historical models is not limited to the `makemigrations` command. When changing the database, it's important to know what state the models are in *at that point*. We are about to create `Tag` data, and when we do so, we will be assuming that only the name and slug values exist. However, in the future, we have no such guarantee. If our migration used a future version of the Tag, neither the name nor slug might exist, or perhaps a new field would be mandatory. Our migration would thus fail to work as expected. We see this in action when we build migrations for NewsLink, and we return to the topic then.

To call our two functions, we simply pass them to RunPython as initializer arguments, as shown in Example 10.6. Note again that add_tag_data() will be used when applying a migration (moving forwards in time), while remove_tag_data() will be used when unapplying a migration (moving backwards in time).

**Example 10.6: Project Code**
organizer/migrations/0002_tag_data.py in d8725d0bf2

```
15    class Migration(migrations.Migration):
 .        ...
21        operations = [
22            migrations.RunPython(
23                add_tag_data,
24                remove_tag_data)
25        ]
```

Actually programming the two functions is pretty easy. We start by creating a tuple with all of the data we want to add (partially printed in Example 10.7).

**Example 10.7: Project Code**
organizer/migrations/0002_tag_data.py in aa0cf8ff69

```
 6    TAGS = (
 7        # ( tag name, tag slug ),
 8        ("augmented reality", "augmented-reality"),
 .        ...
24    )
```

We can first use this new data in add_tag_data(), using Django's object–relational mapping (ORM) exactly as we would in a view or the shell to create Tag objects based on the data structure above. The only trick is how we fetch the Tag model (line 28), as shown in Example 10.8.

**Example 10.8: Project Code**
organizer/migrations/0002_tag_data.py in aa0cf8ff69

```
27    def add_tag_data(apps, schema_editor):
28        Tag = apps.get_model('organizer', 'Tag')
29        for tag_name, tag_slug in TAGS:
30            Tag.objects.create(
31                name=tag_name,
32                slug=tag_slug)
```

We are **not** importing Tag via a Python import (from organizer.models import Tag), and are instead using get_model() method of the Apps instance passed to us to fetch the historical model of Tag. At the moment, the current version of Tag and the historical version that will be used in the migration are identical, so this may seem unnecessary, but we must always remember to use the historical model so that any future changes don't negate our current work.

When we program remove_tag_data(), we similarly use the historical model of Tag, as shown in Example 10.9.

**Example 10.9: Project Code**
organizer/migrations/0002_tag_data.py **in** 080c854868

```
35   def remove_tag_data(apps, schema_editor):
36       Tag = apps.get_model('organizer', 'Tag')
37       Tag.objects.all().delete()
```

I've opted in Example 10.9 to delete all of the Tag objects in the database. The assumption I've made is that because no other migration has created data, no other data apart from this current migration (0002_tag_data.py) exists in the database. This is not actually a safe assumption to make—future migrations might have added data, or else we might have manually added data.

In my experience, I have only had to unapply migrations when something has gone *horribly* wrong. In those instances, indiscriminately deleting data from my database is not what I want. I've gotten into the habit of writing migrations that unapply *exactly* what was applied. In Example 10.10, we want to delete only the Tag data that appears in our data structure.

**Example 10.10: Project Code**
organizer/migrations/0002_tag_data.py **in** d7a5660963

```
35   def remove_tag_data(apps, schema_editor):
36       Tag = apps.get_model('organizer', 'Tag')
37       for _, tag_slug in TAGS:
38           tag = Tag.objects.get(slug=tag_slug)
39           tag.delete()
```

With that done, our migration is ready to be applied! Whenever we create a database from now on, we will automatically have all of the Tag data in our migration file added to the database. Again, this is not typically useful for an actual website, but for a project meant to be used by students learning the framework, it's useful not only because we can now immediately play with the website but also because it allows us to easily break down migrations in this section.

## Django Documentation

For the full list of Django migration operations:

https://dju.link/18/migration-operation

## 10.3.2 Startup Data

Starting in Django 1.8, it became possible to pass the `--name` argument to
`makemigrations`, allowing for the creation of a named empty migration file. Rather than
creating a file (automatically named according to UTC date-time) and then renaming the
file, we can issue a single commmand, as shown in Example 10.11.

**Example 10.11: Shell Code**

```
$ ./manage.py makemigrations --empty --name=startup_data organizer
```

Every data migration is going to feature the structure: We use the `RunPython` operation
to call either a forwards or backwards Python function, as shown in Example 10.12.

**Example 10.12: Project Code**

`organizer/migrations/0003_startup_data.py` **in** f492ab1462

```
132         dependencies = [
133             ('organizer', '0002_tag_data'),
134         ]
135
136         operations = [
137             migrations.RunPython(
138                 add_startup_data,
139                 remove_startup_data)
140         ]
```

You can see on line 133 that Django was able to automatically figure out what our last
migration was. Note how, despite specifying `startup_data` when invoking
`makemigrations`, Django created a file named `0003_startup_data.py`. The numbers
at the front of migration files are not optional!

Before programming our migration files, we create a data structure to contain all of our
startup data, as shown in Example 10.13.

**Example 10.13: Project Code**

`organizer/migrations/0003_startup_data.py` **in** f492ab1462

```
 8     STARTUPS = [
 9         {
10             "name": "Arachnobots",
11             "slug": "arachnobots",
12             "contact": "contact@arachnobots.com",
13             "description":
14                 "Remote-controlled internet-enabled "
15                 "Spider Robots.",
16             "founded_date": date(2014, 10, 31),
17             "tags": ["mobile", "augmented-reality"],
18             "website":
19                 "http://frightenyourroommate.com/",
20         },
 .         ...
```

Both `add_startup_data()` and `remove_startup_data()` must accept two arguments: an instance of `Apps` and an instance of `SchemaEditor`, as shown in Example 10.14.

**Example 10.14: Project Code**

`organizer/migrations/0003_startup_data.py` in f492ab1462

```
104    def add_startup_data(apps, schema_editor):
.     ...
122    def remove_startup_data(apps, schema_editor):
```

In both cases, we need to get the historical model for `Startup`, and in the case of `add_startup_data()`, we also need the historical model for `Tag`, as shown in Example 10.15.

**Example 10.15: Project Code**

`organizer/migrations/0003_startup_data.py` in f492ab1462

```
104    def add_startup_data(apps, schema_editor):
105        Startup = apps.get_model(
106            'organizer', 'Startup')
107        Tag = apps.get_model('organizer', 'Tag')
```

In `add_startup_data()`, we can use Python to loop through the data structure and use model managers to create both `Startup` and `Tag` models, as shown in Example 10.16.

**Example 10.16: Project Code**

`organizer/migrations/0003_startup_data.py` in f492ab1462

```
104    def add_startup_data(apps, schema_editor):
.     ...
108        for startup in STARTUPS:
109            startup_object = Startup.objects.create(
110                name=startup['name'],
111                slug=startup['slug'],
112                contact=startup['contact'],
113                description=startup['description'],
114                founded_date=startup['founded_date'],
115                website=startup['website'])
116            for tag_slug in startup['tags']:
117                startup_object.tags.add(
118                    Tag.objects.get(
119                        slug=tag_slug))
```

The `remove_startup_data()` is exactly the opposite: we use all the same tools to delete exactly what we created, as shown in Example 10.17.

**Example 10.17: Project Code**

`organizer/migrations/0003_startup_data.py` in `f492ab1462`

```
122    def remove_startup_data(apps, schema_editor):
123        Startup = apps.get_model(
124            'organizer', 'Startup')
125        for startup in STARTUPS:
126            startup_object = Startup.objects.get(
127                slug=startup['slug'])
128            startup_object.delete()
```

### 10.3.3  Post Data

The data migration for creating Post objects is almost exactly the same process, but comes with an added difficulty. This migration depends on the existence of the last two migrations we built. There is no way for Django to know this, and so for the first time we will modify the dependecy attribute of the Migration class.

Start by invoking makemigrations with the --empty flag and the --name option on the **blog** app, as shown in Example 10.18.

**Example 10.18: Shell Code**

```
$ ./manage.py makemigrations --empty --name=post_data blog
```

This code creates the `0002_post_data.py` file. Note that previously we had programmed `0002_tag_data.py` and `0003_startup_data.py`. This is not a naming or migration order conflict—previous migrations had been in `organizer/migrations/`, whereas `0002_post_data.py` exists in `blog/migrations/`. Migrations are encapsulated by app, and the order only provides Django with information about the internal order of migration. These numbers cannot help Django figure out how to apply migrations on a project basis.

Django uses the dependency list to determine the absolute (project-wide) order migrations must be applied in. Django builds a tree of migrations and their dependencies and then linearizes the structure.

In the case of our `0002_post_data.py`, we need the Post model to exist as the blog_post table in the database, so we depend on the `0001_initial.py` **blog** migration. However, we also need the data created in **organizer**'s `0002_tag_data.py` and `0003_startup_data.py` migration. Given that `0003_startup_data.py` depends on `0002_tag_data.py` we can simply depend on `0003_startup_data.py` in **blog**'s `0002_post_data.py`. We therefore modify the dependecy attribute to read as shown in Example 10.19.

**Example 10.19: Project Code**

`blog/migrations/0002_post_data.py` in `23dad59b69`

```
131        dependencies = [
132            ('blog', '0001_initial'),
133            ('organizer', '0003_startup_data'),
134        ]
```

This ensures that the data and schemas we depend on in this migration will exist when the migration is applied.

The rest of the work for creating this migration is exactly as before: we use `RunPython` to either apply or unapply a Python function. Both of these functions use the appropriate historical models to add or remove data stored in a data structure in the file. For the purpose of brevity, and because we've already seen this process twice, we skip this code (but remember that it is available in its entirety on Github at https://dju.link/23dad59b69).

## 10.4   Schema Migrations

Creating data migrations are a nice introduction to migrations, but they may be a little too simplistic, mainly because they always rely on a single operation: `RunPython`. Django offers 15 others, and while we won't have the opportunity to see all of them, we are now forced to use some of them to fix a few problems our site has.

When creating `NewsLinkUpdate` (Chapter 9, Section 9.3.2) and `NewsLinkDelete` (Chapter 9, Section 9.4.2) we discovered that we needed a unique way to identify `NewsLink` objects. At the moment, we're using the primary key of each instance, a practice that is frowned upon because it leads to human-unfriendly URLs. Building `NewsLink` without a `SlugField` was thus (intentionally) a mistake that we need to fix—migrations to the rescue!

More problematic, however, is a subtle problem I have not drawn your attention to yet. If you browse to the `Post` create webpage, you'll discover that any `Post` object you try to create *must* be associated with a `Tag` or a `Startup` object. We'll see exactly why this is happening, and then fix the problem, resulting in another schema migration.

### 10.4.1   Making Our Lives Difficult with a Data Migration

Before we actually create a migration for adding a `SlugField` to `NewsLink`, I want to make life more difficult to better replicate real-world conditions. To that end, I want the database to already have `NewsLink` data, which will force us to build our schema migration in the next section with this in mind.

As with `Tag`, `Startup`, and `Post`, we first create the data migration by invoking `makemigrations`, as shown in Example 10.20.

**Example 10.20: Shell Code**

```
$ ./manage.py makemigrations --empty --name=newslink_data organizer
```

This code creates the `0004_newslink_data.py` file in `organizer/migrations/`.

The `NewsLink` data migration is very straightforward: there's no need to change the `dependency` attribute, meaning we just add the `RunPython` operation to the `operations` attribute list. We then need to define two Python functions, `add_newslink_data()` and `remove_newslink_data()`, which both define apps and `schema_editor` parameters to accept instances of `Apps` and `SchemaEditor`. Just as the `Startup` data migration depends on `Tag` data (and therefore uses the historical model for both `Startup` and `Tag` objects), the `NewsLink` data migration depends on `Startup` and necessitates historical models for `NewsLink` and `Startup` objects.

Given how similar the NewsLink data migration is compared to the Startup data migration (code we have already seen), we skip the actual code for this section (but remember that the code is available online: https://dju.link/5754c2acb1).

## 10.4.2 Adding a `slug` to NewsLink

Adding a SlugField to NewsLink is really easy, given Django's declarative syntax, as shown in Example 10.21.

**Example 10.21: Project Code**

`organizer/models.py` in 89c25fd8a8

```
70    class NewsLink(models.Model):
 .       ...
72        slug = models.SlugField(max_length=63)
```

That's it! You're done. (Take heed: we have not set the unique option on the field.)

Mirroring this change in the database and making the lives of your future self and your coworkers easy is a little trickier, especially because we have a database with data in it.

When we call makemigrations, Django compares the current state of our models with the historical models it builds thanks to the Apps and AppConfig classes. It knows that NewsLink has a new field called slug, but it doesn't know how to fill the slug field in for existing data. You can see this as you run makemigrations, as shown in Example 10.22.

**Example 10.22: Shell Code**

```
$ ./manage.py makemigrations
You are trying to add a non-nullable field 'slug' to newslink
without a default; we can't do that (the database needs
something to populate existing rows).
Please select a fix:
 1) Provide a one-off default now (will be set on all existing
    rows)
 2) Quit, and let me add a default in models.py
Select an option: 2
```

In our organizer_newslink table in the database, Django will create a new column called slug. However, given that we already have rows in the table (data we created in the last section with our data migration), Django needs to know what to fill in the slug column of these rows with.

We don't want our slug to have a default—as it's part of our unique identifier (we'll handle this shortly), it's important that there not be a default. We also don't want to create a migration that puts us in an invalid state for our database—we don't want to set a default in our model, migrate, and remove the default, and then migrate again. Instead, we want to build a single migration with multiple operations that will (automatically) bring us from one valid database state to the next.

In this case, we need to use the AddField, RunPython, and AlterField operations. We use AddField to create our SlugField with a default value (the empty string). We then use `RunPython` to define functions that generate the slugs for the existing data in the database. Finally, we use `AlterField` to change the `SlugField` such that it no longer has a default.

To begin, we need a migration file to modify, as shown in Example 10.23.

**Example 10.23: Shell Code**

```
$ ./manage.py makemigrations --empty --name=newslink_slug organizer
```

We start by adding a global variable to help us avoid magic numbers (numbers that are used in code without explanation of their value), as shown in Example 10.24.

**Example 10.24: Project Code**

organizer/migrations/0005_newslink_slug.py **in** 89c25fd8a8

```
7    SLUG_LENGTH = 63
```

We can then add `AddField` to `operations`, as shown in Example 10.25.

**Example 10.25: Project Code**

organizer/migrations/0005_newslink_slug.py **in** 89c25fd8a8

```
38    class Migration(migrations.Migration):
 .        ...
44        operations = [
45            migrations.AddField(
46                model_name='newslink',
47                name='slug',
48                field=models.SlugField(
49                    max_length=SLUG_LENGTH,
50                    default=''),
51            ),
 .        ...
62        ]
```

The use of `AddField` is self-explanatory. We add the `SlugField` (line 48) to `NewsLink` (line 46) as the `slug` attribute (line 47). Any options passed to `SlugField` in `/organizer/models.py` need to be specified here, which is why we define the `max_length` field option on line 49, using the `SLUG_LENGTH` global variable to pass 63, which is the value we used in `/organizer/models.py`. Note that we've also set a `default`, despite not having set this on the model itself. We will change this shortly.

We now need to create the `slug` values in the database. This is tricky, as we need to consider uniqueness when generating these values. The URL we will be using to access `NewsLinkUpdate` is `/<startup_slug>/<newslink_slug>/update/`. Similarly, the URL to access `NewsLinkDelete` is `/<startup_slug>/<newslink_slug>/delete/`. A unique identifier for a `NewsLink` therefore consists of its own `SlugField` and the `Startup` it is associated with. When we generate a slug for an existing `NewsLink`, we need to make sure that another `NewsLink` associated with the same `Startup` doesn't already have the slug we've generated.

In Example 10.26, we define `add_slug_data()` to accept the `Apps` and `SchemaEditor` instances and immediately get the historical model for `NewsLink`. In this case, the historical model is what exists *after* we've run the `AddField` operation, meaning we have access to a `slug` field that has a default (something that never existed and never will exist in our model files).

**Example 10.26: Project Code**

`organizer/migrations/0005_newslink_slug.py` **in** 89c25fd8a8

```
10   def add_slug_data(apps, schema_editor):
11       NewsLink = apps.get_model(
12           'organizer', 'NewsLink')
```

Our goal is now to add a `slug` to every `NewsLink` in the database, as shown in Example 10.27.

**Example 10.27: Project Code**

`organizer/migrations/0005_newslink_slug.py` **in** 89c25fd8a8

```
10   def add_slug_data(apps, schema_editor):
 .       ...
13       query = NewsLink.objects.all()
14       for newslink in query:
```

As detailed in Chapter 3, Section 3.3.1, a slug is a string with alphanumeric characters, a dash, or an underscore. No other characters are allowed. We could write a function to take a string and return a valid string, but Django already has one for us, as shown in Example 10.28.

**Example 10.28: Project Code**

`organizer/migrations/0005_newslink_slug.py` **in** 89c25fd8a8

```
5    from django.utils.text import slugify
```

The `slugify` function first converts a string to ASCII, lowers the case of the string, and then strips out all non-alphanumeric characters, replacing them with dashes. We can use this function on the title of our `NewsLink` objects as a first attempt at creating a slug, as shown in Example 10.29.

**Example 10.29: Project Code**

`organizer/migrations/0005_newslink_slug.py` **in** 89c25fd8a8

```
10   def add_slug_data(apps, schema_editor):
 .       ...
14       for newslink in query:
15           expected_slug = slugify(newslink.title)
```

We then need to make sure that no other `NewsLink` with the same slug shares the same `Startup`. We're not actually interested in whether they exist—we're interested in how many of them there are. For instance, pretend the `Monkey Software` startup already has a `NewsLink` with the slug `django`. We would then want to create the slug `django-2` for the next `NewsLink` titled `Django`. The problem, of course, is that for the next one, we want to create `django-3`. In that case, we need to know the number of `NewsLink` objects related to `Monkey Software` that have a `slug` that starts with `django`. We can use the `count()` method on our model manager to ask the database for this information, as shown in Example 10.30.

**Example 10.30: Project Code**
`organizer/migrations/0005_newslink_slug.py` **in** 89c25fd8a8

```
10    def add_slug_data(apps, schema_editor):
 .        ...
14        for newslink in query:
15            expected_slug = slugify(newslink.title)
16            rivals = (
17                NewsLink.objects.filter(
18                    startup=newslink.startup,
19                    slug__startswith=expected_slug
20                ).count())
```

In the event there is a conflict, we need to add a number to the end of the slug value we've generated and to ensure that the length of this slug is not greater than the length of the `SlugField`, as shown in Example 10.31.

**Example 10.31: Project Code**
`organizer/migrations/0005_newslink_slug.py` **in** 89c25fd8a8

```
10    def add_slug_data(apps, schema_editor):
 .        ...
14        for newslink in query:
 .            ...
21            if rivals > 0:
22                str_len = (
23                    SLUG_LENGTH - len(str(rivals)))
24                newslink.slug = "{}-{}".format(
25                    expected_slug[:str_len - 1],
26                    rivals + 1)
27            else:
28                newslink.slug = expected_slug
```

Generating content like this is hard, and there are all sorts of problems with our approach. For instance, we are looking for any slug that begins with `django`, but this will include false-positives, such as `django-training`, which is not an actual rival. Worse, if the first value that we generate is already 63 characters long, then we will only ever find a single rival even though there may be more to account for. However, our algorithm is Good Enough for the moment.

To finish the job, we save the NewsLink with its new slug, as shown in Example 10.32.

**Example 10.32: Project Code**

organizer/migrations/0005_newslink_slug.py in 89c25fd8a8

```
10    def add_slug_data(apps, schema_editor):
 .        ...
14        for newslink in query:
 .            ...
29            newslink.save()
```

The remove_slug_data() function is far easier, thanks to the use of the update() model manager method, which allows us to update multiple instances at once, as shown in Example 10.33.

**Example 10.33: Project Code**

organizer/migrations/0005_newslink_slug.py in 89c25fd8a8

```
32    def remove_slug_data(apps, schema_editor):
33        NewsLink = apps.get_model(
34            'organizer', 'NewsLink')
35        NewsLink.objects.update(slug='')
```

To make sure these functions are called, we pass them to RunPython in operations, as shown in Example 10.34. Unlike the other times we've used RunPython, in this case I choose to pass the second function as a keyword argument.

**Example 10.34: Project Code**

organizer/migrations/0005_newslink_slug.py in 89c25fd8a8

```
38    class Migration(migrations.Migration):
 .        ...
44        operations = [
 .            ...
52            migrations.RunPython(
53                add_slug_data,
54                reverse_code=remove_slug_data
55            ),
 .            ...
62        ]
```

Finally, we can add the AlterField operation in Example 10.35. The AlterField operation looks exactly like the AddField operation. The sole difference in syntax, in fact, is that the default field option is no longer set.

**Example 10.35: Project Code**
`organizer/migrations/0005_newslink_slug.py` in `89c25fd8a8`

```
38   class Migration(migrations.Migration):
.        ...
44       operations = [
.            ...
56           migrations.AlterField(
57               model_name='newslink',
58               name='slug',
59               field=models.SlugField(
60                   max_length=SLUG_LENGTH),
61           ),
62       ]
```

## 10.4.3   Ensuring a Unique Identifier for NewsLink

In the previous section, we determined that our `NewsLink` objects must be unique according to their `slug` and `startup` fields. However, we are not currently enforcing uniqueness in Django or the database.

Luckily, Django makes it easy to enforce uniqueness according to multiple fields, thanks to the `unique_together` attribute of the nested `Meta` class, as shown in Example 10.36.

**Example 10.36: Project Code**
`organizer/models.py` in `ead1b3cad1`

```
70   class NewsLink(models.Model):
.        ...
77       class Meta:
.            ...
81           unique_together = (('slug', 'startup'),)
```

For convenience, instead of passing a tuple of tuples, Django allows us to pass a single tuple if we're only making a set of fields unique together, as shown in Example 10.37.

**Example 10.37: Project Code**
`organizer/models.py` in `b7c0619244`

```
70   class NewsLink(models.Model):
.        ...
77       class Meta:
.            ...
81           unique_together = ('slug', 'startup')
```

Using the `makemigrations` command in the shell will automatically create the migration file without problems. However, Django won't know how to name the file, so you need to either rename the file or set the `--name` option when invoking the

makemigrations command. The AlterUniqueTogether Django generates for us is
printed in Example 10.38.

**Example 10.38: Project Code**
organizer/migrations/0006_newslink_unique_together_slug_startup.py
**in** 4ffa07c270

```
 7    class Migration(migrations.Migration):
 .        ...
13        operations = [
14            migrations.AlterUniqueTogether(
15                name='newslink',
16                unique_together=set([('slug', 'startup')]),
17            ),
18        ]
```

## 10.4.4  Making Relations Optional in Forms

If you try to submit a Startup with no tags via our Startup create webpage, Django will
error and insist that at least one Tag is mandatory. The same will happen for Post via the
Post create webpage but for both Startup and Tag.

This is a somewhat baffling behavior. We know that many-to-many relationships are a
separate table, and so the database is clearly not what requires this data. Django is enforcing
this behavior. All of our forms are ModelForms, which means that Django is deriving this
form behavior from our models.

Django model fields have a number of field options that change their behavior in a
number of ways. As it turns out, one of these field options, blank, is built almost entirely
for ModelForms. Django requires any field, including many-to-many fields, to be set to
blank=True if the user is allowed to omit the value.

The blank option is not to be confused with the null option. The null option allows
for Django to set values as NULL (the SQL equivalent of Python's None). Where blank is
all about validation and the ModelForm, null is all about the database. What's more,
however, null should never be set to True on any string fields (such as CharField or
SlugField), as these fields already have an empty value: the empty string.

To allow us to create blog posts with no related content, we need to add blank=True
to the many-to-many fields, as shown in Example 10.39.

**Example 10.39: Project Code**
blog/models.py **in** 90a9490877

```
11    class Post(models.Model):
 .        ...
21        tags = models.ManyToManyField(
22            Tag,
23            blank=True,
24            related_name='blog_posts')
```

```
25        startups = models.ManyToManyField(
26            Startup,
27            blank=True,
28            related_name='blog_posts')
```

Calling makemigrations from the shell will automatically generate the migration for us (although you'll have to specify a name yourself—I call the file post_fields_startups_and_tags_optional). Django uses the AlterField operation in this case to change the field above (https://dju.link/90a9490877).

We also want to be able to create Startup objects without related Tag objects, so we add blank to that relation as well, as shown in Example 10.40.

**Example 10.40: Project Code**
organizer/models.py **in** cf7d0519ed

```
36    class Startup(models.Model):
 .        ...
48        tags = models.ManyToManyField(Tag, blank=True)
```

The call to makemigrations works again (without a proper name—I supply the name startup_tag_field_optional), once again using AlterField to mirror our change in the model (hash cf7d0519ed).

If you run the development server (the runserver command), you'll discover you now have the ability to create Post and Startup objects without relations.

Note that we have not used blank on the one-to-many relation between Startup and NewsLink objects because we always want the NewsLink to be associated with a Startup.

### Django Documentation

For Django's model field reference documentation:

https://dju.link/18/fields

# 10.5   Putting It All Together

A migration is a file or script that modifies the database. Typically, our goal when using a migration is to reflect in our models any changes we've made to the structure of our data. The typical workflow for a schema migration is thus as follows:

1.  Modify the model.

2.  Generate or create the migration.

3.  Apply the migration.

With a data migration, given that we are not modifying the migration, the workflow is simply to create and apply the migration.

In Django, a migration is defined by its dependencies and its operations. The dependencies tell Django what we expect to have already happened in the database, while the operations declaratively list the changes we wish to make. Django supplies 16 operations for us to use out of the box. In this chapter, we saw `RunPython`, `AddField`, `AlterField`, and `AlterUniqueTogether`.

In Chapter 1, we discussed how websites can be split according to front end and back end, and we discovered that the back end can further be split into stateful and stateless parts. Despite that Django is a state machine (what with forms and all the rest), we don't care about the application. If it crashes and we lose everything in memory, it's not a huge problem, as we can simply restart the server. However, we care deeply about the data in the database—it contains the long-term state of our web application, and should we lose that, we are in deep trouble.

In many ways, migrations act as the connection between the stateful and the stateless parts of your web application. The Django application is stateless—it doesn't care about the data, it simply computes. The database is stateful—it contains data with meaning that changes. Migrations are a key (with the ORM) that allow for the stateless application to communicate with the stateful data storage and are thus crucial to working with Django.

# 11

# Bending the Rules: The Contact Us Webpage

## In This Chapter

- Send emails from Django
- Display messages across templates
- Review how to build a form without `ModelForm`
- Review Django's core (views)

## 11.1 Introduction

If you were to judge Django on the basis of all the previous content, you might describe the act of building a website as an iterative process where you always

1. Build a model
2. Generate a migration
3. Build webpages by
   a. Creating a template
   b. Creating a view
   c. Creating a URL pattern

While this is a perfectly valid approach to building a website in Django, it is certainly not your only option.

To better aid you in your quest for a holistic understanding of Django, the goal of this chapter is to build a webpage that does not follow the process above. We will build a single webpage that provides a contact form to users, allowing them to send us emails without having us share our email address directly. Along the way, we will use a new part of Django called the messages framework.

At the end, we'll also see that while Django expects you to follow conventions, it is sometimes possible to bend the rules thanks to a little Python.

## 11.2    Creating a `contact` App

We could build our contact page wherever we want, but the functionality doesn't belong in either **organizer** or **blog**. We therefore opt to create a new app, as shown in Example 11.1.

**Example 11.1: Shell Code**

```
$ ./manage.py startapp contact
```

This code creates all the files we expect—but we don't need several of them. We can immediately delete `admin.py` and `models.py`. This app is simply a webpage with a form: there's no need to use any data models! By the same token, we don't need any migrations, so we can delete that directory as well. (If you look at the code on Github at commit `3a35644b28`,[1] you'll observe that I never even commit these files—I delete them right away).

We need to tell our project of the existence of the new app, so we add `contact` to the list of `INSTALLED_APPS` in `suorganizer/settings.py`, as shown in Example 11.2.

**Example 11.2: Project Code**
`suorganizer/settings.py` **in** `0f6243e938`

```
33    INSTALLED_APPS = (
 .       ...
43        'contact',
44    )
```

Finally, we need to configure Django's email settings. We're not actually interested in sending emails at the moment—we just want to be able to see what Django is sending as we develop the website. Django provides a number of back ends for communicating with mail servers, but one of these back ends is the console back end, which simply prints emails to our terminal, as shown in Example 11.3.

**Example 11.3: Project Code**
`suorganizer/settings.py` **in** `c69f4d5f60`

```
88    # Email
89    # https://docs.djangoproject.com/en/1.8/topics/email/
90
91    EMAIL_BACKEND = 'django.core.mail.backends.console.EmailBackend'
```

Django also expects a few more settings before we can get to developing our page, as shown in Example 11.4.

---

1. https://dju.link/3a35644b28

**Example 11.4: Project Code**
`suorganizer/settings.py` **in** `fcf6a14f42`

```
88   # Email
89   # https://docs.djangoproject.com/en/1.8/topics/email/
90
91   EMAIL_BACKEND = 'django.core.mail.backends.console.EmailBackend'
92   SERVER_EMAIL = 'contact@django-unleashed.com'
93   DEFAULT_FROM_EMAIL = 'no-reply@django-unleashed.com'
94   EMAIL_SUBJECT_PREFIX = '[Startup Organizer] '
95   MANAGERS = (
96       ('Us', 'ourselves@django-unleashed.com'),
97   )
```

The DEFAULT_FROM_EMAIL and EMAIL_SUBJECT_PREFIX are exactly what they sound like. If we send an email but don't specify the From header, then Django will default to using the email in DEFAULT_FROM_EMAIL. All emails being sent will have their subjects prefixed by EMAIL_SUBJECT_PREFIX. So, if we send an email with the title "New Content," users will receive "[Startup Organizer] New Content" in their inbox.

The SERVER_EMAIL and MANAGERS settings are a little more cryptic. Django expects websites to have two types of internal users: administrators and managers. Administrators are super users with access to the entire website, whereas managers are privileged users with specific powers. Django enables either of these sets of users to be contacted in the event of a problem. When sending these emails, Django uses the SERVER_EMAIL setting rather than the DEFAULT_FROM_EMAIL setting to set the From header of the email. This allows managers and administrators to tell the difference between routine and critical emails from the website.

We now have a new app and the ability to send emails. It's time to build a form and a view.

> **Django Documentation**
>
> For more about email and email settings in Django:
>
> https://dju.link/18/email

## 11.3 Creating the Contact Webpage

It's time to build a webpage. To start, we build a contact form, which prompts the user for information and then sends that information to us via email. We then build a view and URL pattern to interact with the form, saving the actual templates of the page for last.

The following process for building a data-processing webpage is reproduced for convenience from Chapter 9: Controlling Forms in Views, Section 9.5.

1. Create a form class that inherits ModelForm.

2. Implement any necessary clean functions for the fields of the form.

3. Create a CBV with `get()` and `post()` methods exactly as detailed in the chapter, making sure to specify any desirable attributes (`form_class`, `model`, and `template_name`, being the most common).

4. Create a template that

   a. Defines an HTML form tag, `<form method="post" action=".">`, replacing the `action` attribute value with a value computed by the `url` template tag or that calls a model method to reverse a URL pattern

   b. Defines the `submit` button: `<button type="submit">Submit Button!</button>`

   c. Creates a CSRF token: `{% csrf_token %}`

   d. Generates the form: `{{ form.as_p }}`

This list can act as a set of guidelines, but it's already clear that we cannot adhere to this process in full: we don't have any models and therefore cannot use `ModelForm` to build our form.

## 11.3.1   Contact Form

The goal of the contact page is to enable users to give us feedback on our site. To that end, we want to present users with a form that allows them to write feedback and gives us a way to contact them in the event they want us to. Without a model, we need to build the form as a `Form` (Example 11.5) instead of as a `ModelForm` as we did previously.

**Example 11.5:** Project Code

`contact/forms.py` **in** `3969d84738`

```
 1   from django import forms
 .       ...
 6   class ContactForm(forms.Form):
 .       ...
18       email = forms.EmailField(
19           initial='youremail@domain.com')
20       text = forms.CharField(widget=forms.Textarea)
```

By default, a `forms.CharField` (as opposed to `models.CharField`) presents itself when rendered in a form as a `TextInput` widget (an HTML input tag). In Example 11.5, line 20 overrides the widget, forcing Django to display a `Textarea` widget (an HTML `textarea` tag). This allows the user to write more helpful and descriptive feedback (in theory—the Internet is not always so kind).

If we wanted to make the `email` field optional, we would set the `required` option to `False` (the `blank` and `null` options are only for model fields).

For triage purposes, we also ask that they tell us what kind of message they are sending: a request for support, general feedback, or a correction. The way to achieve this is to use a

ChoiceField. A ChoiceField defines keys and values, where the keys are typically stored in the database and the values are what the user is presented with. To make interacting with a ChoiceField as simple as possible, it's best to create a set of attributes that act as the keys for the field, as shown in Example 11.6.

**Example 11.6: Project Code**
contact/forms.py **in** 3969d84738

```
 6    class ContactForm(forms.Form):
 7        FEEDBACK = 'F'
 8        CORRECTION = 'C'
 9        SUPPORT = 'S'
10        REASON_CHOICES = (
11            (FEEDBACK, 'Feedback'),
12            (CORRECTION, 'Correction'),
13            (SUPPORT, 'Support'),
14        )
15        reason = forms.ChoiceField(
16            choices=REASON_CHOICES,
17            initial=FEEDBACK)
```

This code allows us to call form.CORRECTION rather than referring to the magic string 'C', which might prove problematic in the future.

Finally, we need to program a method on the form to send an email. Previously, we saw that in most cases, forms feature the save() method, as forms typically save information to the database. In many cases, developers create the save() method even when the form is doing something other than storing the data in the database, but this is purely convention, and if need be, we can call the method whatever we'd like, such as send_mail(). Just as for any data-processing form method, however, our first task it to get the validated data from cleaned_data, as shown in Example 11.7.

**Example 11.7: Project Code**
contact/forms.py **in** 3969d84738

```
 6    class ContactForm(forms.Form):
 .        ...
22        def send_mail(self):
23            reason = self.cleaned_data.get('reason')
24            reason_dict = dict(self.REASON_CHOICES)
25            full_reason = reason_dict.get(reason)
26            email = self.cleaned_data.get('email')
27            text = self.cleaned_data.get('text')
28            body = 'Message From: {}\n\n{}\n'.format(
29                email, text)
```

Lines 23 through 25 are a little unusual. The value that will be received by the form will be one of the keys defined as the first value of the tuple in REASON_CHOICES: we will receive one of 'F', 'C', or 'S'. We don't want to send a letter—that's totally unhelpful. We're instead interested in sending 'Feedback', 'Correction', or 'Support'. To get that value, we turn the REASON_CHOICES tuple into a dictionary on line 24 and use the key stored in cleaned_data to fetch the value from the dictionary on line 25.

To actually send the message, we make use of the mail_managers() shortcut that Django provides, which mails all of the emails defined in the MANAGERS setting declared in the last section. The only error Django accounts for with email is the BadHeaderError error, which we will catch and in turn raise a ValidationError, as shown in Example 11.8.

**Example 11.8: Project Code**
contact/forms.py **in** 3969d84738

```
 2    from django.core.exceptions import ValidationError
 3    from django.core.mail import BadHeaderError, mail_managers
 .        ...
 6    class ContactForm(forms.Form):
 .        ...
22        def send_mail(self):
 .            ...
30            try:
31                # shortcut for send_mail
32                mail_managers(full_reason, body)
33            except BadHeaderError:
34                self.add_error(
35                    None,
36                    ValidationError(
37                        'Could Not Send Email.\n'
38                        'Extra Headers not allowed '
39                        'in email body.',
40                        code='badheader'))
41                return False
42            else:
43                return True
```

As we did with save(), we want to provide the caller with extra information about the success of our action. In our case, we opt to always return a Boolean.

## 11.3.2   Contact URL Pattern and View

With a form to work with, we can move straight into building a view and a URL pattern to interact with the form. We anticipate building a class-based view (CBV) called ContactView and therefore create a new file /contact/urls.py to house our URL configuration, as shown in Example 11.9.

**Example 11.9: Project Code**

contact/urls.py **in** 3969d84738

```
1   from django.conf.urls import url
2   from .views import ContactView
3
4
5   urlpatterns = [
6       url(r'^$',
7           ContactView.as_view(),
8           name='contact'),
9   ]
```

We need to point our root URL configuration to this new file, as shown in Example 11.10.

**Example 11.10: Project Code**

suorganizer/urls.py **in** 3969d84738

```
20   from contact import urls as contact_urls
.        ...
25   urlpatterns = [
.        ...
29       url(r'^contact/', include(contact_urls)),
.        ...
31   ]
```

We can now turn our attention to our view. As for any of the views that handle forms, we have a three-state finite-state machine. In the case of our HTTP GET request, we only need to present the form to the user, as shown in Example 11.11.

**Example 11.11: Project Code**

contact/views.py **in** 3969d84738

```
1    from django.shortcuts import redirect, render
2    from django.contrib.messages import success
3    from django.views.generic import View
4    from .forms import ContactForm
5
6
7    class ContactView(View):
8        form_class = ContactForm
9        template_name = 'contact/contact_form.html'
10
11       def get(self, request):
12           return render(request,
13                         self.template_name,
14                         {'form': self.form_class()})
```

In the case of our HTTP POST method, we need to validate the data submitted by the user. If the data is invalid, we present the form again. In the event the data is valid, we send an email to the site managers with the user's feedback.

Our form breaks from previous forms in that Django may fail to send the email. We never considered the possibility that Django may not save the data to the database, as this is usually a problem we cannot recover from. However, with an email, we don't want to ground our site to a stop. Instead, we want to display a quick message to users about whether or not their email was sent.

To that end, we can use the messages framework that Django provides. The messages framework allows us to save a message that we can display on any page, as long as we add this ability in our templates (we do this in the next section). This means that if we redirect to another page, we can effectively still display a message to the user even if we didn't build the template with this purpose in mind.

We've already imported the `success()` shortcut from the message framework on line 2 (shown in the imports in Example 11.11), and we pass it a simple string to display to the user in Example 11.12. The rest of the view is identical to the `post()` methods we built throughout Chapter 9.

**Example 11.12: Project Code**
`contact/views.py` in `3969d84738`

```
 7    class ContactView(View):
 .        ...
16        def post(self, request):
17            bound_form = self.form_class(request.POST)
18            if bound_form.is_valid():
19                mail_sent = bound_form.send_mail()
20                if mail_sent:
21                    # shortcut for add_message
22                    success(
23                        request,
24                        'Email successfully sent.')
25                    return redirect('blog_post_list')
26            return render(request,
27                    self.template_name,
28                    {'form': bound_form})
```

### 11.3.3   Contact Templates

We have two tasks: we need a template to display the contact form, and we need to modify our templates to display messages from the messages framework.

Let's start with the contact template. As with our other apps, it's first in our interest to have a template that inherits from the site's base template and from which all our other app templates inherit. We create two directories, `/contact/templates/` and `/contact/templates/contact/` (for namespacing purposes), and then create `base_contact.html`, as shown in Example 11.13.

**Example 11.13: Project Code**

`contact/templates/contact/base_contact.html` in 3969d84738

```
1   {% extends parent_template|default:"base.html" %}
```

Recall from Section 11.3 the fourth step for building form webpages:

4. Create a template that

    a. Defines an HTML form tag, `<form method="post" action=".">`, replacing the `action` attribute value with a value computed by the `url` template tag or that calls a model method to reverse a URL pattern

    b. Defines the submit button: `<button type="submit">Submit Button!</button>`

    c. Creates a CSRF token: `{% csrf_token %}`

    d. Generates the form: `{{ form.as_p }}`

This list allows us to create the form shown in Example 11.14.

**Example 11.14: Project Code**

`contact/templates/contact/contact_form.html` in 3969d84738

```
 1   {% extends parent_template|default:"contact/base_contact.html" %}
 2
 3   {% block title %}
 4   {{ block.super }} - Contact Us!
 5   {% endblock %}
 6
 7   {% block content %}
 8     <div>
 9       <div>
10         <form
11             action="{% url 'contact' %}"
12             method="post">
13           {% csrf_token %}
14           {{ form.as_p }}
15           <button type="submit">
16             Contact Us!</button>
17         </form>
18       </div>
19     </div>
20   {% endblock %}
```

We can then turn our attention to displaying messages from Django's messages framework. The goal is to enable Django to display a message on any page. The easiest thing to do is to change our site's base template to display any messages added to the template context by the messages framework, as shown in Example 11.15.

**Example 11.15: Project Code**
templates/base.html **in** 3969d84738

```
40              {% if messages %}
41                <div>
42                  <div>
43                    <ul>
44                      {% for message in messages %}
45                        {% if message.tags %}
46                          <li class="{{ message.tags }}">
47                        {% else %}
48                          <li>
49                        {% endif %}
50                        {{ message }}</li>
51                      {% endfor %}
52                  </ul></div></div>
53              {% endif %}
```

Finally, to finish things off, we add a link to our new contact page in the navigation bar of our website, as shown in Example 11.16.

**Example 11.16: Project Code**
templates/base.html **in** 3969d84738

```
24              <nav>
 .                 ...
35                <li>
36                  <a href="{% url 'contact' %}">
37                    Contact</a></li>
```

With that done, we now have a working webpage that allows users to send us emails containing their feedback!

# 11.4　Splitting Organizer `urls.py`

If you open the /organizer/urls.py file, you'll discover that our urlpatterns list is quite long. What's more, we're defining the prefix to many of the URL patterns multiple times: our URL patterns all have regular expression patterns that start with /tag/, /startup/, or /newslink/. That is not desirable.

While Django convention dictates that our app contain all of the URL patterns in a urls.py file, there is absolutely no reason to adhere to this convention if breaking from convention makes our code cleaner. In this section, we split the urls.py file into several smaller modules, resulting in a url package.

To begin, we need to create a url directory in /organizer/ and then create a file called __init__.py in /organizer/urls/. In our new package, we subsequently create the files newslink.py, startup.py, and tag.py, resulting in three modules in our new package, as shown in Example 11.17.

**Example 11.17: Shell Code**

```
$ tree organizer/urls/
organizer/urls/
├── __init__.py
├── newslink.py
├── startup.py
└── tag.py

0 directories, 4 files
```

We can take all of the URL patterns in /organizer/urls.py and move them into one of our new modules, removing the repeated prefixes.

For instance, Example 11.18 shows how the organizer_startup_list URL pattern originally read.

**Example 11.18: Project Code**
organizer/urls.py **in** 3969d84738

```
10    urlpatterns = [
 .        ...
20        url(r'^startup/$',
21            startup_list,
22            name='organizer_startup_list'),
 .        ...
50    ]
```

In our new organizer/urls/startup.py, the organizer_startup_list URL pattern now reads as shown in Example 11.19.

**Example 11.19: Project Code**
organizer/urls/startup.py **in** 2675456e87

```
 7    urlpatterns = [
 8        url(r'^$',
 9            startup_list,
10            name='organizer_startup_list'),
 .        ...
23    ]
```

It is significantly simpler to find the URL pattern for the appropriate object, as we now have them organized in separate modules. What's more, we are better adhering to the DRY principle, as the URL path prefixes to all our URL patterns are now defined in a single place in our project. The root URL configuration had previously read as shown in Example 11.20.

**Example 11.20: Project Code**

`suorganizer/urls.py` **in** 3969d84738

```
21   from organizer import urls as organizer_urls
 .       ...
30       url(r'^', include(organizer_urls)),
```

With our new package, we can change the code above to read as in Example 11.21.

**Example 11.21: Project Code**

`suorganizer/urls.py` **in** 2675456e87

```
21   from organizer.urls import (
22       newslink as newslink_urls,
23       startup as startup_urls, tag as tag_urls)
 .       ...
27   urlpatterns = [
 .       ...
32       url(r'^newslink/', include(newslink_urls)),
33       url(r'^startup/', include(startup_urls)),
34       url(r'^tag/', include(tag_urls)),
35   ]
```

Django's conventions are powerful and useful, but sometimes, it's in our interest to break them. In the preceding code, rather than have a `urls` module, we now have a `urls` package, and our code is cleaner because of this change.

> **Info**
>
> The URL patterns to `NewsLink` webpages have not changed despite that we can now switch from regular expression patterns that use `pk` to those that use the new `slug` field. We will wait until Chapter 17 to change the views and URL patterns of `NewsLink` objects to use the new `SlugField`.

# 11.5   Putting It All Together

We did two things this chapter:

- Split the **organizer** app's `urls` module into a `urls` package with multiple child modules
- Built a webpage to allow users to send us emails

The new `urls` package allowed us to better clean up code and better adhere to DRY despite breaking one of Django's recommended conventions.

Our contact feature behaves unlike anything we've built before. It works without models and doesn't interact with the database in the slightest. The form we built doesn't follow convention by implementing a `save()` method, and we instead built a `send_mail()` method.

In Django, the only thing necessary for basic functionality is a view. Models, templates, forms, messages, and anything else are simply there to help you build better webpages more easily. The basic mechanism of any website is the HTTP request/response cycle, and to that end, you will only ever need the view mechanism that Django provides. The rest may or may not be useful for your purposes.

Django **is** Python. Consequently, it gives you an incredible amount of flexibility and power. Breaking convention and bending the rules is always a possibility, but before you do so, make sure you understand why the convention exists. If the repercussions of your actions are not clear, then breaking from the recommended method is not only inadvisable, it may be dangerous (for your websites security).

# 12

# The Big Picture

## In This Chapter

- Use newfound knowledge to see how Django handles the HTTP request/response cycle in full
- See how models, views, templates, forms, context processors, and middleware all fit together
- Reconsider Model-View-Controller and its application to Django
- Learn about the Model-Template-View concept used to describe Django

## 12.1   Introduction

Congratulations! You have now seen and used the core concepts of Django. From here on out, we can take the training wheels off and really begin to have fun.

Before we dive directly into Django's contributed library and advanced uses of Django's core functionality, we're going to review what we saw in the last 11 chapters and take the opportunity to learn a few new things along the way.

In particular, we take a step back and look at the big picture for Django. We discuss how Model-View-Controller (MVC) architecture falls short of describing how Django actually works, and we talk about the Model-Template-View architecture some developers use to describe Django.

## 12.2   Django's Core

A website is an application that interacts with users via a stateless protocol: HTTP. A user sends a request, and the website returns a response.

At start, Django loads into memory all of the URL patterns we have configured in our URL configuration tree. When Django receives an HTTP request, it translates the data into a Python `HttpRequest` object. It then passes the object to the URL dispatch system, which attempts to match the URL path of the request with one of the regular expression patterns in the URL configuration tree. If one of the regular expressions patterns matches, the dispatch system sends the `HttpRequest` to the view that the URL pattern references. Django, at its most basic, is visualized in Figure 12.1.

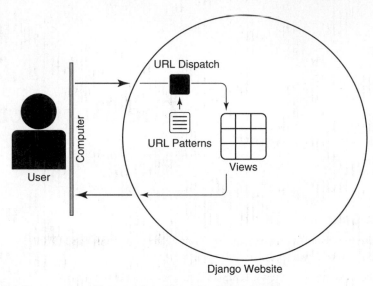

**Figure 12.1:** Django Basic Architecture

Of course, while views and URL patterns are at the heart of Django, it would be difficult to build a website without any other tools. To that end, Django supplies models and templates. Figure 12.2 adds them to the fray.

With models, we can structure data and easily communicate with a number of databases. This turns our application into a system with a stateless (the Django code) and stateful (the database) parts. Especially in today's cloud computing world, this is particularly helpful, as it allows us to quickly change the stateless portion of the application without caring about any of the instances running this code. All of our backup and data protection can thus be entirely focused on the stateful side.

In turn, the template system allows developers to easily dynamically generate front end HTML code, dividing the code so that developers can focus on either the back end or the front end of the website.

At the moment, it may seem as though MVC still applies. However, Figure 12.2 doesn't even take into account forms! We can add a lot of detail to our figure.

In Chapter 5: Creating Webpages with Controllers in Django, we saw that Django can add data to a template's context during the template rendering process. While we did not program our own, we certainly could.

In Chapter 1: Starting a New Django Project, our diagram of Django's architecture introduced the idea of middleware. The concept came up again when discussing cross-site request forgery (CSRF) tokens in Chapter 8: Displaying Forms in Templates. Middleware are Python classes that change `HttpRequest` objects on their way in and modify `HttpResponse` objects on their way out. We can expand on our knowledge by adding them to our diagram, having only mentioned them in passing. Each ring of the middleware section in Figure 12.3 represents a middleware class: middleware is applied in reverse order on the way out when compared to the way in.

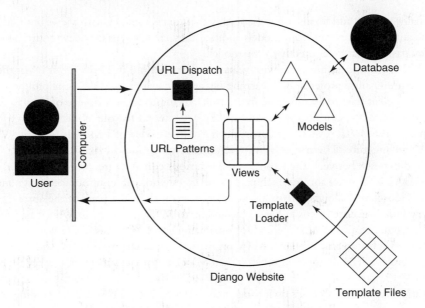

**Figure 12.2:** Django Intermediate Architecture

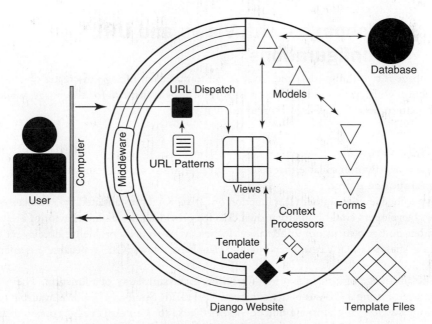

**Figure 12.3:** Django Full Architecture

Finally, we can add forms, noting not only that forms interact with views but that they can be automatically built from models and that they circumvent the view entirely, saving data by passing that data directly to the model.

MVC is a strong architecture with years of history behind it. However, it is not the architecture Django projects use. Learning Django according to MVC is helpful because it provides a great start to learning the framework. Trying to fit every piece of Django within the umbrella of MVC is impossible and will be detrimental to your understanding.

To counter MVC, several developers put forward the idea of a Model-Template-View (MTV) architecture. The names of the two architectures should strike you as similar. The central difference between the two is how the various concepts are coupled together. Whereas MVC is strict about which part of the framework can communicate with another, MTV is looser and allows for communication between all of the parts of the app.

Very little literature discusses Django according to MTV. There is no Wikipedia page and no other framework uses this method for organizing code. Whereas MVC was built to be a generalized solution to a problem, MTV originated as a description of the code inside a Django project. The description is better than MVC, but it lacks many of the key tools seen in Figure 12.3.

Django very much does its own thing, and (once we have a basic understanding of the moving pieces) we no longer need an architecture to describe it. I prefer to think of Django as MVC-inspired and typically try to avoid any discussion of MTV.

# 12.3   Webpages with Views and URL Configurations

A webpage is two things: data and a way to get to that data. Django re-creates this abstraction with views and URL patterns. A view returns the data for a webpage, while the URL pattern defines how and when to use that view.

## 12.3.1   Views

A view is any Python callable that takes an `HttpRequest` instance and returns an `HttpResponse` object.

Typically, views are either (1) a function or (2) an object instantiated by a subclass of `View`. Developers could build their own class for providing the basic behavior of a view, but doing so turns out to be tricky. To best avoid security problems, developers typically stick to using `View` when building class-based views (CBVs) because it is safer and quicker.

The advantage of using a function for a view is the simplicity of a function. The advantage of using a CBV is better adherence to HTTP. Similar behavior is available to developers when programming function views thanks to the `require_http_methods` decorator (and its siblings, such as `require_safe`), but this approach is not quite as powerful. What's more, when building views that share behavior, CBVs become a natural choice, as developers can then use the full power of Python object-oriented programming.

### 12.3.2   URL Patterns and Configurations

To point Django to views, developers build URL patterns.

A URL pattern consists at least of (1) a regular expression pattern and (2) a reference to a view. A URL pattern may additionally define (3) a dictionary, which is passed to the view as keyword arguments, and (4) a name, allowing for the developer to interact with the URL pattern throughout the rest of the site.

The regular expression pattern is used to match a URL path. For instance, a regular expression pattern `^tag/[\w\-]+/$` will match `/tag/django/` and `/tag/video-games/`. If a match occurs, Django calls the view that is associated with the regular expression pattern's URL pattern.

A list of URL patterns is called a **URL configuration**. A URL pattern may include a URL configuration, which results in a conceptual tree of URL patterns. Each node in the tree is a URL configuration. A regular expression pattern `^tag/` could point to a URL configuration with the URL pattern containing the regular expression pattern `^[\w\-]+/$`. Given a URL path `/tag/django/`, Django removes the first slash, resulting in `tag/django/`. Django then attempts to match all of the patterns in the root (of the tree) URL configuration. It matches the `^tag/`, removes the path segment from the URL (resulting in `django/`), and then attempts to match this path segment with the regular expression patterns in this leaf (of the tree). The regular expression pattern `^[\w\-]+/$` matches the URL path `django/`. Django then calls the view associated with this last URL pattern.

The term *URL configuration* is used interchangeably to refer to the lists of URL patterns or else to the tree of all the URL patterns for the website.

# 12.4   Generating Webpages Thanks to Models and Templates

While a URL pattern and a view are all that is necessary for a webpage, the central reason to use Django is for its dynamism. We generate webpages based on data, which allows us to adhere to the Don't Repeat Yourself (DRY) principle.

Pretend we're building a newspaper. Every article webpage looks the same but varies according to the title, author, and content of the article. With Django, we separate the display/layout of the webpage from the content. If we wanted to change the way our articles are displayed, we would make a change in only a single place. In our newspaper website, we would store the content of our articles in Django models, while the layout of our article webpages would be built with Django templates.

### 12.4.1   Structuring and Storing Data in Models

A Django model is a Python class that communicates with a database. We structure the data in the model using Django fields, which are Python classes that contain discrete pieces of data. When represented in the database, a model is a table and fields are columns in the table. A model instance is a row of data in the database.

Django fields map to different kinds of column types. A `CharField` maps to a SQLite3 `varchar` column, while a `DateField` maps to a SQLite3 `date` columns. Django additionally knows how to map fields to PostgreSQL, Oracle, and MySQL databases.

When structuring data in Django, the goal is to start by building models and to let Django generate the database using this data. In no way should developers build a database from scratch and then try to match a Django model to this database.

To further configure the structure and behavior data, models anticipate the definition of a nested `Meta` class with specific attributes. In turn, Django uses methods such as `__str__()` and `get_absolute_url()` if they are defined on the class (and it is recommended that you do so).

Finally, to make modifying models easier in large projects and save developers time, Django provides a migration system. Django migrations are scripts that modify the database and act as version control for the schema and data of the database.

### 12.4.2   Controlling Markup with Django Templates

Developers use templates to control the output of Django. Templates are the only non-Python part of Django. While browsers expect to receive HTML, the Django Template Language (DTL) is built in a language-agnostic manner, allowing developers to generate YAML, XML, JSON, or any other imaginable markup. Templates are **rendered** (generated) using a **context** (a dictionary with data).

The DTL is a domain-specific language with an interesting shortcoming. The language provides loops, conditions, and all the hallmarks of a real programming language, but it lacks the ability to set new long-term variables (I am discounting the creation of scoped variables thanks to loops and the `with` tag, which we have yet to use). The goal of the language is to act on data provided to it (typically, but not always, by the view, as we shall see in Chapter 27: Building Custom Template Tags).

The DTL is split into two types of controls: tags and filters. A filter is a function that acts on a variable, and a tag is for more powerful control. Loops and conditionals occur using template tags, while changing the way the date displays is done via a template filter.

Starting in Django 1.8, the DTL is not the only template language that Django can use to generate output. Out of the box, Django can understand Jinja2 and provides an API for other template languages to hook into. This book uses the DTL exclusively for historical purposes.

## 12.5   Interacting with Data via Forms

HTML comes with the `form` tag, which allows for a webpage to query the user for data and send that data to a web resource. Django supplies the `Form` class to enable developers to quickly generate HTML forms, accept the data they've queried the user for, and determine whether that data is valid and safe.

Forms are complex and are best dealt with as finite-state machines with three states. A form (1) may be empty, (2) may contain invalid or insecure data, or (3) may contain valid data.

Forms are similar to models in that developers build subclasses of `Form`. Form field instances are declared as attributes of the subclass. Much like model fields, form fields are meant to hold a discrete piece of information. However, model fields and form fields are very different. A model field can interact with the database, whereas a form field can be represented in the HTML form by an input field (called a **widget** in Django to avoid further confusion with the word *field*).

Model fields and form fields can be connected through the inheritance of `ModelForm`. Instead of defining a form from scratch, using `ModelForm` allows developers to generate a form to accept data based on the structure of a model.

To control validation of data, developers can define clean methods on the Django form, allowing them to check or modify the data being passed to the form.

Django forms are your go-to tool for allowing users to submit comments, write articles, or upload videos. The difficulty in using forms is that you need to properly understand models, templates, and views before you can fully take advantage of their power.

## 12.6  Intervening in Control Flow

"Don't call us. We'll call you." The Hollywood principle (inversion of control) is the key to understanding how frameworks like Django operate. Sometimes, however, it becomes necessary to change core parts of Django's behavior.

In Part I, we never had the chance to actually use the tools Django provides to inject or modify core behavior, but we've talked about the two major systems developers use to this end: middleware and context processors. A context processor is a function that modifies a context dictionary of a template before the template is rendered with that data. Middleware are classes that modify the `HttpRequest` before it arrives to the URL dispatch system and modify the `HttpResponse` after it is returned from the view. Middleware classes are called in reverse order when dealing with `HttpResponse`: if Middleware A is the first to receive the `HttpRequest`, it will be last to receive the `HttpResponse`.

While middleware and context processors are not necessarily core concepts (as you won't necessarily use them on every single site), they are worth mentioning because they affect the core components of Django on each webpage.

## 12.7  Moving Forward

There are very few websites you could not build with Django given your current knowledge. However, there is still plenty we can learn to make building those websites much easier.

In Part II we discover the contributed library. These are apps (like **organizer** and **blog**) and tools that Django supplies out of the box to make your life a little bit easier.

In Part III we return to Django's core tools to see how to extend and modify them to best take advantage of Django's power.

Before all that, however, I recommend using the tools we have already programmed to build your own website. Here are a few recommendations I have, based on content from my class:

- A poem website (display and add poems; challenge: code snippet website)
- A list website (challenge: to-do lists)
- A poll website (consider Django's tutorial, but skip the sections on Admin, supplementing with content from here)
- A discussion forum (ultra challenge: hierarchical responses)

# II

# Django's Contributed Libraries

Toto, I've a feeling we're not in
Kansas anymore.

Judy Garland as Dorothy Gale
in *The Wizard of Oz* (1939)

# Django's Contributed Library

## In This Chapter

- Dive into Django's source code
- Learn about Django's versions and how they are supported
- Discover Django's contributed library
- See a brief outline of the work we will do in Part II
- Discover the translation framework

## 13.1 Introduction

The focus of Part II is Django's contributed library. Colloquially called *contrib*, the library is a set of premade apps filled with content for developers to use to make building websites as easy and as quick as possible.

This book uses a rather loose definition of the contributed library. As we discover in this chapter, contrib refers to a very select part of Django's source code and to a specific set of tools. Nevertheless, in Part II, we also discuss tools that exist outside of contrib because they provide a means for developers to extend behavior rather than having to customize core behavior (the topic of Part III).

In this chapter, we introduce the contributed library by jumping into Django's actual source code. We see how Django is laid out, where the contributed library exists, and the nature of the library, acting as a jumping board into the rest of Part II. This foundation allows us to talk about a few apps that are not covered in this book.

## 13.2 Django's Source Code (and Versioning)

Django's source code is available for all on Github at https://github.com/django/django/. For beginners, the project is overwhelming, so we break it down here, starting with what Django versions are.

Django versions itself according to major and minor numbers but uses two numbers to represent the major version. Django 1.7 includes the major version, whereas Django 1.7.3 includes the major and minor version numbers. The minor number is incremented for releases that fix bugs or security problems. The major number is incremented when new features are added and when features are deprecated. Deprecated features are removed two versions later: a feature deprecated in Django 1.6 will be fully removed in Django 1.8.

Django supports two major versions. The latest version receives bug fixes of all types, whereas the second-to-last version receives only fixes to security and data-loss problems. Django also marks a version for long-term support (LTS), supporting that version for approximately 3 years, providing bug fixes for security and data-loss problems.

When Django 1.7 was the latest version, Django 1.4 was marked for LTS. Django 1.7 therefore received bug fixes for any sort of problem, while Django 1.6 and 1.4 received bug fixes for only security and data-loss problems. With the release of Django 1.8, Django 1.6 lost support, and Django 1.4 ceased to be LTS. Django 1.8 is marked for LTS, meaning that at the moment only Django 1.8 and 1.7 are supported.

## Ghosts of Django Future

At the time of writing, developers are looking to switch how Django is versioned (to potentially adhere to semantic versioning). Keep an eye out for future versions, as there is a very good chance Django will be playing by different rules starting in version 1.10 (which may then upgrade to 1.11⇒2.0).

All of the versions of Django are represented as branches in the git repository. For instance, you can find the `stable/1.8.x` branch, which contains all of the code and git commits for major version 1.8 of Django. When developers make changes to Django, they typically work on the `development` branch, which contains code meant for the next major release (currently Django 1.9). Any of these changes that fix code in Django 1.8 will be retroactively applied. Any of these changes that fix security or data-loss problems will be further applied to the `stable/1.7.x` branch.

All of the Django code in this book is from the `stable/1.8.x` branch.

If you download the code and step into the first directory level, you'll be greeted with the content in Example 13.1.

**Example 13.1: Shell Code**

```
$ ls
AUTHORS              django
CONTRIBUTING.rst     docs
Django.egg-info      extras
INSTALL              scripts
LICENSE              setup.cfg
MANIFEST.in          setup.py
README.rst           tests
```

Some of this content is simply information for developers looking at the repository. The setup files (`setup.cfg` and `setup.py`) are used for installing Django, and the `tests/` directory contains all of Django's tests. The two directories of interest are `docs/`, which contains all of Django's documentation, and `django/`(shown in Example 13.2), which contains all of the actual source code to run Django.

**Example 13.2: Shell Code**

```
$ ls django/
__init__.py     db              template
apps            dispatch        templatetags
bin             forms           test
conf            http            utils
contrib         middleware      views
core            shortcuts.py
```

Some of the directories shown in Example 13.2 should be familiar. The `http/` directory is where we imported objects like `HttpResponse` and `HttpResponseNotFound` from, while the `db/` directory contains all of the code for models and object-relational mapping (ORM). You can also spot the directory that contains all of the template code we've used.

Despite my claims that models, templates, and even views are a core part of Django, the source code doesn't agree with me and provides a `core/` directory, shown in Example 13.3.

**Example 13.3: Shell Code**

```
$ ls django/core/
__init__.py              paginator.py
cache                    serializers
checks                   servers
context_processors.py    signals.py
exceptions.py            signing.py
files                    urlresolvers.py
handlers                 validators.py
mail                     wsgi.py
management
```

We actually used functionality from `core/` when we loaded tools such as `reverse()` from `urlresolvers.py`. The `urlresolvers.py` file is the system that defines the URL configuration and is definitely part of Django's core. The same can be said about Django's exceptions.

Some of these may surprise you, of course. The `paginator.py` file contains code we won't see until Chapter 14: Pagination(following my loose definition of contrib). All of Django's `manage.py` commands live in the `management` directory, and everything related to sending emails is in `mail/` (tools we used in Chapter 11: Bending the Rules).

Django's source code, now that we've had a quick look, is far more approachable than many give it credit, and the ability to peer into the depths of the framework is an invaluable skill that is well-worth honing. It's huge—there are no two ways about that—and we could spend a lot of time looking at it, but we came here for a reason: let's examine the contributed library.

# 13.3   Django's `contrib` Code

The contributed library is colloquially called *contrib* because that is the name of the directory that houses it, as you can see in Example 13.4.

**Example 13.4: Shell Code**

```
$ ls django/contrib/
__init__.py    gis          sitemaps
admin          humanize     sites
admindocs      messages     staticfiles
auth           postgres     syndication
contenttypes   redirects    webdesign
flatpages      sessions
```

The truth about contrib is very simple: every one of these directories is a Django app. Take, for instance, the flatpages/ directory, shown in Example 13.5.

**Example 13.5: Shell Code**

```
$ ls django/contrib/flatpages/
__init__.py    locale         sitemaps.py
admin.py       middleware.py  templatetags
apps.py        migrations     urls.py
forms.py       models.py      views.py
```

Example 13.5 should look incredibly familiar. Compare it to our own **organizer** app, shown in Example 13.6.

**Example 13.6: Shell Code**

```
$ ls organizer/
__init__.py    migrations    tests       views.py
admin.py       models.py     urls
forms.py       templates     utils.py
```

As we saw in our **contact** app, the definition of an app is simply a Python package that provides at least one piece of Django functionality. In the case of **flatpages** (listed in Example 13.5), we can see that the app provides forms, models, migrations, views, and a URL configuration. However, sometimes an app provides only a single feature; the **webdesign** app (Example 13.7), for instance, contributes only custom template tags (the topic of Chapter 27: Building Custom Template Tags).

**Example 13.7: Shell Code**

```
$ ls django/contrib/webdesign/
__init__.py  apps.py        templatetags
```

We've actually already used a contributed app. In Chapter 11, we used the **messages** app to store messages to be displayed on the next page to be displayed. We can take a quick look at the contents of the directory and see that the app works by using context processors (tools that add data to template contexts, introduced in Chapter 9: Controlling Forms in Views) and middleware (discussed in Chapter 12: The Big Picture) to work as desired (the views.py file is a red herring—it actually provides a mixin class for class-based views [CBVs]). See Example 13.8.

**Example 13.8: Shell Code**

```
$ ls django/contrib/messages/
__init__.py          middleware.py
api.py               storage
apps.py              utils.py
constants.py         views.py
context_processors.py
```

While you don't (yet) have all the tools you need to understand all of the code in the apps in the contributed library, thanks to Part I, you have the majority of the information. Throughout Part II, we examine the structure of apps in the contributed library to better familiarize you with the content and to make the code more approachable. They are, after all, just Django apps.

# 13.4   Content (Not) Covered

As large as this book is, there is a lot of content that we simply do not have the time to cover.

**Example 13.9: Shell Code**

```
$ ls django/contrib/
__init__.py   gis          sitemaps
admin         humanize     sites
admindocs     messages     staticfiles
auth          postgres     syndication
contenttypes  redirects    webdesign
flatpages     sessions
```

In the contributed app, shown in Example 13.9, we will not have the opportunity to use or discuss the following:

- **admindocs**
- **gis**
- **humanize**
- **postgres**
- **redirects**
- **webdesign**

What's more, while we will use the following apps and discuss their basic use, we won't spend any time dedicated to them specifically:

- **contenttypes**
- **messages**
- **sessions**
- **sites**

All in all, the contributed apps we will see are the following:

- **admin** (Chapter 23)
- **auth** (Chapters 19, 20, 21, 22)
- **flatpages** (Chapter 15)
- **sitemaps**
- **staticfiles** (Chapter 16)
- **syndication**

Despite being in contrib, we will wait to use the content of **sitemaps** and **syndication** until Chapter 28: Adding RSS and Atom Feeds and a Sitemap, because it's best to wait until directly before deployment (Chapter 29: Deploy!) to use them.

The rest of Part II is dedicated to parts of Django in the spirit of the contributed library. In Chapter 14, we'll see what tools Django provides to split up long lists of content. In Chapter 17: Understanding Generic Class-Based View, and Chapter 18: Advanced Generic Class-Based View Usage, we'll use a set of views provided by Django (and which very easily could be part of an app in contrib).

## 13.5   Translation

In many of the contributed apps, you will discover the existence of the `locale/` directory. In the code of these apps, you will furthermore run into code that looks like `_('a string value')`. Both the directory and the `_()` function are part of Django's translation framework.

The `_()` is actually a shortcut for the `ugettext()` or `ugettext_lazy()` functions. You may discover this by looking at the imports of the files using the `_()` convention, shown in Example 13.10.

**Example 13.10: Python Code**

```
from django.utils.translation import ugettext_lazy as _
```

Both `ugettext()` and `ugettext_lazy()` mark a string for translation. The translation framework will take all these strings and allow a person to translate them. These translations are then stored in the `locale/` directory.

In an effort not to distract us from the content we are learning, and despite being an integral part of website building, the code in this book does not use the translation framework. Your own project should not do the same. As soon as possible in your projects, you should import `ugettext()` as `_` in your Python code and wrap any string meant to be displayed using `_()`. This should include verbose names in model fields and models' meta, errors displayed on forms, and the text values presented in templates such as form submission buttons (thanks to the `trans` template tag).

If done right away, the cost of using the translation framework is low, as the tools are simple, straightforward, and well documented. However, if you wait until you actually need to translate your entire website, you will put yourself in a position where you have an enormous amount of very simple but tedious work to do.

> **Django Documentation**
> https://dju.link/18/translation

## 13.6   Putting It All Together

Part II is named after Django's contributed library, and while the majority of the code we use in this part belongs to the contributed library, some of it simply follows in the spirit of the contributed library. The true goal of this part is to help fill out our website. While we have basic webpages and the ability to add content, we don't have users or permissions, and the code we've used to build our website is a little too verbose. In Part II, we add complexity, simplify code, and take several very large steps toward building a full website.

Despite that we are building a full website, we are cutting corners to avoid distractions and to focus on one tool at a time. The biggest casualty of this choice is the translation framework, code that integrates into many facets of the website. When building your own website, *do not forego the translation framework*. You won't always need it or use it, but when you already have the code you need integrated, you'll be thankful.

# 14

# Pagination: A Tool for Navigation

## In This Chapter

- Learn about pagination
- Discuss pagination as a means of organizing data
- See how to paginate using different parts of the URL
- Discover optional regular expression patterns and their shortcomings
- Paginate `StartupList` and `TagList` views

## 14.1  Introduction

Pagination is simple: given a list of items, pagination splits up the list across multiple webpages. At the moment, given how little data exists in our database, pagination seems unnecessary. However, as we add data to our database, pagination will become quite useful. For instance, we won't want to show all of our blog posts to the user (particularly if we have 250 of them). Typically, the user will only be interested in seeing the first five. Pagination provides not only a simple way to display the first five items but also the ability to enable the user to navigate our website to see the next five blog posts.

While implementing pagination is simple, deciding whether to implement is not. Pagination is a means of navigation, and as we consider pagination, we must consider many navigation alternatives and how we want the user to view and use our site.

At the moment, we do not have the tools necessary to build a full-featured navigation system in Django, and the problem is mostly a question of usability. Considering the problem at this point is thus counterproductive, and we unfortunately won't have time to deal with the issue in full. We will return to part of the problem in Chapter 17: Understanding Generic Class-Based Views.

In the next section, we paginate our `Tag` and `Startup` object lists as a means of demonstrating how to paginate lists with Django. We paginate each list in a different way. For our `Startup` list, we paginate the list using the query of the URL, creating URLs such as `http://site.django-unleashed.com/startup/?page=2`. Our `Tag` object list will be paginated using the path of the URL, creating `http://site.django-unleashed.com/tag/2/`.

# 14.2   A Word about URLs: Query versus Path

The reason we are building the `Tag` and `Startup` pagination URLs in two different ways is that clients and managers may ask you to paginate in either of the two ways. It is thus helpful to understand each way of implementing pagination.

However, from a purists' approach, one of these methods is *awful*. In the event that you need to make the decision of how to encode pagination for yourself, the information in this section will ensure you understand your choice.

The structure of a URL, as outlined in Chapter 1, is

```
scheme : // network_location / path [? query] [# fragment]
```

The browser uses the scheme and network location to contact a server. Once contacted, the browser asks the server for a resource by sending the path and query (and fragment). The path is a mandatory part of the URL, while the query is not (neither is the fragment). In Part I, we only needed to worry about the path. Now, we are concerned with both the path and the query.

The path contains hierarchical data from most important to least important. The last part of the path is thus the most specific:

```
/milky-way/solar-system/earth/europe/france/paris/
```

The query is reserved for nonhierarchical data and appears as sets of key value pairs:

```
/paris/?order_by=arrondissement
```

The query is meant as an addition, and must work in tandem with the path.

The goal of a URL is to identify a resource permanently (or for as long as possible) and to make sure that identification is obvious to humans. The path `/startup/boundless-software/` is thus excellent, as the user knows to expect a webpage about the Boundless Software startup.

We are about to build pagination in two different ways:

```
/tag/2/
/startup/?page=2
```

The alleged central advantage to the first is that it is prettier, and it seems simpler at first glance. But it is all downhill from there.

The first problem with the first option is that it is not clear what resource we are identifying. What does the digit mean? Does `/tag/1/` identify a tag by the name of `1`? In our case, this is a decent assumption, as `/tag/django/` identifies the webpage about the Django tag. What this means it that our pagination of tags in this case actually conflicts with our tag detail webpages.

To make the URL clearer, some developers advocate the use of `/tag/page/1/`. However, this structure leads to other problems. Each path segment is supposed to be a valid resource. What does the webpage `/tag/page/` display? Is it different from `/tag/`? Some developers instead opt for `/tag/page-1/`. This is quite revealing: the page path segment in all of these cases is acting as the keyword to the number value. This is not hierarchical and is in fact exactly what the query is for.

Django's pagination system, as we are about to discover, essentially assumes that webpages will default to using the URL query, and the documentation provides no information about building pagination with the URL path. Django's development group is not the only one that advocates for the use of the query part of the URL to identify pages: Google does as well. Google's Webmaster Central Blog[1] contains multiple articles on the topic of making pagination easier to index, and in all cases, the authors assume the use of the query part of the URL.

The underlying philosophy in the Google articles is that the path of a URL identifies information, and the query identifies resources: all of the resources at a path modified by a query contain subsets of the information identified by the path. According to Google, the "canonical" URL /tag/ should list all of the tags on our site, and the query should modify the resource to show a subset of this information in different ways: /tag/?page=1 is a direct subset of the list shown at /tag/, and /tag/?page=1&order_by=popularity is a direct modified subset of the list shown at /tag/. Take a moment to look at that last query URL: /tag/?page=1&order_by=popularity. Adding information to a URL path as simply as we have to the URL query is just not possible, hinting at the advantages of the query method as well as how we would eventually build our site navigation (if this book were even longer!).

Before long, the website we are building will adhere to the pagination system described above (information–centric, URL query only). However, because it is useful to know how to paginate using information from the URL query and the URL path, we still build our two paginated lists in two different ways.

## 14.3  Discovering Django Pagination in the Shell

As with all Django tools, the quickest way to discover how to use the tool is to pop open the shell and start fooling around. Use the command in Example 14.1.

**Example 14.1: Shell Code**

```
$ ./manage.py
```

Let's start by splitting up our tag list webpage. At the moment, we have 16 Tag objects in our database, as shown in Example 14.2.

**Example 14.2: Python Interpreter Code**

```
>>> from organizer.models import Tag
>>> Tag.objects.count()
16
```

---

1. http://googlewebmastercentral.blogspot.com/

If we did not know about the `Pagination` class, we could start by slicing our queryset ourselves. In Example 14.3, we ask for all 16 `Tag` objects, and then use a slice to take the first five.

**Example 14.3: Python Interpreter Code**

```
>>> Tag.objects.all()[:5]
[<Tag: Augmented Reality>, <Tag: Big Data>,
 <Tag: Django>, <Tag: Education>, <Tag: Ipython>]
```

This is easy for the first five objects, but what if we need the next five? We would have to manually calculate which set of objects we want for each webpage. This isn't difficult, but it is repetitive work, and we have Django for that. Instead of slicing the queryset ourselves, we can import `Paginator` and ask Django to split our `Tag` objects into groups of five for us, as shown in Example 14.4.

**Example 14.4: Python Interpreter Code**

```
>>> from django.core.paginator import Paginator
>>> paginator = Paginator(Tag.objects.all(), 5)
```

Django will acknowledge the receipt of 16 objects, as shown in Example 14.5.

**Example 14.5: Python Interpreter Code**

```
>>> paginator.count
16
```

To get the first five objects, we can simply ask for the first webpage by passing the number 1 to the `page()` method, as shown in Example 14.6. This creates an instance of the `Page` class, which contains our first five `Tag` objects, as made available to us via the `object_list` attribute.

**Example 14.6: Python Interpreter Code**

```
>>> page1_tags = paginator.page(1)
>>> page1_tags.object_list
[<Tag: Augmented Reality>, <Tag: Big Data>,
 <Tag: Django>, <Tag: Education>, <Tag: Ipython>]
```

At first glance, this might seem problematic. In our tag list template, we are iterating over the `tag_list` variable in a loop to output data for individual tags. If we are now passing in an instance of `Page`, we might think we need to modify this loop variable to `paginated_tag_list.object_list` to properly output our list of tags as before. Fortunately, we don't need to change our templates at all to accommodate this: when iterating over a `Page` instance, the object will automatically supply the objects in the `object_list` attribute, as shown in Example 14.7.

**Example 14.7: Python Interpreter Code**

```
>>> list(page1_tags)
[<Tag: Augmented Reality>, <Tag: Big Data>,
 <Tag: Django>, <Tag: Education>, <Tag: Ipython>]
```

Instances of `Page` are quite clever. On top of the behavior in Example 14.7, they also provide an attribute that points to the paginator that created them. We thus have access to it in the template should we need it. In Example 14.8, we check that the `Paginator` object we instantiated to the `paginator` variable is the same as the one pointed to by the `paginator` attribute of our `Page` instance `page1_tags`.

**Example 14.8: Python Interpreter Code**

```
>>> paginator is page1_tags.paginator
True
```

For instance, if we want to print the number of pages created by the `Paginator`, we can refer to it via our `Page` instance, as shown in Example 14.9.

**Example 14.9: Python Interpreter Code**

```
>>> paginator.num_pages
4
>>> page1_tags.paginator.num_pages
4
```

This is quite useful. While we don't need to change the `tag_list` loop in any way, we do want to add to the template. We want to enable the user to see not just the first five `Tag` objects but also the next five, and so forth. To do so, we must provide a link to webpages that show these `Tag` objects: we must link to webpages displaying other instances of `Page`.

Thankfully, our current `Page` instance knows what its current number is, as shown in Example 14.10.

**Example 14.10: Python Interpreter Code**

```
>>> page1_tags.number
1
```

It also knows whether there are any other pages created by the `Paginator` instance, as shown in Example 14.11.

**Example 14.11: Python Interpreter Code**

```
>>> page1_tags.has_other_pages()
True
```

We see whether this `Page` has a next sibling, and what its number is, in Example 14.12.

**Example 14.12: Python Interpreter Code**

```
>>> page1_tags.has_next()
True
>>> page1_tags.next_page_number()
2
```

Effectively, this tells us that we can create a `Page` by calling `paginator.page(2)` and that it will contain the successive `Tag` elements shown by our current page.

We can do the same with the elements that are listed before the ones we are currently showing: the previous page. `Page` objects are indexed starting at 1, meaning there is no page 0: we are looking at the first five `Tag` objects with page 1. We therefore don't have a previous page, as you can see in Example 14.13.

**Example 14.13: Python Interpreter Code**

```
>>> page1_tags.has_previous()
False
```

If we nonetheless ask for the number of the page, Django will raise an `EmptyPage` exception, informing us that the previous page has no `Tag` objects to display and that the index number may not be less than 1, as shown in Example 14.14.

**Example 14.14: Python Interpreter Code**

```
>>> page1_tags.previous_page_number()
django.core.paginator.EmptyPage: That page number is less than 1
```

We can raise the exact same `EmptyPage` exception by trying to create page 0 ourselves, as shown in Example 14.15.

**Example 14.15: Python Interpreter Code**

```
>>> page0_tags = paginator.page(0)
django.core.paginator.EmptyPage: That page number is less than 1
```

Similarly, Django will raise this exception if we give it a number that is too large, as shown in Example 14.16.

**Example 14.16: Python Interpreter Code**

```
>>> page1000_tags = paginator.page(1000)
django.core.paginator.EmptyPage: That page contains no results
```

Django has a different error for when we pass in a value that makes no sense. In Example 14.17, instead of passing in a number, we pass in the string value A.

**Example 14.17: Python Interpreter Code**

```
>>> pageA_tags = paginator.page('A')
django.core.paginator.PageNotAnInteger:
    That page number is not an integer
```

The problem, however, is not that we are passing in a string, but that we are passing in a non-integer value in the string. In Example 14.18, instead of passing in an integer 1, we pass it in as a string. Django will raise no error, and the Page will work exactly as before.

**Example 14.18: Python Interpreter Code**

```
>>> page1_tags = paginator.page('1')
```

This is quite important: when creating Page instances via Paginator objects, we can forgo catching ValueError and TypeError exceptions and instead focus entirely on EmptyPage and PageNotAnInteger exceptions. Given that URL patterns always pass strings to views, this means that if we get a string containing a number, we do not need to cast it to an integer, as Django does it for us when we call page().

# 14.4  Paginating the Startup List Webpage

With a basic understanding of the Paginator class, we can turn to our startup list webpage and paginate our list. The goal is to allow pagination via the query part of the URL, resulting in http://site.django-unleashed.com/startup/?page=2, for example.

Before we can jump directly into using Pagination and Page, I am going to opt to switch the Startup list page from a function view into a class-based view (CBV). While this is by no means necessary, it will make my life easier in the long run.

We start by replacing the function view with the class shown in Example 14.19.

**Example 14.19: Project Code**
`organizer/views.py` in f0f3d8de64

```
 95   class StartupList(View):
 96       template_name = 'organizer/startup_list.html'
 97
 98       def get(self, request):
 99           startups = Startup.objects.all()
100           context = {'startup_list': startups}
101           return render(
102               request, self.template_name, context)
```

In Example 14.20, we make sure we import our new CBV into our URL configuration, and then point the `organizer_startup_list` URL pattern to the CBV, making sure we call `as_view()`.

**Example 14.20: Project Code**
`organizer/urls/startup.py` in f0f3d8de64

```
 8       url(r'^$',
 9           StartupList.as_view(),
10           name='organizer_startup_list'),
```

We've successfully refactored our code so that it works exactly as before. We can now use our newfound knowledge of `Paginator` to split the list of `Startup` objects. We thus start by importing `Paginator`, as shown in Example 14.21.

**Example 14.21: Project Code**
`organizer/views.py` in ab66617490

```
 1   from django.core.paginator import Paginator
```

To start, let's paginate our list of startups so that we always show the first five `Startup` objects, regardless of anything else. Lines 102 to 105 in Example 14.22 feature this addition.

**Example 14.22: Project Code**
`organizer/views.py` in ab66617490

```
 96   class StartupList(View):
 97       paginate_by = 5   # 5 items per page
 98       template_name = 'organizer/startup_list.html'
 99
100       def get(self, request):
101           startups = Startup.objects.all()
102           paginator = Paginator(
103               startups, self.paginate_by)
```

```
104            page = paginator.page(1)
105            context = {'startup_list': page}
106            return render(
107                request, self.template_name, context)
```

The dictionary passed to render for the template context now takes the Page instance called page on line 105.

If you run the Django development server (./manage.py runserver), you'll be greeted by the output of the first five startups in your database. We've not needed to change our template, as expected. However, we also don't have the ability to view any other pages. Let's change that.

The first thing we can do is inform the user of what page he or she is browsing and how many pages there are. We therefore edit our startup_list.html by using the number attribute of the Page instance and the num_pages attribute of the Paginator instance pointed to by the Page, as shown in Example 14.23.

**Example 14.23: Project Code**
organizer/templates/organizer/startup_list.html **in** 73190831a4

```
40        <li>
41            Page {{ startup_list.number }}
42            of {{ startup_list.paginator.num_pages }}
43        </li>
```

While this is fine, by convention, Django recommends passing the Paginator object directly rather than referencing the object through the Page instance. In our view, we can add the Paginator to the dictionary meant for the RequestContext, as shown in Example 14.24.

**Example 14.24: Project Code**
organizer/views.py **in** 1861a39193

```
105            context = {
106                'paginator': paginator,
107                'startup_list': page,
108            }
```

This allows us to shorten the template code to read as shown in Example 14.25.

**Example 14.25: Project Code**
organizer/templates/organizer/startup_list.html **in** 1861a39193

```
40        <li>
41            Page {{ startup_list.number }}
42            of {{ paginator.num_pages }}
43        </li>
```

We want to print a link to the previous page, but only if our current page has a previous page. We can check whether it does with the `has_previous()` method of the `Page` object. We then create a link, but leave the actual `href` attribute of the anchor tag empty, as shown in Example 14.26.

**Example 14.26: Project Code**

`organizer/templates/organizer/startup_list.html` in 73190831a4

```
34        {% if startup_list.has_previous %}
35          <li>
36            <a href="">
37              Previous</a>
38          </li>
39        {% endif %}
```

In Example 14.27, we can do the same thing for the next page, using `has_next()` instead.

**Example 14.27: Project Code**

`organizer/templates/organizer/startup_list.html` in 73190831a4

```
44        {% if startup_list.has_next %}
45          <li>
46            <a href="">
47              Next</a>
48          </li>
49        {% endif %}
```

We can wrap all of this in a single `ul` tag. Finally, as we only want to print this in the event there are other pages, we can add an if condition. In our `if` template tag, shown in Example 14.28, we check to make sure that `has_other_pages()` returns `True`.

**Example 14.28: Project Code**

`organizer/templates/organizer/startup_list.html` in 73190831a4

```
32        {% if startup_list.has_other_pages %}
33          <ul>
 .          ...
50          </ul>
51        {% endif %}
```

Much like with the reference to `Paginator`, we could opt to be quite lazy. We are always going to call `has_other_pages()`, and we can add the result of the call to `has_other_pages()` in the context dictionary as the `is_paginated` variable, as shown in Example 14.29.

**Example 14.29: Project Code**
organizer/views.py in f355039c13

```
105              context = {
106                  'is_paginated':
107                      page.has_other_pages(),
108                  'paginator': paginator,
109                  'startup_list': page,
110              }
```

Instead of calling startup_list.has_other_pages in the template, we can now simply call is_paginated(), as shown in Example 14.30.

**Example 14.30: Project Code**
organizer/templates/organizer/startup_list.html in f355039c13

```
32      {% if is_paginated %}
33        <ul>
  .         ...
50        </ul>
51      {% endif %}
```

As mentioned at the beginning of the section, we are currently focusing on creating a link to other pages by using the query part of the URL. As such, we need to create a link that's of the format /startup/?page=#. However, because we are already at the /startup/ URL, we only need to specify the query: ?page=#. We thus use the previous_page_number() and next_page_number() methods of the Page object to create these values in the href attribute of out HTML, as shown in Example 14.31.

**Example 14.31: Project Code**
organizer/templates/organizer/startup_list.html in 14d1174c5b

```
36              <a href="?page={{ startup_list.previous_page_number }}">
37                Previous</a>
  .                 ...
46              <a href="?page={{ startup_list.next_page_number }}">
47                Next</a>
```

If we reload the Django development server, we are greeted with a page containing a next link. Navigating to /startup/?page=2 will not change the page output, because our view always returns the first page of Startup objects. We can now return to our view and modify it to use the query information.

In Chapter 9: Controlling Forms in Views, we saw that all of the information passed to our webserver was available in the HttpRequest objects passed to views. We used this information to access the HTTP POST data by accessing request.POST. We can use the same method to access the GET data, which is where URL information is stored. Just like request.POST, the request.GET object acts like a Python dictionary. We can therefore use the get() method to simply ask for the page query, as shown in Example 14.32.

**Example 14.32: Project Code**
organizer/views.py **in** 3109f3f744

```
96    class StartupList(View):
97        page_kwarg = 'page'
98        paginate_by = 5   # 5 items per page
99        template_name = 'organizer/startup_list.html'
 .        ...
101       def get(self, request):
 .           ...
105          page_number = request.GET.get(
106              self.page_kwarg)
107          page = paginator.page(page_number)
```

If you are running your development server and navigate to /startup/?page=1, you will be able to navigate to /startup/?page=2 and be greeted with the next five Startups in our database. This is exactly what we want!

The problem is that if you navigate to /startup/, without the page query information, then you will be greeted by a Django PageNotAnInteger exception. When page is not specified, request.GET.get('page') will return None, which causes the call to paginator.page() to error.

We can modify our code to handle both PageNotAnInteger and EmptyPage exceptions. The first step, shown in Example 14.33, is to import them into our /organizer/views.py file.

**Example 14.33: Project Code**
organizer/views.py **in** ff175264b1

```
1    from django.core.paginator import (
2        EmptyPage, PageNotAnInteger, Paginator)
```

As demonstrated, the main reason PageNotAnInteger will be raised is because page is not specified. In this case, we simply want to display the first page of Startup objects (despite Google's recommendation to display all of them). The EmptyPage exception will be raised if the number passed to page() is below 1 or above the number of pages produced by Paginator. In the first instance, we would want to show the first page, while in the second instance, we would want to show the last page.

While it is possible to pass negative numbers to Django, via URLs such as http://127.0.0.1:8000/startup/?page=-5, the reason EmptyPage is raised is usually that a page number that used to exist is no longer valid. This would only occur if we prune the startup data on our site. Alternatively, a user has taken our URL and entered a number they believe to be the last page. In either case, we want to show the last page of

Startup objects. We therefore return the last page if the `EmptyPage` exception is caught, as shown in Example 14.34.

**Example 14.34: Project Code**
`organizer/views.py` in `ff175264b1`

```
 97   class StartupList(View):
 98       page_kwarg = 'page'
 99       paginate_by = 5   # 5 items per page
100       template_name = 'organizer/startup_list.html'
101
102       def get(self, request):
  .           ...
108           try:
109               page = paginator.page(page_number)
110           except PageNotAnInteger:
111               page = paginator.page(1)
112           except EmptyPage:
113               page = paginator.page(
114                   paginator.num_pages)
```

If you point your browser back to the `/startup/` URL path on the Django development server, you will be greeted by the first five `Startup` objects and working links to other pages, such as `/startup/?page=2` and `/startup/?page=3`. Take note that `/startup/` and `/startup/?page=1` show exactly the same content (ignoring Google's official stance to better illustrate pagination tools).

With this last change, we have successfully paginated our startup list webpage by using the URL query to determine the page number.

The problem with our current implementation is that it's not DRY. We're defining the string `page` for the URL's query part in the view and the template, and a single typo could prevent links from working. Should we wish to change our system to use `p` instead of `page`, we would need to make changes in three places (twice in the template). This is obviously undesirable.

We can generate the links directly in our view, as shown in Example 14.35.

**Example 14.35: Project Code**
`organizer/views.py` in `3bd098b3c8`

```
 97   class StartupList(View):
 98       page_kwarg = 'page'
 99       paginate_by = 5   # 5 items per page
100       template_name = 'organizer/startup_list.html'
101
102       def get(self, request):
  .           ...
115           if page.has_previous():
116               prev_url = "?{pkw}={n}".format(
117                   pkw=self.page_kwarg,
118                   n=page.previous_page_number())
119           else:
120               prev_url = None
```

Remember that we cannot call page.previous_page_number() directly, as it might raise an exception, and that we want the ability to know if the previous or next page exists. We must first check whether the page exists via calls to page.has_previous() and page.has_next(), then set the variable to None if it does not. The process of creating the next page URL is very similar, as shown in Example 14.36.

**Example 14.36: Project Code**
organizer/views.py **in** 3bd098b3c8

```
97    class StartupList(View):
98        page_kwarg = 'page'
99        paginate_by = 5  # 5 items per page
100       template_name = 'organizer/startup_list.html'
101
102       def get(self, request):
   .          ...
121           if page.has_next():
122               next_url = "?{pkw}={n}".format(
123                   pkw=self.page_kwarg,
124                   n=page.next_page_number())
125           else:
126               next_url = None
```

Now we can add these values to our context dictionary, as shown in Example 14.37.

**Example 14.37: Project Code**
organizer/views.py **in** 3bd098b3c8

```
97    class StartupList(View):
98        page_kwarg = 'page'
99        paginate_by = 5  # 5 items per page
100       template_name = 'organizer/startup_list.html'
101
102       def get(self, request):
   .          ...
127           context = {
128               'is_paginated':
129                   page.has_other_pages(),
130               'next_page_url': next_url,
131               'paginator': paginator,
132               'previous_page_url': prev_url,
133               'startup_list': page,
134           }
```

We can then change the conditions and links in our template to use our new URLs, as shown in Example 14.38.

**Example 14.38: Project Code**
`organizer/templates/organizer/startup_list.html` **in** 580794568c

```
34          {% if previous_page_url %}
35            <li>
36              <a href="{{ previous_page_url }}">
37                Previous</a>
38            </li>
39          {% endif %}
   .      ...
44          {% if next_page_url %}
45            <li>
46              <a href="{{ next_page_url }}">
47                Next</a>
48            </li>
49          {% endif %}
```

Our code is a little longer because of DRY, but it is also far cleaner. What's more, we have the ability to split up the functionality of the `get()` method into smaller methods. We take the opportunity to do so in Chapter 17. For the moment, let's paginate our `Tag` object list webpage.

# 14.5   Pagination of Tag List Webpage Using the URL Path

Our goal in this section is to paginate the tag list webpage. Instead of using the query part of the URL, we pass the page number to the path part of the URL. This means that, instead of using `request.GET` to get the information about the query information, we must get it from the URL configuration (just as we get slug information).

Now we are left with a choice. We could create two URL patterns: one to match `/tag/` and one to match `/tag/2/`. Or we could try to use a single URL pattern for both of those URL paths.

As it turns out, we will need to use two URL patterns. We start by trying to use a single regular expression pattern to match both URL path possibilities and discover why we need to use two URL pattens for pagination when passing information via the URL path.

However, before that, I will again opt to switch `Tag` list page to use a class-based view instead of a function view, as shown in Example 14.39.

**Example 14.39: Project Code**
`organizer/views.py` **in** 9a37d33f21

```
168    class TagList(View):
169        template_name = 'organizer/tag_list.html'
170
171        def get(self, request):
172            tags = Tag.objects.all()
```

```
173              context = {
174                  'tag_list': tags,
175              }
176              return render(
177                  request, self.template_name, context)
```

The new URL pattern reads as shown in Example 14.40.

**Example 14.40: Project Code**
organizer/urls/tag.py **in** 9a37d33f21

```
8        url(r'^$',
9            TagList.as_view(),
10           name='organizer_tag_list'),
```

To use a single URL pattern for both /tag/ and /tag/2/, we need to make sure our view can optionally accept the page number passed in the URL path. We thus create an optional keyword parameter page_number as part of get(), as shown in Example 14.41.

**Example 14.41: Project Code**
organizer/views.py **in** 7f4b857b07

```
168   class TagList(View):
  .       ...
171       def get(self, request, page_number=None):
```

Now that we have a page_number parameter, we need to modify our regular expression pattern to optionally pass the page_number value to get(). Our current organizer_tag_list regular expression pattern reads

```
^$
```

This is prefixed in the root URL configuration by the path segment /tag/.

We need to add to this regular expression pattern. To start, we are looking to match any number above 1: we can use \d to match a digit and + to match one or more of them. We then wrap this pattern in a named group called page_number to mirror the view. This leaves us with

```
(?P<page_number>\d+)
```

> **Info**
>
> Remember that regular expression patterns may pass arguments and keyword arguments to functions. Simple groups are passed as arguments, while named groups are passed as keyword arguments. As our get() method has page_number as a keyword argument, we *must* use a named group.

For those confused by how `(?<slug>[\w\-]+)` works with `view_func(request, slug)`, remember that Python allows arguments to be named or not, whereas keyword arguments must be specified. Calling `view_func(req_obj, slug='django')` and `view_func(req_obj, 'django')` are thus both valid.

We always want our URL to end with a slash, so we must append one to this pattern:

```
(?P<page_number>\d+)/
```

The catch with this pattern is that we only want to accept it *sometimes*. This URL pattern must match `/tag/` and `/tag/1/`. We can use the regular expression character ? to make this new partial regular expression pattern optional:

```
((?P<page_number>\d+)/)?
```

We can then insert this regular expression pattern into our original one, resulting in

```
^((?P<page_number>\d+)/)?$
```

## Info

In my Django class, many beginners make the mistake of trying to match this `/tag/` and `/tag/1/` with the following URL pattern:

```
^(?P<page_number>\d+/)?$
```

This is wrong. Here it is side by side with the correct version:

```
^(?P<page_number>\d+/)?$         #wrong!
^((?P<page_number>\d+)/)?$       #correct!
```

The reason the first is wrong is because the value of page_number will always be a digit with a slash at the end. We are passing 2/, not 2, back to our view. Be careful when creating named groups to only match the variable value you want!

Our new URL pattern thus reads as shown in Example 14.42.

**Example 14.42: Project Code**
organizer/urls/tag.py in 5157503073

```
8        url(r'^((?P<page_number>\d+)/)?$',
9            TagList.as_view(),
10           name='organizer_tag_list'),
```

This will correctly pass values to TagList. We can thus browse to /tag/ and /tag/2/, and in the second case, get() will receive page_number=2. However, optional patterns in regular expression patterns cannot be reversed. As it turns out, reverse() is built to ignore optional regular expression patterns. To clarify, we can still use reverse() as before, as shown in Example 14.43.

**Example 14.43: Python Interpreter Code**

```
>>> from django.core.urlresolvers import reverse
>>> reverse('organizer_tag_list')
'/tag/'
```

However, any attempt to set page_number in the URL pattern will result in an exception, as shown in Example 14.44.

**Example 14.44: Python Interpreter Code**

```
>>> reverse('organizer_tag_list', kwargs={'page_number': 3})
django.core.urlresolvers.NoReverseMatch:
    Reverse for 'organizer_tag_list' with arguments '()'
    and keyword arguments '{'page_number': 3}'not found.
    1 pattern(s) tried: ['tag/((?P<page_number>[\\d]+)/)?$']
```

This means that we will be unable to adhere to DRY when creating the navigation links in our template. To paginate our tag list properly, we need two URL patterns.

We can revert our code to use the CBV we originally built, as shown in Example 14.45.

**Example 14.45: Project Code**
organizer/views.py **in** 79bac550f7

```
168    class TagList(View):
  .        ...
171        def get(self, request):
```

The URL pattern for the view is shown in Example 14.46.

**Example 14.46: Project Code**
organizer/urls/tag.py **in** 79bac550f7

```
 8    url(r'^$',
 9        TagList.as_view(),
10        name='organizer_tag_list'),
```

We then create a *new* view, which always takes a page_number named group to pass to the view, as shown in Example 14.47.

**Example 14.47: Project Code**

`organizer/views.py` in 79bac550f7

```
180    class TagPageList(View):
181        template_name = 'organizer/tag_list.html'
182
183        def get(self, request, page_number):
```

For this to work, we create a new URL pattern for our new view, as shown in Example 14.48.

**Example 14.48: Project Code**

`organizer/urls/tag.py` in 79bac550f7

```
14        url(r'^(?P<page_number>\d+)/$',
15            TagPageList.as_view(),
16            name='organizer_tag_page'),
```

We can now turn to the actual act of pagination. As before, we first create a `Paginator` instance, from which we ask for the `Page` we will display. When we ask for the `Page`, we make sure to catch the exceptions the process might raise, as shown in Example 14.49.

**Example 14.49: Project Code**

`organizer/views.py` in c867e96afd

```
181    class TagPageList(View):
182        paginate_by = 5
183        template_name = 'organizer/tag_list.html'
184
185        def get(self, request, page_number):
186            tags = Tag.objects.all()
187            paginator = Paginator(
188                tags, self.paginate_by)
189            try:
190                page = paginator.page(page_number)
191            except PageNotAnInteger:
192                page = paginator.page(1)
193            except EmptyPage:
194                page = paginator.page(
195                    paginator.num_pages)
```

We want to build our links in our view, as we did with `StartupList`. Because we are using the URL configuration, we can use the `url` template tag to reverse our pagination URLs, as shown in Example 14.50.

**Example 14.50: Project Code**
organizer/views.py in c867e96afd

```
181   class TagPageList(View):
182       paginate_by = 5
183       template_name = 'organizer/tag_list.html'
184
185       def get(self, request, page_number):
  .           ...
196           if page.has_previous():
197               prev_url = reverse(
198                   'organizer_tag_page',
199                   args=(
200                       page.previous_page_number(),
201                   ))
202           else:
203               prev_url = None
204           if page.has_next():
205               next_url = reverse(
206                   'organizer_tag_page',
207                   args=(
208                       page.next_page_number(),
209                   ))
210           else:
211               next_url = None
```

Finally, we can use all of this to render our template, as shown in Example 14.51.

**Example 14.51: Project Code**
organizer/views.py in c867e96afd

```
181   class TagPageList(View):
182       paginate_by = 5
183       template_name = 'organizer/tag_list.html'
184
185       def get(self, request, page_number):
  .           ...
212           context = {
213               'is_paginated':
214                   page.has_other_pages(),
215               'next_page_url': next_url,
216               'paginator': paginator,
217               'previous_page_url': prev_url,
218               'tag_list': page,
219           }
220           return render(
221               request, self.template_name, context)
```

In organizer/templates/organizer/tag_list.html, we can now create a navigation menu, as shown in Example 14.52.

**Example 14.52:** Project Code
`organizer/templates/organizer/tag_list.html` **in** 109b027153

```
32      {% if is_paginated %}
33        <ul>
34          {% if previous_page_url %}
35            <li>
36              <a href="{{ previous_page_url }}">
37                Previous</a>
38            </li>
39          {% endif %}
40          <li>
41            Page {{ tag_list.number}}
42            of {{ paginator.num_pages }}
43          </li>
44          {% if next_page_url %}
45            <li>
46              <a href="{{ next_page_url }}">
47                Next</a>
48            </li>
49          {% endif %}
50        </ul>
51      {% endif %}
```

And with that change, we are done!

# 14.6 Putting It All Together

Pagination is a tool for providing navigation to the user by shortening the content on each page. The pagination tools Django provides are mainly about splitting up data in smaller chunks. For most of the necessities around pagination, such as adhering to DRY while creating pagination links, Django expects you to sort out the problem yourself.

In the process of learning to paginate, we discovered that the URL patterns allow regular expression optional patterns but that the `reverse()` function Django provides simply ignores them. They might be useful in certain contexts, but they are typically to be avoided.

We return to pagination in the next chapter and in Chapter 17. For the moment, let's move on to see other display options Django provides.

# Creating Webpages with Django Flatpages

## In This Chapter

- Examine the **flatpages** app
- Learn how to build simple webpages using the app
- Use middleware to change site-wide behavior
- Build the **core** app to house code for interacting with Django's contributed library.

## 15.1 Introduction

When beginners ask if Django allows for the creation of static webpages—simple webpages such as an about or license page that do not need a database to be generated—many developers point these beginners toward the **flatpages** app. However, many beginners are left with the mistaken impression that Django's **flatpages** provides a way to create webpages without a database.

In this section, we use the app to create a very basic about webpage. In doing so, we discover that the **flatpages** contributed app doesn't really create static webpages but instead creates simple—flat—webpages thanks to Django's core system.

## 15.2 Enabling Flatpages

The **flatpages** contributed app is not enabled in Django projects by default. It depends on the **sites** contributed app, which is also not enabled by default.

As we saw in Chapter 1: Starting a New Django Project, to add an app to a project, we need to add the location of the app to our INSTALLED_APPS list in the /suorganizer/ settings.py file. For apps we create, we provide the name of the app. For contributed apps, we provide a Python namespaced string. The existing list of apps, shown in Example 15.1, is thus a list of contributed apps that we are currently using as well as our **blog**, **organizer**, and **contact** apps.

**Example 15.1: Project Code**

`suorganizer/settings.py` **in** `109b027153`

```
34          'django.contrib.admin',
35          'django.contrib.auth',
36          'django.contrib.contenttypes',
37          'django.contrib.sessions',
38          'django.contrib.messages',
39          'django.contrib.staticfiles',
40          'django_extensions',
41          'organizer',
42          'blog',
43          'contact',
44      )
```

## Info

In Example 15.1, you can also see the **django_extensions** app that is used to create IPython notebooks with Django code. The notebooks are available on https://github.com/jambonrose/DjangoUnleashed-1.8/

To enable **sites** and **flatpages**, we simply add `'django.contrib.flatpages'`, and `'django.contrib.sites'`, to the list, as shown in Example 15.2.

**Example 15.2: Project Code**

`suorganizer/settings.py` **in** `09827df6f8`

```
35  INSTALLED_APPS = (
 .          ...
39          'django.contrib.flatpages',
 .          ...
42          'django.contrib.sites',
 .          ...
```

The purpose of the **sites** app is to provide the ability for Django to serve multiple websites using a shared codebase. For instance, if we were creating a service for lawyers and clients, we may wish to create one website for the lawyers and one for the client. The trick is that much of the data and behavior is identical, but some of it is not. The websites would thus appear different and would act as information portals for different individuals, but they would be run by the same instance of Django, which can differentiate between content types thanks to **sites**. We therefore identify the site by providing a `SITE_ID` in settings, as shown in Example 15.3.

**Example 15.3: Project Code**

`suorganizer/settings.py` **in** `09827df6f8`

```
22  SITE_ID = 1
```

With our new apps in our site-wide settings, we need to migrate our database to add any necessary tables, as shown in Example 15.4.

**Example 15.4: Shell Code**

```
$ ./manage.py migrate
Operations to perform:
  Apply all migrations:
    flatpages, sites, contenttypes, auth, admin, blog, sessions, organizer
Running migrations:
  Applying sites.0001_initial... OK
  Applying flatpages.0001_initial... OK
```

We are now ready to begin using **flatpages**.

# 15.3  Anatomy of the App

The **flatpages** app is like any other Django app—it doesn't magically allow for the creation of webpages without a database. In fact, the webpages created by the app are actually instances of the `FlatPage` model class. Flatpages are full webpages that are stored in the database.

For the **flatpages** app to create the illusion of a static page, the app supplies a view to display `FlatPage` instances in. The app also supplies a URL configuration for developers to include in the root URL configuration. Perhaps surprisingly, the app also provides a form to create `FlatPages`, which is mainly used by the **admin** app (which we'll see in Chapter 23: The Admin Library).

The app also provides middleware. Originally, the app used the middleware principally to show `FlatPage` instances. In modern Django, we have the choice as to whether we want to use the URL configuration directly or else to rely on the middleware. In this chapter, we try out both options.

# 15.4  Building an About Webpage

In the next few sections, we explore the use of the `FlatPage` model and include the **flatpage** URL configuration to create a simple about page. We then switch to using middleware to demonstrate its use, before finally switching back to a somewhat customized use of the app.

## 15.4.1  Creating a Template

Before we get started, a quick look at the documentation will tell us that the **flatpage** app expects a template to display the `FlatPage` instances with a `title` field and a `content` field. We first create the template namespace necessary for the flatpage templates, as shown in Example 15.5.

**Example 15.5: Shell Code**

```
mkdir -p templates/flatpages
```

We can then create the `templates/flatpages/default.html` using the code shown in Example 15.6.

**Example 15.6: Project Code**

templates/flatpages/default.html **in** 75c781118d

```
 1   {% extends parent_template|default:"base.html" %}
 2
 3   {% block title %}
 4   {{ block.super }} - {{ flatpage.title }}
 5   {% endblock %}
 6
 7   {% block content %}
 8     <div>
 9       <div>
10         <h1>{{ flatpage.title }}</h1>
11           {{ flatpage.content }}
12       </div>
13     </div>
14   {% endblock %}
```

## 15.4.2   Creating the About `FlatPage`

In Example 15.7, we import the `FlatPage` model into our shell along with the `Site` model from the **sites** app.

**Example 15.7: Python Interpreter Code**

```
>>> from django.contrib.sites.models import Site
>>> from django.contrib.flatpages.models import FlatPage
```

We've taken the name spaced string from our settings, `django.contrib.app_name`, and simply suffixed `models`. The contributed apps that Django supplies follow the same conventions as developer-created apps. Opening either of the files found at `django/contrib/sites/models.py` or `django/contrib/flatpages/models.py` allows us to read the source code for either the `Site` or `FlatPage` model class.

The `Site` model is simple, and we don't actually need to look at the code to use it here. However, as we deal with **flatpages**, we're going to need to use an instance of the `Site` model. We can learn how to use the `Site` model by looking at the existing `Site` object in our database, as shown in Example 15.8. When Django migrated our database, it actually created a site with the ID of 1, which is why we set SITE ID to this value in our settings in Example 15.3.

**Example 15.8: Python Interpreter Code**

```
>>> Site.objects.count()
1
>>> Site.objects.all()
[<Site: example.com>]
>>> Site.objects.values()
[{'name': 'example.com', 'domain': 'example.com', 'id': 1}]
```

In Example 15.9, we grab a reference to the site, which we call `our_site`. We certainly don't have to make any changes to this object, but we're here, so hey, why not?

**Example 15.9: Python Interpreter Code**

```
>>> our_site = Site.objects.all()[0]
>>> our_site.name = 'Startup Organizer'
>>> our_site.domain = 'site.django-unleashed.com'
>>> our_site.save()
```

We can now turn to the **flatpages** app. At the moment, we don't have any `FlatPage` objects in our database, as you can see in Example 15.10.

**Example 15.10: Python Interpreter Code**

```
>>> FlatPage.objects.count()
0
```

To start, we should open `django/contrib/flatpages/models.py` and look at the `FlatPage` model. The required fields of the model are formatted and printed in Example 15.11.

**Example 15.11: Python Code**

```python
class FlatPage(models.Model):
    url = models.CharField(
        _('URL'),
        max_length=100,
        db_index=True)
    title = models.CharField(
        _('title'),
        max_length=200)
    content = models.TextField(
        _('content'),
        blank=True)
```

> **Info**
>
> As briefly mentioned in Chapter 13: Django's Contributed Library, the `_('value')` code is for translation purposes: it is a shortening of `ugettext()` or `ugettext_lazy()`, which both mark strings as items to be translated.

Given the code in Example 15.11, we know a `FlatPage` expects at least an absolute URL, a title, and content. We provide them in Example 15.12.

**Example 15.12: Python Interpreter Code**

```
>>> about_page = FlatPage.objects.create(
...    url='/about/',
...    title='About',
...    content='<p>Organize your content better.</p>',
... )
```

The URL is an absolute path and must always be an absolute path. Don't take my word for it: the **flatpage** app supplies a form in `django/contrib/flatpages/forms.py`, where you'll find a `clean_url()` method, as shown in Example 15.13.

**Example 15.13: Python Code**

```
class FlatpageForm(forms.ModelForm):
    ...
    def clean_url(self):
        url = self.cleaned_data['url']
        if not url.startswith('/'):
            raise forms.ValidationError(
                ugettext("URL is missing a leading slash."),
                code='missing_leading_slash',
            )
```

`FlatPage` instances define the absolute URL where they will be available.

The object we've created is not limited to `url`, `title`, and `content` fields. As Example 15.14 shows, it comes with a number of other values (not printed in the `models.py` code in Example 15.12 to keep the listing short).

**Example 15.14: Python Interpreter Code**

```
>>> about_page
<FlatPage: /about/ -- About>
>>> FlatPage.objects.values()
[{'title': 'About',
  'enable_comments': False,
```

```
'url': '/about/',
'content': 'Organize your content better.',
'template_name': '',
'registration_required': False,
'id': 1}]
```

The tricky part of `FlatPage` instances is that they expect to be associated with at least one `Site` instance in a many-to-many relationship. If you open the `django/contrib/flatpages/models.py` file in Django's source code, you will discover relationship on the `FlatPage` model, shown in Example 15.15.

**Example 15.15: Python Code**

```
class FlatPage(models.Model):
    ...
    sites = models.ManyToManyField(Site)
```

For our `FlatPage` to work properly, we need it to be associated with `our_site` (the instance of the only `Site` object in our database). In the shell, as shown in Example 15.16, we can connect the two.

**Example 15.16: Python Interpreter Code**

```
>>> about_page.sites.all()
[]
>>> about_page.sites.add(our_site)
```

## 15.4.3   Displaying `FlatPage` Objects via the URL Configuration

According to the Django documentation we can display `FlatPage` instances by including the **flatpages** app URL configuration in our own root URL configuration in `suorganizer/urls.py`, as shown in Example 15.17.

**Example 15.17: Project Code**
`suorganizer/urls.py` in 2a02d29ec6

```
18    from django.contrib.flatpages import \
19        urls as flatpages_urls
 .        ...
29    urlpatterns = [
 .        ...
35        url(r'^page', include(flatpages_urls)),
 .        ...
38    ]
```

If you try to run Django's development server via `./manage.py runserver`, you will be unable to reach the about webpage at `/about/`. Instead, the page will be displayed at `/page/about/`.

> ### Warning
>
> If you forget to associate the `FlatPage` with a `Site` instance, it will be completely unavailable.

We've caused a discrepancy in behavior. The `FlatPage` instance thinks that it must be displayed at the `/about/` URL path, but the URL configuration we're including has a prefix of `/page/`. For the curious, attempting to specify `/page/about/` means our about page will be rendered when we request `/page/page/about/`.

In and of itself, this is not terrible, but the problem extends to URL reversal, as shown in Example 15.18.

**Example 15.18:** Python Interpreter Code

```
>>> about_page.get_absolute_url()
'/about/'
>>> reverse('django.contrib.flatpages.views.flatpage',
...         kwargs={'url': about_page.url})
'/page/about/'
```

The `FlatPage` implementation of `get_absolute_url()` just returns the value of the `url` field, while calling `reverse()` actually follows Django convention. Our current implementation blatantly ignores the principle of least surprise, and we need to fix it.

## 15.4.4   Displaying `FlatPage` Objects via Middleware

As discussed in Chapter 9 and Chapter 12, middleware is a class that modifies `HttpRequest` and `HttpResponse` objects. These classes receive the `HttpRequest` before it reaches the view, and then receive the `HttpResponse` that the view has created, as shown in Figure 15.1. The set of middleware classes receive the `HttpResponse` objects in the reverse order from `HttpRequest` objects: the first class to receive the `HttpRequest` will be the last to receive the `HttpResponse` object. The utility of middleware is that it allows information to be added to *every* webpage (this is how the cross-site request forgery [CSRF] token works).

Prior to Django 1.4, the **flatpages** app did not supply a URL configuration; they worked solely through the use of middleware. To enable it, in Example 15.19, we first remove the **flatpages** URL configuration from our root URL configuration in `suorganizer/urls.py`. We then add `FlatpageFallbackMiddleware` to the very end of the `MIDDLEWARE_CLASSES` setting.

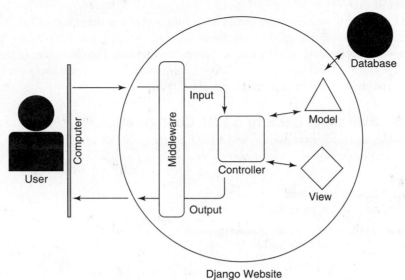

**Figure 15.1:** MVC Diagram with Middleware

**Example 15.19:** **Project Code**
`suorganizer/settings.py` **in** `050d205bc3`

```
50    MIDDLEWARE_CLASSES = (
 .        ...
59        'django.contrib.flatpages.middleware.FlatpageFallbackMiddleware',
60    )
```

We add the middleware to the end of the list because we want it to be the first
middleware to receive the `HttpResponse`. If the `HttpResponse` is a 404 error, the
middleware will see if there are any `FlatPage` instances that match the absolute URL path
that the page had been requesting. For instance, if we request `/about/`, at the moment our
website will raise a 404 error because we don't have any URL patterns that match that path.
The `FlatpageFallbackMiddleware` will catch the `HttpResponseNotFound`. It will
then render the about `FlatPage` in the default template (as opposed to a custom template
defined by the `FlatPage`) using a `RequestContext`, and then replace the
`HttpResponseNotFound` object with an `HttpResponse` containing the newly rendered
page.

If you navigate to `/about/`, this is what Django will be doing on the back end.

There are several key problems with this approach. The `HttpResponseNotFound`
raised in the case above is created by Django's URL system. This means there is an entire set
of middleware classes, called **view middleware**, that will never be called (they are called
between the time the URL system matches the URL path and the time the view is called).
What's more, we're incurring processing cost on every `HttpResponse` despite the fact that

the middleware only works on 404 errors (it ignores 500 or any other sort of error). Middleware are powerful and useful but should be used sparingly, and I don't think a single webpage warrants the cost we are incurring here. What's more, I am not a fan of having a whole slew of URLs that are not in our URL configuration—this seems like a perfect recipe to confuse developers new to the project.

## 15.4.5  Switching Back to a URL Configuration

If we disable the middleware, we can add a URL pattern without a prefix to our root URL configuration to include `FlatPage` objects, as shown in Example 15.20.

**Example 15.20: Project Code**

suorganizer/urls.py **in** 95d9c3ecd9

```
18    from django.contrib.flatpages import \
19        urls as flatpage_urls
  .        ...
29    urlpatterns = [
  .        ...
37        url(r'^', include(flatpage_urls)),
38    ]
```

Prior to Chapter 11, Section 11.4, our **contact** URL configuration was included in the same way, as shown in Example 15.21.

**Example 15.21: Project Code**

suorganizer/urls.py **in** 3969d84738

```
30        url(r'^', include(organizer_urls)),
```

If we had not split our URL configuration in Chapter 11, we'd now have a real problem!

The URL pattern to include the **flatpages** URL configuration must appear as the very last URL pattern in our root URL configuration. The catch-all URL prefix will match *any* URL path and means that any URL patterns below this include will never be reached by Django's URL system.

With this new URL pattern, shown in Example 15.22, our about `FlatPage` not only appears at /about/ but also reverses URLs appropriately and doesn't cause a middleware class to check each and every `HttpResponse`.

**Example 15.22: Python Interpreter Code**

```
>>> about_page.get_absolute_url()
'/about/'
>>> reverse('django.contrib.flatpages.views.flatpage',
...         kwargs={'url': about_page.url})
'/about/'
```

## 15.5  Linking to `FlatPage` Objects

Now that we have a `FlatPage` instance, we need to be able to link to it. While we know that URL reversal works, it's not entirely obvious how to get the information into our webpages.

The **flatpages** app works by providing us with a custom template tag. These tags extend the basic operation of the template and allow for all sorts of new behavior. We will build our own template tags in Chapter 27: Building Custom Template Tags.

To use a custom template tag, we must first load the custom tags. Then we can call `get_flatpages` and set all of the `FlatPage` objects as the `flatpage_list` variable, as shown in Example 15.23.

**Example 15.23: Project Code**

`templates/base.html` in 4b8bef1bdb

```
1   {% load flatpages %}
2   {% get_flatpages as flatpages %}
```

We can then use this list of objects in a loop, printing them out in the navigation list, as shown in Example 15.24.

**Example 15.24: Project Code**

`templates/base.html` in 4b8bef1bdb

```
26          <nav>
27           <ul>
  .            ...
40            {% for page in flatpages %}
41             <li>
42              <a href="{{ page.get_absolute_url }}">
43                 {{ page.title }}</a></li>
44            {% endfor %}
45           </ul>
46          </nav>
```

At this point, any `FlatPage` we add to our database will appear in our navigation menu.

## 15.6  Security Implications of `FlatPages`

Before we go, reexamine our **flatpages** template in `templates/flatpages/default.html`, shown in Example 15.25

**Example 15.25: Project Code**

`templates/flatpages/default.html` in 4b8bef1bdb

```
9           <div>
10           <h1>{{ flatpage.title }}</h1>
11            {{ flatpage.content }}
12          </div>
```

In most cases, we're going to want to store HTML in the `content` field of `FlatPage` objects. As mentioned in Chapter 4: Rapidly Producing Flexible HTML with Django Templates, all of the string variables output in Django templates are escaped. Anything that is a special character in HTML (such as <) will become an HTML entity, as shown in Example 15.26.

**Example 15.26: Python Interpreter Code**

```
>>> template = Template('{{ var }}')
>>> context = Context({'var': '<strong>hello</strong>'})
>>> template.render(context)
'&lt;strong&gt;hello&lt;/strong&gt;'
```

One of the template filters supplied by Django is the `safe` filter, which tells Django that the contents of the string do not need to be escaped, as shown in Example 15.27.

**Example 15.27: Python Interpreter Code**

```
>>> template2 = Template('{{ var|safe }}')
>>> template2.render(c)
'<strong>hello</strong>'
```

The equivalent Python function is the `mark_safe()`, found in `django.utils.html`. When displaying the contents of a `FlatPage`, developers may think it a good idea to use the `safe` template filter, to allow for their HTML code to properly display, as shown in Example 15.28.

**Example 15.28: Project Code**

templates/flatpages/default.html **in** 0f62cac115

```
 9        <div>
10          <h1>{{ flatpage.title }}</h1>
11          {{ flatpage.content|safe }}
12        </div>
```

This practice is totally unnecessary. In the `django/contrib/flatpages/views.py` file in the Django source code, you will discover that the app automatically marks the values of `FlatPage` objects as safe, as shown in Example 15.29.

**Example 15.29: Python Code**

```
f.title = mark_safe(f.title)
f.content = mark_safe(f.content)
```

We can thus remove the `safe` template tag from our template, as shown in Example 15.30.

**Example 15.30: Project Code**
`templates/flatpages/default.html` in `21863e374d`

```
 9      <div>
10        <h1>{{ flatpage.title }}</h1>
11        {{ flatpage.content }}
12      </div>
```

But that's not the key takeaway: this is actually a security risk! If you were considering using the **flatpages** app to allow untrusted users to make webpages, you might have believed that not having the `safe` template tag prevented users from putting HTML or JavaScript on your website. How wrong you would have been! This would have been an exploitable hack on your website.

Use of the **flatpages** app is thus reserved to trusted parties, as HTML escaping is disabled.

# 15.7    Migrations for Sites and Flatpages

We might feel quite satisfied with out work at the moment. However, if we commit it to version control and then push our work to the central repository for our coworker Lora to look at, we're going to run into a problem: the `Site` instance and the `FlatPage` instance we created in this chapter do not exist on Lora's system because they exist only in our database and nowhere in our code.

## 15.7.1   The Core App

The obvious solution to our problem is to create a data migration (as seen in Chapter 10: Revisiting Migrations).

This approach comes with a minor problem: migrations are associated with apps, and the apps we are trying to create migrations for are in Django's source code, not in our own project. We could create the migrations in one of our existing apps, but this approach is frowned upon. Instead, the best-practice is to create a new app whose entire purpose is to handle interaction with Django's contributed library. To that end, in Example 15.31, we create the **core** app with a migrations package to create data migrations for both **sites** and **flatpages**. Rather than use `startapp`, we can simply create a package named `core`, followed by a package named `migrations` (a python package is a directory with the `__init__.py` file inside).

**Example 15.31: Shell Code**

```
$ mkdir core
$ touch core/__init__.py
$ mkdir core/migrations
```

```
$ touch core/migrations/__init__.py
$ tree core
core
├── __init__.py
└── migrations
    └── __init__.py

1 directory, 2 files
```

We then tell our Django project of the existence of this new app, as shown in Example 15.32.

**Example 15.32: Project Code**
`suorganizer/settings.py` **in** d003657fec

```
35   INSTALLED_APPS = (
.        ...
45       'core',
.        ...
49   )
```

## 15.7.2   Data Migration for `Site`

To create a new data migration, we create an empty migration with a custom name, as shown in Example 15.33.

**Example 15.33: Shell Code**

```
$ ./manage.py makemigrations --empty --name=sites_data core
Migrations for 'core':
  0001_sites_data.py:
```

Our first goal is to determine what dependencies our migration has. The **sites** app has a single migration, defined in `django/contrib/flatpages/migrations` in the `0001_initial.py` file. We therefore change our `dependencies` list in Example 15.34.

**Example 15.34: Project Code**
`core/migrations/0001_sites_data.py` **in** 40667a7881

```
36   class Migration(migrations.Migration):
37
38       dependencies = [
39           ('sites', '0001_initial'),
40       ]
```

Next, in Example 15.35, we create a function to apply the migration, and a function to unapply the migration.

**Example 15.35: Project Code**
core/migrations/0001_sites_data.py **in** 40667a7881

```
 8   def add_site_data(apps, schema_editor):
 .       ...
27   def remove_site_data(apps, schema_editor):
```

In both cases, we must accept an instance of Apps and an instance of SchemaEditor. We will use the Apps instance to get the historical model of Site. This may seem unnecessary, because we are never going to modify the Site model. However, there is no guarantee that Django developers won't. If the Django source code modifies Site, we won't have to worry about changing any of this code. The Django source code will provide migrations to change the Site model. We will see how this was done in Chapter 22: Overriding Django's Authentication with a Custom User.

When creating a Site, we need to remember to use the SITE_ID setting, which defines the primary key of the Site that is used by our site. In Example 15.36, we use Python's getattr() built-in to get the value of SITE_ID. If it does not exist, we default to 1.

**Example 15.36: Project Code**
core/migrations/0001_sites_data.py **in** 40667a7881

```
 4   from django.conf import settings
 .       ...
 8   def add_site_data(apps, schema_editor):
 9       Site = apps.get_model('sites', 'Site')
10       new_domain = 'site.django-unleashed.com'
11       new_name = 'Startup Organizer'
12       site_id = getattr(settings, 'SITE_ID', 1)
```

Creating a forward relation for Site data comes with a bit of a catch. In django/contrib/sites/apps.py (a file we will determine the function of in Chapter 23), Django uses a signal (the topic of Chapter 25: Handling Behavior with Signals) to call the create_default_site() function defined in django/contrib/sites/management.py. The net effect of this call is that when we run our data migration, we don't know whether a Site instance exists in the database. In Example 15.37, we structure our forward function to determine whether an instance exists.

**Example 15.37: Project Code**
core/migrations/0001_sites_data.py **in** 40667a7881

```
 8   def add_site_data(apps, schema_editor):
 .       ...
13       if Site.objects.exists():
 .           ...
19       else:
```

In the event the `Site` already exists, we use its primary key to find it and change its values, as shown in Example 15.38.

**Example 15.38: Project Code**

`core/migrations/0001_sites_data.py` **in** `40667a7881`

```
 8   def add_site_data(apps, schema_editor):
 .           ...
14           current_site = Site.objects.get(
15               pk=site_id)
16           current_site.domain = new_domain
17           current_site.name = new_name
18           current_site.save()
```

If the `Site` instance doesn't already exist, we create one, making sure to force its primary key to be the value of the `SITE_ID` setting, as shown in Example 15.39.

**Example 15.39: Project Code**

`core/migrations/0001_sites_data.py` **in** `40667a7881`

```
 8   def add_site_data(apps, schema_editor):
 .           ...
20           current_site = Site(
21               pk=site_id,  # coerce primary key
22               domain=new_domain,
23               name=new_name)
24           current_site.save()
```

Unapplying this migration is much simpler: we know there's a `Site` instance in our database, and we simply revert the values to what `create_default_site()` sets them to, as shown in Example 15.40.

**Example 15.40: Project Code**

`core/migrations/0001_sites_data.py` **in** `40667a7881`

```
27   def remove_site_data(apps, schema_editor):
28       Site = apps.get_model('sites', 'Site')
29       current_site = Site.objects.get(
30           pk=getattr(settings, 'SITE_ID', 1))
31       current_site.domain = 'example.com'
32       current_site.name = 'example.com'
33       current_site.save()
```

For all of this to work, of course, we need to use the `RunPython` migration operation to call the functions we've just created. We do so in Example 15.41.

**Example 15.41: Project Code**

`core/migrations/0001_sites_data.py` **in** `40667a7881`

```
36   class Migration(migrations.Migration):
 .           ...
```

```
42        operations = [
43            migrations.RunPython(
44                add_site_data,
45                remove_site_data,
46            ),
47        ]
```

If we commit and send this code to our other developers, they will now all have the same site data as we have.

### 15.7.3 Data Migration for `FlatPage`

The migration for **flatpages** is actually simpler than the one for sites, as you can see in Example 15.42.

**Example 15.42: Shell Code**

```
$ ./manage.py makemigrations --empty --name=flatpages_data core
Migrations for 'core':
  0001_sites_data.py:
```

There is only a single migration in `django/contrib/flatpages/migrations`, titled `0001_initial.py`, shown in Example 15.43. We depend on it (for the creation of `FlatPages`) as well as on our site data migration.

**Example 15.43: Project Code**
`core/migrations/0002_flatpages_data.py` in 40667a7881

```
62    class Migration(migrations.Migration):
63
64        dependencies = [
65            ('core', '0001_sites_data'),
66            ('flatpages', '0001_initial'),
67        ]
```

In Example 15.44, we create a structure for our data.

**Example 15.44: Project Code**
`core/migrations/0002_flatpages_data.py` in 40667a7881

```
 7    FLATPAGES = [
 8        {
 9            "title": "About",
10            "url": "/about/",
11            "content":
  .        ...
35        },
36    ]
```

Then, in Example 15.45, we create a function to apply the migration.

**Example 15.45: Project Code**

`core/migrations/0002_flatpages_data.py` in 40667a7881

```
 4   from django.conf import settings
 .       ...
39   def add_flatpages_data(apps, schema_editor):
40       FlatPage = apps.get_model(
41           'flatpages', 'FlatPage')
42       Site = apps.get_model('sites', 'Site')
43       site_id = getattr(settings, 'SITE_ID', 1)
44       current_site = Site.objects.get(pk=site_id)
45       for page_dict in FLATPAGES:
46           new_page = FlatPage.objects.create(
47               title=page_dict['title'],
48               url=page_dict['url'],
49               content=page_dict['content'])
50           new_page.sites.add(current_site)
```

Example 15.46 shows a function to unapply the migration.

**Example 15.46: Project Code**

`core/migrations/0002_flatpages_data.py` in 40667a7881

```
53   def remove_flatpages_data(apps, schema_editor):
54       FlatPage = apps.get_model(
55           'flatpages', 'FlatPage')
56       for page_dict in FLATPAGES:
57           page = FlatPage.objects.get(
58               url=page_dict['url'])
59           page.delete()
```

Finally, in Example 15.47, we use `RunPython` to use our functions.

**Example 15.47: Project Code**

`core/migrations/0002_flatpages_data.py` in 40667a7881

```
62   class Migration(migrations.Migration):
 .       ...
69       operations = [
70           migrations.RunPython(
71               add_flatpages_data,
72               remove_flatpages_data,
73           ),
74       ]
```

Other developers on our project will now automatically have an about page the moment they migrate their project.

# 15.8   Putting It All Together

When asked if Django allows for static webpages, people nod their head, say yes, and then tell others to use the **flatpages** app for that purpose. But we now know this is a bald-faced lie. The **flatpages** app, like everything in Django, relies on the MVC architecture provided by Django. The app provides a `FlatPage` model, which stores full webpages in the database, which are rendered in a template, thanks to a view, and pointed to by a URL pattern (or middleware).

The net effect is that, yes, Django provides the tools necessary to store a "static" webpage that a user can then request. However, the page is not truly static—it is being generated, which is desirable! If we change the navigation menu—as we did in this chapter—the menu will change even on our "static" pages because these pages are, in fact, dynamic.

The **flatpages** app is a great example of how being willing to read the Django source code can save you both time and trouble. Reading the code revealed (among other things) the following:

- The app generates content dynamically, storing data in the `FlatPage` model.
- `FlatPage` URLs must be absolute, and are validated via the `clean_url()` method.
- The `safe` template tag is redundant.
- The `content` field is therefore assumed safe, making `FlatPage` unsuitable for public usage.

What's more, because it's based on exactly the same MVC principles we saw in Part I, reading this code is *easy*. Do not be afraid of the Django code! Reading it will reward you—it is the best way to learn Django (besides this book, of course).

The **flatpages** app is not actually a good fit for our project. If we had dozens of `FlatPage` instances, then this app is incredibly useful. But with only a single `FlatPage` instance, it's somewhat overkill. I'm also not a fan of the need for data migrations to keep our webpages in source control. For these reasons, we replace the app in Chapter 17: Understanding Generic Class-Based Views.

# 16

# Serving Static Content with Django

**In This Chapter**

- Use the **static** app to serve CSS and images from our website
- Discover the advantages of the template structure we're using
- Dip your toes into integrating the CSS styles with the HTML in our templates

## 16.1   Introduction

Websites are usually a combination of HTML, CSS, JavaScript, and media. At the moment, our website is HTML only, which means it's rather uninspiring. The goal of this chapter is to add CSS and an image (a site logo) to our website. Django refers to this content as **static content** because Django is not generating the content, unlike HTML (or any other markup).

Adding an image or a CSS file is quite simple: we could simply edit any of our templates to add an HTML tag (img, link, etc.) to connect to our files. The trick, once again, is maintaining DRY. Django provides the **staticfiles** contributed app as a means to organize nongenerated files. Specifically, the app allows us to move these files to different directories: Django will figure out where they are, saving us an enormous amount of time if we need to move them.

To do this, the **staticfiles** app behaves much in the same way the template system does. Static files may be provided to apps or the site, name spaced internally, and used by Django at will. We won't cover the anatomy of the **staticfiles**, because the only thing you need to know is that it supplies custom template tags to do the job.

In this chapter, we use the **staticfiles** contributed app to add CSS and a logo to our website.

# 16.2  Adding Static Content for Apps

The **staticfiles** contributed app is enabled by default in the INSTALLED_APPS list in
suorganizer/settings.py, which means we can jump straight into it.

Much like templates, static files are app-centric by default. In Example 16.1, we create a
static/ directory in each of our apps, and then namespace these directories again, just as
we did our templates.

*dirs for*
*static content*
*in 2 apps*

**Example 16.1: Shell Code**        *Consistent with @ 375*

```
$ mkdir -p organizer/static/organizer
$ mkdir -p blog/static/blog
```
        *↑ apps*

With the directories in place, we can now create CSS files in each of these directories, as
shown in Example 16.2.

*"style.css"*
*for each app*

**Example 16.2: Shell Code**

```
$ touch organizer/static/organizer/style.css
$ touch blog/static/blog/style.css
```

Our style.css filename illustrates the utility of namespacing. In the case above, we
can refer to organizer/style.css and blog/style.css. If we had instead created
organizer/static/style.css and blog/static/style.css, we would be
referring to style.css for each one, and Django would not know which file to actually
load.

We're not going to look at any CSS. This book is about Django and assumes basic
understanding of HTML and CSS. How you style this site is up to you! (Of course, you can
always look at the code supplied on the github repository with all of this code, but be
warned: I am not a CSS developer.) However, remember that the styles in each CSS file
should be limited to whatever app it is styling. The organizer/static/organizer/
style.css style should limit itself to styling the **organizer** templates, and should not style
anything in **blog** or anything in the site-wide templates.

We need to load these CSS files into the templates. To do so, we need the ability to add
HTML link tags in the head of the webpage. We thus need to add a template block in
our generic parent template for our app-specific templates to override. In Example 16.3, we
add a template block named head to the end of the HTML head tag in
templates/base.html.

**Example 16.3: Project Code**
templates/base.html **in** 15cf26b587

```
 6      <head>
 .          ...
18          {% block head %}{% endblock %}
19      </head>
```

Now that we have a block to override in the head, we can add our stylesheets to our templates. The goal is to add the HTML shown in Example 16.4.

**Example 16.4: HTML Code**

```
<link rel="stylesheet" type="text/css" href="" />
```

We want to fill in the `href` attribute of the link with the URL of the stylesheet. To make this easy and adhere to DRY, the **staticfiles** provides a custom template tag `static`, which generates the full path to static content (we create our own custom template tags in Chapter 27: Building Custom Template Tags). We can use the `load` template tag to get the custom template tag, as shown in Example 16.5.

*Access app styles*

**Example 16.5: Django Template Language Code**

```
{% load staticfiles %}
{% static 'organizer/style.css' %}
```

*Get the custom template tag static*
*Employ the static tag*

At the moment, the call to `static` will generate the following HTML:

```
/static/organizer/style.css
```

The reason the call generates this HTML is the `STATIC_URL` setting, provided automatically by Django in `suorganizer/settings.py`, as shown in Example 16.6.

**Example 16.6: Project Code**
`suorganizer/settings.py` **in** 3067246738

```
121    STATIC_URL = '/static/'
```

If we were to override this setting to a different value, such as `'/stylesheets/'`, our call to the `static` template tag above would instead generate

```
/stylesheets/organizer/style.css
```

This is how Django allows us to adhere to DRY. If we need to move our static content in one go, we can, while making only a single change to our site.

Because we have followed best practice when creating templates, we have templates that all of our app templates inherit from:

*Two "base" templates, one per app*

- `base_blog.html`
- `base_organizer.html`

By modifying just these two templates, we add our stylesheets to all of our app templates (ignoring **contact** for the moment). In each one, we simply override the head block we just created. Example 16.7 shows is the code for the base_blog.html template (identical to the base_organizer.html, not printed here).

**Example 16.7: Project Code**
blog/templates/blog/base_blog.html **in** b1165741d5

```
1   {% extends parent_template|default:"base.html" %}
2
3   {% load staticfiles %}
4   {% block head %}
5   <link rel="stylesheet" type="text/css"
6     href="{% static 'blog/style.css' %}" />
7   {% endblock %}
```

Truth be told, I don't actually have any app-specific styles. For our site, I will be deleting all of the work for this section because all of my CSS will be site-wide.

# 16.3   Adding Static Content for the Project

The problem with our code in the previous section is that it was limited to our apps. The /about/ page, for instance, was without any style. To change that, we can create a CSS stylesheet for the entire website.

Just as with templates, we start by creating a directory to store our site-wide templates in the top directory of our project. We can also create the site static namespace in the same command, as shown in Example 16.8.

*dir for site-wide static files*

*cd .../suorganizer*

**Example 16.8: Shell Code**

```
$ mkdir -p static/site
```

*└ consistent with @ 375*

*Additional setting for site-wide static*

In Example 16.9, we add the STATICFILES_DIRS setting to our settings.py file to let Django know to look in this directory for static files.

**Example 16.9: Project Code**
suorganizer/settings.py **in** b4eeb06e86

```
121   STATIC_URL = '/static/'
122   STATICFILES_DIRS = (os.path.join(BASE_DIR, "static"),)
```

Django will be able to see any stylesheet in this directory now (Example 16.10).

**Example 16.10: Shell Code**

```
$ touch static/site/style.css
```

In Example 16.11, we modify our base template to load **staticfiles** template tags and to use the new stylesheet.

**Example 16.11: Project Code**
templates/base.html in 0a56b76e96

*Site wide base.html*
*in suorganizer/templates/base.html*

```
1    {% load staticfiles %}
```

Now we can create a link to our new stylesheet, as shown in Example 16.12.

**Example 16.12: Project Code**
templates/base.html in efb5cff0ac

```
19        <link rel="stylesheet" type="text/css"
20            href="{% static 'site/style.css' %}">
```

Static content is not limited to CSS code, of course. We can add a logo in /static/site/logo.png, and then modify our template to use the static template tag to create a link to the file, as shown in Example 16.13.

**Example 16.13: Project Code**
templates/base.html in 122abbcc16

```
27        <header>
28            <img
29              src="{% static "site/logo.png" %}"
30              alt="Site Logo">
31            <h1>Startup Organizer</h1>
32        </header>
```

Our website will now display a logo on every webpage!

# 16.4  Integrating Real CSS Content

We have a site-wide stylesheet, and we're correctly linking to it. This is a great start, but it's the tip of the iceberg in terms of real work. Modern websites need fairly complicated CSS, and (unless you're an expert) it's best to use a CSS framework to start off a new site.

## Code Repository

To see all of the changes made here, you can view the code at commit 2eee3d5cd6. To see the visual changes to the website, navigate to https://site.django-unleashed.com/2eee3d5cd6.

I tend to prefer lightweight, mobile-friendly frameworks and will opt on this website to use the Skeleton CSS framework[1] with the CSS normalize stylesheet.[2] I add both of these to `static/site/skeleton.css` and `static/site/normalize.css`. I use the `static/site/style.css` file to customize and extend whatever styles I need.

Now that we have site-wide stylesheets, we need to integrate the styles in our HTML. We start by linking to them in our base template, as shown in Example 16.14.

**Example 16.14: Project Code**

templates/base.html **in** 12df61eb6c

```
 7     <head>
 .       ...
19       <link rel="stylesheet" type="text/css"
20         href="{% static 'site/normalize.css' %}">
21       <link rel="stylesheet" type="text/css"
22         href="{% static 'site/skeleton.css' %}">
 .       ...
26     </head>
```

*follows the framework css*

In `style.css`, I've created a style for the logo of the site and opt to replace the previous logo code with the use of the new class, as shown in Example 16.15.

**Example 16.15: Project Code**

templates/base.html **in** 12df61eb6c

```
30         <div class="container">
31           <header class="row">
32             <div class="offset-by-one ten columns">
33               <h1 class="logo">Startup Organizer</h1>
34             </div>
```

The rest of the work will be filling in the classes for all of our HTML elements. To start, we should style all of our pages by changing the code in our base, as shown in Example 16.16.

**Example 16.16: Project Code**

templates/base.html **in** 12df61eb6c

```
58           <div class="row">
59             <div class="twelve columns">
60               <ul class="messages">
```

---

1. http://getskeleton.com/
2. https://necolas.github.io/normalize.css/

We are certainly not limited to the site-wide base template. Our **organizer** templates will all be styled the same way, and so we can use our base_organizer.html file to ensure consistent style.

In Example 16.17, we first create a main section for central content, displayed on both desktop and mobile platforms.

**Example 16.17:** Project Code
organizer/templates/organizer/base_organizer.html **in** 905b187bc8

```
5       <section class="eight columns">
6         {% block org_content %}
7           This is default content!
8         {% endblock %}
9       </section>
```

Then, in Example 16.18, we can create a section for display on only desktop content, where we expect to place buttons to link to the creation forms of objects.

**Example 16.18:** Project Code
organizer/templates/organizer/base_organizer.html **in** 905b187bc8

```
10      <section class="desktop four columns">
11        {% block create_button %}{% endblock %}
12      </section>
```

We wrap the entire thing in a row, as shown in Example 16.19.

**Example 16.19:** Project Code
organizer/templates/organizer/base_organizer.html **in** 905b187bc8

```
4       <div class="row">
.         ...
13      </div>
```

We then create a row across the bottom of the page, where we might add pagination links, as shown in Example 16.20.

**Example 16.20:** Project Code
organizer/templates/organizer/base_organizer.html **in** 905b187bc8

```
14      <div class="row">
15        <div class="twelve columns">
16          {% block content_footer %}{% endblock %}
17        </div>
18      </div>
```

And we wrap the whole thing in a block, as shown in Example 16.21.

**Example 16.21: Project Code**

`organizer/templates/organizer/base_organizer.html` in 905b187bc8

```
 3   {% block content %}
 4     <div class="row">
 5       <section class="eight columns">
 6         {% block org_content %}
 7           This is default content!
 8         {% endblock %}
 9       </section>
10       <section class="desktop four columns">
11         {% block create_button %}{% endblock %}
12       </section>
13     </div>
14     <div class="row">
15       <div class="twelve columns">
16         {% block content_footer %}{% endblock %}
17       </div>
18     </div>
19   {% endblock %}
```

In Example 16.22, in our organizer templates, we now override the org_content block instead of the content block. We use the opportunity to create a button that displays only on mobile platforms.

**Example 16.22: Project Code**

`organizer/templates/organizer/startup_list.html` in 2eee3d5cd6

```
14   {% block org_content %}
15     <h2>Startup List</h2>
16       <div class="mobile">
17         <a
18             href="{% url 'organizer_startup_create' %}"
19             class="button button-primary">
20           Create New Startup</a>
21       </div>
```

For our larger screens, we'll make use of the create_button content block, as shown in Example 16.23.

**Example 16.23: Project Code**

`organizer/templates/organizer/startup_list.html` in 2eee3d5cd6

```
 7   {% block create_button %}
 8     <a
 9         href="{% url 'organizer_startup_create' %}"
10         class="button button-primary">
11       Create New Startup</a>
12   {% endblock %}
```

In both cases, we've changed our links to use the Skeleton button class, which will make our links look like buttons. We use the same styles in our forms and in our **blog** app.

For the most part, integrating CSS with templates is rather straightforward. The exception is the startup_detail.html template. The goal is to have the NewsLink and related Post objects be displayed in two columns next to each other. The difficulty is that not all Startup objects are related to these objects. Some Startup objects are related to one but not the other, while others may not be related to any or may be related to both. The result is complicated conditional logic, a sample of which is shown in Example 16.24.

**Example 16.24: Project Code**

organizer/templates/organizer/startup_detail.html in 2eee3d5cd6

```
48          {% if startup.blog_posts.all %}
49            <section class="meta offset-by-two one-third column">
50          {% else %}
51            <section class="meta offset-by-two two-thirds column">
52          {% endif %}
```

If you browse to a Startup without any NewsLink objects, you'll also discover that we are not displaying a link to create new ones. This is an intentional error that will be fixed in Chapter 20: Integrating Permissions, and that keeps us from writing truly absurd template code. To fix the startup_detail.html code, however, we need the content of Chapter 27.

The bottom line is that, for the most part, styling CSS code is a straightforward, if tedious, endeavor, which is why we're skipping the majority of the code. However, for some tasks, the template tags and filters fall short, and you'll have to turn to more powerful tools.

# 16.5  Putting It All Together

The **staticfiles** app is similar to the template system. Like the template system, the **staticfiles** app organizes non-Python files external to Django according to app or project, namespacing the content. However, whereas the template system will load and use the template files being organized, the **staticfiles** app only refers to them, allowing the template system to point to these files while still adhering to DRY.

When we deploy, we will also discover that the system allows for the collection of all static files, which means that if we adhere to the proper organization, we will be able to very quickly reorganize all of our content for public consumption. Even better, however, is that the use of **staticfiles**, in combination with other tools, will allow for the merging and compression of the CSS and JavaScript files, meaning that instead of making users download several CSS files, we will save them time by making them download a single, small file.

The **staticfiles** app, despite not being core functionality, is a vital part of every Django website, which is why it is enabled by default in all project settings.

# 17

# Understanding Generic Class-Based Views

## In This Chapter

- Learn about generic class-based views, class-based views that Django has already built for us
- Replace the majority of our views with generic class-based views
- Learn when to use generic class-based views

## 17.1 Introduction

Generic class-based views (GCBVs)—alternatively called class-based generic views (CBGVs)—are class-based views (CBVs) that provide behavior commonly needed for websites. They are preprogrammed CBVs that provide *generic* behavior.

We started down the road to creating our own GCBVs but were one step removed. We built the `ObjectCreateMixin`, `ObjectUpdateMixin`, and `ObjectDeleteMixin` classes, allowing for shared behavior between classes. These classes were not GCBVs because we could not invoke these classes as views—they are simply mixins.

Django's GCBVs take the idea of class mixins and CBVs to their logical next step. Django supplies 15 ready-to-use views as well as 30 other classes to work with (once you're advanced enough). These classes allow us to build views that derive the majority of their behavior from the provided classes.

On its own, a GCBV does not have any meaningful behavior. However, by specifying the right variable or overriding the right method, we can benefit from an enormous amount of code.

To best understand GCBVs, rather than use one of Django's right away, we build our own. This exercise allows us to more easily move into using Django's GCBV.

# 17.2   Building Generic Object Detail Pages

The most common task when building a website is to have a page dedicated to displaying the information of a model. At the moment, we have detail pages for Tag, Startup, and Post. The Startup page includes a list of related NewsLink objects.

In this section, we use CBVs to consolidate all of the code in our **organizer** detail views into a single class, resulting in a (custom, as opposed to Django) GCBV.

## 17.2.1   Converting to Class-Based Views

We need to convert the function views for Startup detail and Tag detail into class-based views.

For Tag, use the code in Example 17.1.

**Example 17.1: Project Code**
organizer/views.py **in** 2dfd449f41

```
162   class TagDetail(View):
163
164       def get(self, request, slug):
165           tag = get_object_or_404(
166               Tag, slug__iexact=slug)
167           return render(
168               request,
169               'organizer/tag_detail.html',
170               {'tag': tag})
```

For Startup, use the code in Example 17.2.

**Example 17.2: Project Code**
organizer/views.py **in** 2dfd449f41

```
89    class StartupDetail(View):
90
91        def get(self, request, slug):
92            startup = get_object_or_404(
93                Startup, slug__iexact=slug)
94            return render(
95                request,
96                'organizer/startup_detail.html',
97                {'startup': startup})
```

If any of this code is unfamiliar or confusing, please review Chapter 5: Creating Webpages with Controllers in Django.

In turn, we must update the URL patterns for both views.

For `TagDetail`, use the code in Example 17.3.

**Example 17.3: Project Code**
`organizer/urls/tag.py` **in** 2dfd449f41

```
 3   from ..views import (
 4       TagCreate, TagDelete, TagDetail, TagList,
 5       TagPageList, TagUpdate)
 .       ...
 7   urlpatterns = [
 .       ...
17       url(r'^(?P<slug>[\w\-]+)/$',
18           TagDetail.as_view(),
19           name='organizer_tag_detail'),
 .       ...
26   ]
```

For `StartupDetail`, use the code in Example 17.4.

**Example 17.4: Project Code**
`organizer/urls/startup.py` **in** 2dfd449f41

```
 3   from ..views import (
 4       StartupCreate, StartupDelete, StartupDetail,
 5       StartupList, StartupUpdate)
 .       ...
 7   urlpatterns = [
 .       ...
14       url(r'^(?P<slug>[\w\-]+)/$',
15           StartupDetail.as_view(),
16           name='organizer_startup_detail'),
 .       ...
23   ]
```

And with that, we now have two new CBVs that provide the same behavior as their function view counterparts when an HTTP GET request is issued. Recall that in the event any other HTTP method is used, the CBV will return an HTTP 405 error response (with the exception of HEAD or OPTIONS). This behavior is quite different from that of our function view, which would always behave as if it had received an HTTP GET request. This new behavior is much better.

## 17.2.2 Generic Behavior

If you examine the code in `TagDetail` and `StartupDetail`, you'll notice that the `get()` method is similar. In fact, if our code were less specific and relied on more instance variables, then the `get()` method of both classes would be identical, as shown in Example 17.5.

**Example 17.5: Project Code**

`organizer/views.py` **in** 6b9ce75f10

```
95      def get(self, request, slug):
96          obj = get_object_or_404(
97              self.model, slug__iexact=slug)
98          return render(
99              request,
100             self.template_name,
101             {self.context_object_name: obj})
```

To allow for our classes to both have the method defined in Example 17.5, the declarations of our class and attributes becomes as shown in Example 17.6.

**Example 17.6: Project Code**

`organizer/views.py` **in** 6b9ce75f10

```
89   class StartupDetail(View):
90       context_object_name = 'startup'
91       model = Startup
92       template_name = (
93           'organizer/startup_detail.html')
  .      ...
166  class TagDetail(View):
167      context_object_name = 'tag'
168      model = Tag
169      template_name = (
170          'organizer/tag_detail.html')
```

We now are in violation of DRY, as `TagDetail` and `StartupDetail` each have a method that is identical to the other's. In Example 17.7 in `organizer/utils.py`, we can create a new class, called `DetailView`, which defines the `get()` method.

**Example 17.7: Project Code**

`organizer/utils.py` **in** 1be9f24b68

```
7    class DetailView(View):
8        context_object_name = ''
9        model = None
10       template_name = ''
11
12       def get(self, request, slug):
13           obj = get_object_or_404(
14               self.model, slug__iexact=slug)
15           return render(
16               request,
17               self.template_name,
18               {self.context_object_name: obj})
```

In turn, we can import `DetailView` and inherit the class in `TagDetail` and `StartupDetail`, and delete the `get()` method from each class, as shown in Example 17.8.

**Example 17.8: Project Code**
`organizer/views.py` **in** `1be9f24b68`

```
12    from .utils import (
13        DetailView, ObjectCreateMixin,
14        ObjectDeleteMixin, ObjectUpdateMixin)
 .    ...
89    class StartupDetail(DetailView):
90        context_object_name = 'startup'
91        model = Startup
92        template_name = (
93            'organizer/startup_detail.html')
 .    ...
158   class TagDetail(DetailView):
159       context_object_name = 'tag'
160       model = Tag
161       template_name = (
162           'organizer/tag_detail.html')
```

While neither class now has a `get()` method defined, they both inherit the `get()` method from `DetailView`. The combination of inheritance and class attribute overrides allows both `TagDetail` and `StartupDetail` to behave exactly as before.

This may remind you of our work in Chapter 9: Controlling Forms in Views, when we created `ObjectCreateMixin` and similar mixin classes. However, our `DetailView` class is not a mixin; the inheritance of `DetailView` has replaced `View`, as `DetailView` itself inherits `View`. `DetailView` **is** a CBV!

We could circumvent the creation of `TagDetail` and `StartupDetail` entirely by calling `DetailView` directly with attributes. Remember that we can pass pre-declared attributes to a CBV from the URL pattern by passing keyword arguments to `as_view()`. The URL pattern for our `Tag` detail page could be written as shown in Example 17.9.

**Example 17.9: Project Code**
`organizer/urls/tag.py` **in** `0ab5349753`

```
19        url(r'^(?P<slug>[\w\-]+)/$',
20            DetailView.as_view(
21                context_object_name='tag',
22                model=Tag,
23                template_name=(
24                    'organizer/tag_detail.html')),
25            name='organizer_tag_detail'),
```

The `DetailView` class is a CBV that provides behavior commonly seen in websites. The `DetailView` class we have created is a GCBV. While generic behavior is provided, the class still requires information to work. Without the `context_object_name`, `model`, or `template_name` arguments/attributes, the view *will not work*. This is typical in Django's GCBVs as well.

### 17.2.3   Anticipating Behavior Overrides

Our GCBV, when compared to Django's GCBVs, is somewhat problematic. If we wanted to override behavior, we would be stuck overriding the entirety of the `get()` method, which rather defeats the purposes. Instead, we should provide multiple methods that each provide different behavior.

In the case of an object detail page, we are doing several things:

- Getting an object (`Tag`, `Startup`, etc.) from the database
- Building a dictionary for the template context
- Setting the new object in the template context as a specific variable
- Rendering a specific template

Instead of providing all of this behavior in `get()`, we will split the behavior up into the following new methods:

- `get_object()`
- `get_context_data()`
- `get_context_object_name()`
- `get_template_names()`

The simplest to build is `get_context_object_name()`. The goal is to return the name of the variable as it will be used in the template (`tag` or `startup`). If we've specified the `context_object_name` attribute, we can simply use that. If not, we use the `_meta` attribute on our model instance to get the name of the model type we're using. In this case, we'll assume the creation of the `object` attribute in another method. In the event we cannot figure out the name for the context variable, we return `None`, as shown in Example 17.10.

**Example 17.10: Project Code**
`organizer/utils.py` **in** `cf91f7b080`

```
10   class DetailView(View):
11       context_object_name = ''
 .       ...
34       def get_context_object_name(self):
35           if self.context_object_name:
36               return self.context_object_name
37           elif isinstance(self.object, Model):
38               return self.object._meta.model_name
39           else:
40               return None
```

The get_template_names() works on a similar principle. If the the template_name attribute is overridden, we use that. If not, we generate the template_name based on information for our model instance, which we assign to the object class attribute, as shown in Example 17.11.

**Example 17.11: Project Code**
`organizer/utils.py` in cf91f7b080

```
10    class DetailView(View):
 .       ...
13        template_name = ''
14        template_name_suffix = '_detail'
 .       ...
60        def get_template_names(self):
61            if self.template_name:
62                return self.template_name
63            return "{app}/{model}{suffix}.html".format(
64                app=self.object._meta.app_label,
65                model=self.object._meta.model_name,
66                suffix=self.template_name_suffix)
```

Given a Tag instance, the _meta.app_label returns 'organizer', while _meta.model_name returns 'tag'. Using the new template_name_suffix attribute on line 14 causes the call to format() on lines 63 to 66 to return organizer/tag_detail.html, which is actually where our template exists!

With get_context_object_name(), we can turn our attention to get_context_data(), which checks for the existence of the object attribute, and if it exists, adds the instance to a dictionary with the result of get_context_object_name() (if any), as shown in Example 17.12.

**Example 17.12: Project Code**
`organizer/utils.py` in cf91f7b080

```
10    class DetailView(View):
 .       ...
24        def get_context_data(self):
25            context = {}
26            if self.object:
27                context_object_name = (
28                    self.get_context_object_name())
29                if context_object_name:
30                    context[context_object_name] = (
31                        self.object)
32            return context
```

The get_object() method is the last of our new methods. The goal is to get the instance of our model from the database. In our implementation, this is easy, because in both Tag and Startup we are using a SlugField as a unique identifier. However, GCBVs can't always make this assumption and are in the habit of assigning any keyword arguments received by the view to a kwargs attribute. We follow suit, using the kwargs attribute to get the value of the slug passed to the view, as shown in Example 17.13.

**Example 17.13: Project Code**
organizer/utils.py in cf91f7b080

```
10    class DetailView(View):
 .        ...
42        def get_object(self):
43            slug = self.kwargs.get('slug')
```

If the slug value does not exist, we need to raise an error, as something has gone wrong. In our case, as shown in Example 17.14, we opt for an AttributeError, one of Python's core exceptions used when an expected key is missing.

**Example 17.14: Project Code**
organizer/utils.py in cf91f7b080

```
10    class DetailView(View):
 .        ...
42        def get_object(self):
43            slug = self.kwargs.get('slug')
44            if slug is None:
45                raise AttributeError(
46                    "{c} expects {p} parameter "
47                    " from URL pattern.".format(
48                        c=self.__class__.__name__,
49                        p='slug'))
```

With the value of the slug, we now need to fetch the model instance from the database. To that end, we need to know which model class to use. Unlike what we have for our other attributes, we don't have another attribute to rely on in our class, and so our model attribute is necessary. In the event a GCBV attribute is not specified, instead of using an AttributeError, we should use a Django-specific exception called ImproperlyConfigured, as shown in Example 17.15. This is more descriptive of the problem: the developer is responsible for overriding the attributes of a GCBV, and if the override is done wrong, then the developer has *configured the view improperly*.

**Example 17.15: Project Code**
organizer/utils.py in cf91f7b080

```
 1    from django.core.exceptions import \
 2        ImproperlyConfigured
 .        ...
```

```
10   class DetailView(View):
  ·       ...
42       def get_object(self):
  ·           ...
50           if self.model:
51               return get_object_or_404(
52                       self.model, slug__iexact=slug)
53           else:
54               raise ImproperlyConfigured(
55                   "{c} needs {a} attribute "
56                   " specified to work.".format(
57                       c=self.__class__.__name__,
58                       a='model'))
```

Finally, in Example 17.16, we need to rewrite get() to use these new methods. This is where we create the kwargs and object attributes.

**Example 17.16: Project Code**
organizer/utils.py **in** cf91f7b080

```
10   class DetailView(View):
  ·       ...
16       def get(self, request, **kwargs):
17           self.kwargs = kwargs
18           self.object = self.get_object()
19           template_name = self.get_template_names()
20           context = self.get_context_data()
21           return render(
22                   request, template_name, context)
```

We don't create empty values of the kwargs or object attributes in the class declaration, because we don't want keywords passed to as_view() to conflict with these attributes (only declared class attributes can be overridden by as_view(); for a refresher, please see Chapter 5, Section 5.9). The final class declaration is thus as shown in Example 17.17.

**Example 17.17: Project Code**
organizer/utils.py **in** cf91f7b080

```
10   class DetailView(View):
11       context_object_name = ''
12       model = None
13       template_name = ''
14       template_name_suffix = '_detail'
```

Thanks to all of our work, we can greatly simplify the class declaration of `TagDetail` and `StartupDetail`. Because we derive context and template information directly from the model instance, the only attribute we need to override is the `model` attribute, as shown in Example 17.18.

**Example 17.18: Project Code**
organizer/views.py **in** 677996ceba

```
 89   class StartupDetail(DetailView):
 90       model = Startup
  .       ...
155   class TagDetail(DetailView):
156       model = Tag
```

This simplification is nice, but given all the work we did in this section, it may not seem worth it. However, our ability to customize behavior now far surpasses our original version of `DetailView`. If we simply want to add data to the template context, we originally would have had to override the entire `get()` method, defeating the purpose of having a reusable generic view. If we want to add to the context of `StartupDetail`, thanks to the new structure of `DetailView`, we can define a `get_context_data()` method on `StartupDetail`. Our method would be able to call the version in `DetailView`, grab the current context dictionary, and simply add or modify values in the dictionary before returning it. Our ability to quickly customize behavior in this way is the basis of Chapter 18: Advanced Generic Class–Based View Usage. For the moment, we'll stick to using the functionality Django provides out of the box.

## 17.2.4   Switching to Django's GCBV

Django supplies a GCBV called `DetailView` that does everything our own GCBV does and more. We can thus delete our implementation in `/organizer/utils.py` and replace the import in `/organizer/views.py`, as shown in Example 17.19.

**Example 17.19: Project Code**
organizer/views.py **in** d6268eb17b

```
 7   from django.views.generic import DetailView, View
```

The `DetailView` we built was modeled heavily off of Django's own. The Django GCBV accepts all of the attributes we used (`context_object_name`, `model`, `template_name` and `template_name_suffix`) and contains all of the methods we built (`get()`, `get_context_data()`, `get_context_object_name()`, `get_object()`, `get_template_names()`). We therefore don't need to make any other changes to our code to allow `DetailView`'s inheritance to work correctly with `TagDetail` or `StartupDetail`.

# 17.3   Why Use Classes for Generic Views?

A generic view is a view that provides behavior but that cannot work unless a developer configures it. A GCBV is a generic view that is also class-based. However, Django does not supply generic function views (anymore).

Django introduced the concept of generic views even before version 1.0. At the time, all of the views were functions. The problem with functions as generic views is that they are difficult to override. To demonstrate, we can build our own generic function view.

Our model_list() view, shown in Example 17.20, is built to replace basic listing behavior, as exhibited by TagList or StartupList. As with our custom DetailView, we derive all of the necessary information from the _meta attribute of the model instance, which is passed in via URL pattern dictionary.

**Example 17.20: Project Code**
`organizer/views.py` in 7be2eedcf6

```
17   def model_list(request, model):
18       context_object_name = '{}_list'.format(
19           model._meta.model_name)
20       context = {
21           context_object_name: model.objects.all(),
22       }
23       template_name = (
24           'organizer/{}_list.html'.format(
25               model._meta.model_name))
26       return render(request, template_name, context)
```

The URL pattern to replicate the TagList view with our model_list() generic view is shown in Example 17.21.

**Example 17.21: Project Code**
`organizer/urls/tag.py` in 7be2eedcf6

```
 9       url(r'^$',
10           model_list,
11           {'model': Tag},
12           name='organizer_tag_list'),
```

This approach is very rigid—while our view will be reusable with different models, it's impossible to customize behavior in the way that object-oriented programming does. With DetailView we had the ability override attributes in multiple ways and to use inheritance to replace methods. To replicate this sort of behavior with Python functions would require us to pass lists of functions to other functions, which quickly becomes unwieldy (or to use function composition).

For these reasons, Django 1.3 replaced generic function views with GCBVs. Unfortunately, because CBVs were introduced in the same version, people began confusing CBVs and GCBVs. Hopefully, the difference is now clear:

- A CBV is simply a class that instantiates an object that behaves like a view (request in, response out), and it must be programmed from the ground up.
- A GCBV is a CBV that comes with preprogrammed methods that make use of attributes that must be configured for the view to work properly.

The history behind CBVs and GCBVs explains the mysterious import string for `View`: `from django.views.generic import View`. `View` was built with generic views, and the creators didn't realize that other developers would find the import confusing.

While we now understand the difference between CBV and GCBV and have used a GCBV in our project after building a simpler version of it, we're still going to take the opportunity to build another GCBV just to really get comfortable with the material.

## 17.4  Building Generic Object Create Pages

In this section, we transform `ObjectCreateMixin` into a GCBV.

The `ObjectCreateMixin` class already provides `get()` and `post()` methods, which `TagCreate`, `StartupCreate`, and `NewslinkCreate` all inherit in tandem with `View` to be full-fledged CBVs. To turn `ObjectCreateMixin` into it's own CBV, we can first rename it to `CreateView` and then make it inherit `View`, as shown in Example 17.22.

**Example 17.22: Project Code**
`organizer/utils.py` **in** 6b1f610347

```
7    class CreateView(View):
```

We must thus inherit the new GCBV in the relevant create views, as shown in Example 17.23.

**Example 17.23: Project Code**
`organizer/views.py` **in** 6b1f610347

```
12    from .utils import (
13        CreateView, ObjectDeleteMixin,
14        ObjectUpdateMixin)
 .      ...
17    class NewsLinkCreate(CreateView):
 .      ...
76    class StartupCreate(CreateView):
 .      ...
142   class TagCreate(CreateView):
```

Congratulations! You've now programmed a second GCBV. The process of building a mixin (seen several times in Chapter 9) is only a simple step from having a GCBV.

We could take time to make the class more robust, raising `ImproperlyConfigured` when necessary and splitting the various methods into components, but we're not going to bother. As you may have guessed, Django provides its own `CreateView`, which we can simply replace our own with. We start by deleting the definition of `CreateView` in `/organizer/utils.py` and then changing the import of `CreateView` in `/organizer/views.py`, as shown in Example 17.24.

**Example 17.24: Project Code**
`organizer/views.py` in 58af6fe57d

```
7  from django.views.generic import (
8      CreateView, DetailView, View)
```

# 17.5   Replacing CBVs with GCBVs

We've replaced code in CBVs by inheriting from `DetailView` and `CreateView`. Now we continue to replace behavior that Django provides by changing the inheritance of our classes.

## 17.5.1   Organizer Views

To begin, we can actually delete `organizer/utils.py` in its entirety. We replace `ObjectDeleteMixin` with the `DeleteView` GCBV, and `ObjectUpdateMixin` with `UpdateView`, as shown in Example 17.25.

**Example 17.25: Project Code**
`organizer/views.py` in 3b4975a366

```
  7  from django.views.generic import (
  8      CreateView, DeleteView,
  9      DetailView, UpdateView, View)
      . . .
 80  class StartupDelete(DeleteView):
      . . .
134  class StartupUpdate(UpdateView):
      . . .
146  class TagDelete(DeleteView):
      . . .
213  class TagUpdate(UpdateView):
```

We are replacing not only our mixin classes but also the inheritance of `View`, which we gain via the GCBVs.

As we saw when building our own `DetailView` GCBV, GCBVs are in the habit of filling in data for us, allowing us to omit data. In many cases, we are providing information to the GCBV that the class doesn't need!

As shown in Example 17.26, `StartupDelete` and `TagDelete` no longer need the `template_name` attribute, as the `DeleteView` GCBV derives that information from the `model` attribute (this only works, however, because our templates are named according to Django convention and because we are not overriding `template_name_suffix`).

**Example 17.26: Project Code**
`organizer/views.py` **in** 889de90d7e

```
80    class StartupDelete(DeleteView):
81        model = Startup
82        success_url = reverse_lazy(
83            'organizer_startup_list')
  .       ...
144   class TagDelete(DeleteView):
145       model = Tag
146       success_url = reverse_lazy(
147           'organizer_tag_list')
```

The `model` attribute is one of the more important attributes but is certainly not mandatory. Neither `NewsLinkCreate`, `StartupCreate`, nor `TagCreate` define the `model` attribute, and the effect of using GCBV is that the behavior in Example 17.27 and Example 17.28 are completely identical.

**Example 17.27: Project Code**
`organizer/views.py` **in** 3b4975a366

```
16    class NewsLinkCreate(CreateView):
17        form_class = NewsLinkForm
18        template_name = 'organizer/newslink_form.html'
  .       ...
75    class StartupCreate(CreateView):
76        form_class = StartupForm
77        template_name = 'organizer/startup_form.html'
  .       ...
141   class TagCreate(CreateView):
142       form_class = TagForm
143       template_name = 'organizer/tag_form.html'
```

The use of `model` in Example 17.28 allows the GCBV to derive the name of the template (from Example 17.27), whereas the GCBV doesn't need the model in the case above because we've given it the `form_class` directly.

**Example 17.28: Project Code**
`organizer/views.py` **in** 889de90d7e

```
16    class NewsLinkCreate(CreateView):
17        form_class = NewsLinkForm
18        model = NewsLink
  .       ...
```

```
 75   class StartupCreate(CreateView):
 76       form_class = StartupForm
 77       model = Startup
  .       ...
139   class TagCreate(CreateView):
140       form_class = TagForm
141       model = Tag
```

In the case of UpdateView subclasses, however, we need to specify template_name because we've broken from Django's convention. Django's UpdateView GCBV will try to use {app}/{model}_form.html with UpdateView subclasses. However, our templates are named according to {app}/{model}_form_update.html. We could use the template_name_suffix attribute instead of template_name, and we could remove the model attribute. In Example 17.29, I opt not to change anything here for the moment, as we return to these classes in Chapter 18 to modify their behavior.

**Example 17.29: Project Code**
organizer/views.py in 889de90d7e

```
132   class StartupUpdate(UpdateView):
133       form_class = StartupForm
134       model = Startup
135       template_name = (
136           'organizer/startup_form_update.html')
  .       ...
209   class TagUpdate(UpdateView):
210       form_class = TagForm
211       model = Tag
212       template_name = (
213           'organizer/tag_form_update.html')
```

## 17.5.2  Blog Views

To begin, we can change the inheritance in PostCreate and PostList to use CreateView and ListView, removing all of the methods from those classes, and leaving the attributes as is, as shown in Example 17.30.

**Example 17.30: Project Code**
blog/views.py in 18cf8cb4ed

```
  5   from django.views.generic import (
  6       CreateView, ListView, View)
  .       ...
 12   class PostCreate(CreateView):
 13       form_class = PostForm
 14       model = Post
  .       ...
 53   class PostList(ListView):
 54       model = Post
```

### 17.5.3    Returning to Redirection

In Chapter 5 we built a view to redirect our root URL to our blog post list. This view, thanks to GCBVs, is completely unnecessary. We therefore replace the view and the URL pattern with the `RedirectView` GCBV.

To start, delete the `suorganizer/views.py` file. In `suorganizer/urls.py`, replace the URL pattern referencing `redirect_root` with the code in Example 17.31.

**Example 17.31: Project Code**

`suorganizer/urls.py` **in** b02e39dac0

```
20    from django.views.generic import RedirectView
 .        ...
29        url(r'^$',
30            RedirectView.as_view(
31                pattern_name='blog_post_list',
32                permanent=False)),
```

Thanks to the ability to override CBV attributes and the behavior provided by `RedirectView` GCBV, we are creating a view that redirects to the `blog_post_list` URL pattern directly in the URL configuration. The `permanent` attribute even allows us to choose whether to use an HTTP 301 code (`True`; default) over an HTTP 302 code (`False`).

> **Ghosts of Django Future**
>
> In Django 1.9, the default of the `permanent` attribute will switch from `True` to `False`. It's best to always set this attribute at this point in time.

### 17.5.4    Replacing Flatpages

In Chapter 15: Creating Webpages with Django Flatpages, we used Django's flatpages system to create a simple about page. The problem with this, I complained at the end of the chapter, was that the HTML for our page was hidden away in the database, away from the rest of our templates.

With GCBVs, we can replace our *about* flatpage with a call to `TemplateView`. The `TemplateView` is a GCBV that renders a template with no context data.

We can thus start in Example 17.32 by creating a template called `about.html`. In this example, it is placed in the site-wide directory, but we could also have opted to place it in our `core` app, depending on how we've decided to organize our project.

**Example 17.32: Project Code**

`templates/site/about.html` **in** 99cca2d051

```
1    {% extends parent_template|default:"base.html" %}
2
3    {% block title %}
```

```
 4    {{ block.super }} - About
 5    {% endblock %}
 6
 7    {% block content %}
 .        ...
15    {% endblock %}
```

The actual content in the template is omitted, as it's not important for our purposes (and because you can see it online at https://site.django-unleashed.com/about/).

Much as we did with RedirectView, we call TemplateView directly in the root URL configuration, passing only a single keyword argument: template_name, as shown in Example 17.33.

**Example 17.33: Project Code**
suorganizer/urls.py in 99cca2d051

```
18    from django.views.generic import (
19        RedirectView, TemplateView)
 .        ...
27    urlpatterns = [
 .        ...
32        url(r'^about/$',
33            TemplateView.as_view(
34                template_name='site/about.html'),
35            name='about_site'),
 .        ...
42    ]
```

In our base template, we link to this new URL pattern, as shown in Example 17.34.

**Example 17.34: Project Code**
templates/base.html in 99cca2d051

```
36            <li>
37                <a href="{% url 'about_site' %}">
38                About</a></li>
```

That's all there is to it. That's *much* simpler than the use of flatpages. Speaking of which, we should now disable that system. Start by removing 'django.contrib.flatpages', from INSTALLED_APPS in suorganizer/settings.py. Remove url(r'^', include(flatpage_urls)), (as well as the import from django.contrib.flatpages) from suorganizer/urls.py. Then delete core/migrations/0002_flatpages_data.py and templates/flatpages/default.html.

### 17.5.5   Overriding Methods (in `NewsLinkDelete`)

In Chapter 18, we'll change the URL pattern for `NewsLinkUpdate` and
`NewsLinkDelete` to use `NewsLink`'s new `SlugField`. For now, we keep the URL
pattern as is. This allows for the demonstration of a GCBV that uses `pk` instead of a
`SlugField` (see next chapter), as well as a GCBV that requires a method to be overridden
(right now!).

In most cases, GCBVs can be subclassed by overriding only attributes. However, for
some, method overrides are mandatory. GCBV functionality is split up according to
behavior (similar to how we split our custom `DetailView` in Section 17.2.3), making
method overrides almost as straightforward as attribute overrides.

In `StartupDelete` and `TagDelete`, we were able to set the `success_url` attribute
using `reverse_lazy()` because we simply wanted to redirect to a list page. When deleting
`NewsLink` objects, we want to redirect to the page the user was just on: the detail page of
the `Startup` that the `NewsLink` was associated with. This page cannot be set by an
attribute because it changes from instance to instance. Instead, we can override the
`get_success_url()` method, as shown in Example 17.35.

**Example 17.35: Project Code**
`organizer/views.py` **in** b8cba3bfee

```
21   class NewsLinkDelete(DeleteView):
22       model = NewsLink
23
24       def get_success_url(self):
25           return (self.object.startup
26                      .get_absolute_url())
```

The `get_success_url()` method is called *before* the `NewsLink` instance is deleted
from the database, which is what allows us to call the `object` attribute (created in much
the same way as we created `object` in our custom `DetailView` class) and get the
`NewsLink`'s associated startup. When we delete a `NewsLink`, we will redirect to the page
the user was just on, which is exactly how we want this to work.

The order in which methods in a GCBV are called are crucial to understanding the
GCBV, which is why tools such as Classy Class-Based Views[1] are crucial to using GCBV.

In Chapter 18, we see a lot more about overriding GCBV methods.

## 17.6   Forgoing GCBVs

One of the most difficult tasks when working with GCBV is knowing when and when not
to use a GCBV. For instance, we've left `NewsLinkDelete`, `NewsLinkUpdate`,
`PostDelete`, and `PostUpdate` alone and have not touched the view in the **contact** app.
Our `post_detail` view isn't even a class (yet). This is not an accident! Django does not
supply generic behavior for these views.

---

1. http://ccbv.co.uk

We could replace the current incarnations of `NewsLinkDelete` and `NewsLinkUpdate`, but we're waiting to replace these views in favor of views that use `NewsLink`'s new `SlugField`. Our `NewsLink` model is unique according to the `startup` and to the `slug`, meaning we would need a view that uses both of those fields to fetch the data. However, Django's GCBVs only work with the primary key, a `SlugField` instance, or (starting in Django 1.8) both. We run into the same problem when fetching a `Post` model instance: our view needs to use the month, year, and slug value to get the appropriate `Post` model.

Our `StartupList` could be replaced by a GCBV, but we would lose the code we added in Chapter 14: Pagination, to paginate and to generate the appropriate pagination links (to adhere to DRY). I'm therefore reticent to replace the code with a GCBV without any customization (the topic of Chapter 18).

What's more, because we've completely foregone convention in our **contact** app, no GCBV will come close to working out of the box with our form.

Especially when beginning, it is better to make the mistake of not using a GCBV than to use a GCBV when you should't. We'll see in Chapter 18 that sometimes not understanding what behavior the GCBV supplies can lead to unexpected problems.

# 17.7   Adding Behavior with GCBV

The central advantage of GCBVs is not replacing views: it's how quickly they allow developers to add behavior to the website (if the GCBV meets the requirements for the desired behavior).

In the next section, we add views to our **blog** app to enhance navigation. Our blog post list is helpful for showing the latest views, but it's not particularly helpful for finding a `Post` according to date. The de facto way to handle this is to present date archive pages (rather than, say, pagination). These pages show all of the posts in a year or in a month (of a year).

We will thus build two new views: `PostArchiveYear` and `PostArchiveMonth`. At the end, we will also replace our `PostList` view to better adhere to the standards set forth in our new views.

## 17.7.1   Yearly Archive for `Post`

The `YearArchiveView` GCBV is a view that allows for the organization of objects published in a specific year. The model class used with `YearArchiveView` must therefore have a `DateField` or a `DateTimeField`.

I did not say that the GCBV displays the object list, because that behavior is actually optional. The `YearArchiveView` GCBV exhibits two behaviors. By default, it assumes that developers will wish to list the months that objects were published in a year. If in 2015, we published blog posts in January and March, then `YearArchiveView` will create a template context variable called `date_list` that contains the dates for January 2015 and March 2015, allowing us to link to `MonthArchiveView` subclasses. The second behavior `YearArchiveView` exhibits is the ability to display all of the objects published in a year, but to enable this behavior, we need to override the `make_object_list` attribute.

### 17.7.1.1  Selecting Dates from the Database

YearArchiveView (and other date-based GCBVs) are able to print lists of dates based on lists of objects because of the dates() queryset method. The first argument passed to dates() is the name of the DateField on our model, as shown in Example 17.36.

**Example 17.36: Python Interpreter Code**

```
>>> Post.objects.dates('pub_date', 'year')
[datetime.date(2008, 1, 1),
 datetime.date(2011, 1, 1),
 datetime.date(2013, 1, 1),
 datetime.date(2015, 1, 1),
 datetime.date(2020, 1, 1)]
```

If you compare this example with a call to values_list() (Example 17.37), you'll note that the database has ensured uniqueness of the year in the preceding call, thanks to the second argument passed to dates() (the second parameter is named kind, as in the kind of date we are asking for).

**Example 17.37: Python Interpreter Code**

```
>>> Post.objects.values_list('pub_date')
[(datetime.date(2020, 5, 15),),
 (datetime.date(2015, 4, 8),),
 (datetime.date(2015, 4, 1),),
 (datetime.date(2013, 1, 18),),
 (datetime.date(2011, 2, 21),),
 (datetime.date(2008, 9, 3),)]
```

As Example 17.38 shows, both values_list() and dates() return an instance of ValuesListQuerySet, meaning that regular QuerySet methods such as only(), defer(), and iterator() (methods we explore more thoroughly in Chapter 26: Optimizing Our Site for Speed) and delete() are unavailable.

**Example 17.38: Python Interpreter Code**

```
>>> type(Post.objects.dates('pub_date', 'year'))
django.db.models.query.ValuesListQuerySet
```

dates() accepts a third optional parameter, allowing us to change the order of the ValuesListQuerySet, as shown in Example 17.39. By default, it is set to 'ASC'.

**Example 17.39: Python Interpreter Code**

```
>>> Post.objects.dates('pub_date', 'year', 'DESC')
[datetime.date(2020, 1, 1),
 datetime.date(2015, 1, 1),
```

```
datetime.date(2013, 1, 1),
datetime.date(2011, 1, 1),
datetime.date(2008, 1, 1)]
```

Most important, however, `dates()` allows for the list of dates to be not only `'year'` but also `'month'` or `'day'`. Given that we have no blog posts published on the same day, this list is identical to the one returned by `values_list()`, as shown in Example 17.40.

**Example 17.40: Python Interpreter Code**

```
>>> Post.objects.dates('pub_date', 'month')
[datetime.date(2008, 9, 1),
 datetime.date(2011, 2, 1),
 datetime.date(2013, 1, 1),
 datetime.date(2015, 4, 1),
 datetime.date(2020, 5, 1)]
>>> Post.objects.dates('pub_date', 'day')
[datetime.date(2008, 9, 3),
 datetime.date(2011, 2, 21),
 datetime.date(2013, 1, 18),
 datetime.date(2015, 4, 1),
 datetime.date(2015, 4, 8),
 datetime.date(2020, 5, 15)]
```

Similar to `dates()`, managers and querysets also define the `datetimes()` method, which allows for datetimes to be specified using the following kinds of datetimes: `'year'`, `'month'`, `'day'`, `'hour'`, `'minute'`, or `'second'`.

### 17.7.1.2  View and URL Configuration

We start by using the `YearArchiveView` superclass using its default behavior, and then augment it to use both behaviors.

In Example 17.41, we simply specify a model and then tell the GCBV which field to use for the date.

**Example 17.41: Project Code**
`blog/views.py` in de845a2bcf

```
 5   from django.views.generic import (
 6       CreateView, ListView, View, YearArchiveView)
 .       ...
12   class PostArchiveYear(YearArchiveView):
13       model = Post
14       date_field = 'pub_date'
```

The URL pattern for our view is very straightforward, as you can see in Example 17.42.

**Example 17.42: Project Code**
blog/urls.py **in** de845a2bcf

```
14        url(r'^(?P<year>\d{4})/$',
15            PostArchiveYear.as_view(),
16            name='blog_post_archive_year'),
```

Take note that the URL pattern is not randomly chosen. This is a URL path segment of blog_post_detail, shown in Example 17.43.

**Example 17.43: Project Code**
blog/urls.py **in** de845a2bcf

```
17        url(r'^(?P<year>\d{4})/'
18            r'(?P<month>\d{1,2})/'
19            r'(?P<slug>[\w\-]+)/$',
20            post_detail,
21            name='blog_post_detail'),
```

In anticipation of any links we might need, Example 17.44 creats a method called get_archive_year_url() on Post.

**Example 17.44: Project Code**
blog/models.py **in** de845a2bcf

```
11   class Post(models.Model):
.        ...
47        def get_archive_year_url(self):
48            return reverse(
49                'blog_post_archive_year',
50                kwargs={'year': self.pub_date.year})
```

### 17.7.1.3   Template

Thanks to GCBVs, we've done very little work building a view and a URL pattern. However, creating a template is still as much work as before. We start with Example 17.45.

**Example 17.45: Project Code**
blog/templates/blog/post_archive_year.html **in** de845a2bcf

```
1    {% extends parent_template|default:"blog/base_blog.html" %}
2
3    {% block title %}
4    {{ block.super }} - {{ year|date:"Y" }} Posts
5    {% endblock %}
6
7    {% block content %}
.        ...
37   {% endblock %}
```

By default, the GCBV exhibits only the first behavior described. If we published blog posts in only January and March in 2015, then the 2015 archive view will print a list containing only the months January and March.

**Example 17.46: Project Code**

blog/templates/blog/post_archive_year.html in de845a2bcf

```
 8   <div class="row">
 9     <div class="desktop four columns">
10       <h3>Archives by Month</h3>
11       <ul>
12         {% for m in date_list %}
13         <li><a href="">
14             {{ m|date:"F Y" }}</a></li>
15         {% endfor %}
16       </ul>
17     </div>
18   </div>
```

The links shown in Example 17.46 will bring us to the MonthArchiveView webpages. By default, the date_list_period attribute on YearArchiveView is set to 'month', which is why we list months in date_list using F Y (resulting in strings such as 'January 2015'). We could alternatively set the attribute to 'day' to list all of the days we published (thanks to the DayArchiveView GCBV).

On top of navigating by month, we can also add links to navigate by year (using previous year and next year links). To start, in Example 17.47, we can create the HTML structure to wrap our date pagination system in.

**Example 17.47: Project Code**

blog/templates/blog/post_archive_year.html in de845a2bcf

```
19   <div class="row">
20     <div class="twelve columns">
  .    . . .
35     </div>
36   </div>
```

Django is quite smart about date pagination. Our template context has been given a previous_year and next_year. These are not the mathematical previous/next years, but are instead the year prior to the current year where we published a blog post. If we didn't publish anything in 2014 (shame on us), then the 2015 year will link to the archive view for 2013 (assuming we published content then). The code in Example 17.48 provides this functionality.

**Example 17.48: Project Code**

`blog/templates/blog/post_archive_year.html` **in** de845a2bcf

```
21          <ul class="pagination">
22            {% if previous_year %}
23              <li>
24                <a href="{% url 'blog_post_archive_year'
 .                            previous_year|date:"Y" %}">
25                  ◀ Posts from {{ previous_year|date:"Y" }}</a>
26              </li>
27            {% endif %}
28            {% if next_year %}
29              <li>
30                <a href="{% url 'blog_post_archive_year'
 .                            next_year|date:"Y" %}">
31                  Posts from {{ next_year|date:"Y" }} ▶</a>
32              </li>
33            {% endif %}
34          </ul>
```

It's nice to see which months we published in a year, but if we're looking for a blog post, we may not know which month it was published in. To add the ability to list actual `Post` objects in our template, we can override the `make_object_list` attribute to `True`, as shown in Example 17.49.

**Example 17.49: Project Code**

`blog/views.py` **in** 10c43b4d6f

```
12    class PostArchiveYear(YearArchiveView):
13        model = Post
14        date_field = 'pub_date'
15        make_object_list = True
```

Our template sees the addition of a list of `Post` objects as well as buttons to create, edit, and delete blog posts.

We start by creating the HTML divider to wrap the list in, as shown in Example 17.50.

**Example 17.50: Project Code**

`blog/templates/blog/post_archive_year.html` **in** 10c43b4d6f

```
 9    <div class="eight columns">
 .        ...
50    </div>
```

In Example 17.51, we create a title for the page and loop through all of our `Post` objects in the `post_list` context variable that `YearArchiveView` has created.

**Example 17.51:** Project Code

blog/templates/blog/post_archive_year.html **in** 10c43b4d6f

```
16        <h2>All Posts for {{ year|date:"Y" }}</h2>
17        {% for post in post_list %}
18          <article class="list-item">
  .           ...
48          </article>
49        {% endfor %}
```

For each post in post_list, Example 17.52 enables us to display the title and publication date and to use the truncatewords filter to show the first 20 words of the blog post (effectively mimicking the post_list.html template).

**Example 17.52:** Project Code

blog/templates/blog/post_archive_year.html **in** 10c43b4d6f

```
19            <header>
20              <h3>
21                <a href="{{ post.get_absolute_url }}">
22                  {{ post.title|title }}
23                </a></h3>
  .               ...
36              <p>
37                Written on:
38                <time datetime="{{ post.pub_date|date:"Y-m-d" }}">
39                  {{ post.pub_date|date:"l, F j, Y" }}
40                </time>
41              </p>
42            </header>
43            <p>{{ post.text|truncatewords:20 }}</p>
44            <p class="read-more">
45              <a href="{{ post.get_absolute_url }}">
46                Read more&hellip;
47            </a><p>
```

Below the title, we can add buttons to edit and delete that Post, linking to the UpdatePost and DeletePost views via their URL patterns, as shown in Example 17.53.

**Example 17.53:** Project Code

blog/templates/blog/post_archive_year.html **in** 10c43b4d6f

```
24            <ul class="inline">
25              <li>
26                <a
27                  href="{{ post.get_update_url }}"
28                  class="button">
29                Edit Post</a></li>
30              <li>
```

```
31                          <a
32                              href="{{ post.get_delete_url }}"
33                              class="button">
34                          Delete Post</a></li>
35                  </ul>
```

Finally, in Example 17.54, we add a button to link to PostCreate in two places. The first is displayed only to mobile users, while the second is displayed only to desktop users (directly above the month archive links), thanks to the CSS we created in Chapter 16: Serving Static Content with Django.

**Example 17.54: Project Code**

blog/templates/blog/post_archive_year.html **in** 10c43b4d6f

```
10      <div class="mobile">
11          <a
12              href="{% url 'blog_post_create' %}"
13              class="button button-primary">
14          Write New Blog Post</a>
15      </div>
  .         ...
52          <a
53              href="{% url 'blog_post_create' %}"
54              class="button button-primary">
55          Write New Blog Post</a>
```

The last thing we need to do is link to our MonthArchvieView, but before we can do that, we need it to actually exist.

## 17.7.2   Monthly Archive for Post

Surprisingly, Django's MonthArchiveView GCBV does not work like YearArchiveView GCBV. The MonthArchiveView GCBV does not recognize make_object_list, assuming instead that developers will want to display objects in this template. However, MonthArchiveView also provides the date_list to the template context, created on the basis of the same date_list_period attribute found in YearArchiveView (the default of which is 'day' in MonthArchiveView).

We won't be creating a day archive view for our Post model, as we shouldn't have more than a few blog posts a month. We therefore won't use the date_list context variable. Our view will list only objects published that month.

### 17.7.2.1   View and URL Pattern

In Example 17.55, we add MonthArchiveView to our import list, and then declare a subclass of the GCBV named PostArchiveMonth. We declare the mandatory attributes model and date_field, and override the default month_format attribute to be %m, which will match a number between 1 and 12. The month_format is set to %b on MonthArchiveView; the %b format character matches short month names such as *Sep* and *Oct* (in English).

**Example 17.55: Project Code**
blog/views.py in 7dcd39cac5

```
 5    from django.views.generic import (
 6        CreateView, ListView, MonthArchiveView,
 7        View, YearArchiveView)
 .        ...
13    class PostArchiveMonth(MonthArchiveView):
14        model = Post
15        date_field = 'pub_date'
16        month_format = '%m'
```

In Example 17.56, we then create a new URL pattern.

**Example 17.56: Project Code**
blog/urls.py in 7dcd39cac5

```
 3    from .views import (
 4        PostArchiveMonth, PostArchiveYear, PostCreate,
 5        PostDelete, PostList, PostUpdate, post_detail)
 .        ...
 7    urlpatterns = [
 .        ...
17        url(r'^(?P<year>\d{4})/'
18            r'(?P<month>\d{1,2})/$',
19            PostArchiveMonth.as_view(),
20            name='blog_post_archive_month'),
 .        ...
38    ]
```

Example 17.57 shows that regular expression pattern for the URL pattern is a segment of blog_post_detail. In turn, the regular expression pattern for blog_post_archive_year is a segment of the one in our new blog_post_archive_month URL pattern.

**Example 17.57: Project Code**
blog/urls.py in 7dcd39cac5

```
 7    urlpatterns = [
 .        ...
14        url(r'^(?P<year>\d{4})/$',
15            PostArchiveYear.as_view(),
16            name='blog_post_archive_year'),
 .        ...
21        url(r'^(?P<year>\d{4})/'
22            r'(?P<month>\d{1,2})/'
23            r'(?P<slug>[\w\-]+)/$',
24            post_detail,
25            name='blog_post_detail'),
 .        ...
38    ]
```

As with any URL pattern with regular expression groups, we should create a method on the relevant model class, as shown in Example 17.58.

**Example 17.58: Project Code**
blog/models.py **in** 7dcd39cac5

```
11   class Post(models.Model):
 .      ...
47       def get_archive_month_url(self):
48           return reverse(
49               'blog_post_archive_month',
50               kwargs={'year': self.pub_date.year,
51                       'month': self.pub_date.month})
```

### 17.7.2.2   Template

Due to our use of a GCBV, the bulk of the work occurs in the template, named post_archive_month.html and shown in Example 17.59.

**Example 17.59: Project Code**
blog/templates/blog/post_archive_month.html **in** 7dcd39cac5

```
 1   {% extends parent_template|default:"blog/base_blog.html" %}
 2
 3   {% block title %}
 4   {{ block.super }} - {{ month|date:"F Y" }} Posts
 5   {% endblock %}
 6
 7   {% block content %}
 .       ...
79   {% endblock %}
```

The content for the main page starts on line 8 and goes until 60. From line 61 until line 78, we will add links between month archive views, as shown in Example 17.60.

**Example 17.60: Project Code**
blog/templates/blog/post_archive_month.html **in** 7dcd39cac5

```
 8   <div class="row">
 .       ...
60   </div><!-- row -->
61   <div class="row">
 .       ...
78   </div>
```

As you can see in Example 17.61, pagination is based on the previous_month and next_month variables in the template context.

**Example 17.61: Project Code**

blog/templates/blog/post_archive_month.html **in** 7dcd39cac5

```
62     <div class="twelve columns">
63       <ul class="pagination">
64         {% if previous_month %}
65           <li>
66             <a href="{% url 'blog_post_archive_month'
                              previous_month|date:"Y"
                              previous_month|date:"m" %}">
67                 ◄ Posts from {{ previous_month|date:"F Y" }}</a>
68           </li>
69         {% endif %}
70         {% if next_month %}
71           <li>
72             <a href="{% url 'blog_post_archive_month'
                              next_month|date:"Y"
                              next_month|date:"m" %}">
73               Posts from {{ next_month|date:"F Y" }} ►</a>
74           </li>
75         {% endif %}
76       </ul>
77     </div>
```

In both cases, our call to url 'blog_post_archive_month' necessitates two arguments: one for the year and one for the month. We therefore call previous_month (or next_month on the second link) with the date filter *twice*. Switching the code above with previous_month|date:"Y m" would be incorrect, as in this case date is yielding only a single string argument (with both the year and month, but Django can't infer that!).

The content is split into two sections. The first section is a list of blog posts, and the second section is a list of links to other pages, as shown in Example 17.62.

**Example 17.62: Project Code**

blog/templates/blog/post_archive_month.html **in** 7dcd39cac5

```
9      <div class="eight columns">
         ...
49     </div><!-- eight columns -->
50     <div class="desktop four columns">
         ...
59     </div><!-- four columns -->
```

In the second section (from lines 50 to 59), we create a link to the YearArchiveView for the year of the month being displayed, as well as a link back to the PostList view, as shown in Example 17.63. As with the post_archive_year.html template, we also display two buttons to link to the PostCreate view on our page. The first button (for desktop) is at the top of our links section.

**Example 17.63: Project Code**

`blog/templates/blog/post_archive_month.html` in 7dcd39cac5

```
50      <div class="desktop four columns">
51        <a
52          href="{% url 'blog_post_create' %}"
53          class="button button-primary">
54        Write New Blog Post</a>
55      <p><a href="{% url 'blog_post_archive_year' month|date:"Y" %}">
56        All Posts from {{ month|date:"Y" }}</a></p>
57      <p><a href="{% url 'blog_post_list' %}">
58        Latest Posts</a></p>
59      </div><!-- four columns -->
```

In our first section (from lines 9 to 49), we use a loop over post_list to display all of the blog posts published in the month of the year specified by our URL pattern, as shown in Example 17.64.

**Example 17.64: Project Code**

`blog/templates/blog/post_archive_month.html` in 7dcd39cac5

```
16        <h2>All Posts for {{ month|date:"F Y" }}</h2>
17        {% for post in post_list %}
18          <article class="list-item">
  .         ...
47          </article>
48        {% endfor %}
```

As with the Post list webpage and year archive webpage, we start by displaying a linked title for each blog post as shown in Example 17.65.

**Example 17.65: Project Code**

`blog/templates/blog/post_archive_month.html` in 7dcd39cac5

```
19            <header>
20              <h3>
21                <a href="{{ post.get_absolute_url }}">
22                  {{ post.title|title }}
23              </a></h3>
```

In Example 17.66, we then display the time the Post was published, as well as the first 20 words from the text of the blog post, providing another link for users to see the Post detail webpage.

**Example 17.66: Project Code**

`blog/templates/blog/post_archive_month.html` **in** 7dcd39cac5

```
36              <p>
37                 Written on:
38                 <time datetime="{{ post.pub_date|date:"Y-m-d" }}">
39                    {{ post.pub_date|date:"l, F j, Y" }}
40                 </time>
41              </p>
42           </header>
43           <p>{{ post.text|truncatewords:20 }}</p>
44           <p class="read-more">
45             <a href="{{ post.get_absolute_url }}">
46                 Read more...</a></p>
```

Between the title and the content, we add buttons for editing and deleting the Post
instance, as shown in Example 17.67.

**Example 17.67: Project Code**

`blog/templates/blog/post_archive_month.html` **in** 7dcd39cac5

```
24                <ul class="inline">
25                   <li>
26                     <a
27                        href="{{ post.get_update_url }}"
28                        class="button">
29                     Edit Post</a></li>
30                   <li>
31                     <a
32                        href="{{ post.get_delete_url }}"
33                        class="button">
34                     Delete Post</a></li>
35                </ul>
```

Finally, above the blog post loop, we add the second button to create new Post objects,
as shown in Example 17.68.

**Example 17.68: Project Code**

`blog/templates/blog/post_archive_month.html` **in** 7dcd39cac5

```
10        <div class="mobile">
11           <a
12              href="{% url 'blog_post_create' %}"
13              class="button button-primary">
14           Write New Blog Post</a>
15        </div>
```

### 17.7.2.3 Linking to `PostArchiveMonth`

Now that we have a URL pattern for `PostArchiveMonth`, we can create links in `post_archive_year.html` to link the year archive to month archives, as shown in Example 17.69.

**Example 17.69: Project Code**
`blog/templates/blog/post_archive_year.html` in b716aabd68

```
57        <ul>
58          {% for m in date_list %}
59          <li><a href="{% url 'blog_post_archive_month'
  .                           m|date:"Y" m|date:"n" %}">
60              {{ m|date:"F Y" }}</a></li>
61          {% endfor %}
62        </ul>
```

The use of two arguments, as discussed earlier, is not optional. We cannot change the code to `next_month|date:"Y n"`, as this yields a single string, which Django will use as a single argument when the URL pattern expects two.

In previous iterations of this link, I used the m format character, while in the links above I used the n character. The difference is on a whim: the m character always prints the number of the month as a two-digit number (with a leading zero when necessary), whereas the n character doesn't bother. Django doesn't care either way, and in both cases, the call to `url` will work as desired. We would normally want to be consistent across our website, but I wanted to demonstrate both options, and their potential interoperability, to you.

## 17.7.3 Creating `ArchiveIndexView`

Ideally, we want to link to our new `PostArchiveYear` webpage from the `PostList` page. To do so, we need a list of all of the dates our `Post` objects have been published. We could add the result of `Post.object.dates('pub_date', 'year')` to our template context, modify `post_list.html`, and call it a day. Instead (and despite the fact that this section is about adding GCBV), we will replace `ListView` with `ArchiveIndexView` as `PostList`'s superclass.

Much like `PostList`, `ArchiveIndexView` shows a list of objects. Both may be paginated (a feature we have yet to use on a GCBV). However, `ArchiveIndexView` is meant to be integrated with `MonthArchiveView` and `YearArchiveView` and expects the `DateField` (or `DateTimeField`) to work properly. We specify the `model` and `datefield` options, along with a slew of attributes, in Example 17.70.

**Example 17.70: Project Code**
`blog/views.py` in c5ead7f5f3

```
66    class PostList(ArchiveIndexView):
67        allow_empty = True
68        allow_future = True
69        context_object_name = 'post_list'
```

```
70          date_field = 'pub_date'
71          make_object_list = True
72          model = Post
73          paginate_by = 5
74          template_name = 'blog/post_list.html'
```

To print a list of objects, as opposed to simply printing dates, we override the
make_object_list. By default, the date_list_period is set to 'year', which is
perfect because we will be linking to PostArchiveYear webpages.

By default, ArchiveIndexView subclasses set the context_object_name to
'latest', so we override the option to be 'post_list'. We want the view to use our
existing post_list.html template, and so we override the template_name attribute
(but we could have just set template_name_suffix to '_list').

By default, ArchiveIndexView lists all of the objects for a model. That's not desirable
in our case, and so we paginate the webpage using paginate_by, meaning the page will
display only five items at a time. Django uses the pagination system seen in Chapter 14 to
make this functionality work.

Finally, we specify allow_empty and allow_future pages. By default, if there are no
objects for a model, ArchiveIndexView returns a 404 error. By setting allow_empty,
we disable this behavior. The allow_future attribute defines whether or not objects with
dates in the future are displayed. If you disable it (or don't override it), you'll notice that the
blog post we have scheduled for 2020 disappears.

Take a moment to look at the code in Example 17.70 again. In just 9 lines of code (with
just 8 attributes), we've tapped into an entire set of Django's features. With growing
familiarity of GCBV, this sort of speed and power becomes easy.

Even so, there's no way to avoid our template. Thanks to our switch from PostList to
ArchiveIndexView, we can simply make use of the date_list context variable to
display links to our PostArchiveYear webpages in the sidebar (see Example 17.71).

**Example 17.71: Project Code**
blog/templates/blog/post_list.html in c5ead7f5f3

```
52      <div class="desktop four columns">
  .         ...
57        <h3>Post Archives</h3>
58        <ul>
59          {% for y in date_list %}
60            <li><a href="{% url 'blog_post_archive_year' y|date:"Y" %}">
61              {{ y|date:"Y" }}</a></li>
62          {% endfor %}
63        </ul>
64      </div>
```

We won't be adding links to use the block pagination feature we just enabled. Given the
date pagination we've enabled thanks to PostArchiveYear and PostArchiveMonth,
we don't need any more pagination. Even so, we'll see how to better use pagination in
GCBVs in Chapter 18.

# 17.8   Putting It All Together

Generic class-based views (GCBVs) are class-based views (CBVs) that come with predefined behavior. For this behavior to work correctly, existing attributes on the class must be overridden. Without these overrides, a GCBV will not function.

The major difficulty with GCBVs is the amount of content and overhead there is to learning them. Once understood, they become one of Django's most useful features, as they allow developers to create views quickly and efficiently. It would be silly to try to write your own classes with these behaviors when you can use code that is publicly reviewed and has been in use since 2011 (Django 1.3's release).

The biggest mistake I see beginners make with GCBVs is the attempt to use them everywhere or for behavior that the class is not built for. Don't use a `DetailView` to display a form or a list! If the GCBV doesn't provide the behavior you want, then don't use it! If *none* of the GCBVs have the behavior you desire, then you shouldn't use a GCBV. Use a CBV or a function view.

Of course, once you become familiar with GCBVs, you'll see that the rules are a little less rigid and that, while you shouldn't replace behavior in a GCBV, it becomes fairly easy to bend the behavior to your needs (as we shall see in Chapter 18).

# Advanced Generic Class-Based View Usage

## In This Chapter

- Override generic class-based view internals
- Use multiple inheritance and mixin classes to define behavior once for multiple views
- Restructure URL patterns for NewsLink objects

## 18.1 Introduction

In this chapter, we apply all of our knowledge of class-based views (CBVs) and generic class-based views (GCBVs) to perform a serious upgrade to our website. We do the following:

- Use multiple inheritance in update views to adhere to _form_update standard
- Modify pagination behavior in GCBVs to list Startup and Tag instances according to our own standard
- Inherit and modify DateDetail in PostDetail to display Post objects
- Customize PostUpdate and PostDelete with a mixin
- Switch the URL schemes for NewsLinkUpdate and NewsLinkDelete
- Automate basic behavior in NewsLinkCreate

To get all of this behavior working, we will find ourselves modifying or extending behavior provided by Django's GCBVs. This is a tough chapter. I highly recommend taking it slowly, and using the code on Github to play with the code yourself.

This chapter assumes intermediate Python, such as multiple inheritance and method resolution order. For a primer on this material, please see Appendix B.

# 18.2  Rapid Review of GCBV

Before we jump into the deep end, remind yourself that a GCBV is simply a CBV with predefined behavior that expects to have specific attributes or methods overridden. Using GCBVs allows for rapid development of behavior commonly found on websites.

To remind ourselves of how easy their usage is and to prepare for our modification of `UpdateView`, we can switch `NewsLinkUpdate` to inherit the GCBV, as shown in Example 18.1.

**Example 18.1: Project Code**
`organizer/views.py` **in** `1b77e1ab78`

```
28   class NewsLinkUpdate(UpdateView):
29       form_class = NewsLinkForm
30       model = NewsLink
31       template_name_suffix = '_form_update'
```

If this code is opaque or unfamiliar, please review Chapter 17: Understanding Generic Class-Based Views.

The difficulty with GCBVs is how much overhead there is to using and learning them, which is why the Django community has created tools such as Classy Class-Based Views.[1] What's more, GCBVs allow for the same behavior using different options. In `StartupUpdate` and `TagUpdate`, shown in Example 18.2, we can replace `template_name` with `template_name_suffix` to yield exactly the same behavior (as Django will use the `template_name_suffix` to correctly generate the `template_name` because we have adhered to a naming standard).

**Example 18.2: Project Code**
`organizer/views.py` **in** `d577eee8a7`

```
91    class StartupUpdate(UpdateView):
92        form_class = StartupForm
93        model = Startup
94        template_name_suffix = '_form_update'
  .       ...
167   class TagUpdate(UpdateView):
168       form_class = TagForm
169       model = Tag
170       template_name_suffix = '_form_update'
```

---

1. http://ccbv.co.uk

## 18.3  Globally Setting Template Suffix for Update Views

In TagUpdate, StartupUpdate, and NewsLinkUpdate, we have set the template_name_suffix attributes to be exactly the same value (and we follow suit with PostUpdate in this chapter).

Setting duplicate attributes to use the same resource violates DRY (Don't Repeat Yourself) principles and is very easy to avoid. In a new file, core/utils.py, we can create our own UpdateView GCBV, using Django's own UpdateView GCBV as a base, as shown in Example 18.3.

**Example 18.3: Project Code**
core/utils.py **in** 2825fb7c70

```
1   from django.views.generic import \
2       UpdateView as BaseUpdateView
3
4
5   class UpdateView(BaseUpdateView):
6       template_name_suffix = '_form_update'
```

In organizer/views.py, we remove the import of Django's UpdateView and add an import of our own, as shown in Example 18.4.

**Example 18.4: Project Code**
organizer/views.py **in** 2825fb7c70

```
6   from django.views.generic import (
7       CreateView, DeleteView, DetailView, View)
8
9   from core.utils import UpdateView
```

This import allows us to delete the template_name_suffix from TagUpdate, StartupUpdate, and NewsLinkUpdate but maintain existing behavior. Our code will now more easily follow the standard we've set across our project.

## 18.4  Generating Pagination Links

In Chapter 14: Pagination, we saw that while Django can handle pagination in many ways, it does not build the links for pagination for us. GCBVs follow the same pattern. Given that both TagList and StartupList will use the same kind of pagination, we can extend the pagination behavior of ListView to build the links for our templates.

In organizer/utils.py, we can create a PageLinksMixin class to add the behavior we want, as shown in Example 18.5.

**Example 18.5:** Project Code

`organizer/utils.py` **in** be588e9505

```
1    class PageLinksMixin:
2        page_kwarg = 'page'
```

The basis of all our links is to have a query URL segment with the page variable equal to the number of the page, as shown in Example 18.6.

**Example 18.6:** Project Code

`organizer/utils.py` **in** be588e9505

```
1    class PageLinksMixin:
2        page_kwarg = 'page'
3
4        def _page_urls(self, page_number):
5            return "?{pkw}={n}".format(
6                pkw=self.page_kwarg,
7                n=page_number)
```

Given a Page object, we can generate the link to the previous page if it exists, as shown in Example 18.7.

**Example 18.7:** Project Code

`organizer/utils.py` **in** be588e9505

```
 1    class PageLinksMixin:
 2        page_kwarg = 'page'
 .        ...
 9        def previous_page(self, page):
10            if page.has_previous():
11                return self._page_urls(
12                    page.previous_page_number())
13            return None
```

The code for next_page() is similar, as shown in Example 18.8.

**Example 18.8:** Project Code

`organizer/utils.py` **in** be588e9505

```
 1    class PageLinksMixin:
 2        page_kwarg = 'page'
 .        ...
15        def next_page(self, page):
16            if page.has_next():
17                return self._page_urls(
18                    page.next_page_number())
19            return None
```

We intend to use our mixin class in tandem with subclasses of `ListView`. We can therefore override the `get_context_data()` and use `super()` to call the version of the method found in `ListView`, as shown in Example 18.9. The GCBV will have created the `Page` instance at this point, allowing us to simply pull it out of the dictionary and pass it to the methods we created above as new template context variables.

**Example 18.9: Project Code**

`organizer/utils.py` in be588e9505

```
21        def get_context_data(self, **kwargs):
22            context = super().get_context_data(
23                **kwargs)
24            page = context.get('page_obj')
25            if page is not None:
26                context.update({
27                    'previous_page_url':
28                        self.previous_page(page),
29                    'next_page_url':
30                        self.next_page(page),
31                })
32            return context
```

## 18.4.1 `StartupList` Pagination

We can now use our `PageLinksMixin` in tandem with `ListView` to replace the code for `StartupList`. We therefore change the inheritance to use multiple inheritance of both `PageLinksMixin` and `ListView`, and we keep the `model` and `paginate_by` attributes, as shown in Example 18.10. The rest can be deleted.

**Example 18.10: Project Code**

`organizer/views.py` in 81321265be

```
2    from django.views.generic import (
3        CreateView, DeleteView, DetailView, ListView)
     ...
10   from .utils import PageLinksMixin
     ...
46   class StartupList(PageLinksMixin, ListView):
47       model = Startup
48       paginate_by = 5
```

There's a bit of a gotcha here. In our case, we had been passing the `Page` instance as `startup_list` to make our life easy. However, `ListView` will only pass the `Page` object as `page_obj`. The `startup_list` variable passed to the template by `ListView` is actually `page_obj.object_list` (a Python `list`). Our template code for showing the page number in `startup_list.html` is therefore wrong and must be replaced, as shown in Example 18.11.

**Example 18.11: Project Code**

`organizer/templates/organizer/startup_list.html` **in** 81321265be

```
55          <li>
56            Page {{ page_obj.number }}
57            of {{ paginator.num_pages }}
58          </li>
```

## 18.4.2   `TagList` Pagination

At the end of Chapter 14, we had two CBVs for listing `Tag` objects. `TagList` listed all of the tags in the database on a single page. `TagPageList` paginated the list of tags, using the URL path segment to do so. I'm not a fan of using the URL path to paginate, and so we remove `TagPageList` and paginate `TagList` according to the URL query. With our `PageLinksMixin`, this is quite simple, as you can see in Example 18.12.

**Example 18.12: Project Code**

`organizer/views.py` **in** 81321265be

```
71    class TagList(PageLinksMixin, ListView):
72        paginate_by = 5
73        model = Tag
```

The rest of `TagList` has been removed, and the entirety of `TagPageList` is gone. Best practice is to remove the `organizer_tag_page` URL pattern in `organizer/urls/tag.py` (Python will complain about import errors if you don't).

We need to fix the page number display in `tag_list.html`, as shown in Example 18.13. As with `StartupList`, we had previously been using `tag_list` to store the `Page` instance. The `Page` instance is now stored in `page_obj`, and the `tag_list` template variable is now `page_obj.object_list`.

**Example 18.13: Project Code**

`organizer/templates/organizer/tag_list.html` **in** 81321265be

```
55          <li>
56            Page {{ page_obj.number }}
57            of {{ paginator.num_pages }}
58          </li>
```

## 18.4.3   Pagination Links

In Chapter 16: Serving Static Content with Django we created a template block in `base_organizer.html` for page links in `startup_list.html` and `tag_list.html` to override. However, as the code for page links in both of these templates are created by identical code (which features a condition), we can delete both of these displays and move the code into `base_organizer.html`.

Where the content_footer template block once was (with its surrounding HTML div tags), we now have the code shown in Example 18.14.

**Example 18.14: Project Code**

organizer/templates/organizer/base_organizer.html in b5a75d8dfb

```
14      {% if is_paginated %}
15        <div class="row">
16          <div class="twelve columns">
17            <ul class="pagination">
18              {% if previous_page_url %}
19                <li>
20                  <a href="{{ previous_page_url }}">
21                    Previous</a>
22                </li>
23              {% endif %}
24              <li>
25                Page {{ page_obj.number }}
26                of {{ paginator.num_pages }}
27              </li>
28              {% if next_page_url %}
29                <li>
30                  <a href="{{ next_page_url }}">
31                    Next</a>
32                </li>
33              {% endif %}
34            </ul>
35          </div>
36        </div>
37      {% endif %}
```

### 18.4.4  Extending Pagination Behavior Further

One of the key advantages of our mixin, and the way we are extending GCBV behavior is that it makes it easy to extend behavior across our site. For instance, we might decide to help users navigate pagination by adding first and last links to our pages. Because we've adhered to DRY, we only need to make changes in one Python class and one template.

We can start by modifying PageLinksMixin to generate the first and last links for us, as shown in Example 18.15.

**Example 18.15: Project Code**

organizer/utils.py in 439b4e2f3c

```
1    class PageLinksMixin:
2        page_kwarg = 'page'
.        ...
9        def first_page(self, page):
10           # don't show on first page
11           if page.number > 1:
12               return self._page_urls(1)
13           return None
```

It makes no sense to have a link to the first page if we're on the first page, so we only generate a first page if we're on a different page.

However, this means that on the second page, we would have two links to the first page: both first and previous will point to the first page. We can modify the previous link to generate only if we're not on the first or second page, as shown in Example 18.16.

**Example 18.16:** Project Code

`organizer/utils.py` in 439b4e2f3c

```
 1   class PageLinksMixin:
 2       page_kwarg = 'page'
 .       ...
15       def previous_page(self, page):
16           if (page.has_previous()
17                   and page.number > 2):
18               return self._page_urls(
19                   page.previous_page_number())
20           return None
```

Like the link to the first page, it makes no sense to link to the last page on the last page, so we only display it on other pages, as shown in Example 18.17.

**Example 18.17:** Project Code

`organizer/utils.py` in 439b4e2f3c

```
 1   class PageLinksMixin:
 2       page_kwarg = 'page'
 .       ...
30       def last_page(self, page):
31           last_page = page.paginator.num_pages
32           if page.number < last_page:
33               return self._page_urls(last_page)
34           return None
```

Finally, in Example 18.18, we modify the next link to generate only if the page is not the last or the second to last page (otherwise, we have two links to the last page on the second to last page).

**Example 18.18:** Project Code

`organizer/utils.py` in 439b4e2f3c

```
 1   class PageLinksMixin:
 2       page_kwarg = 'page'
 .       ...
22       def next_page(self, page):
23           last_page = page.paginator.num_pages
24           if (page.has_next()
25                   and page.number < last_page - 1):
```

```
26              return self._page_urls(
27                  page.next_page_number())
28          return None
```

Let's not forget to add our new links to the template context, as shown in Example 18.19.

**Example 18.19: Project Code**
`organizer/utils.py` in 439b4e2f3c

```
 1  class PageLinksMixin:
 .      ...
36      def get_context_data(self, **kwargs):
 .          ...
41          context.update({
42              'first_page_url':
43                  self.first_page(page),
 .          ...
48              'last_page_url':
49                  self.last_page(page),
50          })
```

In the template, we first add a link to the first page, as shown in Example 18.20.

**Example 18.20: Project Code**
`organizer/templates/organizer/base_organizer.html` in 439b4e2f3c

```
18          {% if first_page_url %}
19            <li>
20              <a href="{{ first_page_url }}">
21              First</a>
22            </li>
23          {% endif %}
```

We can then add a link to the last page, as shown in Example 18.21.

**Example 18.21: Project Code**
`organizer/templates/organizer/base_organizer.html` in 439b4e2f3c

```
40          {% if last_page_url %}
41            <li>
42              <a href="{{ last_page_url }}">
43              Last</a>
44            </li>
45          {% endif %}
```

Even if you don't agree with the changes I'm making to the site, you must admit it's quite easy, given the way we've structured our code.

# 18.5   Re-creating `PostDetail` with `DateDetailView`

In Chapter 17, we used `DetailView` to replace the behavior of displaying an object in `TagDetail` and `StartupDetail`, but we left `post_detail()` alone. `DetailView` works only with URL patterns that use a `pk`, a `slug`, or both (starting in Django 1.8). Given that our detail page for `Post` uses the year, month, and slug of the object for uniqueness, it didn't make any sense to use `TagDetail`.

Django provides a GCBV called `DateDetailView` to work with objects that have uniqueness according to a `DateField`, much in the spirit of `ArchiveIndexView` or `YearArchiveView`. The catch is that the GCBV anticipates using the full date: the year, month, and day (on top of the slug). In this section, we not only switch to using the `DateDetailView`, we also modify its behavior to use only the year, month, and slug.

As with any GCBV, actually beginning to use the view is quick and easy, as you can see in Example 18.22.

**Example 18.22: Project Code**
blog/views.py in 17b86e40a6

```
 3   from django.views.generic import (
 4       ArchiveIndexView, CreateView, DateDetailView,
 5       MonthArchiveView, View, YearArchiveView)
 .       ...
51   class PostDetail(DateDetailView):
52       date_field = 'pub_date'
53       model = Post
```

For the view above to work, we need to modify our `blog_post_detail` URL pattern, as shown in Example 18.23.

**Example 18.23: Project Code**
blog/urls.py in 17b86e40a6

```
 3   from .views import (
 4       PostArchiveMonth, PostArchiveYear, PostCreate,
 5       PostDelete, PostDetail, PostList, PostUpdate)
 .       ...
 7   urlpatterns = [
 .       ...
21       url(r'^(?P<year>\d{4})/'
22           r'(?P<month>[\w-]+)/'
23           r'(?P<day>\d{1,2})/'
24           r'(?P<slug>[\w\-]+)/$',
25           PostDetail.as_view(),
26           name='blog_post_detail'),
 .       ...
39   ]
```

Not only does `DateDetailView` anticipate using the day field of the `DateField`, but it anticipates using the month as a string, such as `/blog/2013/jan/18/django-training/`.

For links to continue to work, we need to modify `get_absolute_url()`. Luckily, the Python `%b` format character makes it easy to output month shortnames, as shown in Example 18.24.

**Example 18.24: Project Code**
`blog/models.py` in `17b86e40a6`

```
11   class Post(models.Model):
 .       ...
40      def get_absolute_url(self):
41         return reverse(
42            'blog_post_detail',
43            kwargs={'year': self.pub_date.year,
44                    'month': self.pub_date.strftime('%b').lower(),
45                    'day': self.pub_date.day,
46                    'slug': self.slug})
```

Our first goal is therefore to revert our behavior to using a number for the month. Thankfully (and unsurprisingly), the GCBV supplies the `month_format` attribute that we can override to make this change. In Example 18.25, we set it to the Python `strftime` format character for the number of the month.

**Example 18.25: Project Code**
`blog/views.py` in `e0340da03a`

```
51   class PostDetail(DateDetailView):
52      date_field = 'pub_date'
53      model = Post
54      month_format = '%m'
```

This code allows us to change the regular expression pattern in our month group, as shown in Example 18.26.

**Example 18.26: Project Code**
`blog/urls.py` in `e0340da03a`

```
21      url(r'^(?P<year>\d{4})/'
22         r'(?P<month>\d{1,2})/'
23         r'(?P<day>\d{1,2})/'
24         r'(?P<slug>[\w\-]+)/$',
25         PostDetail.as_view(),
26         name='blog_post_detail'),
```

We also change the code in `get_absolute_url()`, as shown in Example 18.27. (Can you imagine if we didn't have this method?)

**Example 18.27: Project Code**
`blog/models.py` **in** e0340da03a

```
11    class Post(models.Model):
 .        ...
40        def get_absolute_url(self):
41            return reverse(
42                'blog_post_detail',
43                kwargs={'year': self.pub_date.year,
44                        'month': self.pub_date.month,
45                        'day': self.pub_date.day,
46                        'slug': self.slug})
```

Now that we've got the month URL path segment working as desired, we can turn our attention to removing the day part of the URL. In this case, we start with the URL pattern, which is now back to what it was at the beginning of the chapter, as shown in Example 18.28.

**Example 18.28: Project Code**
`blog/urls.py` **in** 018de44b91

```
21        url(r'^(?P<year>\d{4})/'
22            r'(?P<month>\d{1,2})/'
23            r'(?P<slug>[\w\-]+)/$',
24            PostDetail.as_view(),
25            name='blog_post_detail'),
```

Similarly, in Example 18.29, we return `get_absolute_url()` to the code we had at the beginning of the chapter.

**Example 18.29: Project Code**
`blog/models.py` **in** 018de44b91

```
11    class Post(models.Model):
 .        ...
40        def get_absolute_url(self):
41            return reverse(
42                'blog_post_detail',
43                kwargs={'year': self.pub_date.year,
44                        'month': self.pub_date.month,
45                        'slug': self.slug})
```

If you use the documentation or Classy Class-Based Views,[2] you'll discover that the `DayMixin` provides `DateDetailView` with a `get_day()` method and that the `DateMixin` class provides a `_make_single_date_lookup()` method. The latter is where Django actually builds the keyword arguments for the query (to find the object in the database), and so we need to override it to create our own set of parameters for the queryset. The `get_day()` method must be overridden because it will error if it does not find a day variable in the URL pattern—we therefore return a `'1'` for the first day of the month, as shown in Example 18.30.

**Example 18.30: Project Code**
`blog/views.py` **in** `018de44b91`

```
51   class PostDetail(DateDetailView):
52       date_field = 'pub_date'
53       model = Post
54       month_format = '%m'
55
56       def get_day(self):
57           return '1'
58
59       def _make_single_date_lookup(self, date):
60           date_field = self.get_date_field()
61           return {
62               date_field + '__year': date.year,
63               date_field + '__month': date.month,
64           }
```

This code is cryptic, to say the least. Without knowledge of this GCBV, it looks a little like black magic.

The real problem here is that we are removing behavior. While GCBVs are great for modifying and extending behavior, removing behavior gets ugly.

# 18.6  Switching to GCBVs with `PostGetMixin` in `Post` Views

Instead of removing behavior from `DateDetailView`, we should be adding behavior to `DetailView`.

In Chapter 17, we saw that `DetailView` uses the `get_object()` method to actually fetch the object from the database. We can therefore create a mixin class to override the method and use multiple inheritance to override this in `DetailView` and other GCBVs, as shown in Example 18.31.

---

2. http://ccbv.co.uk

**Example 18.31: Project Code**
blog/utils.py **in** a180f20424

```
1   from django.shortcuts import get_object_or_404
2
3   from .models import Post
4
5
6   class PostGetMixin:
7
8       def get_object(self, queryset=None):
9           year = self.kwargs.get('year')
10          month = self.kwargs.get('month')
11          slug = self.kwargs.get('slug')
12          return get_object_or_404(
13              Post,
14              pub_date__year=year,
15              pub_date__month=month,
16              slug__iexact=slug)
```

In blog/views.py, we can replace all of the code for PostDetail, as shown in Example 18.32.

**Example 18.32: Project Code**
blog/views.py **in** a180f20424

```
3   from django.views.generic import (
4       ArchiveIndexView, CreateView, DetailView,
5       MonthArchiveView, View, YearArchiveView)
.       ...
9   from .utils import PostGetMixin
.       ...
52  class PostDetail(PostGetMixin, DetailView):
53      model = Post
```

This is *much* simpler. The rule of thumb when working with GCBVs is to add or change but not to remove behavior.

What's more, we know that PostGetMixin is the right way to tackle the problem because this mixin allows us to shorten our code on PostUpdate and PostDelete.

There is a gotcha here, however. Instead of immediately inheriting PostGetMixin, we start by inheriting just our custom UpdateView in PostUpdate, as shown in Example 18.33. Surprisingly, the view will continue to work exactly as we expect.

**Example 18.33: Project Code**
blog/views.py **in** bb45729858

```
7   from core.utils import UpdateView
.       ...
69  class PostUpdate(UpdateView):
70      form_class = PostForm
71      model = Post
```

Many beginners might make the mistake of thinking that this code is fine. After all, all of the update pages for all our `Post` objects still work! However, they all work only because none of our `Post` objects have slugs that conflict with each other. Remember that slugs in `Post` objects are not unique; the unique identifier for a `Post` instance is the combination of year, month, and slug. If we have a `Post` object published in January 2015 with the slug `django` and a `Post` published in February 2015 with the slug `django`, it should be legal in the database. However, the code above will not know the difference and will return an error about finding two objects in the database because `UpdateView` uses only the `slug` to get objects from the database. It becomes necessary to inherit `PostGetMixin`, which enforces the proper uniqueness identifier, as shown in Example 18.34.

**Example 18.34: Project Code**
blog/views.py in d28c51f2b7

```
69    class PostUpdate(PostGetMixin, UpdateView):
70        form_class = PostForm
71        model = Post
```

Note that this technique only works because `UpdateView` makes use of the `get_object()` method that `PostGetMixin` overrides through multiple inheritance. `DeleteView` works the same way, allowing us to drastically shorten our `DeleteView` code, as shown in Example 18.35.

**Example 18.35: Project Code**
blog/views.py in f9691f7ac0

```
30    class PostDelete(PostGetMixin, DeleteView):
31        model = Post
32        success_url = reverse_lazy('blog_post_list')
```

Our `PostGetMixin` could use some work. For a simple, small tool it does the job, but if we were using it on a larger team, on a larger scale, we would want to better integrate it with the rest of the GCBV system and make it more resilient to problems.

To begin, we should make sure we're always actually receiving the `year`, `month`, and `slug` attributes our class is using. In Example 18.36, we define a dictionary for our error strings (allowing other developers to override our error messages when necessary).

**Example 18.36: Project Code**
blog/utils.py in 7a1a3eda21

```
6    class PostGetMixin:
7
8        errors = {
9            'url_kwargs':
10               "Generic view {} must be called with "
11               "year, month, and slug.",
12        }
```

We can thus check that our attributes exist and raise an exception if they don't, as shown in Example 18.37.

**Example 18.37: Project Code**

`blog/utils.py` in `7a1a3eda21`

```
 6  class PostGetMixin:
 .      ...
14      def get_object(self, queryset=None):
15          year = self.kwargs.get('year')
16          month = self.kwargs.get('month')
17          slug = self.kwargs.get('slug')
18          if (year is None
19                  or month is None
20                  or slug is None):
21              raise AttributeError(
22                  self.errors['url_kwargs'].format(
23                      self.__class__.__name__))
24          return get_object_or_404(
25              Post,
26              pub_date__year=year,
```

Of course, the next step is to allow other developers to override the variable names used in the class, allowing for different variable names in the regular expression named groups of a URL pattern, as shown in Example 18.38.

**Example 18.38: Project Code**

`blog/utils.py` in `29564aca77`

```
 6  class PostGetMixin:
 7      month_url_kwarg = 'month'
 8      year_url_kwarg = 'year'
 .      ...
16      def get_object(self, queryset=None):
17          year = self.kwargs.get(
18              self.year_url_kwarg)
19          month = self.kwargs.get(
20              self.month_url_kwarg)
21          slug = self.kwargs.get(
22              self.slug_url_kwarg)
```

# 18.7  Making `PostGetMixin` Generic

If you examine the current iteration of `PostGetMixin`, you might notice we're only a few steps away from very generic behavior. For our site, falling down the rabbit hole isn't all that helpful. On a larger project, where we might need very specific generic behavior, creating such behavior might prove to be incredibly beneficial. In the interest of uncovering all of the secrets of building your own GCBV classes, we will thus follow the rabbit down the rabbit hole.

The first thing to do is make it so that the pub_date is not hardcoded in the class. In Example 18.39, we introduce the date_field attribute (with a smart default for our own site) and use that attribute in a dictionary that we use for filter arguments in get_object_or_404().

**Example 18.39:** Project Code

blog/utils.py in 2be4df4b8e

```
 6   class PostGetMixin:
 7       date_field = 'pub_date'
 .       ...
17       def get_object(self, queryset=None):
 .           ...
30           date_field = self.date_field
31           slug_field = self.get_slug_field()
32           filter_dict = {
33               date_field + '__year': year,
34               date_field + '__month': month,
35               slug_field: slug,
36           }
37           return get_object_or_404(
38               Post, **filter_dict)
```

And, of course, we've also hardcoded Post. We can easily change that (still maintaining a smart default in the interest of our current site), as shown in Example 18.40.

**Example 18.40:** Project Code

blog/utils.py in 81de62d46d

```
 6   class PostGetMixin:
 7       date_field = 'pub_date'
 8       model = Post
 .       ...
12       errors = {
 .           ...
16           'not_exist':
17               "No {} by that date and slug.",
18       }
 .           ...
40       if queryset is None:
41           queryset = self.get_queryset()
42       queryset = queryset.filter(**filter_dict)
43       try:
44           obj = queryset.get()
45       except queryset.model.DoesNotExist:
46           raise Http404(
47               self.errors['not_exist'].format(
48                   queryset.model
49                   ._meta.verbose_name))
50       return obj
```

To make this setting as robust as possible, we add a new error and build the queryset in an iterative fashion, integrating with the `queryset` parameter used in the majority of GCBVs.

Our mixin could now be used with *any* object that is uniquely identified by year, month, and slug. If this is a common pattern on your site, then this mixin will prove to be incredibly useful.

However, the mixin is still not as flexible as any of Django's GCBVs. In any GCBV, Django typically offers developers the ability to change behavior not just according to attribute but also according to behavior. What if we wanted to change the way the year was handled in just a single subclass? We would have to completely override `get_object()`.

Instead, we can use some of the 30 mixin and base classes that are used to create Django's GCBVs. In Example 18.41, we import the three date mixins relevant to our needs: a mixin for the year, a mixin for the month, and the `DateMixin` class, which defines the `date_field` attribute. These three allow us to create our own `DateObjectMixin`.

**Example 18.41: Project Code**
`blog/utils.py` in `438a2dd48c`

```
40   class DateObjectMixin(
41           YearMixin, MonthMixin, DateMixin):
```

The `DateMixin` provides an implementation of `_make_single_date_lookup()`, but the implementation does not suit our purposes. The implementation in `DateMixin` assumes that the date being passed is a full date: year, month, day. As we have only the first two, we need to override the method.

Despite the fact that our URLs use just the year and month (and slug) as the identifier, the database is storing full dates in the database, including the day. When we search for an object, we therefore need to ask for a range of dates: any object with the following slug, published on or after the first of the month and before the first of the next month.

To build this range, we rely on two existing methods. The `_make_date_lookup_arg()` method defined by `DateMixin` properly sets the timezone if the date is stored in a `DateTimeField`. The `_get_next_month()` method is defined by `MonthMixin` and does exactly what you think it does.

Our `_make_single_date_lookup()` implementation, in Example 18.42, therefore builds one of two ranges: one in the event the dates are stored in a `DateTimeField` and one in the event the dates are stored in a `DateField`. (In our own site we will only ever use the second.) In the case of the latter, we do not need to call `_make_date_lookup_arg()`, as it is used only for `DateTimeField` dates.

**Example 18.42: Project Code**
`blog/utils.py` in `438a2dd48c`

```
40   class DateObjectMixin(
41           YearMixin, MonthMixin, DateMixin):
.        ...
67       def _make_single_date_lookup(self, date):
68           date_field = self.get_date_field()
```

```
69          if self.uses_datetime_field:
70              since = self._make_date_lookup_arg(
71                  date)
72              until = self._make_date_lookup_arg(
73                  self._get_next_month(date))
74              return {
75                  '%s__gte' % date_field: since,
76                  '%s__lt' % date_field: until,
77              }
78          else:
79              return {
80                  '%s__gte' % date_field: date,
81                  '%s__lt' % date_field:
82                      self._get_next_month(date),
83              }
```

We can now turn our attention to actually getting the object in question. In Example 18.43, we start by using methods from our various date mixins to get the date in the URL path (or specified elsewhere, as we'll discover). We then build a queryset, checking permissions on our page and using our _make_single_date_lookup() method to filter the queryset.

**Example 18.43: Project Code**
blog/utils.py **in** 438a2dd48c

```
40  class DateObjectMixin(
41          YearMixin, MonthMixin, DateMixin):
42
43      def get_object(self, queryset=None):
44          year = self.get_year()
45          month = self.get_month()
46          date = _date_from_string(
47              year, self.get_year_format(),
48              month, self.get_month_format(),
49          )
50          if queryset is None:
51              queryset = self.get_queryset()
52          if (not self.get_allow_future()
53                  and date > date.today()):
54              raise Http404(
55                  "Future {} not available because "
56                  "{}.allow_future is False."
57                  .format(
58                      (queryset.model
59                          ._meta.verbose_name_plural),
60                      self.__class__.__name__))
61          filter_dict = (
62              self._make_single_date_lookup(date))
63          queryset = queryset.filter(**filter_dict)
64          return super().get_object(
65              queryset=queryset)
```

The call to the get_queryset() on line 51 assumes we will actually be inheriting a GCBV or mixin that defines this method, as our current class neither defines nor inherits one.

On lines 44 through 49 of Example 18.43, we make use entirely of methods defined on either YearMixin or MonthMixin. We also use _date_from_string() (imported in Example 18.44) to make our lives much easier. Of particular note is that the _date_from_string() function is built to intelligently return dates based on partial information, allowing us to pass a year and a month, in which case it will return the first day of the month of that year.

Django's YearMixin and MonthMixin come with a funny oversight—they do not allow us to override the URL keyword argument being passed. The named groups in the regular expression pattern of the URL pattern must always be year and month (respectively). This feels like something we should correct, and so we will implement these methods in subclasses of the mixins.

In Example 18.44, we change our imports to rename the YearMixin and MonthMixin in our namespace (and to include _date_from_string()).

**Example 18.44: Project Code**

blog/utils.py **in** 438a2dd48c

```
1    from django.http import Http404
2    from django.views.generic.dates import (
3        DateMixin, MonthMixin as BaseMonthMixin,
4        YearMixin as BaseYearMixin, _date_from_string)
```

Django's YearMixin (BaseYearMixin in our namespace) defines the year and year_format attributes. Our subclass adds an attribute for the name of the group in the regular expression pattern of the URL pattern as well as an attribute for the name of a variable in the URL query. This means a year may be (1) set explicitly on a subclass thanks to the year attribute, (2) set in the URL path to an arbitrarily named group, or (3) passed as part of the URL query. We use this knowledge to fetch the year on lines 29 through 34 of Example 18.45.

**Example 18.45: Project Code**

blog/utils.py **in** 438a2dd48c

```
24   class YearMixin(BaseYearMixin):
25       year_query_kwarg = 'year'
26       year_url_kwarg = 'year'
27
28       def get_year(self):
29           year = self.year
30           if year is None:
31               year = self.kwargs.get(
32                   self.year_url_kwarg,
33                   self.request.GET.get(
34                       self.year_query_kwarg))
```

```
35          if year is None:
36              raise Http404("No year specified")
37          return year
```

In our subclass of Django's `MonthMixin`, we follow the same pattern. In Example 18.46, we override the `get_month()` method and allow for developers to set the month in either a subclass (attribute), the URL path, or a URL query. We also override the `month_format` attribute to default to the `%m` format character.

**Example 18.46: Project Code**
`blog/utils.py` in `438a2dd48c`

```
 7    class MonthMixin(BaseMonthMixin):
 8        month_format = '%m'
 9        month_query_kwarg = 'month'
10        month_url_kwarg = 'month'
11
12        def get_month(self):
13            month = self.month
14            if month is None:
15                month = self.kwargs.get(
16                    self.month_url_kwarg,
17                    self.request.GET.get(
18                        self.month_query_kwarg))
19            if month is None:
20                raise Http404("No month specified")
21            return month
```

We've now fully extended the `DateObjectMixin` class (and superclasses), allowing us to return to `blog/views.py` to take full advantage of the behavior we've programmed. We start by importing the class into the file, as shown in Example 18.47.

**Example 18.47: Project Code**
`blog/views.py` in `438a2dd48c`

```
10    from .utils import DateObjectMixin
```

We start by adding the new class as a superclass to `PostDelete`, as shown in Example 18.48. In doing so, we add the attribute for the `date_field` and indicate whether the view may access objects (`Post` objects in this case) published in the future.

**Example 18.48: Project Code**
`blog/views.py` in `438a2dd48c`

```
30    class PostDelete(DateObjectMixin, DeleteView):
31        allow_future = True
32        date_field = 'pub_date'
33        model = Post
34        success_url = reverse_lazy('blog_post_list')
```

The changes to `PostDetail`, shown in Example 18.49, are virtually identical.

**Example 18.49: Project Code**
`blog/views.py` in `438a2dd48c`

```
37   class PostDetail(DateObjectMixin, DetailView):
38       allow_future = True
39       date_field = 'pub_date'
40       model = Post
```

The third time we add these two attributes—to `PostUpdate` in Example 18.50—might make you consider making them defaults. By the same token, we could create a class with intelligent defaults, such as the `model` attribute for all of the views in this file. I won't bother, because I don't think it's needed. What's more, we will override the `allow_future` attribute to be a little more protective in Chapter 20: Integrating Permissions.

**Example 18.50: Project Code**
`blog/views.py` in `438a2dd48c`

```
54   class PostUpdate(DateObjectMixin, UpdateView):
55       allow_future = True
56       date_field = 'pub_date'
57       form_class = PostForm
58       model = Post
```

# 18.8   Fixing `NewsLink` URL Patterns and Form Behavior

In this section, we tackle two problems. We start by changing the URL patterns of `NewsLink` views to adhere idea to the idea of clean, human-readable URLs. We then streamline the process of creating, updating, and deleting `NewsLink` objects.

### 18.8.1   `NewsLink` URL patterns

At the moment, our website uses the primary keys of `NewsLink` objects in the URL patterns of related views. This practice is frowned upon, and we want to switch to using the `SlugField` of the `NewsLink` object, a field we added in Chapter 10: Revisiting Migrations.

The trick to our new URL patterns is that the `slug` does not uniquely identify the `NewsLink` object. Instead, the combination of `startup` and `slug` does. Our URL patterns thus need to use two slugs to identify the `NewsLink`. That's somewhat tricky. All of our pages simply use `slug` as a variable name in regular expression patterns, and now we have to differentiate between `startup_slug` and `newslink_slug` in some instances.

As these views will now be associated with `Startup`, we create the URL patterns in `organizer/urls/startup.py`, deleting the `organizer/urls/newslink.py` file in its entirety, as shown in Example 18.51.

**Example 18.51: Project Code**

`organizer/urls/startup.py` **in** `7dcdf22318`

```
3    from ..views import (
4        NewsLinkCreate, NewsLinkDelete,
5        NewsLinkUpdate, StartupCreate, StartupDelete,
6        StartupDetail, StartupList, StartupUpdate)
```

Remember to also delete the include of the original NewsLink URL configuration and the import of newslink_urls from suorganizer/urls.py.

As Example 18.52 shows, instead of /newslink/create/, our new URL path will be /<startup_slug>/add_article_link/.

**Example 18.52: Project Code**

`organizer/urls/startup.py` **in** `7dcdf22318`

```
18       url(r'^(?P<startup_slug>[\w\-]+)/'
19           r'add_article_link/$',
20           NewsLinkCreate.as_view(),
21           name='organizer_newslink_create'),
```

To delete a NewsLink object, we need to identify it, and therefore we need both the slug for the Startup object as well as the slug for the NewsLink, as shown in Example 18.53.

**Example 18.53: Project Code**

`organizer/urls/startup.py` **in** `7dcdf22318`

```
28       url(r'^(?P<startup_slug>[\w\-]+)/'
29           r'(?P<newslink_slug>[\w\-]+)/'
30           r'delete/$',
31           NewsLinkDelete.as_view(),
32           name='organizer_newslink_delete'),
```

To update a NewsLink, we again identify the object with both slugs, appending the /update/ as a URL path segment, as shown in Example 18.54

**Example 18.54: Project Code**

`organizer/urls/startup.py` **in** `7dcdf22318`

```
33       url(r'^(?P<startup_slug>[\w\-]+)/'
34           r'(?P<newslink_slug>[\w\-]+)/'
35           r'update/$',
36           NewsLinkUpdate.as_view(),
37           name='organizer_newslink_update'),
```

All of our `NewsLink` views—`NewsLinkCreate`, `NewsLinkDelete`,
`NewsLinkUpdate`—will need to learn about the new `startup_slug`, and so we craft
`StartupContextMixin` to get the `Startup` object and add it to the context, thanks to
an override to the `get_context_data()` method, as shown in Example 18.55.

**Example 18.55: Project Code**
`organizer/utils.py` **in** `7dcdf22318`

```
 1    from django.shortcuts import get_object_or_404
 2
 3    from .models import Startup
 .       ...
59    class StartupContextMixin():
60        startup_slug_url_kwarg = 'startup_slug'
61        startup_context_object_name = 'startup'
62
63        def get_context_data(self, **kwargs):
64            startup_slug = self.kwargs.get(
65                self.startup_slug_url_kwarg)
66            startup = get_object_or_404(
67                Startup, slug__iexact=startup_slug)
68            context = {
69                self.startup_context_object_name:
70                    startup,
71            }
72            context.update(kwargs)
73            return super().get_context_data(**context)
```

Of course, none of this will work properly without an override to `get_object()`. We
therefore build another mixin for that purpose, as shown in Example 18.56.

**Example 18.56: Project Code**
`organizer/utils.py` **in** `f4e337f96e`

```
 3    from .models import NewsLink, Startup
 4
 5
 6    class NewsLinkGetObjectMixin():
 7
 8        def get_object(self, queryset=None):
 9            startup_slug = self.kwargs.get(
10                self.startup_slug_url_kwarg)
11            newslink_slug = self.kwargs.get(
12                self.slug_url_kwarg)
13            return get_object_or_404(
14                NewsLink,
15                slug__iexact=newslink_slug,
16                startup__slug__iexact=startup_slug)
```

The only change we need to make to `NewsLinkCreate` is to add the mixins, as shown in Example 18.57.

**Example 18.57: Project Code**
organizer/views.py in f4e337f96e

```
10    from .utils import (
11        NewsLinkGetObjectMixin, PageLinksMixin,
12        StartupContextMixin)
 .        ...
15    class NewsLinkCreate(
16            NewsLinkGetObjectMixin,
17            StartupContextMixin,
18            CreateView):
19        form_class = NewsLinkForm
20        model = NewsLink
```

However, in `NewsLinkDelete`, we need to override the `slug_url_kwarg`, so that the view knows to accept the `newslink_slug` keyword from the regular expression pattern of the URL pattern (instead of the default of `slug`), as shown in Example 18.58.

**Example 18.58: Project Code**
organizer/views.py in 7dcdf22318

```
20    class NewsLinkDelete(
21            StartupContextMixin, DeleteView):
22        model = NewsLink
23        slug_url_kwarg = 'newslink_slug'
```

The same is true for `NewsLinkUpdate`, as shown in Example 18.59.

**Example 18.59: Project Code**
organizer/views.py in f4e337f96e

```
35    class NewsLinkUpdate(
36            NewsLinkGetObjectMixin,
37            StartupContextMixin,
38            UpdateView):
39        form_class = NewsLinkForm
40        model = NewsLink
41        slug_url_kwarg = 'newslink_slug'
```

To make sure that our `SlugField` adheres to the same standards as our other slugs, we should also inherit the `SlugCleanMixin` in `NewsLinkForm`, as shown in Example 18.60.

**Example 18.60: Project Code**

`organizer/forms.py` in `f4e337f96e`

```
19   class NewsLinkForm(
20           SlugCleanMixin, forms.ModelForm):
21       class Meta:
22           model = NewsLink
23           fields = '__all__'
```

With our views, URL patterns, and forms fixed, we should turn our attention to templates. At the moment, all of the links in templates will be throwing errors, because we have radically changed our URLs. Thankfully, because we've followed best practice, we can update all of the links to deleting and modifying `NewsLink` objects by changing `get_delete_url()` and `get_update_url()`, as shown in Example 18.61.

**Example 18.61: Project Code**

`organizer/models.py` in `7dcdf22318`

```
75   class NewsLink(models.Model):
 .       ...
95       def get_delete_url(self):
96           return reverse(
97               'organizer_newslink_delete',
98               kwargs={
99                   'startup_slug': self.startup.slug,
100                  'newslink_slug': self.slug})
```

Similarly, the `get_update_url()` sees only changes to the `kwargs` argument, as shown in Example 18.62.

**Example 18.62: Project Code**

`organizer/models.py` in `7dcdf22318`

```
75    class NewsLink(models.Model):
 .        ...
102       def get_update_url(self):
103           return reverse(
104               'organizer_newslink_update',
105               kwargs={
106                   'startup_slug': self.startup.slug,
107                   'newslink_slug': self.slug})
```

Changing links to `organizer_newslink_create` is a little trickier. Our current template code is {% url 'organizer_newslink_create' %}. Given that we're now using the `Startup`'s `SlugField`, we want to create a method on a model to generate the

URL. Perhaps surprisingly, the simplest thing to do is to create get_newslink_
create_url on the Startup model, as shown in Example 18.63, because the only time
we want the link is on Startup detail pages.

**Example 18.63: Project Code**
organizer/models.py in 7dcdf22318

```
36    class Startup(models.Model):
          ...
62            return reverse('organizer_startup_delete',
63                           kwargs={'slug': self.slug})
64
65        def get_newslink_create_url(self):
66            return reverse(
67                'organizer_newslink_create',
68                kwargs={'startup_slug': self.slug})
69
70        def get_update_url(self):
71            return reverse('organizer_startup_update',
72                           kwargs={'slug': self.slug})
```

Unfortunately, we need to change all of our links in this case. Luckily, they only occur in
two places: first as a link to the actual page, as shown in Example 18.64.

**Example 18.64: Project Code**
organizer/templates/organizer/startup_detail.html in 7dcdf22318

```
54                <p>
55                 <a
56                    href="{{ startup.get_newslink_create_url }}"
57                    class="button">
58                Add Article</a></p>
```

The second occurrence is as the action in the form to create new NewsLink objects, as
shown in Example 18.65.

**Example 18.65: Project Code**
organizer/templates/organizer/newslink_form.html in 7dcdf22318

```
10        <form
11            action="{{ startup.get_newslink_create_url }}"
12            method="post">
```

In our models, we have methods to reverse the URLs for detail pages, delete pages, and
update pages. These are the views that best practice dictates you *must* create methods for.

However, some developers (because of code changes like this last one) will go the extra mile and create methods to reverse the list page, the create form page, and *every* page the model is directly related to. I'm not convinced this is always necessary, but it's certainly not always a bad thing.

## 18.8.2   Automating `Startup` Selection in `NewsLink` Forms

To create a new `NewsLink` object, a user will first browse to a `Startup`'s detail page and then click the `Add Article` link to be brought to the `NewsLinkCreate` view. The form will promptly ask the user which `Startup` he or she would like to create a `NewsLink` for. That's really silly, not only because we just came from the `Startup` we want to create a `NewsLink` for but also because the `slug` of the `Startup` is now in the URL!

There are two ways to fix this problem. In the first, we automatically infer the `Startup` without any outside intervention. In the second, we use a hidden field on the form to submit the slug of the `Startup` to the form.

### 18.8.2.1   Inferring the `Startup`

The slug of the `Startup` we are creating a `NewsLink` object for is in our URL path. We could therefore have the view use the slug to fetch the `Startup` and then pass the `Startup` instance directly to our form in `NewsLinkCreate` or `NewsLinkUpdate`. This is not the recommended way to handle this problem, but we start by looking at this technique because it helps our fundamental understanding of some of Django's moving parts.

GCBVs all use a `form_valid()` method when a form has validated correctly and is ready to save the data. We can create a mixin that overrides `form_valid()`, passing in the `Startup` instance to the form's `save()` method, as shown in Example 18.66.

**Example 18.66: Project Code**
`organizer/utils.py` **in** 15c359e96e

```
 7    class NewsLinkFormMixin():
 8
 9        def form_valid(self, form):
10            startup = get_object_or_404(
11                Startup,
12                slug__iexact=self.kwargs.get(
13                    self.startup_slug_url_kwarg))
14            self.object = form.save(
15                startup_obj=startup)
16            return HttpResponseRedirect(
17                self.get_success_url())
```

Of course, for this to work, we need to override the `save()` method of our `ModelForm` subclass, as shown in Example 18.67. The trick to it is that we first create a `NewsLink` instance without saving it to the database, add the `Startup` to the instance, and then save the new `NewsLink` instance to the database.

**Example 18.67: Project Code**
organizer/forms.py in 15c359e96e

```
19   class NewsLinkForm(
20           SlugCleanMixin, forms.ModelForm):
.        ...
25       def save(self, **kwargs):
26           startup_obj = kwargs.get('startup_obj', None)
27           if startup_obj is not None:
28               instance = super().save(commit=False)
29               instance.startup = startup_obj
30               instance.save()
31               self.save_m2m()
32           else:
33               instance = super().save()
34           return instance
```

The commit=False argument to the save() superclass method tells Django that we want a NewsLink instance without actually saving to the database. This allows us, on line 29, to add the Startup instance to the NewsLink. Without it (if we had tried to save to the database on line 28), the database would have returned an error because the startup field is required.

Saving data in Django is a two-step process. First, Django saves the actual data, and then Django saves any many-to-many relations. This step is only natural: a many-to-many relation exists in a different database table and requires a foreign key to our object (the object's primary key). The primary key is created by the database, not by Django, and does not exist until Django has successfully given the data to the database. For this reason, when overriding the save() method, we first call instance.save() on line 30, and then we save any related data on line 31. Of course, we don't actually have any many-to-many relations on NewsLink objects, but that shouldn't ever stop us from including the save_m2m() call.

For all of this code to work, we of course need to add the new mixin to our views. The addition to NewsLinkCreate is shown in Example 18.68 (but the code for NewsLinkUpdate is not, and we make no changes to NewsLinkDelete because it doesn't need to infer the Startup for the display of a form—it already gets the Startup form StartupContextMixin and simply deletes the NewsLink).

**Example 18.68: Project Code**
organizer/views.py in 15c359e96e

```
10   from .utils import (
11       NewsLinkFormMixin, NewsLinkGetObjectMixin,
12       PageLinksMixin, StartupContextMixin)
13
14
15   class NewsLinkCreate(
16           NewsLinkFormMixin,
17           NewsLinkGetObjectMixin,
18           StartupContextMixin,
19           CreateView):
```

Unfortunately, our current method has a massive hole in it. If we try to save a `NewsLink` with a slug that already exists for that particular `Startup`, the form won't return a nice error warning us of this—the database will error and Django will fail. That is less than desirable.

The problem is that we've entirely removed the `startup` field from being processed by the form. Rather than add the `Startup` instance if the form is valid, we need to hand it off to the form right away for the form to use in its validation phase. Instead of overriding the GCBV's `form_valid()`, we need to override `get_form_kwargs()`, adding the `Startup` object to the data that is given to the form to bind it.

In the `FormMixin` class, Django checks to see if the the HTTP request method is either a POST or PUT. In the event of either, it adds the POST data to the `data` keyword of `kwargs`. Our first step is therefore to call the superclass `get_form_kwargs()` method and take its `kwargs` dictionary, as shown in Example 18.69.

**Example 18.69: Project Code**
`organizer/utils.py` in 57b53a0d2d

```
8        def get_form_kwargs(self):
9            kwargs = super().get_form_kwargs()
```

We want to add our `Startup` instance to `kwargs['data']` if and only if we've received a POST or PUT. In Django, the POST data in an `HttpRequest` object is stored in a `QueryDict`, which is by default immutable. Luckily, Django anticipates that this behavior is not always helpful to developers, and we can use the `copy()` method to copy the `QueryDict` data into a mutable version of itself. Then we can add our `Startup` instance to the POST data, as shown in Example 18.70.

**Example 18.70: Project Code**
`organizer/utils.py` in 57b53a0d2d

```
8        def get_form_kwargs(self):
9            kwargs = super().get_form_kwargs()
10           if self.request.method in ('POST', 'PUT'):
11               self.startup = get_object_or_404(
12                   Startup,
13                   slug__iexact=self.kwargs.get(
14                       self.startup_slug_url_kwarg))
15               data = kwargs['data'].copy()
16               data.update({'startup': self.startup})
17               kwargs['data'] = data
18           return kwargs
```

In our form, we need to intercede in the validation process. We don't want to change any `clean_<field_name>()` methods, but we can override the `clean()` method that is run after any of the field clean methods. In Example 18.71, we first call the superclass `clean()` method to get the `cleaned_data` dictionary, because at this stage of the game, it is not a class attribute yet. We then check to make sure that the `NewsLink` we are about to create is unique.

**Example 18.71: Project Code**
`organizer/forms.py` in `57b53a0d2d`

```
19   class NewsLinkForm(
20           SlugCleanMixin, forms.ModelForm):
 .        ...
25       def clean(self):
26           cleaned_data = super().clean()
27           slug = cleaned_data.get('slug')
28           startup_obj = self.data.get('startup')
29           exists = (
30               NewsLink.objects.filter(
31                   slug__iexact=slug,
32                   startup=startup_obj,
33               ).exists())
34           if exists:
35               raise ValidationError(
36                   "News articles with this Slug "
37                   "and Startup already exists.")
38           else:
39               return cleaned_data
```

Now we can simplify our `save()` method, as shown in Example 18.72.

**Example 18.72: Project Code**
`organizer/forms.py` in `57b53a0d2d`

```
19   class NewsLinkForm(
20           SlugCleanMixin, forms.ModelForm):
 .        ...
41       def save(self, **kwargs):
42           instance = super().save(commit=False)
43           instance.startup = (
44               self.data.get('startup'))
45           instance.save()
46           self.save_m2m()
47           return instance
```

If we submit a new `NewsLink` object or update an existing object, we don't need to tell the form which `Startup` the `NewsLink` is associated with!

### 18.8.2.2  Using a Hidden Field in the HTML Form

The code we wrote to automatically infer a `Startup` in the preceding section is rather complicated and is not the recommended way of doing things. Instead of overriding our classes and form and even changing a `QueryDict`, we can simply change the `startup` field to an HTML hidden input field to the form to pass the value of the startup's slug.

Our first step is to delete `NewsLinkFormMixin` from `organizer/utils.py`, remove it from the inheritance list of `NewsLinkCreate` and `NewsLinkUpdate`, and then remove it's import in `organizer/views.py`. We can then reset `NewsLinkForm` to simpler state, as shown in Example 18.73.

**Example 18.73: Project Code**
organizer/forms.py **in** 10b76285d0

```
19   class NewsLinkForm(
20           SlugCleanMixin, forms.ModelForm):
21       class Meta:
22           model = NewsLink
23           fields = '__all__'
```

To change the startup field to use a hidden input, we simply need to change its widget (its representation in the HTML form, as described in Chapter 7: Allowing User Input with Forms). We can override this in Meta, as shown in Example 18.74.

**Example 18.74: Project Code**
organizer/forms.py **in** 1d610aa072

```
 3   from django.forms.widgets import HiddenInput
 .       ...
20   class NewsLinkForm(
21           SlugCleanMixin, forms.ModelForm):
22       class Meta:
23           model = NewsLink
24           fields = '__all__'
25           widgets = {'startup': HiddenInput()}
```

With the NewsLinkUpdate view, the value of the startup field will be filled in for us. However, in the case of NewsLinkCreate, we need to supply an initial value to the form. Any Django form will accept a dictionary passed to the initial parameter of the form, which acts much like the instance parameter. To accomodate this behavior, GCBVs use a get_initial() method to build the initial dictionary. We can therefore override the method directly in NewsLinkCreate, as shown in Example 18.75, because neither NewsLinkUpdate nor NewsLinkDelete needs this behavior.

**Example 18.75: Project Code**
organizer/views.py **in** 1d610aa072

```
 2   from django.shortcuts import get_object_or_404
 .       ...
16   class NewsLinkCreate(
 .       ...
23       def get_initial(self):
24           startup_slug = self.kwargs.get(
25               self.startup_slug_url_kwarg)
26           self.startup = get_object_or_404(
27               Startup, slug__iexact=startup_slug)
28           initial = {
29               self.startup_context_object_name:
30                   self.startup,
31           }
32           initial.update(self.initial)
33           return initial
```

With this change in place, we no longer need to specify the `Startup` being related to new `NewsLink` objects. `NewsLinkCreate` inherits from `StartupContextMixin`, which also fetches the `Startup` instance the URL path refers to. In `NewsLinkCreate`, we are thus getting the same `Startup` object from the database twice. This is an expensive operation (as we'll discuss in more depth in Chapter 26: Optimizing Our Site for Speed), and we want to avoid doing it twice. As Example 18.76 shows, we can change the code in `StartupContextMixin` to get the object only if it doesn't already exist.

**Example 18.76: Project Code**
`organizer/utils.py` **in** `1d610aa072`

```
72   class StartupContextMixin():
73       startup_slug_url_kwarg = 'startup_slug'
74       startup_context_object_name = 'startup'
75
76       def get_context_data(self, **kwargs):
77           if hasattr(self, 'startup'):
78               context = {
79                   self.startup_context_object_name:
80                       self.startup,
81               }
82           else:
83               startup_slug = self.kwargs.get(
84                   self.startup_slug_url_kwarg)
85               startup = get_object_or_404(
86                   Startup,
87                   slug__iexact=startup_slug)
88               context = {
89                   self.startup_context_object_name:
90                       startup,
91               }
92           context.update(kwargs)
93           return super().get_context_data(**context)
```

Using a hidden field is Django's recommended way of handling the problem of inferring information in a form (or appearing to): it results in less code, allows for easy optimization, but still allows for our best-case in usability. The only catch is that it is arguably less robust, as the user might try to tamper with the data in the hidden field. Given the restrictions we will place on `NewsLink` creation in Chapter 20, this is not a serious concern on our website.

## 18.9   Putting It All Together

In Chapter 17, we saw how to configure GCBVs using attributes or the most basic of methods. In this chapter, we took the idea a step further. We've overridden methods, defined our own, and created our own GCBVs thanks to the base and mixin classes provided by Django.

At the end of the day, all of these classes are just Python classes. They're not magic in any way. They are daunting to beginners only because of all of the overhead it takes to learn how they work, and finding the right method to override can be time consuming. The easiest part is writing the code, once you understand what you're changing.

GCBVs are powerful, and once you know them, they can be instrumental in building a website quickly and efficiently. The trick to it is that you have to learn them first. To that end, when you decide to tackle customizing GCBVs on your own, you will find it necessary to dive deep into the topic. I highly recommend relying first on the ccbv.co.uk documentation, which will lay out the code for you and provide links directly to Django's source code.

# Basic Authentication

## In This Chapter

- Learn about Django's **auth** app and the `User` model
- Use authentication to create login and logout webpages
- Learn about sessions and cookies
- Configure logging of the website
- Learn about `contenttypes` and generic foreign keys

## 19.1 Introduction

When we built our forms in Chapter 7: Allowing User Input with Forms, we enabled anyone visiting our site to submit data to the website. Allowing anyone and anything to submit data to a website is a *terrible* idea. Pseudonymity (and for most users, assumption of anonymity) makes the World Wide Web a bit of a Wild West, and the addition of bots and zombie machines makes unfettered access to a website like ours a very dangerous thing.

To mitigate all of these problems, websites ask visitors who wish to submit data to first log in: visitors **identify** themselves and then **authenticate**, providing secret proof that they are who they claim they are.

Authentication is one of the most difficult and tricky parts of application building (anywhere—not just on the web), because security is *hard*. Luckily, Django provides a slew of tools to help you build a secure website. Most of them are located in Django's **auth** app.

The next four chapters are dedicated to the **auth** app. In this chapter, we learn about how authentication works on the web (sessions and cookies), which apps Django uses in tandem with **auth** to make life easier (**contenttypes**), and how to log information to keep track of everything going on (thanks to Python's `logging` library). Our knowledge will allow us to create users and implement a login and logout system.

In Chapter 20: Integrating Permissions, we use permissions and groups to ensure that only authenticated users can submit data, and we control what content specific types of users can see.

In Chapter 21: Extending Authentication, we allow users to change and reset passwords. We discover how to disable accounts and how to allow visitors to register as new users on the site.

Finally, in Chapter 22: Overriding Django's Authentication with a Custom User, we customize the User model that Django uses to authenticate users and store user data.

This chapter assumes understanding of basic web security principles. Please see Appendix D for a primer on the material. Understanding of cryptographic hashing will also prove helpful.

## 19.2   Configuring Logging

The logging library is a part of Python, and its use is crucial to Django websites. Logging is a functionality whereby the computer records every activity, in sequential order, and stores the record in a file, colloquially called a log file. Developers can refer to the log files to find out exactly what was happening on the server at a given point in time (typically, they want to know what activity took place immediately before something went terribly wrong).

Logging can also be used to discover if parts of the website are not working properly in this case, the log is viewed in real time for quality assurance or troubleshooting. We focus largely on using logging to figure out when a part of Django is not communicating properly with another service (notably, email).

To enable basic logging in Django, we create a dictionary setting called LOGGING in suorganizer/settings.py, as shown in Example 19.1.

**Example 19.1: Project Code**
suorganizer/settings.py **in** effd753184

```
100    LOGGING = {
101        'version': 1,
102        'disable_existing_loggers': False,
103        'handlers': {
  .        ...
107        },
108        'formatters': {
  .        ...
113        },
114        'loggers': {
  .        ...
120        },
121    }
```

Python loggers create LogRecord objects, which are output as strings. When we build a logger to output a record, we think about what will be recorded and where the information will be stored. The handler determines where information is recorded to, while the formatter writes information in a specific format. The logger itself is the combination of handler and formatter, and it is what developers will interact with.

The disable_existing_loggers setting ensures that any other loggers that have already been configured are left alone.

In Example 19.2, we create a handler called `'console'` that uses Python's `StreamHandler` class to log any information sent to `stderr`. All of our logging information will therefore be output to the console. This arrangement is great during development, but keep in mind that during production, we might want to use `FileHandler` or a more persistent storage system.

**Example 19.2: Project Code**
`suorganizer/settings.py` in effd753184

```
100    LOGGING = {
  .        ...
103        'handlers': {
104            'console': {
105                'class': 'logging.StreamHandler',
106            },
107        },
  .        ...
121    }
```

We then specify a Python format string to determine how we want information recorded (or, in our case, output to the console), as shown in Example 19.3.

**Example 19.3: Project Code**
`suorganizer/settings.py` in effd753184

```
96    verbose = (
97        "[%(asctime)s %(levelname)s "
98        "[%(name)s:%(lineno)s] %(message)s")
```

The `asctime` variable prints the time (configured in Example 19.4 as `datefmt`). `levelname` indicates the level at which the problem occurred: debug, info, warning, error, or critical. The `name` is the file name, while `lineno` tells us where the log was written from. Finally, we print the `message` passed to the logger.

In Example 19.4, we use this format string in our definition of the formatter, calling the format `verbose`.

**Example 19.4: Project Code**
`suorganizer/settings.py` in effd753184

```
100    LOGGING = {
  .        ...
108        'formatters': {
109            'verbose': {
110                'format': verbose,
111                'datefmt': "%Y-%b-%d %H:%M:%S"
112            },
113        },
  .        ...
121    }
```

Finally, we can put this code all together in an actual logger. In Example 19.5, we opt to log all information. Loggers will show all of the messages considered equal to or more important than our level. By setting DEBUG, we are opting to see all messages set to the debug, info, warning, error, or critical levels. If we change the setting to WARNING, we would see messages with levels set to warning, error, or critical but none of the messages set to debug or info.

**Example 19.5: Project Code**
suorganizer/settings.py in effd753184

```
100    LOGGING = {
  .        ...
114        'loggers': {
115            'django': {
116                'handlers': ['console'],
117                'level': 'DEBUG',
118                'formatter': 'verbose'
119            },
120        },
121    }
```

On top of handlers and formatters, Python's logger allows for the creation of filters, which selectively filter the particular output of a logger. These are particularly useful if you want a certain level of information but not from all parts of the framework.

For instance, if you delete your database and run ./manage.py migrate, you'll discover that our logger outputs every single SQL command issued to the database. This behavior is highly undesirable. We don't want to change the level to WARNING, but we don't want to see the SQL code during migrations either. We can build a filter to remove this data for us.

In a new file called log_filters.py, we can filter LogRecord objects in a subclass of Filter. The goal is to create a method called filter() that returns a Boolean: True if the information should be recorded, False if not. Luckily, all of the SQL output is created by a function called execute(), and so we can simply filter our LogRecord objects according to whether the record was created by the execute() function, as shown in Example 19.6.

**Example 19.6: Project Code**
suorganizer/log_filters.py in 97c4234a4a

```
1    from logging import Filter
2    from pprint import pprint
3
4
5    class ManagementFilter(Filter):
6
7        def filter(self, record):
8            if (hasattr(record, 'funcName')
9                    and record.funcName == 'execute'):
```

```
10              return False
11          else:
12              return True
```

In Example 19.7, we import our new filter and add it to our LOGGING setting as remove_migration_sql, calling it not in our logger but in our handler.

**Example 19.7: Project Code**
`suorganizer/settings.py` in 97c4234a4a

```
 96    from .log_filters import ManagementFilter
   .      ...
102    LOGGING = {
   .      ...
105        'filters': {
106            'remove_migration_sql': {
107                '()': ManagementFilter,
108            },
109        },
110        'handlers': {
111            'console': {
112                'filters': ['remove_migration_sql'],
113                'class': 'logging.StreamHandler',
114            },
115        },
   .      ...
129    }
```

When writing the code for **auth** (the next four chapters) the logger was instrumental in helping me figure out when emails weren't sending as desired and why. In the next four chapters, we add the logger in all of the places I had it, as it will illustrate where you would want to add the logger in a real site when identifying problems in communication between parts of your website. However, even with all of that, we will be severely under-utilizing the logger.

What's more, there is a lot of work we could do to improve our logger. However, there are entire books written on the topic of logging, and so we will simply leave our logger as is and move on to the rest of the content.

## Python Documentation

For more about the StreamHandler objects and other handlers:

> https://dju.link/18/streamhandler

For more about LogRecord objects (including what a formatter can output and what a filter can use):

> https://dju.link/18/logrecord
> https://dju.link/18/logrecord-attr

# 19.3   Sessions and Cookies

After introducing HTTP in Chapter 1, I asserted that HTTP was a stateless protocol. It transfers data without knowing what the user or the site previously requested or responded with.

Statelessness proves to be a bit of a problem: authentication requires state. We need to know and remember who a specific visitor is so that we may allow them specific access and privileges on the site. Working with a stateless protocol means that we can't rely on the protocol itself to help us with authentication.

To add basic state to the HTTP, developers added cookies to it. A cookie, originally called a magic cookie, stores a uniquely identifying piece of information. When a visitor arrives at a website, the server creates a unique identifier, or **token**, and stores it in a cookie, which it passes back in the HTTP response. For every subsequent request, the visitor attaches the cookie to the HTTP request, voluntarily letting the server know he or she is the same person as before.

Despite the addition of cookies, HTTP is still said to be stateless. Cookies do not confer state—they simply enable the server to create and maintain state by adding a piece of information. What's more, cookies are not the only way to create a session. We could, for instance, create a unique identifier and put it in the URL for the user. If the user remembers to delete his or her history at the end, then this technique is as safe as using a cookie.

Speaking of safety, cookies are not secure by default. They are not encrypted and can easily be duplicated, allowing malicious users to parade around as authenticated users. This is not a huge problem until you are using cookies to identify authenticated users. A user could capture and duplicate a cookie, pretending to be an administrator. Consequently, any site that uses authentication should use Transport Layer Security (TLS) certificates to encrypt all of their traffic. This is also the reason Django uses cryptographic hashing for the cookie's unique identifier: if an attacker can guess the value of another user's cookie, then any encryption is meaningless.

The term **session** can be a little confusing. Originally, a session was any set of requests and responses that happen between a visitor and a server. Today, the formal term refers to a set of request/response cycles when a cookie has been used to establish a pseudonymous identity for a user. A session starts when the website has assigned a user a cookie and lasts until the cookie is changed or destroyed (by either the user or the webserver). Note that none of this implies authentication: we can give an unknown user a cookie for a session, identifying that user pseudonymously. Nevertheless, when talking about sessions, most developers are talking about when a `User id` has been associated with a cookie hash (either in a file or in the database), allowing the website to keep track of an authenticated user.

Django provides utilities in the sessions app for handling sessions (authenticated and not) and cookies (the first relies on the second). The **sessions** app allows our site to use the `SessionMiddleware` and in turn allows the `auth` app to use the `SessionAuthenticationMiddleware`, as shown in Example 19.8.

**Example 19.8: Project Code**
`suorganizer/settings.py` **in** 97c4234a4a

```
35    INSTALLED_APPS = (
 .        ...
39        'django.contrib.sessions',
 .        ...
48    )
 .        ...
50    MIDDLEWARE_CLASSES = (
51        'django.contrib.sessions.middleware.SessionMiddleware',
 .        ...
55        'django.contrib.auth.middleware.SessionAuthenticationMiddleware',
 .        ...
59    )
```

We could use these tools directly (there's actually a `Session` class!), but most of the time we won't need to, as Django does all of the work for us. The point of this section is to inform you of cookies and sessions, and to make you aware of the middleware and **sessions** app. The **auth** app will not work without them!

### Info

For the curious, Netscape introduced the use of cookies in its Mosaic browser in 1994. The idea was to allow Netscape to track whether users had previously visited its site and to allow the company to create an e-commerce store on the web. HTTP had been created in 1989, first documented in 1991, but would only reach version 1 in 1996. The official cookie RFC was first published in 1997 (RFC 2109)[1] and was last updated in 2011 (RFC 6265)[2].

## 19.4   auth App Anatomy: The Basics

The **auth** app, as you might have guessed, is a full-fledged app. It comes equipped with models, forms, views, decorators, URL patterns, and even middleware. It relies heavily on the **sessions** app but also makes use of the **sites** app if it's enabled (we enabled the **sites** app in Chapter 15: Creating Webpages with Django Flatpages). See Example 19.9.

**Example 19.9: Project Code**
`suorganizer/settings.py` **in** 97c4234a4a

```
35    INSTALLED_APPS = (
 .        ...
37        'django.contrib.auth',
 .        ...
```

---

1. https://dju.link/rfc2109
2. https://dju.link/rfc6265

```
41        'django.contrib.sites',
 .        ...
48    )
```

In this chapter, we focus on the `User` Model. Django stores all of the information to identify and authenticate a user/visitor in the model and defines a custom manager on the model (we build our own custom managers in Chapter 24). Notably, the `User` model defines fields for a username, an email, and a password.

The **auth** also gives us a set of working views in `django.contrib.auth.views`:

- `login()`
- `logout()`
- `redirect_to_login()`
- `logout_then_login()`

The `logout_then_login()` logs out any currently authenticated user, and then redirects the user to the `login()` webpage (as opposed to logging the user back in).

By default, the `login()` function view uses `registration/login.html` as a template, and `logout()` uses `registration/logged_out.html`.

In `django.contrib.auth.forms`, Django declares the `AuthenticationForm`, which is the form used by the `login()` view to authenticate returning users (users already in the database).

Finally, the **auth** app defines a few settings:

- `LOGIN_URL`
- `LOGOUT_URL`
- `LOGIN_REDIRECT_URL`

The first two are exactly what they sound like. The third tells Django where to go once a user has successfully authenticated.

## 19.5   Adding Login and Logout Features

The goal of the rest of this chapter is to build two webpages: one to log in the user and the other to log out the user. We know that Django's **auth** app supplies two views to do just this: `login()` and `logout()`. Django even has a URL configuration that uses these views. However, we quickly find out that using the URL configuration poses a few problems, and we switch to using the function views directly.

Before any of that, however, we dive into the shell to interact with the `User` model and see how it works.

### 19.5.1   User in the Shell

The `User` model is rather unusual, because you're not supposed to interact with it as you do with other Django models. Specifically, you should never import it directly, as is done in Example 19.10, for reasons we'll see in Chapter 22.

**Example 19.10: Python Code**

```
# this is not the best way to do this!
>>> from django.contrib.auth.models import User
```

Instead, developers should use the get_user_model() function supplied by **auth** to get the User model, as shown in Example 19.11.

**Example 19.11: Python Code**

```
# optimal
>>> from django.contrib.auth import get_user_model
>>> SiteUser = get_user_model()
>>> SiteUser
<class 'django.contrib.auth.models.User'>
>>> User = SiteUser
```

At its most basic, the User model expects a username, an email, and a password, as shown in Example 19.12.

**Example 19.12: Python Interpreter Code**

```
>>> User.objects.create_user(
... 'andrew', # username
... 'django@jambonsw.com', # email
... 'hunter2') # password
<User: andrew>
```

The username is a CharField with a maximum length of 30 characters and a custom validator that ensures the username is matched by the regular expression ^[\w.@+-]+$. To be clear, that's any alphabet character, any digit, and any of the following: @ . + - _.

The email field is an EmailField. The password is a CharField with a maximum length of 128 characters.

The User model has a lot more fields on it that you might expect, as shown in Example 19.13.

**Example 19.13: Python Interpreter Code**

```
>>> User.objects.values()
[{'date_joined': datetime.datetime(2015, 2, 26, 15, 55, 24, 991925,
                  tzinfo=<UTC>),
  'email': 'django@jambonsw.com',
  'first_name': '',
  'id': 1,
  'is_active': True,
  'is_staff': False,
  'is_superuser': False,
```

```
'last_login': datetime.datetime(2015, 2, 26, 15, 55, 24, 991925,
            tzinfo=<UTC>),
'last_name': '',
'password': 'pbkdf2_sha256$15000$SrJRjeG7K0mZ$8vAACvb+MdU2TWsWjbaJ
            9ffMZPsvpuFWxdLwihiwM4E=',
'username': 'andrew'}]
```

I want to draw your attention to the password field. The $ characters split the field into different pieces of information:

```
<algorithm>$<iterations>$<salt>$<hash>
```

The password above therefore uses 15,000 rounds of the PBKDF2 (Password–Based Key Derivation Function 2) with the sha256 hash. The algorithm's salt (sometimes called an initialization vector, or IV) is SrJRjeG7K0mZ, while the actual hash of the password is

```
8vAACvb+MdU2TWsWjbaJ9ffMZPsvpuFWxdLwihiwM4E=
```

Django removes the pain of thinking about how to store passwords correctly and provides a strong solution out of the gates (the settings for which may be changes in settings.py). What's more, if we opt to strengthen the hash choice (say, by switching to bcrypt or by increasing the number of iterations), then we don't have to worry about changing the passwords in the database. The next time the user logs in, Django will take the opportunity to update the hash stored in the database to whatever standard we have specified.

Of course, this means you never want to interact with the password field directly, which is why we called create_user() on the model manager instead of create(). The User model defines helpful methods for interacting with the password field, as shown in Example 19.14.

**Example 19.14: Python Interpreter Code**

```
>>> andrew.check_password('wrong')
False
>>> andrew.check_password('hunter2')
True
>>> andrew.set_password('quoth.the.server,404')
>>> andrew.password
'pbkdf2_sha256$15000$xxUuqd0WdKmG$OHEEZ3HIguAPXU2CXmBC/DNkhy5HGp/
7LXMLhkGQYkY='
```

We can disable the use of a password thanks to set_unusable_password(), and we can check the status of the password field via has_usable_password().

The User model also provides some basic attributes for role/privilege management, as shown in Example 19.15.

**Example 19.15: Python Interpreter Code**

```
>>> andrew.is_active
True
>>> andrew.is_staff
False
>>> andrew.is_superuser
False
```

The is_active attribute defines whether a user can log in to the site. The is_staff attribute designates whether this user can access the admin site (seen in Chapter 23). The is_superuser attribute means the user has all permissions without any of them being explicitly assigned—we'll see more about that in Chapter 20.

The model also defines two simple methods for interacting with the name fields, as shown in Example 19.16.

**Example 19.16: Python Interpreter Code**

```
>>> andrew = User.objects.get(username='andrew')
>>> andrew.get_username()
'andrew'
>>> andrew.get_full_name()
''
```

The latter method combines the first_name and last_name fields.

Note that when interacting with a user instance, the instance will always be considered authenticated, as shown in Example 19.17.

**Example 19.17: Python Interpreter Code**

```
>>> # always returns True!
>>> andrew.is_authenticated() # method
True
```

This is in direct opposition to whether a user is anonymous, which will always be untrue, as shown in Example 19.18.

**Example 19.18: Python Interpreter Code**

```
>>> andrew.is_anonymous()
False
```

These two methods don't really make sense in the context of a single user instance. They are actually intended to be used in the view when dealing with a user of unknown origin. Django will pass one of the following to a view as part of the HttpRequest:

- A regular user (User instance)
- A superuser (User instance with is_superuser set to True)
- An anonymous user

Let's take a quick look at the superuser. We again avoid calling create() on the manager, and instead call create_superuser(), allowing for simpler interaction with the password field, and automatically setting both is_staff and is_superuser, as shown in Example 19.19.

**Example 19.19:** Python Interpreter Code

```
>>> andrew.delete()  # delete the regular user
>>> andrew = User.objects.create_superuser(
... 'andrew', # username
... 'django@jambonsw.com', # email
... 'hunter2') # password
>>> andrew.is_superuser
True
>>> andrew.is_staff
True
>>> andrew
<User: andrew>
>>> andrew.delete()
```

All of the fields and methods we've seen still apply to the superuser, because the only difference is whether an attribute is True.

We are not limited to the interpreter for creating superusers. manage.py comes equipped with commands for the job (but, surprisingly, does not define a command for creating regular users), as shown in Example 19.20.

**Example 19.20:** Shell Code

```
$ ./manage.py createsuperuser
Username (leave blank to use 'magus'): andrew
Email address: django@jambonsw.com
Password:
Password (again):
Superuser created successfully.
```

A changepassword command is also available.

While the User model acts as both user and superuser, anonymous users are completely different and are stored in Django as instances of AnonymousUser, as shown in Example 19.21.

**Example 19.21:** Python Interpreter Code

```
>>> from django.contrib.auth.models import AnonymousUser
>>> au = AnonymousUser()
```

The class is in no way related to `User`. We can see a list of all of the superclasses of `AnonymousUser` by invoking the method resolution order, as shown in Example 19.22: `AnonymousUser` is its own Python class, inheriting only from `object` (as every Python class does).

**Example 19.22: Python Interpreter Code**

```
>>> AnonymousUser.mro()
[<class 'django.contrib.auth.models.AnonymousUser'>, <class 'object'>]
```

However, each `HttpRequest` object will have either a `User` or an `AnonymousUser` attached to it. The `AnonymousUser` class therefore defines the same interface for us to interact with it, allowing us to ignore whether we have a `User` or `AnonymousUser`, and instead simply asking for the relevant information, as shown in Example 19.23.

**Example 19.23: Python Interpreter Code**

```
>>> au.is_anonymous()
True
>>> au.is_active
False
>>> au.is_staff
False
>>> au.is_superuser
False
```

If we try to call `save()` or `delete()` on an `AnonymousUser`, Django will raise a `NotImplementedError` exception.

Django provides several tools for working with `User` and `AnonymousUser` instances. Much like with passwords, the goal is usually not to interact with the `User` model directly, but instead to use these helper functions. In particular, **auth** provides the `login()` and `logout()` helper functions (not to be confused with the `login()` and `logout()` function views we will be using shortly). These helper functions accept a `User` instance as an argument, and they do the work of creating and destroying sessions for the `User`, allowing us to identify a visitor by username and other information during the rest of his or her visit. Similarly, to get a user from the `HttpRequest` object, Django expects us to use the `get_user()` helper function. When given an `HttpRequest`, the function will return a `User` or `AnonymousUser` instance.

## Django Documentation

For more about the `User` model:

https://dju.link/18/user

## 19.5.2   Creating a User App

Now that we understand the `User` model, we turn our attention to creating a login and logout webpage. We know that the **auth** app supplies a full URL configuration, and we could start by trying to use these URLs for our own site, as shown in Example 19.24.

**Example 19.24: Project Code**
`suorganizer/urls.py` **in** 8c2972bf62

```
18    from django.contrib.auth import urls as auth_urls
 .       ...
27    urlpatterns = [
 .       ...
41       url(r'^user/', include(auth_urls)),
42    ]
```

You might imagine that we now create a template for when the user logs out. By default, the `logout()` view displays this logout-success page at `registration/logged_out.html`, as shown in Example 19.25.

**Example 19.25: Project Code**
`templates/registration/logged_out.html` **in** 8c2972bf62

```
1    {% extends parent_template|default:"base.html" %}
2
3    {% block title %}
4    {{ block.super }} - Logged Out
5    {% endblock %}
6
7    {% block content %}
8    <p>You've successfully logged out.</p>
9    {% endblock %}
```

If you start the development server and browse to `http://127.0.0.1:8000/user/logout/`, you'll discover our template is being completely ignored. Instead, the template from the **admin** app, which already defines the `registration` template namespace, is being used.

By default, our site-wide `/templates/` directory is the last place Django will load a template from. To use our template, we could move the file into an app such as **core** and ensure that **core** appears before **admin** in the `INSTALLED_APPS` settings list. However, then the **admin** app would be using our template too.

The `login()` and `logout()` views allow us to override which template is used thanks to the URL pattern dictionary, but that means that to change the template, we need to call these views directly from our own URL configuration. This in turn implies creating an app for the purpose of storing all user-interaction code (Example 19.26). Creating an entire app for two views may seem like overkill at the moment, but it will make a lot more sense by the end of Chapter 22.

**Example 19.26: Shell Code**

```
$ ./manage.py startapp user
```

In Example 19.27, we add our new app to INSTALLED_APPS in settings.py.

**Example 19.27: Project Code**
suorganizer/settings.py **in** da5e3adca8

```
35   INSTALLED_APPS = (
 .       ...
45       'user',
 .       ...
49   )
```

We then delete the import of django.contrib.auth.urls from suorganizer/urls.py and create a user/urls.py as shown in Example 19.28.

**Example 19.28: Project Code**
user/urls.py **in** 8a685b131d

```
1   urlpatterns = [
2   ]
```

In Example 19.29, we point our root URL configuration to the new app's URL configuration.

**Example 19.29: Project Code**
suorganizer/urls.py **in** 8a685b131d

```
25   from user import urls as user_urls
26
27   urlpatterns = [
 .       ...
41       url(r'^user/', include(user_urls)),
42   ]
```

## 19.5.3 Using Django's Views to Make Login and Logout Pages

If we pop open Django's source code, we can browse to django/contrib/auth/ views.py and look at the definition of login(), shown in Example 19.30.

**Example 19.30: Python Code**

```
# django/contrib/auth/views.py
def login(request, template_name='registration/login.html',
          redirect_field_name=REDIRECT_FIELD_NAME,
          authentication_form=AuthenticationForm,
          current_app=None, extra_context=None):
```

The parameter we're interested in overriding is template_name.

To start, we should import all of the tools we will need for our URL patterns, as shown in Example 19.31.

**Example 19.31: Project Code**
user/urls.py **in** 07122a7dd9

```
1    from django.conf.urls import url
2    from django.contrib.auth import \
3        views as auth_views
4    from django.contrib.auth.forms import \
5        AuthenticationForm
6    from django.views.generic import RedirectView
```

I'm not importing login() or logout() directly, and I am instead importing django.contrib.auth.views as a module (renamed auth_views). Throughout the book, I've imported views directly into the URL configuration file because (in my experience) beginners find it easier to keep track of all of the views that way. However, projects typically just import the views module and then call views as attributes of this module. In our **user** app, we'll get a taste of that. To create the URL pattern, we therefore call auth_views.login, passing a template_name key with the value of our own template, as shown in Example 19.32.

**Example 19.32: Project Code**
user/urls.py **in** 07122a7dd9

```
 8    urlpatterns = [
 .        ...
13        url(r'^login/$',
14            auth_views.login,
15            {'template_name': 'user/login.html'},
16            name='login'),
 .        ...
23    ]
```

The process for building a URL pattern is the same, because the function signature is nearly the same, as shown in Example 19.33.

**Example 19.33: Python Code**

```python
def logout(request, next_page=None,
           template_name='registration/logged_out.html',
           redirect_field_name=REDIRECT_FIELD_NAME,
           current_app=None, extra_context=None):
```

However, I want to display the login form (an instance of `AuthenticationForm`) on the logout page, to make it easier for users to log right back in. We could automatically redirect to the login page after logging out by setting next_page in the URL dictionary, but I explicitly want to have a login form on the `logged_out.html` template.

If we look at the context dictionary in `login()`, shown in Example 19.34, we can see that the form is included.

**Example 19.34: Python Code**

```python
#django/contrib/auth/views.py login
context = {
    'form': form,
    redirect_field_name: redirect_to,
    'site': current_site,
    'site_name': current_site.name,
}
```

However, in `logout()` this is not the case, as shown in Example 19.35.

**Example 19.35: Python Code**

```python
context = {
    'site': current_site,
    'site_name': current_site.name,
    'title': _('Logged out')
}
```

In both `login()` and `logout()`, we can pass a dictionary to the extra_content parameter, and the content of this dictionary will be added to the form, as shown in Example 19.36.

**Example 19.36: Python Code**

```python
#django/contrib/auth/views.py
    if extra_context is not None:
        context.update(extra_context)
```

To override the template and add `AuthenticationForm` to the context of the `logged_out.html` template, we therefore define our URL pattern, as shown in Example 19.37.

**Example 19.37: Project Code**

user/urls.py **in** 07122a7dd9

```
 8   urlpatterns = [
 .       ...
17       url(r'^logout/$',
18           auth_views.logout,
19           {'template_name': 'user/logged_out.html',
20            'extra_context':
21                {'form': AuthenticationForm}},
22           name='logout'),
23   ]
```

We could run off to create our templates, but we'd discover a problem with our URL configuration. We've just created a URL pattern named `login` and a URL pattern named `logout`. However, these patterns conflict with the **admin** app, which also defines URL patterns named `login` and `logout` in django/contrib/admin/sites.py. Consequently, we must change the inclusion of user URLs in the root URL configuration in order to use a namespace for the user URLs, as shown in Example 19.38.

**Example 19.38: Project Code**

suorganizer/urls.py **in** 07122a7dd9

```
25   from user import urls as user_urls
26
27   urlpatterns = [
 .       ...
41       url(r'^user/',
42           include(
43               user_urls,
44               app_name='user',
45               namespace='dj-auth')),
46   ]
```

By adding the `app_name` and `namespace` arguments to the call to `include()`, we've informed Django that we're pointing to the **user** app and that we'd like all of the names of the URL patterns in the app to be preceded by `dj-auth`. So, instead of referring to `login`, we now refer to `dj-auth:login`. We can see this in action in our call to `RedirectView`, as shown in Example 19.39.

**Example 19.39: Project Code**

user/urls.py **in** 07122a7dd9

```
 8   urlpatterns = [
 9       url(r'^$',
10           RedirectView.as_view(
11               pattern_name='dj-auth:login',
12               permanent=False)),
 .       ...
23   ]
```

We've successfully defined a webpage for both /user/login/ and /user/logout/, and the call to RedirectView creates a redirect for the /user/ URL path. We can now turn our attention to templates.

As with any new app, we start by creating a base app template, which extends the project base template, as shown in Example 19.40.

**Example 19.40: Project Code**
user/templates/user/base_user.html in 07122a7dd9

```
1    {% extends parent_template|default:"base.html" %}
```

We know we're going to create a form in both login.html and logged_out.html and that in both cases we'll be displaying the AuthenticationForm and sending the information to dj-auth:login. Rather than creating the form twice in two different places, we can create the form in a single template and use the include template tag to render the form and then display it within our other templates.

We therefore create the login_form.html and just print a basic template with a few basic variables, as shown in Example 19.41.

**Example 19.41: Project Code**
user/templates/user/login_form.html in 07122a7dd9

```
1    <form
2        action="{% url 'dj-auth:login' %}"
3        method="post">
4    {% csrf_token %}
5    {{ form.as_p }}
6    <button type="submit">
7        {{ login_button|default:'Log in' }}</button>
8    </form>
```

We then create our login.html template and include the template in Example 19.41 in the template in Example 19.42. I want to stress: the template login_form.html will be rendered *first*, before it is added as HTML code to the template in Example 19.42 when our templates system renders the login.html template. All of the context variables available to login.html will be available to login_form.html.

**Example 19.42: Project Code**
user/templates/user/login.html in 07122a7dd9

```
1    {% extends parent_template|default:"user/base_user.html" %}
2
3    {% block title %}
4    {{ block.super }} - Login
5    {% endblock %}
```

```
 6
 7   {% block content %}
 8     <div class="row">
 9       <div class="offset-by-two five columns">
10         {% include "user/login_form.html" %}
11       </div>
12     </div>
13   {% endblock %}
```

The include template tag allows for extra context variables to be defined via the with token. For example, we can use with to override the login_button value, not normally found in the context of the logged_out.html template. The ability to define extra context variables allows us to take our code from templates/registration/ logged_out.html and replace it with the code in Example 19.43.

**Example 19.43: Project Code**
user/templates/user/logged_out.html **in** 07122a7dd9

```
 1   {% extends parent_template|default:"user/base_user.html" %}
 2
 3   {% block title %}
 4   {{ block.super }} - Logged Out
 5   {% endblock %}
 6
 7   {% block content %}
 8     <div class="row">
 9       <div class="offset-by-two eight columns">
10         <p>You've successfully logged out.</p>
11         {% include "user/login_form.html"
 .           with login_button='Log Back In' %}
12       </div>
13     </div>
14   {% endblock %}
```

We finish by adding a small status indicator at the top of our base template, linking to our new pages in the process, as shown in Example 19.44.

**Example 19.44: Project Code**
templates/base.html **in** 07122a7dd9

```
29         <div class="status row">
30           <div class="offset-by-eight four columns">
31             <ul class="inline">
32               {% if user.is_authenticated %}
33                 <li><a href="{% url 'dj-auth:logout' %}">
34                   Log Out</a></li>
```

```
35                    {% else %}
36                      <li><a href="{% url 'dj-auth:login' %}">
37                        Log In</a></li>
38                    {% endif %}
39                </ul>
40              </div>
41            </div>
```

### 19.5.4  Post-Authentication Redirection

If you log in to the website, you'll discover that Django tries to redirect us to the
/accounts/profile/ URL path segment, a webpage that doesn't exist. That's rather silly.

We can change this behavior by overriding the LOGIN_REDIRECT_URL. In
Example 19.45, we also define the LOGIN_URL and LOGOUT_URL settings, which will be
useful in Chapter 20.

**Example 19.45: Project Code**
suorganizer/settings.py in a4c0b0aec0

```
166    from django.core.urlresolvers import reverse_lazy
167
168    LOGIN_REDIRECT_URL = reverse_lazy('blog_post_list')
169    LOGIN_URL = reverse_lazy('dj-auth:login')
170    LOGOUT_URL = reverse_lazy('dj-auth:logout')
```

This is a great start, but we can do much better. Users are able to log in and be redirected
to the page they were on before they decided to log in. This functionality is very useful: if I
spot a typo on the startup detail page, after I log in, I want to be back at the startup detail
page, not at the blog list!

Luckily for us, both login() and logout() views will look for a submitted value to
redirect. By default, this is set to 'next' (Example 19.46) but can be additionally
overridden by the URL pattern dictionary via the key redirect_field_name.

**Example 19.46: Python Code**

```
# django/contrib/auth/__init__.py
REDIRECT_FIELD_NAME = 'next'
```

If we set the URL query next variable to a URL path, the login() or logout()
view will add the next variable with its value to the template. It anticipates that a user will
add a next hidden field on the form. When the view receives next as part of the POST
data, the view will redirect to that page.

To use this functionality, we simply add a next HTML hidden input field to our login
form, as shown in Example 19.47.

**Example 19.47: Project Code**

`user/templates/user/login_form.html` **in** e0bb647e02

```
 6      {% if next %}
 7        <input
 8          type="hidden"
 9          name="next"
10          value="{{ next }}">
11      {% endif %}
```

Then, to make sure that the `next` variable is always in the URL query, we can change our links in our base template, as shown in Example 19.48.

**Example 19.48: Project Code**

`templates/base.html` **in** 8de327c521

```
33              <li><a href="{% url 'dj-auth:logout' %}?
.                         next={{ request.path }}">
.                  . . .
36              <li><a href="{% url 'dj-auth:login' %}?
.                         next={{ request.path }}">
```

If you click on the login link on any page and successfully log in, Django will now redirect you to the page you were previously on. This only works, however, because we are using `'RequestContext'` for all of our views, as Django is adding the `'request'` object for us.

# 19.6    Putting It All Together

This chapter is the tip of the iceberg when it comes to **auth**. We learned about sessions and cookies, took a quick look at some of the tools provided by the **auth** app, and then built two very straightforward webpages.

The `User` model is the heart of the **auth** app, and while we did not interact with it directly, both the `login()` and `logout()` views are manipulating the user data sent as part of the `HttpRequest` object. The views will receive either a `User` or an `AnonymousUser`.

When `login()` receives the POST data from `AuthenticationForm`, it finds a user by the same username and then uses the `check_password()` method provided by the `User` class. In the event the password matches the hash stored in the database, then the `login()` view uses the `login()` function to create a session, associating the `User` instance with a cookie.

The `logout()` view passes the `HttpRequest` object to the `get_user()` helper function to retrieve the `User` (or `AnonymousUser`) instance. In essence, the `get_user()` function is a tool for asking the `HttpRequest` for the `User` of the session of the cookie sent as part of the HTTP request. This allows the `logout()` view to call the `logout()` helper function, which destroys the user's session.

# Integrating Permissions

## In This Chapter

- Learn about **auth**'s `Permission` and `Group` models
- Limit who can use our create, update, and delete webpages via permissions
- Set permissions on views using decorators
- Control what is displayed in templates
- Conditionally display `Post` objects depending on when they are published

## 20.1 Introduction

In security, a **permission** is a rule that determines whether a user has the right to perform an operation, usually on an object (e.g., file, socket, etc.). In this chapter, we create and use permissions to control access to some of our webpages and limit access to specific data.

## 20.2 Understanding `contenttypes` and Generic Relations

By default, Django includes the `contenttypes` contributed app in every new project, as shown in Example 20.1.

**Example 20.1: Project Code**
`suorganizer/settings.py` **in** 97c4234a4a

```
35    INSTALLED_APPS = (
 .        ...
38        'django.contrib.contenttypes',
 .        ...
48    )
```

The app keeps track of all of the types of content in our project, as shown in Example 20.2.

**Example 20.2: Python Interpreter Code**

```
>>> from django.contrib.contenttypes.models import ContentType
>>> ContentType.objects.all()
[<ContentType: log entry>,
 <ContentType: permission>,
 <ContentType: group>,
 <ContentType: user>,
 <ContentType: content type>,
 <ContentType: session>,
 <ContentType: site>,
 <ContentType: tag>,
 <ContentType: startup>,
 <ContentType: news article>,
 <ContentType: blog post>]
```

Listing the `ContentType` objects allows us to see which model is defined on which app, as shown in Example 20.3.

**Example 20.3: Python Interpreter Code**

```
>>> ContentType.objects.values()
[{'app_label': 'admin', 'id': 1, 'model': 'logentry'},
 {'app_label': 'auth', 'id': 2, 'model': 'permission'},
 {'app_label': 'auth', 'id': 3, 'model': 'group'},
 {'app_label': 'auth', 'id': 4, 'model': 'user'},
 {'app_label': 'contenttypes', 'id': 5, 'model': 'contenttype'},
 {'app_label': 'sessions', 'id': 6, 'model': 'session'},
 {'app_label': 'sites', 'id': 7, 'model': 'site'},
 {'app_label': 'organizer', 'id': 8, 'model': 'tag'},
 {'app_label': 'organizer', 'id': 9, 'model': 'startup'},
 {'app_label': 'organizer', 'id': 10, 'model': 'newslink'},
 {'app_label': 'blog', 'id': 11, 'model': 'post'}]
```

The powerful part of the **contenttypes** app is that it easily allows us to use data in the database to fetch an actual model class, and then interact with that object, as shown in Example 20.4.

**Example 20.4: Python Interpreter Code**

```
>>> post_ct = ContentType.objects.get(app_label='blog')
>>> Post = post_ct.model_class()
>>> Post.objects.count()
6
```

This may seem odd at first, but it turns out to be incredibly useful. In our models, all of the relations are associated with another specific model. What if we wanted to be able to have a relation with *any* other model? For instance, our `Tag` model is related to `Startup` and `Post` objects specifically. Why not allow it to be related to *any* object?

A one-to-many relation is created by a foreign key: a number that identifies data in another table by its primary key. What if instead of knowing which table that was, we identified each table by a number. We would thus have a number for the primary key (the foreign key) and a number for the table. The number for the table is what each `ContentType` object supplies. The use of a foreign key and a table key is called a **generic relation**.

To make interacting with a generic relation in Python as simple as possible, the **contenttypes** app supplies the `GenericForeignKey` field. We create a one-to-many relationship with the `ContentType` model (the table key) and define a `PositiveIntegerField` (to act as a foreign key). The `GenericForeignKey` expects the names of both of these fields to define a generic one-to-many relation with any other model in our project, as shown in Example 20.5.

**Example 20.5: Python Code**

```
from django.contrib.contenttypes.fields import GenericForeignKey

class MyModel(models.Model):
    ...
    content_type = models.ForeignKey(ContentType)
    object_id = models.PositiveIntegerField()
    content_object = GenericForeignKey('content_type', 'object_id')
```

In Python, we can therefore create a relation thanks to the the content_object field rather than defining the table key and foreign key ourselves, as shown in Example 20.6.

**Example 20.6: Python Code**

```
an_instance = AnotherModel.objects.all()[0]
mymodel_intance = MyModel(content_object=an_instance)
```

What's more, the **contenttypes** app also supplies the `GenericRelation` field to define the reverse of a one-to-many relation, as shown in Example 20.7.

**Example 20.7: Python Code**

```
from django.contrib.contenttypes.fields import GenericRelation

class AnotherModel(models.Model):
    ...
    mymodel = GenericRelation(MyModel)
```

Unfortunately, `contenttypes` doesn't support the creation of generic many-to-many relations. Of course, given that a many-to-many relationship is a table with two foreign keys, we could build our own model with a foreign key (to `Tag` objects, for instance) and a generic foreign key for any other object. Or, if we wanted to associate any row of data with any other object, we could even create a table with two generic relations. (I do not recommend or condone this course of action.)

Generic relations are the basis for how Django deals with permissions. Django has a `Permission` model that may be associated with any other model in our project, thanks to `GenericForeignKey`. When interacting with the `Permission` model, we will unsurprisingly find ourselves interacting with `ContentType` as well as `GenericForeignKey` fields.

# 20.3   auth App Anatomy: Permission and Group Models

Taking a page from UNIX's security policy, Django's **auth** app defines not only a `User` model but also `Permission` and `Group` models. These two new models are the central focus of this chapter.

`User`, `Permission`, and `Group` are all related by many-to-many relations. A `User` may belong to a `Group`, and a `Group` may be related to multiple `User` instances. Similarly, we can define `Permission` instances to limit behavior on both `User` and `Group` instances.

`Permission` instances are often described code by the string format `'<app>.<behavior>_<model>'`, where behavior is one of `add`, `change`, or `delete`. For instance, the string `'blog.change_post'` is the permission to modify `Post` objects. A `Permission` limits control to behavior at the model level. Given the `'blog.change_post'` permission, a `User` will be able to modify any `Post` instance. We discuss object-level permissions (where a permission can control whether a `User` has access to a specific instance) shortly.

On top of these new models, we use Python decorators in this chapter. The **auth** app supplies three decorators meant to be applied to function views (not just any type of view!): `@login_required` `@permission_required()` and `@user_passes_test`. We even use these decorators to build our own for our class-based views.

Before that, we turn to the shell to familiarize ourselves with our new models.

## 20.3.1   Permissions in the Shell

At the moment, we have a single superuser in our database. Having a superuser is not particularly helpful, because the superuser by default has access to all permissions. We can use the `has_perm()` method on the `User` model to check this with all of the permissions automatically generated for our **blog** app, as shown in Example 20.8.

**Example 20.8: Python Interpreter Code**

```
>>> andrew = User.objects.get(username='andrew')
>>> andrew.is_superuser
True
>>> andrew.has_perm('blog.add_post')
True
>>> andrew.has_perm('blog.change_post')
```

```
True
>>> andrew.has_perm('blog.delete_post')
True
```

For each model, the **auth** app generates a permission to control whether the user can create, modify, or delete that type of model instance. By default, regular users do not have any permissions, as shown in Example 20.9.

**Example 20.9: Python Interpreter Code**

```
>>> from django.contrib.auth import get_user_model
>>> User = get_user_model()
>>> ada = User.objects.create_user(
... 'ada',  # username
... 'ada@djangogirls.org',  # (fake) email
... 'algorhythm')  # password
>>> ada
<User: ada>
>>> ada.has_perm('blog.add_post')
False
>>> ada.has_perm('blog.change_post')
False
>>> ada.has_perm('blog.delete_post')
False
```

> ## Warning!
>
> Django Girls is a real and very cool organization, but it is not affiliated with this book and the email above is **not** a real one. Use of their name is for illustrative purposes only.

The many-to-many relation between the User model and the Permission model is defined as user_permissions on the User model, as shown in Example 20.10, to differentiate from the permissions relation of the Group model (seen next section).

**Example 20.10: Python Interpreter Code**

```
>>> ada.user_permissions.all()
[]
>>> ada.user_permissions
<django.db.models.fields.related.create_many_related_manager.<locals>.
  ManyRelatedManager object at 0x10ad79780>
```

The superuser doesn't have any permissions by default either—it's just that the is_superuser field on the User model tells the has_perm() method to always return True, as shown in Example 20.11.

**Example 20.11: Python Interpreter Code**

```
>>> andrew.user_permissions.all()
[]
```

To add permissions to our regular users, we of course need our `Permission` model. With four models, you might expect 12 permissions—but you've forgotten all of the models in the contributed apps! They include `Site`, `Session`, and of course `User`, `Permission`, and `Group`, as shown in Example 20.12.

**Example 20.12: Python Interpreter Code**

```
>>> from django.contrib.auth.models import Permission
>>> Permission.objects.count()
42
```

To be able to set permissions on any and all models, the `Permission` model defines a `GenericForeignKey` to the `ContentType` model from the **contenttypes** app. We can use the `content_type` field to limit the number of `Permission` objects in a queryset, as shown in Example 20.13.

**Example 20.13: Python Interpreter Code**

```
>>> from django.contrib.contenttypes.models import ContentType
>>> from blog.models import Post
>>> blog_content_type = ContentType.objects.get_for_model(Post)
>>> Permission.objects.filter(content_type=blog_content_type)
[<Permission: blog | blog post | Can add blog post>,
 <Permission: blog | blog post | Can change blog post>,
 <Permission: blog | blog post | Can delete blog post>]
```

On top of the `content_type` field, the `Permission` model defines a field for the name of the permission as well as a code name, as shown in Example 20.14. The code name of generated permissions is of the format `'<behavior>_<model>'` and is one part of the `Permission` identifier: `'<app>.<behavior>_<model>'`. Of course, like all models, instances also store a primary key named `id` (with a shortcut to pk).

**Example 20.14: Python Interpreter Code**

```
>>> Permission.objects.filter(content_type=blog_content_type).values()
 [{'codename': 'add_post',
  'content_type_id': 10,
  'id': 28,
  'name': 'Can add blog post'},
 {'codename': 'change_post',
  'content_type_id': 10,
  'id': 29,
  'name': 'Can change blog post'},
 {'codename': 'delete_post',
  'content_type_id': 10,
  'id': 30,
  'name': 'Can delete blog post'}]
```

The real power with permissions, of course, is that we can create new ones to best suit our needs. In Example 20.15, we create a new permission to control whether a user can read unpublished `Post` instances, where an unpublished instance is any instance with a `pub_date` defined in the future.

**Example 20.15: Python Interpreter Code**

```
>>> new_permission = Permission.objects.create(
... codename='view_future_post',
... name='Can view unpublished Post',
... content_type=blog_content_type)
>>> new_permission
<Permission: blog | blog post | Can view unpublished Post>
```

A key problem of having data in the database is that none of your coworkers share that data. To solve this problem, permissions are not typically created as in Example 20.15. We delete this new permission in Example 20.16.

**Example 20.16: Python Interpreter Code**

```
>>> new_permission.delete()
```

Instead, permissions can be defined on the model they apply to. In Example 20.17, we define the same permission as above by adding a tuple to a tuple of new permissions. The inner tuple defines the `codename` and the `name` of the permission.

**Example 20.17: Project Code**
`blog/models.py` **in e2046b3a15**

```
11    class Post(models.Model):
  .        ...
30        class Meta:
  .            ...
34            permissions = (
35                ("view_future_post",
36                 "Can view unpublished Post"),
37            )
```

With a change to a model comes a new migration. In this case, we don't have to worry about it, as Django generates exactly what we want, as shown in Example 20.18.

**Example 20.18: Shell Code**

```
$ ./manage.py makemigrations --name=add_view_future_post_permission blog
$ ./manage.py migrate
```

If you reload your shell, you'll be able to get our new permission, as shown in Example 20.19.

**Example 20.19: Python Interpreter Code**

```
>>> Permission.objects.get(codename='view_future_post')
<Permission: blog | blog post | Can view unpublished Post>
```

## 20.3.2   Groups in the Shell

Groups are an easy way to organize permissions. Typically, it's best not to assign permissions to users directly. Instead, you create groups (such as administrator, manager, etc.) that have different levels of permissions. Users who belong to these groups inherit the permissions of the group.

Developers often confuse the `is_staff` and `is_superuser` fields on the `User` model with `Group` instances. By default, there are no groups defined, as shown in Example 20.20.

**Example 20.20: Python Interpreter Code**

```
>>> from django.contrib.auth.models import Group
>>> Group.objects.all()
[]
```

Our site is going to need capable users whom we trust to update the website with valid information. We can create a group called `'contributors'` to contain all of these users, as shown in Example 20.21.

**Example 20.21: Python Interpreter Code**

```
>>> Group.objects.create(name='contributors')
<Group: contributors>
>>> Group.objects.values()
[{'id': 1, 'name': 'contributors'}]
```

The many-to-many relation on the `Group` model is accessible via the `permissions` attribute, as shown in Example 20.22. As you might expect, there are no permissions by default.

**Example 20.22: Python Interpreter Code**

```
>>> contributor.permissions.all()
[]
>>> contributor.permissions
<django.db.models.fields.related.create_many_related_manager.<locals>.
   ManyRelatedManager object at 0x10ae70748>
```

To begin, we want to make sure our contributors can see all of our `Post` instances and that they can write blog posts of their own, as shown in Example 20.23.

**Example 20.23: Python Interpreter Code**

```
>>> Permission.objects.get(codename='view_future_post')
<Permission: blog | blog post | Can view Post>
>>> contributor.permissions.add(
... Permission.objects.get(codename='view_future_post')
... Permission.objects.get(codename='add_post')
>>> contributor.permissions.all()
[<Permission: blog | blog post | Can add blog post>,
 <Permission: blog | blog post | Can view Post>]
```

To use our group, we need to add actual users, as shown in Example 20.24.

**Example 20.24: Python Interpreter Code**

```
>>> ada = User.objects.get(username='ada')
>>> ada.groups
<django.db.models.fields.related.create_many_related_manager.<locals>.
   ManyRelatedManager object at 0x10ae78470>
>>> ada.groups.add(contributor)
>>> ada.groups.all()
[<Group: contributors>]
```

If you try to check Ada's permissions right away, you'll be surprised to discover that nothing appears to have changed, as shown in Example 20.25.

**Example 20.25: Python Interpreter Code**

```
>>> ada.has_perm('blog.view_post')
False
>>> ada.has_perm('blog.add_post')
False
```

Django caches permissions. If permissions change, it becomes necessary to reload the object in its entirety to see the object's current permission set, as shown in Example 20.26.

**Example 20.26: Python Interpreter Code**

```
>>> ada = User.objects.get(username='ada')
>>> ada.has_perm('blog.view_post')
True
>>> ada.has_perm('blog.add_post')
True
```

Conveniently, it's possible to list a users's permissions, as shown in Example 20.27.

**Example 20.27: Python Interpreter Code**

```
>>> ada.get_group_permissions()
{'blog.add_post', 'blog.view_post'}
>>> ada.get_all_permissions()
{'blog.add_post', 'blog.view_post'}
```

It's also possible to check multiple permissions at once, as shown in Example 20.28. This turns out to be a gotcha: the User model defines has_perm and has_perms. If has_perms is not passed a list, it simply returns False, which can lead to some rather confusing behavior.

**Example 20.28: Python Interpreter Code**

```
>>> ada.has_perms('blog.view_post')
False
>>> ada.has_perms('blog.add_post', 'blog.view_post')
False
>>> ada.has_perms(['blog.add_post'])
True
```

Finally, it's possible to check whether a User has any permissions in an app, as shown in Example 20.29. This is not comprehensive: Ada does not have all of the permission in **blog**, just a few.

**Example 20.29: Python Interpreter Code**

```
>>> ada.has_module_perms('blog')
True
>>> ada.has_module_perms('organizer')
False
```

While we could add more permissions, it will be useful for us not to add anymore to best understand the code in the next section. We return to the topic at the end of the chapter.

### 20.3.3   Object-Level Permissions

The group and permission system in place for Django is very basic—permissions control a type of object (models). Django does not provide the code necessary to checking permissions on specific objects. However, Django does anticipate that you might want this behavior. The definition of many of the permission-checking methods allows for an optional obj argument, as shown in Example 20.30.

**Example 20.30: Python Code**

```
has_perm(perm, obj=None)
has_perms(perm_list, obj=None)
get_group_permissions(obj=None)
get_all_permissions(obj=None)
```

The documentation states that "if obj is passed in, this method won't check for a permission for the model, but for this specific object." This statement unfortunately confuses many beginners, as they think it implies that Django provides this behavior, leading to code similar to Example 20.31.

**Example 20.31: Python Interpreter Code**

```
>>> p = Post.objects.all()[0]
>>> ada.has_perm('blog.view_post')
True
>>> ada.has_perm('blog.view_post', p)
False
```

The problem, of course, is that Django has no way of determining how developers and systems would like to handle object permissions, as there are dozens of ways it can be arranged. The documentation clarifies: "Django's permission framework has a foundation for object permissions, though there is no implementation for it in the core."

Django expects that you might need object-level permissions, but because it doesn't know how your models are built or how you want object permissions organized, it simply can't make intelligent choices about your desired behavior. Instead, the best solution is to use one of the many object-related tools provided as third-party apps. We discuss this topic in more depth in Chapter 30: Starting a New Project Correctly.

## Django Documentation

For more on using **auth**:

https://dju.link/18/auth

For the documentation about object-level permissions and a sneak peek at the next two chapters:

https://dju.link/18/auth-custom

# 20.4   Protecting Views with Permissions

Now that we understand permissions and groups, and we have a contributor group to help add content to the website, we need to protect the webpages that affect data such that only contributors and superusers can access the page. In HTTP, if a page is inaccessible, we return a 403 Not Authorized error.

To start, we can use the @login_required decorator to protect a view and force visitors to authenticate. Unfortunately, decorators are aimed specifically at functions, which means we can't apply them to any of our classes or even our methods. With that said, because class-based views (CBVs) actually generate a function view (the inner view() function; see Chapter 5: Creating Webpages with Controllers in Django, Section 5.9.3, for a refresher), we can use the decorator as a function (it's true nature!) in the URL pattern. In Example 20.32, we use the decorator on the organizer_tag_create URL pattern.

**Example 20.32: Project Code**
organizer/urls/tag.py **in** 208760340d

```
 2   from django.contrib.auth.decorators import \
 3       login_required
 .       ...
 9   urlpatterns = [
 .       ...
13       url(r'^create/$',
14           login_required(
15               TagCreate.as_view()),
16           name='organizer_tag_create'),
 .       ...
26   ]
```

I really don't like this solution. A webpage is two things: data and a path to that data. At the moment, we are protecting the path to the data rather than the data itself. If we were to add the URL pattern elsewhere, or refactor the code, it would be easy to forget the decorator. For this reason, I am firmly of the opinion that security in Django should be applied directly to the view and not in the URL pattern.

Consequently, we need some way to use the function-only @login_required decorator on a method. Luckily, Django anticipates this need and supplies the @method_decorator(), which takes a function decorator and allows it to work with methods. Now all we need is a method, which we do not have in the case of TagCreate because we are using a generic class-based view (GCBV) (Chapter 17: Understanding Generic Class-Based Views).

If we want to protect a single HTTP method on a CBV, we can protect only that method; to protect the data shown via GET request, we could add the @login_required with the @method_decorator() to the get() method. Typically, however, we want to protect all of the methods that access the CBV. In this case, we might consider overriding as_view() or dispatch(). Because as_view() is a class method, it isn't actually passed an HttpRequest object, which is what @login_required depends on. We therefore add our decorators to an overridden dispatch() method, which simply calls the same method in the superclass. We demonstrate this in TagCreate, having removed the decorator from organizer_tag_create, as shown in Example 20.33.

**Example 20.33: Project Code**
`organizer/views.py` **in** ca03d7cd10

```
1    from django.contrib.auth.decorators import \
2        login_required
.        ...
5    from django.utils.decorators import \
6        method_decorator
.        ...
86   class TagCreate(CreateView):
87       form_class = TagForm
88       model = Tag
89
90       @method_decorator(login_required)
91       def dispatch(self, request, *args, **kwargs):
92           return super().dispatch(
93               request, *args, **kwargs)
```

Forcing users to log in is swell and all, but it doesn't check that they actually have permission to do what they want to do. Instead, we use the `@permission_required()` decorator, as shown in Example 20.34.

**Example 20.34: Project Code**
`organizer/views.py` **in** abedd94330

```
1    from django.contrib.auth.decorators import \
2        permission_required
.        ...
86   class TagCreate(CreateView):
.        ...
90       @method_decorator(
91           permission_required(
92               'organizer.add_tag',
93           ))
94       def dispatch(self, request, *args, **kwargs):
95           return super().dispatch(
96               request, *args, **kwargs)
```

This code actually results in some odd and frustrating behavior. If we log in with our Ada user account, who does not have have permissions to create tags, we will then be prompted to log in. But we are logged in!

Instead of prompting the user to log in, we can set the `raise_exception` parameter to `True` when using the `@permission_required()` decorator to raise an HTTP 403 error, as shown in Example 20.35.

**Example 20.35:** Project Code

`organizer/views.py` in 9f7b45e4c2

```
86    class TagCreate(CreateView):
   .      ...
90        @method_decorator(
91            permission_required(
92                'organizer.add_tag',
93                raise_exception=True
94            ))
95        def dispatch(self, request, *args, **kwargs):
96            return super().dispatch(
97                request, *args, **kwargs)
```

## Warning!

Both the @permission_required() decorator and @login_required decorator
are based on the @user_passes_test(), which allows us to write arbitrary
functions to test whether a user has permission to access a webpage. This sometimes
leads developers to write code that tests whether the user belongs to a group, as
demonstrated in Example 20.36.

**Example 20.36:** Project Code

`organizer/views.py` in fadd9ce54a

```
  1    from django.contrib.auth import PermissionDenied
  2    from django.contrib.auth.decorators import \
  3        user_passes_test
   .      ...
 87    def in_contrib_group(user):
 88        if user.groups.filter(
 89                name='contributors').exists():
 90            return True
 91        else:
 92            raise PermissionDenied
   .      ...
 95    class TagCreate(CreateView):
   .      ...
 99        @method_decorator(
100            user_passes_test(
101                in_contrib_group
102            ))
103        def dispatch(self, request, *args, **kwargs):
104            return super().dispatch(
105                request, *args, **kwargs)
```

This practice is not a good idea. For one, the superusers are not guaranteed to pass the
test, despite that we want them to be able to access *everything* on the site. When
building permissions, stick to checking permissions unless you are certain that's not
good enough.

If we're logged in with Ada, browsing to the `TagCreate` page will now return a 403 error. However, if we log out (becoming an anonymous user), we will also see a 403 error.

Compare this behavior with that of the `@login_required`, added in Example 20.37 to the `TagUpdate` view. Here, we will always be prompted to log in, even if we already are.

**Example 20.37: Project Code**
`organizer/views.py` in 95f226887f

```
  1   from django.contrib.auth import PermissionDenied
  2   from django.contrib.auth.decorators import (
  3       login_required, user_passes_test)
  .       ...
123   class TagUpdate(UpdateView):
124       form_class = TagForm
125       model = Tag
126
127       @method_decorator(login_required)
128       def dispatch(self, request, *args, **kwargs):
129           return super().dispatch(
130               request, *args, **kwargs)
```

Ideally, we want the best of both worlds. If we are not logged in, we want to be prompted to log in. Only then can Django actually use permissions to check whether we can access the page. However, if we are authenticated and not permitted, we want Django to tell us rather than prompting us with a login.

The trick is to chain the decorators together, as shown in Example 20.38.

**Example 20.38: Project Code**
`organizer/views.py` in 4c4ad42d6c

```
  1   from django.contrib.auth.decorators import (
  2       login_required, permission_required)
  .       ...
 86   class TagCreate(CreateView):
  .       ...
 90       @method_decorator(login_required)
 91       @method_decorator(
 92           permission_required(
 93               'organizer.add_tag',
 94               raise_exception=True,
 95           ))
 96       def dispatch(self, request, *args, **kwargs):
 97           return super().dispatch(
 98               request, *args, **kwargs)
```

If you browse to `/tag/create/`, you will be prompted to log in. If you log in as Ada, you'll be greeted with a 403 error. However, log in as Andrew (the superuser) and you'll see our tag form webpage.

### 20.4.1   Custom Decorators

Having to override `dispatch()` in each and every one of our views is an unacceptable method for adding permissions. We should be able to use decorators on our class-based views directly. Even though Django doesn't supply this behavior, because this is all Python, we can create our own decorators.

Decorators are one of Python's trickier techniques, and even though Appendix B provides a primer on the material, we will take this slowly. To begin, we recreate the `@login_required` decorator a new file called `user/decorators.py`, as shown in Example 20.39.

**Example 20.39: Project Code**

`user/decorators.py` in `47885ef1d7`

```
 1   from django.conf import settings
 2   from django.contrib.auth import get_user
 3   from django.shortcuts import redirect
 4
 5
 6   def custom_login_required(view):
 7       # view argument must be a function
 8
 9       def new_view(request, *args, **kwargs):
10           user = get_user(request)
11           if user.is_authenticated():
12               return view(request, *args, **kwargs)
13           else:
14               url = '{}?next={}'.format(
15                   settings.LOGIN_URL,
16                   request.path)
17               return redirect(url)
18
19       return new_view
```

The goal of a decorator is to take a callable, such as a function, and to return a new callable. Typically, this new callable modifies or uses the original in some way. In our `@custom_login_required` decorator, we create a new view called `new_view()`, which checks whether the user is authenticated. If the user is authenticated, the view being decorated is called. If the user is not authenticated, we redirect to the login page, setting the next URL query to allow the login page to return the user to this view.

Like `@login_required`, `@custom_login_required` is built only to work with functions, meaning we still need `@method_decorator()` applied to `dispatch()`, as shown in Example 20.40.

**Example 20.40: Project Code**

`organizer/views.py` in `47885ef1d7`

```
117   class TagUpdate(UpdateView):
  .       ...
121       @method_decorator(custom_login_required)
```

```
122      def dispatch(self, request, *args, **kwargs):
123          return super().dispatch(
124              request, *args, **kwargs)
```

It's best practice to use the `@wraps()` decorator when building your own. This decorator will make the `new_view()` look like the original `view()`, adding attributes like document strings. To make this easier, Django also supplies the `available_attrs()` function to find all of the attributes you might want to add to the decorator, as shown in Example 20.41.

**Example 20.41: Project Code**
`user/decorators.py` **in** 546a4681aa

```
1    from functools import wraps
 .       . . .
6    from django.utils.decorators import \
7        available_attrs
 .       . . .
10   def custom_login_required(view):
 .       . . .
13       @wraps(view, assigned=available_attrs(view))
14       def new_view(request, *args, **kwargs):
```

Effectively, if we introspect the code in the shell, `new_view()` will look identical to `view()`.

Of course, it's very silly of us to reprogram behavior that Django provides, and we should instead use `@login_required` for the behavior above (including `@wraps()`), as shown in Example 20.42.

**Example 20.42: Project Code**
`user/decorators.py` **in** 813eca7544

```
1    from django.contrib.auth.decorators import \
2        login_required
3
4
5    def custom_login_required(view):
6        # view argument must be a function
7        decorated_view = login_required(view)
8        return decorated_view
```

We can then integrate `@method_decorator()` directly into our own decorator, as shown in Example 20.43.

**Example 20.43: Project Code**

user/decorators.py **in** 338d1961d8

```
3   from django.utils.decorators import \
4       method_decorator
.       ...
7   def custom_login_required(view):
8       # view argument must be a method
9       decorator = method_decorator(login_required)
10      decorated_view = decorator(view)
11      return decorated_view
```

With @method_decorator in place, we can remove @method_decorator() from
TagUpdate, as shown in Example 20.44.

**Example 20.44: Project Code**

organizer/views.py **in** 338d1961d8

```
117   class TagUpdate(UpdateView):
.         ...
121       @custom_login_required
122       def dispatch(self, request, *args, **kwargs):
```

We now want to create a decorator that combines @login_required and
@permission_required(). However, whereas @login_required does not take any
arguments, @permission_required() does. In this instance, we need to create a
function that accepts a string (the permission identifier) and returns a decorator (which
accepts a callable and returns a callable), as shown in Example 20.45.

**Example 20.45: Project Code**

user/decorators.py **in** b1ebb780f2

```
1    from django.contrib.auth.decorators import (
2        login_required, permission_required)
.        ...
14   def require_authenticated_permission(permission):
15
16       def decorator(view):
17           # view must be a function
18           check_auth = login_required
19           check_perm = (
20               permission_required(
21                   permission, raise_exception=True))
22
23           decorated_view = (
24               check_auth(check_perm(view)))
25           return decorated_view
26
27       return decorator
```

We can use this new decorator to replace the two decorators on `TagCreate`, as shown in Example 20.46.

**Example 20.46: Project Code**

`organizer/views.py` **in** `b1ebb780f2`

```
87   class TagCreate(CreateView):
 .      ...
91       @method_decorator(
92           require_authenticated_permission(
93               'organizer.add_tag'
94           ))
95       def dispatch(self, request, *args, **kwargs):
```

As before, we can use `@method_decorator()` directly in our decorator to avoid having to call it at all points in the rest of our code, as shown in Example 20.47.

**Example 20.47: Project Code**

`user/decorators.py` **in** `b121f6fe99`

```
14   def require_authenticated_permission(permission):
15
16       def decorator(view):
17           # view must be a method
18           check_auth = (
19               method_decorator(login_required))
20           check_perm = (
21               method_decorator(
22                   permission_required(
23                       permission,
24                       raise_exception=True)))
25
26           decorated_view = (
27               check_auth(check_perm(view)))
28           return decorated_view
29
30       return decorator
```

This shortens the decorator code of `TagCreate` again, as shown in Example 20.48.

**Example 20.48: Project Code**

`organizer/views.py` **in** `b121f6fe99`

```
85   class TagCreate(CreateView):
 .      ...
89       @require_authenticated_permission(
90           'organizer.add_tag')
91       def dispatch(self, request, *args, **kwargs):
```

The original goal of this section was to build decorators that allow us to avoid overriding dispatch() in all of our views. In Example 20.49, let's replace @custom_login_required with a new decorator @class_login_required that replaces dispatch() for us in any class that is decorated by it.

**Example 20.49: Project Code**
user/decorators.py **in** add65f2c2b

```
 3   from django.core.exceptions import \
 4       ImproperlyConfigured
 .       ...
 7   from django.views.generic import View
 .       ...
10   def class_login_required(cls):
11       if (not isinstance(cls, type)
12               or not issubclass(cls, View)):
13           raise ImproperlyConfigured(
14               "class_login_required"
15               " must be applied to subclasses "
16               "of View class.")
17       decorator = method_decorator(login_required)
18       cls.dispatch = decorator(cls.dispatch)
19       return cls
```

The easy stuff is on lines 17 and 18. We simply use the @login_required with @method_decorator() to create a decorator, which we then call as a function on the dispatch() method, replacing the original method by assigning the new method to cls.dispatch.

The condition on lines 11 and 12 is trickier. In Python, everything is an object—including classes. They're objects created by the type object. To make sure that we are applying our decorator to a class, we therefore ask if we're applying the decorator to an instance of type on line 11. Then, to make sure that dispatch() actually exists, we make sure that the class is a subclass of View, Django's CBV. In the event one of these is false, we raise an ImproperlyConfigured exception.

In Example 20.50, we can remove our override of dispatch() from TagUpdate and decorate the class with our new decorator.

**Example 20.50: Project Code**
organizer/views.py **in** add65f2c2b

```
  7   from user.decorators import (
  8       class_login_required,
  9       require_authenticated_permission)
  .       ...
111   @class_login_required
112   class TagUpdate(UpdateView):
113       form_class = TagForm
114       model = Tag
```

Of course, that's just a simple login, and our end goal is to protect CBVs with first a login and then a permission check. This decorator is a little bit longer than the first.

Our new @require_authenticated_permission() needs to know which permission it's checking and then return a decorator that applies to a class, as shown in Example 20.51.

**Example 20.51:** Project Code
user/decorators.py in 627a30c341

```
22   def require_authenticated_permission(permission):
23
24       def decorator(cls):
 .           ...
43       return decorator
```

The inner decorator raises an exception if it's not been applied to a subclass of View, as shown in Example 20.52.

**Example 20.52:** Project Code
user/decorators.py in 627a30c341

```
22   def require_authenticated_permission(permission):
23
24       def decorator(cls):
25           if (not isinstance(cls, type)
26                   or not issubclass(cls, View)):
27               raise ImproperlyConfigured(
28                   "require_authenticated_permission"
29                   " must be applied to subclasses "
30                   "of View class.")
```

In Example 20.53, we then combine Django's existing decorators to get the desired behavior we want, applying the new decorators to dispatch() and replacing the original method on the class. We then return the class, as expected of our decorator.

**Example 20.53:** Project Code
user/decorators.py in 627a30c341

```
22   def require_authenticated_permission(permission):
23
24       def decorator(cls):
 .           ...
31           check_auth = (
32               method_decorator(login_required))
33           check_perm = (
34               method_decorator(
35                   permission_required(
36                       permission,
37                       raise_exception=True)))
```

```
38
39              cls.dispatch = (
40                  check_auth(check_perm(cls.dispatch)))
41          return cls
```

In Example 20.54, we remove our dispatch() override from TagCreate and switch
to using our new decorator to ensure that only authenticated users with the organizer.
add_tag permission ever use the webpage.

**Example 20.54: Project Code**
organizer/views.py **in** 627a30c341

```
85   @require_authenticated_permission(
86       'organizer.add_tag')
87   class TagCreate(CreateView):
88       form_class = TagForm
89       model = Tag
```

With our new decorator, it becomes easy to protect all of the views that create, modify,
or delete objects. For instance, as shown in Example 20.55, we can start by replacing the
decorators on TagUpdate (as it only checks for whether a user is authenticated, not for
permission).

**Example 20.55: Project Code**
organizer/views.py **in** 8fea49bb90

```
121   @require_authenticated_permission(
122       'organizer.change_tag')
123   class TagUpdate(UpdateView):
124       form_class = TagForm
125       model = Tag
```

It takes only two lines to protect our StartupUpdate view, as shown in
Example 20.56.

**Example 20.56: Project Code**
organizer/views.py **in** 8fea49bb90

```
90   @require_authenticated_permission(
91       'organizer.change_startup')
92   class StartupUpdate(UpdateView):
93       form_class = StartupForm
94       model = Startup
```

We can import the decorator from our **user** app into our **blog** views.py file to protect
the views here as well. PostCreate and its new decorator are shown in Example 20.57.

**Example 20.57: Project Code**
`blog/views.py` in dd45d1ed9e

```
 7   from user.decorators import \
 8       require_authenticated_permission
 .       ...
27   @require_authenticated_permission(
28       'blog.add_post')
29   class PostCreate(CreateView):
30       form_class = PostForm
31       model = Post
```

I'll stop there. The code to protect our views is short, simple, and available online, but seeing each and every application would be tedious.

## 20.4.2 Future Posts Mixin

We've limited the use of permissions to a Boolean that determines whether a user can or cannot see and use a webpage. While this is the simplest way to use permissions, remember that Django provides the ability to use permissions on single objects. We won't use the permissions for individual objects, but we can use a permission to create a separate class of object.

Earlier in the chapter, we created the `view_future_post` permission with the intent that it would limit the display of `Post` objects with `pub_date` fields set to future dates. We want to make it so that only users with the permission can see unpublished `Post` objects. This means not only limiting specific `Post` detail webpages but also changing which `Post` objects are displayed in `PostList`.

If we were writing our own CBVs, we would want to check the permission on the user and then filter the queryset as appropriate. However, we're using GCBVs for all of our `Post` views. We've seen GCBV's `allow_future` attribute. GCBVs usually supply both an attribute and a method for behavior, and so it shouldn't surprise you that there is also a `get_allow_future()` method. We can directly integrate the `view_future_post` permission in the `get_allow_future()` method via the `AllowFuturePermissionMixin` class mixin, as shown in Example 20.58.

**Example 20.58: Project Code**
`blog/utils.py` in 0f8aad165a

```
 7   class AllowFuturePermissionMixin():
 8
 9       def get_allow_future(self):
10           return self.request.user.has_perm(
11               'blog.view_future_post')
```

Any GCBV with this method will use the method to change the queryset for us. We can thus integrate the method in `PostDelete`, `PostDetail`, and `PostUpdate` by adding the mixin to the inheritance of the `DateObjectMixin` as shown in Example 20.59.

**Example 20.59: Project Code**

`blog/utils.py` **in** `0f8aad165a`

```
47    class DateObjectMixin(
48            AllowFuturePermissionMixin,
49            YearMixin, MonthMixin, DateMixin):
```

We therefore delete the `allow_future` attribute from `PostDelete`, `PostDetail`, and `PostUpdate`.

We also need to inherit `AllowFuturePermissionMixin` in `PostArchiveMonth`, `PostArchiveYear`, and `PostList`, removing `allow_future` wherever it has been defined. `PostList` is printed in Example 20.60.

**Example 20.60: Project Code**

`blog/views.py` **in** `0f8aad165a`

```
52    class PostList(
53            AllowFuturePermissionMixin,
54            ArchiveIndexView):
55        allow_empty = True
56        context_object_name = 'post_list'
57        date_field = 'pub_date'
58        make_object_list = True
59        model = Post
60        paginate_by = 5
61        template_name = 'blog/post_list.html'
```

Our use of permissions is still Boolean: a user can or cannot behave a certain way. However, instead of applying the permission to an entire model, we've limited it to a subset of model instances.

## 20.5   Conditionally Displaying Template Links

While our webpages are now fully protected, many of our templates still link to these protected views. We will be displaying links to views that unauthenticated users cannot reach, which is misleading.

Thankfully, as shown in Example 20.61, we can check permissions in the template thanks to the `perms` variable, added in by context processor (therefore requiring `RequestContext`).

**Example 20.61: Python Code**

```
{% if perms.organizer.add_tag %}
{% if perms.organizer.change_tag %}
{% if perms.organizer.delete_tag %}
```

Much as we did with the CSS conditional checks we created in Chapter 16: Serving Static Content with Django, we can use basic logic to change how our webpages are displayed thanks to permissions, as shown in Example 20.62.

**Example 20.62: Project Code**
`organizer/templates/organizer/tag_detail.html` in `cc3b638cdb`

```
9    {% if perms.organizer.change_tag or perms.organizer.delete_tag %}
```

The permissions better allow us to take control of our templates. When we left our templates in Chapter 16, we were no longer displaying the link to `NewsLinkCreate`. This is because our condition to display the entire section was limited to the existence of related objects, as reprinted in Example 20.63.

**Example 20.63: Project Code**
`organizer/templates/organizer/startup_detail.html` in `2eee3d5cd6`

```
44    {% if startup.newslink_set.all
.        or startup.blog_posts.all %}
```

With our permissions, we can add a condition to check wether the user has access to the `NewsLinkCreate` webpage, displaying the section with a link to the webpage in the event they have the permission, as shown in Example 20.64.

**Example 20.64: Project Code**
`organizer/templates/organizer/startup_detail.html` in `cc3b638cdb`

```
50    {% if startup.newslink_set.all
.        or startup.blog_posts.all
.        or perms.organizer.add_newslink %}
```

We will skip the display of the rest of this conditional logic, because the application is simple but very tedious.

# 20.6 Displaying Future Posts in the Template

When we created the `AllowFuturePermissionMixin` class, we successfully limited the `Post` views to only display future blog posts to users with the `blog.view_future_post` permission. However, we have `Post` objects listed in the `tag_detail.html` and `startup_detail.html` templates, and these are not using the permission system.

In the template, we therefore create a condition to check whether the user has the permission and the display either all of the posts or all of the published posts. By design, the template system cannot pass arguments to methods. We therefore cannot create a queryset for published posts in the template, and nor would we want to, given the philosophy of "fat models, thin templates." To that end, we need a new `published_posts()` method that takes no arguments (apart from `self`) and returns the right queryset. Example 20.65 presents the implementation on `Tag` (virtually identical to the one on `Startup`).

**Example 20.65: Project Code**
`organizer/models.py` **in** 790403c3ab

```
1    from datetime import date
2
3    from django.core.urlresolvers import reverse
4    from django.db import models
5
.        ...
11   class Tag(models.Model):
.        ...
37       def published_posts(self):
38           return self.blog_posts.filter(
39               pub_date__lt=date.today())
```

We therefore start by creating a new condition to check the permission in `tag_detail.html`, as shown in Example 20.66.

**Example 20.66: Project Code**
`organizer/templates/organizer/tag_detail.html` **in** 790403c3ab

```
44   {% if perms.blog.view_future_post %}
.        ...
60   {% else %}
.        ...
76   {% endif %}
```

If we're printing all of the `Post` objects related to our `Tag`, we simply use the code that already existed in our template (created originally in Chapter 4). The new code to only print published `Post` objects related to the tag is shown in Example 20.67.

**Example 20.67: Project Code**
`organizer/templates/organizer/tag_detail.html` **in** 790403c3ab

```
61       {% if tag.published_posts|length > 0 %}
62         <section>
63           <h3>Blog Post{{ tag.published_posts|pluralize }}</h3>
64           <ul>
65             {% for post in tag.published_posts %}
66               <li><a href="{{ post.get_absolute_url }}">
67                 {{ post.title|title }}
68               </a></li>
69             {% endfor %}
70           </ul>
71         </section>
72       {% endif %}
```

In Chapter 4, we created a check to display a short sentence to the user in the event the
`Tag` was not related to any content. Our permission condition necessitates that this check
exists twice: once for when we are checking all of the blog posts and once for when we are
checking the published blog posts, as shown in Example 20.68.

**Example 20.68: Project Code**
`organizer/templates/organizer/tag_detail.html` **in** 790403c3ab

```
57        {% if not tag.startup_set.all and not tag.blog_posts.all %}
58           <p>This tag is not related to any content.</p>
   .         ...
73        {% if not tag.startup_set.all and not tag.published_posts %}
74           <p>This tag is not related to any content.</p>
75        {% endif %}
```

We now turn to the `startup_detail.html` template. At first glace, the work seems to
be quite a bit more complicated. However, we can take advantage of the fact that the and
Boolean operator takes high precedence over the or Boolean operator. For every instance
of `startup.blog_posts.all` in a condition, we can start by transforming that into
`perms.blog.view_future_post` and `startup.blog_posts.all`. We then want to
use the or operator with `startup.published_posts|length > 0`. This will
effectively check for whether there are any posts if the user has the right permission or else
check the number of objects returned by `published_posts()` before displaying a section.

With these new conditions in place (throughout the template), we can actually print
related published `Post` objects by adding the code in Example 20.69.

**Example 20.69: Project Code**
`organizer/templates/organizer/startup_detail.html` **in** 790403c3ab

```
114       {% if perms.blog.view_future_post
   .         and startup.blog_posts.all %}
124       {% elif startup.published_posts|length > 0 %}
125          <h3>Blog Post{{ startup.published_posts|pluralize }}</h3>
126          <ul>
127            {% for post in startup.published_posts %}
128             <li>
129              <a href="{{ post.get_absolute_url }}">
130                 {{ post.title|title }}</a>
131             </li>
132            {% endfor %}
133          </ul>
134       {% endif %}
```

Lines 115 to 123 comprise the code we added originally in Chapter 4. I recommend
looking at the full set of changes: https://dju.link/790403c3ab.

## 20.7   Putting It All Together

In this chapter, we saw how to use the `Permission` and `Group` models to build a basic class-level (as opposed to object-level) security system. We used the permissions to control access to our views and to modify what was displayed in our templates.

The `User`, `Permission`, and `Group` models are all related, thanks to many-to-many relations, which allows us to check for individual permissions on a `User` via the `has_perm()` method. These permissions are identified by strings such as `blog.add_post` and are actually instances of `Permission`, stored in the database. While Django generates add, change, and delete permissions for every model, we can also create our own, typically by defining the `permissions` attribute in the nested `Meta` class on a model.

In the template, context processors defined by the **auth** app add the `perms` variable, which allows us to use attributes to check for individual permissions, such as `perms.blog.view_future_post`. This also allowed us to change the output of our templates, limiting the links to protected views.

To protect views, we saw that **auth** supplies a number of decorators. Based on the `@user_passes_test()`, the `@login_required` and `@permission_required()` decorators allow for function views to be protected appropriately. We saw that, ideally, we wanted to use both decorators: the first to ask users to log in, and the second to verify whether the authenticated user had permission to interact with the page (thanks to the `raise_exception` parameter). In tandem with `@method_decorator()`, we used these decorators to create our own decorators to be applied directly to CBVs.

Using authentication to control behavior according to permissions is an integral part of security, and now that our website controls what is and what isn't available, we are several very large steps closer to having a real website.

# Extending Authentication

## In This Chapter

- Allow users to change and reset their passwords
- Create views to allow visitors to create and disable accounts
- See how Django builds cryptographic tokens to protect users during the password reset system
- Use Django's cryptographic tokens to create a view to activate new user accounts

## 21.1 Introduction

Having a login and logout page, as well as webpages with permissions enforced, doesn't mean a lot if we don't have users and controls for users.

In this chapter, we finish using Django's basic authentication features by extending the functionality of the **auth** app. We create webpages for visitors to sign up as new users and for users to disable their accounts if they no longer wish to have an account. We add templates to allow users to change their passwords as well as templates to allow users to reset forgotten passwords. The goal, overall, is to allow users to control their accounts on our site.

## 21.2 auth App Anatomy: Password Views

Much as it does for `login()` and `logout()`, Django supplies all of the views necessary for interacting with passwords. All we need to do is add these views to our URL patterns and create the templates these views will use by default.

Django's views for changing passwords, as well as the templates, are as follows:

- `password_change()`
  - `registration/password_change_form.html`
- `password_change_done()`
  - `registration/password_change_done.html`

The `password_change()` is the view that displays the `PasswordChangeForm`, allowing users to change their passwords. The `password_change_done()` displays a success message when a user does so.

Resetting passwords follows the same pattern but is a little more involved. To reset a password, we want to make sure the user is who he or she claims to be, so we email a link to a password reset page to the email we have in the database for that user. This means we need a webpage to allow users to request this email as well as a webpage to reset the password. In both cases, the **auth** app supplies success webpages.

The four views are

- `password_reset()`
- `password_reset_done()`
- `password_reset_confirm()`
- `password_reset_complete()`

The `password_reset()` view prompts the user for his or her email address, sends the user an email, and then redirects to `password_reset_done()`. The email provides a link to `password_reset_confirm()`. To help ensure that malicious or unauthorized users cannot reset other users' passwords, the `password_reset_confirm()` checks for a token in the URL path. If the token is correct, it displays a form for the user to reset his or her password. If the token is incorrect, the view displays an error. In the first case, after the user resets the password, `password_reset_confirm()` redirects to `password_reset_complete()`.

The password reset views require quite a few templates. The `password_reset()` expects a template to display to the user as well as two templates for the email it will send to the user: one for the email's subject and one for the email's content:

- `password_reset()`
  - `registration/password_reset_form.html`
  - `registration/password_reset_email.html`
  - `registration/password_reset_subject.txt`

The rest of the password reset templates expect a single template each:

- `password_reset_done()`
  - `registration/password_reset_done.html`
- `password_reset_confirm()`
  - `registration/password_reset_confirm.html`
- `password_reset_complete()`
  - `registration/password_reset_complete.html`

In all, these views will be using three forms provided by the **auth** app:

- `PasswordResetForm` (used by `password_reset()` view)
- `SetPasswordForm` (used by `password_reset_confirm()` view)
- `PasswordChangeForm` (used by `password_change()` view)

These are not the only forms we will be interacting with. While Django does not supply any views for creating and disabling user accounts, the **auth** app provides two forms:

- `UserCreationForm`
- `UserChangeForm`

There is also the `AdminPasswordChangeForm`, but that is reserved for the **admin** app. In this chapter, we only need to use the `UserCreationForm` to build the webpages we want.

## 21.3    Changing Passwords

The goal of this section is to use the following views in our URL configuration:

- `password_change()`
- `password_change_done()`

To that end, we also build the following two templates.

- `user/password_change_form.html`
- `user/password_change_done.html`

To begin, in Example 21.1, we create a separate URL configuration in the `user/urls.py`. Given that all of our password URLs start with `/password/`, this step will keep our URLs DRY.

**Example 21.1: Project Code**
`user/urls.py` in `c1d1ef5767`

```
1    from django.conf.urls import include, url
.        ...
24   urlpatterns = [
.        ...
39       url(r'^password/', include(password_urls)),
40   ]
```

The new `password_urls` URL configuration is simply a list above the **user** URL configuration, as shown in Example 21.2.

**Example 21.2: Project Code**
user/urls.py **in** c1d1ef5767

```
 9  password_urls = [
 .      ...
22  ]
```

In Example 21.3, in the new URL configuration, we start by adding password_
change(). We need to override the path to the template, as the registration
namespace will conflict with the registration namespace defined by the **admin** app.
We therefore pass the template_name key in the URL dictionary to the function view.
We also need to tell the view where password_change_done() view is located, passing it
the name of the URL pattern we will build for it. Note that because our **user** URL
configuration is namespaced, so are our password_urls URL patterns, as they are a child
configuration of the **user** URL configuration, and therefore must be preceded by the same
dj-auth namespace.

**Example 21.3: Project Code**
user/urls.py **in** c1d1ef5767

```
 6  from django.core.urlresolvers import reverse_lazy
 .      ...
 9  password_urls = [
10      url(r'^change/$',
11          auth_views.password_change,
12          {'template_name':
13              'user/password_change_form.html',
14           'post_change_redirect': reverse_lazy(
15              'dj-auth:pw_change_done')},
16          name='pw_change'),
 .      ...
22  ]
```

The password_change_done() view URL pattern is even simpler, and we only need
to pass the template_name keyword argument to the view, as shown in Example 21.4.

**Example 21.4: Project Code**
user/urls.py **in** c1d1ef5767

```
17      url(r'^change/done/$',
18          auth_views.password_change_done,
19          {'template_name':
20              'user/password_change_done.html'},
21          name='pw_change_done'),
```

With our views both in place, we need to build the actual templates they will use.
The confirmation page is easiest, as shown in Example 21.5.

**Example 21.5: Project Code**

user/templates/user/password_change_done.html in c1d1ef5767

```
1   {% extends parent_template|default:"user/base_user.html" %}
2
3   {% block title %}
4   {{ block.super }} - Change Password
5   {% endblock %}
6
7   {% block content %}
8     <div class="row">
9       <div class="offset-by-two eight columns">
10        <p>Password successfully changed.</p>
11      </div>
12    </div>
13  {% endblock %}
```

The password_change_form.html is much like our other forms. We start with the general outline of our template, as shown in Example 21.6.

**Example 21.6: Project Code**

user/templates/user/password_change_form.html in c1d1ef5767

```
1   {% extends parent_template|default:"user/base_user.html" %}
2
3   {% block title %}
4   {{ block.super }} - Change Password
5   {% endblock %}
6
7   {% block content %}
8     <div class="row">
9       <div class="offset-by-two eight columns">
.         ...
18      </div>
19    </div>
20  {% endblock %}
```

We then build the form itself, remembering the cross-site request forgery (CSRF) token, the action, the method, and the submission button, as shown in Example 21.7.

**Example 21.7: Project Code**

user/templates/user/password_change_form.html in c1d1ef5767

```
10        <form
11            action="{% url 'dj-auth:pw_change' %}"
12            method="post">
13          {% csrf_token %}
14          {{ form.as_p }}
```

```
15              <button type="submit">
16                  Change Password</button>
17          </form>
```

Users will now be able to change their password! We'll add links to these pages soon.

## 21.4   Resetting Passwords

The process for resetting passwords is the same as for changing passwords, but it is a little more involved. We have four views:

- `password_reset()`
- `password_reset_done()`
- `password_reset_confirm()`
- `password_reset_complete()`

For these views, we will build six templates.

- `user/password_reset_form.html`
- `user/password_reset_email.html`
- `user/password_reset_subject.txt`
- `user/password_reset_done.html`
- `user/password_reset_confirm.html`
- `user/password_reset_complete.html`

Before we jump into the code, let's talk about `password_reset_confirm()`. The goal of the view is to allow users to reset their password. This is a potential security vulnerability: we need to make sure the user is who he or she claims to be, lest we let a malicious user reset the password of a legitimate user. To mitigate this possibility, the `password_reset()` view creates a very specific link to the `password_reset_done()`, telling the view which user this password reset is for and providing a unique identifier so that `password_reset_done()` can verify the link was created by our website. The `password_reset_done()` view expects the URL pattern to pass it two keyword arguments named `uidb64` and `token`.

The `uidb64` is simply the primary key of the user in base64 (User ID Base 64), allowing the view to know which user it is resetting a password for. The `token` is much more complicated, as it is what proves to the view that it is allowed to change the password. A valid token might look like this: `405-6241343f9abe37f8c58b`

To begin, we want to make sure that any link created by `password_reset()` is valid only for a certain period of time. We don't want these links to be valid forever—a malicious user might get his or her hands on an old link (for example, in the history of a browser) and then be able to change the user's password at will. The first part of the token (the `405` before the hyphen in the preceding example) is therefore a representation of the date: it tells the view when the link was created by listing the number of days since 2001-1-1 in base 36.

The second part of the token is a cryptographic hash. It is created by hashing the values of fields from the User instance and the current timestamp. Specifically, it uses the primary key, the password, and the date from the last time the user logged in. By using the internal state of the User instance, Django ensures that this token is invalid the moment the user changes his or her password. The base-36 number of days is protection for old, unused links. To make it difficult for an attacker to guess any of these fields, the data is hashed using SHA1 (a secure hash algorithm) with two salts. The first is simply a string that is the same on every Django project (seen in django/contrib/auth/tokens.py). The second (used in django/utils/crypto.py) is the SECRET_KEY value of the website (found in suorganizer/settings.py in our case). To shorten the SHA1 hash from 40 characters to 20 (as in our example—the characters after the hyphen), Django picks every other character of the hash.

The net effect is that

- We can trust that malicious attackers will have a *very* difficult time resetting the password of another user.
- Our URL pattern for password_reset_done() needs a regular expression group for uidb64 and one for token.
- The email sent by password_reset() must provide the uidb64 and token values in a link for the user.

As the uidb64 is merely a base-36 number, the regular expression pattern is

```
(?P<uidb64>[0-9A-Za-z_\-]+)
```

You might consider using \w to replace the pattern match above. However, it is less precise, as \w includes all roman Unicode characters (including, for instance, accented characters).

In django/contrib/auth/urls.py, we can see how Django builds the token regular expression group for its own URL configuration:

```
(?P<token>[0-9A-Za-z]{1,13}-[0-9A-Za-z]{1,20})
```

This is a *very* forward-looking and flexible URL pattern. The hyphen splits the date and the hash. In our hash example, the date was three digits, but the URL pattern allows for 13 digits. The number of days since January 1, 2001, in base 36 will be three digits until the year 2121, and we could easily limit the length of that pattern to three and be confident of our choice for the next 100 years. Django sticks with 13 because that is the number of digits needed to represent any 64-bit integer in base 36. In fact, the limit is placed not only on the URL pattern but also on the actual function to convert base-36 numbers to base-10 integers.

What's more, we could also limit the hash to exactly 20 characters because a SHA1 hash is always 40 characters, and Django always takes every other character from the hash.

Even though we could theoretically change the regular expression groups to be more precise, I opt to use Django's (I can't help but wonder if they know something I don't).

Now that we are clear on what `uidb64` and `token` are, we can create our URL patterns. The URL pattern for `password_reset()`, named `pw_reset_start`, passed quite a few arguments to the function view via the URL dictionary, as shown in Example 21.8.

**Example 21.8:** Project Code

`user/urls.py` **in** d364bb5761

```
22        url(r'^reset/$',
23            auth_views.password_reset,
24            {'template_name':
25                'user/password_reset_form.html',
26             'email_template_name':
27                'user/password_reset_email.txt',
28             'subject_template_name':
29                'user/password_reset_subject.txt',
30             'post_reset_redirect': reverse_lazy(
31                'dj-auth:pw_reset_sent')},
32            name='pw_reset_start'),
```

These come as no real surprise. We knew we had to provide three templates and that we had to provide the URL to the `password_reset_done()` view. We can create the `pw_reset_sent` URL pattern for this view in Example 21.9.

**Example 21.9:** Project Code

`user/urls.py` **in** d364bb5761

```
33        url(r'^reset/sent/$',
34            auth_views.password_reset_done,
35            {'template_name':
36                'user/password_reset_sent.html'},
37            name='pw_reset_sent'),
```

This leads us to the `password_reset_confirm()` view. In Example 21.10, we create a regular expression pattern with `uidb64` and `token`, passing the view the new template as well as the URL path to the `password_reset_complete()` view.

**Example 21.10:** Project Code

`user/urls.py` **in** d364bb5761

```
38        url(r'^reset/'
39            r'(?P<uidb64>[0-9A-Za-z_\-]+)/'
40            r'(?P<token>[0-9A-Za-z]{1,13}'
41            r'-[0-9A-Za-z]{1,20})/$',
42            auth_views.password_reset_confirm,
43            {'template_name':
44                'user/password_reset_confirm.html',
45             'post_reset_redirect': reverse_lazy(
46                'dj-auth:pw_reset_complete')},
47            name='pw_reset_confirm'),
```

Finally, in Example 21.11, we create the pw_reset_complete URL pattern for the password_reset_complete() view. I opt not only to pass a new template_name but also to add the AuthenticationForm to the template context. This form allows us to tell users their password has been changed and to immediately allow them to log in.

**Example 21.11: Project Code**
user/urls.py in d364bb5761

```
48      url(r'reset/done/$',
49          auth_views.password_reset_complete,
50          {'template_name':
51              'user/password_reset_complete.html',
52           'extra_context':
53              {'form': AuthenticationForm}},
54          name='pw_reset_complete'),
```

Now we are left with our templates:

- user/password_reset_form.html
- user/password_reset_email.html
- user/password_reset_subject.txt
- user/password_reset_done.html
- user/password_reset_confirm.html
- user/password_reset_complete.html

As with any form template, we start with the outline of the template, as shown in Example 21.12.

**Example 21.12: Project Code**
user/templates/user/password_reset_form.html in d364bb5761

```
 1    {% extends parent_template|default:"user/base_user.html" %}
 2
 3    {% block title %}
 4    {{ block.super }} - Reset Password
 5    {% endblock %}
 6
 7    {% block content %}
 .        ...
22    {% endblock %}
```

We then turn our attention to the form itself, wrapping it in the appropriate div tags, as shown in Example 21.13. Don't forget the action, method, CSRF token, and the submission button.

**Example 21.13: Project Code**
user/templates/user/password_reset_form.html **in** d364bb5761

```
 8    <div class="row">
 9      <div class="offset-by-two eight columns">
10        <div class="center">
11          <p>Reset your password by email.</p>
12        </div>
13        <form
14            action="{% url 'dj-auth:pw_reset_start' %}"
15            method="post">
16          {% csrf_token %}
17          {{ form.as_p }}
18          <button type="submit">
19            Send Me Reset Instructions</button>
20        </form>
21    </div></div>
```

The password_reset() view uses the form above to send an email to a user. To do so, the view renders two templates as an email: the first is the subject of the email, and the second is the body of the email. The subject is easiest, as you can see in Example 21.14.

**Example 21.14: Project Code**
user/templates/user/password_reset_subject.txt **in** d364bb5761

```
 1    {{ site_name }} Password Reset
```

The content is a little trickier, because we don't know what's in the context. With a little poking around django/contrib/auth/views.py, you would discover that the view adds not only the User instance for the supposed person asking for a reset but also the name of our site, which protocol the site uses by default (http or https), and our domain name. This information is all for the purpose of building a full link to our website for the password_reset_confirm() view, done on line 9 in Example 21.15.

**Example 21.15: Project Code**
user/templates/user/password_reset_email.txt **in** d364bb5761

```
 1    Hello from {{ site_name }}!
 2
 3    We've received a request to reset {{ user.get_username }}'s password.
 4
 5    If you did not request a password reset, please ignore this message.
 6
 7    To reset your password, please navigate to:
 8
 9    {{ protocol }}://{{ domain }}{% url 'dj-auth:pw_reset_confirm' uid
 .        token %}
```

We then build the template to inform users that we've sent them an email, as shown in Example 21.16.

**Example 21.16:** Project Code
user/templates/user/password_reset_sent.html **in** d364bb5761

```
1    {% extends parent_template|default:"user/base_user.html" %}
2
3    {% block title %}
4    {{ block.super }} - Password Reset Sent
5    {% endblock %}
6
7    {% block content %}
8      <div class="row">
9        <div class="offset-by-two eight columns">
10         <p>Password reset email sent!</p>
11         <p>Please check your inbox and spam box.</p>
12       </div>
13     </div>
14   {% endblock %}
```

This brings us to the template for password_reset_confirm(). If the uidb36 and token are valid, then we need to provide the SetPasswordForm for users to change their password. If the uidb36 and token are invalid, we present an error and prompt the user to request another link to the page (this time with a still-valid token).

We start with an outline of the template, as shown in Example 21.17.

**Example 21.17:** Project Code
user/templates/user/password_reset_confirm.html **in** d364bb5761

```
1    {% extends parent_template|default:"user/base_user.html" %}
2
3    {% block title %}
4    {{ block.super }} - Reset Password
5    {% endblock %}
6
7    {% block content %}
.      ...
29   {% endblock %}
```

In Example 21.18, we fill in the edges of the content block with HTML div tags for style.

**Example 21.18:** Project Code
user/templates/user/password_reset_confirm.html **in** d364bb5761

```
8      <div class="row">
9        <div class="offset-by-two eight columns">
.        ...
28     </div></div>
```

We can then use the `validlink` variable to check whether the `uidb36` and `token` passed to the view are valid, as shown in Example 21.19.

**Example 21.19: Project Code**

user/templates/user/password_reset_confirm.html **in** d364bb5761

```
10          {% if validlink %}
 .          ...
22          {% else %}
 .          ...
27          {% endif %}
```

If the link is valid, we display the `SetPasswordForm` form, as shown in Example 21.20. (Take a look at the form `action` for a different technique from our usual templates. This only works if the `password_reset_confirm()` is rendering the template.)

**Example 21.20: Project Code**

user/templates/user/password_reset_confirm.html **in** d364bb5761

```
11          <p>Enter a new password below.</p>
12          <form
13            action="{{ request.path }}"
14            method="post">
15          {% csrf_token %}
16          {{ form.as_p }}
17          <button
18            class="button-primary"
19            type="submit">
20          Save New Password</button>
21          </form>
```

If the link is invalid, we inform the user, and provide a link to `password_reset()`, as shown in Example 21.21.

**Example 21.21: Project Code**

user/templates/user/password_reset_confirm.html **in** d364bb5761

```
23          <p>This reset link is no longer valid.</p>
24          <p>Please request a new reset email
25            <a href="{% url 'dj-auth:pw_reset_start' %}">
26              here</a>.</p>
```

Finally, once the user submits the form in `password_reset_confirm.html`, the `password_reset_confirm()` view redirects the user to `password_reset_complete()`, which renders the `password_reset_complete.html` template, as shown in Example 21.22.

**Example 21.22: Project Code**
`user/templates/user/password_reset_complete.html` **in** d364bb5761

```
 1  {% extends parent_template|default:"user/base_user.html" %}
 2
 3  {% block title %}
 4  {{ block.super }} - Password Reset Successful
 5  {% endblock %}
 6
 7  {% block content %}
 8    <div class="row">
 9      <div class="offset-by-two eight columns">
10        <p>Your password has been reset.</p>
11        <p>Log in below using your new password.</p>
12        {% include "user/login_form.html" %}
13      </div>
14    </div>
15  {% endblock %}
```

To make this feature immediately accessible, I add the link to the `login.html` page, as shown in Example 21.23. I could very well add it to the `logout.html` page as well, given that it also displays a login form.

**Example 21.23: Project Code**
`user/templates/user/login.html` **in** d364bb5761

```
12      <div class="three columns">
13        <ul class="task-list">
14          <li><a href="{% url 'dj-auth:pw_reset_start' %}">
15            Forgotten password?</a></li>
16        </ul>
17      </div>
```

# 21.5  Disabling Accounts

Before we create new user accounts, we first see how to disable user accounts.

When building a website, the ideal in usability is to first disable a user account and then delete the account some time later. Disabling an account means ensuring the user may no longer log in. Out of the box, Django immediately supports both disabling and deleting user accounts. Deleting an account is so straightforward and simple (particularly in our case), that we look only at disabling an account.

Unlike what it does for password management, Django does not supply any views for us to rely on when it comes to disabling a user account, so we must build our own view (Example 21.24). The idea is to build a page that disables the account of the currently authenticated user and to log out the user in the process.

**Example 21.24: Project Code**

`user/views.py` in 7d14beca7a

```
 1  from django.conf import settings
 .     ...
12  from django.views.generic import View
 .     ...
15  class DisableAccount(View):
16      success_url = settings.LOGIN_REDIRECT_URL
17      template_name = (
18          'user/user_confirm_delete.html')
```

To properly build this view, we will need a number of tools, shown in Example 21.25.

**Example 21.25: Project Code**

`user/views.py` in 7d14beca7a

```
 2  from django.contrib.auth import get_user, logout
 3  from django.contrib.auth.decorators import \
 4      login_required
 5  from django.shortcuts import redirect
 6  from django.template.response import \
 7      TemplateResponse
 8  from django.utils.decorators import \
 9      method_decorator
10  from django.views.decorators.csrf import \
11      csrf_protect
```

The @login_required and @method_decorator() should be familiar after Chapter 20: Integrating Permissions. The logout() function is not the view but the function to destroy the current user's session (assuming the user is authenticated). The get_user() function takes an HttpRequest object and returns the User (or AnonymousUser) instance.

The @csrf_protect decorator is perhaps the most confusing part of the process. We already have CSRF tokens, added thanks to a context processor and middleware. Why do we need a CSRF decorator on top of these? At the moment, given the other tools, we don't. However, if the middleware or context processor are ever accidentally disabled, we *absolutely* want to ensure that our view still has the CSRF token. We are using the belt and braces approach: we probably don't need the decorator, but we will be very glad if it is here when something goes pear-shaped.

Finally, we have the TemplateResponse class, which is a replacement for the HttpResponse object. The difference is in mutability. Once the template is rendered and passed to the HttpResponse, the object is a set, static piece of data. This is in direct contrast to TemplateResponse, which will remain a mutable equivalent to HttpResponse with discrete data until it is transformed into an actual HTTP response. Truth be told, we probably don't need to use it in this instance, but as the majority of **auth**'s views use the TemplateResponse, it seemed as good a time as any to introduce the object.

## Django Documentation
https://dju.link/18/template-response

These tools allow us to write a very simple get() method, as shown in Example 21.26.

**Example 21.26:** Project Code
`user/views.py` in 7d14beca7a

```
15    class DisableAccount(View):
16        success_url = settings.LOGIN_REDIRECT_URL
17        template_name = (
18            'user/user_confirm_delete.html')
19
20        @method_decorator(csrf_protect)
21        @method_decorator(login_required)
22        def get(self, request):
23            return TemplateResponse(
24                request,
25                self.template_name)
```

Our post() method, shown in Example 21.27, is a little more complicated. We first grab the current User, which thanks to the @login_required we know cannot be an AnonymousUser. We disable the user, terminate the session to log the user out, and return our now-anonymous visitor to the front page of our website (currently defined as the list of blog posts in suorganizer/settings.py).

**Example 21.27:** Project Code
`user/views.py` in 7d14beca7a

```
15    class DisableAccount(View):
16        success_url = settings.LOGIN_REDIRECT_URL
17        template_name = (
18            'user/user_confirm_delete.html')
.         ...
27        @method_decorator(csrf_protect)
28        @method_decorator(login_required)
29        def post(self, request):
30            user = get_user(request)
31            user.set_unusable_password()
32            user.is_active = False
33            user.save()
34            logout(request)
35            return redirect(self.success_url)
```

The act of disabling the user occurs on lines 31 to 33. On line 31, we disable the password, and on the next line, we disable the account proper. We then save these changes on line 33. This code ensures twice over that they cannot log into our site.

We can now add a URL pattern for our new view, as shown in Example 21.28.

**Example 21.28: Project Code**
user/urls.py in 7d14beca7a

```
 9    from .views import DisableAccount
 .        ...
64        url(r'^disable/$',
65            DisableAccount.as_view(),
66            name='disable'),
```

Finally, we create the template for the view to display the confirmation to disable the account.

We start with the outline of the account, as shown in Example 21.29.

**Example 21.29: Project Code**
user/templates/user/user_confirm_delete.html in 7d14beca7a

```
 1    {% extends parent_template|default:"user/base_user.html" %}
 2
 3    {% block title %}
 4    {{ block.super }} - Disable Account
 5    {% endblock %}
 6
 7    {% block content %}
 8      <div class="row">
 9        <div class="offset-by-two eight columns">
 .          ...
19        </div>
20      </div>
21    {% endblock %}
```

Then, in Example 21.30, we create a basic form for the user to submit.

**Example 21.30: Project Code**
user/templates/user/user_confirm_delete.html in 7d14beca7a

```
10          <p>Disable your account?</p>
11          <p>This cannot be undone.</p>
12          <form
13              action="{% url 'dj-auth:disable' %}"
14              method="post">
15            {% csrf_token %}
16            <button type="submit">
17              Disable Account</button>
18          </form>
```

# 21.6 Creating Accounts

Creating a `User` account is easily the most difficult and complicated part of this chapter. When we create a new `User`, we want to check that the email address supplied by the user is valid. We therefore create a disabled `User` and send the user an email to confirm the existence of his or her email account. This email contains a link to an activation webpage, which when accessed enables the `User`. To make sure that this process works securely, we use a cryptographic hash in the URL pattern of the activation page.

If this process sounds familiar, it's because it is: we are effectively re-creating the password reset system but for the purpose of creating a new user. The key difference is that we need the ability to resend an activation link (because if the `token` expires, we can't re-create a `User` with the same email address). We therefore need webpages to

- Create an account
- Confirm creation of the account
- Activate the account
- Resend the activation email

We don't have an activation confirmation view, because we will instead use the **messages** app to display a message on the login page, which the activation page redirects to on success.

Given that we can use a `TemplateView` GCBV for the account-creation confirmation page, we need to create three views:

- `CreateAccount`
- `ActivateAccount`
- `ResendActivationEmail`

In the event the `CreateAccount` runs into problems, it will redirect not to the confirmation page but instead to `ResendActivationEmail`. Also, given that `ActivateAccount` will redirect to `login()` on success, we only need our template to show what happens if the activation link is invalid.

We need to build two forms for our views:

- `UserCreationForm`
- `ResendActivationEmailForm`

Thanks to Django's own `UserCreationForm`, the first form will be easier than if we had to build it from scratch.

Both of our forms share behavior, because both `CreateAccount` and `ResendActivationEmail` share behavior. In both, we need to send an email. To make our code DRY (and our lives simpler), we start by building a form mixin to send emails. For our forms, we therefore build the `ActivationMailFormMixin`. To make interacting with the form as simple as possible, we also build the `MailContextViewMixin`, which does some of the work of interacting with the form in `CreateAccount` and `ResendActivationEmail` views.

### 21.6.1   Mixins for Sending and Logging Emails

The goal of our `ActivationMailFormMixin` is to send an account activation email to a new user. To that end, we must provide the string for an error in the form in the event the email is not sent. In Example 21.31, we create a `mail_validation_error` attribute for subclasses of the mixin to override, allowing developers to specify the output of the error in their own class.

**Example 21.31: Project Code**
user/utils.py **in** 0cbcf42d4f

```
23   class ActivationMailFormMixin:
24       mail_validation_error = ''
```

While we use parts of the form's validation system to inform Django whether email was sent or not, we also want to be able to check this on the go. We therefore create a `mail_sent` property on the class, as shown in Example 21.32.

**Example 21.32: Project Code**
user/utils.py **in** 0cbcf42d4f

```
23   class ActivationMailFormMixin:
 .       ...
52       @property
53       def mail_sent(self):
54           if hasattr(self, '_mail_sent'):
55               return self._mail_sent
56           return False
```

We also create a `setter` for the property, disabling developers from overriding the `mail_sent` attribute, as shown in Example 21.33.

**Example 21.33: Project Code**
user/utils.py **in** 0cbcf42d4f

```
23   class ActivationMailFormMixin:
 .       ...
58       @mail_sent.setter
59       def set_mail_sent(self, value):
60           raise TypeError(
61               'Cannot set mail_sent attribute.')
```

Much like with `password_reset()`, our view will render two templates to create an email. We can render the message from these templates in our `get_message()` method using `render_to_string()`, as shown in Example 21.34.

**Example 21.34:** Project Code

user/utils.py **in** 0cbcf42d4f

```
14    from django.template.loader import \
15        render_to_string
 .        ...
23    class ActivationMailFormMixin:
 .        ...
63        def get_message(self, **kwargs):
64            email_template_name = kwargs.get(
65                'email_template_name')
66            context = kwargs.get('context')
67            return render_to_string(
68                email_template_name, context)
```

In Example 21.35, we use the same technique in get_subject() to render the subject. We ensure that the subject is a single line long to avoid the BadHeader exception.

**Example 21.35:** Project Code

user/utils.py **in** 0cbcf42d4f

```
23    class ActivationMailFormMixin:
 .        ...
70        def get_subject(self, **kwargs):
71            subject_template_name = kwargs.get(
72                'subject_template_name')
73            context = kwargs.get('context')
74            subject = render_to_string(
75                subject_template_name, context)
76            # subject *must not* contain newlines
77            subject = ''.join(subject.splitlines())
78            return subject
```

In both get_message() and get_subject(), we are rendering templates with a context that is passed to the methods. In get_context_data(), we actually build that context. We begin in Example 21.36 by allowing the method to accept a context argument (useful if we wish to override the method in a subclass). If the parameter is not set, we create our own dictionary.

**Example 21.36:** Project Code

user/utils.py **in** 0cbcf42d4f

```
23    class ActivationMailFormMixin:
 .        ...
80        def get_context_data(
81                self, request, user, context=None):
82            if context is None:
83                context = dict()
```

Once we have a dictionary, we need to build the values necessary for the templates. We saw the values we needed for this in the `password_reset_email.txt` email. To build these values, we need a few extra tools, as shown in Example 21.37.

**Example 21.37: Project Code**
`user/utils.py` in `0cbcf42d4f`

```
 7   from django.contrib.auth.tokens import \
 8       default_token_generator as token_generator
 9   from django.contrib.sites.shortcuts import \
10       get_current_site
 .       ...
16   from django.utils.encoding import force_bytes
17   from django.utils.http import \
18       urlsafe_base64_encode
```

The `token_generator()` function is the tool Django uses to build the `token` hash seen in the password reset views. Cryptography is hard, and given how easily we can reuse Django's own crypto, it'd be silly not to take advantage of it here.

Much as we did with the regular expression pattern for the `pw_reset_confirm` URL pattern, we use not only `token` but also `uidb64`. To build the base-64 number, we need to pass the new user's primary key to `urlsafe_base64_encode()`. However, as the function expects `bytes` (as opposed to a `str` objects), we import the `force_bytes()` function to help us out.

Finally, when given an `HttpRequest` object, the `get_current_site()` function will tell us which `Site` object is being used on this site. Given that our Django project has only a single `Site` object (as we're only building a single website), this seems silly, but it makes the code much more robust in the long run.

With these new tools, we return to `get_context_data()` and create the values our email templates will need, as shown in Example 21.38.

**Example 21.38: Project Code**
`user/utils.py` in `0cbcf42d4f`

```
23   class ActivationMailFormMixin:
 .       ...
80       def get_context_data(
81           self, request, user, context=None):
 .           ...
84           current_site = get_current_site(request)
85           if request.is_secure():
86               protocol = 'https'
87           else:
88               protocol = 'http'
89           token = token_generator.make_token(user)
90           uid = urlsafe_base64_encode(
91               force_bytes(user.pk))
```

Finally, we add these values into the context variable by updating the dictionary (either the one we created or the one passed to the method), as shown in Example 21.39.

**Example 21.39: Project Code**
user/utils.py **in** 0cbcf42d4f

```
 23    class ActivationMailFormMixin:
  .         ...
 80        def get_context_data(
 81            self, request, user, context=None):
  .             ...
 92            context.update({
 93                'domain': current_site.domain,
 94                'protocol': protocol,
 95                'site_name': current_site.name,
 96                'token': token,
 97                'uid': uid,
 98                'user': user,
 99            })
100            return context
```

To tie it all together, we create two methods for sending email. The first, _send_mail() will actually send the email, while the send_mail() call will handle calls from views. Let's start with the first.

To begin, _send_mail() needs to build the context and render the email templates. We do all this in a dictionary, as shown in Example 21.40.

**Example 21.40: Project Code**
user/utils.py **in** 0cbcf42d4f

```
  6    from django.conf import settings
  .         ...
 23    class ActivationMailFormMixin:
  .         ...
102        def _send_mail(self, request, user, **kwargs):
103            kwargs['context'] = self.get_context_data(
104                request, user)
105            mail_kwargs = {
106                "subject": self.get_subject(**kwargs),
107                "message": self.get_message(**kwargs),
108                "from_email": (
109                    settings.DEFAULT_FROM_EMAIL),
110                "recipient_list": [user.email],
111            }
```

In a try...except block, we use Django's send_mail function to attempt to send the email, passing in the dictionary we just built, as shown in Example 21.41.

**Example 21.41: Project Code**
user/utils.py **in** 0cbcf42d4f

```
 12   from django.core.mail import (
 13       BadHeaderError, send_mail)
  .       ...
 23   class ActivationMailFormMixin:
  .       ...
102       def _send_mail(self, request, user, **kwargs):
  .           ...
112           try:
113               # number_sent will be 0 or 1
114               number_sent = send_mail(**mail_kwargs)
115           except Exception as error:
  .               ...
125           else:
```

We never want the current user to know if there's a problem, so we catch all of the exceptions this raises. We then use the log_mail_error() (which we will program shortly) to keep track of the problem. We return a tuple informing the send_mail() method that the email was not sent (False), and providing an error code to describe the problem, based on the kind of exception that might be raised, as shown in Example 21.42.

**Example 21.42: Project Code**
user/utils.py **in** 0cbcf42d4f

```
  4   from smtplib import SMTPException
  .       ...
 23   class ActivationMailFormMixin:
  .       ...
102       def _send_mail(self, request, user, **kwargs):
  .           ...
115           except Exception as error:
116               self.log_mail_error(
117                   error=error, **mail_kwargs)
118               if isinstance(error, BadHeaderError):
119                   err_code = 'badheader'
120               elif isinstance(error, SMTPException):
121                   err_code = 'smtperror'
122               else:
123                   err_code = 'unexpectederror'
124               return (False, err_code)
```

Given that we're returning a tuple pair here, it's best to always return a tuple pair throughout the rest of _send_mail(), even if there is no error.

In the event the email does send, we make sure that the number of emails that was sent is greater than zero, and then return a tuple pair where True signifies that the email was sent. Of course, there is still the (slim and unlikely) chance that we don't raise an exception and that we don't send an email. In this case, we again log the problem and return a tuple with False and an error code, as shown in Example 21.43.

**Example 21.43: Project Code**
user/utils.py **in** 0cbcf42d4f

```
 23    class ActivationMailFormMixin:
   .       ...
102        def _send_mail(self, request, user, **kwargs):
   .           ...
125            else:
126                if number_sent > 0:
127                    return (True, None)
128            self.log_mail_error(**mail_kwargs)
129            return (False, 'unknownerror')
```

Now, in Example 21.44, we build the send_mail() method, which is what developers will actually call to send an email. The main goal of the method is to call the _send_mail() method and to act on the result.

**Example 21.44: Project Code**
user/utils.py **in** 0cbcf42d4f

```
 23    class ActivationMailFormMixin:
   .       ...
131        def send_mail(self, user, **kwargs):
   .           ...
142        self._mail_sent, error = (
143            self._send_mail(
144                request, user, **kwargs))
```

To be able to call _send_mail(), we always need the HttpRequest object, so we ensure that the object is passed to us. If the method is not given an HttpRequest object, we need to tell the developer by logging the problem. This can be one of the most frustrating errors to get: being told that the call to the method doesn't include the right value is great, but it's completely unhelpful if you don't know how that call was made. This is particularly true of a mixin—we don't even know which form will be using this method. When we log the problem, we will therefore include the Python traceback, as shown in Example 21.45, which shows all of the calls that occurred before this one, allowing us to gather far more information about which part of our website isn't calling the method properly.

**Example 21.45: Project Code**
user/utils.py **in** 0cbcf42d4f

```
  2    import traceback
   .       ...
 11    from django.core.exceptions import ValidationError
   .       ...
 23    class ActivationMailFormMixin:
   .       ...
```

```
131        def send_mail(self, user, **kwargs):
132            request = kwargs.pop('request', None)
133            if request is None:
134                tb = traceback.format_stack()
135                tb = ['  ' + line for line in tb]
136                logger.warning(
137                    'send_mail called without '
138                    'request.\nTraceback:\n{}'.format(
139                        ''.join(tb)))
140                self._mail_sent = False
141                return self.mail_sent
142            self._mail_sent, error = (
143                self._send_mail(
144                    request, user, **kwargs))
```

However, if the `HttpRequest` is included, then we will successfully call `_send_mail()` on lines 142 to 144. We use the newly set `mail_sent` attribute to see if the email has been sent. If it hasn't been, we add an error to our form, allowing for display of errors as on any other form. The error displayed will be the `mail_validation_error` string attribute declared on line 24. In all cases, we return the `mail_sent` attribute, as shown in Example 21.46.

**Example 21.46: Project Code**
user/utils.py in 0cbcf42d4f

```
 23    class ActivationMailFormMixin:
 24        mail_validation_error = ''
  .        ...
131        def send_mail(self, user, **kwargs):
  .            ...
145            if not self.mail_sent:
146                self.add_error(
147                    None,  # no field - form error
148                    ValidationError(
149                        self.mail_validation_error,
150                        code=error))
151            return self.mail_sent
```

The core behavior of our mixin is done, but we still need to create the `log_mail_error()` method that logs most of the problems in our class. For all of these to work (including the log with the traceback), we need to import Python's logging system and declare the logger, which is defined in our site settings, as shown in Example 21.47.

**Example 21.47: Project Code**
user/utils.py in 0cbcf42d4f

```
  1    import logging
  .        ...
 20    logger = logging.getLogger(__name__)
```

The method itself will also pass a similar message, displaying all of the information passed to Django's `send_mail()` function, as shown in Example 21.48.

**Example 21.48: Project Code**
`user/utils.py` in `0cbcf42d4f`

```
23    class ActivationMailFormMixin:
 .        ...
26        def log_mail_error(self, **kwargs):
27            msg_list = [
28                'Activation email did not send.\n',
29                'from_email: {from_email}\n'
30                'subject: {subject}\n'
31                'message: {message}\n',
32            ]
```

To this string, in Example 21.49, we add the list of recipients (despite the fact that we always expect there to be exactly one recipient).

**Example 21.49: Project Code**
`user/utils.py` in `0cbcf42d4f`

```
23    class ActivationMailFormMixin:
 .        ...
26        def log_mail_error(self, **kwargs):
 .            ...
33            recipient_list = kwargs.get(
34                'recipient_list', [])
35            for recipient in recipient_list:
36                msg_list.insert(
37                    1, 'recipient: {r}\n'.format(
38                        r=recipient))
```

We then get the `Exception` subclass passed to the method as the `error` keyword and add it to the message, as shown in Example 21.50. This also allows us to set the severity of the log record. In the event the `error` key is not set, we have *very* unexpected behavior, and so we set the level to `CRITICAL`.

**Example 21.50: Project Code**
`user/utils.py` in `0cbcf42d4f`

```
 3    from logging import CRITICAL, ERROR
 .        ...
23    class ActivationMailFormMixin:
 .        ...
26        def log_mail_error(self, **kwargs):
 .            ...
39            if 'error' in kwargs:
40                level = ERROR
```

```
41                    error_msg = (
42                        'error: {0.__class__.__name__}\n'
43                        'args: {0.args}\n')
44                    error_info = error_msg.format(
45                        kwargs['error'])
46                    msg_list.insert(1, error_info)
47            else:
48                level = CRITICAL
```

Finally, we turn the list into a string and format it with the contents of kwargs, which contains all of the same variables we would use in an email template. We then log this message into a record, as shown in Example 21.51.

**Example 21.51: Project Code**
user/utils.py in 0cbcf42d4f

```
23   class ActivationMailFormMixin:
     ...
26       def log_mail_error(self, **kwargs):
             ...
49           msg = ''.join(msg_list).format(**kwargs)
50           logger.log(level, msg)
```

And now we breathe. The functionality to send an email with templates is not simple to begin with, but when we try to make it as robust as possible, the process can be quite complex. Thankfully, we've split all of it up into separate functions—this would be far worse as a monolith.

Before we build our forms and view, we create the MailContextViewMixin class for views to inherit from. The send_mail() method on ActivationMailFormMixin expects specific keyword arguments, and we shouldn't need to remember what they are. The MailContextViewMixin will do that for us.

To begin, we declare the mixin with the names of the templates we anticipate using, as shown in Example 21.52.

**Example 21.52: Project Code**
user/utils.py in 0cbcf42d4f

```
154   class MailContextViewMixin:
155       email_template_name = 'user/email_create.txt'
156       subject_template_name = (
157           'user/subject_create.txt')
```

This allows us to build a dictionary with the keyword arguments that send_mail() expects, as shown in Example 21.53.

**Example 21.53:** Project Code
user/utils.py in 0cbcf42d4f

```
154    class MailContextViewMixin:
  .        ...
159        def get_save_kwargs(self, request):
160            return {
161                'email_template_name':
162                    self.email_template_name,
163                'request': request,
164                'subject_template_name':
165                    self.subject_template_name,
166            }
```

In our views, we will be able to use this code to quickly call send_mail().

## 21.6.2  Creation Form

Now that we have the ActivationMailFormMixin class, we can build our forms. For the moment, we'll stick to UserCreationForm.

The reason we are not using Django's own UserCreationForm is that it only prompts users for a username and a password (twice over), but it does not prompt for their email address. Thankfully, however, we can use the form. Django's UserCreationForm defines two fields, password1 and password2, and uses ModelForm inheritance to add the username field from the User model.

### Ghosts of Django Past

The UserCreationForm prior to Django 1.8 defines the username field explicitly, meaning that our override here (and most of the code in the next chapter) will not work in versions earlier than Django 1.8. Instead, you will have to create this class from scratch. Take a look at the Putting It All Together section of this chapter before you do so, as the information there will change the way you attack this problem in a real project.

We first import **auth**'s UserCreationForm and rename it to BaseUserCreation Form. We import our form mixin and inherit both of these classes in a new User CreationForm, as shown in Example 21.54.

**Example 21.54:** Project Code
user/forms.py in 9af8a05373

```
 2    from django.contrib.auth.forms import \
 3        UserCreationForm as BaseUserCreationForm
 4
 5    from .utils import ActivationMailFormMixin
  .        ...
 8    class UserCreationForm(
 9            ActivationMailFormMixin,
10            BaseUserCreationForm):
```

To properly restructure UserCreationForm to use the fields in
BaseUserCreationForm, we need to change the Meta class where the ModelForm
behavior is defined. This Meta class therefore inherits the Meta class in
BaseUserCreationForm, overriding the model with get_user_model() and adding
the email form to the field, as shown in Example 21.55.

**Example 21.55: Project Code**
user/forms.py **in** 9af8a05373

```
 1   from django.contrib.auth import get_user_model
 .      ...
 8   class UserCreationForm(
 9          ActivationMailFormMixin,
10          BaseUserCreationForm):
 .      ...
16       class Meta(BaseUserCreationForm.Meta):
17           model = get_user_model()
18           fields = ('username', 'email')
```

In Example 21.56, we define the mail_validation_error attribute, overriding the
empty string value defined in ActivationMailFormMixin.

**Example 21.56: Project Code**
user/forms.py **in** 9af8a05373

```
 8   class UserCreationForm(
 9          ActivationMailFormMixin,
10          BaseUserCreationForm):
11
12       mail_validation_error = (
13           'User created. Could not send activation '
14           'email. Please try again later. (Sorry!)')
```

Finally, in Example 21.57, we override the save() method in multiple steps, declaring
it to accept keyword arguments we will pass to send_mail(). To start, we create a User
instance from the data without saving it to the database. If it already has a primary key, then
the data is already in the database, and we don't need to send an account activation email. If
the primary key is not set, we disable the account and plan to send an activation email.

**Example 21.57: Project Code**
user/forms.py **in** 9af8a05373

```
 8   class UserCreationForm(
 9          ActivationMailFormMixin,
10          BaseUserCreationForm):
 .      ...
20       def save(self, **kwargs):
21           user = super().save(commit=False)
```

```
22          if not user.pk:
23              user.is_active = False
24              send_mail = True
25          else:
26              send_mail = False
```

Now that we know whether or not to send an email, we can save the `User` instance to the database, remembering to save any many-to-many relations using the `save_m2m()` method. In the event we needed to send an email, we call the `send_mail()` method defined in the `ActivationMailFormMixin` class. Following best practice, we then return the new or updated object, as shown in Example 21.58.

**Example 21.58: Project Code**
user/forms.py in 9af8a05373

```
 8   class UserCreationForm(
 9           ActivationMailFormMixin,
10           BaseUserCreationForm):
 .       ...
20       def save(self, **kwargs):
21           user = super().save(commit=False)
 .           ...
27           user.save()
28           self.save_m2m()
29           if send_mail:
30               self.send_mail(user=user, **kwargs)
31           return user
```

### 21.6.3 Views for Creating and Activating Accounts

Now that we have our `UserCreationForm`, we can build the views to create and activate new users. To begin, we can create the `CreateAccount` view, starting in the user/ urls.py file. We first import the necessary tools and views, as shown in Example 21.59.

**Example 21.59: Project Code**
user/urls.py in 9af8a05373

```
 7   from django.views.generic import (
 8       RedirectView, TemplateView)
 9
10   from .views import (
11       ActivateAccount, CreateAccount,
12       DisableAccount)
```

We can then create a very simple URL pattern for `CreateAccount`, as shown in Example 21.60.

**Example 21.60: Project Code**

user/urls.py **in** 9af8a05373

```
73        url(r'^create/$',
74            CreateAccount.as_view(),
75            name='create'),
```

In user/views.py, we declare the CreateAccount class, defining the attributes we expect to use, as shown in Example 21.61.

**Example 21.61: Project Code**

user/views.py **in** 9af8a05373

```
 9    from django.core.urlresolvers import reverse_lazy
      ...
26    from .forms import UserCreationForm
27    from .utils import MailContextViewMixin
      ...
62    class CreateAccount(MailContextViewMixin, View):
63        form_class = UserCreationForm
64        success_url = reverse_lazy(
65            'dj-auth:create_done')
66        template_name = 'user/user_create.html'
```

Our get() method adheres to the belt and braces philosophy, using the @csrf_protect decorator as a caution, as shown in Example 21.62.

**Example 21.62: Project Code**

user/views.py **in** 9af8a05373

```
62    class CreateAccount(MailContextViewMixin, View):
      ...
68        @method_decorator(csrf_protect)
69        def get(self, request):
70            return TemplateResponse(
71                request,
72                self.template_name,
73                {'form': self.form_class()})
```

We then build our post() method in Example 21.63. The declaration of the view sees the addition of the @sensitive_post_parameters() decorator, which marks specific data as sensitive. Django will not cache or store this data, and it will filter the data out of any error reporting. We are thus making extra sure that our users' passwords are not accidentally displayed to developers or to other users in the event of an error.

**Example 21.63: Project Code**

`user/views.py` in 9af8a05373

```
22   from django.views.decorators.debug import \
23       sensitive_post_parameters
 .       ...
62   class CreateAccount(MailContextViewMixin, View):
 .       ...
75       @method_decorator(csrf_protect)
76       @method_decorator(sensitive_post_parameters(
77           'password1', 'password2'))
78       def post(self, request):
```

## Django Documentation

For more information about filtering sensitive information:

https://dju.link/18/sensitive-info

The outline of our `post()` method is similar to many of our other form-processing views. We begin by binding the form with data, and then checking whether the data is valid. In the event the data is invalid, we redisplay the bound form with errors, as shown in Example 21.64.

**Example 21.64: Project Code**

`user/views.py` in 9af8a05373

```
62   class CreateAccount(MailContextViewMixin, View):
 .       ...
78       def post(self, request):
79           bound_form = self.form_class(request.POST)
80           if bound_form.is_valid():
 .               ...
92           return TemplateResponse(
93               request,
94               self.template_name,
95               {'form': bound_form})
```

If the data is valid, we save the new `User`, passing in the result of `get_save_kwargs()` defined in the `MailContextViewMixin` class, as shown in Example 21.65. This action also sends the user the activation email. We verify that it was sent and redirect only if it was.

**Example 21.65: Project Code**

`user/views.py` in 9af8a05373

```
62   class CreateAccount(MailContextViewMixin, View):
 .       ...
80           if bound_form.is_valid():
81               # not catching returned user
```

```
82              bound_form.save(
83                  **self.get_save_kwargs(request))
84              if bound_form.mail_sent:  # mail sent?
85                  return redirect(self.success_url)
86              else:
87                  errs = (
88                      bound_form.non_field_errors())
89                  for err in errs:
90                      error(request, err)
91              # TODO: redirect to email resend
```

In the event the email isn't sent, we pull the error message out of the form and use the error() function defined by the **messages** app to store the message. Once we have a page to resend an activation link, we redirect the user to that page, removing as much friction as possible from the process (of course, ideally, we'll simply send the user an email). The **messages** app ensures that the user sees the error and is aware of what happened.

In Example 21.66, we now build a webpage for confirmation of user creation (and correct behavior for sending an email). We can use a simply GCBV for this page, as it simply displays a template.

**Example 21.66: Project Code**
user/urls.py **in** 9af8a05373

```
76          url(r'^create/done/$',
77              TemplateView.as_view(
78                  template_name=(
79                      'user/user_create_done.html')),
80              name='create_done'),
```

Our next webpage is the activation webpage, shown in Example 21.67. As we did for our password_reset_confirm() view, we use the uidb64 and token URL path segments to check that the user accessing the page actually received a link in his or her email.

**Example 21.67: Project Code**
user/urls.py **in** 9af8a05373

```
67          url(r'^activate/'
68              r'(?P<uidb64>[0-9A-Za-z_\-]+)/'
69              r'(?P<token>[0-9A-Za-z]{1,13}'
70              r'-[0-9A-Za-z]{1,20})/$',
71              ActivateAccount.as_view(),
72              name='activate'),
```

We can then declare the actual view class in user/views.py, as shown in Example 21.68.

**Example 21.68: Project Code**

`user/views.py` **in** `9af8a05373`

```
30   class ActivateAccount(View):
31       success_url = reverse_lazy('dj-auth:login')
32       template_name = 'user/user_activate.html'
```

The class-based view (CBV) will have only a single method: `get()`. The goal of `get()` is to use the `uidb64` and `token` arguments to activate an account. We use the `uidb64` to identify the user according to primary key, and we then check to see if the `token` is valid (that we created it). If the token was successfully created, we activate the account and redirect to the login page. If the token was not successfully created, we display the `user_activate.html`, which informs the user that the account could not be activated.

One of the techniques we will see for speeding up our website (in Chapter 26: Optimizing Our Site for Speed) is caching—the act of remembering and reusing the results of a computation. The problem with caching is that sometimes it leads us to display information that has expired or is wrong. In the case of our `ActivateAccount`, we know that every time a user visits the page, we want to compute the view from scratch—we will never, ever want to use the cache for this webpage. To begin, we therefore import the `@never_cache` decorator and decorate our `get()` method with it, as shown in Example 21.69.

**Example 21.69: Project Code**

`user/views.py` **in** `9af8a05373`

```
18   from django.views.decorators.cache import \
19       never_cache
 .       ...
30   class ActivateAccount(View):
 .       ...
34       @method_decorator(never_cache)
35       def get(self, request, uidb64, token):
```

To get the code to work inside of `get()`, we need the model that represents the user (currently Django's `User` model class) and a way to turn the base-64 `uidb64` number into a base-10 number for us to use with the model. We can use the `get_user_model()` function for the first and the `urlsafe_base64_decode()` function for the second. Much like `urlsafe_base64_encode()`, which we used to turn the primary key into the base-64 `uidb64` variable, `urlsafe_base64_decode()` returns `bytes`, and so we use the `force_text()` utility function to turn that into a Python `str` object. In Example 21.70, we import all of our tools.

**Example 21.70: Project Code**

`user/views.py` **in** `9af8a05373`

```
2    from django.contrib.auth import (
3        get_user, get_user_model, logout)
 .       ...
```

```
15    from django.utils.encoding import force_text
16    from django.utils.http import \
17        urlsafe_base64_decode
```

In get(), we start by getting the User model and attempting to get the User instance that is to be activated. In the event any of the process goes wrong, we simply set our user variable to None and keep going, as shown in Example 21.71.

**Example 21.71:** Project Code
user/views.py **in** 9af8a05373

```
30    class ActivateAccount(View):
 .        ...
35        def get(self, request, uidb64, token):
36            User = get_user_model()
37            try:
38                # urlsafe_base64_decode()
39                #     -> bytestring in Py3
40                uid = force_text(
41                    urlsafe_base64_decode(uidb64))
42                user = User.objects.get(pk=uid)
43            except (TypeError, ValueError,
44                    OverflowError, User.DoesNotExist):
45                user = None
```

We then want to check whether we found a user and whether the token in the URL path is valid. In the event one of these is False, we display the template for the view, as shown in Example 21.72.

**Example 21.72:** Project Code
user/views.py **in** 9af8a05373

```
 6    from django.contrib.auth.tokens import \
 7        default_token_generator as token_generator
 .        ...
30    class ActivateAccount(View):
 .            ...
46            if (user is not None
47                    and token_generator
48                    .check_token(user, token)):
 .            ...
56            else:
57                return TemplateResponse(
58                    request,
59                    self.template_name)
```

In the event we have a User instance and a valid token, we redirect to the login page, using the **messages** app to display a message informing the user that his or her account has been activated, as shown in Example 21.73.

**Example 21.73: Project Code**
`user/views.py` in 9af8a05373

```
 8   from django.contrib.messages import error, success
 .       ...
30   class ActivateAccount(View):
 .           ...
49           user.is_active = True
50           user.save()
51           success(
52               request,
53               'User Activated! '
54               'You may now login.')
55           return redirect(self.success_url)
```

When building this view, I debated whether or not to use a template at all. In the event the URL is invalid (typically because `token` has expired), I thought about simply redirecting the user to the webpage that prompts the user to resend an activation email. I would have used the `error()` function from the **messages** app to warn the user that the account had not been activated. I opted to use a template here, mainly because the resend activation page doesn't exist yet. In your own project, you might choose to do any of these tasks differently.

### 21.6.4  Account Creation Templates

Now that we have URL patterns and views, we need our templates:

- `user_create.html`
- `subject_create.txt`
- `email_create.txt`
- `user_create_done.html`
- `user_activate.html`

The `user_create.html` displays a form to create a new user. We start with the outline of the template, as shown in Example 21.74.

**Example 21.74: Project Code**
`user/templates/user/user_create.html` in 9af8a05373

```
 1   {% extends parent_template|default:"user/base_user.html" %}
 2
 3   {% block title %}
 4   {{ block.super }} - Create Account
 5   {% endblock %}
 6
 7   {% block content %}
 8     <div class="row">
 9       <div class="offset-by-two eight columns">
 .           ...
18       </div>
19     </div>
20   {% endblock %}
```

We then create the actual form, as shown in Example 21.75.

**Example 21.75: Project Code**
user/templates/user/user_create.html **in** 9af8a05373

```
10          <form
11              action="{% url 'dj-auth:create' %}"
12              method="post">
13          {% csrf_token %}
14          {{ form.as_p }}
15          <button type="submit">
16              Create New Account</button>
17          </form>
```

Once the user fills out UserCreationForm in user_create.html, the CreateAccount view saves UserCreationForm, which uses the methods we created in ActivationMailFormMixin to send an email. For this to work, we need to build the subject_create.txt template and the email_create.txt template. The first is simple, as you can see in Example 21.76.

**Example 21.76: Project Code**
user/templates/user/subject_create.txt **in** 9af8a05373

```
1   {{ site_name }} Account Activation
```

The get_context_data() in ActivationMailFormMixin defines all of the context variables we expect in our context, allowing us to create a link to the ActivateAccount view, as shown in Example 21.77.

**Example 21.77: Project Code**
user/templates/user/email_create.txt **in** 9af8a05373

```
1   Hello from {{ site_name }}!
2
3   We've received a request to create an account for this email.
4
5   If you did not request a user account, please ignore this message.
6
7   To activate your account, please navigate to:
8
9   {{ protocol }}://{{ domain }}{% url 'dj-auth:activate' uid token %}
```

After sending this email, we display a confirmation of the process, as shown in Example 21.78.

**Example 21.78: Project Code**

`user/templates/user/user_create_done.html` **in** `9af8a05373`

```
 1  {% extends parent_template|default:"user/base_user.html" %}
 2
 3  {% block title %}
 4  {{ block.super }} - Account Created
 5  {% endblock %}
 6
 7  {% block content %}
 8    <div class="row">
 9      <div class="offset-by-two eight columns">
10        <p>Your account has been created!</p>
11        <p>Please check your email for
12          the activation link.</p>
13      </div>
14    </div>
15  {% endblock %}
```

Finally, in Example 21.79, we create the template that `ActivateAccount` displays if the `uidb64` or `token` are invalid.

**Example 21.79: Project Code**

`user/templates/user/user_activate.html` **in** `9af8a05373`

```
 1  {% extends parent_template|default:"user/base_user.html" %}
 2
 3  {% block title %}
 4  {{ block.super }} - Account Activation Failed
 5  {% endblock %}
 6
 7  {% block content %}
 8    <div class="row">
 9      <div class="offset-by-two eight columns">
10        <p>This activation link is no longer valid.</p>
11      </div>
12    </div>
13  {% endblock %}
```

With our pages completed, we can now link to them, as shown in Example 21.80. I opt to add a link to the user creation page in the project base template, displayed only if the user is not authenticated.

**Example 21.80: Project Code**

`templates/base.html` **in** `9af8a05373`

```
36            <li><a href="{% url 'dj-auth:create' %}">
37                Register</a></li>
```

I also add a link directly below the login form on the login page, as shown in Example 21.81.

**Example 21.81: Project Code**

user/templates/user/login.html **in** 9af8a05373

```
14              <li><a href="{% url 'dj-auth:create' %}">
15                 Register New Account</a></li>
```

## 21.6.5   Resending Activation

If a user creates an account but then forgets to click the activation link in his or her email until after the number of days set in the PASSWORD_RESET_TIMEOUT_DAYS setting, the user will be unable to activate the account. The user's email is already in our database, and so creating another account is out of the question. Instead, we need the user to be able to request another activation email.

To start, we create the ResendActivationEmailForm. Like the UserCreation Form, it uses the ActivationMailFormMixin to send the User an email. However, unlike the UserCreationForm, we won't be creating an account.

We start by importing our logging tools and Django's form package, as shown in Example 21.82.

**Example 21.82: Project Code**

user/forms.py **in** e17aa4bb0c

```
1   import logging
2
3   from django import forms
.      ...
10  logger = logging.getLogger(__name__)
```

In Example 21.83, we can then create our form. Unlike we did for UserCreation Form, we are not using a ModelForm superclass. Our form has only a single field: the user's email. We also override the mail_validation_error attribute declared in ActivationMailFormMixin.

**Example 21.83: Project Code**

user/forms.py **in** e17aa4bb0c

```
13  class ResendActivationEmailForm(
14          ActivationMailFormMixin, forms.Form):
15
16      email = forms.EmailField()
17
18      mail_validation_error = (
19          'Could not re-send activation email. '
20          'Please try again later. (Sorry!)')
```

We then define the `save()` method on our form. This method comes with a quirk: it always claims success in keeping with Django's default behavior. When a user gives an email to the `password_reset()` view, the view will always tell the user that it has sent a reset email to that address, even if there is no user in the database with that email address. This precaution prevents malicious users and robots from figuring out which emails are in the database.

This can be *very* frustrating to users. If a user has several email accounts and cannot remember which email address he or she used on the website, having the website show success even if it's not actually sending an email can be infuriating, as the user is expecting an email that will never arrive.

There are other ways to handle this problem. For instance, our website could limit the number of requests an IP address makes to the reset/resend-activation pages, and we could use a CAPTCHA system to try and make sure there is an actual human asking for the reset/activation. Both of these solutions rely on systems outside of Django, however, and as our goal is to use *just* Django in this book, we won't have the time to dive into these options. However, it's important to understand the usability shortcoming here, made in favor of stronger security.

The exception to our default success is if we have a valid user but we are unable to send the email. In this case, we assume that the user is not malicious (an incredibly dangerous assumption), and we warn the user that there was a problem on our end.

Our `save()`, shown in Example 21.84, function thus attempts to find a user by the email submitted, and if that user exists, it sends the user a new activation email. If not, we simply log the problem without raising any validation errors.

**Example 21.84: Project Code**
`user/forms.py` in e17aa4bb0c

```
13   class ResendActivationEmailForm(
14           ActivationMailFormMixin, forms.Form):
 .       ...
22       def save(self, **kwargs):
23           User = get_user_model()
24           try:
25               user = User.objects.get(
26                   email=self.cleaned_data['email'])
27           except:
28               logger.warning(
29                   'Resend Activation: No user with '
30                   'email: {} .'.format(
31                       self.cleaned_data['email']))
32               return None
33           self.send_mail(user=user, **kwargs)
34           return user
```

While our form will never display an error if the email is not sent or if a user does not exist, it is still possible for the form to be invalid. For instance, if the user does not submit a value to `email` or submits a value to `email` that does not validate as one (e.g., `'%%%'`), then the form will be invalid.

We use the form in the `ResendActivationEmail`, for which we create a simple URL pattern, as shown in Example 21.85.

**Example 21.85: Project Code**
`user/urls.py` in e17aa4bb0c

```
10   from .views import (
11      ActivateAccount, CreateAccount,
12      DisableAccount, ResendActivationEmail)
.      ...
73      url(r'^activate/resend/$',
74          ResendActivationEmail.as_view(),
75          name='resend_activation'),
```

In Example 21.86, we then declare `ResendActivationEmail`, making use of the `MailContextViewMixin` class we built earlier this chapter to make dealing with the form easier.

**Example 21.86: Project Code**
`user/views.py` in e17aa4bb0c

```
 26   from .forms import (
 27      ResendActivationEmailForm, UserCreationForm)
  .      ...
122   class ResendActivationEmail(
123          MailContextViewMixin, View):
124      form_class = ResendActivationEmailForm
125      success_url = reverse_lazy('dj-auth:login')
126      template_name = 'user/resend_activation.html'
```

Our view will handle requests using both the HTTP GET and POST methods. In the case of our `get()` method, shown in Example 21.87, we simply render a template, using `TemplateResponse` instead of `HttpResponse` in keeping with the rest of **auth**.

**Example 21.87: Project Code**
`user/views.py` in e17aa4bb0c

```
122   class ResendActivationEmail(
123          MailContextViewMixin, View):
  .      ...
128      @method_decorator(csrf_protect)
129      def get(self, request):
130          return TemplateResponse(
131              request,
132              self.template_name,
133              {'form': self.form_class()})
```

We use the belt and braces approach on both `get()` and `post()`, decorating both with the `@csrf_protect` decorator, as shown in Example 21.88.

**Example 21.88: Project Code**
`user/views.py` in e17aa4bb0c

```
122    class ResendActivationEmail(
123           MailContextViewMixin, View):
  .       ...
135           @method_decorator(csrf_protect)
136           def post(self, request):
```

In `post()`, as shown in Example 21.89, we check to see if the form was valid, and in all cases, we redirect to the login page, displaying the message that the email was successfully sent (even if it was not!).

**Example 21.89: Project Code**
`user/views.py` in e17aa4bb0c

```
122    class ResendActivationEmail(
123           MailContextViewMixin, View):
  .       ...
136           def post(self, request):
137               bound_form = self.form_class(request.POST)
138               if bound_form.is_valid():
  .           ...
154               success(
155                   request,
156                   'Activation Email Sent!')
157           return redirect(self.success_url)
```

In the case the form was actually valid, we attempt to resend the activation email by calling `save()` on the form, using the `get_save_kwargs()` method defined on `MailContextViewMixin` to pass in the right arguments, as shown in Example 21.90.

**Example 21.90: Project Code**
`user/views.py` in e17aa4bb0c

```
122    class ResendActivationEmail(
123           MailContextViewMixin, View):
  .       ...
136           def post(self, request):
  .           ...
138               if bound_form.is_valid():
139                   user = bound_form.save(
140                       **self.get_save_kwargs(request))
```

We then handle our exception: if we have a valid user, and if we expected to send an email but could not, we must let the user know there was a problem. We therefore check to see if we have a `User` instance and whether or not the email was sent. Recall that `ActivationMailFormMixin` will have added a form error in this case, which we can pop from the list in `non_field_errors()`, as shown in Example 21.91.

**Example 21.91: Project Code**
`user/views.py` in e17aa4bb0c

```
122    class ResendActivationEmail(
123            MailContextViewMixin, View):
 .        ...
136        def post(self, request):
 .            ...
138            if bound_form.is_valid():
 .                ...
141                if (user is not None
142                        and not bound_form.mail_sent):
143                    errs = (
144                        bound_form.non_field_errors())
```

Instead of displaying the errors of the form, we display the errors in messages, indiscriminately removing all of the form-wide (as opposed to field-specific) errors from the form afterward, as shown in Example 21.92. Some developers will frown at this choice. However, as we listed errors this way when redirecting from the `CreateAccount` view, it will keep our UI consistent on this page.

**Example 21.92: Project Code**
`user/views.py` in e17aa4bb0c

```
122    class ResendActivationEmail(
123            MailContextViewMixin, View):
 .        ...
136        def post(self, request):
 .            ...
138            if bound_form.is_valid():
 .                ...
141                if (user is not None
142                        and not bound_form.mail_sent):
 .                    ...
145                    for err in errs:
146                        error(request, err)
147                    if errs:
148                        bound_form.errors.pop(
149                            '__all__')
```

In Example 21.93, we then redisplay the template with our `ResendActivation` `EmailForm`, prompting the user to reuse the form to retry (as we scramble on the other end of the Internet to try to fix whatever is wrong with our email system).

**Example 21.93:** Project Code

`user/views.py` in `e17aa4bb0c`

```
122    class ResendActivationEmail(
123            MailContextViewMixin, View):
  .        ...
136        def post(self, request):
  .            ...
138            if bound_form.is_valid():
  .                ...
141                if (user is not None
142                        and not bound_form.mail_sent):
  .                    ...
150                    return TemplateResponse(
151                        request,
152                        self.template_name,
153                        {'form': bound_form})
```

We can now actually build the template our view will use. We start with the outline of the template, as shown in Example 21.94.

**Example 21.94:** Project Code

`user/templates/user/resend_activation.html` in `e17aa4bb0c`

```
 1    {% extends parent_template|default:"user/base_user.html" %}
 2
 3    {% block title %}
 4    {{ block.super }} - Resend Activation E-Mail
 5    {% endblock %}
 6
 7    {% block content %}
 8      <div class="row">
 9        <div class="offset-by-two eight columns">
  .          ...
21      </div></div>
22    {% endblock %}
```

And then we build the form, as shown in Example 21.95.

**Example 21.95:** Project Code

`user/templates/user/resend_activation.html` in `e17aa4bb0c`

```
10          <div class="center">
11            <p>Resend your account activation email.</p>
12          </div>
13          <form
14              action="{% url 'dj-auth:resend_activation' %}"
15              method="post">
16            {% csrf_token %}
17            {{ form.as_p }}
```

```
18              <button type="submit">
19                  Resend Activation E-Mail</button>
20          </form>
```

And, of course, we link to our new page on the login page, as shown in Example 21.96.

**Example 21.96: Project Code**
user/templates/user/login.html **in** e17aa4bb0c

```
18          <li><a href="{% url 'dj-auth:resend_activation' %}">
19              Lost Activation E-Mail?</a></li>
```

In Example 21.97, I opt to link to our new view on the page that creates new accounts, as well.

**Example 21.97: Project Code**
user/templates/user/user_create.html **in** e17aa4bb0c

```
10          <div class="center">
11            <a href="{% url 'dj-auth:resend_activation' %}">
12              Lost Activation E-Mail?</a>
13          </div>
```

Finally, in Example 21.98, we can return to our CreateAccount view and redirect the user to our ResendActivationEmail in the event there is a problem.

**Example 21.98: Project Code**
user/views.py **in** 954f641460

```
63   class CreateAccount(MailContextViewMixin, View):
 .       ...
79       def post(self, request):
 .               ...
92                  return redirect(
93                      'dj-auth:resend_activation')
```

## 21.7   URL Cleanup

Before we finish, we should take a quick look at our URL patterns. You'll discover that we're not fully adhering to a clean URL path policy. We have URLs with the path prefix /user/password/ but no view for the actual path. We can use a simple GCBV to fix that, as shown in Example 21.99.

**Example 21.99: Project Code**
user/urls.py **in** 541375e172

```
14    password_urls = [
15        url(r'^$',
16            RedirectView.as_view(
17                pattern_name='dj-auth:pw_reset_start',
18                permanent=False)),
 .      ...
64    ]
```

Similarly, our activation webpage uses the /activate/ URL path prefix, but we don't have an actual page for /activate/ or even for /activate/<uidb64>/. To catch all of the URLs that use /activate/ but that don't match the activate URL pattern, we can use the code shown in Example 21.100.

**Example 21.100: Project Code**
user/urls.py **in** 541375e172

```
 66    urlpatterns = [
 .      ...
 80        url(r'^activate',
 81            RedirectView.as_view(
 82                pattern_name=(
 83                    'dj-auth:resend_activation'),
 84                permanent=False)),
 .      ...
107    ]
```

Of course, as this code is a catch-all (we never use the $ to limit the URL pattern), we need it to appear below the activate URL pattern.

# 21.8 Anatomy of the App: Full Dissection

The **auth** app is the most full-featured app we tackle in this book: models, forms, views, middleware, context processors, decorators. In many ways, it could be easier to describe the app by talking about what parts of Django it doesn't use.

The app ships with three models and custom managers for each of them:

- User
- Permission
- Group

The app also supplies a number of forms to interact with these models:

- AuthenticationForm (used by login() view)
- PasswordResetForm (used by password_reset() view)

- `SetPasswordForm` (used by `password_reset_confirm()` view)
- `PasswordChangeForm` (used by `password_change()` view)
- `UserCreationForm`
- `UserChangeForm`
- `AdminPasswordChangeForm`

In turn, **auth** defines a number of views in `django.contrib.auth.views`. To begin, it supplies the basics for authenticating users, using the **sessions** app to store state:

- `login()` (`registration/login.html`)
- `logout()` (`registration/logged_out.html`)
- `redirect_to_login()`
- `logout_then_login()`

It has two views for changing passwords:

- `password_change()` (`registration/password_change_form.html`)
- `password_change_done()` (`registration/password_change_done.html`)

And finally, four views are provided to reset passwords:

- `password_reset()`
  - `registration/password_reset_form.html`
  - `registration/password_reset_email.html`
  - `registration/password_reset_subject.txt`
- `password_reset_done()`
  - `registration/password_reset_done.html`
- `password_reset_confirm()`
  - `registration/password_reset_confirm.html`
- `password_reset_complete()`
  - `registration/password_reset_complete.html`

All of these views are used in a URL configuration in `django.contrib.auth.urls`, but changing their behavior proved impossible (and detrimental to learning this material), so we built our own.

Finally, the **auth** app defines a set of settings that the user may or may not wish to override:

- `LOGIN_URL`
- `LOGOUT_URL`
- `LOGIN_REDIRECT_URL`
- `PASSWORD_RESET_TIMEOUT_DAYS`

Perhaps unbelievably, we are still not done with this app. So far, we have used basic behavior by providing a login/logout system and protecting pages with permissions. We have extended the behavior of the app with our own forms and views. We have yet to customize the behavior of this app.

# 21.9   Putting It All Together

Extraordinarily, there is an enormous amount of work we could still do. We could use the `activate` URL pattern to reactivate disabled user accounts, and we could add a system to prune unactivated or disabled accounts from the database. We could rewrite the `password_reset()` and `ResendActivationEmailForm` to not default to success. We could prompt users to change their passwords every year and warn them when their password is weak. We will do none of these things

The *terrible* truth of the last three chapters is that you will rarely write your own authentication views.

The **auth** system provides the ability to build and use custom back ends. These back ends, usually third-party apps (Django apps not provided by Django or you but available free online), will come with all of the desired behavior for an authentication system and essentially allow most developers to simply plug in existing code to get all of the work we just did. Some, such as `django-registration`,[1] provide a basic authentication system like the one we built in the last three chapters. Others allow login using Twitter, Facebook, and Google Plus.

The problem with any of these back ends, of course, is that if you do not understand what Django supplies, it becomes hard to work with the extra code, as it will never be clear how it works. Thanks to the last three chapters, one of the most crucial aspects of your website will hold absolutely no secrets for you.

---

1. https://github.com/macropin/django-registration

# 22

# Overriding Django's Authentication with a Custom User

## In This Chapter

- Create a public profile for users
- Create a custom `User` model
- Integrate the new model with our website, modifying forms, templates, and migrations in the process
- Use the new model to add an `author` field to blog posts

## 22.1 Introduction

Once the basics of authentication have been handled, most developers seek to add information about users. Perhaps they want a birth date, or perhaps they want to connect with their users on Twitter or Facebook. Regardless of the purpose, they want to store extra information about the user, and given what we know about **auth** so far, there is no clear and obvious approach to this problem.

In this chapter, we explore two possibilities for adding user information. We first create a `Profile` model to store extra information, tying it to the **auth**'s `User` model. Then, we build our own `User` model to be able to change behavior and actually remove information from the model rather than adding fields. By the end, we'll see that the best use-case for user management is an extremely simple `User` model that changes as little as possible and a `Profile` model that the developer may change in whatever way he or she wishes.

This chapter uses some of the material reserved for Chapter 24: Creating Custom Managers and Querysets, and Chapter 25: Handling Behavior with Signals. While you don't need the material from those chapters, it will certainly clarify a few of the concepts found in this chapter.

## 22.2   Creating a User Profile

The user profile is a fairly common website feature. It allows users to list their location, birth date, favorite pizza toppings, and whatever else the developer allows them to add. In the next few sections, we create a very simple Profile model for the user to display. We create a page to display the user's own profile as well as a page to display profiles to other users. While these two pages use different views, they rely on the same template. We therefore also create a webpage to allow users to update their profile, but we ensure that each user has a profile as soon as the User instance is created.

### 22.2.1   The Profile Model

The Profile model itself is nothing fancy or interesting, with the exception of the relation to User, as shown in Example 22.1.

**Example 22.1: Project Code**
user/models.py in 23e819627f

```
 1   from django.conf import settings
 2   from django.db import models
 3
 4
 5   class Profile(models.Model):
 6       user = models.OneToOneField(
 7           settings.AUTH_USER_MODEL)
 8       slug = models.SlugField(
 9           max_length=30,
10           unique=True)
11       about = models.TextField()
12
13       def __str__(self):
14           return self.user.get_username()
```

The one-to-one relation to the user is created by the OneToOneField. When building code in other sections of the website, we used the get_user_model() to get the User model class. When building relations, we use the setting.AUTH_USER_MODEL, as it acts the same way. By default, the AUTH_USER_MODEL setting points to auth.User. However, we don't know which model is being used to represent the user (for reasons we will discover shortly), and using these settings is the best practice.

The slug field on Profile is for displaying the Profile publicly to other users. Any other field is purely for display.

To create a table in the database, we use the migration system, as shown in Example 22.2.

**Example 22.2: Shell Code**

```
$ ./manage.py makemigrations user
$ ./manage.py migrate
```

I leave the work of creating a data migration to create `Profile` instances for existing users as an exercise for you (as it is certainly not necessary in our case, and we've seen more than enough data migrations to get the job done).

We want `Profile` instances to be created at the same time as `User` accounts, and so we return to the `UserCreationForm` class in `user/forms.py` to add this functionality.

In Example 22.3, we generate the `slug` of the profile using the `username` field on the `User` model. This means that the `username` is now limited to specific values: we cannot allow username values that will clash with URL paths at the same level as the `Profile`. If we anticipate creating the profile at the `/user/<username>/` path, none of the path prefixes in the **user** URL configuration may be used. To be clear: we have a webpage at `/user/login/`, so if a user creates an account with the username `'login'`, then their profile will be accessible only at `/user/login/`, causing a clash. We therefore create the `clean_username()` method on the form to ensure that none of the path segments prefixing the URL patterns in the user URL configuration are ever used. We lie to the user in the event they try this.

**Example 22.3: Project Code**
`user/forms.py` **in** 6b8d9ef930

```
 7    from django.core.exceptions import ValidationError
 8    from django.utils.text import slugify
 9
10    from .models import Profile
  .      ...
40    class UserCreationForm(
41            ActivationMailFormMixin,
42            BaseUserCreationForm):
  .      ...
52        def clean_username(self):
53            username = self.cleaned_data['username']
54            disallowed = (
55                'activate',
56                'create',
57                'disable',
58                'login',
59                'logout',
60                'password',
61                'profile',
62            )
63            if username in disallowed:
64                raise ValidationError(
65                    "A user with that username"
66                    " already exists.")
67            return username
```

We can then create the `Profile` object in the `save()` method of `UserCreationForm`. We wait until after we save the `User` instance and the many-to-many relations to create the `Profile`, whereupon we use the `update_or_create()` method. The method tries to find an existing `Profile` for this user, using the keyword argument passed to it. In the event the `Profile` exists, the method uses the dictionary passed to the `defaults` keyword to update those values, in this case updating just the `slug` field. In the event `update_or_create()` cannot find a `Profile` for this user, it creates one, filling in both the `user` and `slug` fields, as shown in Example 22.4.

**Example 22.4: Project Code**
`user/forms.py` in 6b8d9ef930

```
40    class UserCreationForm(
41            ActivationMailFormMixin,
42            BaseUserCreationForm):
  .     ...
69        def save(self, **kwargs):
  .         ...
76            user.save()
77            self.save_m2m()
78            Profile.objects.update_or_create(
79                user=user,
80                defaults={
81                    'slug': slugify(
82                        user.get_username()),
83                })
```

## 22.2.2  Implementing `ProfileDetail`

Creating a public profile view is quite straightforward, so I opt to take on the stranger case first. In the case of our `ProfileDetail` view, shown in Example 22.5, we want to show the user's own profile at a static (without regular expression character sets) URL: `/user/profile/`.

**Example 22.5: Project Code**
`user/urls.py` in de5e3e356d

```
10    from .views import (
11        ActivateAccount, CreateAccount,
12        DisableAccount, ProfileDetail,
13        ResendActivationEmail)
  .     ...
67    urlpatterns = [
  .     ...
108       url(r'^profile/$',
109           ProfileDetail.as_view(),
110           name='profile'),
111   ]
```

To properly display the profile of the current User, we need to take the authenticated `User` from the `HttpRequest` object and then use it to return the related `Profile`. In anticipation of needing `Profile` in multiple views, we create the `ProfileGetObjectMixin`, implementing the `get_object()` commonly used by GCBVs, as shown in Example 22.6.

**Example 22.6: Project Code**
`user/utils.py` **in** de5e3e356d

```
  7    from django.contrib.auth import get_user
  .       ...
170    class ProfileGetObjectMixin:
171
172        def get_object(self, queryset=None):
173            current_user = get_user(self.request)
174            return current_user.profile
```

We can use this mixin with the `DetailView` GCBV to quickly create our `ProfileDetail` view, as shown in Example 22.7. To ensure that there is always an actual user accessing the page, we use the `@class_login_required` decorator we created in Chapter 20: Integrating Permissions (if we do not, anonymous visitors will cause the `get_object()` to attempt to get the `profile` attribute on `AnonymousUser` instances, which will error).

**Example 22.7: Project Code**
`user/views.py` **in** de5e3e356d

```
 24    from django.views.generic import DetailView, View
 25
 26    from .decorators import class_login_required
  .       ...
 29    from .models import Profile
 30    from .utils import (
 31        MailContextViewMixin, ProfileGetObjectMixin)
  .       ...
126    @class_login_required
127    class ProfileDetail(
128          · ProfileGetObjectMixin, DetailView):
129        model = Profile
```

Finally, we can create our template, as shown in Example 22.8.

**Example 22.8: Project Code**
`user/templates/user/profile_detail.html` **in** de5e3e356d

```
 1    {% extends parent_template|default:"user/base_user.html" %}
 2
 3    {% block title %}
 4    {{ block.super }} -
 5    {{ profile.user.get_username }}'s Profile
 6    {% endblock %}
 7
 8    {% block content %}
```

```
 9      <div class="row">
 .        ...
26      </div><!-- row -->
27    {% endblock %}
```

Line 5 may seem odd: Why are we not using request.user? We will be using this template for both ProfileDetail and PublicProfileDetail and therefore need to always fetch user information through the Profile object.

With the outline of the template, we then create two columns in our row, as shown in Example 22.9.

**Example 22.9: Project Code**
user/templates/user/profile_detail.html **in** de5e3e356d

```
10          <div class="offset-by-two five columns">
 .            ...
15          </div><!-- columns -->
16
17          <div class="three columns">
 .            ...
24          </div>
```

The first column displays the actual profile and acts as the main content for the page, as shown in Example 22.10.

**Example 22.10: Project Code**
user/templates/user/profile_detail.html **in** de5e3e356d

```
12          <h2>About {{ profile.user.get_username }}</h2>
13          {{ profile.about|default:"No Profile"|linebreaks }}
```

The second column provides links to the user, allowing the user to change his or her password or disable his or her account, as shown in Example 22.11. We return to handle permissions once we build PublicProfileDetail.

**Example 22.11: Project Code**
user/templates/user/profile_detail.html **in** de5e3e356d

```
18          <ul class="task-list">
19            <li><a href="{% url 'dj-auth:pw_change' %}">
20              Change Password</a></li>
21            <li><a href="{% url 'dj-auth:disable' %}">
22              Disable Account</a></li>
23          </ul>
```

Finally, in Example 22.12, we link to our new profile from the base template, displaying the link for all authenticated users.

**Example 22.12: Project Code**
`templates/base.html` **in** de5e3e356d

```
33                          <li><a href="{% url 'dj-auth:profile' %}">
34                          View Profile</a></li>
```

## 22.2.3 Profile Update

A user profile is meaningless if the user can't control it, and so we create `ProfileUpdate` for users to change their profile as they see fit.

Thanks to `ProfileGetObjectMixin`, creating the view is very simple. We also gain the benefit of our own `UpdateView` GCBV, as shown in Example 22.13.

**Example 22.13: Project Code**
`user/views.py` **in** 83167965e8

```
 26    from core.utils import UpdateView
   .       ...
134    @class_login_required
135    class ProfileUpdate(
136            ProfileGetObjectMixin, UpdateView):
137        fields = ('about',)
138        model = Profile
```

Unlike with many of our other `UpdateView` subclasses, we are not setting the `form_class` attribute and are instead using the `fields` attribute. The view will generate a form for us using `ModelForm` inheritance, passing the `fields` attribute to this form, just as we have seen on all our own `ModelForm` subclasses.

We can then create the URL pattern for our view, as shown in Example 22.14.

**Example 22.14: Project Code**
`user/urls.py` **in** 83167965e8

```
 10    from .views import (
 11        ActivateAccount, CreateAccount,
 12        DisableAccount, ProfileDetail, ProfileUpdate,
 13        ResendActivationEmail)
   .       ...
 67    urlpatterns = [
   .       ...
111        url(r'^profile/edit/$',
112            ProfileUpdate.as_view(),
113            name='profile_update'),
114    ]
```

Finally, we create the template in Example 22.15.

**Example 22.15: Project Code**

`user/templates/user/profile_form_update.html` in 83167965e8

```
1    {% extends parent_template|default:"user/base_user.html" %}
2
3    {% block title %}
4    {{ block.super }} - Update Profile
5    {% endblock %}
6
7
8    {% block content %}
9      <div class="row">
10       <div class="offset-by-two eight columns">
.        ...
19       </div>
20     </div>
21   {% endblock %}
```

The HTML form is par for the course, as shown in Example 22.16.

**Example 22.16: Project Code**

`user/templates/user/profile_form_update.html` in 83167965e8

```
11          <form
12              action="{{ profile.get_update_url }}"
13              method="post">
14           {% csrf_token %}
15           {{ form.as_p }}
16           <button type="submit">
17             Update Profile</button>
18          </form>
```

With a full webpage, we can create a get_update_url() method on the Profile model, as shown in Example 22.17.

**Example 22.17: Project Code**

`user/models.py` in 83167965e8

```
2    from django.core.urlresolvers import reverse
.        ...
6    class Profile(models.Model):
.        ...
17       def get_update_url(self):
18           return reverse('dj-auth:profile_update')
```

Now we can quickly get the link in the `profile_detail.html` template, allowing users to access the form from their own profile page, as shown in Example 22.18.

**Example 22.18: Project Code**

`user/templates/user/profile_detail.html` **in** 83167965e8

```
19                 <li><a href="{{ profile.get_update_url }}">
20                     Edit Your Profile</a></li>
```

## 22.2.4 Public Profile

As opposed to the `ProfileDetail` page, the `PublicProfileDetail` webpage shows the profiles of other users, meaning that we use the `slug` field on the `Profile` model to find the `Profile` and then display it. The `PublicProfileDetail` webpage is thus simple, because the view is just a `DetailView` subclass, as you can see in Example 22.19.

**Example 22.19: Project Code**

`user/views.py` **in** a1d420b17a

```
134    class PublicProfileDetail(DetailView):
135        model = Profile
```

The URL is also exactly what you'd expect, as you can see in Example 22.20.

**Example 22.20: Project Code**

`user/urls.py` **in** a1d420b17a

```
 10    from .views import (
 11        ActivateAccount, CreateAccount,
 12        DisableAccount, ProfileDetail, ProfileUpdate,
 13        PublicProfileDetail, ResendActivationEmail)
   .       ...
 67    urlpatterns = [
   .       ...
114        url(r'^(?P<slug>[\w\-]+)/$',
115            PublicProfileDetail.as_view(),
116            name='public_profile'),
117    ]
```

We've already created the `profile_detail.html`, but we now need to modify it. We only ever want to show the side column (with the links to change passwords and disable the account) in the event the user accessing the page is the owner of the profile, so we wrap the column in a condition, as shown in Example 22.21.

**Example 22.21: Project Code**
`user/templates/user/profile_detail.html` **in** a1d420b17a

```
21        {% if user.pk == profile.user.pk %}
 .        ...
32        {% endif%}
```

If the side column does not exist, then we can expand the main content column to be larger, as shown in Example 22.22.

**Example 22.22: Project Code**
`user/templates/user/profile_detail.html` **in** a1d420b17a

```
10        {% if user.pk == profile.user.pk %}
11          <div class="offset-by-two five columns">
12        {% else %}
13          <div class="offset-by-two eight columns">
14        {% endif%}
```

The utility of our template is that the side column will be shown not only when the `ProfileDetail` view is used but also when the `PublicProfileDetail` renders the template for the owner of the profile. If my user `'andrew'` visits /user/andrew/, then the side column will still be shown to me, just as if I had visited /user/profile/, but it will not be shown if Ada visits my public profile page. This is because none of our variables care which view or URL was used to render the template and instead rely on information about the owner of the `Profile` object.

Finally, in Example 22.23, we take the opportunity to create a model method to easily link to our new webpage.

**Example 22.23: Project Code**
`user/models.py` **in** a1d420b17a

```
 6    class Profile(models.Model):
 .        ...
17        def get_absolute_url(self):
18            return reverse(
19                'dj-auth:public_profile',
20                kwargs={'slug': self.slug})
```

# 22.3   Custom User

Creating a `Profile` model is great when we need to add information, but it becomes woefully unhelpful if we want to change or remove information. I am not a fan of the fact that our current implementation uses both a `username` and an `email` field on the `User` model. If we want to use only the `email` field, we must change the `User` model itself.

The User model is actually a very thin model that inherits from AbstractUser, where most of the user fields are defined. However, this class in turn inherits from AbstractBaseUser and PermissionsMixin. The AbstractBaseUser defines the heart of the User model, supplying the password and last_login field as well as the methods to interact with the password field. The PermissionsMixin defines the many-to-many relations to the Group and Permission models as well as the is_superuser field.

If we wanted to extend the User model, we would want to inherit from AbstractUser. But as we are looking to simplify the model and remove fields, we instead inherit from AbstractBaseUser and PermissionsMixin, as shown in Example 22.24.

**Example 22.24: Project Code**
user/models.py **in** 3d4b58d6e3

```
2    from django.contrib.auth.models import (
3        AbstractBaseUser, PermissionsMixin)
```

## Warning!

Starting this section, and until we generate our migrations, the check command for manage.py is going to be very unhappy with you. It will warn you of things like the following:

```
auth.User.groups: (fields.E304)
Reverse accessor for 'User.groups' clashes with
reverse accessor for 'User.groups'.
```

These warnings occur because PermissionsMixin defines the related_name option on the relations to Group and Permission. The user_set attribute on Group doesn't know whether to use the **auth** User model or our custom User model.

Our User model, shown in Example 22.25, is very simple. While most permissions are handled on top of our email field, we need to define is_staff and is_active. Without the first, our users won't be able to use the **admin** app, seen in Chapter 23: The Admin Library, and without the second, we won't be able to disable accounts (AbstractBaseUser defines is_active as always being True, meaning that if we didn't override it, we'd still be able to log in).

**Example 22.25: Project Code**
user/models.py **in** 3d4b58d6e3

```
28   class User(AbstractBaseUser, PermissionsMixin):
29       email = models.EmailField(
30           'email address',
31           max_length=254,
32           unique=True)
```

```
33        is_staff = models.BooleanField(
34            'staff status',
35            default=False,
36            help_text=(
37                'Designates whether the user can '
38                'log into this admin site.'))
39        is_active = models.BooleanField(
40            'active',
41            default=True,
42            help_text=(
43                'Designates whether this user should '
44                'be treated as active. Unselect this '
45                'instead of deleting accounts.'))
```

For our interactions with other parts of Django to work, we need to set the USERNAME attribute, which informs Django which of our fields is to be used for logins and the like, as shown in Example 22.26.

**Example 22.26: Project Code**
user/models.py **in** 3d4b58d6e3

```
28   class User(AbstractBaseUser, PermissionsMixin):
 .       ...
47        USERNAME_FIELD = 'email'
```

In Example 22.27, we then define __str__() and get_absolute_url(), as we do for any model.

**Example 22.27: Project Code**
user/models.py **in** 3d4b58d6e3

```
28   class User(AbstractBaseUser, PermissionsMixin):
 .       ...
49        def __str__(self):
50            return self.email
51
52        def get_absolute_url(self):
53            return self.profile.get_absolute_url()
```

To finish, we add two new fields to Profile: name and joined, as shown in Example 22.28. AbstractUser (not AbstractBaseUser, which we are inheriting from) defines fields for first_name, last_name, and date_joined. The last one is added because of its utility in demonstrating a feature in Chapter 23. The first two are meant to draw your attention to the fact that splitting the name into first and last is perfectly normal in most of the western world, but it doesn't fly in a lot of other places. While this will depend largely on your audience, it's increasingly considered good practice to simply supply a single field for the name and to let the user do the work.

**Example 22.28: Project Code**
user/models.py **in** 271c91a607

```
 8   class Profile(models.Model):
 .       ...
11       name = models.CharField(
12           max_length=255)
 .       ...
17       joined = models.DateTimeField(
18           "Date Joined",
19           auto_now_add=True)
```

The utility is also that we get to define get_full_name() get_short_name() on User, making our model's API as similar as possible to the original (Example 22.29).

**Example 22.29: Project Code**
user/models.py **in** 271c91a607

```
36           max_length=254,
 .       ...
60       def get_full_name(self):
61           return self.profile.name
62
63       def get_short_name(self):
64           return self.profile.name
```

## 22.3.1   Creating a Custom Manager for User

When we interacted with the **auth**'s User model, we found that the manager has been changed to make interacting with passwords easier. Unfortunately, because we've created our own custom User, we no longer have access to the UserManager provided by **auth**.

Creating custom managers is the topic of Chapter 24, and so we're jumping the gun a little bit in this section. However, we don't need full understanding of managers in this section, because the changes in this section are really easy. The **auth**'s UserManager inherits from BaseUserManager and defines the create_user() and create_superuser() methods we want to use. Therefore, we can create a class that inherits from BaseUserManager and define our own create_user() and create_superuser() methods.

To create the new manager, we import BaseUserManager and inherit it in the new class we declare, as shown in Example 22.30. I set the use_in_migrations to True so that the migrations system will use the manager when interacting with User.

**Example 22.30: Project Code**

`user/models.py` **in** 9c6001c36d

```
2   from django.contrib.auth.models import (
3       AbstractBaseUser, BaseUserManager,
4       PermissionsMixin)
.       ...
34  class UserManager(BaseUserManager):
35      use_in_migrations = True
```

Given that both `create_user()` and `create_superuser()` create a user, we create a helper function that does the majority of the work, called `_create_user()`.

To start, we rely on the `normalize_email()` method provided by the `BaseUserManager` class to standardize the case of the domain in the email. We then get expected values from `kwargs` and set intelligent defaults (`False`) if they don't exist. Finally, we use the `model` attribute to create the `User` instance, set a password, and save the object to the database, as shown in Example 22.31.

**Example 22.31: Project Code**

`user/models.py` **in** 9c6001c36d

```
34  class UserManager(BaseUserManager):
.       ...
37      def _create_user(
38              self, email, password, **kwargs):
39          email = self.normalize_email(email)
40          is_staff = kwargs.pop('is_staff', False)
41          is_superuser = kwargs.pop(
42              'is_superuser', False)
43          user = self.model(
44              email=email,
45              is_active=True,
46              is_staff=is_staff,
47              is_superuser=is_superuser,
48              **kwargs)
49          user.set_password(password)
50          user.save(using=self._db)
51          return user
```

> **Info**
>
> It is possible the password passed to our `_create_user` will be None. In the event `set_password` is passed None, the User instance will not have a valid password, as shown by the `has_usable_password()` method. This is perfectly valid and will not be a problem. However, should we wish to create a password, we could rely on the `make_random_password()` method.

Example 22.32 makes the implementation of `create_user()` very straightforward, as we simply call `_create_user()`.

**Example 22.32: Project Code**
`user/models.py` in 9c6001c36d

```
34    class UserManager(BaseUserManager):
 .       ...
53       def create_user(
54             self, email, password=None,
55             **extra_fields):
56          return self._create_user(
57             email, password, **extra_fields)
```

The implementation of `create_superuser()` is similarly straightforward, but we make sure in this instance to set `is_staff` and `is_superuser` to True, as shown in Example 22.33. We also make the `password` argument mandatory in this case, as opposed to `create_user()` where the field was optional.

**Example 22.33: Project Code**
`user/models.py` in 9c6001c36d

```
34    class UserManager(BaseUserManager):
 .       ...
59       def create_superuser(
60             self, email, password,
61             **extra_fields):
62          return self._create_user(
63             email, password,
64             is_staff=True, is_superuser=True,
65             **extra_fields)
```

Usually, Django generates managers for models automatically. If we want our own, we can simply override the `objects` attribute in the model. To connect our `UserManager` to the `User` model, we do just that in Example 22.34.

**Example 22.34: Project Code**
`user/models.py` in 9c6001c36d

```
68    class User(AbstractBaseUser, PermissionsMixin):
 .       ...
89       objects = UserManager()
```

We now have the ability to call `User.objects.create_user()` again!

## 22.3.2    Swapping the User Model

We have a new `User` model and a new `UserManager`—now we need to replace the **auth** versions. The code to do so is surprisingly easy: we just need to define a variable in our settings and tell it the location of the new `User` model, as shown in Example 22.35.

**Example 22.35: Project Code**

`suorganizer/settings.py` in 19560085fc

```
83   # User
84   # https://docs.djangoproject.com/en/1.8/topics/auth/customizing/
85
86   AUTH_USER_MODEL = 'user.User'
```

This black magic is actually one of Django's secret, undocumented features, called **swappable models**. In anticipation of our desire to override the `User` class, the Django team set out to allow *any* model to be swapped with another. For a model to be swappable, the `swappable` attribute on the `Meta` nested class needs to be defined, declaring the setting that will allow the model to be replaced, as shown in Example 22.36.

**Example 22.36: Python Code**

```
# django/contrib/auth/models.py
class User(AbstractUser):
    ...
    class Meta(AbstractUser.Meta):
        swappable = 'AUTH_USER_MODEL'
```

*Any* model you build can be set to be swapped. When building a large project meant to be reused by others, this feature can be powerful and useful. However, you use it at your own peril: the reason the feature is undocumented is because, while in actual use, the feature is subject to change.

The other problem with swappable models is that they don't play well with migrations. If you try to create a migration for our new `User` model, Django will error in several different, cryptic ways. The issue is that we have migrations applied for the **auth**'s `User` model, and the relations with other models no longer make sense to Django.

If we had a production database at this point, we would be in *real* trouble. We would have to unload all our data (using fixtures, seen in Chapter 24), rebuild the database, and structure our data to be loaded back in. This would be a lot of work (work we usually avoid because of migrations!).

We thankfully don't have a production database, and all of the important data in our site is generated in data migrations, so we can simply delete the database, as shown in Example 22.37.

**Example 22.37: Shell Code**

```
rm db.sqlite3
```

This is only the first step to correcting our problem. At the moment, our initial **user** migration creates the `Profile` model in the database as the `user_profile` table. This model has a one-to-one relation with `User`, which means the `user_profile` table has a column pointing to the `user_user` table—which doesn't exist. We need the migration of the `User` model to appear before the `Profile` model. In fact, Django's documentation states that the migration for a swappable model must be the first migration in the app. We therefore delete the current migration and create a new one, as shown in Example 22.38.

**Example 22.38: Shell Code**

```
rm user/migrations/0001_initial.py
./manage.py makemigrations user
```

This code creates the `user/migrations/0001_initial.py` migration file, which will use the `CreateModel` operation twice to create first the `User`, then the `Profile` (don't use the original `Profile` migration: it will be invalid because of the name and `joined` fields we added). Given that the `User` model being swapped in is considered special, we opt to remove the `CreateModel` operation for `Profile` and move it into its own migration file. We rename the first migration as well, leaving us with two files, as shown in Example 22.39.

**Example 22.39: Shell Code**

```
$ tree user/migrations/
user/migrations/
├── 0001_user.py
├── 0002_profile.py
└── __init__.py

0 directories, 3 files
```

To recreate our database, we can simply use `migrate`, as shown in Example 22.40.

**Example 22.40: Shell Code**

```
$ ./manage.py migrate
```

All of our `Tag`, `Startup`, `NewsLink`, and `Post` will be right back in the database thanks to our data migrations. However, any users we had previously created are now missing. We could invoke the Django shell and use our new `UserManager` to create them, but we'll opt to wait, as we'll be creating data migrations for our users.

## Warning!

As of right now, the create_superuser command for manage.py doesn't work as desired. The command will still correctly create a user, but will not create a Profile, resulting in some unexpected site behavior. We will fix this in Chapter 24.

### 22.3.3    Integrating Forms and Templates

When we created our new User model, we removed the username field, choosing to use only the email field for user authentication. This is a bit of a problem because the UserCreationForm uses the username to create the Profile object. The profile_detail.html also needs to be changed because it calls get_username(), which will now display the email and needs to instead use get_full_name().

This transition away from username is made possible largely because of the name field added to the Profile model. Our goal is thus to ask the user for a value for the name field and then to use it to create the Profile, including the generation of the slug field on Profile.

Our first change to UserCreationForm is thus to add a manual name field, as shown in Example 22.41.

**Example 22.41: Project Code**
user/forms.py in f84d897b92

```
40    class UserCreationForm(
41            ActivationMailFormMixin,
42            BaseUserCreationForm):
43
44        name = forms.CharField(
45            max_length=255,
46            help_text=(
47                "The name displayed on your "
48                "public profile."))
```

We then want the field to appear before the email, so in Example 22.42, we use it in the fields attribute of the nested Meta class (it will appear at the bottom of the form if we don't do this).

**Example 22.42: Project Code**
user/forms.py in f84d897b92

```
40    class UserCreationForm(
41            ActivationMailFormMixin,
42            BaseUserCreationForm):
 .        ...
54        class Meta(BaseUserCreationForm.Meta):
55            model = get_user_model()
56            fields = ('name', 'email')
```

We rename clean_username() to clean_name() and change any instance of username to name, as shown in Example 22.43.

**Example 22.43: Project Code**
user/forms.py **in** f84d897b92

```
40    class UserCreationForm(
41            ActivationMailFormMixin,
42            BaseUserCreationForm):
  .        ...
58        def clean_name(self):
59            name = self.cleaned_data['name']
  .            ...
69            if name in disallowed:
70                raise ValidationError(
71                    "A user with that name"
72                    " already exists.")
73            return name
```

Finally, in Example 22.44, we change the call to update_or_create() in the save() method to use the new name field.

**Example 22.44: Project Code**
user/forms.py **in** f84d897b92

```
40    class UserCreationForm(
41            ActivationMailFormMixin,
42            BaseUserCreationForm):
  .        ...
75        def save(self, **kwargs):
  .            ...
82            user.save()
83            self.save_m2m()
84            Profile.objects.update_or_create(
85                user=user,
86                defaults={
87                    'name': self.cleaned_data['name'],
88                    'slug': slugify(
89                        self.cleaned_data['name']),
90                })
91            if send_mail:
92                self.send_mail(user=user, **kwargs)
```

The change to the template is far simpler: we just change the call in the title of the page to use get_full_name(), as shown in Example 22.45.

**Example 22.45: Project Code**
user/templates/user/profile_detail.html **in** 390536ebb8

```
 5    {{ profile.user.get_full_name }}'s Profile
  .        ...
16        <h2>About {{ profile.user.get_full_name }}</h2>
```

## 22.4   Data Migrations

When we erased our database, we removed all of the users we had previously added. I'm lazy, and if I know I need those users on my website, I am loathe to create them again every time. I'm therefore going to create a data migration to create basic user accounts.

Please take a moment to consider that what I am doing is a **huge security risk**. If this code is available publicly (it is) or unchanged at production (`https://site .django-unleashed.com` does not have these users), then these accounts are attack vectors and provide the bad people and bad robots with access to our website. In a normal website, you probably don't want to do what I am about to. However, this website isn't really a production website—it's a website to learn Django in a book. As such, being able to download the code and create a database with existing users and passwords is in your interest and provides a learning opportunity.

The problem with a `User` migration is that we rely on the existence of permissions. In particular, we will be relying on the `Post` object permissions: we will create both `andrew` and `ada` users again, and we will assign `ada` to the `contributor` group, with permissions to add, edit, and view future `Post` objects. These permissions existed in our database before we deleted it, but when creating a new database (for example, each time we use the test suite, unfortunately not covered in this book), they are only generated by Django after all of the migrations have been applied, thanks to the `create_permissions()` function in the **auth** app. Before we can create a `User` migration, we must create a migration that ensures the existence of these permissions. We thus create two data migrations: the first to force the generation of `Post` object permissions, and the second to create the actual `User` and `Group` instances, as shown in Example 22.46.

**Example 22.46: Shell Code**

```
$ ./manage.py makemigrations --empty --name='post_permissions' blog
$ ./manage.py makemigrations --empty --name='user_data' user
```

In our new `0005_post_permissions.py`, we jump straight into the `generate_ permissions()` function, which will be used when we apply the migration. We fetch the historical `Permission` model, and we check whether or not any of the expected permissions exists, as shown in Example 22.47.

**Example 22.47: Project Code**
blog/migrations/0005_post_permissions.py in 5454084e88

```
 4    from django.contrib.auth.management import \
 5        create_permissions
 .        ...
 9    def generate_permissions(apps, schema_editor):
10        Permission = apps.get_model(
11            'auth', 'Permission')
```

```
12         try:
13             Permission.objects.get(
14                 codename='add_post',
15                 content_type__app_label='blog')
16         except Permission.DoesNotExist:
```

In the event an exception is raised, we wish to use the create_permissions() function to generate the permissions, just as Django would do normally. At this point, our code gets a little strange, as you can see in Example 22.48.

**Example 22.48: Project Code**
blog/migrations/0005_post_permissions.py **in** 5454084e88

```
 9     def generate_permissions(apps, schema_editor):
 .         ...
16         except Permission.DoesNotExist:
17             models_module = getattr(
18                 apps, 'models_module', None)
19             if models_module is None:
20                 apps.models_module = True
21                 create_permissions(apps, verbosity=0)
22                 apps.models_module = None
23             else:
24                 raise
```

In Chapter 10: Revisiting Migrations, we discussed how the migration system relies on the Apps structure, which is a list of AppConfig objects, containing information about every app in our project. In the preceding code, we appear to be pulling the models_module attribute from the Apps instance, asserting that it is *always* None, and then setting it to True for create_permissions() and reverting the attribute to None. This is strange indeed, especially if you consult the documentation, which will tell you that the models_module should typically point to the models.py file in each app. Why, then, are we so sure the models_module is None, when we are certain that the **blog** app contains a models.py file?

## Django Documentation

For the actual documentation being referenced:

https://dju.link/18/models-module

The migrations system doesn't actually use Apps or AppConfig and instead subclasses the two of them into slightly different creatures to more easily calculate the historical models: StateApps and AppConfigStub. Unlike AppConfig, the AppConfigStub class avoids the use of models_module. When we assert that models_module is None, we are effectively checking that the migrations system is being used and that it has not changed.

However, the `create_permissions()` is meant to be run and called with a full `AppConfig`, and it checks for the existence of the `models_module`. After all, without any models, it won't need to generate any permissions on that app. This proves to be a problem with `AppConfigStub`, where the attribute is always `None` and will always fail the check. However, this is merely a check, and `create_permissions()` relies on `get_models()`, defined on `AppConfigStub`, to actually do the work. Therefore, we can simply set `models_module` to `True` to pass the internal check, and `create_permissions()` will correctly generate permissions with `AppConfigStub`.

This technique is a little bit dangerous, of course. We are creating permissions for the historical blog app. If this app changes greatly over the course of our project, or if Django changes its internal use of the `create_permissions()` function, this migration may get us into more trouble than it's worth. Django doesn't supply a way to call `create_permissions()` before the migrations are done, and so this code is very much considered a workaround. Because most developers frown upon creating users in data migrations (it's a security risk!), this is also not likely to change anytime soon.

With our forward function, we can build the function that will be used when unapplying the migration. The catch, of course, is that we have absolutely no work to do, as you can see in Example 22.49.

**Example 22.49: Project Code**

`blog/migrations/0005_post_permissions.py` **in** `5454084e88`

```
27   def reverse_code(apps, schema_editor):
28       pass
```

It might seem like a good idea to forgo the creation of this function and simply leave the `reverse_code` parameter of the `RunPython` operation blank. However, if we do so, unapplying the migration will error. It's therefore best to always define a function to reverse the migration, even if that function does nothing.

Our migration relies not only on the rest of our **blog** migration but also on the ability to create the `Permission` object. In Example 22.50, we therefore add a dependency to the latest migration in the **auth** app (this is the latest in Django 1.8—it is certainly not the latest in Django 1.7, and may not be the one to use in Django 1.9 or later. You will need to check as appropriate.)

**Example 22.50: Project Code**

`blog/migrations/0005_post_permissions.py` **in** `5454084e88`

```
31   class Migration(migrations.Migration):
32
33       dependencies = [
34           ('auth',
35            '0006_require_contenttypes_0002'),
36           ('blog',
37            '0004_add_view_future_post_permission'),
38       ]
```

Finally, in Example 22.51, we can actually call the RunPython operation with our function.

**Example 22.51: Project Code**
blog/migrations/0005_post_permissions.py **in** 5454084e88

```
31   class Migration(migrations.Migration):
 .       ...
40       operations = [
41           migrations.RunPython(
42               generate_permissions,
43               reverse_code,
44           )
45       ]
```

Now we can turn our attention to the 0003_user_data.py migration in the **user** app, where we'll create two functions to apply and unapply the migration, as shown in Example 22.52.

**Example 22.52: Project Code**
user/migrations/0003_user_data.py **in** 5454084e88

```
 4   from django.contrib.auth.hashers import \
 5       make_password
 .       ...
 9   def add_user_data(apps, schema_editor):
 .       ...
64   def remove_user_data(apps, schema_editor):
```

We make sure to depend on our new 0005_post_permissions.py migration as well as the other **user** migrations, and we use the two methods to generate data, as shown in Example 22.53.

**Example 22.53: Project Code**
user/migrations/0003_user_data.py **in** 5454084e88

```
79   class Migration(migrations.Migration):
80
81       dependencies = [
82           ('blog', '0005_post_permissions'),
83           ('user', '0002_profile'),
84       ]
85
86       operations = [
87           migrations.RunPython(
88               add_user_data,
89               remove_user_data)
90       ]
```

We won't actually see the code in the forwards and backwards functions. The code uses the material we learned in Chapter 10 and in Chapter 19: Basic Authentication, and it doesn't present anything new, so we will skip it. Of course, the code is in the repository online in case you're curious or stuck on anything.

## 22.5   Adding an Author to Blog Posts

Given that we are allowing specific users to write blog posts, it would be nice if we identified which blog post was written by which user. We can connect our `Post` to the `User` model exactly as if we had never customized it, as shown in Example 22.54.

**Example 22.54: Project Code**
`blog/models.py` in 9515ba8ede

```
 1    from django.conf import settings
 .        ...
12    class Post(models.Model):
 .        ...
18        author = models.ForeignKey(
19            settings.AUTH_USER_MODEL,
20            related_name='blog_posts')
```

Hopefully, our dependency on the use of `get_user_model()` and relations built using the `setting.AUTH_USER_MODEL` is a lot clearer than before. We won't always know which model is being used to represent a user account because the `User` model supplied by **auth** is a swappable model. By relying on these tools, we limit the code we will have to modify if the swappable model is changed, and we can write more generic Django code that more easily integrates with projects (we still cannot avoid the problem of migrations with swappable models, sadly).

To create a migration for the new field, we can invoke `makemigrations`, as shown in Example 22.55. Django will ask us at that point what value we wish to fill into the column for the existing `Post` object.

**Example 22.55: Shell Code**

```
$ ./manage.py makemigrations
You are trying to add a non-nullable field 'author' to post without
    a default; we can't do that (the database needs something to populate
    existing rows).
Please select a fix:
 1) Provide a one-off default now (will be set on all existing rows)
 2) Quit and let me add a default in models.py
Select an option: 1
Please enter the default value now, as valid Python
The datetime and django.utils.timezone modules are available, so you can
    do, e.g., timezone.now()
```

As we've added a relation, we need to pass in a primary key value. I know that I'm the first User in the database, so I pass the primary key of 1 to point all existing blog posts to the Andrew user, as shown in Example 22.56.

**Example 22.56: Shell Code**

```
>>> 1
Migrations for 'blog':
  0006_post_author.py:
    - Add field author to post
```

We can then apply the new blog/migrations/0006_post_author.py file, as shown in Example 22.57.

**Example 22.57: Shell Code**

```
$ ./manage.py migrate
```

When users write a blog post, we want Django to fill in the author field for them (so that they can't write an inflammatory article and then blame someone else). We therefore exclude the new field from the PostForm form, as shown in Example 22.58.

**Example 22.58: Project Code**
blog/forms.py **in** 9515ba8ede

```
2    from django.contrib.auth import get_user
.        ...
7    class PostForm(forms.ModelForm):
8        class Meta:
9            model = Post
10           exclude = ('author',)
```

When we save this form, we want Django to infer which user is submitting the form. We can use the content seen in Chapter 18: Advanced Generic Class–Based View Usage, Section 18.8.2, to build this functionality. We create a mixin class for GCBVs to pass the HttpRequest object to the form when calling save(), allowing the form to get the currently authenticated user submitting the data.

We start by overriding the save() method, as shown in Example 22.59. We accept the HttpRequest object and create a Post instance without saving to the database. In the event we are creating the object (it does not yet have a primary key), we use the HttpRequest object to get the currently authenticated user who is submitting the data, and add that user as the author field. We then save the form, and remember to call save_m2m() to save related Tag and Startup data that might have changed (in our form, we deal only with the Post, so this won't be terribly important, but if our form were more complicated, it would be crucial).

**Example 22.59: Project Code**

blog/forms.py **in** 9515ba8ede

```
 7   class PostForm(forms.ModelForm):
 .       ...
15       def save(self, request, commit=True):
16           post = super().save(commit=False)
17           if not post.pk:
18               post.author = get_user(request)
19           if commit:
20               post.save()
21               self.save_m2m()
22           return post
```

We can then create a mixin for our Post GCBVs. In Example 22.60, we override the form_valid() method, called when the form (defined in the form_class or generated by the fields attribute) is bound and valid.

**Example 22.60: Project Code**

blog/utils.py **in** 9515ba8ede

```
  1   from django.http import (
  2       Http404, HttpResponseRedirect)
  .       ...
 95   class PostFormValidMixin:
 96
 97       def form_valid(self, form):
 98           self.object = form.save(self.request)
 99           return HttpResponseRedirect(
100               self.get_success_url())
```

Example 22.61 allows us to inherit the behavior in both PostCreate and PostUpdate.

**Example 22.61: Project Code**

blog/views.py **in** 9515ba8ede

```
12   from .utils import (
13       AllowFuturePermissionMixin, DateObjectMixin,
14       PostFormValidMixin)
 .       ...
35   class PostCreate(PostFormValidMixin, CreateView):
 .       ...
67   class PostUpdate(
68           PostFormValidMixin,
69           DateObjectMixin,
70           UpdateView):
```

Now that we have an author for our blog posts, we can show the posts written by the user on his or her profile.

In preparation for the related content we will display on the user's profile page, we create a published_posts() method on the User model, as shown in Example 22.62, imitating the methods by the same name on Tag and Startup models, implemented in Chapter 20.

**Example 22.62: Project Code**
user/models.py in 8dc8c71baf

```
  1    from datetime import date
  .       ...
 70    class User(AbstractBaseUser, PermissionsMixin):
  .        ...
105        def published_posts(self):
106            return self.blog_posts.filter(
107                pub_date__lt=date.today())
```

In Example 22.63, we first create a condition for what to display in the template, checking both permissions and the existence of content.

**Example 22.63: Project Code**
user/templates/user/profile_detail.html in 8dc8c71baf

```
 19        {% if perms.blog.view_future_post and profile.user.blog_posts.all %}
  .          ...
 30        {% elif profile.user.published_posts|length > 0 %}
  .          ...
 41        {% endif %}
```

In the second condition clause, in Example 22.64, we use the new published_posts() method to show all of the related Post instances.

**Example 22.64: Project Code**
user/templates/user/profile_detail.html in 8dc8c71baf

```
 31            <section>
 32              <h3>Blog Post{{ profile.user.published_posts|pluralize }}</h3>
 33              <ul>
 34                {% for post in profile.user.published_posts %}
 35                  <li><a href="{{ post.get_absolute_url }}">
 36                    {{ post.title|title }}
 37                  </a></li>
 38                {% endfor %}
 39              </ul>
 40            </section>
```

The code for the first clause is not displayed because it is very similar, using `profile.user.blog_posts.all` instead of `published_posts()`.

## 22.6   Putting It All Together

When changing the information about the user in Django, we have two choices. If we want to add information, we can create a `Profile` model to add the information. If we wish to remove or change information or behavior, we need to customize the `User` model, made possible because it is a swappable model.

Determining what information the product needs to work is one of the first questions a developer should ask when building a website in Django, largely because changing the `User` model affects the migration system in a very disruptive manner (we *deleted* our database because that was the best option—this option will not always be available to you).

In modern Django, best practice is to have as little information as possible on the `User` model and then to *never, ever* change it. This attitude exists mainly because of the migration problems. All of the extraneous data not related to authentication and permissions is therefore set on `Profile`, which can be much more easily changed. This is effectively what we have by the end of the chapter: our `User` model has an `email` and a `password` field for authentication, and all of the other fields—`is_staff`, `is_superuser`, and `is_active`—are for permissions. In fact, only the `last_login` field appears to be extraneous. The field is defined in `AbstractBaseUser` and actually pertains to security, because it is used by the token generation parts of **auth** to reset passwords, as discussed in Chapter 21. As such, there is *nothing* we could remove from our `User` model and still have authentication work. This is in contrast to `Profile`, which really only needs the `slug` and user fields to be used by Django. The rest is purely for human consumption.

With the swap of the `User` model and the creation of the `Profile`, we have finished with the **auth** app. In the last four chapters, we created login pages, enabled permissions on our website, allowed users to manage their account, and then streamlined the user model. The **auth** app has absolutely no secrets anymore.

In an actual website, you likely won't interact with the **auth** in the way we have. You'll rely on third-party apps to provide object-level permissions or else on authentication with other services such as Twitter and Facebook. However, when using these apps, any problem that occurs will be far more accessible to you because you will understand the layer that each of these apps in built on.

# 23

# The Admin Library

## In This Chapter

- Configure the **admin** app to work with the rest of our project
- Use the **admin** to quickly build webpages to list, create, and edit objects
- Add extra properties to objects in the admin
- Configure inline instances of other objects
- Build a custom admin action allowing multiple objects to be processed simultaneously

## 23.1  Introduction

A lot of the work of building a website revolves around the webpages used to create, update, and delete content. The purpose of the **admin** app is to easily provide these webpages. The catch to the **admin** is that it is targeted at administrators and managers and is not meant to be used by website visitors. Furthermore, the automatic generation of pages in the **admin** comes at the cost of simplicity and ease of use.

Colloquially called the **admin**, this app is one of Django's most advertised (and used) features, because it works out of the box and plugs into any existing app. In this chapter, we use the **admin** app to quickly build pages to create, modify, and delete blog posts and users.

> ### Warning!
>
> This chapter requires an active `User` instance with the `is_staff` field set to `True`. We created such users in migrations in the last chapter. Alternatively, invoke `./manage.py createsuperuser` and follow the on-screen instructions. (Beware: This command will create a user, but until Chapter 24, it will not create a `Profile`, resulting in some strange site behavior.)

## 23.2  A First Look

Django automatically enabled the **admin** app when we created our project, including a URL configuration in our root URL configuration, as shown in Example 23.1.

**Example 23.1: Project Code**

`suorganizer/urls.py` **in** `38bc0b6d91`

```
17   from django.contrib import admin
 .        ...
30   urlpatterns = [
 .        ...
39       url(r'^admin/', include(admin.site.urls)),
 .        ...
49   ]
```

Most of our interactions with the **admin** app will be configuring the app to interact with the rest of our project as we desire. To begin with, in Example 23.2, we can change the header and title of the admin webpages. The header is the text displayed in the body of the webpage, while the title refers to the HMTL `title` tag in the `head` tag.

**Example 23.2: Project Code**

`suorganizer/urls.py` **in** `38bc0b6d91`

```
27   admin.site.site_header = 'Startup Organizer Admin'
28   admin.site.site_title = 'Startup Organizer Site Admin'
```

The full title for our site will be

```
Site administration | Startup Organizer Site Admin
```

If we run the development server and navigate to `http://127.0.0.1:8000/admin/`, we are greeted by the login page shown in Figure 23.1.

If we sign in with any `User` instance with the `is_staff` field set to `True`, we are greeted by the admin panel, shown in Figure 23.2. By default, this page allows us to interact

**Figure 23.1:** Admin Front in 38bc0b6d91

with any model that Django knows about. If we had not created our own `User` instance in
Chapter 22: Overriding Django's Authentication with a Custom User, Django would be
listing the **auth** app's default model here.

If we click on the site link, we are greeted with a list of `Site` instances, shown in
Figure 23.3.

Clicking on the `Site` instance displays the values we set for our site in Chapter 15:
Creating Webpages with Django Flatpages, as shown in Figure 23.4.

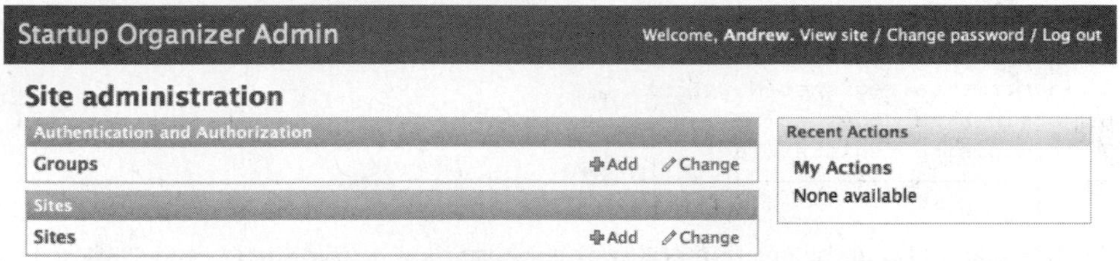

**Figure 23.2:** Admin Panel in 38bc0b6d91

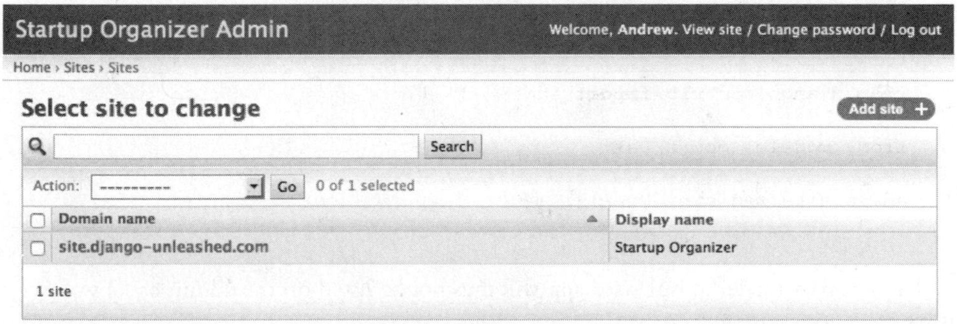

**Figure 23.3:** Site List in 38bc0b6d91

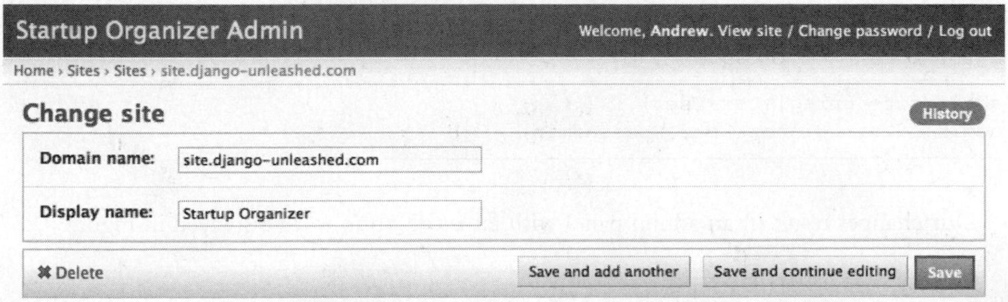

**Figure 23.4:** Site Detail in 38bc0b6d91

To add models from the rest of our project, we can use the `admin.py` files that we've been ignoring in our apps. We import the models from our app, and then register them with the **admin** app so that it knows where these models exist. In `organizer/admin.py`, this looks like Example 23.3.

**Example 23.3: Project Code**
`organizer/admin.py` **in** `88dc0f7049`

```
1    from django.contrib import admin
2
3    from .models import NewsLink, Startup, Tag
4
5    admin.site.register(NewsLink)
6    admin.site.register(Startup)
7    admin.site.register(Tag)
```

This code results in the creation of `NewsLinkAdmin`, `StartupAdmin`, and `TagAdmin`. The process is the same in `user/admin.py` and `blog/admin.py`. The first is printed in Example 23.4.

**Example 23.4: Project Code**
`user/admin.py` **in** `88dc0f7049`

```
1    from django.contrib import admin
2
3    from .models import User
4
5    admin.site.register(User)
```

The `Profile` model in our **user** app will thus not be listed on the admin panel webpage, as we have not registered it.

If we did not have our own custom `User` model but wanted to create a custom `UserAdmin` (which we would declare manually, as we will do shortly), we would have to first unregister the `User` model, as shown in Example 23.5.

**Example 23.5: Python Code**

```
admin.site.unregister(User)
admin.site.register(User, UserAdmin)
```

Our changes result in an admin panel with far more options, as displayed in Figure 23.5.

## Django Documentation

For all of the options available to configuring the **admin**, see

https://dju.link/18/admin

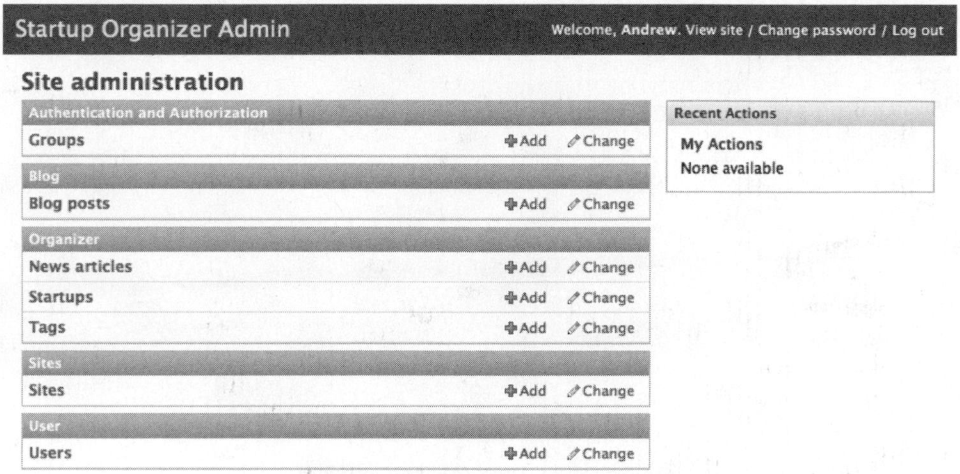

**Figure 23.5:** Admin Panel in 88dc0f7049

# 23.3 Modifying the Admin Controls for Blog Posts

For each model, the **admin** app provides four webpages: a list page, a creation page (typically called the *add view*), an edit page (called the *change view*), and a delete confirmation page. The majority of the options available to developers when working with the **admin** app pertain to configuring one of these webpages. To configure our PostAdmin, we start by configuring our list page. We then configure the creation and edit webpages together. Finally, we return to the list page and extend the webpage's behavior.

## 23.3.1 Configuring the List of Post Objects

Instead of letting the **admin** app generate PostAdmin for us through a call to site.register(), we can instead use the @register() decorator on a subclass of ModelAdmin, allowing us to configure the set of admin pages using expected attributes. To begin, we can set the list_display attribute, defining which fields in PostAdmin we want displayed, as shown in Example 23.6. Figure 23.6 shows the result of this change.

**Example 23.6: Project Code**
blog/admin.py **in** 14e2d2282b

```
6   @admin.register(Post)
7   class PostAdmin(admin.ModelAdmin):
8       list_display = ('title', 'pub_date')
```

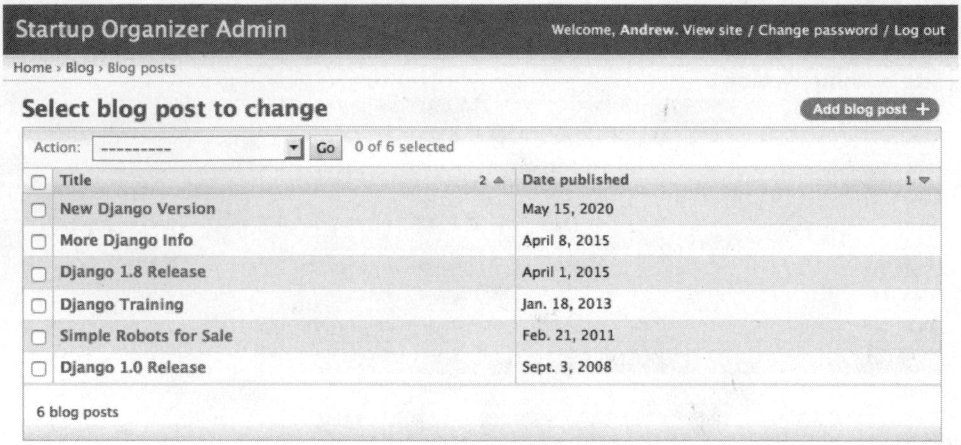

**Figure 23.6:** Post List in 14e2d2282b

This change has no effect on the add page, shown in Figure 23.7, or on the edit page, shown in Figure 23.8.

The **admin** app uses the permissions defined by the **auth** app. If we log in with the account for Ada, we'll discover that the links to delete Post objects are missing and that we don't have the ability to create Tag or Startup objects. The changes are small, but if you look at Figure 23.9, you'll note the delete button at the bottom left is gone and that the plus sign buttons next to the list of Tag and Startup objects are also missing.

With this in mind, we can continue to change our list page. In Example 23.7, we add the date_hierarchy attribute, defining the field on Post to use to show a list of relevant dates at the top of the list page.

**Example 23.7: Project Code**
blog/admin.py **in** 7dd2c1d9b9

```
7    class PostAdmin(admin.ModelAdmin):
8        date_hierarchy = 'pub_date'
```

In Example 23.8, we then define the list_filter attribute, which tells Django to allow for these fields to be filtered in the user interface. This code provides a set of links that present navigational tools, depending on the kind of field specified.

**Example 23.8: Project Code**
blog/admin.py **in** 942c448247

```
7    class PostAdmin(admin.ModelAdmin):
.        ...
10       list_filter = ('pub_date',)
```

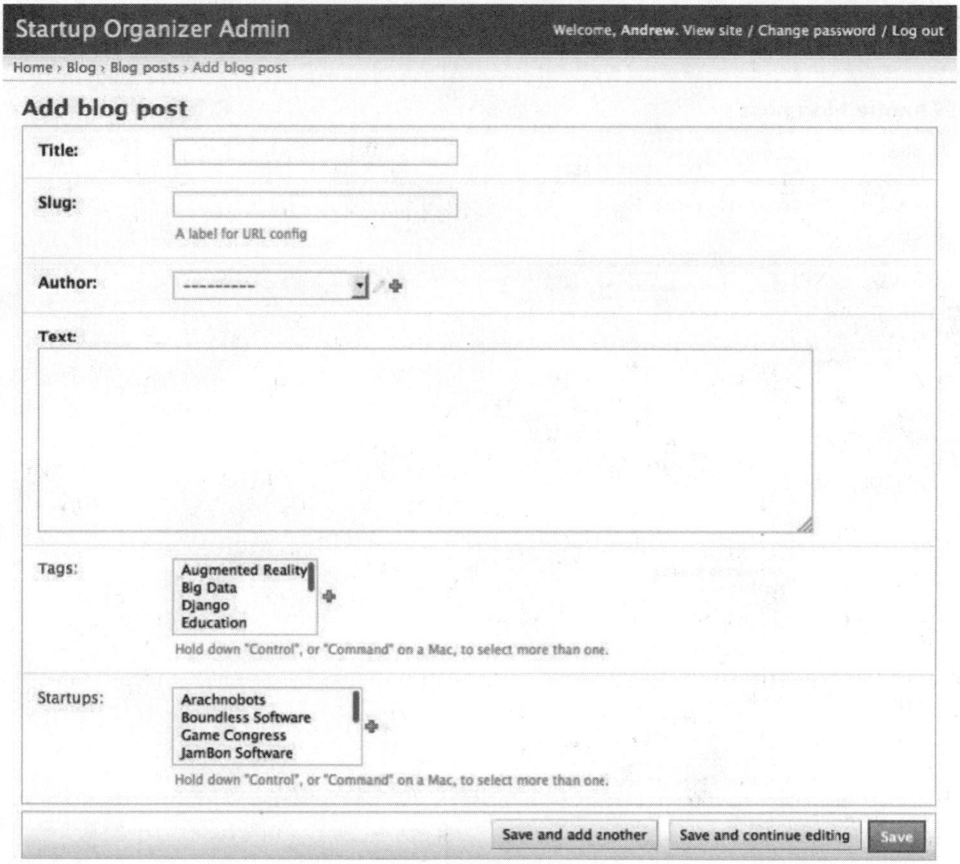

**Figure 23.7:** Post Add in 14e2d2282b

Finally, in Example 23.9, we can add a search bar, specifying which fields we want to search over in the search_fields attribute.

**Example 23.9: Project Code**
blog/admin.py **in** 172f27bece

```
 7    class PostAdmin(admin.ModelAdmin):
 .        ...
11        search_fields = ('title', 'text')
```

The result of these changes is displayed in Figure 23.10. To be clear, the date_hierarchy option is what creates the list of years directly below the search bar, while the list_filter tuple generates the entire right sidebar.

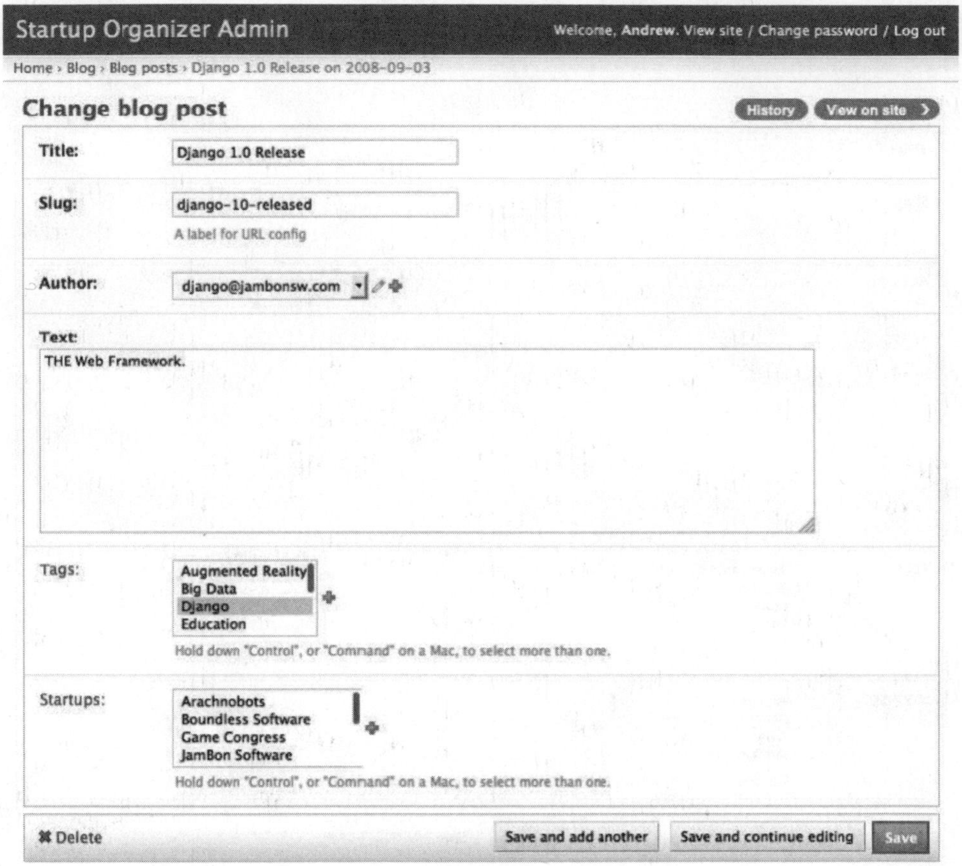

**Figure 23.8:** Post Edit in 14e2d2282b

## 23.3.2   Configuring the Add and Edit Pages

Even though the add and edit pages are different, many of the **admin**'s options configure
both pages. The fieldsets option, for instance, allows us to define which fields are
available on the forms in each page and further allow us to organize the fields, as shown in
Example 23.10.

**Example 23.10:** Project Code

blog/admin.py **in** 478395e75c

```
 7    class PostAdmin(admin.ModelAdmin):
 .        ...
13        # form view
14        fieldsets = (
15            (None, {
```

```
16              'fields': (
17                  'title', 'slug', 'author', 'text',
18              )}),
19          ('Related', {
20              'fields': (
21                  'tags', 'startups')}),
22      )
```

The result of the code above is shown in Figure 23.11.

The **admin** app supplies a number of powerful options for manipulating fields. One of the most popular options is the `prepopulated_fields` option. Given a dictionary of fields, the **admin** uses JavaScript to fill in a field using the value of another field. For example, we can use the `title` field to prepopulate the `slug` field, as shown in Example 23.11.

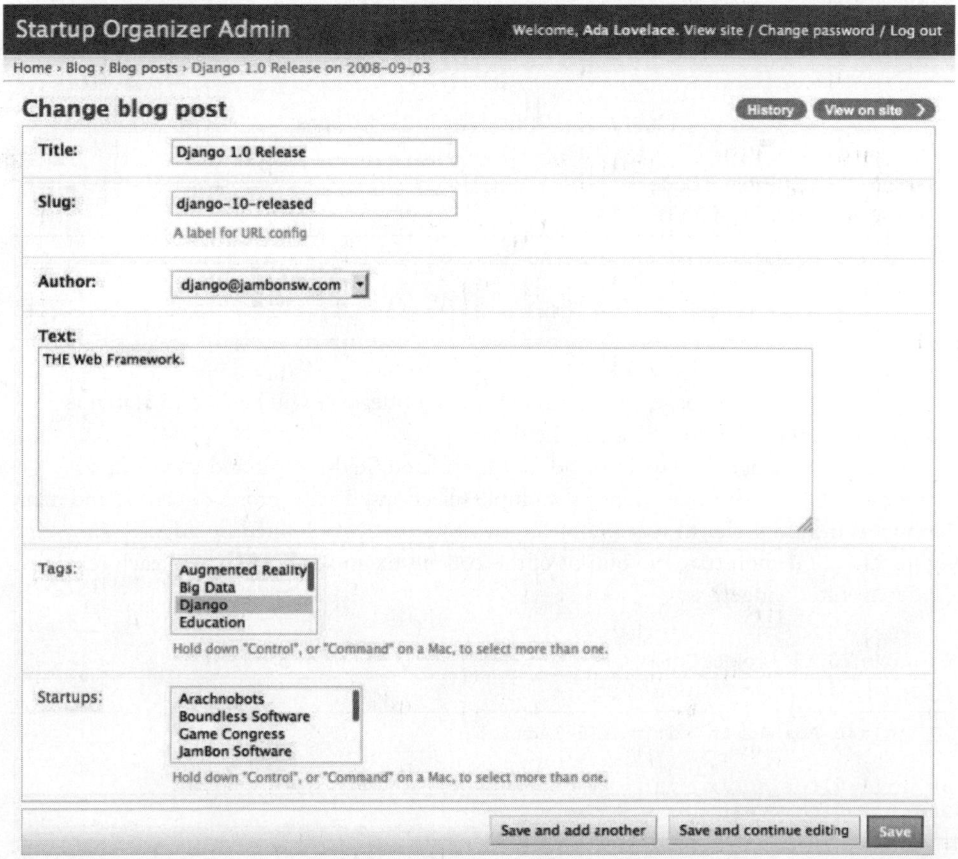

**Figure 23.9:** Ada's Post Edit

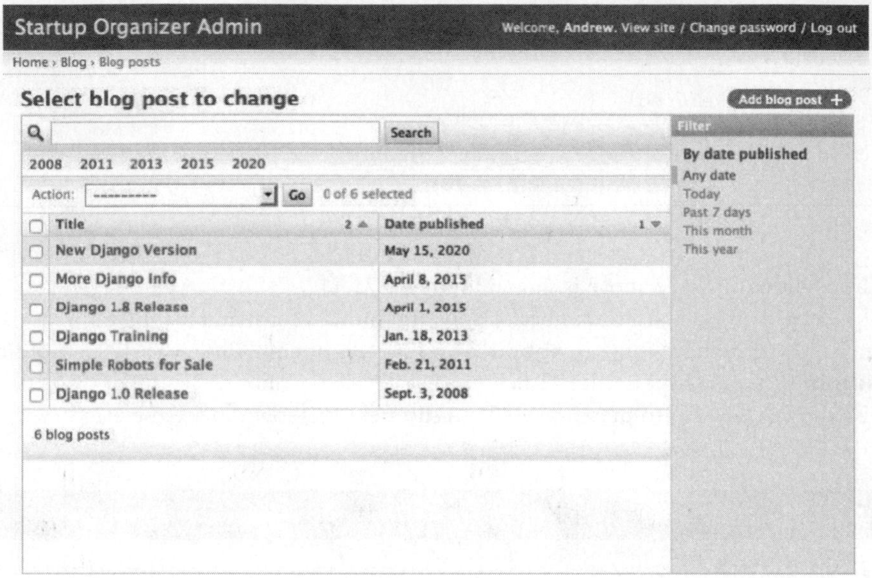

**Figure 23.10:** Post List in 172f27bece

**Example 23.11: Project Code**

blog/admin.py **in** 74953edb04

```
 7    class PostAdmin(admin.ModelAdmin):
 .        ...
23        prepopulated_fields = {"slug": ("title",)}
```

If you navigate to the page and begin typing in a title, you will be able to watch as Django fills in the value for the slug field.

We can also change the layout of fields. Our related fields, tags and startups, currently appear in a list that supports multiple selections. This is prone to errors, and many developers instead prefer to use one of the two filter widgets defined by **admin**. In Figure 23.12, I demonstrate the output of the code in Example 23.12, where each relation is a different filter widget.

**Example 23.12: Project Code**

blog/admin.py **in** 09aeae50ec

```
 7    class PostAdmin(admin.ModelAdmin):
 .        ...
23        filter_horizontal = ('startups',)
24        filter_vertical = ('tags',)
```

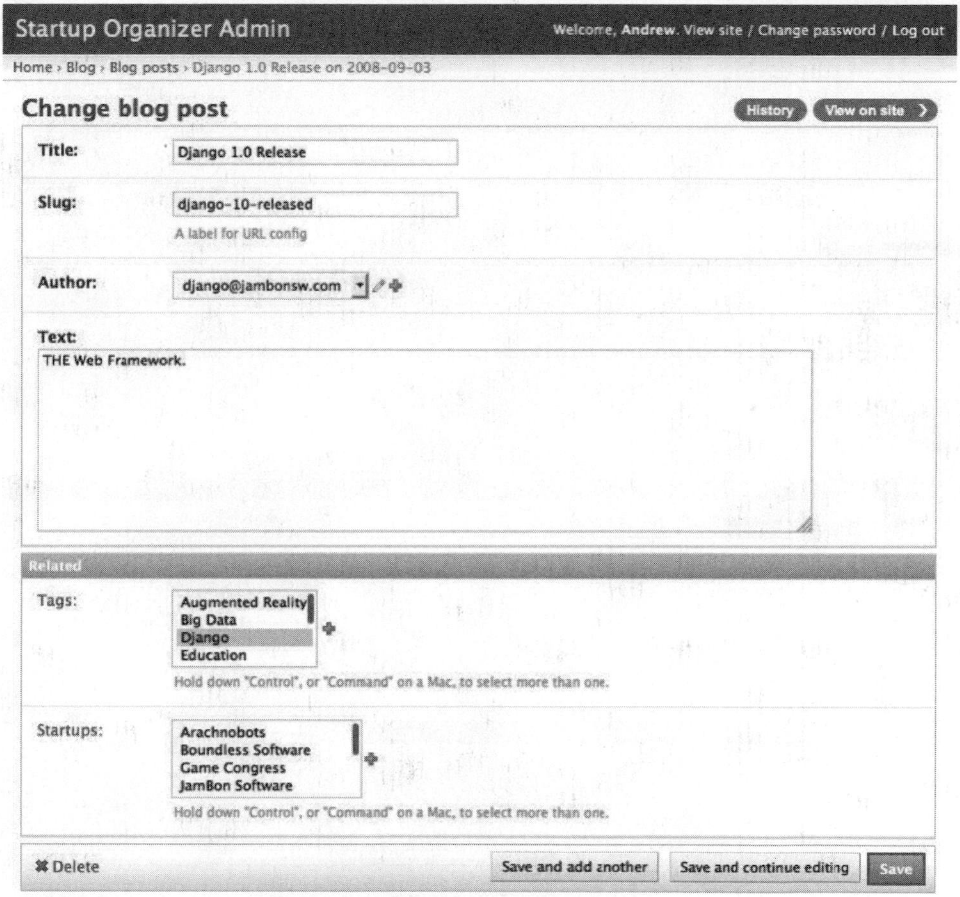

**Figure 23.11:** Post Edit in 478395e75c

I prefer the horizontal filter, so in Example 23.13, we switch the tags field to use the horizontal filter widget as well.

**Example 23.13: Project Code**
blog/admin.py **in** 9fec06c6ac

```
 7    class PostAdmin(admin.ModelAdmin):
 .        ...
23        filter_horizontal = ('tags', 'startups',)
```

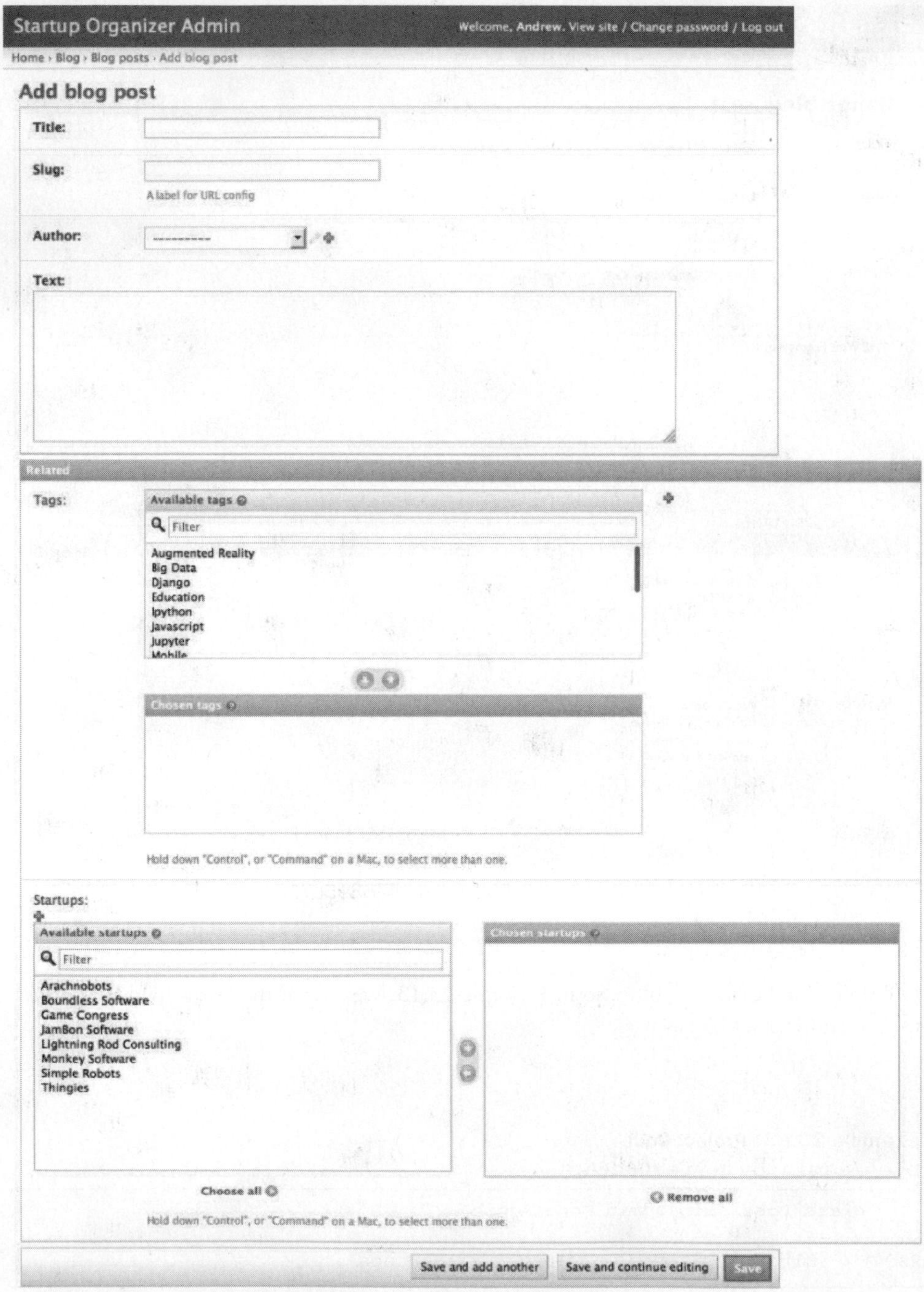

**Figure 23.12:** Post Add in 09aeae50ec

### 23.3.3 Adding Extra Information to the List View

The **admin** app is rather rigid. There are four pages for every app, and every page has a set number of options to configure that page. The list page, in particular, focuses on presenting data that is contained in the fields of the model. To try and mitigate this limitation, the **admin** provides a number of options for extending the data in the list view.

The list page allows for the display of object properties. On our `Post` model, shown in Figure 23.12, we can create a property to display the number of tags the instance is related to, as shown in Example 23.14.

**Example 23.14:** Project Code

`blog/models.py` **in** `07ce477dd1`

```
12    class Post(models.Model):
 .        ...
80        @property
81        def tag_count(self):
82            return self.tags.count()
```

In `PostAdmin`, we can use this new property in the list page, as shown in Example 23.15. The result of this change is displayed in Figure 23.13.

**Example 23.15:** Project Code

`blog/admin.py` **in** `07ce477dd1`

```
 7    class PostAdmin(admin.ModelAdmin):
 .        ...
10        list_display = (
11            'title', 'pub_date', 'tag_count')
```

There are two problems with this new field. First, we can't sort the field, and second, we've created a new property in our `Post` model which is only used in the **admin**. It would be much cleaner to have this property defined in `PostAdmin`. As it turns out, we can do just that, as shown in Example 23.16.

**Example 23.16:** Project Code

`blog/admin.py` **in** `4c270031d9`

```
 7    class PostAdmin(admin.ModelAdmin):
 .        ...
27        def tag_count(self, post):
28            return post.tags.count()
29        tag_count.short_description = 'Number of Tags'
```

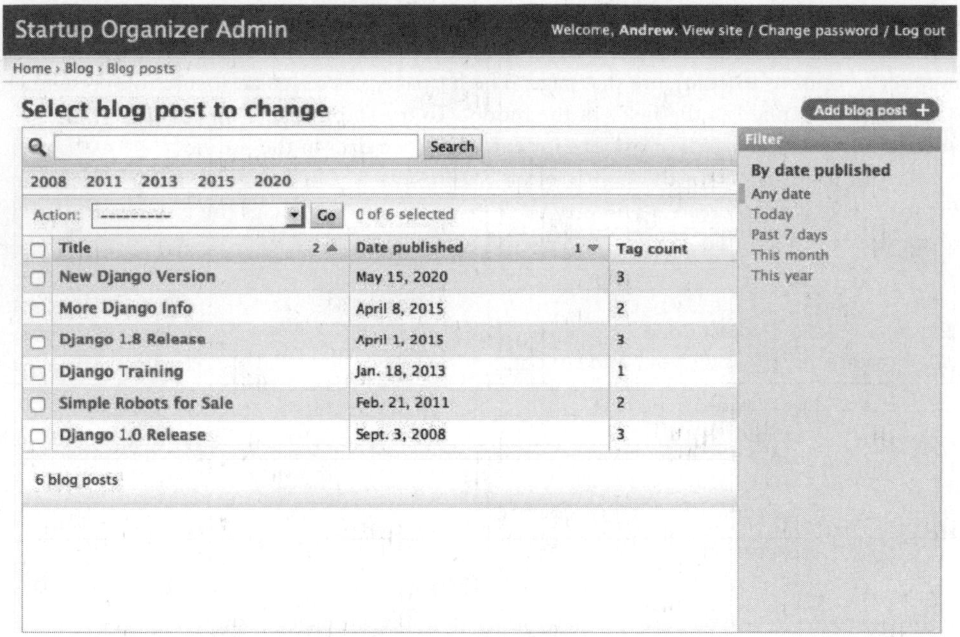

**Figure 23.13:** Post List in 07ce477dd1

The method expects to be given the actual Post object, thanks to its existence in the
list_display attribute. The short_description attribute on the method actually
changes the text in the column header. Instead of Tag Count, the list will now display
Number of Tags.

## Warning!

The short_description attribute works with methods in list_display as long
as the @property decorator is **not** used. For more information:

https://dju.link/18/list-display

As we'll discuss in Chapter 26, calling the database is an expensive operation. That's bad
news for us, because our current code results in a call to the database for each object in our
list. That is *very* expensive, and we can do better.

A little bit like GCBV's get_object() method, subclasses of admin.ModelAdmin
will be using the get_queryset() method to actually build the list of objects displayed in
the list page. We can override this method, using the aggregate functions of the
object-relational mapping (ORM).

The aggregate functions allow us to perform calculations directly in the database. For example, we can ask the database for the Max or Min or simply to Count rows. In combination with the annotate queryset method, we can Count all of the tags related to each and every Post in a single query to the database, assigning the number to a variable called tag_number. Example 23.17 shows the code for this query.

**Example 23.17: Project Code**
blog/admin.py **in** 4c949cd171

```
 2   from django.db.models import Count
 .       ...
 8   class PostAdmin(admin.ModelAdmin):
 .       ...
28       def get_queryset(self, request):
29           queryset = super().get_queryset(request)
30           return queryset.annotate(
31               tag_number=Count('tags'))
32
33       def tag_count(self, post):
34           return post.tag_number
35       tag_count.short_description = 'Number of Tags'
36       tag_count.admin_order_field = 'tag_number'
```

Each Post instance will now have this number, allowing us not only to access it directly in the tag_count() but also to add the admin_order_field attribute on the method, allowing Django to sort the column in the list page.

As mentioned at the beginning of the chapter, the **admin** app respects the default permissions generated by the **auth** app. This is apparent if we log in with Ada's account, as shown in Figure 23.14, because the **admin** app allows Ada to access only the PostAdmin pages, following the permissions assigned to her by the contributor group.

Our blog.view_future_post permission is not included in the list of permissions that the **admin** will automatically use. We can modify get_queryset() to use the permission to filter out unpublished Post instances, as shown in Example 23.18.

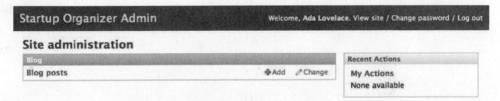

**Figure 23.14:** Ada's Admin Panel in b62b6bbf95

**Example 23.18: Project Code**
`blog/admin.py` in b62b6bbf95

```
 1    from datetime import datetime
 .        ...
 9    @admin.register(Post)
 .        ...
30        def get_queryset(self, request):
31            queryset = super().get_queryset(request)
32            if not request.user.has_perms(
33                    'view_future_post'):
34                queryset = queryset.filter(
35                    pub_date__lte=datetime.now())
36            return queryset.annotate(
37                tag_number=Count('tags'))
```

If you log in with Ada's account, you'll see that our blog post announcing the latest Django version in 2020 is no longer in the list. This page is displayed in Figure 23.15. To contrast this, Figure 23.16 shows the superuser view. This figure also modifies the order of the list via the Number of Tags column (and we could very easily have done this in Ada's account).

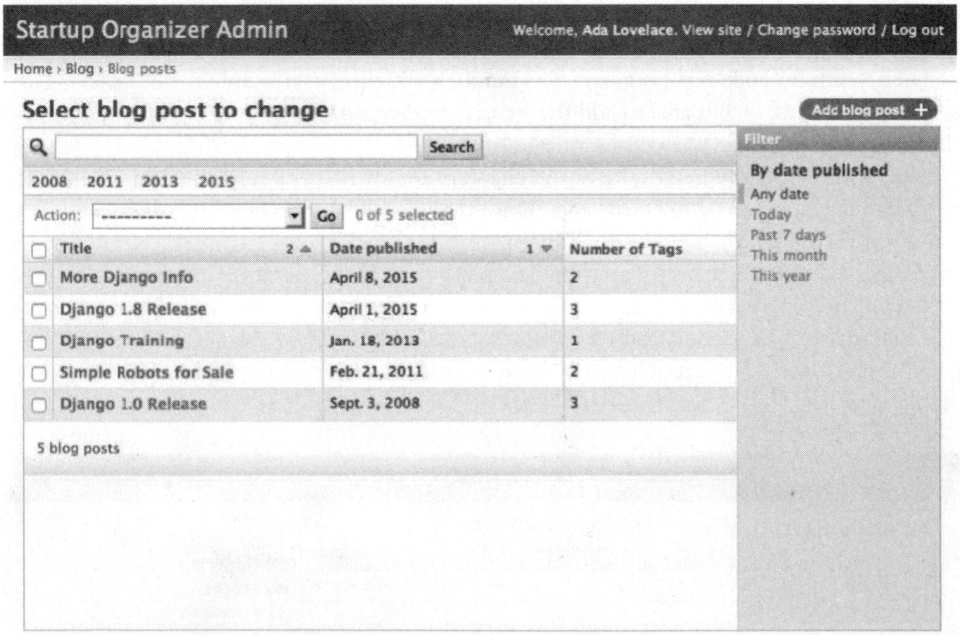

**Figure 23.15:** Ada Post List in b62b6bbf95

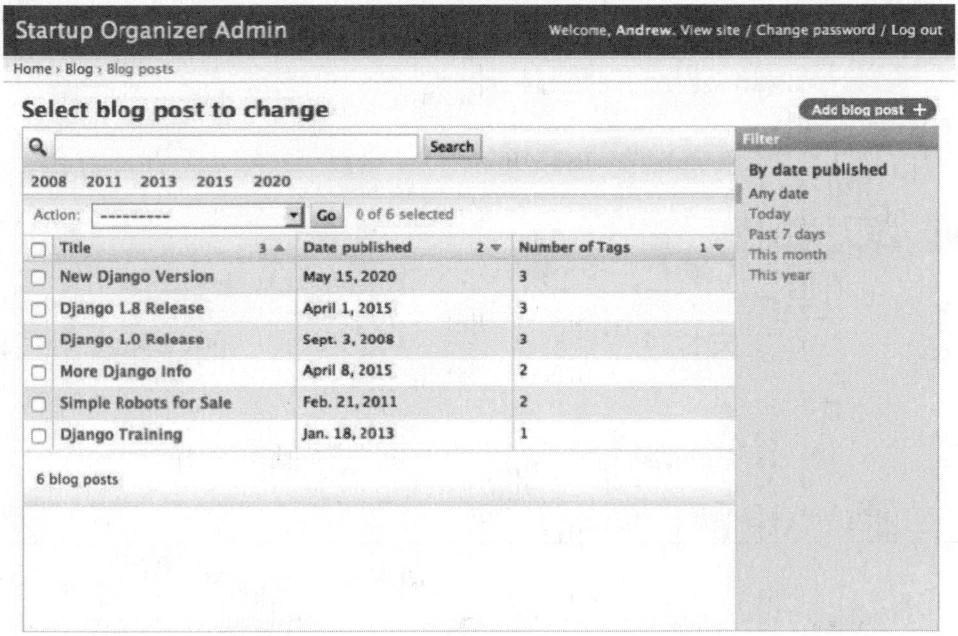

**Figure 23.16:** Post List Sorted by Tag in b62b6bbf95

# 23.4 Configuring the Admin for the User Model

The `PostAdmin` was a very straightforward process. We first configured the list page and then used options to configure both the add and edit pages. Finally, we saw how to extend data displayed in the list view.

The `UserAdmin` is anything but straightforward. While the list page is very simple, our add and edit pages are problematic. In the case of our `User` model, we want these pages to be quite different, and by default, Django does not supply the tools to achieve this end. Even worse, we want to create a page to change passwords, causing us to take control of the `UserAdmin`'s more integral features. Once we have our pages for properly dealing with the `User` model, we will change our views to use inline instances, allowing us to control the `Profile` model at the same time as the `User` model.

## 23.4.1 Configuring the List Page

In Example 23.19, we start by declaring the `UserAdmin`, using the `@register()` decorator to associate it with our `User` model. We define the `list_display`, `list_filter`, and `search_fields` attributes seen on `PostAdmin`.

**Example 23.19: Project Code**
user/admin.py in f44c761f37

```
 1   from django.contrib import admin
 2
 3   from .models import User
 4
 5
 6   @admin.register(User)
 7   class UserAdmin(admin.ModelAdmin):
 8       # list view
 9       list_display = (
10           'email',
11           'is_staff',
12           'is_superuser')
13       list_filter = (
14           'is_staff',
15           'is_superuser',
16           'profile__joined')
17       search_fields = ('email',)
```

In Example 23.20, we add the `ordering` attribute to set the default ordering on the list (when the page is first loaded).

**Example 23.20: Project Code**
user/admin.py in ebba310de0

```
 7   class UserAdmin(admin.ModelAdmin):
 .       ...
17       ordering = ('email',)
```

We can extend the data displayed to use the `joined` `DateTimeField` on the `Profile` model by creating the `get_date_joined()` method. We add the method to the `list_display` attribute on line 11, and then use Django's relations on line 22 to get the actual value, as shown in Example 23.21.

**Example 23.21: Project Code**
user/admin.py in f118d1c3cb

```
 7   class UserAdmin(admin.ModelAdmin):
 .       ...
 9       list_display = (
10           'email',
11           'get_date_joined',
12           'is_staff',
13           'is_superuser')
 .       ...
```

```
21        def get_date_joined(self, user):
22            return user.profile.joined
23        get_date_joined.short_description = 'Joined'
24        get_date_joined.admin_order_field = (
25            'profile__joined')
```

The short_description attribute on the method (line 23) replaces the column header text, while the admin_order_field attribute is the value Django will use to order the Joined column. Note that while list_display cannot display fields on related models, the admin_order_field attribute on the get_date_joined() method has no problem processing it.

We follow the same process to add the name field also found on the Profile object of the User instance, as shown in Example 23.22.

**Example 23.22: Project Code**
user/admin.py **in** 7c65017fa1

```
7    class UserAdmin(admin.ModelAdmin):
.        ...
9        list_display = (
10           'get_name',
11           'email',
12           'get_date_joined',
13           'is_staff',
14           'is_superuser')
.        ...
28       def get_name(self, user):
29           return user.profile.name
30       get_name.short_description = 'Name'
31       get_name.admin_order_field = 'profile__name'
```

Finally, in Example 23.23, we pass a subset of the items in list_display to list_display_links via a tuple. All of the values in these fields will become links, linking to the edit page for the instance of the User.

**Example 23.23: Project Code**
user/admin.py **in** fec0e16edb

```
7    class UserAdmin(admin.ModelAdmin):
.        ...
15       list_display_links = ('get_name', 'email')
```

The result of all our work above is displayed in Figure 23.17.

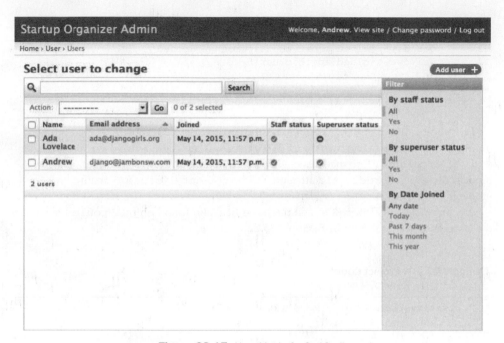

**Figure 23.17:** User List in fec0e16edb

## 23.4.2   Configuring the Add and Edit Pages

We can use the fieldsets attribute to take control of the output of the forms in both the add and edit pages of our admin, as shown in Example 23.24.

**Example 23.24: Project Code**
user/admin.py **in** 3dc9075fbf

```
 7    class UserAdmin(admin.ModelAdmin):
 .        ...
22        # form view
23        fieldsets = (
24            (None, {'fields': ('email', 'password')}),
25            ('Permissions', {
26                'fields': (
27                    'is_active',
28                    'is_staff',
29                    'is_superuser',
30                    'groups',
31                    'user_permissions')}),
32            ('Important dates', {
33                'fields': ('last_login',)}),
34        )
```

We can then also use horizontal filter widgets on our related fields, as shown in Example 23.25.

**Example 23.25: Project Code**
user/admin.py **in** 3dc9075fbf

```
 7    class UserAdmin(admin.ModelAdmin):
 .        ...
35        filter_horizontal = (
36            'groups', 'user_permissions',)
```

The result of these changes is shown in Figure 23.18.

Our form views are really cluttered. Django's **admin** app supplies two styles we can apply to fieldsets sections, wide and collapse, as shown in Example 23.26. The wide is more or less what we already have. The collapse CSS style hides the section for us, allowing us to reveal it by clicking the arrow. The effect of this change is shown in Figure 23.19.

**Example 23.26: Project Code**
user/admin.py **in** 797c12d24b

```
 7    class UserAdmin(admin.ModelAdmin):
 .        ...
23        fieldsets = (
24            (None, {
25                'classes': ('wide',),
26                'fields': ('email', 'password')}),
27            ('Permissions', {
28                'classes': ('collapse',),
29                'fields': (
30                    'is_active',
31                    'is_staff',
32                    'is_superuser',
33                    'groups',
34                    'user_permissions')}),
35            ('Important dates', {
36                'classes': ('collapse',),
37                'fields': ('last_login',)}),
38        )
```

Simplifying our webpages reveals a problem. If we look at an existing user account on the edit page, as shown in Figure 23.20, we can see that the password field is completely unusable.

This makes sense. We discovered when using the **auth** app that we should never interact with the password field directly because of the way passwords are stored and that we should instead use the many methods on the User and UserManager classes to deal with passwords.

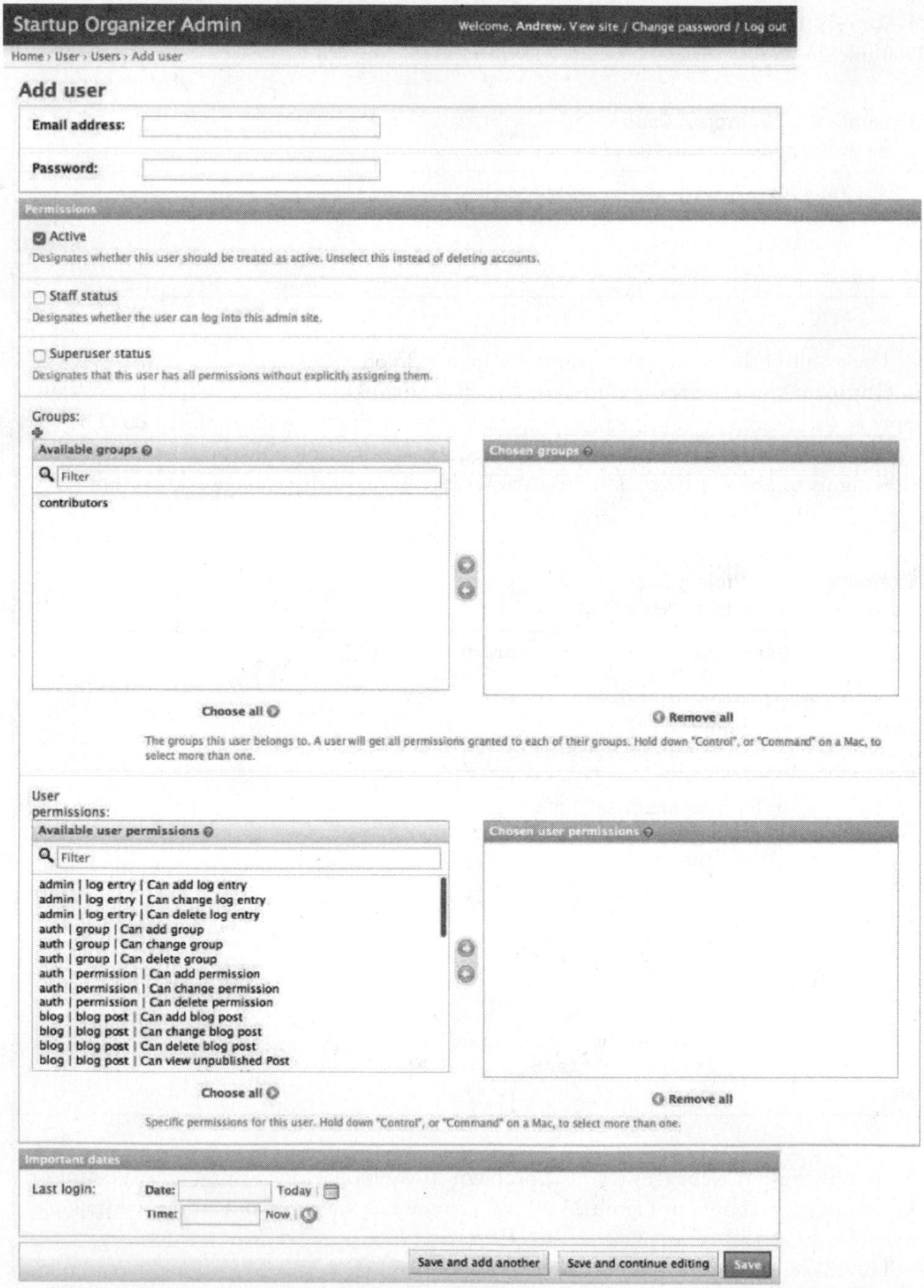

## Startup Organizer Admin

Welcome, **Andrew**. View site / Change password / Log out

Home › User › Users › Add user

## Add user

**Email address:**

**Password:**

### Permissions

☑ **Active**
Designates whether this user should be treated as active. Unselect this instead of deleting accounts.

☐ **Staff status**
Designates whether the user can log into this admin site.

☐ **Superuser status**
Designates that this user has all permissions without explicitly assigning them.

**Groups:**
✛

| Available groups ⊘ | Chosen groups ⊘ |
|---|---|
| 🔍 Filter | |
| contributors | |

**Choose all** ⊘                 ⊙ **Remove all**

The groups this user belongs to. A user will get all permissions granted to each of their groups. Hold down "Control", or "Command" on a Mac, to select more than one.

**User permissions:**

| Available user permissions ⊘ | Chosen user permissions ⊘ |
|---|---|
| 🔍 Filter | |
| admin | log entry | Can add log entry | |
| admin | log entry | Can change log entry | |
| admin | log entry | Can delete log entry | |
| auth | group | Can add group | |
| auth | group | Can change group | |
| auth | group | Can delete group | |
| auth | permission | Can add permission | |
| auth | permission | Can change permission | |
| auth | permission | Can delete permission | |
| blog | blog post | Can add blog post | |
| blog | blog post | Can change blog post | |
| blog | blog post | Can delete blog post | |
| blog | blog post | Can view unpublished Post | |

**Choose all** ⊘                 ⊙ **Remove all**

Specific permissions for this user. Hold down "Control", or "Command" on a Mac, to select more than one.

### Important dates

**Last login:**   Date: _____ Today | 📅

Time: _____ Now | ⊙

[ Save and add another ]  [ Save and continue editing ]  [ Save ]

**Figure 23.18:** User Create in 3dc9075fbf

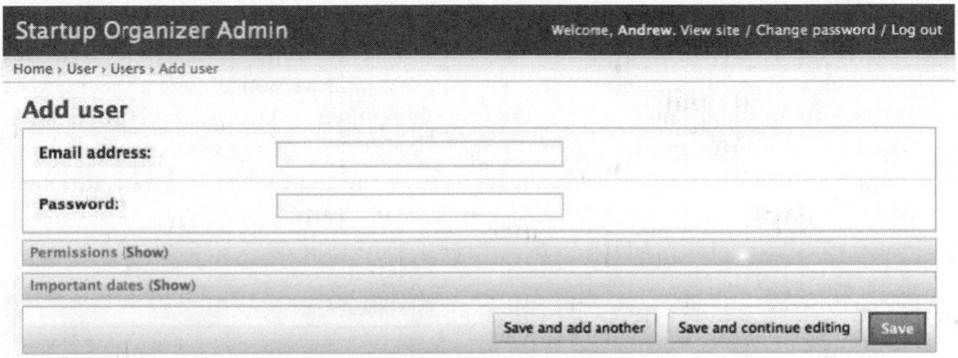

**Add user**

| | |
|---|---|
| **Email address:** | |
| **Password:** | |

Permissions (Show)

Important dates (Show)

Save and add another · Save and continue editing · Save

Figure 23.19: User Create in 797c12d24b

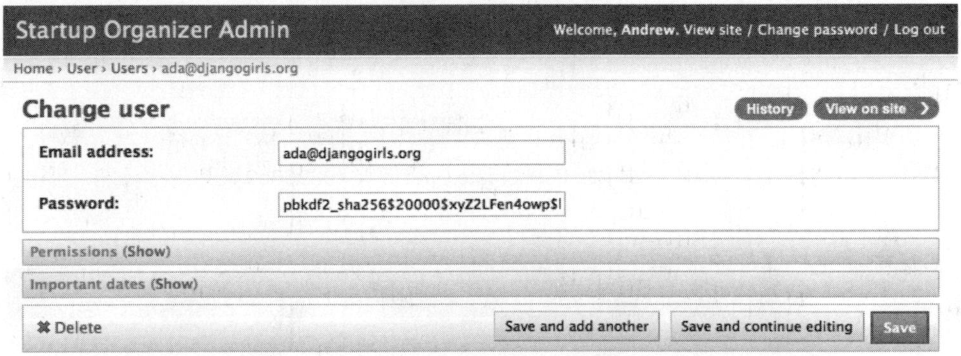

**Change user** · History · View on site ›

| | |
|---|---|
| **Email address:** | ada@djangogirls.org |
| **Password:** | pbkdf2_sha256$20000$xyZ2LFen4owp$l |

Permissions (Show)

Important dates (Show)

✖ Delete · Save and add another · Save and continue editing · Save

Figure 23.20: User Edit in 797c12d24b

An easy fix would be to remove the `password` field from the form entirely, as we do in Example 23.27.

**Example 23.27: Project Code**
`user/admin.py` **in** 40493966b9

```
 7    class UserAdmin(admin.ModelAdmin):
 .        ...
23        fieldsets = (
 .            ...
26            'fields': ('email',)}),
```

Perhaps surprisingly, Django will not complain if we create a new user account with this limited form. We need only supply an email address, as shown in Figure 23.21, and Django will then redirect us back to the list page, displaying a message using the **messages** app at the top informing us of the success of the operation (and listing the new user). This page is displayed in Figure 23.22.

If we look at Russell's account in the list in Figure 23.22, we notice quite a few fields of information are missing. This is because the form being used by Django at this point is generated by the **admin** app. Instead, we should use our `UserCreationForm` that we worked so hard for. We therefore delete the `fieldsets` and `filter_horizontal` attributes, and add the code shown in Example 23.28.

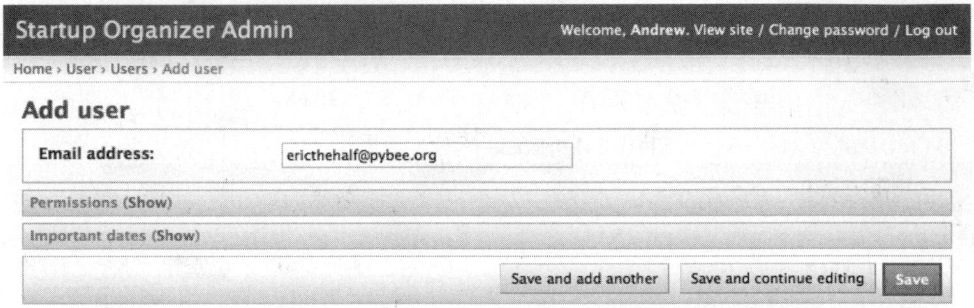

**Figure 23.21:** User Create Data in 40493966b9

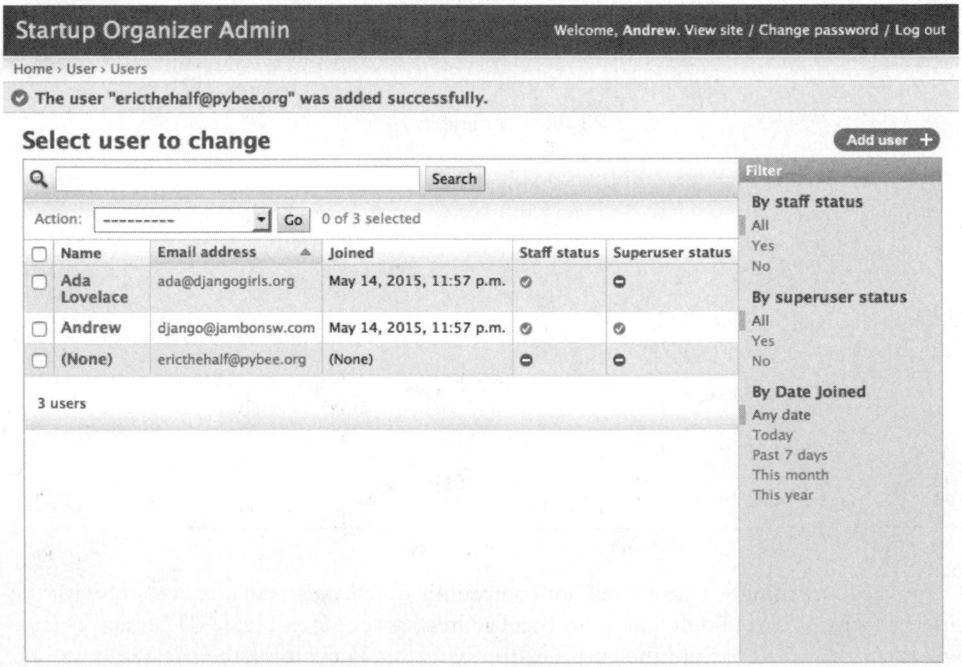

**Figure 23.22:** User Create Complete in 40493966b9

**Example 23.28: Project Code**
user/admin.py **in** 9fabdc7f2f

```
 3    from .forms import UserCreationForm
 .       ...
 8    class UserAdmin(admin.ModelAdmin):
 .       ...
24        form = UserCreationForm
```

This change looks great in the add page, as shown in Figure 23.23, but the edit page, shown in Figure 23.24, is less helpful.

**Figure 23.23:** User Create Data in 9fabdc7f2f

**Figure 23.24:** User Edit in 9fabdc7f2f

The truth is that we're only interested in using the `UserCreationForm` when creating a new account. The **admin** doesn't handle this action by default. However, because the **admin** is Django, and Django is Python, we're not going to let that stop us. In Example 23.29, we can assign our form to the `add_form`, which we have made up (the `ModelAdmin` will not use the attribute by default). We can then override the `getform()` method defined by `ModelAdmin` as the method for getting the form in both the add and edit pages. If the object already exists, then we are creating an object, and so we use `UserCreationForm`. If not, we use the **admin** app's default.

**Example 23.29: Project Code**
user/admin.py **in** e0418c1204

```
 8   class UserAdmin(admin.ModelAdmin):
 .       ...
24       add_form = UserCreationForm
 .       ...
37       def get_form(
38           self, request, obj=None, **kwargs):
39         if obj is None:
40             kwargs['form'] = self.add_form
41         return super().get_form(
42             request, obj, **kwargs)
```

The `ModelAdmin`'s default is a `ModelForm` from the `User` model, which we were customizing with the `fieldsets` attribute. We therefore re-create the `fieldsets` attributes to change the look of the form on the edit page, removing the `password` filed in the process, as shown in Example 23.30.

**Example 23.30: Project Code**
user/admin.py **in** 1bf70e07b1

```
 8   class UserAdmin(admin.ModelAdmin):
 .       ...
24       fieldsets = (
25           (None, {
26               'fields': ('email',)}),
27           ('Permissions', {
28               'classes': ('collapse',),
29               'fields': (
30                   'is_active',
31                   'is_staff',
32                   'is_superuser',
33                   'groups',
34                   'user_permissions')}),
35           ('Important dates', {
36               'classes': ('collapse',),
37               'fields': ('last_login',)}),
38       )
```

We also redefine the `filter_horizontal` attribute to change the widgets on the groups and permissions fields, as shown in Example 23.31.

**Example 23.31: Project Code**
`user/admin.py` **in** `1bf70e07b1`

```
 8    class UserAdmin(admin.ModelAdmin):
 .        ...
39        filter_horizontal = (
40            'groups', 'user_permissions',)
```

The net effect of these attributes is shown in Figure 23.25.

We don't have to limit our use of the `fieldsets` attribute to the edit page. We can also create our own `add_fieldsets` attribute for use with the fields in `UserCreationForm`, as shown in Example 23.32.

**Example 23.32: Project Code**
`user/admin.py` **in** `1bf70e07b1`

```
 8    class UserAdmin(admin.ModelAdmin):
 .        ...
41        add_fieldsets = (
42            (None, {
43                'classes': ('wide',),
44                'fields': (
45                    'name',
46                    'email',
47                    'password1',
48                    'password2')
49            }),
50        )
```

| Startup Organizer Admin | Welcome, **Andrew**. View site / Change password / Log out |
|---|---|

Home › User › Users › ada@djangogirls.org

## Change user                    ( History )  ( View on site  › )

| **Email address:** | ada@djangogirls.org |
|---|---|

Permissions (Show)

Important dates (Show)

✖ Delete          ( Save and add another )  ( Save and continue editing )  ( **Save** )

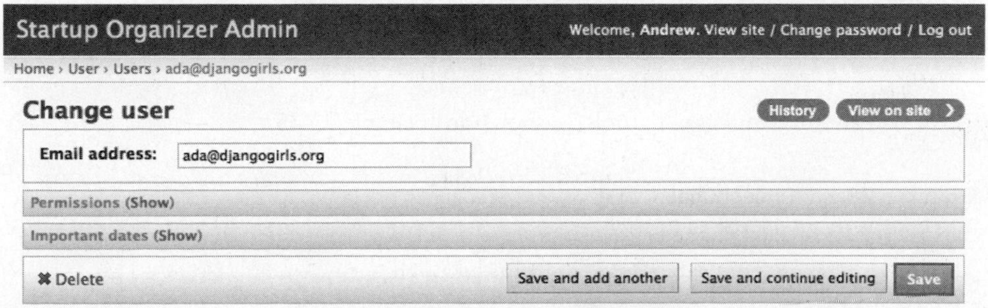

**Figure 23.25:** User Edit in `1bf70e07b1`

Of course, this works only if we apply it ourselves, as the `ModelAdmin` will not use it by default. We can override the `get_fieldsets()` method in Example 23.33 to conditionally use `add_fieldsets` or `fieldsets`, depending on whether the object already exists.

**Example 23.33: Project Code**
user/admin.py in 1bf70e07b1

```
64        def get_fieldsets(self, request, obj=None):
65            if not obj:
66                return self.add_fieldsets
67            return super().get_fieldsets(request, obj)
```

### 23.4.3   Adding a Change Password Page

While we can now easily add a user with a new password and a profile, we are currently unable to change a password in the **admin**. The goal of this section is to create a new page to change passwords. Creating a change password page is surprisingly difficult and requires a complete override of the `ModelAdmin` subclass.

To begin, we import a set of familiar tools, as shown in Example 23.34.

**Example 23.34: Project Code**
user/admin.py in 3ca4f2fbf7

```
 1    from django.conf.urls import url
 .        ...
10    from django.contrib.messages import success
11    from django.core.exceptions import \
12        PermissionDenied
13    from django.http import (
14        Http404, HttpResponseRedirect)
15    from django.template.response import \
16        TemplateResponse
17    from django.utils.decorators import \
18        method_decorator
19    from django.utils.encoding import force_text
 .        ...
21    from django.views.decorators.debug import \
22        sensitive_post_parameters
```

We will also need a few new tools, as shown in Example 23.35.

**Example 23.35: Project Code**
user/admin.py in 3ca4f2fbf7

```
 3    from django.contrib.admin.options import \
 4        IS_POPUP_VAR
 5    from django.contrib.admin.utils import unquote
```

```
 6   from django.contrib.auth import \
 7       update_session_auth_hash
 8   from django.contrib.auth.forms import \
 9       AdminPasswordChangeForm
 .       ...
20   from django.utils.html import escape
```

The IS_POPUP_VAR is a constant in the **admin** app and is used to tell if the current window is a pop-up window. The **admin** typically creates pop-up windows for related content. For example, when creating a new Post object in the **admin**, should we want to create a new Tag object for the Post instance, clicking the plus sign will result in a pop-up window, using the add page from TagAdmin.

The unquote() is the opposite of quote(), which is used by Django's **admin** to escape any representation of a primary key to make it safe for use in a URL pattern. The unquote() must therefore be used on any incoming primary key for an object. In our case, we use it on the primary key for the User instance we are editing.

If we change a user's password, we want that user to be logged out of the system if he or she were already logged in, forcing the user to use the new password to log back in. To force a user to log out, we need to change the user's session, which is what the update_session_auth_hash() function is for.

The AdminPasswordChangeForm is much like the PasswordChangeForm we used in Chapter 21, but it is aimed at being used in the **admin**. If we had not used a custom User model, Django would be using this form in a custom page for exactly the same functionality.

The escape() function is meant to take a string and make it safe to be printed in an HTML page, replacing characters such as & with &amp.

We can declare the AdminPasswordChangeForm as an attribute for quick access (and better adherence to DRY) and create a new change_user_password_template attribute as well, as shown in Example 23.36.

**Example 23.36: Project Code**
user/admin.py **in** 3ca4f2fbf7

```
29   class UserAdmin(admin.ModelAdmin):
 .       ...
73       # password
74       change_password_form = AdminPasswordChangeForm
75       change_user_password_template = (
76           'admin/auth/user/change_password.html')
```

With all the tools we need to get started, our first goal is to add a new page to the URL configuration of **admin**. To properly generate URL patterns for objects, the **admin** forgoes Django convention and builds the URL configuration internally in each ModelAdmin subclass. To add to the URL configuration, we therefore need to override the get_urls() method, adding a new URL pattern to the configuration generated by the ModelAdmin superclass, as shown in Example 23.37.

**Example 23.37: Project Code**

user/admin.py **in** 3ca4f2fbf7

```
 29    class UserAdmin(admin.ModelAdmin):
  .        ...
101        def get_urls(self):
102            password_change = [
103                url(r'^(.+)/password/$',
104                    self.admin_site.admin_view(
105                        self.user_change_password),
106                    name='auth_user_password_change'),
107            ]
108            urls = super().get_urls()
109            urls = password_change + urls
110            return urls
```

The URL for this page will be admin/user/user/<id>/password/, where id is the primary key for the User instance, matched by the (unnamed) group above.

To create the view for this URL pattern, we create a method named user_change_password, which accepts a request, the id of the object, and a form_url keyword parameter, which is meant to be passed to the template context and is used as the action attribute of the HTML form tag. As we are setting passwords (the form will have two fields, password1 and password2, just like PasswordChangeForm), we use the @sensitive_post_parameters() decorator to ensure that the passwords are never printed in the logs or in any debug statements, as shown in Example 23.38.

**Example 23.38: Project Code**

user/admin.py **in** 3ca4f2fbf7

```
 29    class UserAdmin(admin.ModelAdmin):
  .        ...
112        @method_decorator(sensitive_post_parameters())
113        def user_change_password(
114                self, request, user_id, form_url=''):
```

Within user_change_password(), our first goal is to make sure that the authenticated user using the **admin** has the right to change a password. If they do not, we raise a PermissionDenied exception, as shown in Example 23.39.

**Example 23.39: Project Code**

user/admin.py **in** 3ca4f2fbf7

```
 29    class UserAdmin(admin.ModelAdmin):
  .        ...
113        def user_change_password(
114                self, request, user_id, form_url=''):
115            if not self.has_change_permission(
116                    request):
117                raise PermissionDenied
```

To go any further, we need to get the User object that we will be changing the password for. The unquote() function ensures any changes to the id made by the **admin** are reversed, and rather than use the ORM directly, we rely on the ModelAdmin's method to get the instance, as shown in Example 23.40.

**Example 23.40: Project Code**
user/admin.py **in** 3ca4f2fbf7

```
 29     class UserAdmin(admin.ModelAdmin):
  .         ...
113         def user_change_password(
114               self, request, user_id, form_url=''):
  .             ...
118             user = self.get_object(
119                 request, unquote(user_id))
120             if user is None:
121                 raise Http404(
122                     '{name} object with primary key '
123                     '{key} does not exist.'.format(
124                         name=force_text(
125                             self.model
126                             ._meta.verbose_name),
127                         key=escape(user_id)))
```

We then follow the convention of forms in function views (seen last in Chapter 9: Controlling Forms in Views), by checking whether the HTTP request uses the POST method. If it does, then we process the form and act accordingly. If we do not receive a POST request we assume we've received a GET request and work on presenting the form. The form, in this case, is the change_password_form attribute, which is currently set to use the AdminPasswordChangeForm, as shown in Example 23.41.

**Example 23.41: Project Code**
user/admin.py **in** 3ca4f2fbf7

```
 29    class UserAdmin(admin.ModelAdmin):
  .         ...
112         @method_decorator(sensitive_post_parameters())
113         def user_change_password(
  .             ...
128             if request.method == 'POST':
129                 form = self.change_password_form(
130                     user, request.POST)
```

In the event we receive a POST request and the data provided is valid, we save the form, which changes the user's password. We then create a message to tell the **admin** of our success, as shown in Example 23.42. This message is displayed in the "Recent Actions" box on the admin panel page, allowing for quick access to make the change again. Figure 23.26 shows what this looks like when creating a new user.

**Example 23.42: Project Code**

user/admin.py **in** 3ca4f2fbf7

```
 29    class UserAdmin(admin.ModelAdmin):
  .        ...
112        @method_decorator(sensitive_post_parameters())
113        def user_change_password(
  .            ...
131            if form.is_valid():
132                form.save()
133                change_message = (
134                    self.construct_change_message(
135                        request, form, None))
136                self.log_change(
137                    request, user, change_message)
138                success(
139                    request, 'Password changed.')
140                update_session_auth_hash(
141                    request, form.user)
142                return HttpResponseRedirect('..')
```

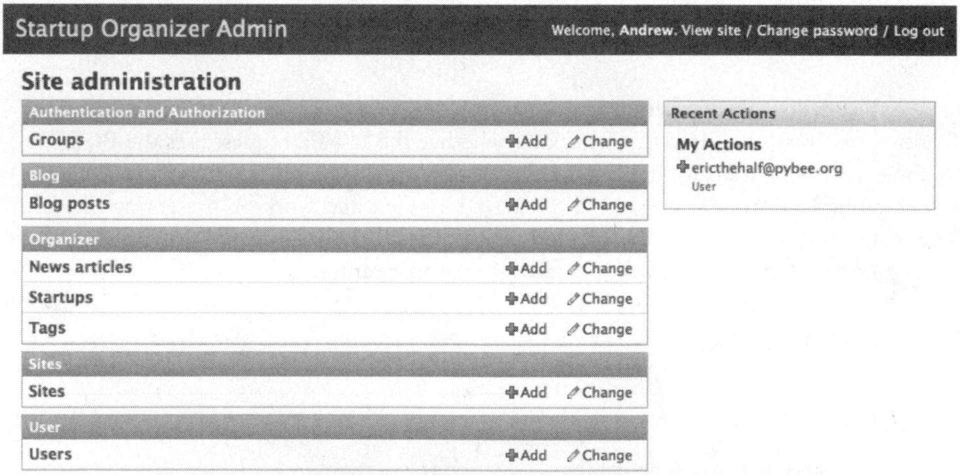

**Startup Organizer Admin**    Welcome, **Andrew**. View site / Change password / Log out

## Site administration

| Authentication and Authorization | | |
|---|---|---|
| **Groups** | ✚Add | ⊘ Change |

| Blog | | |
|---|---|---|
| **Blog posts** | ✚Add | ⊘ Change |

| Organizer | | |
|---|---|---|
| **News articles** | ✚Add | ⊘ Change |
| **Startups** | ✚Add | ⊘ Change |
| **Tags** | ✚Add | ⊘ Change |

| Sites | | |
|---|---|---|
| **Sites** | ✚Add | ⊘ Change |

| User | | |
|---|---|---|
| **Users** | ✚Add | ⊘ Change |

**Recent Actions**

**My Actions**

✚ ericthehalf@pybee.org
  User

**Figure 23.26:** Admin Panel After User Creation in 3ca4f2fbf7

In the event of a GET request, we create an unbound form, as shown in Example 23.43.

**Example 23.43: Project Code**

user/admin.py **in** 3ca4f2fbf7

```
 29    class UserAdmin(admin.ModelAdmin):
  .        ...
113        def user_change_password(
```

```
114                 self, request, user_id, form_url=''):
  .             ...
143             else:
144                 form = self.change_password_form(user)
```

The rest of the code is in the event the data submitted is invalid or in the event of a GET request. The form stored in `form` is thus either (1) unbound or (2) bound and invalid.

We must then build the template context for the template. We give the template a `title` and pass in not only the `form` but also the new `adminForm`. We also include the `form_url` passed to the view. Finally, we make use of the IS_POPUP_VAR attribute to see if our current window is a pop-up (admittedly, this should never be the case with our view). We pass the `User` instance as the `original` variable, and give the model options to `opts` (so that it may use attributes like `verbose_name`), as shown in Example 23.44.

**Example 23.44: Project Code**
`user/admin.py` in 3ca4f2fbf7

```
 29     class UserAdmin(admin.ModelAdmin):
  .         ...
113         def user_change_password(
114                 self, request, user_id, form_url=''):
  .             ...
146             context = {
147                 'title': 'Change password: {}'.format(
148                     escape(user.get_username())),
149                 'form_url': form_url,
150                 'form': form,
151                 'is_popup': (
152                     IS_POPUP_VAR in request.POST
153                     or IS_POPUP_VAR in request.GET),
154                 'opts': self.model._meta,
155                 'original': user,
156             }
```

Finally, in Example 23.45, we update the context with the title and header of the site, thanks to the `eachcontext()` method.

**Example 23.45: Project Code**
`user/admin.py` in 3ca4f2fbf7

```
 29     class UserAdmin(admin.ModelAdmin):
  .         ...
113         def user_change_password(
114                 self, request, user_id, form_url=''):
  .             ...
157             context.update(
158                 admin.site.each_context(request))
```

For proper resolution of namespaced URLs, we need to add the `current_app` attribute to our `HttpRequest` object. We can then create a `TemplateResponse` with our context, using our expected template, as shown in Example 23.46.

**Example 23.46: Project Code**
user/admin.py **in** 3ca4f2fbf7

```
 29    class UserAdmin(admin.ModelAdmin):
  .       ...
113        def user_change_password(
114                self, request, user_id, form_url=''):
  .            ...
160            request.current_app = self.admin_site.name
161
162            return TemplateResponse(
163                request,
164                self.change_user_password_template,
165                context)
```

## Django Documentation

For more about why we are assigning `current_app` to the `HttpRequest` object, please see

https://dju.link/18/namespaces

We will now be able to access the password change page by browsing to `admin/user/user/<id>/password/`. For instance, `admin/user/user/2/password/` should bring you to the password change page for Ada's user account, as shown in Figure 23.27. If we change the password, we'll be redirected to Ada's account edit page,

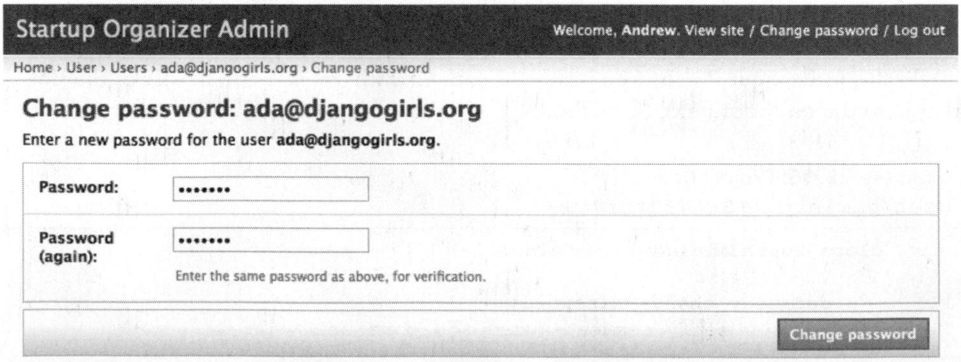

**Startup Organizer Admin**   Welcome, **Andrew.** View site / Change password / Log out

Home › User › Users › ada@djangogirls.org › Change password

### Change password: ada@djangogirls.org

Enter a new password for the user **ada@djangogirls.org**.

| Password: | •••••• |
|---|---|
| Password (again): | •••••• |
| | Enter the same password as above, for verification. |

Change password

**Figure 23.27:** User Password Edit in 3ca4f2fbf7

with a message confirming the change, as shown in Figure 23.28. If we browse to the admin panel, we'll see our change in the "Recent Actions" box, as shown in Figure 23.29.

This is exactly what we want, but at the moment, we don't have a link to our new password change page. We could simply add a small link on the edit page of the `UserAdmin`, but it turns out that the **auth** app allows much better. In `django/contrib/auth/forms.py`, the app defines a `ReadOnlyPasswordHashWidget`, which displays the password in a friendly, read-only format and allows us to easily link to our new page (it was built for this purpose). The widget is used in the `ReadOnlyPasswordHashField`, which in turn is used as the only field in the

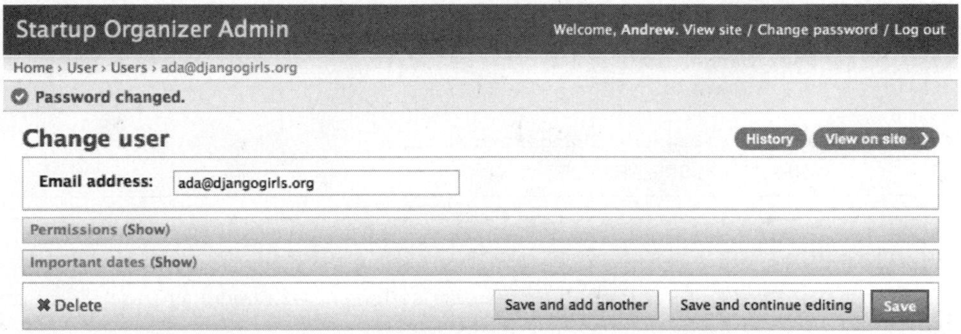

**Figure 23.28:** User Password Edit Complete in 3ca4f2fbf7

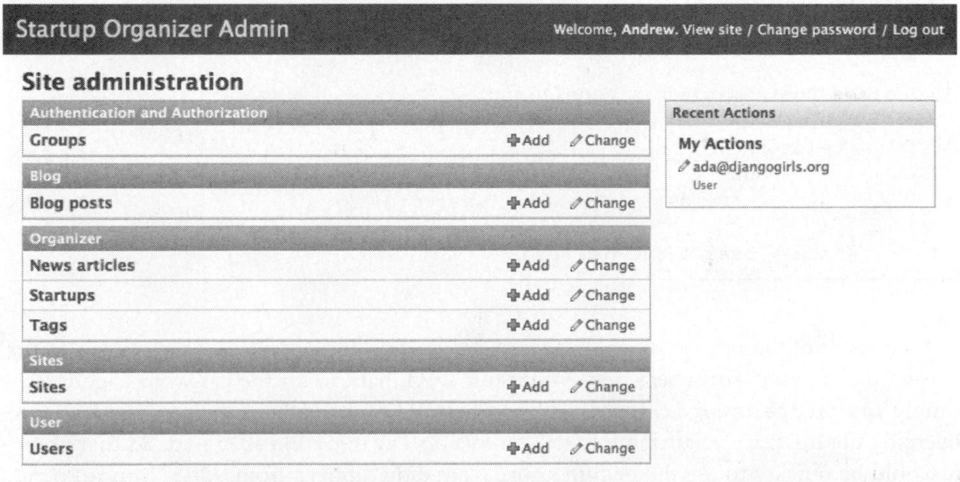

**Figure 23.29:** Admin Panel after Password Change in 3ca4f2fbf7

UserChangeForm, which is a subclass of ModelForm. Rather than have to plug in the
widget of the field, we can simply use the form in the UserAdmin.

The ModelForm inherited by UserChangeForm points the class to **auth**'s User model.
We want the form to use the User model we created. We can therefore inherit
UserChangeForm in our own form class and change the Meta nested class to use our
User model instead of **auth**'s. I opt to do this in user/forms.py, as shown in
Example 23.47.

**Example 23.47: Project Code**
user/forms.py **in** bc2c7a99ff

```
 5    from django.contrib.auth.forms import (
 6        UserChangeForm as BaseUserChangeForm,
 7        UserCreationForm as BaseUserCreationForm)
 .        ...
41    class UserChangeForm(BaseUserChangeForm):
42        """For UserAdmin."""
43
44        class Meta(BaseUserChangeForm.Meta):
45            model = get_user_model()
```

In UserAdmin, we can change the fieldsets attribute to include the ReadOnly-
PasswordHashField in our UserChangeForm, so long as we remember to set form to
UserChangeForm, as shown in Example 23.48.

**Example 23.48: Project Code**
user/admin.py **in** bc2c7a99ff

```
24    from .forms import (
25        UserChangeForm, UserCreationForm)
 .        ...
30    class UserAdmin(admin.ModelAdmin):
 .        ...
46        fieldsets = (
47            (None, {
48                'fields': ('email', 'password')}),
 .        ...
74        form = UserChangeForm
```

The result of this code is shown in Figure 23.30. The link provided in the widget to the
password page only works because we built our URL pattern for the password page to
simply append /password/. If we had built the URL in any other way, we would need to
override the help_text attribute of the ReadOnlyPasswordHashField. At that point,
it would be quicker to use the field in a form that didn't inherit from UserChangeForm.

**Figure 23.30:** User Edit in bc2c7a99ff

### 23.4.4    Adding `Profile` to `UserAdmin` Thanks to Inline Instances

Our `User` model is associated with our `Profile` model on a one-to-one basis. When we create a user, both in the **admin** and elsewhere, we automatically create a `Profile`. It would be really nice if the `Profile` instance associated with the `User` instance were displayed while we edited a `User`.

To allow for the display of other objects in the form pages (add and edit pages), the **admin** provides inline objects: `InlineModelAdmin` and its two subclasses, `TabularInline` and `StackedInline`. The difference between the two is how they are displayed.

To display the `Profile` instance, we can create a class that inherits from either `TabularInline` or `StackedInline` and declare the `model` attribute to `Profile`, as shown in Example 23.49. I opt for the `StackedInline` class. Because we want to display the inline options only on the edit page, we also override the `get_inline_instances()` method, displaying the inline only if a user instance is passed to the method.

**Example 23.49: Project Code**
`user/admin.py` **in** 589d2324f7

```
26    from .models import Profile, User
27
28
29    class ProfileAdminInline(admin.StackedInline):
30        model = Profile
  .       ...
```

```
 34    class UserAdmin(admin.ModelAdmin):
  .       ...
107            def get_inline_instances(
108                self, request, obj=None):
109            if obj is None:
110                return tuple()
111            inline_instance = ProfileAdminInline(
112                self.model, self.admin_site)
113            return (inline_instance,)
```

The result of the code in Example 23.49 is shown in Figure 23.31.

Much like `ModelAdmin` subclasses, `InlineModelAdmin` comes with a number of attributes and methods that we can declare and override. The result of the code in Example 23.50 is displayed in Figure 23.32.

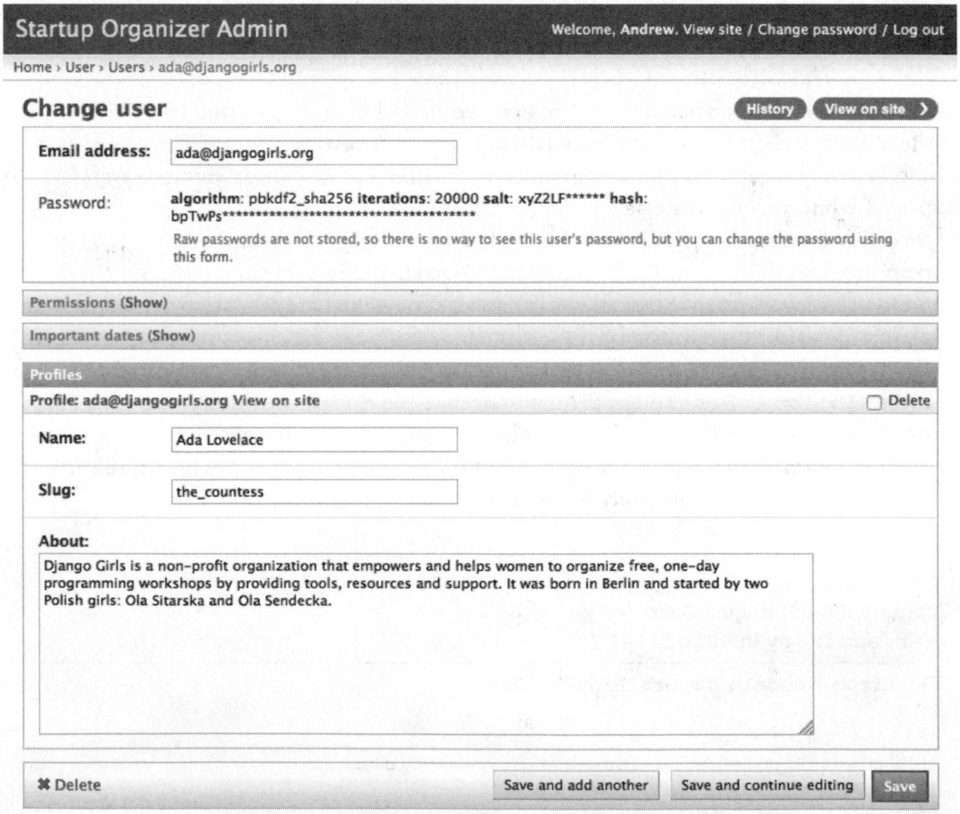

**Figure 23.31:** User Edit in 589d2324f7

**Figure 23.32:** User Edit in 96c33e21f6

**Example 23.50:** Project Code

user/admin.py **in** 96c33e21f6

```
29   class ProfileAdminInline(admin.StackedInline):
30       can_delete = False
31       model = Profile
32       exclude = ('slug',)
33
34       def view_on_site(self, obj):
35           return obj.get_absolute_url()
```

And with that, we've successfully configured UserAdmin to behave exactly how we'd like it to.

## Django Documentation

For the documentation relating to InlineModelAdmin and all of the options available when using any subclasses, please see

https://dju.link/18/inline

## 23.5   Creating Admin Actions

An **admin** action is a method that changes one or more objects. For instance, it may be useful to be able to select multiple users and change their is_staff field to True, to allow them access to the **admin** site. This counts as an action.

Thanks to the ORM, given a queryset from the User model with multiple User instances, we can simply use the update() method to change the information on all of those User objects. The qs.update(is_staff=True) will update all of the User instances selected by the queryset to be True. To disable every User from having access, we could use the code shown in Example 23.51.

**Example 23.51: Python Code**

```
User.objects.all().update(is_staff=False)
# the all() is actually unnecessary, but drives the point home
```

We can create a method called make_staff() in UserAdmin to take a queryset and change the is_staff field on every user in that queryset. To tell the class of the existence of this new method, we add it to a list, assigned to the actions attribute, as shown in Example 23.52.

**Example 23.52: Project Code**
user/admin.py **in** dd5127fb11

```
 38    @admin.register(User)
 39    class UserAdmin(admin.ModelAdmin):
 40        # list view
 41        actions = ['make_staff']
  .        ...
186
187        def make_staff(self, request, queryset):
188            rows_updated = queryset.update(
189                is_staff=True)
190            if rows_updated == 1:
191                message = '1 user was'
192            else:
193                message = '{} users were'.format(
194                    rows_updated)
195            message += ' successfully made staff.'
196            self.message_user(request, message)
197        make_staff.short_description = (
198            'Allow user to access Admin Site.')
```

The actual work is done on lines 188 and 189. The rest is just to display information to the user. We create a message on lines 190 to 196, and then display the message at the top of the list page using message_user(), which in turn uses the **messages** app.

If we select our new User and select the action, as shown in Figure 23.33, and then hit Go, we will be greeted with the page shown in Figure 23.34, confirming the change in Russell's status. The advantage to using message_user() is that the message is displayed not only here, but also in the "Recent Actions" list on the **admin** panel, as shown in Figure 23.35.

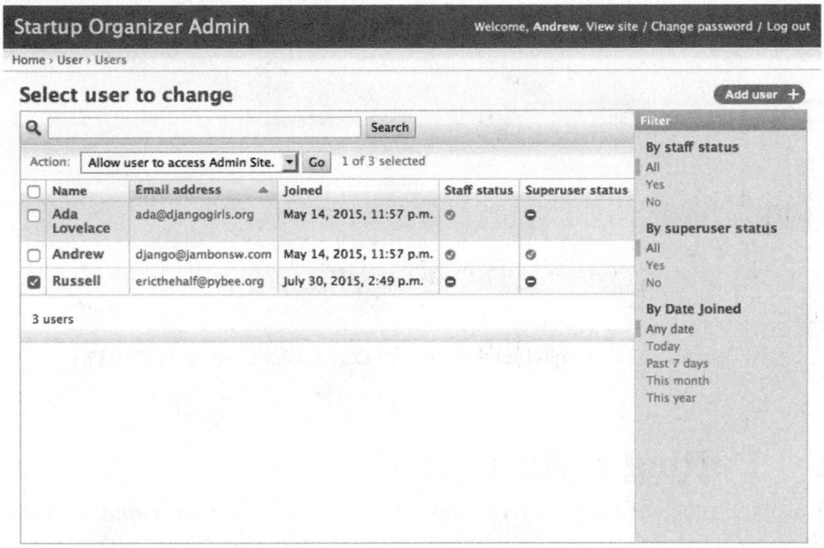

**Figure 23.33:** Selecting the Staff Change Action in dd5127fb11

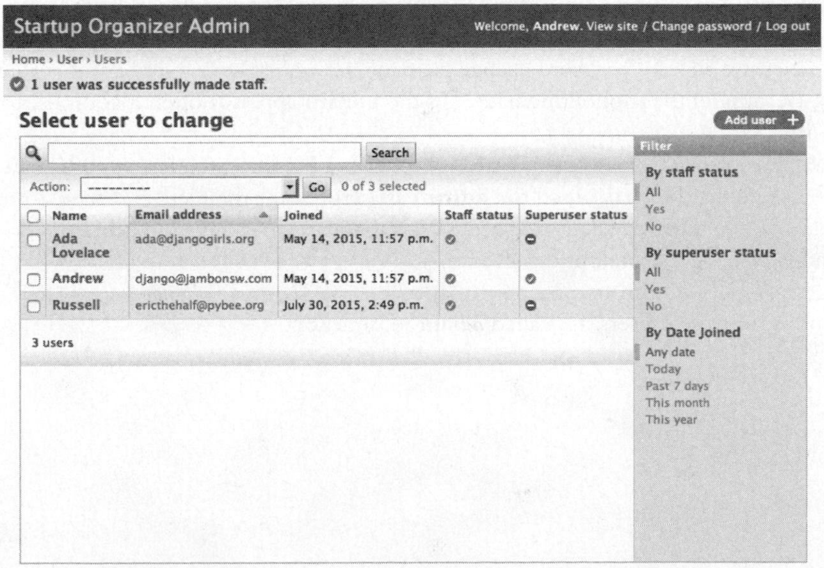

**Figure 23.34:** User List after Staff Change Action in dd5127fb11

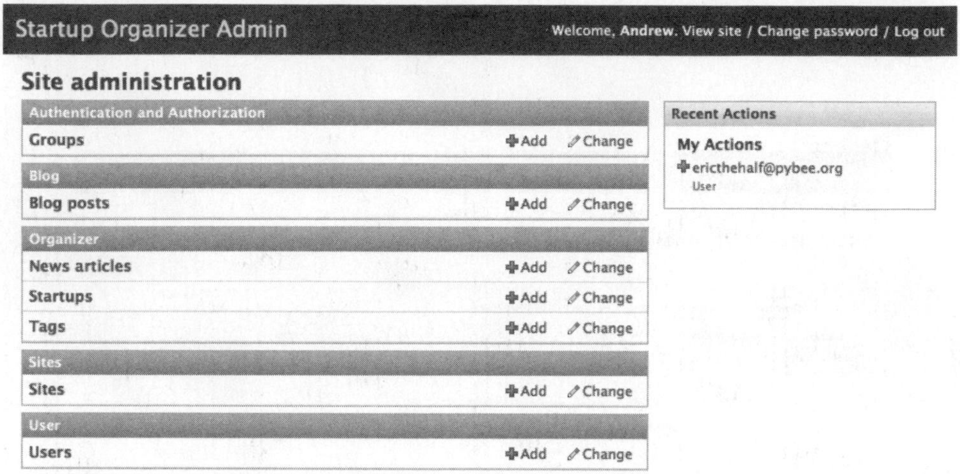

**Figure 23.35:** Admin Panel after Staff Change Action in dd5127fb11

# 23.6   Putting It All Together

The **admin** app is one of Django's most popular apps because getting started with the app is easy, and it provides an enormous amount of functionality out of the box. It's appealing, and to many beginners, it looks to solve many of their problems. Just think, with the **admin**, you could skip all of the code in Chapters 7, 8, and 9, and then some of the code in Chapter 17. You do so at the expense of control (and the learning process), but it is certainly a way to get started.

Customizing the **admin** beyond simply declaring attributes is where things begin to fall apart. The **admin** is limited, expecting there to be only four pages, and adding a page, as we did when we added a password change page for UserAdmin, got very complicated, very quickly. Because of the monolithic nature of the **admin** app, it is often a complex tool to work with.

When all is said and done, the **admin** is useful, but I caution beginners to be careful, as more than one developer has used the **admin** as a crutch for their site and then come to regret it. Use the **admin** when your site is getting started, but limit the **admin** to simple tasks and easy-to-configure options even then.

Finally, only let administrators and managers near it. Do not—*do not*—use it for your anonymous, untrusted users. It's called *admin* for a reason.

# III

# Advanced Core Features

Because, after all, real
developers ship.

Jeff Atwood

24

# Creating Custom Managers and Querysets

## In This Chapter

- Create custom managers and querysets
- Use fixtures to serialize data
- Write custom management commands

## 24.1 Introduction to Part III

In Part III, we return to Django's core and take full control of tools surrounding models, templates, and views. The ultimate goal of this part is to deploy a full website, which we do in Chapter 29: Deploy! The last chapter, Chapter 30: Starting a New Project Correctly, discusses how we would have started our project in Chapter 1 if we had known what we now know.

We start in this chapter by creating custom model managers to make interacting with the database even easier. We see how to loosely couple behavior across our site in Chapter 25: Handling Behavior with Signals, and perform basic optimization of our site in Chapter 26: Optimizing Our Site for Speed. We then greatly simplify our template code and enforce consistency in our webpages thanks to template tags in Chapter 27: Building Custom Template Tags. Finally, we create RSS and Atom feeds for visitors to more easily get our news and create a sitemap for Google to more easily index our site in Chapter 28: Adding RSS and Atom Feeds and a Sitemap. Only then will we deploy.

## 24.2 Introduction to Chapter 24

While views are the heart of Django, many see the object-relational mapper (ORM) and the easy interaction with the database as Django's most important features. Developers interact with the ORM almost as often as they do with views, and the process saves developers hours of work, so it's no surprise such an emphasis is put on models, managers, and migrations.

Model managers are the main ORM tool developers interact with when handling data. We saw in Chapter 22: Overriding Django's Authentication with a Custom User, how easy it is to add our own methods (`createuser()` and `createsuperuser()`) to managers, because they are simply Python classes. In this chapter, we see how to modify and change behavior, gaining greater control over how we interact with data in Django.

In the process, we also explore Django's fixtures and management commands, as both pertain to data handling and very often interact with the ORM. The fixtures system allows for easy serialization of data in a few formats, such as JSON and YAML, allowing developers to easily dump or load data from the database. The management commands allow developers to create commands for `manage.py`, allowing for increased control of data and the website from within the terminal.

## 24.3   Custom Managers and Querysets

A manager is any Python class that inherits from the `Manager` class defined in Django's `db.models` package. Django automatically generates a manager for a model class unless the `objects` attribute is explicitly declared.

To create and connect our custom `PostManager`, we simply declare it as a subclass of `Manager` and then add it as the `objects` attribute on `Post`. In Example 24.1, we also add the `published()` method to find all `Post` objects with a `pub_date` from before today's date, much like the `published()` method defined in `Tag` and `Startup`.

**Example 24.1: Project Code**

blog/models.py **in** 74627b7014

```
 1   from datetime import date
 .       ...
14   class PostManager(models.Manager):
15
16       def published(self):
17           return self.get_queryset().filter(
18               pub_date__lte=date.today())
 .       ...
21   class Post(models.Model):
 .       ...
43       objects = PostManager()
```

Interacting with our new manager works great, but our code has a rather large shortcoming, as shown in Example 24.2.

**Example 24.2: Python Interpreter Code**

```
>>> from blog.models import Post
>>> Post.objects.published()
[<Post: Django Consulting on 2015-01-28>,
 <Post: Boundless Software on 2013-05-15>,
 <Post: Django 1.0 Release on 2008-09-03>]
>>> Post.objects.all().published()
AttributeError: 'QuerySet' object has no attribute 'published'
```

A manager merely returns a queryset, and at the moment, our queryset doesn't have a published() method defined on it.

Much like a manager, a queryset is simply a class that inherits the QuerySet class defined in django.db.models. We can similarly create a PostQuerySet and define published() on the class, as shown in Example 24.3.

**Example 24.3: Project Code**
blog/models.py **in** c6380cab2c

```
14   class PostQueryset(models.QuerySet):
15
16       def published(self):
17           return self.filter(
18               pub_date__lte=date.today())
```

There are several ways to connect PostManager to PostQuerySet. The original method, shown in Example 24.4, involves overriding the get_queryset() method in Manager, changing it so that it uses our new class. In this case, we can also change the manager's published() method to use the queryset's code, resulting in a much more DRY implementation.

**Example 24.4: Project Code**
blog/models.py **in** c6380cab2c

```
21   class PostManager(models.Manager):
22
23       def get_queryset(self):
24           return PostQueryset(
25               self.model, using=self._db)
26
27       def published(self):
28           return self.get_queryset().published()
```

The second method is to use the manager class as a base class. The Manager class defines a from_queryset() method, which creates a new class from the manager based on the queryset class. We can thus delete the get_queryset() method from PostManager and use the from_queryset() method to create a new connected PostManager class, as shown in Example 24.5. We then use this class as the actual manager.

**Example 24.5: Project Code**
blog/models.py **in** 4f02c0b814

```
27   ConnectedPostManager = PostManager.from_queryset(PostQueryset)
 .       ...
30   class Post(models.Model):
 .       ...
52       objects = ConnectedPostManager()
```

The third way to create a manager is to entirely derive it from a queryset, thanks to the as_manager() method defined in QuerySet starting in Django 1.8. We delete the PostManager class and create the manager entirely with PostQueryset, as shown in Example 24.6.

**Example 24.6: Project Code**
blog/models.py **in** 3ead47bd4b

```
21    class Post(models.Model):
 .        ...
43        objects = PostQueryset.as_manager()
```

In each case above, the call Post.objects.all().published() will work exactly as desired.

# 24.4   Fixtures

A **fixture** is simply a file with data built to be loaded in the database. Django allows for serialization of data (putting data into a flat file for storage) into JSON or XML out of the box, but it can also use YAML if the PyYAML package is installed.

The utility of fixtures is broad because they become useful anytime you need data outside of the database. When we switched to a new User model in Chapter 22, had we had a production database, one approach to the problem would have been to serialize our data, modify the JSON, and then load the data into a restructured database. If we needed to pass data to another developer for testing purposes, or any other internal use, fixtures would be the solution.

By default, Django looks for fixtures in the <app>/fixtures/ directory. To create fixtures, we use the dumpdata command with manager.py. On its own, it will output all of the data in the database. The command allows for the data to be limited to an app or even a model. In Example 24.7, we output all of the Post instances in our database as JSON (the default). I set the indent level of the output to two spaces.

**Example 24.7: Shell Code**

```
$ ./manage.py dumpdata --indent=2 blog.post
```

This will print everything to stdout (the terminal window). To put this information in a file, we can use file redirection (a feature of the shell, not of Django or Python). I output all of the data for each model to a separate file, as shown in Example 24.8.

**Example 24.8: Shell Code**

```
$ mkdir blog/fixtures
$ mkdir organizer/fixtures
$ ./manage.py dumpdata --indent=2 blog.post > \
> blog/fixtures/post_data.json
```

```
$ ./manage.py dumpdata --indent=2 organizer.tag > \
> organizer/fixtures/tag_data.json
$ ./manage.py dumpdata --indent=2 organizer.startup > \
> organizer/fixtures/startup_data.json
$ ./manage.py dumpdata --indent=2 organizer.newslink > \
> organizer/fixtures/newslink_data.json
```

Much like templates or static files, Django allows for site-wide content (as opposed to app-specific) as long as we add a setting telling Django where the content is added, as shown in Example 24.9.

### Example 24.9: Project Code
suorganizer/settings.py in e1978560da

```
167    FIXTURE_DIRS = (os.path.join(BASE_DIR, 'fixtures'),)
```

Now that Django knows where we will put our site-wide fixtures, we can actually generate them by invoking dumpdata, as shown in Example 24.10.

### Example 24.10: Shell Code

```
$ mkdir fixtures
$ ./manage.py dumpdata --indent=2 sites > \
> fixtures/sites_data.json
$ ./manage.py dumpdata --indent=2 user auth.Group > \
> fixtures/user_data.json
```

A key problem with serialized data is that it's usually hard to read and manipulate. Relations are output exactly as they are in the database: as foreign keys, as shown in Example 24.11.

### Example 24.11: JSON

```
"tags": [ 3, 11, 15 ],
```

When interacting with data, it would be nice if the data were a little more human-friendly. Django calls this data "natural," and it looks like that shown in Example 24.12.

### Example 24.12: JSON

```
"tags": [ [ "django" ], [ "python" ], [ "web" ] ],
```

Django's serialization system relies on code in models and managers to make this work. When dumping data, Django uses the natural_key() method on the model to output data. When loading data, Django uses the get_by_natural_key() method on managers to find objects by their natural key, allowing for relations like the one above.

A natural key is a unique identifier consisting of one or more fields. We can use the fields we use for our URL patterns as the natural keys for our objects.

To output natural Post data, we define the natural_key() method to return the year and month of the pub_date field and the slug field, as shown in Example 24.13.

**Example 24.13: Project Code**
blog/models.py in a1dd2a227b

```
 33    class Post(models.Model):
  .        ...
103        def natural_key(self):
104            return (
105                self.pub_date,
106                self.slug)
```

It is possible to tell Django that certain models depend on other data. For example, if we output a fixture with startups and tags, we know that we must load our tags into the database first because our startups rely on them. We can define an attribute on the natural_key() method to let Django know of these dependencies, as shown in Example 24.14.

**Example 24.14: Project Code**
blog/models.py in a1dd2a227b

```
 33    class Post(models.Model):
  .        ...
103        def natural_key(self):
104            return (
105                self.pub_date,
106                self.slug)
107        natural_key.dependencies = [
108            'organizer.startup',
109            'organizer.tag',
110            'user.user',
111        ]
```

Django only respects dependencies within a single file. If we load a file for tags and a file for startups, Django will ignore the startup's dependencies on tag data. We will have to load our separate fixture files one by one, in order of dependency.

To find Post data according to natural keys, we create the get_by_natural_key() on a newly declared BasePostManager class, as shown in Example 24.15.

**Example 24.15:** Project Code

blog/models.py in a1dd2a227b

```
21    class BasePostManager(models.Manager):
22
23        def get_by_natural_key(self, pub_date, slug):
24            return self.get(
25                pub_date=pub_date,
26                slug=slug)
```

We want the get_by_natural_key() to exist on the manager, and not on the queryset, so we define our own manager, as shown in Example 24.16. While we can no longer use PostQueryset.as_manager() in this instance, we can still rely on from_queryset() to make our lives a little simpler.

**Example 24.16:** Project Code

blog/models.py in a1dd2a227b

```
29    PostManager = BasePostManager.from_queryset(
30        PostQueryset)
```

We use our generated manager class as our Post model's manager, as shown in Example 24.17.

**Example 24.17:** Project Code

blog/models.py in a1dd2a227b

```
33    class Post(models.Model):
.         ...
55        objects = PostManager()
```

Creating the natural_key() and get_by_natural_key() for the rest of our models and managers (Tag, Startup, NewsLink, User, Profile) is exactly like the code above, and so we skip seeing it in the book (the changes I make are in the same commit as the changes in the preceding code examples).

# 24.5 Management Commands

When we swapped the User model in Chapter 22, we discovered that we had effectively broken the UserManager, and we extended the **auth** app's implementation with our own createuser() and createsuperuser() methods.

When we did so, we partially broke the createsuperuser command for manage.py, called the createsuperuser management command. In this section, we fix that by creating our own custom management commands to create users and superusers. Before we jump into these commands, we first ease into the process by building a simpler command: `createtag`.

## 24.5.1  The `createtag` Management Command

The goal is to create a simple management command that will create a new `Tag` object, as shown in Example 24.18.

**Example 24.18: Shell Code**

```
$ ./manage.py createtag "django unleashed"
```

Commands are stored in the `commands` package of the management package of apps, as shown in Example 24.19.

**Example 24.19: Shell Code**

```
$ mkdir -p organizer/management/commands
$ touch organizer/management/__init__.py
$ touch organizer/management/commands/__init__.py
$ touch organizer/management/commands/createtag.py
$ tree organizer/management/
organizer/management/
├── __init__.py
└── commands
    ├── __init__.py
    └── createtag.py

1 directory, 3 files
```

The command call is based on the name of the file, as shown in Example 24.20.

Django supplies the `BaseCommand` for custom commands to inherit (Django eats its own dog food and uses the command internally as well).

**Example 24.20: Project Code**

`organizer/management/commands/createtag.py` in 8003bd8f2b

```
1  from django.core.management.base import (
2      BaseCommand, CommandError)
3  from django.utils.text import slugify
4
5  from ...models import Tag
```

The `CommandError` exception is exactly what it sounds like.

When we invoke `createtag`, Django looks in all of the `/commands/` subdirectories for the `createtag.py` file, inside of which it will look for the `Command` class. We can create a new `Command` class by inheriting `BaseCommand`. We then define basic help text for the command, as shown in Example 24.21.

**Example 24.21: Project Code**
`organizer/management/commands/createtag.py` **in** `8003bd8f2b`

```
8    class Command(BaseCommand):
9        help = 'Create new Tag.'
```

Our first task it to tell the command what kind of arguments it should expect, which we do in Example 24.22. The `BaseCommand` class expects us to define the `add_arguments()` method, to which the `Command` will pass an `ArgumentParser` object, part of Python's `argparse` package.

**Example 24.22: Project Code**
`organizer/management/commands/createtag.py` **in** `8003bd8f2b`

```
8    class Command(BaseCommand):
.        ...
11       def add_arguments(self, parser):
```

## Ghosts of Django Past

The use of `argparse` is new as of Django 1.8. In Django 1.7 and earlier, the `BaseCommand` will pass an `OptionParser` object, part of Python's `optparse`. Django switched to `argparse` because `optparse` was deprecated in Python 3.2.

https://dju.link/18/optparse

## Python Documentation

For more information about the `ArgumentParser`, please see

https://dju.link/18/argumentparser

To inform our `Command` that it expects a string (which it will use to create a new `Tag` object), we call the `add_argument()` command on the `ArgumentParser` object, as shown in Example 24.23.

**Example 24.23: Project Code**
`organizer/management/commands/createtag.py` **in** `8003bd8f2b`

```
8    class Command(BaseCommand):
.        ...
11       def add_arguments(self, parser):
12           parser.add_argument(
13               'tag_name',
14               default=None,
15               help='New tag name.')
```

## Python Documentation

For more information about the add_argument() method on ArgumentParser, please see

https://dju.link/18/add-argument

When the command is actually invoked, it uses the handle() method to use the expected arguments, which are passed to the function as a set of keyword arguments, typically called options instead of kwargs in Django's Command classes. We named our argument tag_name in add_argument(), and so we can retrieve it from the dictionary using that key, as shown in Example 24.24.

**Example 24.24: Project Code**

organizer/management/commands/createtag.py in 8003bd8f2b

```
 8   class Command(BaseCommand):
 .       ...
17       def handle(self, **options):
18           tag_name = options.pop('tag_name', None)
19           Tag.objects.create(
20               name=tag_name,
21               slug=slugify(tag_name))
```

The command in Example 24.25 will now work!

**Example 24.25: Shell Code**

```
$ ./manage.py createtag "django unleashed"
```

## 24.5.2  The createuser and createsuperuser Commands

The createuser and createsuperuser commands are much more involved than the createtag command, but the principle is the same. In /user/management/commands/ we create a file called createuser.py for the createuser command and a file called createsuperuser.py for the createsuperuser command. In both files, we declare a Command class, which inherits from BaseCommand. Our goal is to define the add_arguments() and handle() methods.

We take this a step further and imitate the createsuperuser.py command supplied by **auth**. The command has two ways of working: interactively and non-interactively. If you checkout a commit in the git repo from before Chapter 22, you'll be able to see this for yourself. To see all of the options, you can invoke the command with the -h flag, as shown in Example 24.26.

**Example 24.26:** Shell Code

```
$ ./manage.py createsuperuser -h
```

To use the command interactively, we can simply call the command with no arguments, and the command will prompt us for values, as shown in Example 24.27.

> **Info**
>
> When I use the NewUser information, I mean that this data does not already exist in the database.

**Example 24.27:** Shell Code

```
$ ./manage.py createsuperuser
Username (leave blank to use 'andrew'): NewUser
Email address: newuser@django-unleashed.com
Password:
Password (again):
Superuser created successfully.
```

The command will enter a semi-interactive state if we specify a username and an email. The command will still take the opportunity to prompt us for a password, as shown in Example 24.28.

**Example 24.28:** Shell Code

```
$ ./manage.py createsuperuser \
> --username NewUser \
> --email newuser@django-unleashed.com
Password:
Password (again):
Superuser created successfully.
```

For a fully noninteractive experience, we can pass the --noinput flag to the command, as shown in Example 24.29.

**Example 24.29:** Shell Code

```
$ ./manage.py createsuperuser \
> --username NewUser \
> --email newuser@django-unleashed.com \
> --noinput
Superuser created successfully.
```

Our own command will work very similarly, except instead of username and email, we will have name and email. Our command will use the name argument to create a

Profile for the new user. In Example 24.30, we mimic the original command with the noinput flag.

**Example 24.30: Shell Code**

```
$ ./manage.py createuser \
> --name NewUser \
> --email newuser@django-unleashed.com \
> --noinput
```

Without the noinput flag, we prompt for a password, as shown in Example 24.31.

**Example 24.31: Shell Code**

```
$ ./manage.py createuser \
>  --name NewUser \
> --email newuser@django-unleashed.com
Password:
Password (again):
```

And, of course, we provide a fully interactive version, as shown in Example 24.32.

**Example 24.32: Shell Code**

```
$ ./manage.py createuser
Email address: newuser@django-unleashed.com
Name: NewUser
Password:
Password (again):
```

In the event the email or name values passed already exist when in noninteractive mode, we return an error, as shown in Example 24.33.

**Example 24.33: Shell Code**

```
$ ./manage.py createuser \
> --name NewUser \
> --email django@jambonsw.com \
> --noinput
CommandError: That Email address is already taken.
```

If we are in interactive mode, we will be able to accept values but prompt the developer in the event the values are incorrect or already taken. Finally, using Control-C during interactive mode will cause the command to end, as demonstrated in Example 24.34.

**Example 24.34: Shell Code**

```
$ ./manage.py createuser \
> --name Andrew \
> --email django@jambonsw.com
Error: That email address is already taken.
Error: That name is already taken.
Email address: ^C
Operation cancelled.
```

This is a key difference between our `createtag` command and our new commands. Our `createuser` and `createsuperuser` commands will be far more robust and will check the validity of the data as we submit it rather than blindly add it to the database. To do this, we actually use the fields on the `User` and `Profile` model to validate the data and use our managers to check that the values we are submitting do not conflict with current data in the database.

To begin, we import the `sys` and `getpass` Python package in Example 24.35. The `sys` package allows us to end the process if we need to, while the `getpass` package is built exclusively for asking for passwords in consoles.

**Example 24.35: Project Code**
`user/management/commands/createuser.py` in 51406f9ea8

```
1    import getpass
2    import sys
```

We then import our tools from Django in Example 24.36. The two new tools are `force_str()` and `cap_first()`. The first is a utility to convert `bytes` or similar structures into native Python strings, while the second simply capitalizes the first letter in a string.

**Example 24.36: Project Code**
`user/management/commands/createuser.py` in 51406f9ea8

```
4    from django.contrib.auth import get_user_model
5    from django.core.exceptions import (
6        ObjectDoesNotExist, ValidationError)
7    from django.core.management.base import (
8        BaseCommand, CommandError)
9    from django.utils.encoding import force_str
10   from django.utils.text import capfirst, slugify
11
12   from user.models import Profile
```

We declare our command and provide help text, as shown in Example 24.37.

**Example 24.37: Project Code**

user/management/commands/createuser.py **in** 51406f9ea8

```
15   class Command(BaseCommand):
16       help = 'Create new User with Profile.'
```

To make our lives easier, we add commonly accessed pieces of data as attributes to our class by overriding the __init__() method, as shown in Example 24.38. We therefore add our User model, the EmailField from the User model, and the CharField in the Profile model to store the name. The two fields allow us to check that the values being passed are valid for the database, thanks to their clean methods.

**Example 24.38: Project Code**

user/management/commands/createuser.py **in** 51406f9ea8

```
15   class Command(BaseCommand):
.        ...
21       def __init__(self, *args, **kwargs):
22           super().__init__(*args, **kwargs)
23           self.User = get_user_model()
24           self.name_field = (
25               Profile._meta.get_field('name'))
26           self.username_field = (
27               self.User._meta.get_field(
28                   self.User.USERNAME_FIELD))
```

We also override the execute() method, as shown in Example 24.39. Internally, execute() is what the Command class uses to run the command. We don't actually want to change anything here—we simply want to grab the stdin keyword argument, as we will use it in the interactive mode to make sure we can actually behave interactively.

**Example 24.39: Project Code**

user/management/commands/createuser.py **in** 51406f9ea8

```
15   class Command(BaseCommand):
.        ...
30       def execute(self, *args, **options):
31           self.stdin = options.get(
32               'stdin', sys.stdin)
33           return super().execute(*args, **options)
```

With all our tools ready to go, we can now program add_arguments() and handle(), as shown in Example 24.40. We start with the first, adding an argument for the the name field on the Profile model, using the attributes we saved for ourselves in the __init__() method.

**Example 24.40: Project Code**
user/management/commands/createuser.py in 51406f9ea8

```
15   class Command(BaseCommand):
 .        ...
35       def add_arguments(self, parser):
36           parser.add_argument(
37               '--{}'.format(self.name_field.name),
38               dest=self.name_field.name,
39               default=None,
40               help='User profile name.')
```

The next argument is for the email field in our User model. Following Django convention, I will refer to this data as the username, as our EmailField acts as the username for our User model (as defined in the USERNAME_FIELD attribute on the model). However, even if I refer to it in the rest of the code, given that the USERNAME_FIELD is titled email, the actual keyword destination of the argument will be email. We'll be sure to use the self.User.USERNAME_FIELD to keep this standard, as shown in Example 24.41.

**Example 24.41: Project Code**
user/management/commands/createuser.py in 51406f9ea8

```
15   class Command(BaseCommand):
 .        ...
35       def add_arguments(self, parser):
 .            ...
41           parser.add_argument(
42               '--{}'.format(
43                   self.User.USERNAME_FIELD),
44               dest=self.User.USERNAME_FIELD,
45               default=None,
46               help='User login.')
```

The interactive argument is a little different from our others. The default of the argument is True, but if the flag is specified, the action tells the ArgumentParser to change the interactive value to False (store_false), as shown in Example 24.42.

**Example 24.42: Project Code**
user/management/commands/createuser.py in 51406f9ea8

```
15   class Command(BaseCommand):
 .        ...
35       def add_arguments(self, parser):
 .            ...
47           parser.add_argument(
48               '--noinput',
49               action='store_false',
50               dest='interactive',
```

```
51                  default=True,
52                  help=(
53                      'Do NOT prompt the user for '
54                      'input of any kind. You must use '
55                      '--{} with --noinput, along with '
56                      'an option for any other '
57                      'required field. Users created '
58                      'with --noinput will not be able '
59                      'to log in until they\'re given '
60                      'a valid password.'.format(
61                          self.User.USERNAME_FIELD)))
```

In the **auth**'s version of `createsuperuser`, it is possible to supply a `database` argument, which will tell the command which database to use in situations where the website has multiple databases. We only have one, so I'm not going to worry about it. However, it may be beneficial for you to read Django's source code if you want to see how to create and use such an argument.

Before we jump into implementing `handle()`, we're going to build two functions to help us in the long run: `clean_value()` and `check_unique()`. In the rest of the code, we will find ourselves repeating the task of validating the information provided to us. To shorten our code, we build these two functions to do all of the expected validation. The first uses the `clean()` method on our fields to check submitted values. The second checks to see if the data already exists in the database.

Our `clean_value()` accepts the field and the value the developer has submitted, and runs the field `clean()` method on the value within a `try...except` block. If there are no problems with validation, we return the value, as shown in Example 24.43.

**Example 24.43: Project Code**
user/management/commands/createuser.py in 51406f9ea8

```
15    class Command(BaseCommand):
 .        ...
63        def clean_value(
64                self, field, value, halt=True):
65            try:
66                value = field.clean(value, None)
67            except ValidationError as e:
 .            ...
76            else:
77                return value
```

In the event validation fails, we want to respond in one of two ways. If we are in interactive mode, we simply want to print an error and then prompt the user for another value. If we are in non-interactive mode, we want to print an error and then halt the program. For the latter, we can use `CommandError`, as the exception will cause a command to end. For the first, however, we use the `self.stderr`, which allows us to write() to the console's stderr (versus stdout). To tell clean_value() which behavior to follow, we use the halt Boolean, as shown in Example 24.44.

**Example 24.44: Project Code**
user/management/commands/createuser.py in 51406f9ea8

```
15    class Command(BaseCommand):
 .        ...
63        def clean_value(
64                self, field, value, halt=True):
 .            ...
67            except ValidationError as e:
68                if halt:
69                    raise CommandError(
70                        '; '.join(e.messages))
71                else:
72                    self.stderr.write(
73                        "Error: {}".format(
74                            '; '.join(e.messages)))
75                return None
```

The check_unique() method works similarly. In Example 24.45, we check for the value of the field in the database, wrapping the attempt in a try...except block. If the value does not exist, we return the value (this is what we want!).

**Example 24.45: Project Code**
user/management/commands/createuser.py in 51406f9ea8

```
15    class Command(BaseCommand):
 .        ...
79        def check_unique(
80                self, model, field, value, halt=True):
81            try:
82                q = '{}__iexact'.format(field.name)
83                filter_dict = {q: value}
84                model.objects.get(**filter_dict)
85            except ObjectDoesNotExist:
86                return value
87            else:
 .                ...
99                return None
```

If the values does exist in the database (we successfully were able to retrieve it), we again rely on halt to know whether or not we need to halt the program. If we end the program, we raise a CommandError, and if not, we output to stderr, in both cases informing the developer that the value for the field of that model already exists, as shown in Example 24.46.

**Example 24.46: Project Code**

`user/management/commands/createuser.py` in `51406f9ea8`

```
15   class Command(BaseCommand):
.        ...
79       def check_unique(
80               self, model, field, value, halt=True):
.            ...
87           else:
88               if halt:
89                   raise CommandError(
90                       "That {} is already taken."
91                       .format(
92                           capfirst(
93                               field.verbose_name)))
94               else:
95                   self.stderr.write(
96                       'Error: That {} is '
97                       'already taken.'.format(
98                           field.verbose_name))
99           return None
```

The ultimate goal of this exercise, of course, is to create a simple user and to tie this new User instance to a Profile object. Despite all of the work we do, because we cannot guarantee there won't be any clashes with the slug field in the Profile (calls to slugify() with inputs super man and super-man are identical), we wrap the creation of a new Profile object in a try...except block, as shown in Example 24.47.

**Example 24.47: Project Code**

`user/management/commands/createuser.py` in `51406f9ea8`

```
15   class Command(BaseCommand):
.        ...
212      def create_user(
213              self, name, username, password):
214          new_user = self.User.objects.create_user(
215              username, password)
216          try:
217              Profile.objects.create(
218                  user=new_user,
219                  name=name,
220                  slug=slugify(name))
221          except Exception as e:
222              raise CommandError(
223                  "Could not create Profile:\n{}"
224                  .format('; '.join(e.messages)))
```

Finally, we can turn to handle(). In some instances, we will have all of our arguments, and in some instances, we will have none, depending entirely on how the developer has called createuser. We pop the possible arguments, assigning None in the event they do not exist, as shown in Example 24.48.

**Example 24.48: Project Code**

user/management/commands/createuser.py **in** 51406f9ea8

```
 15    class Command(BaseCommand):
   .       ...
226       def handle(self, **options):
227           name = options.pop(
228               self.name_field.name, None)
229           username = options.pop(
230               self.User.USERNAME_FIELD, None)
231           password = None
```

In Example 24.49, we then check the noinput flag, which has been assigned to interactive. If we are in interactive mode, we call handle_interactive(), and if not, we call handle_non_interactive(). We write both of these methods shortly. We make sure they return the values we expect, and then call the create_user() method we just implemented.

**Example 24.49: Project Code**

user/management/commands/createuser.py **in** 51406f9ea8

```
 15    class Command(BaseCommand):
   .       ...
226       def handle(self, **options):
   .           ...
233           if not options['interactive']:
234               name, username = (
235                   self.handle_non_interactive(
236                       name, username, **options))
237           else:
238               name, username, password = (
239                   self.handle_interactive(
240                       name, username, **options))
241
242           self.create_user(name, username, password)
```

Of the two methods, handle_non_interactive() is much simpler. In this case, we must have been passed both an email and a name. Our first job is to check this is the case and to error if not, as shown in Example 24.50.

**Example 24.50: Project Code**

user/management/commands/createuser.py **in** 51406f9ea8

```
 15    class Command(BaseCommand):
   .       ...
 18       required_error = (
 19           'You must use --{} with --noinput.')
   .           ...
101       def handle_non_interactive(
102               self, name, username, **options):
```

```
103              if not username:
104                  raise CommandError(
105                      self.required_error.format(
106                          self.User.USERNAME_FIELD))
107              if not name:
108                  raise CommandError(
109                      self.required_error.format(
110                          self.name_field.name))
```

If we have been given these values, we must then make sure that we can use them. We can use our `clean_value()` and `check_unique()` utility methods to perform our validation, as shown in Example 24.51. We are not setting `halt` on any of our calls, meaning they will default to `True`, causing our command to raise `CommandError` and halt in the event of a problem.

**Example 24.51: Project Code**

user/management/commands/createuser.py **in** 51406f9ea8

```
 15    class Command(BaseCommand):
  .        ...
101        def handle_non_interactive(
102                self, name, username, **options):
  .            ...
111            username = self.clean_value(
112                self.username_field, username)
113            name = self.clean_value(
114                self.name_field, name)
115            username = self.check_unique(
116                self.User,
117                self.username_field,
118                username)
119            name = self.check_unique(
120                Profile, self.name_field, name)
121            return (name, username)
```

Before we implement `handle_interactive()`, we create a helper function called `get_field_interactive()`. The method's job is to prompt the user for input and verify that the input is correct. We start by defining the `value` and the prompt, called `input_msg`, as shown in Example 24.52.

**Example 24.52: Project Code**

user/management/commands/createuser.py **in** 51406f9ea8

```
 15    class Command(BaseCommand):
  .        ...
123        def get_field_interactive(self, model, field):
124            value = None
125            input_msg = '{}: '.format(
126                capfirst(field.verbose_name))
```

Until the input is correct (`value` is no longer None), we continue to show the prompt to the user. Once we have the user's input, we check that it is valid for the field using our `clean_value()` helper method. We then use our `check_unique()` helper method to check that the value doesn't already exist in the database, as shown in Example 24.53.

**Example 24.53: Project Code**

`user/management/commands/createuser.py` in `51406f9ea8`

```
 15    class Command(BaseCommand):
   .        ...
123        def get_field_interactive(self, model, field):
   .            ...
127            while value is None:
128                value = input(input_msg)
129                value = self.clean_value(
130                    field, value, halt=False)
131                if not value:
132                    continue
133                value = self.check_unique(
134                    model, field, value, halt=False)
135                if not value:
136                    continue
137            return value
```

The `handle_interactive()` method is the most complicated method in this class. We start in Example 24.54 by declaring it and creating the `password` variable for later use.

**Example 24.54: Project Code**

`user/management/commands/createuser.py` in `51406f9ea8`

```
 15    class Command(BaseCommand):
   .        ...
139        def handle_interactive(
140                self, name, username, **options):
141
142            password = None
```

Our first job is to make sure that we *can* behave interactively. We use the `stdin` attribute that we assigned in the `execute()` method to check that the management command is being called from an interactive shell, as shown in Example 24.55. If it is not, we raise an error, as none of our prompts in the rest of this method will work.

**Example 24.55: Project Code**

`user/management/commands/createuser.py` in `51406f9ea8`

```
 15    class Command(BaseCommand):
   .        ...
139        def handle_interactive(
140                self, name, username, **options):
   .            ...
```

```
144             if (hasattr(self.stdin, 'isatty')
145                     and not self.stdin.isatty()):
146                 self.stdout.write(
147                     'User creation skipped due '
148                     'to not running in a TTY. '
149                     'You can run 'manage.py '
150                     'createuser' in your project '
151                     'to create one manually.')
152                 sys.exit(1)
```

We then check the username argument, as shown in Example 24.56. It is possible for createuser to be called with certain parameters set noninteractively, and at the moment, we don't know which information we have (we don't know what handle() has passed to handle_interactively()). If the username argument was passed, we check it first for valid data and then for existence in the database using our helper methods.

**Example 24.56: Project Code**

user/management/commands/createuser.py in 51406f9ea8

```
 15    class Command(BaseCommand):
   .        ...
139        def handle_interactive(
140                self, name, username, **options):
   .            ...
154            if username is not None:
155                username = self.clean_value(
156                    self.username_field,
157                    username,
158                    halt=False)
159                if username is not None:
160                    username = self.check_unique(
161                        self.User,
162                        self.username_field,
163                        username,
164                        halt=False)
```

In Example 24.57, we do exactly the same thing for the name argument.

**Example 24.57: Project Code**

user/management/commands/createuser.py in 51406f9ea8

```
 15    class Command(BaseCommand):
   .        ...
139        def handle_interactive(
140                self, name, username, **options):
   .            ...
165            if name is not None:
166                name = self.clean_value(
167                    self.name_field, name, halt=False)
168                if name is not None:
```

```
169                    name = self.check_unique(
170                        Profile,
171                        self.name_field,
172                        name,
173                        halt=False)
```

At this point, we have checked all of the values passed by `handle()`, and we are ready to begin interactively. Our first step is to wrap all of our interactive code in a `try...except` block, as shown in Example 24.58. We want to make sure that, at any point, the developer may hit `Control-C` to end the program and that if he or she does, we simply terminate. Python comes with an exception to handle `Control-C`: `Keyboard Interrupt`. We rely on Python's `sys` package to actually exit the program.

**Example 24.58: Project Code**

user/management/commands/createuser.py in 51406f9ea8

```
 15    class Command(BaseCommand):
   .       ...
139        def handle_interactive(
140                self, name, username, **options):
   .           ...
175            try:
   .               ...
207            except KeyboardInterrupt:
208                self.stderr.write(
209                    "\nOperation cancelled.")
210                sys.exit(1)
```

Within the `try` section, we first check for the existence of `username` and `name`. If they do not exist, we prompt the developer for these values, relying on the `get_field_interactive()` method to do the job, as shown in Example 24.59.

**Example 24.59: Project Code**

user/management/commands/createuser.py in 51406f9ea8

```
 15    class Command(BaseCommand):
   .       ...
139        def handle_interactive(
140                self, name, username, **options):
   .           ...
175            try:
176                if not username:
177                    username = (
178                        self.get_field_interactive(
179                            self.User,
180                            self.username_field))
181                if not name:
182                    name = self.get_field_interactive(
183                        Profile,
184                        self.name_field)
```

This finally allows us, in Example 24.60, to prompt the developer for the password, thanks to Python's `getpass` package. The use of `getpass` ensures that the strings provided are never printed in the shell, allowing us to adhere to best security practices.

**Example 24.60: Project Code**

`user/management/commands/createuser.py` in 51406f9ea8

```
 15    class Command(BaseCommand):
  .        ...
139        def handle_interactive(
140                self, name, username, **options):
  .            ...
175            try:
  .                ...
186                while password is None:
187                    password = getpass.getpass()
188                    password2 = getpass.getpass(
189                        force_str(
190                            'Password (again): '))
```

In Example 24.61, we make sure the two password strings we've prompted the developer for are the same, or else we set the `password` variable to None and restart the loop to prompt the developer for totally new strings.

**Example 24.61: Project Code**

`user/management/commands/createuser.py` in 51406f9ea8

```
 15    class Command(BaseCommand):
  .        ...
139        def handle_interactive(
140                self, name, username, **options):
  .            ...
175            try:
  .                ...
186                while password is None:
  .                    ...
191                    if password != password2:
192                        self.stderr.write(
193                            "Error: Your "
194                            "passwords didn't "
195                            "match.")
196                        password = None
197                        continue
```

We also need to make sure the password values are not simply empty, as shown in Example 24.62.

**Example 24.62: Project Code**

user/management/commands/createuser.py in 51406f9ea8

```
15     class Command(BaseCommand):
  .        ...
139        def handle_interactive(
140            self, name, username, **options):
  .            ...
175            try:
  .                ...
186                while password is None:
  .                    ...
198                    if password.strip() == '':
199                        self.stderr.write(
200                            "Error: Blank passwords "
201                            "aren't allowed.")
202                        password = None
203                        continue
```

Finally, in Example 24.63, we return the name, username, and password to handle(), which uses these values to call create_user().

**Example 24.63: Project Code**

user/management/commands/createuser.py in 51406f9ea8

```
15     class Command(BaseCommand):
  .        ...
139        def handle_interactive(
140            self, name, username, **options):
  .            ...
175            try:
  .                ...
186                while password is None:
  .                    ...
205                return (name, username, password)
```

If you run the createuser command in the shell, it will now work exactly how I described and demonstrated at the beginning of this section.

The command we coded in this section comes with several major shortcomings. First and foremost, we assume that the name field in Profile is unique, which is not true! The slug must be unique, but because of how much more complicated ensuring that condition makes this script (while accepting nonunique names), I opted to present a far simpler script (which may be hard to believe, given the complexity seen here). The goal, after all, was not to build a robust, fool-proof script but to demonstrate all the key parts that you need to build such a script.

Luckily, because of all our hard work, creating createsuperuser is far, far easier, but it comes with a catch.

We can create the file for the command, as shown in Example 24.64

**Example 24.64: Shell Code**

```
touch user/management/commands/createsuperuser.py
$ tree user/management/
user/management/
├── __init__.py
└── commands
    ├── __init__.py
    ├── createsuperuser.py
    └── createuser.py

1 directory, 4 files
```

In Example 24.65, you can see we need far fewer tools for this command, because we can use the Command class we just built in `createuser.py` as our BaseCommand class.

**Example 24.65: Project Code**

user/management/commands/createsuperuser.py **in** a3f3f522d8

```
1    from django.utils.text import slugify
2
3    from user.models import Profile
4
5    from .createuser import Command as BaseCommand
```

To do so, we only need to override the `create_user()` method in the class. The key difference is that we use the UserManager's `create_superuser()` method instead of `create_user()`, as shown in Example 24.66. That's all!

**Example 24.66: Project Code**

user/management/commands/createsuperuser.py **in** a3f3f522d8

```
8    class Command(BaseCommand):
9        help = 'Create new Super User with Profile.'
10
11       def create_user(
12               self, name, username, password):
13           new_user = (
14               self.User.objects.create_superuser(
15                   username, password))
```

The call to create the Profile, shown in Example 24.67, is exactly the same, wrapped in a `try...except` block so that we don't shower the developer in information when something goes wrong (some developers will disagree with this choice, but because they have to drop into the shell to fix the problem regardless, I see no real problem).

**Example 24.67:** Project Code
`user/management/commands/createsuperuser.py` in `a3f3f522d8`

```
 8    class Command(BaseCommand):
 .        ...
11        def create_user(
12                self, name, username, password):
 .            ...
16            try:
17                Profile.objects.create(
18                    user=new_user,
19                    name=name,
20                    slug=slugify(name))
21            except Exception as e:
22                raise CommandError(
23                    "Could not create Profile:\n{}"
24                    .format('; '.join(e.messages)))
```

Our command is correct, but if you try to invoke it, you'll be surprised to discover that the `createsuperuser` command behaves exactly like the one in **auth**. That's because Django is still using the command in **auth** instead of the one in our **user** app. Django uses the order of apps in `INSTALLED_APPS` to find commands, and if there are commands with duplicate names, it picks the first one. To prioritize our command over the one in **auth**, we can simply move the location of our **user** app to precede **auth** in the list, as shown in Example 24.68.

**Example 24.68:** Project Code
`suorganizer/settings.py` in `a3f3f522d8`

```
35    INSTALLED_APPS = (
36        'user',
37        'django.contrib.admin',
38        'django.contrib.auth',
39        'django.contrib.contenttypes',
40        'django.contrib.sessions',
41        'django.contrib.messages',
42        'django.contrib.sites',
43        'django.contrib.staticfiles',
44        'django_extensions',
45        'core',
46        'organizer',
47        'blog',
48        'contact',
49    )
```

The command will now work, creating a proper `User` instance with `Profile` object.

# 24.6   Putting It All Together

This chapter is a whirlwind tour of managers, querysets, fixtures, and commands. The last two rely heavily on the first two, making managers and querysets the central focus of the chapter, despite the amount of time we spent creating a full management command.

A manager can be extended to add new methods but can also be modified for seamless interaction with custom querysets. The tools to do this are

- `QuerySetClass.as_manager()`
- `ManagerClass.from_queryset(QuerySetClass)`
- overriding `get_queryset()` in `ManagerClass` to use `QuerySetClass`

One of the most common reasons to override managers and querysets is to enable natural keys in fixtures. By creating a `natural_key()` method in the model, and `get_by_natural_key()`, fixtures created or loaded by the management commands `dumpdata` or `loaddata` will be human readable and easier to manipulate or modify on the fly.

While we did not use the natural key methods in our own command, Django uses the natural key methods in many of the management commands made available by its contributed apps. It becomes an easy way to get data and, when programmed, can be used all over the place: including in views, which often rely on exactly the same data. This is an uncommon but strong way to adhere to DRY.

We could easily have replaced some of the methods for finding published `Post` objects with the use of our new managers. I have not done so because we will be returning to the topic in Chapter 26, when we optimize our website.

25

# Handling Behavior with Signals

## In This Chapter

- Directly interact with `Apps` objects and `AppConfig` objects
- Learn about loose coupling with signals
- Implement signal handlers to display login status and automatically assign `Tag` instances to `Post` objects

## 25.1  Introduction

Signals are a little bit of an oddity for Django. Everything in the core parts of the framework is tightly coupled. It would be difficult to change the HTTP request/response cycle, just as it would be difficult to replace Django's object-relational mapper (ORM) with a third-party ORM.

There are several exceptions. Django provides loose coupling for templates. The template system, starting in Django 1.8, allows for other template engines (such as Jinja2) to be plugged right into Django. This is one kind of loose coupling.

The other major exception is signals, and this is a different kind of loose coupling, much more in line with the **messages** app's loose coupling. Based on Python's own `signal` package, the system allows for event handling. In the code, a developer will opt to issue or send a signal. Any of the signal handlers (callables) that have been registered to the system will be called with this signal. This approach allows for loose coupling of behavior, as it allows us to define behavior in one part that may be called by multiple other parts of Django (if and when they send a signal).

In Chapter 1: Starting a New Django Project, we set out to create a blog system that would be able to inherit `Tag` objects. If we create a blog post about a specific `Startup`, then any of the `Tag` objects related to the `Startup` should automatically be related to the `Post` object. Achieving this goal without signals is rather tedious: we would have to handle it when a `Post` object is created, when a `Post` is related to `Startup` (via the `Post` model and the `startups` field), and when a `Startup` is related to a `Post` (via the `Startup` model and the `blog_posts` field). We would be duplicating code in at least three places. Instead, we can define a single signal handler method to do all the work for us.

Before we jump into building signal handlers, we first see the AppConfig object. We've interacted with it and come across it multiple times, but this is the first time we will actually have to understand it to make our code work.

## 25.2  `Apps` **and** `AppConfig`

In Chapter 1, we discovered that a Django project is a website and that a Django app is a feature of the website. A Django project is actually just the agglomeration of apps, provided by Django, ourselves, or other developers (such as the **django_extensions** app we used for the IPython notebooks in the github repository). The full list of apps belonging to a project is found in the `settings.py` file of the project, declared as the `INSTALLED_APPS` variable. If you are ever brought onto an existing project, looking at the `INSTALLED_APPS` is a great way to see all of the tools that the website uses to work.

When the server starts, Django loads the settings defined for the project, allowing it to configure the site. For example, it uses this time to load the URL configurations defined by the apps and build the tree structure of URL configurations. Before it can do these tasks, however, it must know which apps are available to it. It takes the `INSTALLED_APPS` and loads or generates an `AppConfig` object for each app, which it then stores in an `Apps` structure. This instance of the `Apps` class is called the master registry: it is the app registry for a project as the project runs.

The master registry is in direct contrast to other instances of `Apps` (other app registries). The migration system uses a subclass of `Apps` to build historical lists of `AppConfig` objects. This feature is quite powerful, as it means we could create our own app registries with our own custom `AppConfig` objects. I admit to being completely unsure *why* you might need to, but that's beside the point: you *could* if you needed to.

In Example 25.1 we interact with the master registry in the shell, and use it to get apps in our project.

**Example 25.1: Python Interpreter Code**

```
>>> from django.apps import apps as suorganizer_apps
>>> organizer_app = suorganizer_apps.get_app_config('organizer')
>>> auth_app = suorganizer_apps.get_app_config('auth')
```

AppConfig objects come with two notable attributes: `name` and `label`. The second is usually derived from the first, which must be declared on any custom AppConfig class. On **organizer**, the difference is not at all clear, but the **auth** app (in Example 25.2) shows the difference between the two.

**Example 25.2: Python Interpreter Code**

```
>>> organizer_app.name
'organizer'
>>> organizer_app.label
'organizer'
```

```
>>> auth_app.name
'django.contrib.auth'
>>> auth_app.label
'auth'
```

The name attribute is the only attribute that must be set. It must be the Python import path to the app from the project's base. To import organizer we only need to use import organizer, but for **auth** we need to use django.contrib.auth. The label is automatically generated from the name in the event it is not explicitly declared. Both are used to refer to AppConfig objects. The INSTALLED_APPS uses the name of the AppConfig to find the app, while migrations files use the label of the app. When interacting with Apps and AppConfig options in the shell, Django uses label (as seen in get_app_config()).

Unsurprisingly—given our knowledge of migrations—the AppConfig allows for direct interaction with the models in the app, as demonstrated in Example 25.3.

**Example 25.3: Python Interpreter Code**

```
>>> organizer_app.get_models()
<generator object get_models at 0x10e951a68>
>>> list(organizer_app.get_models())
[organizer.models.Tag, organizer.models.Startup,
 organizer.models.NewsLink]
>>> organizer_app.get_model('Startup')
organizer.models.Startup
```

Django convention is to create custom AppConfig objects in the file <app>/apps.py. We create a file called blog/apps.py shortly. However, Django will not actually look inside of files named apps.py by default. Anytime we create an AppConfig in apps.py, we need to inform Django of its existence by setting the default_app_config variable in the __init__.py file for that app.

The key reason to override an AppConfig is to implement the ready() method. When Django loads the project and apps, the ready() method is called on the AppConfig, allowing us to add or change any of our existing setup. We use the ready() method to tell Django of our signal handlers, so that Django knows of their existence. Think of ready() as being the final line of defense for inversion of control (even though it is the first thing called). If we cannot integrate it with the rest of our tightly integrated site and system (in the views, templates, or models), then we can turn to AppConfig.ready() to let Django know of the existence of the tool (assuming we then also use it in appropriate situations—Django cannot infer information! We're still just filling in the blanks in a game of Mad Libs!)

The AppConfig and Apps are powerful, but they can cause some funny errors, especially with URL configurations and the translation system. If the app has not been loaded yet, then none of the code inside of it will work. Attempting to load or run code inside of an app before Django has fully loaded it will cause problems, which is why the lazy version of some tools exist. In particular, the `reverse_lazy()` (for reversing URL patterns) and the `ugettext_lazy()` (for translating text) are all about waiting until the apps and URL configurations are loaded and ready before attempting to call and use these features. For example, we must use `reverse_lazy()` in code implemented directly in the URL configuration, or else Django will attempt to reverse a URL pattern before the URL configuration has actually loaded, which is problematic. Bear this in mind when you attempt to write code in places that may be used before apps are loaded (such as `AppConfig` and URL configurations).

### Ghosts of Django Past

The organization of apps changed drastically in Django 1.7, and this chapter only details how this code is organized in Django 1.7 and after. For a comparison of the older and newer systems, you may be interested in my article series, http://andrewsforge.com/presentation/upgrading-django-to-17/, which provides a section about the differences between apps and migrations in Django 1.6 and in Django 1.7.

The shortlink URL to the article series is http://afrg.co/updj17/.

### Info

The **admin** app's *multiple* `AppConfig` classes are a great way to dive further into the topic and to see some of the power afforded by `AppConfig` classes.

## 25.3   Signals

To create loosely coupled behavior, we can rely on signals and create a signal handler to be activated when a specific signal has been sent. For Django to know of the existence of our signal handler, we can override the `ready()` method in our `AppConfig`, loading and registering the signal handler as soon as the website is started.

There are *many* signals used by Django. Django sends signals before a model is instantiated, after a model is instantiated, before a model is saved, and after a model is saved. There are signals for migrations: the generation of permissions in `create_permissions()`, which we took control of in Chapter 22: Overriding Django's Authentication with a Custom User, waits for a `post_migrate` signal to run, which is why we called it directly in our own migration when we needed that data to exist beforehand. There are signals for requests and responses and a signal for template rendering. And then, several of the Django contributed apps also have their own signals. We could even define our own.

In the next two sections, we build two signal handlers. The first catches the `user_logged_in` and `user_logged_out` signals defined in the **auth** app and displays a message to users via the **messages** app to let them know they have successfully logged in or out of the site.

The second signal handler catches any change to the relations on a Post object. When we relate a Startup to a Post object, we will add all of the Tag objects related to the Startup to the Post object.

## 25.3.1  Informing the User of Login/Logout Actions

To begin, we can create a new file under user/signals.py.

Our first goal is to import our necessary tools. We need the actual signals from **auth** as well as the success() function from the **messages** app. We then import the @receiver() decorator, which allows us to register our function to be called when a specific signal is sent, as shown in Example 25.4.

**Example 25.4: Project Code**
user/signals.py in 4bd73cbe74

```
1   from django.contrib.auth.signals import (
2       user_logged_in, user_logged_out)
3   from django.contrib.messages import success
4   from django.dispatch import receiver
```

In Example 25.5, we first program display_login_message(), a function that displays a message when the user authenticates. We use the @receiver() decorator to register the function with the user_logged_in signal on line 7, turning the function into a signal handler: this function will be called each time the user_logged_in signal is sent (in our site, the **auth**-supplied login() view we are using from our URL configuration issues the signal). We need to accept the sender (the issuer of the signal—login()) as well as a set of keyword arguments. One of the keyword arguments passed is the HttpRequest object and the User instance, both of which we use with success().

**Example 25.5: Project Code**
user/signals.py in 4bd73cbe74

```
7    @receiver(user_logged_in)
8    def display_login_message(sender, **kwargs):
9        request = kwargs.get('request')
10       user = kwargs.get('user')
11       success(
12           request,
13           "Successfully logged in as {}".format(
14               user.get_short_name()),
15           fail_silently=True)
```

We tell the **messages** framework to fail silently in the event success() goes wrong. There's nothing we'd be able to do from this position, and the functionality we are creating is convenient but nonessential.

By the end of this section, the preceding code will result in the visual display of a message to the user, as shown in Figure 25.1.

**Figure 25.1:** Message for Logging In

The `display_logout_message()` function is even more straightforward, as shown in Example 25.6. We simply want to tie the function to the `user_logged_out` signal, which is only issued by the `logout()` view in our project. We use the function to display a message informing the visitor of our site that he or she has successfully logged out.

**Example 25.6: Project Code**
`user/signals.py` **in** `4bd73cbe74`

```
18   @receiver(user_logged_out)
19   def display_logout_message(sender, **kwargs):
20       request = kwargs.get('request')
21       success(
22           request,
23           "Successfully logged out",
24           fail_silently=True)
```

At the end of the section, the code results in the display shown in Figure 25.2.

The `@receiver()` decorator makes it easy for us to register signal handlers, but this only works if the code in the module is loaded by Python. Django does not load any file by default (with arguably the `settings.py` file as the exception), meaning that our self-contained code will never be loaded and our signal handlers never registered.

To change that, we can create a custom `AppConfig` for our **user** app. We create the `user/apps.py` file, and inside, declare an `AppConfig` class. We must define the `name` attribute to be the value Django will use to load the app (it is the same string as in `INSTALLED_APPS`). We can then implement the `ready()` method, whose only goal is to load the `signals.py` file, so that Python will run the `@receiver()` decorator, as shown in Example 25.7.

Register Log In

# Startup Organizer

**ABOUT    BLOG    STARTUPS    TAGS    CONTACT**

Successfully logged out

## More Django Info

Written on: Wednesday, April 8, 2015 by Andrew

Remember that the official websites for Django and this
book contain a number of extra resources.
https://djangoproject.com https://django-unleashed.com
Want more ...
Read more...

## Post Archives

○ 2015

○ 2013

○ 2011

○ 2008

**Figure 25.2:** Message for Logging Out

**Example 25.7: Project Code**
user/apps.py in 4bd73cbe74

```
1   from django.apps import AppConfig
2
3
4   class UserConfig(AppConfig):
5       name = 'user'
6
7       def ready(self):
8           import user.signals
```

Django does not know by default to load apps.py. In Example 25.8, we tell it to do so
by setting the default_app_config variable in our package's init module.

**Example 25.8: Project Code**
user/__init__.py in 4bd73cbe74

```
1   default_app_config = 'user.apps.UserConfig'
```

## Django Documentation

For more information about **auth** signals:

https://dju.link/18/auth-signals

## 25.3.2 **Automatically Assigning** `Tag` **Objects to** `Post` **Instances**

In this section, we implement a signal handler to assign `Tag` objects to `Post` instances whenever a `Post` and `Startup` are related.

A `Post` may be related to a `Startup` in various ways, as shown in Example 25.9.

**Example 25.9: Python Code**

```
post_object.startups.add(startup_object1, startup_object2)
startup_object.blog_posts.add(post_object1, post_object2)
```

Even though a many-to-many relationship is symmetric (if you are someone's friend, then they are also your friend), Django defines the first relation as the forward relation, while the second is the reverse relation. Django uses this definition in our signal handler, too.

To start, we need to import our tools, as shown in Example 25.10. We need the `@receiver()` decorator again, as well as our `Tag` and `Post` models (but surprisingly, not our `Startup` model). The signal we will receive (or catch) will be the m2m signal, which is sent whenever a many-to-many relationship changes.

**Example 25.10: Project Code**
`blog/signals.py` in 4f89e70ac1

```
1    from django.db.models.signals import m2m_changed
2    from django.dispatch import receiver
3
4    from organizer.models import Tag
5
6    from .models import Post
```

In a database, a many-to-many relationship must be defined as a separate table with at least two foreign keys: one for each row in another table. Django names these many-to-many tables as **through tables**. The table for the many-to-many relationship for `Post` objects and `Startup` objects is identified by `Post.startups.through` (and may also be identified as `Startup.blog_posts.through`). This is pertinent information, as we need to know the sender of the m2m signal to behave appropriately.

On top of limiting our signal handler to a single signal (m2m), we can also limit to call according to the sender. When we decorate our function with `@receiver()`, as shown in Example 25.11, we can set the `sender` attribute. Our signal handler function will be called only when the m2m signal is sent from the `Post.startups.through` table (the through table will emit a signal when we relate or unrelate a `Startup` to or from a `Post`).

**Example 25.11: Project Code**
`blog/signals.py` in 4f89e70ac1

```
 9    @receiver(m2m_changed,
10              sender=Post.startups.through)
11    def assign_extra_tags(sender, **kwargs):
12        action = kwargs.get('action')
```

The keywords passed to our `assign_extra_tags()` signal handler will be quite different from our previous signal handlers. The `action` keyword is key, as it tells us when the signal was sent. There are several options (taken directly from the documentation):

- `pre_add`
  - Sent before one or more objects are added to the relation.
- `post_add`
  - Sent after one or more objects are added to the relation.
- `pre_remove`
  - Sent before one or more objects are removed from the relation.
- `post_remove`
  - Sent after one or more objects are removed from the relation.
- `pre_clear`
  - Sent before the relation is cleared.
- `post_clear`
  - Sent after the relation is cleared.

We only want to act if a relation has been created, so we limit our signal handler to only when the `action` of the signal is `post_add`. We then need to know whether the relation is a forward relation or a backward relation. Despite the symmetric nature of the relation, whether it is a forward or backward relation not only changes what has been assigned to various variables in `kwargs` but also tells us the potential number of items being affected. In a forward relation, we have a single `Post` and at least one `Startup`, while in a reverse relation, we have a single `Startup` and at least one `Post` item. All of this information is available to us via the Boolean variable named `reverse`, as shown in Example 25.12.

**Example 25.12: Project Code**
`blog/signals.py` in 4f89e70ac1

```
11    def assign_extra_tags(sender, **kwargs):
12        action = kwargs.get('action')
13        if action == 'post_add':
14            reverse = kwargs.get('reverse')
15            if not reverse:
.             ...
25            else:
```

In the event of a forward relation (`post_object.startups.add()`), the `Post` instance is assigned to the `instance` keyword, while the `Startup` model is assigned to the `model` keyword. The list of `Startup` primary keys being assigned to the `Post` object is passed to the `pk_set` keyword. We can use this `pk_set` list to find all of our `Tag` objects, thanks to some tricky manager calls.

The `in` lookup available to managers and querysets finds all of the values in a list. We could use it with any field, as demonstrated in Example 25.13.

**Example 25.13: Python Interpreter Code**

```
>>> Profile.objects.filter(name__in=['Andrew', 'Ada'])
```

In our case, we wish to use the in lookup on the Tag model to find all of the tags related to the Startup objects with the primary keys in the pk_set list. We cannot use the startup_set manager, because it is defined on Tag instances. Instead, as shown in Example 25.14, we can use the startup field, which is defined on the Tag model but is inaccessible from instances.

**Example 25.14: Python Interpreter Code**

```
>>> Tag._meta.get_all_field_names()
['name', 'blog_posts', 'id', 'slug', 'startup']
>>> Tag.objects.filter(startup__in=[1,2,3])
[<Tag: Augmented Reality>,
 <Tag: Big Data>,
 <Tag: Mobile>,
 <Tag: Video Games>]
```

The numbers used to filter the startup field are foreign keys (Startup primary keys).

On top of the in lookup in the filter(), we chain our queryset to use the values_set() method to give us a flat list of primary keys. We use the distinct() method to make sure the primary keys are unique/distinct, and we then call iterator(). The iterator() method is primarily used for optimization and is a taste of things to come in Chapter 26. We use it here to make sure that Django does not cache our queryset. With an iterator object that will output tag primary keys, we can call the post.tags.add() method to add these primary keys to the many-to-many relationship between Post and Tag objects, as shown in Example 25.15.

**Example 25.15: Project Code**

blog/signals.py **in** 4f89e70ac1

```
11   def assign_extra_tags(sender, **kwargs):
.          ...
15          if not reverse:
16              post = kwargs.get('instance')
17              # Startup = kwargs.get('model')
18              startup_pk_set = kwargs.get('pk_set')
19              tag_pk_set = (
20                  Tag.objects.filter(
21                      startup__in=startup_pk_set)
22                  .values_list('pk', flat=True)
23                  .distinct().iterator())
24              post.tags.add(*tag_pk_set)
```

What Django passes to instance, model, and pk_set changes if the reverse relation is used, and reverse changes as well. In the event the reverse keyword is True, the instance will be a Startup instance, the model will be the Post model, and the pk_set will be a list of Post primary keys.

While the fact that we have a Startup instance makes getting the related Tag objects far easier, it also means we have to relate the objects to multiple Post instances, as we do in Example 25.16. We can use the in_bulk() queryset method to load the Post objects with the primary keys in pk_set. The in_bulk() method is a little quirky, and instead of returning a queryset object, it simply returns an enumerated dictionary. We get the actual Post objects by using the values() dictionary method. We use this method to iterate through the dictionary of Post objects, assigning our list of Tag primary keys to each one.

**Example 25.16: Project Code**
blog/signals.py in 4f89e70ac1

```
11    def assign_extra_tags(sender, **kwargs):
 .            ...
25            else:
26                startup = kwargs.get('instance')
27                tag_pk_set = tuple(
28                    startup.tags.values_list(
29                        'pk', flat=True).iterator())
30                PostModel = kwargs.get('model')
31                post_pk_set = kwargs.get('pk_set')
32                posts_dict = (
33                    PostModel.objects.in_bulk(
34                        post_pk_set))
35                for post in posts_dict.values():
36                    post.tags.add(*tag_pk_set)
```

Our signal handler will be called only when the m2m signal is issued by the Post.startups.through model, and it will handle both forward and reverse relation changes after a new relation has been created (post_add).

Django will not know to load the file, and Python will therefore not run the @receiver() decorator to register our function. To change this, we override the ready() method of the AppConfig, remembering to define the name attribute of the class, as shown in Example 25.17.

**Example 25.17: Project Code**
blog/apps.py in 4f89e70ac1

```
1    from django.apps import AppConfig
2
3
4    class BlogConfig(AppConfig):
5        name = 'blog'
6
7        def ready(self):
8            import blog.signals
```

We then point Django to our new file in the init file of the package, as shown in Example 25.18.

**Example 25.18: Project Code**
blog/__init__.py **in** 4f89e70ac1

```
1   default_app_config = 'blog.apps.BlogConfig'
```

## 25.4    Putting It All Together

Loose coupling behavior requires a slightly different mindset from the regular approach.

Developers sometimes refer to loose coupling in terms of asynchronous events. This terminology can be misleading, as it implies that signal handlers will be called independently of the HTTP request/response loop. *This is not the case.* If your signal handler function takes time, it will slow down the entire response time of your webpage.

A better way to think of signals and loosely coupled behavior is according to the basics of actor model theory. The idea is that software is split into independent actors that send messages to each other, where none of the actors can guarantee any behavior of another actor. (The origins of object-oriented programming (OOP) can be found in the actor model. See messages in SmallTalk and Objective-C for actor model implementations of OOP.) In Python, signal handlers are guaranteed to receive signals they are registered to, but it is dangerous to rely heavily on behavior in a signal handler, as it is difficult to recover from errors in the limited scope of the signal handler. Signal handlers can be incredibly useful but should be used judiciously.

# 26

# Optimizing Our Site for Speed

## In This Chapter

- Learn about website optimization
- Learn about profiling websites
- Limit the number of database queries made

## 26.1 Introduction

In certain computational environments, *performance* is a nuanced term that can refer to time and space constraints. How performant software is might refer to how much memory is needed to run it or how many operations are used per object to run a computation.

On the web, performance is one thing: speed. When we talk about optimizing performance on a website, what we are talking about is making the site take less time to return information to the user. The rule of thumb is to take less that 200 milliseconds to receive, compute, and return data to the user. Two hundred milliseconds is not a lot of time, and sometimes, following this rule of thumb can be quite challenging.

When discussing performance and optimization, developers often talk about the act of scaling a website. As the number of visitors to a website (and therefore the number of data requests) increases, the server—if not scaled to accommodate the increased traffic—becomes overwhelmed with requests and either slows or fails. This limitation is at the root of the denial-of-service (DOS; pronounced *daws*) attack as well as the distributed denial-of-service (DDOS; pronounced *dee-daws*) attack. Scaling a website is the act of making it more robust to more visitors.

Developers sometimes state that a language, framework, or database is "web-scale" or "not web-scale." The idea that a tool might automatically scale or that it might not allow you to scale is a bit of a silly notion. No matter what tool you use, your website will require work in different areas to enable it to handle increases in user traffic. Different tools support different problems, and some work better than others, which is why the first task in optimizing any website is to determine where the website is taking the most time to compute and return data. The act of analyzing a computer process is called **profiling**.

# 26.2   Profiling

There are numerous ways to profile software. Some profilers dig directly into system memory, while others are Python tools that aggregate all the information of your process, providing an in-depth look at all that is going on in Python's bytecode.

For our purposes, such tools are overkill. We don't have any users: we don't know what our most viewed webpages are, or what our most used features are. It makes no sense to profile at such a low level when we can't even target the right webpage or feature. When it comes to profiling and optimization, information is key. Without it, you are usually wasting your time pre-optimizing your code.

Even so, there are several basic optimizations that we can make before we launch our website. One of the slowest operations on computers generally is the process of loading data from disk and is referred to as IO (input/output). IO occurs not only every time we load a template form disk but also every time we ask the database for information, which we've been quite liberal about doing.

In many instances, we can simply cache information. Caching is the act of saving information for reuse. Typically, the cache is stored in memory (as opposed to disk), but on very large sites, the cache may be stored on entirely different computers.

The goal of this chapter is to limit the number of database queries we make and cache database results when possible, as well as to use caching to limit the number of times we load and render templates.

To aid us, we use a popular third-party Django app called the **debug_toolbar**. To install it, you may use `pip`, following the guide in Appendix G. Once installed, the app can be added to our project in the `INSTALLED_APPS` list, as shown in Example 26.1.

**Example 26.1: Project Code**
`suorganizer/settings.py` in eb0dc1e1d1

```
35   INSTALLED_APPS = (
 .       ...
44       'debug_toolbar',
 .       ...
50   )
```

## Warning!

The **debug-toolbar** app is an incredible tool, and we should be incredibly grateful for all the work that developers have put into it. When using it, however, be wary that it will slow down your site and that some of the numbers for how quickly the site takes to load should be taken with a grain of salt.

Remember that the actual number of milliseconds it takes to return data is not what counts. The real goal is to make it *feel* fast for users. On top of profiling, usability testing goes a long, long way.

# 26.3 Limiting Database Queries

In this section, we focus solely on limiting the number of database queries, either by caching queries for reuse or by modifying and combining database queries.

## 26.3.1 Understanding the Problem

Every time we use a model manager to get data, we are fetching data from the database. This was perhaps obvious in our views, where that was rather the point. However, it is also true in our templates, where we use model manager methods *liberally*.

The problem is not that we are fetching data—we *have* to fetch data by necessity. The problem is that in many cases we are fetching the same information multiple times. Instead of fetching the related blog posts of a startup once, we're fetching them a half-dozen times.

A key complication is that the actual number of queries Django makes in some of these templates changes depending on whether or not we're authenticated with privileges. In our startup detail template, the `view_future_post` changes how the template gets related blog posts, meaning that we must take care to check our optimizations with different permissions.

Finally, on top of fetching the same information several times, the holy grail is to make a *single* query to the database. Not only does fetching data from disk cost a bundle (IO), but so does the actual connection being made to the database. If we can get all of the information we need in a single request, we should. Most of the time, of course, we can't. We instead settle for accessing a table in the database a single time for each webpage.

To improve this situation, we start by removing redundant queries by caching information in our models, templates, and views. We then see how to change querysets in our views to get multiple types of information.

## 26.3.2 Template Short-Circuiting

Before we make any changes to our code, it's worth noting that we have already made a few optimizations to our website. The least obvious of the bunch is the order of condition checks in templates.

The Django Template Language (DTL) is rife with clever optimizations. One of the most powerful is condition short-circuiting. In Example 26.2, for instance, consider the condition in `startup_detail.html`.

**Example 26.2: Project Code**

`organizer/templates/organizer/startup_detail.html` in eb0dc1e1d1

```
114          {% if perms.blog.view_future_post and startup.blog_
   .             posts.all %}
```

The order of conditions in the DTL matter. In the preceding code, Django first checks our privileges, which are always loaded and should be considered a sunk cost. Thanks to the and operator, the manager method is called *only* if the permission is `True`. If not, then we do not incur the cost of a call to the database. This would not be the case if the conditions were switched. In the event the manager method came first, we would *always* incur the cost of a query to the database, even if we were not going to use the query because the permission were False.

When writing conditions in the template, it's always worth considering the impact of the condition on the code. A quick rule of thumb is to always use a permission check first, as permissions are always loaded.

### 26.3.3   Caching Properties

One of the easiest optimizations is to cache a database query as a property on a model. Take, for instance, the published_posts() method on Startup. In our startup_detail.html template, we call the method seven times: the first four times changes the layout of the template, while the last two are for printing the list of published blog posts. This method currently results in multiple separate calls to the database for exactly the same information. By caching the results of the first database query, we can avoid the rest entirely.

If you browse the development server to /startup/simple-robots/, you'll be able to click on the debug-toolbar on the right, and then the SQL button, to reveal that our site currently makes 11 queries for this page alone (or 14 if you're authenticated) every time it is loaded. If you examine the code closely, you'll see that our published_posts() method is called five times.

To cache our published_posts() queries, as shown in Example 26.3, we can rely on Django's @cached_property decorator, which turns any method into a property and will cache the result after the first call. This cache lasts until the HTTP response is sent to the visitor.

**Example 26.3: Project Code**
organizer/models.py **in** ce3492c31e

```
  5    from django.utils.functional import \
  6        cached_property
  .        ...
 61    class Startup(models.Model):
  .        ...
101        @cached_property
102        def published_posts(self):
103            return self.blog_posts.filter(
104                pub_date__lt=date.today())
```

If you browse back to /startup/simple-robots/, you'll see that the number of queries has dropped to seven. We've taken the five calls to published_posts() and ensured only the first results in a database query ($11 - 5 + 1 = 7$).

The @cached_property decorator works only on methods with no arguments (ignoring the mandatory self argument) and saves the results of the first call as a property to the instance. As long as our Startup exists, we will only make a single database call to this method, storing the queryset to the object.

This turns out to be a bit of a problem in certain instances. Querysets are lazy and wait until the last moment to be evaluated. Normally, this behavior is incredibly useful because it avoids unnecessary queries to the database. However, by caching a queryset, we open ourselves to the possibility that the queryset will be evaluated multiple times. The template system is clever enough to know not to reevaluate the property, but this is not necessarily true of the rest of Django. For instance, accessing the property in the shell causes Django to re-evaluate the queryset each time. To avoid reevaluation, we can force evaluation of the queryset and store a tuple instead, as shown in Example 26.4.

**Example 26.4: Project Code**
`organizer/models.py` in b3d28d3115

```
 61    class Startup(models.Model):
   .        ...
101        @cached_property
102        def published_posts(self):
103            return tuple(self.blog_posts.filter(
104                pub_date__lt=date.today()))
```

Using tuples in this case is desirable not only because we avoid queryset evaluation but also because tuples have a smaller memory footprint than `QuerySet` objects.

We then replicate these changes on the `published_posts()` method on the `Tag` model.

## 26.3.4 Caching Template Variables

Caching properties in our model is a great start to optimizing the `Startup` detail views, but it only works for unauthenticated users. If you authenticate as a superuser and browse to `/startup/simple-robots/`, the **debug-toolbar** will tell you that Django is making 14 queries to display all of the data on this page. That is the same number we had at the beginning of last section and means that the page has not benefitted from our `@cached_property` decorator, which makes sense: the `published_posts()` is only called when the visitor doesn't have the `view_future_post` permission. As an authenticated superuser, we have this permission, so our page is instead calling `startup.blog_posts.all()` to render the page.

The problem is still exactly the same: we are making multiple calls to the database for identical information, and we should be caching this information.

There are two places we can cache this information. By far the more powerful option is to do so in the view, as we shall see shortly. However, before we do, it's worth seeing how to cache variables in templates, allowing for smaller, more local optimizations.

The DTL supplies the `with` template tag, which allows for the creation of a scoped variable based on the existence of another. In our `startup_detail.html` template, as shown in Example 26.5, we're interested in limiting the number of times `startup.blog_posts.all()` is called, so we can assign the query returned by the manager method to a variable, which I call `post_list`. Anything within the `with` block may now use `post_list` instead of `startup.blog_posts.all()`.

**Example 26.5: Project Code**

`organizer/templates/organizer/startup_detail.html` in 892c9f1263

```
115             {% with post_list=startup.blog_posts.all %}
116                 <h3>Blog Post{{ post_list|pluralize }}</h3>
    .               ...
118                 {% for post in post_list %}
    .               ...
125             {% endwith %}
```

The pluralization and the loop no longer use `startup.blog_posts.all()`—that would result in another database call. However, because both use the scoped `post_list`, we are avoiding calls to the database.

We can do the same thing with the `Tag` relation in the same template, as shown in Example 26.6.

**Example 26.6: Project Code**

`organizer/templates/organizer/startup_detail.html` in 4761714f3f

```
38      {% with tag_list=startup.tags.all %}
39          <dt>Tag{{ tag_list|pluralize }}</dt>
40          {% for tag in tag_list %}
    .       ...
45      {% endwith %}
```

The use of `with` is not reserved for manager methods or querysets. It can be used to store any value. For instance, as shown in Example 26.7, we could use it to store the result of `published_posts()` in `tag_detail.html`. Because we're using the `@cached_property`, this isn't really an optimization, just a demonstration of the `with` template tag.

**Example 26.7: Project Code**

`organizer/templates/organizer/tag_detail.html` in df50a95120

```
44      {% if perms.blog.view_future_post %}
45          {% with tag_list=tag.blog_posts.all %}
    .       ...
61          {% endwith %}
62      {% else %}
63          {% with tag_list=tag.published_posts %}
    .       ...
78          {% endif %}
79      {% endwith %}
```

The problem with the `with` tag is that it can really complicate a template. In the case of both `tag_detail.html` and `startup_detail.html`, the optimizations we've been able to perform are small. If we wanted to truly optimize all of the redundant queries, we would have to use the `with` tag across the entirety of the template (we would have to put lines 52 to 143 of `startup_detail.html` within the `with` block). What's more, we would have multiple, nested `with` template blocks, which easily leads to confusion (when is a variable valid?). This work simply isn't worth it, because doing the same amount of work in views directly with querysets is far easier.

### 26.3.5 Introspecting Optimization in the Shell

Using the shell in Django can help us learn not only how to optimize querysets but also how to profile our querysets to improve them.

#### 26.3.5.1 Basic Introspection and Optimization

While the debug-toolbar is an incredibly useful tool for seeing the global state of a webpage created by Django, it is not equipped to examine querysets granularly. Luckily, Django is. Every `QuerySet` object comes with a `query` attribute, as shown in Example 26.8, which prints the SQL code that Django uses to get the information from the database.

**Example 26.8: Python Interpreter Code**

```
>>> posts = Post.objects.all()
>>> print(posts.query)
```

Because of the length of the actual SQL, I do not put the output of these commands in the book. The IPython notebook for Chapter 26 contains all of the output, and may be viewed at

https://dju.link/18/optimize-notebook

The SQL query is exactly what you'd expect. Django uses a `SELECT` operation on the `blog_post` table to get the list of all blog posts, ordered by `pub_date` and `title` (as coded in the nested `Meta` class defined on `Post`).

The utility of query is that we can use it to learn about manager methods meant for optimizations. One of the most useful is `select_related()`, which allows us to use a single query to fetch a list of items and a one-to-many relation. For example, to fetch a list of `Post` objects, as well as all the `User` objects that are related to the `Post` object as authors, we can use the Python code shown in Example 26.9.

**Example 26.9: Python Interpreter Code**

```
>>> Post.objects.select_related('author')
```

Adding a `.query` to the end will print the SQL Django will use, which reveals that Django is using an `INNER JOIN` with `blog_post` and `user_user` to get the related data. This approach is much, much quicker than asking for a specific user for each `Post` object we display in a template, which is what we are currently doing.

Beware that `select_related()` only works from one end of the relation. We can use it with `Post` objects and the `author` field, but we cannot use it with a `User` list and the `blog_post` field (one `User` for multiple `Post`; `select_related()` is for finding the one). For that, we have the `prefetch_related()` method (one `User` for multiple `Post`; `prefetch_related` is for finding the many). The method may also be used to fetch related data in many-to-many relations. For instance, we can get all of the `Startup` objects related to our `Post` objects using the method, as shown in Example 26.10.

**Example 26.10:** Python Interpreter Code

```
>>> Post.objects.prefetch_related('startups')
```

As it turns out, using the `query` attribute here is of no help to us, as shown in Example 26.11.

**Example 26.11:** Python Interpreter Code

```
>>> posts = Post.objects.all()
>>> posts_startups = Post.objects.prefetch_related('startups')
>>> list(posts_startups) == list(posts)
True
>>> str(posts.query) == str(posts_startups.query)
True
```

At a glance, we might assume that our `prefetch_related()` method has had no effect. The truth is that the method does not change the query to get the `Post` objects. Instead, it results in another query to get a subset of the `Startup` objects, related via an `INNER JOIN` to the table containing the relation, `blog_post_startups`. A grossly simplified version of the SQL query is shown in Example 26.12.

**Example 26.12:** SQL Code

```
SELECT ...
FROM "organizer_startup"
INNER JOIN "blog_post_startups"
ON ( "organizer_startup"."id" = "blog_post_startups"."startup_id" )
WHERE "blog_post_startups"."post_id" IN (...)
```

Django is quite explicit: it lists all of the fields it wants and provides a full list of all of the primary keys of the `Post` objects that it got from the first query. This means that the `Startup` list we are retrieving is a subset of the full list.

Don't take my word for it! We can use Django's connection list to see the last queries Django issued to the database, as shown in Example 26.13.

**Example 26.13:** Python Interpreter Code

```
>>> from django.db import reset_queries
>>> reset_queries()
>>> posts_startups = list(
...     Post.objects.prefetch_related('startups'))
>>> from django.db import connection
>>> connection.queries[-1]['sql']
>>> connection.queries[-2]['sql']
```

We use the `reset_queries()` function to erase the list in `connection`. We then fetch our `Post` objects with their related `Startup` objects. This allows us to see only the queries used in our single queryset. The use of `list()` is not optional: we are forcing evaluation of the queryset because the queries are lazy and will not touch the database until the last possible moment. Without `list()`, the `connection` list will be empty. The first connection query will print the SQL used to get the list of `Post` objects. The second will print the result of the `prefetch_related()`.

You might also be interested in using Python's pretty print package to print the entirety of `connection`, as shown in Example 26.14.

**Example 26.14:** Python Interpreter Code

```
>>> from pprint import pprint
>>> pprint(connection.queries)
```

The `prefetch_related()` method is actually one of Django's most powerful tools because of how often it comes into play. To begin, it allows for multiple relations to be referred to and uses lookup syntax to fetch relations of relations. For instance, if we wanted the tags related to the startups related to the blog posts, we could code as shown in Example 26.15.

**Example 26.15:** Python Interpreter Code

```
>>> Post.objects
...     .prefetch_related(
...         'startups__tags')
```

This code predictably results in three queries: one for blog posts, one for startups, and one for tags. Django associates all of the necessary data in Python. The queryset in Example 23.15 is therefore equivalent to the one in Example 26.16.

**Example 26.16:** Python Interpreter Code

```
>>> Post.objects
...     .prefetch_related(
...         'startups',
...         'startups__tags',
... )
```

However, it is different from the code in Example 26.17, where we chain
`prefetch_related()`.

**Example 26.17:** Python Interpreter Code

```
>>> Post.objects
...      .prefetch_related(
...          'startups'
...      ).prefetch_related(
...          'tags'
...      )
```

In Example 26.17, the `organizer_tag` table will be connected via `INNER JOIN` to
the `blog_post_tags` table—which houses the relation of blog posts to tags—whereas the
use of the `startups__tags` causes the `INNER JOIN` to be on the `organizer_`
`startup_tags` table. The subset of `Tag` objects being fetched from the database will be
different. Depending on what data we need, we want to be very careful about how we
structure our `prefetch_related()` calls.

### 26.3.5.2  The `Prefetch` Object

To further complicate matters (and empower us), Django provides the `Prefetch` object.
We can use it directly with the `prefetch_related()` method, just as we would a normal
call to the method, as shown in Example 26.18.

**Example 26.18:** Python Interpreter Code

```
>>> from django.db.models import Prefetch
>>> Post.objects.prefetch_related(
...     Prefetch('startups__tags'),
... )
```

The utility of the `Prefetch` object is that it allows us to change the queries that Django
will issue based on the call to `prefetch_related()` by overriding the queryset used to
get the object. It also allows us to assign the results to a particular attribute, as shown in
Example 26.19.

**Example 26.19:** Python Interpreter Code

```
>>> post_list = list(
...     Post.objects.prefetch_related(
...         Prefetch(
...             'startups__tags',
...             queryset=Tag.objects.all(),
...             to_attr='cached_tags',
...         ),
...     )
... )
```

Example 26.19 still results in three queries: one for all of our `Post` objects, one for the subset of `Startup` objects related to our `Post` objects, and one for the subset of `Tag` objects related to the subset of `Startup` objects. To be clear: my use of the `all()` in the queryset above does not change the fact that Django is using an `INNER JOIN` to fetch a subset of `Tag` objects.

Provided a `post` from the `post_list`, we can access the startups associated via `post.startups.all()`, as we normally would. The `post.startups` attribute is a model manager, but Django has cached the queryset returned by `all()`, allowing us to get the related startups without touching the database. Given one of these `Startup` objects, we can use the new `cached_tags` attribute we created (thanks to `to_attr`) to access any of the related `Tag` objects without incurring another database call. However, should we call `startup.tags.all()`, we will force Django to query the database, because we are not using the `cached_tags` attribute (which is a `list` object).

The use of `prefetch_related()` and `Prefetch` is incredibly powerful, and can save us computation time, but it is not without pitfalls. Let's see a much more complex query, as shown in Example 26.20.

**Example 26.20: Python Code**

```python
startup_list = list(
    Startup.objects.prefetch_related(
        Prefetch(
            'blog_posts',
            queryset=(
                Post.objects
                .select_related(
                    'author__profile')),
            to_attr='cached_posts'),
        Prefetch(
            'cached_posts__tags',
            to_attr='cached_post_tags'),
        Prefetch(
            'tags',
            to_attr='cached_tags'),
        Prefetch(
            'cached_tags__startup_set')))
```

Example 26.20 results in five queries:

1. One for all the `Startup` objects in our database
2. One for the subset of related `Post` objects with related `User` and `Profile` objects (thanks to `select_related` passed to the queryset argument)
3. One for the subset of `Tag` objects related to the subset of `Post` objects
4. One for the subset of `Tag` objects related to the `Startup` objects
5. One for the `Startup` objects related to the subset of `Tag` objects

Item 5 should give you pause. This information is redundant! We already know all of the relations between `Startup` and `Tag` objects because of item 4. We don't need that information, right? Unfortunately, we do. Without it, the call to `tag.startup_set.all()` in Example 26.21 results in a query for each `Tag` object.

**Example 26.21: Python Code**

```python
for startup in startups:
    print(
        '{} has the following competitors:'
        .format(startup))
    for tag in startup.cached_tags:
        for competitor in tag.startup_set.all():
            if competitor.pk != startup.pk:
                print(
                    '        {}'
                    .format(competitor))
```

The next pitfall is the use of attributes created via the `to_attr` parameter. If we create an attribute, we must use that attribute for subsequent related calls. When we created the `cached_posts` attribute for `blog_posts`, to get the `Tag` objects related to our `Post` objects, we used `cached_posts__tags` instead of `blog_posts__tags`. Had we instead used `blog_posts__tags` in this situation (with the attribute), we would have incurred an extra query for nothing.

However, without the use of `to_attr`, we would be fine calling `blog_posts__tags`. The following two calls are thus equivalent:

```python
startup_list = list(
    Startup.objects.prefetch_related(
        Prefetch(
            'blog_posts',
            to_attr='cached_posts'),
        Prefetch('cached_posts__tags')))
startup_list = list(
    Startup.objects.prefetch_related(
        Prefetch('blog_posts'),
        Prefetch('blog_posts__tags')))
```

### 26.3.5.3   Limiting Fields

In most of our queries, we ask for the database to give us all of the data related to an object. This can be quite expensive, depending on the table.

We saw in Chapter 3: Programming Django Models and Creating an SQLite Database, that it was possible to use the `values()` and `values_list()` methods to select a specific set of fields, but they are not the only tools available to us. Managers and querysets also give us the `defer()` and `only()` methods, shown in Example 26.22, which allow us to either ignore or select fields.

**Example 26.22: Python Code**

```
Tag.objects.only('name')   # get only name
Tag.objects.defer('slug')  # get all but slug
```

Because the `Tag` model has only two fields, the two queries created by Django in Example 26.22 are actually identical.

There are two pitfalls with these new methods. The first is that they will always fetch the primary key of the object. Any attempt to call `defer('id')` will simply be ignored. What's more, whereas `get()` and `filter()` provide a shortcut to the primary key field via the `pk` variable (`Tag.objects.get(pk=1)`), any attempt to refer to `pk` with `defer()` will result in an error (unless, of course, you've defined a `pk` field; this does not apply to `only()`, which is happy with `pk`).

Finally, the `values()` and `values_list()` methods do not play well with the `defer()` and `only()` methods. In fact, `values()` and `values_list()` will override prior calls to `defer()` and `only()`, while attempting to call `defer()` and `only()` on a `ValuesQuerySet` results in a `NotImplementedError`.

## 26.3.6  Using Migrations to Learn about Optimization

We could now jump into our views and begin optimizing our webpages there. Before we do, however, I want to draw your attention to our migration files.

By default, when you run tests (when, not if) Django creates a new database based on migrations files. Despite living in memory, this process can be quite time consuming. A fun exercise for learning to optimize code is to take the code in our migrations and attempt to speed them up. This exercise also provides the opportunity for us to use the `Q` object.

> **Info**
>
> It is possible to disable migrations during tests. If you have a large number of migrations, disabling them for your tests may be advisable.

When we programmed our `Tag` data migration in Chapter 10: Revisiting Migrations, we used a loop over a tuple to create and save a `Tag` object for each item in the tuple, as shown in Example 26.23. This results in as many queries as there are items in our tuple.

**Example 26.23: Project Code**
`organizer/migrations/0002_tag_data.py` **in** d7a5660963

```
27  def add_tag_data(apps, schema_editor):
28      Tag = apps.get_model('organizer', 'Tag')
29      for tag_name, tag_slug in TAGS:
30          Tag.objects.create(
31              name=tag_name,
32              slug=tag_slug)
```

Instead of creating each `Tag` separately, we can create a bunch of `Tag` instances, load them into a list, and then use the `bulk_create()` manager method, as shown in Example 26.24. This technique will always result in a single query.

**Example 26.24: Project Code**

`organizer/migrations/0002_tag_data.py` **in** ed667175f4

```
27   def add_tag_data(apps, schema_editor):
28       Tag = apps.get_model('organizer', 'Tag')
29       tag_list = []
30       for tag_name, tag_slug in TAGS:
31           tag_list.append(
32               Tag(name=tag_name, slug=tag_slug))
33       Tag.objects.bulk_create(tag_list)
```

Take note the `bulk_create()` method does not handle any sort of relation, making it a somewhat specialized tool (this is because relations require primary keys, which are created by the database—primary keys won't exist until *after* the call to `bulk_create()`).

We can also optimize the `remove_tag_data()` function in our migration file. When we last left it, the code read as in Example 26.25.

**Example 26.25: Project Code**

`organizer/migrations/0002_tag_data.py` **in** d7a5660963

```
35   def remove_tag_data(apps, schema_editor):
36       Tag = apps.get_model('organizer', 'Tag')
37       for _, tag_slug in TAGS:
38           tag = Tag.objects.get(slug=tag_slug)
39           tag.delete()
```

I want to remind you that querysets have a `delete()` method and that, in the event we have a queryset with multiple objects, we can use the method to delete all of the objects. Our code might look as shown in Example 26.26.

**Example 26.26: Project Code**

`organizer/migrations/0002_tag_data.py` **in** 1d25f5b72b

```
36   def remove_tag_data(apps, schema_editor):
37       Tag = apps.get_model('organizer', 'Tag')
38       for _, tag_slug in TAGS:
39           Tag.objects.filter(slug=tag_slug).delete()
```

The trick is thus to be able to create a queryset with all of the objects that we want. Given our current knowledge, that is impossible. However, Django provides the ability to run multiple queries with the Q object. We can then combine these objects using Boolean operators. For instance,

```
>>> from django.db import Q
>>> Tag.objects.filter(
...     Q(slug='django') | Q(slug='mobile')
... )
[<Tag: Django>, <Tag: Mobile>]
```

Thanks to some of Python's functional tools, we can create a list of Q objects and then combine them. The reduce() tool (sometimes called fold in functional languages) combines a list according to a function. In combination with the operator package, we can work some very cool magic. To demonstrate, we can use these tools to sum a list of numbers, as shown in Example 26.27.

**Example 26.27: Python Interpreter Code**

```
>>> from functools import reduce
>>> from operator import add
>>> reduce(add, [1,1,1])
3
```

Instead of the operator.add() function, we instead use the or_() function, which preforms a Boolean or operation on items. The two querysets in Example 26.28 are thus equivalent.

**Example 26.28: Python Interpreter Code**

```
>>> Tag.objects.filter(
...     Q(slug='django') | Q(slug='mobile')
... )
>>> Tag.objects.filter(
...     reduce(
...         or_,
...         [Q(slug='django'), Q(slug='mobile')],
...     )
... )
[<Tag: Django>, <Tag: Mobile>]
```

We start by importing our tools, as shown in Example 26.29.

**Example 26.29: Project Code**
`organizer/migrations/0002_tag_data.py` **in** e8b093f29e

```
4   from functools import reduce
5   from operator import or_
.       ...
8   from django.db.models import Q
```

In our `remove_tag_data()`, we first start by declaring a list. We append Q objects to the list with the parameters we want. We then use `reduce()` and `or_` to combine all of the Q objects, allowing us to find and delete all of those objects in a single query to the database, as shown in Example 26.30.

**Example 26.30: Project Code**
`organizer/migrations/0002_tag_data.py` in e8b093f29e

```
40   def remove_tag_data(apps, schema_editor):
41       Tag = apps.get_model('organizer', 'Tag')
42       query_list = []
43       for _, tag_slug in TAGS:
44           query_list.append(
45               Q(slug=tag_slug))
46       query = reduce(or_, query_list)
47       Tag.objects.filter(query).delete()
```

This code is complete overkill in this instance. However, the point is that Python and Django provide a number of tools to optimize your database queries, and some of them are found in unexpected places.

## 26.3.7   Optimizing Views with Related Content

We've seen `select_related()`, `prefetch_related()`, Q and `Prefetch` objects, and we know how to profile with `queryset.query` and `connection`. It's time to put all our tools to work.

In our generic class-based views (GCBVs), we have used the `model` attribute to tell our views which model to fetch. Most GCBVs also allow for the use of the `queryset`, which enables us to define the queryset used on the `model` (which now doesn't need to be set). We can, for instance, use the `select_related()` method in `PostDetail` to fetch both the Post object and the User object related by the `author` field, as shown in Example 26.31.

**Example 26.31: Project Code**
`blog/views.py` in 17ac1d0e95

```
48   class PostDetail(DateObjectMixin, DetailView):
49       date_field = 'pub_date'
50       queryset = (
51           Post.objects
52           .select_related('author')
53       )
```

This is a good start, but we should remember that the User `get_absolute_url()` method (used on the display of the blog posts's author) uses information from the `Profile`. We can therefore fetch the related `Profile` object as well, as shown in Example 26.32.

**Example 26.32:** Project Code

`blog/views.py` **in** 2c824f25a9

```
48   class PostDetail(DateObjectMixin, DetailView):
49       date_field = 'pub_date'
50       queryset = (
51           Post.objects
52           .select_related('author')
53           .select_related('author__profile')
54       )
```

As with the `prefetch_related()` method earlier, the call to both `author` and `author__profile` is redundant. We can simply specify the latter, as it implies the former, as shown in Example 26.33.

**Example 26.33:** Project Code

`blog/views.py` **in** 039ca49313

```
48   class PostDetail(DateObjectMixin, DetailView):
49       date_field = 'pub_date'
50       queryset = (
51           Post.objects
52           .select_related('author__profile')
53       )
```

Speaking of `prefetch_related()`, we can use the method to immediately fetch the related `Startup` and `Tag` objects, as shown in Example 26.34.

**Example 26.34:** Project Code

`blog/views.py` **in** 7275afba58

```
48   class PostDetail(DateObjectMixin, DetailView):
49       date_field = 'pub_date'
50       queryset = (
51           Post.objects
52           .select_related('author__profile')
53           .prefetch_related('startups')
54           .prefetch_related('tags')
55       )
```

If you browse to `blog/2013/1/django-training/` before and after these changes, the debug-toolbar will show you we've dropped the number of queries for an unauthenticated user from 12 to 3. For an authenticated user, the number goes from 14 to 5. We can do no better. The three are for each model: `Post`, `Startup`, and `Tag`. When authenticated, we have two extra queries: one for the session for the authenticated user and one for the `User` instance of the authenticated user.

We won't always want to use the `prefetch_related()` method indiscriminately. Take, for instance, our `StartupDetail` view, shown in Example 26.35. We cannot simply add a `prefetch_related()` for `Post` object, because which objects we want depends on the user's permissions. If we simply add `prefetch_related('blog_post')`, we might be saving time, but we might also be incurring a query for nothing.

**Example 26.35: Project Code**
`organizer/views.py` in 87e4424d4a

```
81    class StartupDetail(DetailView):
82        queryset = (
83            Startup.objects.all()
84            .prefetch_related('tags')
85            .prefetch_related('newslink_set')
86            # below omitted because of with tag
87            # and conditional display based on time
88            # .prefetch_related('blog_posts')
89        )
```

We could override the `get_object()` or `get_queryset()` methods available on GCBVs. However, we'll discover in the next chapter that the display of related blog posts is a perfect job for custom template tags, and so for the moment I won't bother to optimize this.

We could keep going, adding `select_related()` and `prefetch_related()` to all of our views, such as `TagDetail`, as shown in Example 26.36.

**Example 26.36: Project Code**
`organizer/views.py` in d0864d3eac

```
119    class TagDetail(DetailView):
120        queryset = (
121            Tag.objects
122            .prefetch_related('startup_set')
123        )
```

The work to optimize the rest of our site is straightforward and not particularly thrilling. You have the tools to do it, and so we won't optimize the rest of our site. The last thing I leave you with is that pagination results in a call to count, so any paginated list will always result in an extra query.

## 26.3.8    Optimizing `Manager` and `QuerySet` Classes Directly

If you find yourself changing all of your views and templates in the same way, it's worth considering the fact that you can use `select_related()` and `prefetch_related()` directly in a manager or queryset. For instance, we could *always* fetch the related `User` and `Profile` objects when fetching `Post` objects, as shown in Example 26.37.

**Example 26.37: Project Code**
blog/models.py in 54840cbbb8

```
21    class BasePostManager(models.Manager):
22
23        def get_queryset(self):
24            return (
25                PostQueryset(
26                    self.model,
27                    using=self._db,
28                    hints=self._hints)
29                .select_related('author__profile'))
```

The using parameter tells Django which database to use if we have several databases, while the hints parameter provides database hints, which allow for instruction on how to execute a query.

Take into account that by doing this, we will *always* incur a more complicated query when fetching Post objects. If we were always displaying the author of Post objects, then this might make sense. But in both startup_detail.html and tag_detail.html, we only list the title of the Post, which means our query will be more complicated than it needs to be. I would not normally use this technique here but will leave it in the code for your benefit.

### 26.3.9 Optimizing Admin Pages

Our views and templates are not the only places we should consider optimization. In the **admin**, our list of User objects lists the name and joined fields on the related Profile object, resulting in a database query for each User in the list at the moment. We can reduce all of these queries to a single one thanks to the list_select_related, which will use select_related() with any parameters we pass to the tuple, as shown in Example 26.38.

**Example 26.38: Project Code**
user/admin.py in 3e60afbdbe

```
39    class UserAdmin(admin.ModelAdmin):
 .        ...
53        list_select_related = ('profile',)
```

If we wanted to be able to use prefetch_related(), we would have to do so in the get_queryset() method of the ModelAdmin subclass. Keep in mind that the use of annotate and Count in blog/admin.py are technically optimizations.

## 26.4  Changing Database Behavior Internally

We've focused entirely on limiting the number of queries we make, but sometimes the problem is how long a query takes to run.

Databases rely on indexing to speed queries up. In Chapter 3, we saw in passing that Django automatically indexes database columns that it expects to access often. Primary key and `SlugField` columns are indexed so that any time we ask for a value from those columns the database returns a value as quickly as possible.

In some instances, this isn't good enough. When finding a `Post` object, Django isn't asking the database to search for just a particular `slug` but is instead asking for a particular slug in association with a year and month. The unique identifier for the `Post` object is the combination of `slug` and `pub_date`. The database is not optimized to make these queries quick. To speed up every query involving both `slug` and `pub_date`, we want to index the two in the database.

Following what we learned in Chapter 3, changing the database directly should *always* be a last resort. It becomes untenable quickly, as it forces developers to manually replicate changes to the database and can usually be avoided. Instead, we should always see if we can first make a change to our model. If that doesn't work, we should try to construct a migration to make the change for us. Migrations supply the `RunSQL` operation, which mirrors the `RunPython` operation, but for making changes directly to the database in raw SQL.

As it turns out, we won't need this knowledge here. Django provides the ability to create any number of indexes with any arbitrary fields in the nested `Meta` class on models via the `index_together` attribute. We can therefore add a tuple to the attribute to index `slug` and `pub_date` together, as shown in Example 26.39.

**Example 26.39: Project Code**
`blog/models.py` **in** 2f2a41581b

```
41    class Post(models.Model):
 .        ...
65        class Meta:
 .            ...
73            index_together = (
74                ('slug', 'pub_date'),
75            )
```

For this change to take affect, we need to create a migration and then apply the migration, as shown in Example 26.40.

**Example 26.40: Shell Code**

```
$ ./manage.py makemigrations --name=index_together_slug_pubdate blog
$ ./manage.py migrate
```

## Django Documentation

For more about `RunSQL` migration operation:

https://dju.link/18/runsql

# 26.5 Changing Performance Globally

We can affect the performance of our website not only webpage by webpage but also on a project-wide basis.

In software, any sort of IO is costly. Whenever we load a template, we are currently loading it from disk, rendering it, and then throwing that information away. In the next few sections, we see how to cache our template files and then how to cache the rendered results of our views.

## 26.5.1 Caching Template Files

Instead of loading templates each time we need one, we can cache any template we load into memory. This means that any subsequent load and render of the template will avoid any disk IO and will instead load the template file from memory. This approach is much, much quicker.

All of the settings for templates can be found in the `TEMPLATES` setting in `suorganizer/settings.py`. By default, Django does not list the template loaders used to get and fetch files. Instead, it supplies the key-value `'APP_DIRS': True`, which is a shortcut to the `app_directories.Loader` we are about to add in Example 26.41. If we delete the `APP_DIRS` key, we can then explicitly set the values for `loaders` under `OPTIONS`.

**Example 26.41: Project Code**
`suorganizer/settings.py` **in** ebc040b0d7

```
65    TEMPLATES = [{
 .        ...
70        'OPTIONS': {
 .            ...
77            'loaders': [
78                'django.template.loaders.filesystem.Loader',
79                'django.template.loaders.app_directories.Loader',
80            ],
81        },
82    }]
```

This change makes no changes to our website behavior! It just makes our settings more explicit.

To cache any templates Django loads, we can use the `cached.Loader`, passing in any of the other loaders that we want Django to use, as shown in Example 26.42.

**Example 26.42: Project Code**
`suorganizer/settings.py` **in** 25c1937f74

```
65    TEMPLATES = [{
 .        ...
70        'OPTIONS': {
 .            ...
77            'loaders': [
```

```
78                    ('django.template.loaders.cached.Loader', [
79                        'django.template.loaders.filesystem.Loader',
80                        'django.template.loaders.app_directories.Loader',
81                    ]),
82                ],
83            },
84    }]
```

With this little change, we have enabled caching on all our template files.

## Ghosts of Django Past

All of the settings surrounding templates changed in Django 1.8. If you are using
Django 1.7 or earlier, you will need to look at the TEMPLATE_LOADERS setting.

## 26.5.2   Caching Entire Webpages

Why optimize queries or cache template files when we can cache the results of our
computations? Django allows us to easily cache the output of views, with templates
rendered and middleware already having worked their magic.

Django provides several kinds of caches. For our purposes, we use the local memory
cache, which simply keeps computer webpages in memory. When we deploy, we will switch
to using a cache for memcache.

It is possible to define multiple different caches, each of which might fulfill a different
purpose. In our case, we simply define a single cache called default. The BACKEND key
tells the cache what kind of cache it is, while the location gives the cache a unique identifier
(used separately from the default name), which we could omit in this case (as we only
have a single local memory cache). Finally, we tell the cache how long we want it to
remember each webpage for, as shown in Example 26.43.

**Example 26.43: Project Code**
`suorganizer/settings.py` in a754dcd00b

```
89    # Caches
90    # https://docs.djangoproject.com/en/1.8/topics/cache/
 .                #local-memory-caching
91
92    CACHES = {
93        'default': {
94            'BACKEND': 'django.core.cache.backends.locmem.LocMemCache',
95            'LOCATION': 'unique-snowflake',
96            'TIMEOUT': 600,  # seconds == 10 minutes
97        }
98    }
99    CACHE_MIDDLEWARE_ALIAS = 'default'
```

The easiest way to use this cache is via middleware, as shown in Example 26.44. We first tell our middleware which cache to use by defining the CACHE_MIDDLEWARE_ALIAS setting.

We then add two middleware classes to our middleware list. The UpdateCache Middleware adds a webpage to the cache, while the FetchFromCacheMiddleware gets a webpage from the cache.

We want the FetchFromCacheMiddleware to be the last middleware called, so that the other middleware can change the request before Django sees whether the webpage for that request is cached. We therefore add FetchFromCacheMiddleware to the bottom of the middleware list.

Similarly, we want to let all of the other middleware modify the response before Django caches it, meaning UpdateCacheMiddleware should be the last to be called during the response phase. The order in which middleware are called in the response phase is the reverse of that in the request phase, so we add UpdateCacheMiddleware to the top of the list such that it is called last.

**Example 26.44: Project Code**
`suorganizer/settings.py` **in** 87488a01b5

```
52    MIDDLEWARE_CLASSES = (
53        'django.middleware.cache.UpdateCacheMiddleware',
 .        ...
62        'django.middleware.cache.FetchFromCacheMiddleware',
63    )
```

Any website accessed multiple times within 10 minutes will now be computed only once. The view will not be called, the templates will not be rendered, and no database queries will occur. If you visit a page with the debug-toolbar and then reload the page, you will be able to watch the computation time drop by an enormous amount. The webpages on my local site first load at just over 200 ms. With the cache, the total load time of these pages drops to around 25 ms.

Caching can be our friend, but it's best to remember the following advice from an unknown source:

There are three things that are difficult in computer science:

1. Naming
2. Caching
3. Off-by-one errors

It is possible to build a cache that doesn't actually help your site. Remember to profile your project and to analyze your traffic so that you know how to best cache your project. What's more, take into account that while we are caching all our webpages, Django allows for much more granular control of caches, enabling developers to control which webpages are cached and even to cache parts of templates.

Remember the `@never_cache` decorator from Chapter 21: Extending Authentication? Its opposite is the `@cache_page()` decorator.

> ## Django Documentation
>
> For more about caching in Django:
>
> https://dju.link/18/cache

### 26.5.3    Development

While some of the changes in this section will make our website really fast, they also complicate development quite a bit. In this section, we turn them off and replace them with development-friendly tools that mimic these tools.

To start, in Example 26.45, we replace the global local memory cache with a dummy cache. A dummy cache will make it look like there is a cache but still always results in computation.

**Example 26.45: Project Code**

`suorganizer/settings.py` in eb97deeb6a

```
94    CACHES = {
95        'default': {
96            'BACKEND': 'django.core.cache.backends.dummy.DummyCache',
97        }
98    }
99    CACHE_MIDDLEWARE_ALIAS = 'default'
```

We then want to make sure our templates are always loaded: if we change a template, we don't want to have to restart the development server to destroy the cache in order to see our changes. To do this, we simply comment out the cache loader, as shown in Example 26.46.

**Example 26.46: Project Code**

`suorganizer/settings.py` in 9597770828

```
67    TEMPLATES = [{
 .        ...
72        'OPTIONS': {
 .            ...
79            'loaders': [
80                # ('django.template.loaders.cached.Loader', [
81                    'django.template.loaders.filesystem.Loader',
82                    'django.template.loaders.app_directories.Loader',
83                # ]),
84            ],
85        },
86    }]
```

We can now get back to developing the rest of the website.

# 26.6   Putting It All Together

Optimizing a website, making it more performant, is all about making the website fast. The way to do this is to make sure we are doing as little work as possible. We request information from the database only if we don't already have it, and we opt for more complex queries over multiple queries.

We also rely on caching. The idea is simple: if we've already done it, we don't do it again until we need to. It's a bit more difficult to figure out *when* to cache, which is why most beginning caches simply work on a time basis.

On the web, speed is key. Users are known to leave websites that take too long to load, and the definition of too long is over 200 ms. We used the **debug-toolbar** app to look at our page speeds, but this is not the only tool you should rely on. Remember to perform traffic analytics and to use external tools to check page speeds.

### Django Documentation

For more about about performance, optimization, and profiling:

https://dju.link/18/optimization
https://dju.link/18/performance
https://dju.link/profiling

# Building Custom Template Tags

## In This Chapter

- Learn to better adhere to DRY with custom template tags
- Obfuscate emails with a template filter
- Build a template tag to print related blog posts
- Use a template tag to inject variables into the current template tags
- Automatically generate website forms by including external templates

## 27.1   Introduction

When discussing Model–View–Controller (MVC) architecture (which Django is only very loosely based on, as we saw in Chapter 12: The Big Picture), developers advocate for fat models, thin controllers, and even thinner views. Django follows a similar principle: logic surrounding data should be placed in models as much as possible, while the controller should handle only logic related to rendering webpages. The templates should be limited entirely to displaying content.

At the moment, some of our templates are overly complicated. The way we compute how to display related blog posts is long and complicated. What's more, our templates are in violation of Don't Repeat Yourself (DRY) principles in multiple places: most of our forms follow exactly the same structure and really should be centralized to make changes easier.

We can use custom template tags to fix all of these problems. A custom template tag is simply a tag that we have defined in the Django Template Language (DTL). In many ways, custom template tags are the final piece of the puzzle when it comes to breaking any semblance of MVC adherence in Django. While we are removing logic from our actual template files and placing the logic in Python, we won't be adhering to the fat models principle. Instead, we are creating a tool that allows for communication completely outside of anything MVC defines.

To this point, the book is written in a bottom to top fashion. We start with the lowest level and then we see the shortcuts. This chapters breaks from the mold and chooses to teach top to bottom. We start with the simplest tools, using shortcuts to achieve our goals. Only in our very last example do we need to use Django's full power for our goals.

This chapter assumes basic compiler knowledge. Understanding the purposes of lexers and parsers will be instrumental in our last example. Appendix F covers this material.

## 27.2   Custom Template Filters

Before jumping into building custom template tags, we detour and create a custom template filter. A filter is simply a tool that changes a string in the template. We saw the `length`, `pluralize`, `title`, `date`, and `linebreaks` filters (as well as a few others) in Chapter 4: Rapidly Producing Flexible HTML with Django Templates. In this section, we create our own filter.

The goal of our filter, called `obfuscate`, is to take an email and change it. Robots are known for scrapping the web in an attempt to find information, and by printing people's emails on our website, we are doing them a disservice. Instead, we will print a string that is human understandable but (hopefully) unintelligible to robots. We will use it in `startup_detail.html`, as shown in Example 27.1.

**Example 27.1: Project Code**

`organizer/templates/organizer/startup_detail.html` **in** 68d0947cd5

```
 2    {% load obfuscate_email %}
 .          ...
37            <dd>{{ startup.contact|obfuscate }}</dd>
```

When we used custom template tags in other chapters (such as Chapter 15: Creating Webpages with Django Flatpages), we saw that we had to first load the custom template tags (or filters). On line 2 in Example 27.1, the code we define in Example 27.2 is loaded. We first create a directory in our **organizer** app called `templatetags`, and within our new directory we create the `obfuscate_email.py` file. Django looks for any custom template tags in the `templatetags` directory and treats them as a namespace. A custom tag in one app is available to all apps. The name of the file is the name we use to load our custom template filter in the template.

To begin, in Example 27.2, we need to import our tools.

**Example 27.2: Project Code**

`organizer/templatetags/obfuscate_email.py` **in** 68d0947cd5

```
1    from django import template
2    from django.template.defaultfilters import (
3        stringfilter)
```

We import the entirety of Django's `template` package, then import the `@stringfilter` decorator. This decorator is a shortcut that allows us to build our filter quickly. It tells Django that our function accepts a string as our only argument.

When it loads our file in the template, Django expects to find a valid template library, with tags and filters registered to that library. For this to work, in Example 27.3, we create a `Library` instance, which we then use to register our custom tags and filters.

**Example 27.3: Project Code**

`organizer/templatetags/obfuscate_email.py` **in** 68d0947cd5

```
7   register = template.Library()
```

We can then build our filter in Example 27.4. The goal is simple: given an email address in a string, we remove the `'@'` and replace it with `' at '`. We replace any instance of `'.'` with `' dot '`. The (fake) email `'django@jambonsw.com'` will thus become `'django at jambonsw dot com'`.

*↓ Project*

*''' /organizer/ templatetags /obfuscate_email.*
*py*

**Example 27.4: Project Code**

`organizer/templatetags/obfuscate_email.py` **in** 68d0947cd5

```
9    @register.filter('obfuscate', is_safe=False)
10   @stringfilter
11   def obfuscate_email(value):
12       return (value
13               .replace('@', ' at ')
14               .replace('.',' dot '))
```

The function itself is very straightforward. The new material is on lines 9 and 10. On line 9, we register the function as the filter called `obfuscate`. We inform Django that the string being returned is not safe: we have not escaped any HTML special characters or ensured there is no malicious code in the string being returned. On line 10, we use the `@stringfilter` decorator so that Django knows that the `obfuscate` filter can only be applied to a string, allowing it to handle any type errors on its own.

And that's it! We are now protecting (to some extent) the emails on our site.

## Info

In Chapter 3, we saw the capitalization of `Startup` objects was undesirable, because it caused startup names like *JamBon* to be incorrectly transformed to *Jambon*. A similar problem has been happening with our `Tag` objects, where instead of displaying *IPython* and *PHP*, our website is displaying *Ipython* and *Php*. We would want to use a filter to fix all of this behavior.

We won't build such a template filter. The implementation is tedious and detail oriented, but it doesn't actually teach very much about Django or template filters. What's more, there are several Django packages built specifically to handle this task. We discuss how to find packages such as these in Chapter 30.

# 27.3   Custom Template Tags

Template tags come in a variety of shapes and sizes. A template tag is separated from the rest of the markup by the {% %} delimiters and may create scope (like `block` or `with`) or may simply be a command (like `load` or `url`). Tags may take any number of arguments and keyword arguments and can either change control flow (like `if` or `for`) or print values.

In the next few sections, we build several template tags. In all cases, our tags will be simple commands (we will not build scope) and will always print values (rather than change flow of control).

To start, we build a template tag to display related blog posts. This allows us to greatly simplify our `tag_detail.html` and `startup_detail.html` webpages. We then see how to replace all of our forms with a template tag, and finally, we use a tag to print the latest blog posts on all of our webpages.

## 27.3.1   Displaying Related Posts

The goal is to build a template tag that allows us to quickly and easily print the blog posts of any related object. Our final custom template tag is a bit complex, so we start with a very simple tag.

The goal is to first load our template tag via Example 27.5.

**Example 27.5: Project Code**

`organizer/templates/organizer/startup_detail.html` in 573488aa97

*load cus tom template* (margin note)

```
3   {% load partial_post_list %}
```

We then replace the entirety of the template to print related blog posts in `startup_detail.html` with the code in Example 27.6.

**Example 27.6: Project Code**

`organizer/templates/organizer/startup_detail.html` in 573488aa97

```
118         {% if perms.blog.view_future_post and startup.blog_posts.all %}
119           {% with post_list=startup.blog_posts.all %}
120             <h3>Blog Post{{ post_list|pluralize }}</h3>
121             {% format_post_list post_list %}
122           {% endwith %}
123         {% elif startup.published_posts|length > 0 %}
124             <h3>Blog Post{{ startup.published_posts|pluralize }}</h3>
125             {% format_post_list startup.published_posts %}
126         {% endif %}
```

On lines 121 and 125, we are using our custom template tag to print the list of `Post` objects passed to our template tag (having removed the loops that were there previously).

*templatetags/ dir in app*

In our **blog** app, we create the `templatetags/` directory, and inside, we create the `partial_post_list.py` file. The name of our file is what we pass to the `load` template tag.

In Example 27.7, we import our `Post` model and the Django `template` package. We also import the `StringIO` class, which is an object that allows us to store strings as if we were writing to a file.

**Example 27.7: Project Code**
blog/templatetags/partial_post_list.py **in** 27c1a17765

```
1    from io import StringIO
2
3    from django import template
```

In Example 27.8, we create the tag `Library` Django expects, which allows us to register our custom template tag.

**Example 27.8: Project Code**
blog/templatetags/partial_post_list.py **in** 27c1a17765

```
7    register = template.Library()
```

On line 10 in Example 27.9, we register the tag with the `@simple_tag` decorator. This decorator allows us to use a single function that accepts any number of arguments to create a template tag that acts as a single command.

**Example 27.9: Project Code**
blog/templatetags/partial_post_list.py **in** 27c1a17765

```
10   @register.simple_tag
11   def format_post_list(post_list):
12       indent = '    '
13       output = StringIO()
14       output.write('<ul>\n')
```

Just as the name of the file must be the same as what we call `load` with, the name of our function here must be the same as the tag we use in the template.

We prepare to create HTML output in a `StringIO` object by first instantiating the class and then adding the beginning of an HTML unordered list to the object. This then allows us to loop over the `post_list` argument passed to the template tag, as shown in Example 27.10.

**Example 27.10: Project Code**

blog/templatetags/partial_post_list.py **in** 27c1a17765

```
11    def format_post_list(post_list):
 .        ...
15        for post in post_list:
16            output.write(
17                '{}<li><a href="{}">\n'.format(
18                    indent, post.get_absolute_url()))
19            output.write('{}{}\n'.format(
20                indent * 2, post.title.title()))
21            output.write('{}</a></li>\n'.format(
22                indent))
23        output.write('</ul>\n')
24        return output.getvalue()
```

If you load a `StartupDetail` webpage, our webpage will still display related blog posts just as before.

Our method of generating this markup is terrible. The entire purpose of templates was to allow us to avoid such code. One of the most common forms of custom template tags is the inclusion tag, which loads another template, renders it, and then places the result inside the template using the tag. To make our code significantly cleaner, we will switch our current simple tag to an inclusion tag.

First, we need a template to use with the inclusion tag. By convention, we create an `includes/` directory in `/blog/templates/blog/` to store all of our inclusion templates. We then create the `partial_post_list.html` template, as shown in Example 27.11.

**Example 27.11: Project Code**

blog/templates/blog/includes/partial_post_list.html **in** 8ae4396137

```
1    <ul>
2      {% for post in post_list %}
3        <li><a href="{{ post.get_absolute_url }}">
4          {{ post.title|title }}
5        </a></li>
6      {% endfor %}
7    </ul>
```

In `partial_post_list.py`, we remove all of the contents of `format_post_list()`. We change the decorator from `@simple_tag` to `@inclusion_tag()`, passing the decorator the path to our new template (using the template namespace because there is no `/blog/templates/` at the beginning of the path). The only thing we need to do is return a dictionary that will be used as context in our inclusion template, as shown in Example 27.12.

**Example 27.12:** **Project Code**

`blog/templatetags/partial_post_list.py` in 8ae4396137

```
 8   @register.inclusion_tag(
 9       'blog/includes/partial_post_list.html')
10   def format_post_list(post_list):
11       return {
12           'post_list': post_list,
13       }
```

Once again, if you visit any `StartupDetail` page, you will discover that the output is unchanged.

We can, of course, do better. First, we want to remove all redundancy in the template: we should not have two different instances where we print the title for our list of blog posts. Second, we don't want to check whether the user has the right permissions. Essentially, we simply want to make the call shown in Example 27.13.

**Example 27.13:** **Project Code**

`organizer/templates/organizer/startup_detail.html` in 2114ec3f93

```
112          {% format_post_list startup %}
```

There is no other code! No condition, no loops, we just want to print the right list of blog posts in our template.

To begin, we can modify our template to check for the existence of a list of blog posts, and then to add the title for the list, as shown in Example 27.14.

**Example 27.14:** **Project Code**

`blog/templates/blog/includes/partial_post_list.html` in 2114ec3f93

```
 1   {% if post_list %}
 2     <section>
 3       <h3>Blog Post{{ post_list|pluralize }}</h3>
 .       ...
11     </section>
12   {% endif %}
```

In our `format_post_list()` tag (Python function), we check user permissions and provide the inclusion template with the correct list of blog posts. For this to work, we need the `HttpRequest` object so that we might have access to the user. We don't need to change the call in our template; we can change the decorator to give us the context of the template calling our tag by setting the `takes_context` parameter to `True`, as we do on line 10 in Example 27.15.

**Example 27.15: Project Code**

blog/templatetags/partial_post_list.py **in** 2114ec3f93

```
 8   @register.inclusion_tag(
 9       'blog/includes/partial_post_list.html',
10       takes_context=True)
11   def format_post_list(context, detail_object):
12       request = context.get('request')
13       future_perms = request.user.has_perm(
14           'blog.view_future_post')
15       if future_perms:
16           post_list = detail_object.blog_posts.all()
17       else:
18           post_list = detail_object.published_posts
19       return {
20           'post_list': post_list,
21       }
```

Our function signature has changed to accept the context, which is passed as the
first argument. Our new second argument is no longer the list of blog posts,
but instead, the object being displayed. We use this object (a `Startup` in the case of
`startup_detail.html`) and our permissions to get the right list of blog posts, which we
return in our context dictionary.

In `tag_detail.html`, we can use our new template tag to replace 22 lines of code, as
shown in Example 27.16.

**Example 27.16: Project Code**

organizer/templates/organizer/tag_detail.html **in** 2114ec3f93

```
 2   {% load partial_post_list %}
 .   ...
46   {% format_post_list tag %}
```

Of course, our tag doesn't print the nice warning about a lack of content, but this is
easily remedied, as shown in Example 27.17.

**Example 27.17: Project Code**

organizer/templates/organizer/tag_detail.html **in** 2114ec3f93

```
48   {% if not perms.blog.view_future_post or not tag.blog_posts.all %}
49       {% if not tag.published_posts|length > 0 %}
50           {% if not tag.startup_set.all %}
51             <p>This tag is not related to any content.</p>
52           {% endif %}
53       {% endif %}
54   {% endif %}
```

We could call it a day, but if you load any of the pages we've changed, you'll notice that our Cascading Style Sheet (CSS) is completely out of order. That makes sense: a lot of the work we did previously was checking which CSS class to use in the HTML `section` tag around our blog post list.

In all cases, the blog post list was always the second column if there was other related content. Related content appeared for two reasons: either there was a list of items or there was a button to link to the webpage to create such an item.

We can easily change our custom template tag to accommodate us. We first need to know whether we have a list of other items to display. We call these items `opposite` (as in opposite column). We also need to know whether the current visitor has the ability to see a button in the opposite column. We call this `perm_button`. In both cases, there might not be any values, so our new information will be passed as keywords to our templates.

We won't need any of these features in `tag_detail.html`, but the call to list related blog posts in `startup_detail.html` is printed in Example 27.18.

**Example 27.18: Project Code**
`organizer/templates/organizer/startup_detail.html` **in** 5da4484859

```
112    {% format_post_list startup opposite=startup.newslink_set.all
  .           perm_button=perms.organizer.add_newslink %}
```

In our template, we add a template variable to our HTML `section` tag, where we will print the CSS class if applicable, as shown in Example 27.19.

**Example 27.19: Project Code**
`blog/templates/blog/includes/partial_post_list.html` **in** 5da4484859

```
2    <section {{ section_attr }}>
```

Because we will be passing raw HTML to our template, we need to make sure that Django won't escape the string we pass. We import `mark_safe()` for that purpose, as shown in Example 27.20.

**Example 27.20: Project Code**
`blog/templatetags/partial_post_list.py` **in** 5da4484859

```
2    from django.utils.text import mark_safe
```

Finally, in `format_post_list()`, we change our function signature to accept `args` and `kwargs`. From the `kwargs` dictionary, we attempt to pop the `opposite` and `perm_button` keywords, as shown in Example 27.21. By default, if one of the keywords does not exist, Python will set the variable to `None`.

**Example 27.21: Project Code**

blog/templatetags/partial_post_list.py **in** 5da4484859

```
12  def format_post_list(
13          context, detail_object, *args, **kwargs):
 .      ...
15      opposite = kwargs.get('opposite')
16      perm_button = kwargs.get('perm_button')
```

If we don't have an opposite column, we don't need a class. If there is an opposite column with values or a button, we assign the one-third CSS class. If there is a column but no values, we assign the two-thirds CSS class and offset the column by two, as shown in Example 27.22.

**Example 27.22: Project Code**

blog/templatetags/partial_post_list.py **in** 5da4484859

```
12  def format_post_list(
13          context, detail_object, *args, **kwargs):
 .      ...
23      if opposite is None:
24          section_attr = ''
25      elif opposite or perm_button:
26          section_attr = mark_safe(
27              'class="meta one-third column"')
28      else:  # opposite is an empty list
29          section_attr = mark_safe(
30              'class="meta offset-by-two '
31              'two-thirds column"')
```

Finally, in Example 27.23, we remember to pass the value we've assigned as part of the template context dictionary.

**Example 27.23: Project Code**

blog/templatetags/partial_post_list.py **in** 5da4484859

```
12  def format_post_list(
13          context, detail_object, *args, **kwargs):
 .      ...
32      return {
33          'section_attr': section_attr,
34          'post_list': post_list,
35      }
```

We can finish the job in Example 27.24 by using the template tag in profile_detail.html, resulting in 22 fewer lines of template code and assured consistency between our templates.

**Example 27.24: Project Code**

`user/templates/user/profile_detail.html in` 93159331ac

```
 2    {% load partial_post_list %}
 .       ...
20          {% format_post_list profile.user %}
```

We are currently using our `format_post_list` template tag in the `startup_detail.html`, `tag_detail.html`, and `profile_detail.html` templates. If you navigate to any webpage generated with one of these templates and activate the **debug_toolbar** as discussed in Chapter 26, the tool will reveal that we are making multiple queries to the database to load our blog posts (for both authenticated and unauthenticated users). This is particularly obvious on the user profile page, because we never applied the `@cached_property` decorator to the `published_posts()` method on the `User` model.

We don't want to rely on the `published_posts()` method in our Python code the way we currently are. Instead, we should always be using the manager methods. Note that the `published()` queryset method we created in Chapter 24 exists not only on the `Post` model manager but also for all related managers (i.e., `startup.blog_posts`). We can therefore use the method in our template tag function, as shown in Example 27.25.

**Example 27.25: Project Code**

`blog/templatetags/partial_post_list.py in` 17c2e6ec2e

```
19        if future_perms:
20            post_list = detail_object.blog_posts.all()
21        else:
22            post_list = detail_object.blog_posts.published()
```

Now that we have a queryset in `post_list`, no matter the conditions, we can use the `values()` method to fetch only the data we wish to have, as shown in Example 27.26.

**Example 27.26: Project Code**

`blog/templatetags/partial_post_list.py in` 17c2e6ec2e

```
32        return {
33            'section_attr': section_attr,
34            'post_list': post_list.values(
35                'title', 'slug', 'pub_date'),
36        }
```

We are displaying the `title`, but we also provide a link to the `PostDetail` page, which requires both `slug` and `pub_date`.

Django will stop issuing a database query every time we access the `post_list` in our inclusion template because we are using a `ValuesQuerySet` instead of a `QuerySet`.

*Now* our custom template tag is complete and will properly print related blog post tags in a consistent manner in any template we want.

## 27.3.2  Displaying Create and Update Forms

All of the HTML forms to create or update objects that we created in this book followed a formula. Instead of constantly building these forms, it would have been far simpler for us to create an inclusion tag to display the form with certain parameters.

In our **core** app, we create the `templatetags` directory and a `display_form.py` file. In it, we import our tools and create the template library, as shown in Example 27.27.

**Example 27.27: Project Code**

core/templatetags/display_form.py **in** 95d56b7b4f

```
1    from django.core.exceptions import \
2        ImproperlyConfigured
3    from django.core.urlresolvers import reverse
4    from django.template import (
5        Library, TemplateSyntaxError)
6
7    # https://docs.djangoproject.com/en/1.8/howto/custom-template-tags/
8    register = Library()
```

The only new import is the `TemplateSyntaxError`, which we will raise when we or another developer uses a template tag in an unexpected or incorrect fashion.

Our `form` template tag includes the template at `core/includes/form.html` and uses the context from the template calling it, as shown in Example 27.28.

**Example 27.28: Project Code**

core/templatetags/display_form.py **in** 95d56b7b4f

```
11   @register.inclusion_tag(
12       'core/includes/form.html',
13       takes_context=True)
14   def form(context, *args, **kwargs):
```

We expect the possibility of three arguments, which we allow to be passed as either arguments or keyword arguments. In Example 27.29, we also take the Django form from the context of the template calling our template tag.

**Example 27.29: Project Code**

core/templatetags/display_form.py **in** 95d56b7b4f

```
14   def form(context, *args, **kwargs):
15       action = (args[0] if len(args) > 0
16                    else kwargs.get('action'))
17       button = (args[1] if len(args) > 1
18                    else kwargs.get('button'))
19       method = (args[2] if len(args) > 2
20                    else kwargs.get('method'))
21       form = context.get('form')
```

In the event action is not set, we raise an error. We then simply return these values as context to the template being included, as shown in Example 27.30.

**Example 27.30: Project Code**
core/templatetags/display_form.py **in** 95d56b7b4f

```
14   def form(context, *args, **kwargs):
 .       ...
22       if action is None:
23           raise TemplateSyntaxError(
24               "form template tag requires "
25               "at least one argument: action, "
26               "which is a URL.")
27       return {
28           'action': action,
29           'button': button,
30           'form': form,
31           'method': method}
```

The template is *exactly* like all our other forms. We start by surrounding the form with CSS, as shown in Example 27.31.

**Example 27.31: Project Code**
core/templates/core/includes/form.html **in** 95d56b7b4f

```
 1   <div class="row">
 2     <div class="offset-by-two eight columns">
 .       ...
14     </div>
15   </div>
```

We then declare a form with an action and a method, using the context to define these values. We use the default template filter to set the method to post if no value is provided, as shown in Example 27.32.

**Example 27.32: Project Code**
core/templates/core/includes/form.html **in** 95d56b7b4f

```
 3       <form
 4           action="{{ action }}"
 5           method="{{ method|default:'post' }}">
 .           ...
13       </form>
```

In Example 27.33, we use the csrf_token tag, display the form, and print a button using the value passed to button or a default of 'Submit'.

**Example 27.33: Project Code**

`core/templates/core/includes/form.html` **in** 95d56b7b4f

```
 6          {% csrf_token %}
 7          {{ form.as_p }}
 8          <button
 9              class="button-primary"
10              type="submit">
11            {{ button|default:'Submit' }}
12          </button>
```

To use our tag, we first load it and then simply call `form`, passing in the URL for the action and the string for the submission button, as shown in Example 27.34.

**Example 27.34: Project Code**

`blog/templates/blog/post_form_update.html` **in** b3295872e1

```
 2   {% load display_form %}
 .       ...
 8   {% block content %}
 9     {% form post.get_update_url 'Update Blog Post' %}
10   {% endblock %}
```

In the event the URL must be reversed first, we can use the `as` to save the value of the computation and then pass that new variable to our template tag, as shown in Example 27.35.

**Example 27.35: Project Code**

`blog/templates/blog/post_form.html` **in** b3295872e1

```
 2   {% load display_form %}
 .       ...
 8   {% block content %}
 9     {% url 'blog_post_create' as form_url %}
10     {% form form_url 'Create Blog Post' %}
11   {% endblock %}
```

All of the changes to our templates will look like one of the last two examples, and we are therefore able to use our new tag in the following templates:

- `contact_form.html`
- `newslink_form.html`
- `newslink_form_update.html`
- `startup_form.html`
- `startup_form_update.html`
- `tag_form.html`

- `tag_form_update.html`
- `password_change_form.html`
- `password_reset_form.html`
- `profile_form_update.html`

### 27.3.3 Displaying Delete Confirmation Forms

In the previous section, we created a template tag for forms that create or update objects. What about the forms to confirm deletion of an object?

I encourage you to take the opportunity to see if you can build your own template tag to display forms in our delete templates:

- `newslink_confirm_delete.html`
- `post_confirm_delete.html`
- `startup_confirm_delete.html`
- `tag_confirm_delete.html`
- `user_confirm_delete.html`

We won't see the code here, but the principle is exactly the same as in the previous two sections. Commit 9877981c74 in the project github provides a possible solution.

### 27.3.4 Listing the Latest Blog Posts

When we want to build a more complicated template tag, Django cannot provide a decorator to make our life easier. Instead, we must deal with the objects that Django uses internally.

For a template tag, Django expects the creation of a function and a subclass of the `Node` class. The function we create can be thought of loosely as a function to lex and parse the call to the template tag. The `Node` subclass is what Django uses in the abstract syntax list (yes, that's right—it is not a tree but a list).

From within a node, we can do most of anything available to Python within the confines of a template. One of the more powerful features is the ability to add data to the template. In this section, we create a custom template tag that adds a list of the most recent blog posts to our template context.

We start by importing our tools, as shown in Example 27.36.

**Example 27.36: Project Code**
`blog/templatetags/blog_latest.py` in ee6a14897a

```
1   from django.template import (
2       Library, Node, TemplateSyntaxError)
3
4   from ..models import Post
5
6   # https://docs.djangoproject.com/en/1.8/howto/custom-template-tags/
7   register = Library()
```

By convention, most template tag function start with do. We therefore create a function titled do_latest_post, which accepts the template parser as well as a single string with all of the arguments passed to the tag. We register the tag to the template library, naming it in the process, as shown in Example 27.37.

**Example 27.37: Project Code**
blog/templatetags/blog_latest.py **in** ee6a14897a

```
10   @register.tag(name="get_latest_post")
11   def do_latest_post(parser, token):
12       return LatestPostNode()
```

In the case of our current template tag, we are going to ignore everything and simply return an instance LatestPostNode, which is a Node subclass.

The node itself defines the render() method, which accepts a template context and then prints a value. In this case, we are not interested in displaying anything, and we instead want to add a value to the context. We therefore append the latest blog post to the context and return an empty string, as shown in Example 27.38.

**Example 27.38: Project Code**
blog/templatetags/blog_latest.py **in** ee6a14897a

```
15   class LatestPostNode(Node):
16
17       def render(self, context):
18           context['latest_post'] = (
19               Post.objects.published().latest())
20           return str()
```

This code creates a perfectly valid template tag. In base_organizer.html, we can load the custom template library, invoke the tag on line 13, and then display the latest_post object we added to the template context, as shown in Example 27.39.

**Example 27.39: Project Code**
organizer/templates/organizer/base_organizer.html **in** ee6a14897a

```
 2   {% load blog_latest %}
 .       ...
11       <section class="desktop four columns">
12         {% block create_button %}{% endblock %}
13         {% get_latest_post %}
14         <section class="latest_post">
15           <h4>Latest Post</h4>
16           <p><a href="{{ latest_post.get_absolute_url }}">
17             {{ latest_post.title }}</a></p>
18         </section>
19       </section>
```

We can now extend this basic behavior. For our next set of changes, we want to add a list of blog post items. We call the template tag with the number of items we want, as in Example 27.40.

**Example 27.40: Project Code**
`organizer/templates/organizer/base_organizer.html` in f93977f2c5

```
13          {% get_latest_posts 5 %}
14          <section class="latest_posts">
15            <h4>Latest Posts</h4>
16            <ul>
17              {% for latest_post in latest_posts_list %}
18                <li><a href="{{ latest_post.get_absolute_url }}">
19                  {{ latest_post.title }}</a></li>
20              {% endfor %}
21            </ul>
22          </section>
```

I opt to create a totally separate Node and function for this behavior (mainly to leave the first Node available in the code at all times for your perusal).

The LatestPostsNode has the render() method as before, where we again add to the context. For this to work, we expect the class to be instantiated with the number of items to fetch from the database, as shown in Example 27.41.

**Example 27.41: Project Code**
`blog/templatetags/blog_latest.py` in f93977f2c5

```
42    class LatestPostsNode(Node):
43
44        def __init__(self, number_of_posts):
45            self.num = number_of_posts
46
47        def render(self, context):
48            context['latest_posts_list'] = (
49                Post.objects.published()[:self.num])
50            return str()
```

In our function, we need to get this number. All of the tag call is passed as a string in an object. The string is accessible as the content attribute on token. The string at the moment is `"get_latest_posts 5"`. In Example 27.42, we can use a helper function to return the tuple (`"get_latest_posts"`, `"5"`).

**Example 27.42: Project Code**
`blog/templatetags/blog_latest.py` in f93977f2c5

```
23    @register.tag(name="get_latest_posts")
24    def do_latest_posts(parser, token):
```

```
25      try:
26          tag_name, number_of_posts_str = (
27              token.split_contents())
28      except ValueError:
29          raise TemplateSyntaxError(
30              "get_latest_posts takes 1 argument: "
31              "number of posts to get")
```

Using `split_contents()` is the most robust option available to us. We should use it over `token.content.split()`, because `split_contents()` respects variables grouped by quotation marks. The call to imaginary template tag `{% fiction "hello there" %}` will be split by `split_contents()` as `("fiction", "hello there")`, whereas `token.content.split()` will make the mistake of returning `("fiction", '"hello', 'there"',)`.

Now that we have the argument passed to our template tag, we can cast it to an integer, and then pass it to `LatestPostsNode` during instantiation, as shown in Example 27.43.

**Example 27.43: Project Code**
`blog/templatetags/blog_latest.py` in f93977f2c5

```
24  def do_latest_posts(parser, token):
 .      ...
32      try:
33          number_of_posts = int(number_of_posts_str)
34      except ValueError:
35          raise TemplateSyntaxError(
36              "tag '{tag_display}' sole argument "
37              "must be an integer".format(
38                  tag_display=tag_name))
39      return LatestPostsNode(number_of_posts)
```

If we load any of the pages in the **organizer** app, we will be greeted by the five most recent blog posts.

As a final step, we implement the use of the `as` token seen in many of Django's template tags. It allows us to set the name of the variable being added to the context. Our template code would thus read as shown in Example 27.44.

**Example 27.44: Project Code**
`organizer/templates/organizer/base_organizer.html` in e2738eb8b2

```
13          {% get_latest_posts 5 as custom_post_list %}
 .          ...
17              {% for latest_post in custom_post_list %}
```

In our `Node` subclass, we would thus pass the name of the variable we should set during instantiation. When we render the node, we add the number of blog posts either to `latest_posts_list` or else to the variable specified after the as token, as shown in Example 27.45.

**Example 27.45:** Project Code

`blog/templatetags/blog_latest.py` in `e2738eb8b2`

```
43   class LatestPostsNode(Node):
44
45       def __init__(self, number_of_posts, asvar):
46           self.num = number_of_posts
47           self.asvar = asvar
48
49       def render(self, context):
50           objs = Post.objects.published()[:self.num]
51           if self.asvar is None:
52               context['latest_posts_list'] = objs
53           else:
54               context[self.asvar] = objs
55           return str()
```

Our lex and parse functions must be more flexbile than before, as we don't know whether or not the tag is being called with as. Thanks to Python 3's extended unpacking features, we can grab the name of the tag and then any other arguments (if any) to the tokens list, as shown in Example 27.46. The use of as must always be the last thing to occur, making it easy to pull off the variable being specified (as well as the as token, thrown away in the _ variable unpacked on line 28).

**Example 27.46:** Project Code

`blog/templatetags/blog_latest.py` in `e2738eb8b2`

```
24   def do_latest_posts(parser, token):
25       asvar = None
26       tag_name, *tokens = token.split_contents()
27       if len(tokens) >= 2 and tokens[-2] == 'as':
28           *tokens, _, asvar = tokens
```

Our list of tokens should contain only a single token at this point: the number of items to display, as shown in Example 27.47.

**Example 27.47:** Project Code

`blog/templatetags/blog_latest.py` in `e2738eb8b2`

```
24   def do_latest_posts(parser, token):
 .       ...
29       if len(tokens) != 1:
30           raise TemplateSyntaxError(
31               "'{name}' takes 1 argument:"
32               "the number of posts.".format(
33                   name=tag_name))
```

We make sure that the only token is an integer, and we then instantiate `LatestPostsNode` with the number of integers to display, as well as the variable to add to the context (or None if it was not specified), as shown in Example 27.48.

**Example 27.48: Project Code**

`blog/templatetags/blog_latest.py` in e2738eb8b2

```
24   def do_latest_posts(parser, token):
.         ...
34       try:
35           number_of_posts = int(tokens.pop())
36       except ValueError:
37           raise TemplateSyntaxError(
38               "'{name}' expects argument to be "
39               "an integer.".format(name=tag_name))
40       return LatestPostsNode(number_of_posts, asvar)
```

This change allows for far greater control of our templates.

Take into consideration that this is a demonstration of a template tag, but if we actually wanted to simply add data to our templates, we could just as easily have created a custom context processor (a topic not covered in the book because of how simple it is).

### Python Documentation

For the PEP describing extended unpacking features in Python:

https://dju.link/pep3132

# 27.4   Putting It All Together

Custom template tags are incredibly useful, as they allow us to take control of the DTL in a way that was previously unavailable to us. We can control the display of variables using filters, and the power afforded to us by template tags means we can change display, control flow, and almost anything imaginable.

Custom template tags are also an excellent way to circumvent views' centralized power. Instead of needing a view to give the template context, template tags allow us to reach directly to models (or any other part of the system) to do exactly what we want. When discussing why Django doesn't adhere to MVC architecture, most developers cite custom template tags as their first example.

# Adding RSS and Atom Feeds and a Sitemap

## In This Chapter

- Implement RSS and Atom feeds for our blog and for the Startup news links
- Create Google sitemaps for the full site structure

## 28.1 Introduction

We are a step away from deployment. We have all our features, we've optimized our site for speed, and we've kept our code as clean as reasonably possible while learning a framework.

Before we actually deploy, however, we should add a few features to the website.

The first feature are RSS and Atom feeds. Users may subscribe to these feeds to automatically be updated anytime we write a new blog post or if a startup adds news to their page.

The second feature is a sitemap, which will allow search engines to better index our website for searching.

Django provides tools for building both of these features, making our life very, very easy.

Before we dive into the actual code, I will add an RSS icon to the project in commit 1dbc13a2d3,[1] taken from the feedicons.com website. I won't actually use the icon in the HTML and instead will use our Cascading Style Sheet (CSS) to add it to the appropriate links.

## 28.2 RSS and Atom Feeds

RSS and Atom are two competing formats for feeds. A feed is simply a list of items typically updated and sorted by date. In many ways, the work we will be doing is similar to using the `ListView` if the generic class-based view (GCBV) didn't use a template but still output XML that was fully compliant with feed formats.

---

1. https://dju.link/1dbc13a2d3

One of the neat things is that Django supports multiple formats but allows us to only implement a single class for use for both kinds of feeds. To that end, however, we start by extending our model to make the code in the feed a little bit cleaner. We add two methods on `Post` to format fields in the model, as shown in Example 28.1.

**Example 28.1: Project Code**
`blog/models.py` **in** 3b20644562

```
 41    class Post(models.Model):
   .        ...
124        def formatted_title(self):
125            return self.title.title()
126
127        def short_text(self):
128            if len(self.text) > 20:
129                short = ' '.join(self.text.split()[:20])
130                short += ' ...'
131            else:
132                short = self.text
133            return short
```

This allows us to create new file `feeds.py` where we import the `Feed` view, as shown in Example 28.2.

**Example 28.2: Project Code**
`blog/feeds.py` **in** 3b20644562

```
1    from datetime import datetime
2
3    from django.contrib.syndication.views import Feed
4    from django.core.urlresolvers import reverse_lazy
5    from django.utils.feedgenerator import (
6        Atom1Feed, Rss201rev2Feed)
7
8    from .models import Post
```

The `Feed` class, despite being both a view and a class, is not considered a class-based view (CBV) because it is completely unassociated with the `View` class. It is, in fact, a different and very specialized beast, but much like with GCBVs, our goal is to override the right methods. In Example 28.3, apply `Atom1Feed` and `Rss201rev2Feed` to subclasses of the `Feed` view, which will in turn tell the class which methods to expect.

**Example 28.3: Project Code**
`blog/feeds.py` **in** 3b20644562

```
32    class AtomPostFeed(BasePostFeedMixin, Feed):
33        feed_type = Atom1Feed
  .        ...
36    class Rss2PostFeed(BasePostFeedMixin, Feed):
37        feed_type = Rss201rev2Feed
```

The actual logic of the feeds will thus be created in our `BasePostFeedMixin` class. We start by defining attributes for the name of the feeds and provide a description, as shown in Example 28.4. The link will take the user to the HTML page that displays the same (or similar) information as the list in these feeds.

**Example 28.4: Project Code**
`blog/feeds.py` **in** 3b20644562

```
11    class BasePostFeedMixin():
12        title = "Latest Startup Organizer Blog Posts"
13        link = reverse_lazy('blog_post_list')
14        description = subtitle = (
15            "Stay up to date on the "
16            "hottest startup news.")
```

While both RSS and Atom feeds typically print the same information, Django will expect us to use different attributes and methods for each one, despite the fact that they frequently serve the same purpose. In the case of our description, the `description` attribute is for the RSS feed, while the `subtitle` attribute is for the Atom feed.

In both feed types, we define the `items()` method, which provides the list of items listed in the feed, as shown in Example 28.5.

**Example 28.5: Project Code**
`blog/feeds.py` **in** 3b20644562

```
11    class BasePostFeedMixin():
 .        ...
18        def items(self):
19            # uses Post.Meta.ordering
20            return Post.objects.published()[:10]
```

For each item, we provide a title, a description, and a link to the actual item, as shown in Example 28.6.

**Example 28.6: Project Code**
`blog/feeds.py` **in** 3b20644562

```
11    class BasePostFeedMixin():
 .        ...
22        def item_title(self, item):
23            return item.formatted_title()
24
25        def item_description(self, item):
26            return item.short_text()
27
28        def item_link(self, item):
29            return item.get_absolute_url()
```

In Example 28.7, in `suorganizer/urls.py`, we start by creating a separate URL configuration of our new feeds (which could arguably be placed in `blog/urls.py` instead of here).

**Example 28.7: Project Code**
`suorganizer/urls.py` **in** 3b20644562

```
22   from blog.feeds import AtomPostFeed, Rss2PostFeed
 .       ...
31   sitenews = [
32       url(r'^atom/$',
33           AtomPostFeed(),
34           name='blog_atom_feed'),
35       url(r'^rss/$',
36           Rss2PostFeed(),
37           name='blog_rss_feed'),
38   ]
```

We then link to this URL configuration from the root URL configuration in the same file, as shown in Example 28.8.

**Example 28.8: Project Code**
`suorganizer/urls.py` **in** 3b20644562

```
40   urlpatterns = [
 .       ...
52       url(r'^sitenews/', include(sitenews)),
 .       ...
60   ]
```

Finally, in Example 28.9, we add links to our feeds. We start in the HTML `head`, where we can tell the browser of the existence of these feeds. Most browsers use this information to add an icon to the address bar letting the user know these feeds exist.

**Example 28.9: Project Code**
`templates/base.html` **in** 3b20644562

```
23       <link rel="alternate" title="Blog News RSS"
24           type="application/rss+xml"
25           href="{% url 'blog_rss_feed' %}">
26       <link rel="alternate" title="Blog News Atom"
27           type="application/atom+xml"
28           href="{% url 'blog_atom_feed' %}">
```

Not all browsers use this information, and so I recommend adding links to the pages in the footer of our base template, as shown in Example 28.10.

**Example 28.10: Project Code**
`templates/base.html` in 3b20644562

```
108        <ul>
109          <li>
110            <a
111                href="{% url 'blog_rss_feed' %}"
112                class="feed">
113              Blog RSS Feed</a>
114          </li>
115          <li>
116            <a
117                href="{% url 'blog_atom_feed' %}"
118                class="feed">
119              Blog Atom Feed</a>
120          </li>
121        </ul>
```

We've create feeds for a global list of objects, but we're certainly not limited to that. We now create a feed for each `Startup` instance, where the feed of the object lists the related `NewsLink` objects. In anticipation of needing a small description for each `NewsLink` instance, we can add a method onto the class that tells us a little about it, as shown in Example 28.11.

**Example 28.11: Project Code**
`organizer/models.py` in 38520bcf7a

```
  2    from urllib.parse import urlparse
  .        . . .
131    class NewsLink(models.Model):
  .        . . .
174        def description(self):
175            return (
176                "Written on "
177                "{0:%A, %B} {0.day}, {0:%Y}; "
178                "hosted at {1}".format(
179                    self.pub_date,
180                    urlparse(self.link).netloc))
```

To create our feeds, we start by creating the `feeds.py` file in the **organizer** app and by importing the tools shown in Example 28.12.

**Example 28.12: Project Code**
`organizer/feeds.py` in 38520bcf7a

```
1    from datetime import datetime
2
3    from django.contrib.syndication.views import Feed
```

```
4   from django.core.urlresolvers import reverse_lazy
5   from django.shortcuts import get_object_or_404
6   from django.utils.feedgenerator import (
7       Atom1Feed, Rss201rev2Feed)
8
9   from .models import Startup
```

The goal, like last time, is to create an RSS feed and an Atom feed, both of which inherit their behavior from a shared superclass, as shown in Example 28.13.

**Example 28.13: Project Code**
organizer/feeds.py **in** 38520bcf7a

```
46   class AtomStartupFeed(BaseStartupFeedMixin, Feed):
47       feed_type = Atom1Feed
 .       . . .
50   class Rss2StartupFeed(BaseStartupFeedMixin, Feed):
51       feed_type = Rss201rev2Feed
```

Unlike our last feeds, these feeds are based on a single object. Our first goal is therefore to get that object. We can do this by overriding the get_object() method, as shown in Example 28.14. This method is not like the get_object() method found in GCBVs; it is more similar to the get() method found on CBVs.

**Example 28.14: Project Code**
organizer/feeds.py **in** 38520bcf7a

```
12   class BaseStartupFeedMixin():
 .       . . .
18       def get_object(self, request, startup_slug):
19           # equivalent to GCBV get() method
20           return get_object_or_404(
21               Startup,
22               slug__iexact=startup_slug)
```

When provided an object, the Feed class will pass the object to the items() method, allowing us to use our Startup instance in the method to get the related NewsLink objects, as shown in Example 28.15.

**Example 28.15: Project Code**
organizer/feeds.py **in** 38520bcf7a

```
12   class BaseStartupFeedMixin():
 .       . . .
24       def items(self, startup):
25           return startup.newslink_set.all()[:10]
```

As before, we write methods to display each of these items, as shown in Example 28.16.

**Example 28.16: Project Code**
`organizer/feeds.py` **in** 38520bcf7a

```
12   class BaseStartupFeedMixin():
.        . . .
27       def item_description(self, newslink):
28           return newslink.description()
29
30       def item_link(self, newslink):
31           return newslink.link
32
33       def item_title(self, newslink):
34           return newslink.title
```

Unlike with our previous feeds, we don't want to set a static description in our feed class, because the description of each `Startup` feed should change according to `Startup`. Luckily, we don't have to set these attributes and can instead implement methods to provide these values in the feed, as shown in Example 28.17. Note that, as last time, the `subtitle()` value simply uses the `description()` value.

**Example 28.17: Project Code**
`organizer/feeds.py` **in** 38520bcf7a

```
12   class BaseStartupFeedMixin():
.        . . .
14       def description(self, startup):
15           return "News related to {}".format(
16               startup.name)
.        . . .
36       def link(self, startup):
37           return startup.get_absolute_url()
38
39       def subtitle(self, startup):
40           return self.description(startup)
41
42       def title(self, startup):
43           return startup.name
```

As we want to create a feed for each `Startup` object, we create the URL patterns for our feeds, as shown in Example 28.18.

**Example 28.18: Project Code**
`organizer/urls/startup.py` **in** 38520bcf7a

```
3   from ..feeds import (
4       AtomStartupFeed, Rss2StartupFeed)
.        . . .
```

```
10   urlpatterns = [
 .       ...
24       url(r'^(?P<startup_slug>[\w\-]+)/atom/$',
25           AtomStartupFeed(),
26           name='organizer_startup_atom_feed'),
 .       ...
30       url(r'^(?P<startup_slug>[\w\-]+)/rss/$',
31           Rss2StartupFeed(),
32           name='organizer_startup_rss_feed'),
 .       ...
46   ]
```

This in turn allows us to create model methods to easily reverse the URL patterns, as shown in Example 28.19.

**Example 28.19: Project Code**
organizer/models.py **in** 38520bcf7a

```
 63   class Startup(models.Model):
  .       ...
 94       def get_feed_atom_url(self):
 95           return reverse(
 96               'organizer_startup_atom_feed',
 97               kwargs={'startup_slug': self.slug})
 98
 99       def get_feed_rss_url(self):
100           return reverse(
101               'organizer_startup_rss_feed',
102               kwargs={'startup_slug': self.slug})
```

Finally, in Example 28.20, we can add a link to these feeds in the startup_detail .html template.

**Example 28.20: Project Code**
organizer/templates/organizer/startup_detail.html **in** 38520bcf7a

```
32       <dl>
 .         ...
49         <dt>Feeds</dt>
50           <dd>
51             <a href="{{ startup.get_feed_atom_url }}">
52               Atom</a></dd>
53           <dd>
54             <a href="{{ startup.get_feed_rss_url }}">
55               RSS</a></dd>
56
57       </dl>
```

Now, users who are interested in a specific startup will be able to follow their feed and immediately be updated when any news about the company is listed on our website.

# 28.3  Sitemaps

A sitemap is a list of all the webpages that a search engine should know about. Originally proposed by Google, the idea is that we can tell Google where all our pages are and rank them by importance so that Google can best determine what to show users searching the web or our site.

Technically, the ability to provide sitemaps is an app in the Django contributed library, and this content actually belongs in Part II. However, we don't want to build sitemaps until the very last moment before we deploy, and so I've bent the rules a little.

To begin, we therefore need to add the **sitemaps** app to our INSTALLED_APPS list, as shown in Example 28.21.

**Example 28.21: Project Code**
`suorganizer/settings.py` in b1f09978d6

```
35    INSTALLED_APPS = (
  .      ...
43        'django.contrib.sitemaps',
  .      ...
51    )
```

The **sitemaps** app defines two views for us to use: index() and sitemap(). In both cases, we pass a dictionary containing instances of subclasses of the Sitemap class. The sitemap() view is meant to display the relevant data for a single one of those classes, while the index() view lists all of the sitemap() views (the index() view lists the keys in the dictionary passed).

## 28.3.1  Post **Sitemap**

We therefore need a Sitemap subclass. We can start with our **blog** app, creating a sitemaps.py file where we import our tools, as shown in Example 28.22.

**Example 28.22: Project Code**
`blog/sitemaps.py` in b1f09978d6

```
1    from datetime import date
2
3    from django.contrib.sitemaps import Sitemap
4
5    from .models import Post
```

We then declare our subclass in Example 28.23. The goal is to provide a list of *all* of the pages in our **blog** app. Because we've implemented get_absolute_url() on Post, this turns out to be surprisingly easy: we just need to return a list of Post objects in the items() method. We can also tell the search engine when the Post instance was modified thanks to the lastmod() method.

**Example 28.23: Project Code**

blog/sitemaps.py **in** b1f09978d6

```
 8   class PostSitemap(Sitemap):
 9       changefreq = "never"
10       priority = 0.5  # default value
11
12       def items(self):
13           return Post.objects.published()
14
15       def lastmod(self, post):
16           return post.pub_date
```

The changefreq attribute defines the frequency with which the items will change. We don't anticipate our blog posts being edited after publication, and so their change frequency is never. The priority attribute tells the search engine how important each webpage is.

Now that we have a Sitemap subclass, we need a sitemap dictionary. This is a site-wide feature, so we create a sitemaps.py file under the suorganizer/ directory, adding our new PostSitemap to a dictionary, as shown in Example 28.24.

**Example 28.24: Project Code**

suorganizer/sitemaps.py **in** b1f09978d6

```
1   from blog.sitemaps import PostSitemap
2
3   sitemaps = {
4       'posts': PostSitemap,
5   }
```

In our site URL configuration file, we import the views provided by the **sitemaps** app as well as our sitemaps_dict, as shown in Example 28.25.

**Example 28.25: Project Code**

suorganizer/urls.py **in** b1f09978d6

```
18   from django.contrib.sitemaps.views import (
19       index as site_index_view,
20       sitemap as sitemap_view)
  .      ...
31   from .sitemaps import sitemaps as sitemaps_dict
```

In Example 28.26, we then add URL patterns for these new views, passing in the dictionary we've created.

**Example 28.26: Project Code**

`suorganizer/urls.py` **in** b1f09978d6

```
57      url(r'^sitemap\.xml$',
58          site_index_view,
59          {'sitemaps': sitemaps_dict},
60          name='sitemap'),
61      url(r'^sitemap-(?P<section>.+)\.xml$',
62          sitemap_view,
63          {'sitemaps': sitemaps_dict},
64          name='sitemap-sections'),
```

If you browse to the path `/sitemap.xml` on the development server (the `index()` view), you'll be greeted with an XML file with a single link to the `/sitemap-posts.xml` page. This page (the `sitemap()` view) displays information about each and every blog post on our site.

Most search engines search for the sitemap index at the `/sitemap.xml` path, just as we've specified. Nevertheless, in Example 28.27, we add a link to the sitemap in the footer of our base template.

**Example 28.27: Project Code**

`templates/base.html` **in** b1f09978d6

```
109         <li>
110           <a href="{% url 'sitemap' %}">
111             Sitemap</a>
112         </li>
```

Depending on who you ask, the priority attribute of each webpage is either the most or least important part of the sitemap. We'll pretend for a moment that it's the most important. We therefore want to create a priority number for each blog post webpage. The integer 1 is given the most priority, whereas 0 is given none, and 0.5 is normal priority, as shown in Example 28.28.

**Example 28.28: Project Code**

`blog/sitemaps.py` **in** 34231c9cee

```
 2    from math import log10
 .        ...
 9    class PostSitemap(Sitemap):
 .        ...
18        def priority(self, post):
19            """Returns numerical priority of post.
20
21            1.0 is most important
22            0.0 is least important
23            0.5 is the default
24            """
```

We can define the priority according to date, as shown in Example 28.29. If our blog post was just published, we want it to have priority of 1. Once it's 3 months old, it should be normal priority.

**Example 28.29: Project Code**
`blog/sitemaps.py` in 34231c9cee

```
 9    class PostSitemap(Sitemap):
 .          ...
25          period = 90  # days
26          timedelta = date.today() - post.pub_date
27          # 86400 seconds in a day
28          # 86400 = 60 seconds * 60 minutes * 24 hours
29          # use floor division
30          days = timedelta.total_seconds() // 86400
```

We could make this gradual change linear, but where is the fun in that? Instead, we can make the drop-off from 1 to 0.5 be logarithmic—we drop very quickly from 1 but ease into 0.5, as shown in Example 28.30.

**Example 28.30: Project Code**
`blog/sitemaps.py` in 34231c9cee

```
 9    class PostSitemap(Sitemap):
 .          ...
31          if days == 0:
32              return 1.0
33          elif 0 < days <= period:
34              # n(d) = normalized(days)
35              # n(1) = 0.5
36              # n(period) = 0
37              normalized = (
38                  log10(period / days) /
39                  log10(period ** 2))
40              normalized = round(normalized, 2)
41              return normalized + 0.5
42          else:
43              return 0.5
```

The math in Example 28.30 will result in a drop off like the one shown in Figure 28.1.

None of the blog posts were written in the last 3 months, but if you write your own blog post, you'll be able to watch the number drop over the next few days.

## 28.3.2  Tag Sitemap

Not all sitemaps need be as complicated as the one for `Post` objects. Django anticipates, that, in a lot of cases, we'll simply be overriding the `items()` method of the `Sitemap` subclass and nothing else. To make this easy, the **sitemaps** app supplies the

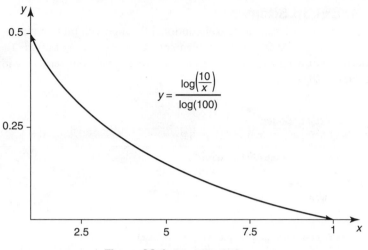

**Figure 28.1:** Logarithmic Curve

GenericSitemap class, which can be passed a dictionary of items to automatically generate a Sitemap subclass, as shown in Example 28.31.

**Example 28.31: Project Code**
organizer/sitemaps.py **in** e58a4cc3ba

```
1    from django.contrib.sitemaps import (
2        GenericSitemap, Sitemap)
3
4    from .models import Startup, Tag
5
6    tag_sitemap_dict = {
7        'queryset': Tag.objects.all(),
8    }
9
10
11   TagSitemap = GenericSitemap(tag_sitemap_dict)
```

To add our new TagSitemap to the rest, we can simply import it in suorganizer/sitemaps.py and add it to the dictionary, as shown in Example 28.32.

**Example 28.32: Project Code**
suorganizer/sitemaps.py **in** e58a4cc3ba

```
1    from blog.sitemaps import PostSitemap
2    from organizer.sitemaps import TagSitemap
3
4    sitemaps = {
5        'posts': PostSitemap,
6        'tags': TagSitemap,
7    }
```

### 28.3.3 `Startup` **Sitemap**

Most of the values in a sitemap are actually optional (Django will fill them in for you). In our `StartupSitemap`, we can simply implement `items()`. The `lastmod()` implementation is not necessary, but it is a nice way to associate our startups with a date, as shown in Example 28.33.

**Example 28.33: Project Code**

`organizer/sitemaps.py` **in** `aabf064551`

```
14   class StartupSitemap(Sitemap):
15
16       def items(self):
17           return Startup.objects.all()
18
19       def lastmod(self, startup):
20           if startup.newslink_set.exists():
21               return (
22                   startup.newslink_set.latest()
23                   .pub_date)
24           else:
25               return startup.founded_date
```

Of course, we add the new sitemap to the dictionary, as shown in Example 28.34.

**Example 28.34: Project Code**

`suorganizer/sitemaps.py` **in** `aabf064551`

```
1   from blog.sitemaps import PostSitemap
2   from organizer.sitemaps import (
3       StartupSitemap, TagSitemap)
4
5   sitemaps = {
6       'posts': PostSitemap,
7       'startups': StartupSitemap,
8       'tags': TagSitemap,
9   }
```

### 28.3.4 **Blog Post Archive Sitemap**

For the webpages that list `Post` objects according to date, I want to do something a little different. I want to list pages for both the year and the month archives, and I want these pages to be sorted according to date, so that the month archives appear before the year archives (for the same year). These requirements seem a little silly, but they force us to customize the `Sitemap` a little more than before.

To start, we can get all of the dates for the `Post` objects, first according to year, and then according to month, as shown in Example 28.35.

**Example 28.35: Project Code**
blog/sitemaps.py **in** 477533df0e

```
49   class PostArchiveSitemap(Sitemap):
50
51       def items(self):
52           year_dates = (
53               Post.objects.published().dates(
54                   'pub_date', 'year', order='DESC',
55               ).iterator())
56           month_dates = (
57               Post.objects.published().dates(
58                   'pub_date', 'month', order='DESC',
59               ).iterator())
```

We can then add each date to a tuple, noting which tuple was from the year query and which was from the month query, as shown in Example 28.36. This may seem a little strange at the moment, but it will make sense when we tackle the next method.

**Example 28.36: Project Code**
blog/sitemaps.py **in** 477533df0e

```
49   class PostArchiveSitemap(Sitemap):
50
51       def items(self):
 .           ...
60           year_tuples = map(
61               lambda d: (d, 'y'),
62               year_dates)
63           month_tuples = map(
64               lambda d: (d, 'm'),
65               month_dates)
```

We need a few tools to progress, as shown in Example 28.37.

**Example 28.37: Project Code**
blog/sitemaps.py **in** 477533df0e

```
2   from itertools import chain
.       ...
4   from operator import itemgetter
.       ...
7   from django.core.urlresolvers import reverse
```

To sort all of our dates together, we use Python's sorted() function, which notably respects place. We first use the chain() function to build a single iterable from both tuples to sort through. Because sorted() is in place, we pass the month tuple to chain first (as we want any month pages for a year to appear before the year page). We only want to sort the tuples according to the date, which is the first item in the tuple. We use the itemgetter() function to give sorted() that date from the tuple. Finally, we want the latest dates first, so we ask for the reverse sort, as shown in Example 28.38.

**Example 28.38: Project Code**

blog/sitemaps.py **in** 477533df0e

```
49    class PostArchiveSitemap(Sitemap):
50
51        def items(self):
.            ...
66            return sorted(
67                chain(month_tuples, year_tuples),
68                key=itemgetter(0),
69                reverse=True)
```

In our previous Sitemap subclasses, the links, or locations, for all of these pages were being created because we defined the get_absolute_url method on the models whose instances we were passing as items. In the case of our dates, we don't have items, and so we need to implement the location() method.

In Example 28.39, the method will be called with one of the tuples from the sorted list, meaning we will receive a tuple with a date and a string, where the string is either 'm' or 'y'.

**Example 28.39: Project Code**

blog/sitemaps.py **in** 477533df0e

```
49    class PostArchiveSitemap(Sitemap):
.        ...
71        def location(self, date_tuple):
72            archive_date, archive_type = date_tuple
```

The second item in the tuple can therefore be used to indicate which URL pattern to reverse, as shown in Example 28.40.

**Example 28.40: Project Code**

blog/sitemaps.py **in** 477533df0e

```
49    class PostArchiveSitemap(Sitemap):
.        ...
71        def location(self, date_tuple):
.            ...
73            if archive_type == 'y':
74                return reverse(
75                    'blog_post_archive_year',
76                    kwargs={
77                        'year': archive_date.year})
78            elif archive_type == 'm':
79                return reverse(
80                    'blog_post_archive_month',
81                    kwargs={
82                        'year': archive_date.year,
83                        'month': archive_date.month})
```

In the unlikely event we receive a value that is neither `'m'` or `'y'`, we raise an error, as shown in Example 28.41.

**Example 28.41: Project Code**
`blog/sitemaps.py` in 477533df0e

```
49    class PostArchiveSitemap(Sitemap):
 .        ...
71        def location(self, date_tuple):
 .            ...
84            else:
85                raise NotImplementedError(
86                    "{} did not recognize "
87                    "{} denoted '{}'.".format(
88                        self.__class__.__name__,
89                        'archive_type',
90                        archive_type))
```

Finally, in Example 28.42, we can add our new sitemap to the dictionary.

**Example 28.42: Project Code**
`suorganizer/sitemaps.py` in 477533df0e

```
 1    from blog.sitemaps import (
 2        PostArchiveSitemap, PostSitemap)
 .        ...
 6    sitemaps = {
 7        'post-archives': PostArchiveSitemap,
 .        ...
11    }
```

## 28.3.5 Other Pages Sitemap

The sitemaps we've built so far cover all of the dynamic pages in our website, but none of them cover basic pages like the about page or our list pages. To remedy this, we can create a sitemap that lists these pages. As these pages are quite important, we give them a slightly higher than normal priority, as shown in Example 28.43.

**Example 28.43: Project Code**
`suorganizer/sitemaps.py` in bb71d3562d

```
 1    from django.contrib.sitemaps import Sitemap
 2    from django.core.urlresolvers import reverse
 .        ...
10    class RootSitemap(Sitemap):
11        priority = 0.6
```

We can then simply define a list of URL pattern names to be returned in `items()` and use each URL pattern name in `location()` as the argument to `reverse()`, as shown in Example 28.44.

**Example 28.44: Project Code**

`suorganizer/sitemaps.py` **in** `bb71d3562d`

```
10    class RootSitemap(Sitemap):
 .        ...
13        def items(self):
14            return [
15                'about_site',
16                'blog_post_list',
17                'contact',
18                'dj_auth:login'
19                'organizer_startup_list',
20                'organizer_tag_list',
21            ]
22
23        def location(self, url_name):
24            return reverse(url_name)
```

Finally, we add this new sitemap to the sitemap dictionary, as shown in Example 28.45.

**Example 28.45: Project Code**

`suorganizer/sitemaps.py` **in** `bb71d3562d`

```
27    sitemaps = {
28        'post-archives': PostArchiveSitemap,
29        'posts': PostSitemap,
30        'roots': RootSitemap,
31        'startups': StartupSitemap,
32        'tags': TagSitemap,
33    }
```

# 28.4   Putting It All Together

Feeds and sitemaps are by no means necessary for a website, but they are incredibly useful. RSS feeds make it easier for people to keep up with news, while sitemaps make it easier for search engines to index our site.

Now that we have both of these, we can turn to the next task at hand: getting our work into the hands of users and search engines!

# 29

# Deploy!

## In This Chapter

- Shared hosts, virtual servers, cloud servers, and managed cloud services, oh my!
- Deploy our website to Heroku's managed cloud platform
- Enable email, logging, and caching on Heroku's platform

## 29.1 Introduction: Understanding Modern Deployments

### Warning!

Of all the content in this book, this chapter will be obsolete the quickest. While the process will be the same no matter when you read this, any commands and specifics may have changed. Please use this chapter as a set of guidelines for deployment, and double check the specifics in the relevant documentation.

Deploying a website means to make it accessible to its targeted market. This might be an internal part of a company or the entire population on the internet.

Originally, deploying involved buying hardware, building a computer, connecting the computer to the internet, securing it, and then making its contents available to the public. To handle all the incoming crowds if the website was popular, developers had to repeat the process (referred to as scaling the website, as briefly discussed in Chapter 26: Optimizing Our Site for Speed).

Because of the complexity of deploying a website, companies began to handle this task for customers. Shared hosting or virtual private servers became great starting options for small websites, allowing them to simply switch services when they needed to accommodate more users. However, much larger websites still needed to build their own datacenters to handle their enormous loads. Companies such as Amazon and Rackspace stepped in, offering the computing power to handle these much larger loads. These new services were dubbed **cloud computing** (much to the confusion of other companies, such as IBM, who had offered warehouses of general computers since long before cloud computing).

The difficulty with cloud computing services is that they can be overwhelming and time consuming. Companies have entire teams of engineers whose sole jobs it is to handle deployment (called **development operations**, or **devops**). For individuals and small teams without the resources for dedicated devops engineers, managed cloud hosting is a powerful alternative. Companies that offer these services provide tools to make interacting with larger clouds simpler and faster.

One such company is Heroku: it provides a set of tools to make deploying websites to the Amazon cloud easy. In this chapter, we use Heroku's platform to deploy our website to the public internet.

I want to emphasize that I am not associated with Heroku or Amazon in any way. There are many other options that might suit your needs: PythonAnywhere, Gondor, Rackspace, Linode, and more. It is worth your time to take a look around the internet as to see what options are available to you.

Originally, this book attempted to deploy to Amazon directly, as Amazon is currently considered the leader in the field of cloud hosting for websites. The deploy to Amazon proved time consuming and detail oriented. Using Heroku's platform is far quicker and easier to understand, but it is also more expensive. I urge you to weigh your options when considering which host/cloud to use and to look at other services such as Rackspace. With that said, my opinion is that a managed cloud solution (like Heroku) is worth the extra cost compared to an unmananged cloud solution (like Amazon) up until the managed cloud costs the same as a devops team.

## 29.2   Preparing for Deployment

Once you've picked a company to host your website with, it's time to dive into the documentation.

If you're following along with the site on Github and deploying to Heroku, you won't actually need to read much of Heroku's documentation, but its "Getting Started with Python"[1] will be very helpful.

Heroku works with dynos and add-ons. A **dyno**, sometimes called a worker, is an increment of power. The more dynos you have, the more visitors you can handle. Internally, a dyno is simply a Linux container with the website and all dependencies, allowing Heroku to quickly create dynos as well as pass dynos around from computer to computer (as they fail or are added to Heroku's internal system). A dyno is the code of our website and should therefore be treated as stateless and expendable.

Heroku's dynos are built to interact with Django via WSGIs (Web Server Gateway Interfaces), which is considered the best way to run Django today. Heroku recommends using the gunicorn server, and so we plan to do just that.

Heroku charges according to the dyno, so you want to be extra careful to run only as many dynos as you need (there is a feature to autoscale dynos, but we won't see that in this book).

Heroku also works with **add-ons**, sometimes called backing services.[2] If the dyno is the stateless code of our website, the add-ons are all the stateful parts as well as anything outside

---

1. https://dju.link/heroku-start
2. https://dju.link/heroku-backing

basic HTTP interaction: a database, logging, email, and caching, for example. We use add-ons for each of these features in this chapter.

Once we understand all of the tools we will use for deployment, we need to make sure our Django code is in a state ready for deployment. Django supplies documentation about deployment,[3] as well as a deployment checklist[4] that is quite useful.

Combined with Heroku's documentation, we know we need to do the following:

- Add HTML error pages to our Django app.
- Install Heroku's toolbelt and integrate the tools in our project.
- Prepare our settings for a production environment.

We also discuss what happens to our development server when we make all of these changes, as a website is quite often a work in progress.

## 29.2.1 Creating Error Pages

As we were developing, anytime we asked for a page that didn't exist or that caused the server to error horribly, Django would catch the error and then tell us what was going on internally. Leaking this information to a stranger on the internet is a terrible idea. In the next section, we disable this behavior by changing the DEBUG setting to False. However, when we do, Django will begin to look for templates that we have not created yet.

These templates will be loaded and rendered with a RequestContext whenever a problem occurs. When a URL path that doesn't match a URL pattern is received by Django, Django will load and render the 404.html in the root of our template namespace. We therefore create the templates/404.html template, as shown in Example 29.1.

**Example 29.1: Project Code**
templates/404.html **in** f5b5b484de

```
 1   {% extends parent_template|default:"base.html" %}
 2
 3   {% block title %}
 4   Page Not Found
 5   {% endblock %}
 6
 7   {% block content %}
 8     <div class="row">
 9       <div class="offset-by-two eight columns">
10         <h1>Page Not Found</h1>
11         <p>The path {{ request.path }} is not a
12            webpage on this site!</p>
13       </div>
14     </div>
15   {% endblock %}
```

---

3. https://dju.link/18/deploy
4. https://dju.link/18/deploy-checklist

Django will do the same for HTTP 400 (Bad Request), 403 (Permission Denied), and 500 (Internal Server Error) errors as well. We therefore create the following templates:

- `templates/400.html`
- `templates/403.html`
- `templates/500.html`

The templates are just as straightforward as `404.html` and are therefore not printed here. As always, the code is available in the public Github repository.

## 29.2.2  Deployment Tools

Heroku supplies a command-line interface (CLI) for interacting with its platform and a number of Python tools for our site to more easily interact with its add-ons and dynos.

To download the CLI, browse to https://toolbelt.heroku.com/, download the package for your system, and install it. The CLI enables you to interact with the `heroku` command in the terminal. The toolbelt also installs the `foreman` tool, which you can read more about at http://theforeman.org/.

In our project, we need to install the Python package called `django-toolbelt`. The `django-toolbelt` is different from Heroku's toolbelt CLI. The toolbelt is a command-line interface for interacting with Heroku, while the `django-toolbelt` Python package is a set of tools built entirely for Django, which we will use to integrate our website with Heroku's dynos. Before we do any of that, however, we need to restructure our `requirements.txt`.

The `requirements.txt` file is discussed in Chapter 3: Programming Django Models and Creating a SQLite Database. In a nutshell, it lists the projects needed for our website to work. Heroku uses the file to determine what tools are necessary for running the website in the cloud.

In the github repository, the requirements file currently lists the tools shown in Example 29.2.

**Example 29.2: Project Code**
`requirements.txt` in `f5b5b484de`

```
1   Django>=1.8,<1.9
2   django-debug-toolbar
3   django-extensions
4   ipython[notebook]
```

While Django is required for our site to run, none of the other tools are. The `debug-toolbar` is for development purposes only, and so we don't want Heroku to use it. The `django-extensions` tools provide the tools necessary to create Django IPython notebooks, which are in turn installed by `ipython[notebook]`. You might want these on your website to expand the shell functionality, but I will be removing these as well and placing them in the `dev_requirements.txt` file in the root of our project, as shown in Example 29.3.

**Example 29.3: Project Code**
`dev_requirements.txt` **in** ee87540b2b

```
1    django-debug-toolbar
2    django-extensions
3    ipython[notebook]
```

For our site to work, we need not only the Python package `django-toolbelt` but also `psycopg2` and `whitenoise`, as shown in Example 29.4.

**Example 29.4: Project Code**
`requirements.txt` **in** ee87540b2b

```
1    Django>=1.8,<1.9
2    django-toolbelt
3    psycopg2
4    whitenoise
```

Our site at the moment uses the SQLite database that Django configures by default. In a production environment, we absolutely do not want to use SQLite, because while the database is a wonderful tool for small projects, it cannot handle many simultaneous connections. For public websites in the cloud, we want to use either MySQL or PostgreSQL. The current favorite, because it is feature-packed, open source, and originally designed with the help of Turing Award-winner Michael Stonebraker, is PostgreSQL. What's more, Heroku automatically gives us a PostgreSQL database because it assumes we want one. For our website to communicate with PostgreSQL, we need the `psycopg2` tool.

In cloud computing, our goal is always to separate state from behavior, content from code. Ideally, all of our static assets (CSS, images, JavaScript) would be stored on a separate server (such as Amazon's S3 service or Rackspace's CloudFiles service) and pointed to by our stateless Django code. We are not going the full nine yards because of time constraints. Instead, we host our static assets with our Heroku dyno with our code (mixing stateful with stateless). We use the `whitenoise` tool to allow for this to work.

To install all of these tools locally, we can issue the command shown in Example 29.5.

**Example 29.5: Shell Code**

```
$ pip install -r requirements.txt
```

The `psycopg2` may require you to actually have a PostgreSQL server locally (despite the fact that we will continue to use SQLite locally—we'll discuss why this is a terrible idea in Chapter 30, but we do it anyway in this chapter).

### 29.2.3  Preparing Django Settings

When we deploy to production, there are several changes we must always remember to make. The two largest are: keep the SECRET_KEY in the project setting secret and set DEBUG to False.

The problem with changing these settings is that it makes it harder to actually develop the website, where you want DEBUG to be True and you simply want the development server to run, never mind the security key.

To handle both development, production, and any other possible environment, developers split the settings.py file into multiple files. We thus delete suorganizer/settings.py and create the suorganizer/settings/ directory with multiple files. The dev.py file contains all of the settings specific to development, while the production.py contains all of the settings specific to the production server. For settings shared by both, we create a base.py file for the two to inherit. Our file reorganization is shown in Example 29.6.

**Example 29.6: Shell Code**

```
$ tree suorganizer/
suorganizer/
├── __init__.py
├── log_filters.py
├── settings
│   ├── __init__.py
│   ├── base.py
│   ├── dev.py
│   └── production.py
├── sitemaps.py
├── urls.py
└── wsgi.py

1 directory, 9 files
```

When we change the location of our settings, we have to change the paths to all of our project directories, such as the site-wide template directory and the site-wide static directory. Because we've been using os.join() with the BASE_DIR variable, we can change the BASE_DIR to take an extra call to dirname(), as shown in Example 29.7.

**Example 29.7: Project Code**
suorganizer/settings/base.py **in** 3c73f989ea

```
8    BASE_DIR = os.path.dirname(os.path.dirname(os.path.dirname(__file__)))
```

The installed apps and middleware in base.py are the ones used in both development and production. In Example 29.8, we also take the opportunity to add the BrokenLink EmailsMiddleware, which will send administrators emails when the URL path is not matched by a URL pattern.

**Example 29.8: Project Code**

`suorganizer/settings/base.py` **in** `3c73f989ea`

```
28   MIDDLEWARE_CLASSES = (
 .       ...
31       'django.middleware.common.BrokenLinkEmailsMiddleware',
 .       ...
40   )
```

## Django Documentation

For more about the `BrokenLinkEmailsMiddleware` and error reporting, please
see

https://dju.link/18/errors

We also add all of the configuration related to login pages, most email settings, and our
static page content to `base.py`.

For static content to work, we also need to add the `STATIC_ROOT` setting, as shown in
Example 29.9.

**Example 29.9: Project Code**

`suorganizer/settings/base.py` **in** `3c73f989ea`

```
110   STATICFILES_DIRS = (os.path.join(BASE_DIR, "static"),)
```

This code tells Django where to put all our static content when running the website.
We'll see it in action shortly.

In `dev.py`, we can simply append our development tools to the list, as shown in
Example 29.10.

**Example 29.10: Project Code**

`suorganizer/settings/dev.py` **in** `3c73f989ea`

```
14   INSTALLED_APPS += (
15       'debug_toolbar',
16       'django_extensions',
17   )
```

The code in Example 29.11 works only because of the way we are importing our base
settings, using the star to import them all directly into the Python namespace. This practice
is normally frowned upon, but it turns out to be incredibly useful for us.

**Example 29.11: Project Code**

`suorganizer/settings/dev.py` **in** `3c73f989ea`

```
5   from .base import *
```

In `dev.py`, we also add our not-so-secret key, as well as DEBUG, as shown in Example 29.12.

**Example 29.12:** Project Code

`suorganizer/settings/dev.py` **in** 3c73f989ea

```
 8   SECRET_KEY = '1)zht&^pddidsyqe$+09%se1*ba2#b_q-!j0^v$(-3c-=-vmq4'
 9
10   DEBUG = True
11
12   ALLOWED_HOSTS = []
```

We add the current SQLite database to development. We also add our `DummyCache` and `console.EmailBackend` settings to `dev.py`, as well as our logging settings (we'll change this last bit shortly).

The `production.py` settings file is where things get a little strange, because we begin to use tools from Heroku's toolbelt. One of the tools `django-toolbelt` installed was the `dj_database_url`, which allows our website to easily configure communication with the PostgreSQL server provided by Heroku (to clarify: `dj_database_url` configures our settings; Django will still use `psycopg2` to actually communicate).

We start by importing our base settings and by importing `dj_database_url`, as shown in Example 29.13.

**Example 29.13:** Project Code

`suorganizer/settings/production.py` **in** 3c73f989ea

```
4   import os
5
6   import dj_database_url
7
8   from .base import *
```

While not specified in `base.py`, we want to make sure all our debugging settings are off. We also need a secret key, but we will not put this in our code (as it is a security vulnerability). Instead, we will define it in the runtime, and we can use Python's os package to get the secret key, as shown in Example 29.14.

**Example 29.14:** Project Code

`suorganizer/settings/production.py` **in** 3c73f989ea

```
13   DEBUG = False
14   TEMPLATE_DEBUG = False
15
16   SECRET_KEY = os.environ.get('SECRET_KEY')
```

We then use `dj_database_url` to configure the connection to the PostgreSQL database, as shown in Example 29.15.

**Example 29.15: Project Code**
`suorganizer/settings/production.py` **in** `3c73f989ea`

```
20    DATABASES = {'default': dj_database_url.config()}
```

If we were using a PostgreSQL database in development (we should be—we discuss this topic in Chapter 30), we could use the `config()` method in `base.py`, as it allows developers to pass a `default` keyword with configuration for when the site is run off of Heroku.

When we first deploy to Heroku, we will be assigned a server, typically of the format `https://<appname>.herokuapp.com`. For this to work, we need to specify the `ALLOWED_HOSTS` to recognize this server, as shown in Example 29.16. To make this easy, I will simply set the star parameter to accept *any* host. In a real deploy, you should limit this setting to your own domain, or if you don't yet have that configured with Heroku (not covered here), then use `['appname.herokuapp.com']`.

**Example 29.16: Project Code**
`suorganizer/settings/production.py` **in** `3c73f989ea`

```
18    ALLOWED_HOSTS = ['*']
```

For `https://<appname>.herokuapp.com` to work properly, we also need to allow for the use of Transport Layer Security (TLS). We would eventually want to use our own TLS certificates, but for the moment we can rely on Heroku's. For that to work, we add the setting shown in Example 29.17.

**Example 29.17: Project Code**
`suorganizer/settings/production.py` **in** `3c73f989ea`

```
22    SECURE_PROXY_SSL_HEADER = ('HTTP_X_FORWARDED_PROTO', 'https')
```

Finally, we need to enable `whitenoise` so that our static content is loaded in production properly. We start by informing the **static** app of the existence of `whitenoise`, as shown in Example 29.18.

**Example 29.18: Project Code**
`suorganizer/settings/production.py` **in** `3c73f989ea`

```
24    STATICFILES_STORAGE = 'whitenoise.django.GzipManifestStaticFilesStorage'
```

Because we're breaking a rule by providing stateful content in our stateless dyno, we need to modify the application being run. We need to open /suorganizer/wsgi.py, import DjangoWhiteNoise, and wrap our WSGI app with it. The new code is on lines 13 and 18 in Example 29.19.

**Example 29.19: Project Code**

suorganizer/wsgi.py **in** f100faade7

```
10    import os
11
12    from django.core.wsgi import get_wsgi_application
13    from whitenoise.django import DjangoWhiteNoise
14
15    os.environ.setdefault("DJANGO_SETTINGS_MODULE", "suorganizer.settings")
16
17    application = get_wsgi_application()
18    application = DjangoWhiteNoise(application)
```

Now that we have our settings properly split, we can finally configure the foreman, which was installed by Heroku's CLI toolbelt. The goal is to tell the foreman, which will be used in Heroku's dyno's, to run our Django website using gunicorn.[5]

By default, foreman (and Heroku) will look for this information in a file called Procfile. We therefore create the file, and code as shown in Example 29.20.

**Example 29.20: Project Code**

Procfile **in** 5bae91924a

```
1    web: gunicorn --env DJANGO_SETTINGS_MODULE=suorganizer.settings.
.    production suorganizer.wsgi --log-file -
```

The web command we have defined is the one Heroku invokes by default. In our case, it will call gunicorn (installed in our dyno by default) and direct the server to run the Django app via the WSGI interface in suorganizer.wsgi (the wsgi.py in our /suorganizer/ directory). We want to make sure it uses the settings defined in production.py, and so we override the DJANGO_SETTINGS_MODULE environment variable to point to that file. Finally, we tell gunicorn to direct any logs captured from the Django project to stdout (defined as the - in the command).

Finally, we create the runtime.txt file, as shown in Example 29.21.

**Example 29.21: Project Code**

runtime.txt **in** 2dbbea4acd

```
1    python-3.4.3
```

---

5. https://dju.link/18/gunicorn

By default, Heroku will use Python 2.7. We don't want this: we've programmed a modern Django app using Python 3.4, and we want to use that on our server. This runtime file ensures Heroku uses 3.4 instead of the (totally outdated) default.

Congratulations! You are officially ready to deploy! Before deploying, however, we'll see how our changes affect our local servers.

### 29.2.4 Running Django's Development Server

If you try to run Django's development server, Django will inform you it doesn't know where the settings file is anymore. When we invoke it, we can inform Djange of our `dev.py` file by specifying the `settings` flag, as shown in Example 29.22.

**Example 29.22: Shell Code**

```
$ ./manage.py runserver --settings=suorganizer.settings.dev
```

Specifying the flag in each and every call to management commands is undesirable. Instead, in Example 29.23, we can set the `DJANGO_SETTINGS_MODULE` environment variable, which Django will use instead.

**Example 29.23: Shell Code**

```
export DJANGO_SETTINGS_MODULE=suorganizer.settings.dev
$ ./manage.py runserver
```

Our development server, and every other command, will now work in this shell. Unfortunately, anytime we create a new shell, we have to set the `DJANGO_SETTINGS_MODULE` environment variable again. Many developers solve this by writing bash/zfs/Python scripts to automatically determine the value based on their toolset. Depending on your system, terminal, and shell, the answer to this problem will be different, and most are easily Googled, so we do not discuss the large number of possibilities here.

### 29.2.5 Running Foreman's Server

When we installed Heroku's toolbelt CLI, we also installed the foreman server (http://theforeman.org/). The foreman will be used by Heroku in the cloud, and having it on our server locally provides the ability to test our production settings. Many development teams will create an entire server or cloud instance to test production settings. These servers or instances are called **staging servers**. In our case, we can create a simple staging server by running foreman.

The problem with our staging server, if we run it, is that our production settings are currently intended to work with Heroku, and not with our local setup. The production settings don't define a secret key and cryptically define a database. We need to fix them for our local staging server to work

Before we do, however, we need to collect our static content into a single location, as shown in Example 29.24. This is usually used to send the content to a different server or service.

**Example 29.24: Shell Code**

```
$ ./manage.py collectstatic --noinput
```

Next, we need to create a secret key, as shown in Example 29.25. In our production settings, we fetch the secret key from the environment variable SECRET_KEY, and so to allow for our Django website to run in staging and production, we need this key to exist.

**Example 29.25: Shell Code**

```
$ export SECRET_KEY='xC(7"56MT-sVb9bh!8F!#1714B4"e#0M5*0AL(0w6(W) Ti6NtD'
```

You will want to randomly generate the 50-character key above. There are three easy ways to do this: with django_extensions, in the Python interpreter, or in the shell (bash, zfs, etc.).

If you have django_extensions installed and enabled in the project (I added it to enable IPython notebooks in the project repository), then you can simply use the generate_secret_key management command, as shown in Example 29.26.

**Example 29.26: Shell Code**

```
$ ./manage.py generate_secret_key
```

In the Django shell (./manage.py shell), we can use the same tools Django does to create a secret key, as shown in Example 29.27.

**Example 29.27: Python Interpreter Code**

```
>>> from django.utils.crypto import get_random_string
>>> chars = 'abcdefghijklmnopqrstuvwxyz0123456789!@#$%^&*(-_=+)'
>>> get_random_string(50, chars)
```

In the shell, we can use OpenSSL (assuming you have it installed), as shown in Example 29.28.

**Example 29.28: Shell Code**

```
openssl rand -base64 39 | head -c50 | xargs echo
```

## Info

The 39 integer is the number of bytes we are requesting: 39 bytes is 312 bits
($39 * 8 = 312$). In base 64, each character is represented by 6 bits ($2^6 = 64$), which
means we will output 52 characters ($\frac{312}{6}$). We use head to limit the key to 50
characters.

We do not need to change the DJANGO_SETTINGS_MODULE variable (set to the
development settings) because the command in Procfile forcibly uses the production
settings.

Finally, in Example 29.29, we need to allow the database to work. The purpose of
dj_database_url is to take the DATABASE_URL environment variable and to generate a
proper configuration dictionary for the site settings. We could, therefore, create a local
DATABASE_URL environment variable.

**Example 29.29: Shell Code**

```
$ export DATABASE_URL=sqlite:///'pwd'/db.sqlite3
```

The alternative is to define a default in our production.py, as shown in
Example 29.30.

**Example 29.30: Project Code**
suorganizer/settings/production.py in 76410be420

```
20   DATABASES = {
21       'default': dj_database_url.config(
22           default='sqlite:///{}'.format(
23               os.path.abspath(
24                   os.path.join(
25                       BASE_DIR, 'db.sqlite3'))),
26       ),
27   }
```

In either case, this allows us to start the foreman server, as shown in Example 29.31.

**Example 29.31: Shell Code**

```
$ foreman start web
```

We have successfully created an environment that simulates most of our production server
environment. Eventually, we'll want to have a staging server that mimics the environment
entirely (and many simply use actual Heroku instances to that end). However, for the
moment, we will be content that our site works flawlessly on foreman and that it's ready to
be deployed.

### 29.2.6    Checking Our Production Settings

We saw in passing in Chapter 3 that Django (as of version 1.7) supplies a `check` management command. The command acts as a method to supply a specific kind of test to our project. Powerfully, the check framework allows for checks to apply to specific portions of the project. There is an entire section of checks dedicated to deployment.

We set appropriate environment settings in Example 29.32.

---

**Example 29.32: Shell Code**

```
$ export SECRET_KEY='8$2(j1asy+2t113v%7%#qdntydt_@voxs3rz#7)&2u+66i!y0f'
$ export DJANGO_SETTINGS_MODULE=suorganizer.settings.production
```

---

We can then use the the `check` command with the `deploy` flag, as shown in Example 29.33.

---

**Example 29.33: Shell Code**

```
./manage.py check --deploy
```

---

Yikes! That's a lot of errors!

Most of the work of dealing with these errors involves reading the documentation, seeing if you want or need the setting (in most cases, you do), and changing your setting as appropriate. Many of these settings pertain to TLS and certificate security, which will only make sense once you have your own domain and certificates set up in Heroku. The work of getting your settings in order is tedious but straightforward: we skip the actual work in the book.

## 29.3    Deploying to Heroku

Preparing for deployment is the hardest part of deploying to Heroku. Actually deploying is incredibly simple.

Start by logging into the service using the toolbelt CLI, as shown in Example 29.34.

---

**Example 29.34: Shell Code**

```
$ heroku login
```

---

We then create a new Heroku app, as shown in Example 29.35.

---

**Example 29.35: Shell Code**

```
$ heroku create
```

---

This command creates a cloud instance and connects our git hub repository to Heroku. Heroku assigns your app a random name, but you can rename the app to whatever you wish, as shown in Example 29.36.

**Example 29.36: Shell Code**

```
$ heroku apps:rename newname
```

If you are deploying your own website, you may want to change the app name. If you are deploying the **suorganizer** project, I urge you **not** to rename the app from whatever name Heroku has assigned you. You don't want malicious users to find your website, especially given that the passwords for the users in the website are publicly available on github and in this book. What's more, the app name is used in the Heroku URL: `https://<appname>.herokuapps.com`. If you call the app `suorganizer`, you will clash with anyone else naming it `suorganizer` (you are [I hope] not the only one reading this book), and you will make your site a target for malicious users. In Example 29.37 we use git to see the remotes that Heroku added to our repository.

**Example 29.37: Shell Code**

```
$ git remote -v
heroku   https://git.heroku.com/suorganizer.git (fetch)
heroku   https://git.heroku.com/suorganizer.git (push)
origin   git@github.com:jambonrose/DjangoUnleashed-1.8.git (fetch)
origin   git@github.com:jambonrose/DjangoUnleashed-1.8.git (push)
```

Before we push our project code to Heroku via git, we should configure the environment. We start by setting a secret key, as shown in Example 29.38.

**Example 29.38: Shell Code**

```
$ heroku config:set SECRET_KEY='l)zht&^pddidsyqe$+09
    %sel*ba2#b_q-!j0^v$(-3c-=-vmq4'
```

While the foreman already knows of the location of our settings because of the command in `Procfile`, nothing else does. If we run management commands directly on Heroku, we won't want to worry about it, so we define the DJANGO_SETTINGS_MODULE variable in Example 29.39.

**Example 29.39: Shell Code**

```
$ heroku config:set DJANGO_SETTINGS_MODULE=suorganizer.settings
    .production
```

Finally, in Example 29.40, we set the PYTHONHASHSEED variable to random to strengthen our security by trying to enforce generation of cryptographically-strong pseudorandom numbers.

**Example 29.40: Shell Code**

```
$ heroku config:set PYTHONHASHSEED=random
```

We can see all our variables by simply invoking config, as shown in Example 29.41.

**Example 29.41: Shell Code**

```
$ heroku config
```

Before we deploy, remember that the site in the code repository is not safe. You should be using your own secret key, and while this is an excellent step to securing the site, it doesn't matter because *the passwords for pregenerated users of the website in this book are publicly available.* I recommend deleting the 0003_user_data.py migration before you keep going and changing the URL pattern to the **admin** interface (or removing the app entirely if you're not going to use it).

To actually deploy, we simply push to the server, as shown in Example 29.42.

**Example 29.42: Shell Code**

```
$ git push heroku master
```

We can then assign two dynos to work on our website, as shown in Example 29.43.

**Example 29.43: Shell Code**

```
$ heroku ps:scale web=2
```

Take heed: we are now officially spending money. To spend less money, you can drop the number of dynos, as shown in Example 29.44.

**Example 29.44: Shell Code**

```
$ heroku ps:scale web=1
```

We can open a browser to our website (no matter the name of the Heroku app) by invoking the open command, as shown in Example 29.45.

**Example 29.45: Shell Code**

```
$ heroku open
```

I'm sure you'll be disappointed to be greeted by our HTTP 500 error page. The reason is quite simple: we don't have a database. Thanks to migrations, this error is easy to fix. We simply run the migrate command on Heroku, as shown in Example 29.46.

**Example 29.46: Shell Code**

```
$ heroku run python manage.py migrate
```

If you reload the page, you'll discover that the webserver now runs smoothly. Congratulations! You've successfully deployed a website.

# 29.4   Adding Backing Services

Our website is now running and available publicly, but we're missing many of the key features we need for it. Referred to as **backing services**, or colloquially as **add-ons**, these tools are typically run by other companies on the Heroku platform. This means, however, that we will be paying these companies to manage the services we sign up for. As long as we're incurring a cost that is less than what it costs to dedicate an engineer or a team to the task of managing the services, then we are benefitting from the service. For a startup or a small website, the cost is typically well worth it.

In the next three subsections we do the following:

1. Add logging to our production site

2. Enable transactional emails

3. Enable caching

To do these tasks, I have chosen the services available from Papertrail, Postmark, and Memcachier. I am not affiliated with any of these services, and there are many competing services available on Heroku that may better suit your needs. I will point out some of your other options as we go. The utility of these sections is less about the tools and more about the process.

> **Info**
>
> At the time of writing, Heroku lists its backing services in two locations:
>
> - https://addons.heroku.com/
> - https://elements.heroku.com/addons

## 29.4.1   Logging with Papertrail

Heroku, by default, will store logs about our service, as shown in Example 29.47.

**Example 29.47: Shell Code**

```
$ heroku logs --tail
```

The feature comes with basic filtering, allowing us to see output from Heroku itself or just our app, as shown in Example 29.48.

**Example 29.48: Shell Code**

```
$ heroku logs --tail --source heroku
$ heroku logs --tail --source app
```

Heroku's log feature is limited to 1,500 messages, and according to Heroku's documentation, it is built more for routing messages and less for storage. We therefore add a service for storing our logs long term. There are three companies on Heroku's platform: FlyData, Papertrail, and Logentries. I opt to use Papertrail, but the competing services may better suit your needs.

## Info

For more about Heroku's logging service:

https://devcenter.heroku.com/articles/logging

To read more about how the Papertrail add on works, we can use the `addons` command, as shown in Example 29.49.

**Example 29.49: Shell Code**

```
$ heroku addons:docs papertrail
```

To use the service, we can issue the command shown in Example 29.50

**Example 29.50: Shell Code**

```
$ heroku addons:create papertrail
```

If we open our Papertrail interface (Example 29.51), we'll be greeted by a blank screen, because we have nothing to log.

**Example 29.51: Shell Code**

```
$ heroku addons:open papertrail
```

At the moment, all of our logging settings are in `dev.py`. We can move the settings to `base.py` so that we are logging in both development and production.

By default, Python's `StreamHandler` (in our `handler` setting) outputs to `stderr`. This is a bit of a problem, because Papertrail only watches `stdout` for logging purposes. To redirect `StreamHandler` output, we can add the `stream` option on line 134 in Example 29.52.

**Example 29.52: Project Code**
`suorganizer/settings/base.py` **in** `3081b1e4d2`

```
  5    import sys
  .       ...
123    LOGGING = {
  .       ...
131        'handlers': {
132            'console': {
133                'filters': ['remove_migration_sql'],
134                'class': 'logging.StreamHandler',
135                'stream': sys.stdout,
136            },
137        },
  .       ...
151    }
```

If you push our changes via github, all of the logs will appear in our Papertrail user interface, and anytime our app sends information to the log, Papertrail will record it.

**Info**

For more options for logging options, please see

https://addons.heroku.com/#logging

## 29.4.2  Sending Emails with Postmark

**Warning!**

Actually setting up an email service requires a registered domain and for the domain to be configured to receive email. If you are following along with the **suorganizer** project (rather than your own), it is best to read this section and not actually issue the commands here.

Our website currently has no way to send emails. We can't verify new users (we can't send activation emails) or reset passwords, which is rather a large problem. These emails are referred to as **transactional emails** as opposed to bulk emails (such as newsletters and mailing lists).

There are *many* email service providers on the Heroku platform. The leaders in the field at the time of writing are Sendgrid, with Mandrill and Mailgun as popular options. I opt to use Postmark because it specializes in transactional email (let's be honest: it's because Postmark's marketing sells me and I like their interface—Sendgrid, Mandrill, and Mailgun are likely just as good at transactional email). Note that Postmark is more expensive that any of its competitors and that the service *does not* support bulk email. This is fine for us at the moment, as we're not interested in sending bulk emails.

In Example 29.53, we start by reading Postmark's documentation.

**Example 29.53: Shell Code**

```
$ heroku addons:docs postmark
```

We can then add the service to our app and open the interface, as shown in Example 29.54.

**Example 29.54: Shell Code**

```
$ heroku addons:create postmark:10k
$ heroku addons:open postmark
```

Postmark requires a little bit of configuration and further requires that we verify the email address we're sending from, which may require even more setup. I do not cover the setup process here, as I can't possibly know which email service you're using or which DNS registrar you've registered your domain with.

Once the service is configured, we must configure our Django project to use it, as shown in Example 29.55. We do this via the environment variables that Postmark added when we enabled the service.

**Example 29.55: Shell Code**

```
$ heroku config
```

There are typically two ways to interact with email services: by API and by SMTP. For Django, given that the default email system is SMTP, it's easiest to use the SMTP options. Following Postmark's documentation allows us to add the following settings to our production settings, as shown in Example 29.56.

**Example 29.56: Project Code**
suorganizer/settings/production.py **in** 0f5887f2f2

```
34    EMAIL_HOST = os.environ.get('POSTMARK_SMTP_SERVER')
35    EMAIL_PORT = 587
36    EMAIL_HOST_USER = os.environ.get('POSTMARK_API_TOKEN')
37    EMAIL_HOST_PASSWORD = os.environ.get('POSTMARK_API_TOKEN')
38    EMAIL_USE_TLS = True
```

Make sure the setting for the console email system is in the development settings (and not in base.py), as shown in Example 29.57. This ensures Django uses the SMTP default in our production settings.

**Example 29.57: Project Code**
`suorganizer/settings/dev.py` in `3c73f989ea`

```
81  EMAIL_BACKEND = 'django.core.mail.backends.console.EmailBackend'
```

If you push to the server, new users will now have the ability to register, as we will officially be able to send them an activation email.

## Django Documentation

For more about Django's SMTP email back end:

https://dju.link/18/smtp

### 29.4.3   Caching with Memcache

In Chapter 26, we discussed how to limit the amount of work our website has to do. One way to avoid work is to cache results. At the end of the chapter, we disabled our site-wide caching settings to make development easier. In this section, we reenable caching and configure our caching to work with one of the industry's fastest out-of-the-box in-memory caches: Memcache.

At the time of writing, there are two services that provide access to managed memcache services on the Heroku platform: the Memcached Cloud and Memcachier. I opt to use Memcachier. The first step, as always, is to read the documentation (Example 29.58).

**Example 29.58: Shell Code**

```
$ heroku addons:docs memcachier
```

## Info
For more caching services:

https://addons.heroku.com/#caching

In Example 29.59, we can then add the service to our app, and see what variables the service has added to environment.

**Example 29.59: Shell Code**

```
$ heroku addons:create memcachier:dev
$ heroku config
```

To run on Heroku, we need to add the `pylibmc` and `django-pylibmc` Python package, as shown in Example 29.60.

**Example 29.60: Shell Code**

```
$ echo "pylibmc" >> requirements.txt
$ echo "django-pylibmc" >> requirements.txt
$ sort -u requirements.txt -o requirements.txt
```

Our requirements for running our website thus read as shown in Example 29.61.

**Example 29.61: Project Code**
requirements.txt **in** 176077d4aa

```
1    Django>=1.8,<1.9
2    django-pylibmc
3    django-toolbelt
4    psycopg2
5    pylibmc
6    whitenoise
```

To run these locally, we would need the libmemcached C library. I do not provide instructions to install this library.

With the Memcachier service running on Heroku, we can turn to the task of reenabling our cache.

To begin, we can cache any template file that we load, as shown in Example 29.62.

**Example 29.62: Project Code**
suorganizer/settings/production.py **in** 176077d4aa

```
40    TEMPLATES[0]['OPTIONS']['loaders'] = [
41        ('django.template.loaders.cached.Loader', [
42            'django.template.loaders.filesystem.Loader',
43            'django.template.loaders.app_directories.Loader',
44        ]),
45    ]
```

Of course, for any caching to work, we need to define the CACHE setting. Because we have caching in production, but not in staging (assuming that libmemcached is not installed and that we have not added environment variables to our own local memcache instance) we need this setting to work when memcache is available as well as when it isn't. We can define a function to return our settings and use a try...except block to handle cases where memcache doesn't exist, as shown in Example 29.63.

**Example 29.63: Project Code**
suorganizer/settings/production.py **in** 176077d4aa

```
48    def get_cache():
49        try:
  .        ...
```

```
62          except:
63              return {
64                  'default': {
65                      'BACKEND': 'django.core.cache.backends.locmem.
 .                                 LocMemCache'
66                  }
67              }
68
69   CACHES = get_cache()
```

For when Django is running in production on Heroku, we follow the documentation and load the environment variables Memcachier added to our app, as shown in Example 29.64. We assign these variables as MEMCACHE_* variables, because they are what django-pylibmc will use to find the memcache instance.

**Example 29.64:** Project Code
`suorganizer/settings/production.py` in 176077d4aa

```
48   def get_cache():
49       try:
50           os.environ['MEMCACHE_SERVERS'] = (
51               os.environ['MEMCACHIER_SERVERS'].replace(',', ';'))
52           os.environ['MEMCACHE_USERNAME'] =
 .               os.environ['MEMCACHIER_USERNAME']
53           os.environ['MEMCACHE_PASSWORD'] =
 .               os.environ['MEMCACHIER_PASSWORD']
```

We can then use configure our cache instance using django-pylibmc, as shown in Example 29.65.

**Example 29.65:** Project Code
`suorganizer/settings/production.py` in 176077d4aa

```
48   def get_cache():
49       try:
 .           ...
54           return {
55               'default': {
56                   'BACKEND': 'django_pylibmc.memcached.PyLibMCCache',
57                   'TIMEOUT': 500,
58                   'BINARY': True,
59                   'OPTIONS': {'tcp_nodelay': True},
60               }
61           }
```

If we push the changes to Heroku and reload the page a few times, the service interface we open with the command in Example 29.66 will inform us that the cache is working.

**Example 29.66: Shell Code**

```
$ heroku addons:open memcachier
```

At the time of writing, there is a little bug that requires a bit of a workaround (and is documented in Memcachier's documentation). In the interface in Example 29.66, you might notice that the number of connections is increased with every page load. At the moment, this is because Django is reconnecting to our cache every single time we load a new page. This is not scalable, as creating the connection is an expensive operation. To get around this, we can override the method that closes the connection to avoid this bug, as shown in Example 29.67.

**Example 29.67: Project Code**
`suorganizer/wsgi.py` **in** 6e01872f46

```
12   from django.core.cache.backends.memcached import \
13       BaseMemcachedCache
.        ...
19   BaseMemcachedCache.close = lambda self, **kwargs: None
```

Now our cache will work as desired and will make our website much quicker. With that said, caching and optimization is all about profiling a website and using the cache where needed. I recommend taking a look through Memcachier's documentation on Heroku, as it demonstrates several key ways to optimize a Django website with memcache that are not discussed in the book.

# 29.5   Putting It All Together

You have learned to use Django, used its core and its contributed library, and extended it to take full command of its power. And now you have deployed it—fully-featured—to the cloud. Congratulations!

Our website is now publicly available with logging, email, and caching, and we were able to do it with very little effort thanks to a managed cloud solution. We could keep adding services. There are services for monitoring performance, catching exceptions, and performing split testing to see what our visitors prefer. It all depends on what we need and where we want to go from here.

In many ways, building a website is only the first step to a much larger, longer journey—a journey you are now prepared for.

Well. Almost. Chapter 30 is here to get you started on your next project the right way.

# Starting a New Project Correctly

## In This Chapter

- Reconsider the URL scheme for our website
- Discover resources for selecting third-party apps to Django projects
- Outline a proper attack plan for your next project, including a change in database and the inclusion of testing

## 30.1 Introduction

This chapter is all about starting a project now that you understand Django through and through. We'll talk about how to create a specification for a website. We discuss the creation of the URL scheme, look at how to pick third-party apps to lessen the amount of work we have to do, and list the items we need to tackle right away.

## 30.2 Preparing a Project

Before writing a single line of code, you should outline your project; define behavior, data structures, and a URL scheme; and choose third-party apps to lessen the amount of work you need to do.

### 30.2.1 Project Specification

The view is the heart of Django, and the purpose of the view is to handle HTTP. A modern website is defined by behavior, and the first goal when building a website is always to ask: What does it do?

In the case of Startup Organizer, the answer is that this website organizes news and information about startup companies. The behavior is to provide lists of information and to allow users to find related content and to be kept up to date about a world that is constantly on the move.

Once we understand behavior, we can ask: What data do we need to achieve our goal? Obviously, we need information about startups, and to list news, we must create links to external articles. To organize them and make it easy to navigate the site, we can add tags. Startups, tags, and article links are the heart of the site and would have constituted our minimum-viable product if we were an actual startup business (as opposed to a book). To complicate matters in the book, I added a blog, allowing us to list news about our own site as well as provide a place for us to talk about startups among ourselves. This extra feature would have waited for version 2 of our project in normal circumstances.

With data in mind, we can design our models.

When building a model, we need to know how the data is accessed. A key question is always: Does this model need a slug?

To fully answer the question of data access, we should always design our URL scheme. The URL scheme forces us to consider the data as well as the behavior. Crucially, we want our URLs to be consistent and to last for as long as possible. If our site URLs change, then any links to our webpages made elsewhere will fail, which is totally undesirable. The W3C provides a discussion of building clean, long-term URLs at https://dju.link/uri.

We dipped our toes into building URLs in Chapter 1: Starting a New Django Project, but we were nowhere near as thorough as we should have been. We can tackle the problem by organizing URLs according to model and CRUD: how do we list, create, read, update, and delete objects? With our `Tag` model, we would write out the following:

- `/tag/`
- `/tag/<tag_name>/`
- `/tag/<tag_name>/delete/`
- `/tag/<tag_name>/update/`
- `/tag/create/`

We would *immediately* see that `/create/` was going to conflict with `<tag_name>`. Similarly, we would have know right off the bat that our `NewsLink` model would require a `SlugField`. We would never have started with the following:

- `newslink/create/`
- `newslink/delete/<pk>/`
- `newslink/update/<pk>/`

We would immediately have been able to design our website with the `/startup/` path segment prefix. What's more, we would have had a choice:

- D1: `/startup/<startup_name>/delete_newslink/<newslink_title>/`
- D2: `/startup/<startup_name>/<newslink_title>/delete/`
- U1: `/startup/<startup_name>/update_newslink/<newslink_title>/`
- U2: `/startup/<startup_name>/<newslink_title>/update/`

The goal when designing URL paths is to ensure that every path segment is a valid page. In the case of U1 and D1, we would need to define pages for

- `/startup/<startup_name>/delete_newslink/`
- `/startup/<startup_name>/update_newslink/`

As it's not at all clear what to display on those pages, we choose the second option, which is also why we opt for URL paths like `/tag/create/` instead of `/create/tag/`; `/create/tag/` avoids the `create` conflict, but what does `/create/` do?

By combining our `NewsLink` URL paths with `Startup` model URLs, we would anticipate needing the following paths:

- `/startup/`
- `/startup/<startup_name>/` # Read for `Startup` and List for `NewsLink`
- `/startup/<startup_name>/<newslink_title>/delete/`
- `/startup/<startup_name>/<newslink_title>/update/`
- `/startup/<startup_name>/add_article_link/`
- `/startup/<startup_name>/delete/`
- `/startup/<startup_name>/update/`
- `/startup/create/`

We immediately know that no `Startup` may have a slug of `create`, and we further know that the `NewsLink` model needs a slug and that the slug—based on the `NewsLink`'s `title` field—may not be `add_article_link`, `delete`, or `update`.

The reason I intentionally avoided laying this all out is so we could fix the problem with migrations.

If we had followed the process above, we would also have predicted the existence of the archive pages at the following URLs:

- `/blog/<year>/`
- `/blog/<year>/<month>/`

By creating a specification that defines behavior, data, and a URL scheme, we set ourselves up with a very clear plan of how to proceed when building the website.

## 30.2.2  Picking Third-Party Apps

Once you understand what your site does (what behavior and data structure you need), your next step is to see if someone has already done the work for you. One of Django's greatest assets is the ability to easily plug in apps built by other developers. The difficulty is finding the right tool for the job.

To get you started, http://awesome-django.com/ contains a curated list of some of Django's most popular packages.

Then, there's https://www.djangopackages.com/, which attempts to organize the overwhelming number of packages for Django.

When picking a package, remember that one of the most important aspects is whether it's up to date and maintained. If you have several choices for a package, you want the one that best suits your purposes, but you also want the one that is actively maintained and up to date, as that will make your life much easier.

In the event the package is no longer maintained, consider contributing to the project (you should consider contributing even if the package is maintained). In many cases, it will be quicker than building a new feature from scratch, and it provides an excellent learning opportunity. By contributing to a package, you will be not only building your project but also providing others with your work. In turn, people using the package will help make the package better, which will make your own project better. Contributing is a win–win for everyone!

It admittedly takes a little bit of effort to turn an app into a reusable app or package, and we won't see how to do so in this book. I recommend reading relevant chapters in the book *Two Scoops of Django* and following the packaging guide put out by the Python Packaging Authority (PyPA). Google will also be your friend for this adventure.

### 30.2.3    The `User` Model

When building a website in Django, the user requires some extra consideration. The swappable nature of the `User` model and the way it affects our migrations means that it is the next thing we want to consider and one of the first pieces of code to tackle (or at least prepare for). We want to make sure the `User` model is as lean as possible, but everything else is in the air:

- Username or email?
- Password or external service (such as Twitter, Google, or Facebook, or even an organization-specific service)?

Any information not related to authentication should be placed in other model(s). This topic is tied in not only with URL scheme design but also with third-party apps, as there are many, many apps to handle user authentication and make it as easy for you as possible.

Consider in particular that users are not fond of registering for new accounts and that anything you can do to reduce the friction of sign-up is a good step to take. The apps listed under Authorization and Authentication on http://awesome-django.com/ are worth looking into. These sections also list third-party tools for enabling object-level permissions in Django.

## 30.3    Building the Project

Now that you know what to build, you have to actually build it. If this were an intermediate Django book, some of the content would have been very different. We would have added tests at every opportunity and immediately started with generic views, and our model methods would have been a little different.

### 30.3.1 Testing

The most glaring omission in this book is testing. There is simply no way to build a website as large as the one in this book without tests, and the website we built was not particularly difficult in the grand scheme of things. Test-driven development (TDD) and behavior-driven development (BDD) are both considered great ways to add testing to projects, and Harry Percival's *Test-Driven Development with Python* teaches TDD while building a Django site. Had this been an intermediate book, we would have added multiple tests for each of our views, as well as tests for forms, and a few very simple tests for model methods.

### 30.3.2 PostgreSQL

It is a bad idea to use a different database in production than the database used in development. When starting a project, you will want to switch immediately to the database you will be using in production, and to that end, I strongly recommend using PostgreSQL for your relational database (to say nothing of your nonrelational database requirements).

There are many guides to getting started with a PostgreSQL database with Django (including one at https://django-unleashed.com under the Extras section), and so we will not demonstrate the setup here.

### 30.3.3 Starting with Generic Views

If we had started our site with generic class-based views (GCBVs), this book would have been much, much shorter (and far more opaque). When building a view, use Django's documentation and https://ccbv.co.uk/ and ask yourself: Does a GCBV already provide the majority of the behavior I want? If the answer is yes, then you should definitely use a GCBV.

In the event the answer is no, then you are left with the choice of building a view with a class-based view (CBV) or else a function view (FV). In the event you need reusable behavior, you should absolutely use a CBV, as it affords you all of the power of object-oriented programming. However, if you don't need reusable behavior, you are still left with the choice between a CBV and an FV. At this point, it becomes pure preference. If you do opt for the FV, remember that the HTTP specification is not respected and that to handle HTTP methods properly, you should use the `@require_http_methods()` decorator.

### 30.3.4 Reconsidering Reverse Methods

Throughout the code in the book, we routinely defined `get_absolute_url()`, `get_delete_url()`, and `get_update_url()`. On some sites, you may find it beneficial to implement the `get_create_url()` and `get_list_url()` methods.

### 30.3.5 Optimization

Entire books could be (and have been) written about optimization, performance, and caching. We saw how to optimize querysets but didn't discuss denormalization of databases. We cached entire webpages but did not have time to see that Django provides ways to cache querysets, views, sections of templates, and just about anything. We did not even begin to discuss how to optimize Python code.

A great introduction to a more thorough understanding of the problems of optimization and performance is Peter Baumgartner and Yann Malet's *High Performance Django*.

### 30.3.6   Building REST APIs

Websites consist of a front end and a back end, and a lot of the time you will want to build websites where the two communicate with each other. In most circumstances, enabling the JavaScript front end to communicate with the Django back end will involve building a REST API.

The most popular tool today for building REST APIs in Django is the Django REST Framework, and I recommend you take a look at how it works (and what a REST API is), as it will prove instrumental in helping you rapidly build modern websites.

## 30.4   The Road Ahead

I would tell you that you are now capable of building the back end to any website, but that's not quite right. You are now capable of building any website that works on HTTP (which is the vast majority of websites on the Internet). As of 2011, the World Wide Web has been playing with a new protocol called Websockets. Its use is far more limited than HTTP, but in key instances, it is a powerful and useful alternative to HTTP. Django has yet to add the tools required to properly handle the new protocol (few frameworks have), but discussion is under way to Get It Right and to continue to make Django the incredible project it is. As such, I will congratulate you on being able to use Django to build 95% of all the possible websites you might consider building.

Django is an amazing tool to have under your belt, and it is my go-to choice for building websites. However, it is only a piece of the puzzle. If you want to specialize in web work, then some knowledge of JavaScript (the front end) is a good idea. However, it is by no means required, and a strong background in Django and back end work is all you might want or need. You might instead decide to expand your knowledge of caching, optimization, or even Python. Learning to use a different tool, such as Tornado or Twisted, might prove valuable as well.

I will be routinely updating https://django-unleashed.com with more writing related to this book. You can find more of my writing and work at https://andrewsforge.com.

Thank you for reading my book. I hope it has helped you in your quest to learn Django.

# IV

# Appendixes

Mad Hatter: "Why is a raven like a writing-desk?"
"Have you guessed the riddle yet?" the Hatter said, turning to Alice again.
"No, I give it up," Alice replied: "What's the answer?"
"I haven't the slightest idea," said the Hatter.

*Alice in Wonderland*
by Lewis Carroll

# A

# HTTP

The HyperText Transfer Protocol was built to transfer files written in the HyperText Markup Language (HTML; HTTP was later extended to be for "hypermedia"). There are multiple versions of HTTP, including the up-and-coming HTTP version 2.0. This document concerns itself with HTTP version 1.1, usually written as HTTP/1.1.

HTTP defines two types of users: a client and a server. HTTP uses the request/response model: the client **requests** data, and the server **responds** with data. To request data, the client sends an HTTP method (and any related data) to a specific URL. The most common method is the GET method, shown in Example A.1.

**Example A.1: HTTP**

```
GET /tag/ HTTP/1.1
```

The server responds with an HTTP return code as well as any relevant data. On the Foreman server at the end of the book, the request above results in the response shown in Example A.2, where the 200 OK is the response code.

**Example A.2: HTTP**

```
HTTP/1.1 200 OK
Server: gunicorn/19.3.0
Date: Sat, 01 Aug 2015 16:10:56 GMT
Connection: close
Transfer-Encoding: chunked
Last-Modified: Sat, 01 Aug 2015 16:10:56 GMT
Cache-Control: max-age=600
```

```
Vary: Cookie
Expires: Sat, 01 Aug 2015 16:20:56 GMT
X-Frame-Options: SAMEORIGIN
Content-Type: text/html; charset=utf-8

<html>
<!-- truncated -->
```

The full HTML page is also transmitted in the response, but it is removed from the output in this example to save space on the page.

The 200 response code signifies that the request was valid and that the information could be found. The numeral in the hundreds position (the 2) tells us the most about the response code.

- 100s are typically information responses
- 200s are for successful responses
- 300s are for redirections
- 400s are for errors on the client side
- 500s are for errors on the server side

Django concerns itself primarily with the following:

- 200 OK—the resource was found and returned correctly
- 400 Bad Request—the server did not understand the request
- 403 Forbidden—the client isn't allowed to access this information
- 404 Not Found—there is no resource at that URL
- 405 Method Not Allowed—the HTTP method used is not allowed to be used at that URL
- 500 Internal Server Error—something went wrong on the server's end, and the server could not return any data

If we ask for a URL that does not exist, our server will respond with a 404 error code, as shown in Example A.3.

**Example A.3: HTTP**

```
GET /nonexistent/ HTTP/1.1

HTTP/1.1 404 NOT FOUND
Server: gunicorn/19.3.0
Date: Sat, 01 Aug 2015 16:51:08 GMT
Connection: close
Transfer-Encoding: chunked
Vary: Cookie
X-Frame-Options: SAMEORIGIN
Content-Type: text/html; charset=utf-8
```

In the book, we primarily used the GET method, which simply asks for a resource at a page, and the POST method, which sends information to the server for it to use. In a few sections, it became useful to know about the HEAD and OPTIONS methods.

- HEAD is a truncated version of GET that returns the meta-information without the actual resource (the 200 OK response to our GET in Example A.3 prints only what the HEAD method would have returned, removing the actual HTML resource to save space in the book).

- OPTIONS asks the server for the list of methods that may be used at that URL (and is heavily tied to the 405 error message).

HTTP request methods can be categorized in a few different ways. The most common way is according to whether they are safe or unsafe methods. The GET, HEAD, and OPTIONS methods are safe because they do not change any data on the server, and they simply return whatever resource is being requested. The POST method is unsafe because it creates data.

When building Django websites, it is useful to know about the DELETE and PUT methods (and specifically how PUT differs from POST). Because we did not deal with these methods in the book, I do not cover that material here. (I intentionally avoided it because of the subtleties of dealing with POST and PUT, choosing a simpler approach to always use POST so that we might focus on Django).

## Documentation

For a more thorough discussion of HTTP, I recommend the resources available at the W3C, as well as the articles on Wikipedia.

- http://www.w3schools.com/tags/ref_httpmethods.asp
- https://en.wikipedia.org/wiki/Hypertext_Transfer_Protocol
- https://en.wikipedia.org/wiki/Hypertext_Transfer_Protocol#Request_methods
- https://en.wikipedia.org/wiki/List_of_HTTP_status_codes

# B

# Python Primer

Python is an object-oriented language with functional tools. Everything in Python is an object.

Many, many, many beginner's guides to Python have been written. A great place to start is the *Beginner's Guide to Python* at https://wiki.python.org/moin/BeginnersGuide.

Zed Shaw's *Learn Python the Hard Way* is a very popular book, and I further recommend David Beazley's *Python Essential Reference* as an excellent book to have on hand.

There are nonetheless a few topics not frequently covered in many beginner's guides that will prove useful while reading this book.

## B.1 Decorators

A decorator changes the input and output of a callable. It encapsulates or wraps a callable. A decorator is simply another callable that replaces the first and that calls the callable being decorated. It works because Python has first-class functions (read: functions are objects).

For instance, we have a function f() that accepts and returns an integer. If we wanted (for whatever reason) to modify the integer being returned, we could create a new function with the intent of decorating the method, as shown in Example B.1.

**Example B.1: Python Code**

```python
def f(i):
    return i

def g(func):
    def new_f(i):
        r = func(i)
        return r+10
    return new_f
```

We can see this in action in the Python interpreter, shown in Example B.2.

**Example B.2: Python Interpreter Code**

```
>>> f(5)
5
>>> # the code below decorates f()
>>> f = g(f)
>>> f(5)
>>> 15
```

Python defines syntactic sugar that makes it easier to decorate a function, as shown in Example B.3.

**Example B.3: Python Code**

```
@g
def h(i):
    return i
```

In Example B.4, the h() function has been decorated by g() (written as @g in this book to demonstrate intent).

**Example B.4: Python Interpreter Code**

```
>>> h(5)
15
```

# B.2   Multiple Inheritance

In Python, it is possible for a class to inherit multiple classes. The difficulty with multiple inheritance is that it becomes difficult to know where behavior is being inherited from.

The classic problem is the diamond inheritance problem, which is illustrated in Figure B.1. If class D inherits from B and C, which in turn inherit from A, and A and C define different values of an attribute, what is the value of the attribute inherited by D?

In modern Python (post version 2.3), the answer is that the x attribute will be True in instances of D. To allow for this, Python linearizes inheritance graphs into a list, allowing for a simple way of determining which attribute or method to inherit directly from. This list is called the **method resolution order**, and any class or object can provide the developer with this list thanks to the mro() method.

When working with Django's class-based views and especially generic class-based views, understanding the linearization of graph inheritance structures and where information is being inherited from is crucial.

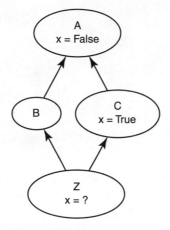

**Figure B.1:** Diamond Problem

# C

# Relational Database Basics

The goal of a database is to store data in discrete, organized pieces. What we colloquially call a database is actually a database and a database manager. A database manager is the interface used to interact with the database, which is the actual data storage mechanism. Relational databases are organized like spreadsheets. A database may have multiple spreadsheets, called **tables**. A table has columns and rows. Each cell (or entry) in the table is a discrete piece of information. The columns determine the meaning of the cell; in Table C.1, each cell in the Department column is the name of a department. Each row in the table is a collection of information that makes up a whole: in Table C.1, each row is a different class, made up of three pieces of information: department, class number, and title.

Relational databases use relations to tie discrete pieces of information together, allowing for information to be stored in only a single place in the database. To do this, relational databases assign each row a unique identifier, called a **primary key**, shown in the first column of Table C.2.

**Table C.1: Class Table**

| Department | Number | Title |
| --- | --- | --- |
| Math | 101 | Calculus |
| Math | 111 | Linear Algebra |
| Physics | 101 | Kinematics |
| French | 144 | Theater |
| English | 105 | Shakespeare |
| English | 143 | Book Writing |

**Table C.2: Class Table**

| PK | Department | Number | Title |
|----|-----------|--------|-------|
| 1 | Math | 101 | Calculus |
| 2 | Math | 111 | Linear Algebra |
| 3 | Physics | 101 | Kinematics |
| 4 | French | 144 | Theater |
| 5 | English | 105 | Shakespeare |
| 6 | English | 143 | Book Writing |

**Table C.3: Department Table**

| PK | Department Name |
|----|-----------------|
| 1 | Math |
| 2 | Physics |
| 3 | French |
| 4 | English |

**Table C.4: Class Table**

| PK | Dept. | Number | Title |
|----|-------|--------|-------|
| 1 | 1 | 101 | Calculus |
| 2 | 1 | 111 | Linear Algebra |
| 3 | 2 | 101 | Kinematics |
| 4 | 3 | 144 | Theater |
| 5 | 4 | 105 | Shakespeare |
| 6 | 4 | 143 | Book Writing |

For instance, instead of listing the department in the row, we can create a separate table for departments, as shown in Table C.3.

We can then use the primary key of the department in the class table. When using a primary key of another table, we call the unique identifier a **foreign key**. The foreign key relates data in one table to data in another, as you can see in Table C.4.

If we ever wish to change the name of a department, we will only need to do so in a single location. The act of making data unique and discrete is called **normalization**.

When using a foreign key, we create a one-to-many relationship. Every class will relate to a department (one), but every department will relate to multiple classes (many).

It is also possible to create many-to-many relations. For example, many students may take many classes. We create a table of students in Table C.5.

**Table C.5: Student Table**

| PK | Student ID | First N. | Last Name |
|----|-----------|----------|-----------|
| 1  | Smth77    | John     | Smith     |
| 2  | Ndrcvr80  | Elias    | Undercover |
| 3  | Tbls83    | Robert   | Tables    |

**Table C.6: Student–Class M2M Relationship Table**

| PK | Student FK | Class FK |
|----|-----------|----------|
| 1  | 1         | 4        |
| 2  | 2         | 4        |
| 3  | 3         | 4        |
| 4  | 1         | 5        |
| 5  | 2         | 5        |
| 6  | 3         | 6        |
| 7  | 1         | 3        |
| 8  | 2         | 3        |

A simple column in a table does not provide enough information for a many-to-many relationship (m2m); a column in a table can be used only for one-to-many relationships (or one-to-one if uniqueness is enforced by the database on the column). Instead, we need an entire table for the job, as shown in Table C.6.

In Table C.6, our first relation tells us that John Smith is taking Theater 144. The Department column in the class table further tells us that the class is related to the French department. If we ever need to change information about a student, we only change it in the student table. The same is true for classes and departments.

There are other kinds of databases out there, such as graph databases, but relational databases should be your go-to, as they provide the right tools to structure and store data for a website.

# D

# Security Basics

The main tenet of security on the Internet can be boiled down to one sentence: **Don't trust the user.**

Security, more than anything, is a mindset. Assume that every user is out to break your site and steal your data. The goal is to figure out what data is important, who you're protecting the data from, and how to do so.

Django provides many protections from well-known attacks. The ORM (object-relational mapper)—seen in Chapter 3—is built to protect from database injection attacks, which is when the user crafts data in GET or POST to try to modify your database or retrieve data from the website. To prevent injection attacks, the ORM escapes any input to avoid possible confusion with SQL syntax.

The vulnerability that Django developers must think about most prevalently is the cross-site request forgery (CSRF) attack, because Django requires developer cooperation to successfully protect from the attack. The attack consists of using an innocent user to attack a website. Imagine an attacker wants to transfer funds to a bank account on a specific bank website. He or she can write JavaScript code to issue the transfer and inject the code on a different website (this is an attack in and of itself). Any user who is logged into the bank website and then visits the webpage with the injected code will be transferring money from his or her account to the attackers' account. (Did I mention you shouldn't trust *any* of your users?)

To protect against CSRF, we need to protect our own site in two ways: we don't want to be attacked as part of a CSRF, and we don't want to be the attack vector website where the attacker has injected code.

Preventing code from being injected into our webpages is easy: we escape HTML elements in anything being printed in templates. Django's Template Language does this to a certain extent by default, but using the `bleach` and `django-bleach` projects to add to this behavior is typically recommended.

To prevent data being sent to our site from other websites requires a little more work. When submitting data, a user typically uses an HTML form on a website. To enforce the use of forms on only our website, we can generate a random token, display it on the form, and then accept data only if a valid token is sent with the submitted data.

This action mitigates CSRF attacks but does not prevent them. Injected code could still ask for the form, fill it out, and then pass it back with the proper token. Modern browsers mitigate this risk with the same-origin policy, wherein browsers and servers use the Origin and Referer HTTP headers to check where the data came from. In tandem with the CSRF token, the same-origin policy strongly mitigates the CSRF attack.

When building forms for data submission in Django, it's crucial to use the CSRF token and to ensure that CSRF middleware is enabled. For essential views, it's best to use a belt and braces approach and to use the `@csrf_protect` decorator. The CSRF token, middleware, and decorator are all used in the main content of the book.

One topic not seen in the book is the use of Transport Layer Security (TLS), which is the Secure Socket Layer (SSL)'s successor but is still commonly referred to as SSL. TLS allows for the encryption of data between the server and the client.

When building websites, it's best to keep an eye on the latest vulnerabilities and to keep up to date with Django. For a full encyclopedia of attacks and how to mitigate them, see `https://www.owasp.org`. For Django's latest updates (including security advisories), see the blog at `https://www.djangoproject.com/weblog/`.

### Info

I recommend reading the OWASP and Django documentation about the cross-site scripting (XSS), cross-site request forgery (CSRF), database injection, and clickjacking attacks. They describe the attacks with far greater detail and precision than what I might provide.

# E

# Regular Expressions

## Warning!

Entire books have been written on this topic. Rather that attempt to cover the content of a book in a few pages, this primer hopes to introduce the material and provide the absolute least amount of knowledge needed to get started with *Django Unleashed*. I recommend using a full reference when programming or if any of this information proves to be unclear.

A regular expression answers a binary question: Does this string meet a set of requirements? These requirements are created by regular expression patterns. A regular expression pattern will either match (true) or reject (false) a string. These patterns look arcane but are actually quite simple.

Imagine we have a list of first names mixed in with pseudonyms, and we want to weed out all of the pseudonyms as best we can. We can start by identifying all of the names with the regular expression pattern `'^.+$'`. The circumflex accent (^) defines the beginning of a string, and the dollar sign defines the end of the string. The period matches any character, and the plus sign modifies the character so that the pattern will match at least one character. This pattern will this match *any* string of length 1 or more. If we use the pattern with the regular expression system of any language, this pattern will match *Lora*, *James*, but also *l33th4xx0r*.

## Info

If we wanted to match a string of any length, including a string of length 0 (the empty string `''`), we would switch the plus sign to the star sign, resulting in `'.*'`.

We return to the problem of *l33th4xx0r* in a moment. Let's pretend we want to find all of the names starting with *L* and *J*. If we change our pattern to `'^L.+$'`, we will match any string that starts with *L*. If we change our pattern to `'^J.+$'`, we will match any string that starts with *J*. To get both, we can use a character set, which is defined by brackets. Any character in a character set can be matched. The pattern `'^[JL].+$'` thus matches *James*, *Lora* and *Lindsay* (and will match *l33th4xx0r* if the regular expression system is run in case-insensitive mode). The character set is not modified by either the plus sign or the star sign, meaning that it is being used to match a single character (a *J* or an *L*). The new pattern will not match names like *Andrew*, because the string does not start with either a *J* or an *L*.

Human names don't typically use numbers, and so to avoid matching pseudonyms, we can change the pattern to reject strings that contain numbers. We can do this in two ways: we can explicitly match alphabet characters, or we can match anything but numbers.

To explicitly match only alphabet characters, we would change the pattern from `'^.+$'` to `'^[a-z]+$'` or `'^[A-Za-z]+$'` depending on whether we were in case-sensitive mode or not. The dash character defines a range of characters: anything in the range is valid. `'^[a-z]$'` is thus a match for any single lowercase alphabet character (unless we're in case-insensitive mode, in which case it matches any basic roman character). By adding a plus, we are matching at least one alphabet character.

To match anything but numbers, we could change the pattern from `'^.+$'` to `'^[^0-9]+$'`. The character set defines a range of all numbers and uses the circumflex accent to negate the range (match the opposite). To be clear: when used outside character sets, the circumflex accent defines the beginning of the string; when used inside a character set, the circumflex accent negates or inverses the selection.

While neither of our new patterns will match *l33th4xx0r*, they are not equivalent. This is where regular expressions get a little tricky. If you're thinking in terms of the basic roman English alphabet (the ASCII encoding), these two patterns are equivalent. Today, we no longer use ASCII (thank goodness), and instead use the Unicode standard. The Unicode standard allows for names like *Raphaël* and 黒澤明. The `'^[a-z]+$'` pattern will match neither *Raphaël* nor 黒澤明, whereas `'^[^0-9]+$'` *will*.

Different languages will define shortcuts for various ranges. For instance, Python defines the `'\w'` and `'\D'` shortcuts. Some developers focus (because it's easier) on the fact that `'\w'` is equivalent to `'[a-zA-Z0-9_]'` in ASCII, and they forget that Python's actual definition of `'\w'` is "Matches Unicode word characters; this includes most characters that can be part of a word in any language." Similarly, `'\D'` is not truly equivalent to `'[^0-9]'`, because `'\D'` actually matches "any character which is not a Unicode decimal digit." In the case of our attempt to weed out pseudonyms from a list of names, we would want to use the pattern `'^\D+$'`, as it would allow for names such as *Raphaël*, but weed out names with digits (including Roman numeral like Ⅴ, Chinese/Japanese/Korean ideographs like 四 and 匃 and even Thai, Ethiopic, and Bengali glyphs [to name but a few]).

Regular expressions themselves are not difficult (they are actually quite simple). Dealing with encoding while writing regular expressions can be quite tricky (because encodings are tricky).

## Python Documentation

For more about regular expressions in Python:
https://docs.python.org/3.4/library/re.html

# F

# Compilation Basics

## Warning!

Entire books have been written on this topic. Rather that attempt to cover the content of a book in a few pages, this primer hopes to introduce the material and provide the absolute least amount of knowledge needed to get started with *Django Unleashed*. I recommend using a full reference when programming or if any of this information proves to be unclear.

The process of compilation is far outside the scope of this book. However, when dealing custom template tags—Chapter 27: Building Custom Template Tags—it becomes useful to understand the big picture of compilers.

The goal of a compiler is to take one programming language and convert it into another (typically machine code). In some ways, this is a form of translation: developers write in a language that the machine doesn't actually understand but that the compiler can translate into a form that the computer can use.

To translate code from one language to another, a compiler first **lexes** the file containing the code into discrete pieces called tokens. It then **parses** the tokens into an **abstract syntax tree (AST)**. From here, a compiler might output an intermediate programming language and/or optimize the code. Finally, the compiler outputs its target language.

The act of lexing is splitting up the programming into meaningful tokens. The goal is to take a file of code and figure out what all the individual parts are. For instance, `for` is a token, just as an equals sign is a token.

With all of the tokens in a list, the compiler begins to assign meaning to the code. It parses the list of tokens, determining the meaning of combinations of tokens. The parser helps validate the code; e.g., does the variable used in the assignment actually exist? As it parses the code, the compiler turns the list of tokens into a tree (the AST) that outlines the possible paths the program might take.

With the AST in place, the compiler now understands (as much as any computer program can) the purpose of the code. It then walks the tree, outputting new code that provides the behavior the developer specified in the original code.

When building custom template tags, compilation basics come into play if the tags are built from scratch (the very end of the chapter). Django expects the developer to provide the lexing, parsing, and target code output. Django hands the developer a call to a template tag, and the developer is expected to tokenize the full input for that tag. The developer further defines a node in the abstract syntax list (parsing; Django's templates do not use a tree but instead use a list) and use this node to specify the output of the template tag (the output to target code). Having a basic understanding of compilers and the steps one must take when building a custom template tag goes a long way when writing intermediate Python code.

### Info

I don't recommend trying to slog through a compiler book on your own. While the topic is fascinating and well worth the effort, it is detail-oriented work and can be confusing and a little bit tedious. Take a class on the subject if you can! You won't regret it.

# G

# Installing Python, Django, and Your Tools

This appendix is less about how to install your toolset and more about which tools to install. I do not provide install instructions because each tool has far better and more recent instructions than I could hope to provide. Instead, I point you toward software and provide the process by which to install your tools. The goal is to give you the tools used by Python and Django developers during real development.

## G.1   Package Management

If you're on Linux distribution or a BSD flavor, then you already have a package (or port) manager, and you're all set. If you're developing on Windows or Mac OS X, however, you'll want to add one to your system, as it will make your life much easier.

On Mac OS X, your two main choices are MacPorts and Homebrew. I favor MacPorts because it's been around longer and has a much larger package library, but it's a little bit more difficult to use than Homebrew, whose goal is to be as simple as possible (sometimes to your detriment).

On Windows, you have a choice between Chocolatey or Cygwin in tandem with the `apt-cyg` package manager (similar to Debian's `apt-get` package manager). Windows 10 also ships with the PackageManagement tool, which is based on the OneGet open-source project and allows users to pull from multiple package management solutions.

Once you have a package manager, your next step is to familiarize yourself with the commands.

## G.2   Version Control

With a package manager, you will be able to install a distributed version control system. This book uses `git`, but it is certainly not the only option available. Using version control in software projects makes your life significantly easier and allows you to share your code or contribute to online projects on websites such as Github.

## G.3   Python

With a package management tool, it is very easy to install Python. You'll want to first search the package repository for the package you want. It might be listed either as `python`, `python3`, or `python-34`. You can then issue the install command for your package manager.

The next step is a little confusing: you want another package manager. Most package managers for systems provide large package repositories for software specific to that system. We want a package manager for just Python packages, specifically from the `pypi.python.org` website. Using your system package manager, you will want to install `pip` (which stands for "Pip Installs Packages" or "Pip Installs Python").

## G.4   Virtual Environments

One of the advantages to the setup described is the ability to quickly add and remove packages. One of the most useful is `virtualenvwrapper`. It allows for the creation of specific development environments. For instance, if you're working on two projects, and one requires Django 1.7 but the other uses Django 1.8, you can easily run both on your system thanks to the virtual environment wrapper, as shown in Example G.1.

**Example G.1: Shell Code**

```
$ pip install virtualenvwrapper
```

### Django Documentation

For more about `virtualenvwrapper`:
https://virtualenvwrapper.readthedocs.org/en/latest/

## G.5   Django

With both Python and `pip` installed on your system, and a virtual environment for your project you can now install Django, as shown in Example G.2.

**Example G.2: Shell Code**

```
$ pip install Django
```

Similarly, this will allow you to quickly install any third-party apps or Python tools needed for your project, as briefly discussed in Chapter 30: Starting a New Project Correctly.

On some systems, you will also need to install SQLite, which is used as the default database in Django (on other systems, such as Mac OS X, the database manager is already installed). You will need to use the system package manager installed in the first step to do this (`pip` cannot help you).

# G.6   Syntax Tools and Testing

A few new tools are incredibly useful when using Python. When testing, the `coverage` tool shows you how much of your code is actually being tested. The `flake8` tool allows you to check the syntax of your Python files and adhere to best practices. The `isort` tool sorts your Python imports to adhere to best practices.

Finally, one of the most common questions I get is which IDE to use. The truth is that your IDE doesn't matter; choose one you are comfortable with and go from there. The PyCharm IDE is a very popular option, and I've seen recommendations for the Atom editor for beginners. However, I tend to favor `vim` because it is open source and (somewhat) easily extensible, and it allows me to work in a number of programming languages while only having to learn a single IDE. That said, even with a slew of plugins, `vim`'s Python, HTML, and CSS code completion is not as good as that of tools dedicated to the task, and I frequently find myself using Espresso by MacRabbit for my CSS code.

# Index